MW00638900

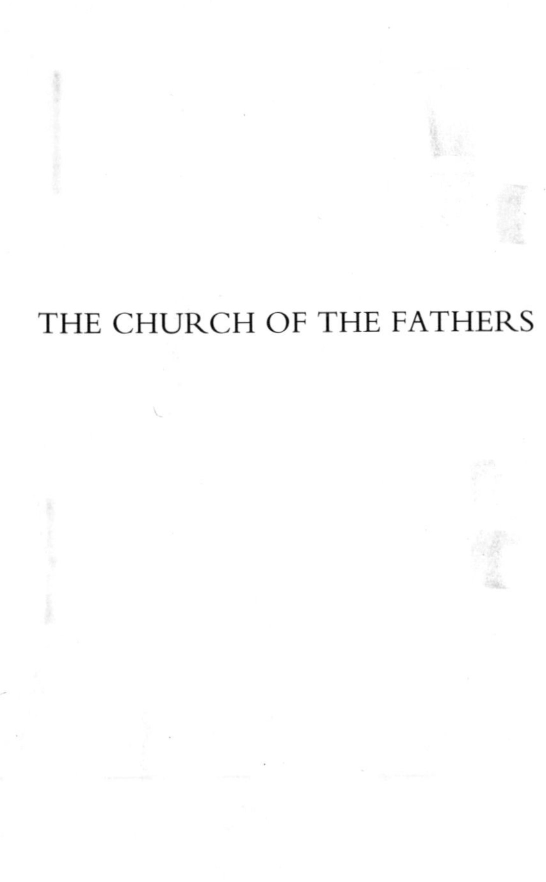

THE CHURCH OF THE FATHERS

THE WORKS OF

CARDINAL JOHN HENRY NEWMAN

BIRMINGHAM ORATORY

MILLENNIUM EDITION

VOLUME V

SERIES EDITOR

JAMES TOLHURST DD

First published in 1840 by
J. G. F. and J. Rivington
and
in 1872–3 by
Basil Montague Pickering
Published in the Birmingham Millennium Oratory Edition in 2002
jointly by

Gracewing
2 Southern Avenue
Leominster
Herefordshire HR6 0QF

University of Notre Dame Press
310 Flanner Hall
Notre Dame
IN 46556 USA

UK ISBN 0 85244 447 8
US ISBN 0 268 00279 8

A CIP record for this book has been applied for
and will be available from the Library of Congress

Additional typesetting by Action Publishing Technology Ltd,
Gloucester, GL1 5SR
Printed in England by MPG Books Ltd, Bodmin, PL31 1EG

THE CHURCH OF THE FATHERS

BY

JOHN HENRY CARDINAL NEWMAN

with an Introduction and Notes by

FRANCIS McGRATH FMS

Gracewing.

NOTRE DAME

CONTENTS

NOTE ON THE TEXT

The Church of the Fathers

In this Millennium Edition, the text on pp. 1–210 follows the uniform Longmans Edition of HISTORICAL SKETCHES, VOL. II, published by Longmans, Green & Co., London, 1888.

Primitive Christianity

In this Millennium Edition, the text on pp. 333–446 follows the uniform Longmans Edition of HISTORICAL SKETCHES, VOL. I, published by Longmans, Green & Co., London, 1876.

Taking the text from two separate volumes of HISTORICAL SKETCHES has created the variance in pagination from pp. 210–333.

ACKNOWLEDGEMENTS

I wish to acknowledge and thank the Fathers of the Birmingham Oratory for allowing me access to the resources both in their library and in the Newman archive, in particular, their Provost, the Very Reverend Paul Chavasse, Father Gregory Winterton, Father Guy Nicholls and Father Dermot Fenlon.

I am most grateful to Michael Hill, FMS, former provincial of the Sydney province of the Marist Brothers, for his unfailing support and encouragement throughout this long project. I am indebted to the current provincial, John Thompson FMS, and to my own Marist community at Ashgrove in Brisbane who quietly encouraged and supported me. At this point, I wish also to acknowledge affiliated member, Father Frank Comerford, CSSp. for his comments.

I am indebted to the Marist Community in Wolverhampton with whom I stay when working at the Birmingham Oratory, in particular, Wilfrid Harrison, FMS, Pat Sheils, FMS, Robert Lee, FMS, Joseph Lavelle, FMS and the late Henry Jackson, FMS. For many years now, 99A Old Fallings Lane has been my home away from home. I am thankful to the Series Editor of the Millennium Edition, the Reverend James Tolhurst, DD. I am also thankful to Mark Farrow from MAP graphics, Brisbane, for producing two maps in Appendix 1, as I am to John Crowson, Ipswich, to John Coles, my former Brisbane colleague, and to Professor James J. O'Donnell, Provost of Georgetown University, D.C., who located some ancient cities, now long gone, which Newman mentions in his chapters on Augustine of Hippo.

Finally, I am particularly indebted to Gerard Tracey, Librarian and Archivist at the Birmingham Oratory, whose unique insights into and monumental knowledge of Newman and the age he lived in is a continual source of surprise. I am also very appreciative of his unfailing readiness and generosity in sharing that knowledge. I thank him for his invaluable advice, support and friendship.

F.McG.

ABBREVIATIONS

Abbreviations used for the works by Newman are those listed in Joseph Rickaby, SJ, *Index to the Works of John Henry Cardinal Newman* (London, 1914), with some additions. Unless stated otherwise, references to works included by Newman in the uniform edition are always to that edition, which began in 1868 with *Parochial and Plain Sermons* and which concluded in 1881 with *Select Treatises of St. Athanasius*.

Apo.	*Apologia pro Vita Sua*
Ari.,	*Arians of the Fourth Century*
Ath., I, II	*Select Treatises of St. Athanasius*, 2 volumes
A.W.	*John Henry Newman: Autobiographical Writings*
D.A.	*Discussions and Arguments on Various Subjects*
Dev.	*An Essay on the Development of Christian Doctrine*
Diff., I, II	*Certain Difficulties felt by Anglicans in Catholic Teaching*, 2 volumes
Ess. I, II	*Essays Critical and Historical*, 2 volumes
G.A.	*An Essay in Aid of a Grammar of Assent*

H.S., I, II	*Historical Sketches*, 3 volumes
Idea	*The Idea of a University defined and illustrated*
Jfc.	*Lectures on the Doctrine of Justification*
K.C.	*Correspondence of John Henry Newman with John Keble and Others, 1839–1845*
L.G.	*Loss and Gain: the story of a Convert*
Mir.	*Two Essays on Biblical and on Ecclesiastical Miracles*
Mix.	*Discourses addressed to Mixed Congregations*
O.S.	*Sermons preached on Various Occasions*
P.S., I–VIII	*Parochial and Plain Sermons*
S.D.	*Sermons bearing on Subjects of the Day*
T.T.	*Tracts Theological and Ecclesiastical*
U.S.	*Fifteen Sermons preached before the University of Oxford*
V.M. I, II	*The Via Media*, 2 volumes
V.V.	*Verses on Various Occasions*
A.S., I, II	*Anglican Sermons*, 2 volumes
L.D., I–XXXI	*The Letters and Diaries of John Henry Newman*
T.P., I, II	*The Theological Papers of John Henry Newman*, 2 volumes
P.N. I, II	*John H. Newman, the Philosophical Notebook*, 2 volumes
C.F.	*The Church of the Fathers*
P.C.	*Primitive Christianity*
BOA	Birmingham Oratory Archives

INTRODUCTION

I. HISTORICAL BACKGROUND

This 'cursed Irish Spoliation bill'

On 12 February 1833, the Whig Chancellor of the Exchequer in the Grey government, tabled the much anticipated Irish Church Temporalities Bill into a newly reformed House of Commons at Westminster.[1] Among its measures, the bill proposed to abolish ten of twenty-two sees in the established Church of Ireland; to downgrade the archbishoprics of Cashel and Tuam to the status of ordinary bishoprics; to trim the endowments of the wealthiest sees, Armagh and Derry; to cancel future appointments to parishes where no service had been held for three years; to abolish church cess;[2] and to allow tenants of church lands to convert leases into permanent freehold. The purpose of the bill was to appropriate the Church's

[1] Lord Althorp (1782–1845) was the Chancellor and Earl Grey (1764–1845) the Prime Minister.

[2] Church cess was an unpopular tax imposed on locals, irrespective of creed, to maintain the parish church in good repair.

surplus revenue for educational purposes on the principle that church property was not private property but property held in trust, subject to the satisfactory performance of certain duties. The Whigs argued that the Church's endowment was to serve the 'moral and religious instruction' of *all* parties and not just its own members. As one government spokesman put it, the trust was for the 'well-being and harmony of the state' and for the benefit of its citizens generally.[3] In catering to a minority population, the Whigs argued that the Church of Ireland was not fulfilling its part of the bargain.[4] Therefore, parliament had every right to 'interfere in its administration' and every right to 'ensure that the terms of the trust were met'.[5]

As was to be expected, the bill met with a mixed reception. Many backbenchers, particularly Irish and radical MPs, were delighted. It was a step in the right direction. On the other hand, conservatively-minded churchmen were outraged. Some dubbed it the 'Irish Church Robbery Bill'. Newman himself was equally appalled. He kept referring to it variously as the 'Sacrilege Bill', the 'Spoliation Bill', the 'Erastian Bill', and the 'Irish Sees extinction Bill'.[6] The dedicated Protestant MP representing the University of Oxford said that dismantling half the Church of Ireland was as

[3] Lord John Russell (1792–1878) in his speech to the House of Commons.

[4] One official source estimated that the Protestant minority in Ireland was roughly one tenth of the total population.

[5] R. Brent, *Liberal Anglican Politics: Whiggery, Religion, and Reform 1830–1841*, Oxford 1987, pp. 65–6.

[6] *The Letters and Diaries of John Henry Newman* (*L.D.*) IV, p. 9, letter to Henry Wilberforce, 16 July 1833; Newman also referred to the bill as the 'Spoliation Bill', the 'Erastian Bill' (ibid., p. 17), and the 'Irish Sees extinction Bill' (ibid., p. 175).

good as destroying it altogether.[7] The Bishop of Durham deplored the legislation as 'utterly subversive of every rational view of an Established Church'.[8] It was sounding ominously like the death knell for the Church of England.[9]

At the time the bill was being debated in parliament, Newman was out of England on a seven-month tour of the Mediterranean with a friend and the friend's father.[10] One of his first reactions to the legislation came while he was in Malta: 'How awful seems the crime (to me here) of demolition in England! All I can say of Whigs, Radicals and the rest is, that they know not what they do.'[11] Later, from Naples, after hearing more details of the 'Irish Church Reform Bill', he again exploded: 'well done, my blind Premier [Earl Grey], confiscate and rob, till, like Samson, you pull down the political structure on your own head, tho' without his deliberate purpose and his good cause!'[12] By the time he got to Rome, his anger against this 'atrocious Irish sacrilege bill' continued unabated. He now hated the Whigs 'more bitterly than ever'.[13] Having had no letters from home since leaving, he was curious to know 'what various individuals in England think of this cursed Irish spoliation

[7] Sir Robert Inglis (1786–1855) who represented Oxford University from 1829 to 1854.

[8] William Van Mildert (1765–1836).

[9] E.A. Varley, *The Last of the Prince Bishops: William Van Mildert and the High Church Movement of the early nineteenth century*, Cambridge 1992, p. 185.

[10] Richard Hurrell Froude (1803–36), fellow of Oriel College, and his father, Archdeacon Robert Hurrell Froude (1770–1859).

[11] *L.D.* III, p. 206, letter to Mrs Newman, 26 January 1833.

[12] ibid., p. 224, letter to Mrs Newman, 28 February 1833.

[13] ibid., p. 242, letter to Thomas Mozley, 9 March 1833.

bill.'[14] He had also picked up rumours that the government, once the Church of Ireland had had its house set in order, was going to make sure that the Church of England was to be reformed.[15] He was also critical of the king's role in the affair.[16] He has 'literally betrayed us'. By becoming the 'creature of an Infidel Parliament', our sovereign had forfeited his royal right to appoint bishops.[17] 'If I were a Bishop', he threatened, 'the first thing I would do would be to excommunicate Lord Grey and a half a dozen more, whose names it is almost a shame and a pollution for a Christian to mention.'[18]

Newman returned to Oxford on 9 July 1833. On the following Sunday morning,[19] John Keble preached his celebrated Assize sermon on 'National Apostasy' at St Mary the University Church, Oxford, a fortnight before the bill passed successfully through the House of Lords.[20] In front of visiting judges, Keble denounced the government's sacrilegeous treatment of the Church of Ireland.[21] In cutting back on the number of bishoprics in Ireland, the State was violating the ancient doctrine of Apostolical Succession. In a preface to the printed sermon, Keble

[14] ibid., p. 247, letter to Henry Wilberforce, 9 March 1833.

[15] ibid., p. 259, letter to Edward Bouverie Pusey, 19 March 1833.

[16] William IV (1765–1837).

[17] ibid., p. 300, letter to H.A. Woodgate, 17 April 1833.

[18] *L.D.* IV, p. 32, letter to J.W. Bowden, 20 August 1833.

[19] 14 July 1833.

[20] 30 July 1833. The Irish Church Temporalities Bill became law on 14 August 1833. Like Newman, John Keble was a fellow of Oriel College. After Newman's conversion to Rome in 1845, the two friends did not meet for another twenty years.

[21] Assize was an assembly of judges from the courts of Westminster which held sessions in certain regional centres twice a year.

asked how loyal Anglicans could be expected to 'continue their communion' with the Established Church, '(hitherto the pride and comfort of their lives,) without any taint of those Erastian Principles on which she is now avowedly to be governed? What answer can we make henceforth to the partisans of the Bishop of Rome, when they taunt us with being a mere Parliamentary Church? And how, consistently with our present relations with *the State*, can even the doctrinal purity and integrity of the MOST SACRED ORDER be preserved?'[22] In Newman's later opinion, Keble's 'National Apostasy' sermon marked the beginning of the Oxford Movement.[23]

From a political and economic point of view, there was, indeed, a strong case for reforming the Church of Ireland. From a theological point of view, however, many Churchmen, including Newman himself, saw the move as indefensible. Doctrinal truth must never bow to political and economic expedience. The Church's position was unique for it was not just another arm of government ruled from and answerable to the whim of any political alliance that happened to be in office at the time. With the passing of the bill, ten Irish bishoprics had been abolished and indignant High Churchmen were told to be thankful that more drastic measures had not been enacted. It was at this point that a small group of High Churchmen took decisive action.

[22] John Keble, 'National Apostasy', p. iv, *Sermons Academical, and Occasional*, Oxford 1848, p. 128. 'Erastianism, – that is, the union of . . . Church and State' *Apologia pro Vita Sua* (*Apo.*, p. 39).

[23] *Apo.*, p. 35.

Tractarian Countermeasures

A meeting was held at a rectory in Hadleigh, Suffolk, the home of the highly respectable and well-connected Hugh James Rose, to discuss tactics in July 1833.[24] It decided on two courses of action: establish a number of committees to promote High Church principles; and organise a petition to the Archbishop of Canterbury.[25] Newman thought the strategies, good as they were, did not go far enough. Stronger action was needed. Since living 'movements do not come from committees', he proposed to a group of friends that they form an informal alliance to publish and distribute a series of tracts to fellow clergy round the country.[26] This briefly was the beginning of the celebrated *Tracts for the Times* which were to have such an impact on the Church of England over the next few decades.[27] Newman kicked off the project by writing the first three tracts. They were short, sharp trumpet blasts to remind clergy that the Church of England was separate from and independent of the State. *Tract* 1 focused on the question of Apostolical Succession which, Newman insisted, was a divine gift handed down from the Apostles in trust to the present generation of bishops who alone had the right to govern itself without outside interference. Politicians have no right to meddle in Church affairs. If they

[24] Newman himself did not attend. Among those who did were Richard Hurrell Froude and William Palmer of Worcester College.

[25] In the end, an address of 7000 clergy was presented to the Archbishop, William Cowley, on 6 February 1834.

[26] *Apo.*, p. 39. The group included John Keble and Richard Hurrell Froude.

[27] Between 1833 and 1841, ninety tracts were written, printed and distributed.

think they can, then they labour under the illusion that the 'test of your Divine commission' boils down to performance and popularity. To sit idly on the side lines 'much longer will be itself to take part'. Therefore, gentleman, '*Choose* your side' since, sooner or later, you will have to. Neutrality is not an option in these 'troublous times'.[28] Are you satisfied to be turned into puppets of the State, like other civil servants? 'Did the State make us? can it unmake us? can it send out missionaries? can it arrange dioceses?' Paul the Apostle would have put up a fight if some Roman bureaucrat had decided to appoint Timothy Bishop of Miletus while he was still Bishop of Ephesus. Nor, for that matter, would Timothy have sat idly by. Of twenty tracts printed in 1833, Newman wrote, or had a hand in writing, eleven.[29]

Having, at that time, no other formal duties than Vicar of St Mary's, Newman threw himself whole-

[28] *Tracts for the Times*, London 1834, Volume I, *Tract* 1: 'Thoughts on the Ministerial Commission', p. 4, 9 September 1833.

[29] ibid., *Tract* 2: 'The Catholic Church', p. 2, 9 September 1833. Other Newman tracts included: *Tract* 3: 'Thoughts respectfully addressed to the Clergy on Alterations in the Liturgy', 5 pp.; 'The Burial Service', 3 pp.; 'The Principle of Unity [Episcopal Authority], 9 September; 1 p.; *Tract* 6: 'The Present Obligation of Primitive Practice', 3 pp.; 'A Sin of the Church' [infrequent celebration of the Eucharist], 1 p., 29 October; *Tract* 7: 'The Episcopal Church Apostolical', 4 pp., 29 October; *Tract* 8: 'The Gospel a Law of Liberty', 3 pp.; 'Church Reform' [need for 'godly discipline'], 1 p., 31 October; *Tract* 10: 'Heads of a Week-Day Lecture, delivered to a Country Congregation' [Bishops the successors of the Apostles], 6 pp., 4 November; *Tract* 11: 'The Visible Church', Letters I and II, 8 pp., 11 November; *Tract* 15: 'On the Apostolical Succession in the English Church', 11 pp., 13 December; *Tract* 19: 'On arguing concerning the Apostolical Succession. On Reluctance to confess the Apostolical Succession', 4 pp., 23 December; *Tract* 20: 'The Visible Church', Letter III, 4 pp., 24 December (see *L.D.* IV, pp. 385–7).

heartedly into the campaign. Throughout the next few months, he and others rode about the countryside, distributing parcels of tracts and visiting parsonages.[30] In addition to maintaining a large correspondence, he managed to fit in meetings, lunches, dinners and soirées to alert people to the danger facing the Church from an Erastian-minded government. In spite of the hectic pace, he still managed to fit in his study of the Church Fathers.

1833 saw the Whig government at the peak of its popularity. But, as its influence waned, so too did the threat of state interference in church affairs for the time being. As the threat faded, it was natural for the movement to turn its sights on current liberal Anglicans. Like Froude, Newman was of the opinion that Erastianism was the 'parent, or if not the parent, the serviceable and sufficient tool, of liberalism'. And until that union was severed, 'Christian doctrine never could be safe'.[31] What alarmed Newman and his colleagues about these liberals was their habit of hewing and chiselling Christianity into 'an intelligible human system', which they then presented, 'when thus mutilated', as 'remarkable evidence of the truth of the Bible, an *evidence* level to the reason, and superseding the *testimony* of the Apostles'.[32] In Oxford, there was a group of liberal Anglicans who became known as 'Noetics' and who looked, at one stage of

[30] Each of the early tracts sold for 1*d*. Later longer tracts sold for as much as 1*s*. 3*d*. By November of 1833, the first printing of Tract 1 had completely sold out.

[31] *Apo.*, p. 39.

[32] *Tracts for the Times*, *Tract* 73, 'On the Introduction of Rationalistic Principles into Religion', p. 14. See *Essays Critical and Historical* I, p. 48.

their career, as if they would be the moving force in the government of the Church of England.[33] In reality, they turned out to be the rearguard of a school of apologists which had its origins in the writings of John Locke (1632–1704), the father of British rationalism.[34] They included figures such as Renn Dickson Hampden, Thomas Arnold, Baden Powell, Edward Hawkins, Edward Copleston and Richard Whately.

Rationalism, enlightened common sense and private judgment were the tools they used to present anew traditional Christian teaching. They were suspicious of dogmatic certainty, primitive Christianity, ancient creeds, catechisms, the sacramental system, general councils, monasticism, celibacy, miracles, the priesthood and episcopal authority. To them, time-honoured definitions of the Trinity and the Incarnation were products of the human mind, and based on the 'tyranny of authority' rather than on what was rational, sensible and practical.[35] Once Newman and his colleagues became aware of the harm their principles were doing to the faith of ordinary Churchgoers, they went on the offensive. As he pointed out to his former mentor, Richard Whately, he strongly objected, among other

[33] The term 'Noetic' is derived from Aristotle's *Nicomachean Ethics* (Book VI). Originally, Noetics were individuals who exercised their intellectual faculties to the highest possible degree in contrast to those who did not.

[34] Locke's *Essay Concerning Human Understanding* (1690) influenced the course of European thought for the next one hundred years.

[35] R.D. Hampden, *The Scholastic Philosophy Considered in its Relation to Christian Theology* (Oxford 1833), p. 13. Throughout the Middle Ages, scholasticism, with its worldview derived from Aristotle and Arabian philosophers, had been a controlling factor in the way philosophers, scientists and theologians had traditionally tried to make sense of the world they lived in.

things, to his 'dangerous' undervaluing of 'antiquity', to his over-confident trust in his own 'reasonings, judgments' and 'definitions', and to his rejection of 'authority and precedent'.[36] Thus it was that many of the later longer tracts were aimed at the corrosive influence of liberal Anglican thought on traditional Anglo-Catholic principles.[37]

In addition to writing and distributing tracts, Newman also came up with the idea of looking at the writings of the Church Fathers to see whether parallels might not exist between what had happened in primitive Christianity in the fourth century and what was happening in the Church of England in the 1830s.[38] The idea soon snowballed into a series of articles on the fourth-century Church which he began submitting to a periodical called the *British Magazine* founded in 1832 to promote Anglo-Catholic principles and to oppose radical Whig reforms.[39] By mid-August, he sent four completed articles to its editor, Hugh James Rose, who agreed to start publishing them as a series, beginning with the October issue.[40] But the

[36] *L.D.* IV, p. 358, letter to Richard Whately, Archbishop of Dublin, 11 November 1834.

[37] For example, Newman wrote *Tract* 73, 'On the introduction of rationalistic principles into religion', 56 pp, 2 February 1836; and *Tract* 85, 'Lectures in the Scripture Proof of the Doctrines of the Church', 115 pp., 21 September 1838.

[38] *L.D.* IV, p. 24, letter to Thomas Mozley, 5 August 1833.

[39] *The British Magazine and Monthly Register of Religious and Ecclesiastical Information, Parochial History, and Documents Respecting the State of the Poor, Progress of Education, &c.*

[40] *L.D.* IV, p. 30, letter H.J. Rose to Newman, 20 August 1833. This was the same Hugh James Rose at whose Suffolk rectory in July 1833 it was decided to present a petition to the Archbishop of Canterbury protesting about government interference in church affairs. Although initially sympathetic to the Tractarian movement, he later became wary of it.

cautious Rose, realising the controversial nature of the material, decided to relegate them to the correspondence section under the general title, 'Letters on the Church of the Fathers' and prefaced with the following editorial comment: 'The Editor begs to remind his readers that he is not responsible for the opinions of his Correspondents'. And it was from there that he continued publishing them anonymously on a regular basis from October 1833 to February 1838.[41] The first three letters focused on Ambrose's stormy relationship with the imperial court at Milan which was forever meddling in Church affairs. The fourth letter concentrated on the emperor Valens' jealous attempts to neutralise as much as possible the influence of Basil the Great as exarch of Cappadocia. Altogether, Newman wrote twenty-one so-called 'letters'.[42] They ranged over a variety of topics – from Church-State issues to celibacy and monasticism; from miracles and relics to episcopal authority and the Apostolical Canons.

The *Church of the Fathers* is very frequently

[41] Rose's decision to relegate the articles to the correspondence section must have rankled with Newman for many years. At the beginning of the unfortunate *Rambler* affair in 1859, he reflected that all 'through my life I have been plucked. My first book, the Arians, was plucked by Rose and Lyell [Lyall]. My Church of the Fathers [1833], instead of being . . . part of the [[British]] Magazine, appeared among the correspondence (*L.D.* XIX, p. 181, letter to Henry Wilberforce, 20 July 1859).

[42] In 1834, Newman wrote a further letter for inclusion in the *British Magazine* on the martyrs Gervasius and Protasius, but, for one reason or another, withdrew it from the series. A different essay on the same topic appeared in *The Church of the Fathers* in 1840 and subsequent editions. He also published an account of the martyrs in his second essay on ecclesiastical miracles in *Essays on Miracles* under the title 'Recovery of the Blind Man by the Relics of St. Gervasius and St. Protasius at Milan', Section VIII, pp. 348–68. For the original Gervasius and Protasius letter, see Appendix 6.

described as one of Newman's Anglican Works, even when reference is being made to (or even quotation being made from) the *Historical Sketches*. In reality, there is both an Anglican *Church of the Fathers* (that of 1840 and subsequent editions), and a Catholic *Church of the Fathers* (those of 1868 and 1873). In places, many passages and even long series of pages are almost identical, while elsewhere, the contrast is striking; and, of course, there are many excisions, some of considerable length. Newman's evocation of the spiritual and moral ethos of the early Church is perhaps more successful in the Catholic text, but that text also loses much of the Tractarian acerbity. Indeed, a great deal of the strategy and agenda of the movement is to be found in the 1840 edition.[43]

II. TEXTS AND CRITICAL RESPONSES

'Letters on the Church of the Fathers': 1833–1838

The first of the 'Letters on the Church of the Fathers' focuses on Ambrose of Milan's celebrated clash with the pro-Arian empress, Justina, and her son, the boy emperor, Valentinian II. Newman wanted to remind ordinary Churchgoers of his day that, as the early Church had to rely on the laity for its survival in its struggle with the State, the present Church may well have to do the same again in the 1830s, now that its bishops and clergy had been left high-and-dry by the

[43] It is unfortunate that, in a biography that is so comprehensive in its scope (and so rightly and hugely admired), Ian Ker's *John Henry Newman* (Oxford 1988) relies exclusively on the 1873 text when discussing the work in its Tractarian setting.

State. The opening lines draw attention to the parallels he saw between the early Church's uneasy relationship with the State in Ambrose's day and the Church of England's uneasy relationship with the government alliance of his day:

> No considerate person will deny that there is much in the spirit of the times, and in the actual changes which the British constitution has lately undergone, which makes it probable, or not improbable, that a material alteration will soon take place in the relations of the church towards the state, to which it has been hitherto united. I do not say it is out of the question that things may return to their former quiet and happy course, as in the good old time of king George III.; but the very chance that that they will not, makes it a practical concern for each churchman to prepare himself for a change, and a practical question for the clergy, by *what instruments* the authority of religion is to be supported, when the protection and recommendation of the government are withdrawn. ... My question concerns *the church*, that peculiar institution which Christ set up as a visible home and memorial of truth; and which, being of this world, must be supported by means of this world.[44]

In former times, the Anglican clergy had 'the *state*' to depend on, but now, and 'I shall disgust many men when I say, we must *look to the people*'.[45] It is not us who have deserted the State, rather the other

[44] *Brit. Mag.*, Volume IV, No. I, 421–3, October 1833.
[45] ibid., p. 422.

way round. Thus, present circumstances have forced us 'back on those below us, because those above us will not support us'.[46] One has only to look at the early Church for parallels where we come face to face with the 'undeniable fact' that the Church was always at its 'purest and most powerful' when it looked to ordinary people for support. To illustrate this particular parallel, he launches into an 'account of certain ecclesiastical proceedings in the city of Milan, AD 385, during the holy season of Lent,' when Ambrose was leader of the Church in Milan, and the empress Justina and her son were the 'reigning powers' of the State.[47]

Later letters bring out, with great gusto and energy, other issues such as the importance of monasticism and celibacy in the early Church. At this point, Newman begins to have second thoughts about their reception by the public. He has 'some misgivings' whether or not he has been 'too bold in the June Magazine' which looks at early monasticism.[48] The second paragraph, deleted from all subsequent editions of *The Church of the Fathers*, contained statements which would have shocked the sensitivities of the average Churchgoer of the 1830s – statements which suggest that the monastic way of life is *not* necessarily *incompatible* with Gospel values, as was generally believed. To argue that monasticism *is* incompatible simply on the grounds that there is nothing about it in the Gospels, 'is as about as sensible as to say there is nothing about deans and chapters, rich rectors,

[46] ibid.
[47] ibid., pp. 422–3.
[48] *L.D.* V, pp. 99–100, letter to Richard Hurrell Froude, 16 July 1835.

bishops in parliament; nothing (much more) about the lawfulness of commerce, the rights of man':

> Certainly it is as accordant with Scripture that a Christian should live in prayer and fasting, poverty and almsgiving, as that he should pass all his best days in making money, gain a patent of peerage, and found a family. It is not more culpable, *in the nature of things*, for a given individual to take a vow of celibacy, than to take a vow in marriage; though of course it is as sinful in a father to force a daughter into a convent as it is to force her to a marriage she dislikes, and as inexpedient to take a monastic vow hastily, as to marry before one has come to years of discretion. And if people lift up their hands and eyes and cry out this is Popery, I beg to ask them in which of the Articles monasticism is condemned? and, since I do not force them to agree with me, I claim that liberty of 'private judgment' in indifferentials which I accord to them.[49]

In retrospect, he wonders whether he may not be 'not burdening my well-wishers with too heavy a load, when I oblige them to take up and defend these opinions too'. Even some of his supporters thought that he was out of step with current thinking on the issue. His reply was to ally himself with the thinking of the early Church and to throw 'myself on the general Church, and avow (as I do) that if anyone will show me any opinion of mine which the primitive Church condemned I will renounce it – any which it

[49] 'Letters on the Church of the Fathers', No. XII, *Brit. Mag*, Volume 7, June 1835, p. 663.

did not insist on, I will not insist on it.'[50] Towards the end of that year, Rose was able to reassure him that the general feedback about the 'Letters on the Church of the Fathers' had been very favourable, in fact, they have probably 'done more good than almost anything which has come forth of late – and heartily do I wish it could go on.'[51]

Apart from the general title, 'Letters on the Church of the Fathers', only Letter XVI, for some reason or other, was given a specific title – namely, 'Church of the Fathers. – No. XVI. Apollinaris'. They focused on:

1. Ambrose of Milan versus the empress Justina (October 1833).
2. Ambrose of Milan versus the emperor Valentinian II (November 1833).
3. Ambrose of Milan versus the emperor Theodosius I (December 1833).
4. Basil the Great versus the emperor Valens (December 31, 1833).
5. Basil the Great's chequered career as Bishop of Caesarea and exarch of Cappadocia (February 1834).
6. Further trials and tribulations of Basil the Great (June 1834).
7. Basil the Great's deteriorating relationship with Gregory of Nazianzus (July 1834).
8. Gregory's rise and fall (August 1834).
9. Gregory of Nazianzus as Patriarch of Constantinople (September 1834).

[50] *L.D.* V, pp. 99–100, letter to Richard Hurrell Froude, 16 July 1835.
[51] ibid., p. 178, 1n.

10. Augustine of Hippo versus the Vandals (October 1834).
11. Augustine's conversion (May 1835).
12. Augustine in Roman north Africa (June 1835).
13. Trials and tribulations of Antony of Egypt, the father of monasticism (July 1835).
14. Further trials and tribulations of Antony (August 1835).
15. Antony the man (September 1835).
16. Life and ideas of the heresiarch, Apollinaris (July 1836).
17. Apollinaris versus the great Athanasius (August 1836).
18. Jovinian, the unorthodox monk, versus Cyril, orthodox Patriarch of Jerusalem (September 1836).
19. Authority of the Apostolical Canons of the early Church I (April 1837).
20. Authority of the Apostolical Canons of the early Church II (May 1837).
21. Authority of the Apostolical Canons of the early Church III (February 1838).

First and second editions: 1840, 1842

About a year after the appearance of the last 'Letters on the Church of the Fathers' in the *British Magazine* in 1838, Newman decided to publish a revised version in book form with the title, *The Church of the Fathers.* As the date of publication drew near in March 1840, he once again became 'very anxious' about the contents which he described as 'strong meat'. So nervous was he that he withheld his name from the cover. 'I suppose I must expect a clamour', he wrote resignedly, 'unless persons are tired of clamouring'.[52] In the meantime, he was rewriting and reshaping large portions of it.[53] At one point, he thought the whole thing was 'so dreadfully monastic, that I have some tremours what will happen to me'.[54] Once, however, he had an advance copy from the publishers in his hands, he relaxed and changed his tune. It was now, he thought, the '*prettiest* book I have done', which, when one thinks about it, was not surprising as it contained nothing more 'than the words and works of the Fathers'. He continued to be nervous about the public reaction on reading the views of the Fathers on celibacy, miracles, and the like.[55] He dedicated the book to his friend, Isaac Williams, fellow Tractarian, poet and his former curate at St. Mary, the University Church, Oxford:[56]

TO MY DEAR AND MUCH ADMIRED
ISAAC WILLIAMS, B.D.,
FELLOW OF TRINITY COLLEGE, OXFORD,
THE SIGHT OF WHOM
CARRIES BACK HIS FRIENDS
TO ANCIENT, HOLY, AND HAPPY TIMES.[57]

As he explained in the preface, his aim was 'to illustrate, as far as they go, the tone and modes of thought,

[52] *L.D.* VII, p. 202, letter to J.W. Bowden, 5 January 1840.
[53] ibid., pp. 213; 223, letter to his sister Jemima, 14 January 1840; letter to Henry Wilberforce, 21 January 1840.
[54] ibid., p. 218, letter to H.A. Woodgate, 17 January 1840.
[55] *L.D.* VII, p. 241, letter to J.W. Bowden, 21 February 1840.
[56] Isaac Williams (1802–65) had been Newman's curate at St. Mary the Virgin, University Church, Oxford and its sister church at nearby Littlemore.
[57] In the 1857 and 1868 editions, Newman added a date to the dedication: '*Feb.* 21, 1840.'

the habits and manners' of the early Church. His intended audience was the general public, and not a specialist one.[58] He added four new chapters: one on Vincent of Lerins; two on Martin of Tours; and one on the martyrs Gervasius and Protasius which was a completely different essay from the one he had withdrawn in 1834. As it turned out, there were twenty-one chapters in all – the same number as had appeared in the *British Magazine*, but arranged somewhat differently. Some remained untouched, while others underwent modification of one sort or another. The chapters were as follows:

I. Ambrose and Justina
II. Ambrose and Valentinian
III. The martyrs Gervasius and Protasius
IV. The penitence of Theodosius
V. Basil the Great
VI. Trials of Basil
VII. Labours of Basil
VIII. Basil and Gregory
IX. Rise and fall of Gregory
X. Vincentius of Lerins
XI. Apollinaris
XII. Augustine and the Vandals
XIII. Conversion of Augustine
XIV. Demetrias
XV. Jovinian and his companions
XVI. Canons of the Apostles
XVII. Canons of the Apostles
XVIII. Antony in conflict

[58] *The Church of the Fathers*, 1840 edition, pp. iv; vii.

XIX. Antony in calm
XX. Martin, the Apostle of Gaul
XXI. Martin and Priscillian

As it turned out, *The Church of the Fathers* proved popular with Tractarians of 'both sexes, who found in it for the first time the inspiration of the lives of the saints, as real and human as if they were still alive, as indeed they were to Newman'.[59] A second edition appeared in 1842, again without his name on the cover.[60]

Critical response

As expected, *The Church of the Fathers* did draw criticism from certain quarters. One irate clergyman from Lichfield could not believe how Newman could 'offend and alienate' so 'many really thoughtful men' by his sneering attitude towards the Established Church and by his provocative statements on the invocation of the saints and celibacy. In reply, an unapologetic Newman admitted that, in saying what he did, he probably did get some people offside, 'but on the other hand I know perfectly (if one must appeal to *results*) that I gain ardent and superior minds by the very things by which the persons to whom you allude might be offended'. It was difficult to please everybody – in fact, downright impossible. 'I utterly despair of pleasing all persons, and find that, as I conciliate one, I offend another.' Ever since he and his

[59] Meriol Trevor, *Pillar of the Cloud*, p. 231, London 1962.

[60] On the title page of both the 1840 and 1842 editions, Newman inserted a quote from the Song of Solomon (6: 10) from the King James' Version: 'Who is she that looketh forth as the morning, fair as the moon, clear as the sun, and terrible as an army with banners?'

friends had begun writing on such subjects, 'to which the Church of the Fathers relates':

> ... we have been exclaimed against, reprobated, *and followed*. If you had our experience of the *indignation* and *horror* which has been the process through which men have been persuaded and converted[,] how they protested against points which can now be quietly assumed as first principles, how we are accused of intemperance and rancour for writings which are now blamed as plausible, artful, and affectedly dispassionate, you would not wonder that I cannot help anticipating that some persons who just now are startled at the 'Church of the Fathers' may end in allowing its statements, if not in approving them. The newest Tract or Volume has always been *the* indiscreet one, and our last point but one has been that at which we ought to have stopped.[61]

As an example of Newman's sneering attitude to the Church of England, the same irate gentleman had singled out his comments on Gregory of Nazianzus' panegyric on Basil the Great.[62] Newman pointed out that he also knew several people 'who have been much taken with those pages of my book, who see in them no "sneer" at our church,' and 'who feel in them nothing repugnant to their Anglo-catholic principles.'[63] As for his comments on the invocation of

[61] *L.D.* VII, p. 330, letter to Henry Moore, Vicar of St. Mary's, Lichfield north of Birmingham in Staffordshire. 21 May 1840.

[62] see *Historical Sketches* II, p. 75ff.

[63] *L.D.* VII, pp. 330–1.

saints, he was convinced that his views were similar to the correspondent's own views, namely, that invoking the saints, 'though not abstractedly wrong, has been proved by experience to be dangerous':

> At the same time surely it is a great principle of our church, as expressed in the Canons of 1603, that 'usam non tollit abusus' ['the abuse of a thing doth not take away the lawful use of it']; whereas to urge the abuse against the use is the very ground of the Puritans, which Hooker is at such pains to invalidate. Scripture is as silent about kneeling at the reception of the Elements or crossing in Baptism, as about making mention of the saints, after St Gregory's manner; on the other hand in our daily service we say, 'O ye spirits and souls of the righteous, O Ananias, Azarias, and Misael, bless ye the Lord,' which would seem to show that there are invocations which are not 'Romish.'[64]

As for the reverend gentleman's views on celibacy and the married state, does not the notion that the celibate life 'is not a holier state than matrimony' smack somewhat of Pelagianism?[65]

An Oriel colleague of Newman, William James, then Vicar of Rawmarsh in Yorkshire, wrote to him telling of the 'great pleasure' *The Church of the Fathers* had given

[64] Virtually up to the time of his conversion to Rome in 1845, Newman adopted a cautious approach to the invocation of saints. While frowning on the practice of praying *to* a particular saint, he saw nothing wrong in asking a saint to intercede on a person's behalf, but was very much aware that the practice was open to abuse. See *Loss and Gain*, pp. 238–40.

[65] ibid., p. 331.

him, 'particularly the first part'.[66] He did, however, have one or two reservations. He thought that the chapters on the so-called "Canons of the Apostles" lacked conviction.[67] For one reason or another, he was left with the impression that Newman was trying to say that they were authoritative documents and were *still* binding on the Church today. In reply, Newman said that he never dreamt of implying anything of the sort. First and foremost, he was interested in examining the Apostolical Canons collectively and not individually in order to show 'the *sort of religion*' which was practised in the early Church with the hope of ascertaining whether any trace of 'Protestantism, as the word is popularly understood', ever existed in primitive Christianity. Next, he was interested in determining the 'kind of religion' bequeathed to the early Church by the Apostles. Furthermore, he was implying that the so-called Canons were simply examples of received usage in those times.[68] Finally, there was a vast difference between church rules and church principles. Church rules, such as the rules of fasting are subject to alteration, while church principles, such as the sacraments, are absolutely *unalterable*.[69]

[66] William James (1787–1861) was a fellow of Oriel College from 1809 to 1837. It was he who first taught Newman about the doctrine of Apostolical Succession.

[67] *L.D.* VIII, p. 494, 1n. It was a lengthy and detailed letter to Newman, 12 March 1842.

[68] Although Newman did add: 'though I think on the whole they *were* Canons'. Although attributed to the Apostles, the 85 Canons were compiled as a concluding chapter to the *Apostolical Constitutions* in the late fourth century. They dealt mainly with ordination matters plus clerical duties and responsibilities. Many eventually found their way into the early canon law of the western Church.

[69] *L.D.* VIII, pp. 494–5, letter to William James, Easter Monday, 28 March 1842.

Third and fourth editions: 1857 and 1868

At the time of the third edition of *The Church of the Fathers* in 1857, Newman was a Roman Catholic priest. For this particular edition, he withdrew eight of the original chapters – the four chapters on Ambrose, the two on the Apostolical Canons, and the two on Vincent of Lerins and Jovinian. Apart from that, the material remained the same as in the 1840 edition 'with such trivial alterations, as were rendered necessary by the circumstances under which they were written.'[70] But he was quite aware that no number of alterations would completely wipe clean 'the polemical character of a work directed originally against Protestant ideas':

> And this consideration must plead for certain peculiarities, which it exhibits, such as its freedom in dealing with saintly persons, the gratuitous character of some of its assertions, and the liberality of many of its concessions. It must be recollected, that, in controversy, a writer grants all that he can afford to grant, and makes use of all that he can get granted: – in other words, if he seems to admit, it is mainly 'for argument's sake'; and if he seems to affirm, it is mainly as an 'argumentum ad hominem'. As to positive statements of his own, he commits himself to as few as he can; just as a soldier on campaign takes no more baggage than is enough, and considers the conveniences of home only *impedimenta* in his march.[71]

[70] At that stage, Newman was still a member of the Church of England.
[71] *The Church of the Fathers*, third edition, Dublin 1857, pp. vii–viii.

The structure of the 1857 edition was as follows:

Introduction
I. Basil the Great
II. Trials of Basil
III. Labours of Basil
IV. Basil and Gregory
V. Rise and Fall of Gregory
VI. Apollinaris
VII. Antony in Conflict
VIII. Antony in Calm
IX. Augustine and the Vandals
X. Conversion of Augustine
XI. Demetrias
XII. Martin, the Apostle of Gaul

Unfortunately, in the 1857 preface, Newman forgot to specify *which* eight chapters were deleted or *why* they were deleted. The 1868 preface now rectified the oversight and explained which ones were deleted and why. The chapters on Ambrose were withdrawn because he had been planning a re-write 'at some future day with care and pains less unworthy of the great Saint commemorated in them'. As for the chapter on Gervasius and Protasius, he had since written a new account in his *Essay on Ecclesiastical Miracles* and did not want to repeat himself.[72] He withdrew the chapter on Vincent of Lerins because it also had been superseded in 'one of the Oxford Tracts (*Records of the Church*), and

[72] *Two Essays on Biblical and on Ecclesiastical Miracles*, Essay II, 'The Miracles of Early Ecclesiastical History', Chapter V, 'On the Evidence for Particular Alleged Miracles', Section VIII, 'Recovery of the Blind Man by the Relics of the Martyrs', pp. 348–68.

by the Oxford Edition of the work.'[73] As for the chapters on Jovinian and the Apostolical Canons, he withdrew them 'on account of their controversial and antiquarian character, which made them uninteresting to the general reader.' Finally, the two chapters on Martin of Tours were merged into one chapter.[74] The table of contents for the 1868 edition remained virtually the same as in the previous edition, except that Chapter XII, 'Martin, the Apostle of Gaul' now became 'Martin and Maximus'.

For both editions, Newman replaced the King James' version of the Song of Solomon (6: 10) with the Latin Vulgate, Canticle of Canticles (6: 9):

> QUÆ EST ISTA, QUÆ PROGREDITUR, QUASI AURORA CONSURGENS, TERRIBILIS UT CASTRORUM ACIES ORDINATA.[75]

Although retaining the Isaac Williams dedication, he added a new one, this time to another friend, Robert Isaac Wilberforce (1802–57):

[73] *Records of the Church* was published concurrently with the *Tracts for the Times* and sold as separate pamphlets. 'Vincentius of Lerins on the Tests of Heresy and Error' was Number XXIV in the series and prefaced with the words: 'The Holy Church Throughout All the World Doth Acknowledge Thee'. It was published in 1835, sold for twopence and was eight pages long. As for the 1837 Oxford edition of the Vincent's *Commonitory*, Newman specifically refers to it in *Historical Sketches* I, p. 382, 1n.

[74] *The Church of the Fathers*, fourth edition, London 1868, pp. xiii–xiv.

[75] 'Who is she that cometh forth as the morning rising ... terrible as an army set in array'.

TO A FRIEND,
WHO IS AS DEAR TO ME NOW,
AS WHEN HIS NAME STOOD HERE,
AND THREW LIGHT OVER MY PAGES;
WHOSE HEART IS IN GOD'S HAND,
TO BRING INTO THAT SACRED HERITAGE,
WHICH IS BOTH THE CHURCH OF THE FATHERS,
AND THE HOME OF THE CHILDREN.

March 25, 1857[76]

Wilberforce was the second eldest son of the reformer, philanthropist and Evangelical leader, William Wilberforce (1759–1833). A competent theologian, his treatise on the Incarnation in 1848 was one of the outstanding achievements of the Oxford Movement. He became a Catholic in 1854, went to Rome to study for the priesthood, but died of fever a few weeks before ordination. He was fifty-five. His brothers, Henry and William, also became Catholics while another brother, Samuel, became Anglican Bishop of Oxford and later of Winchester. The 1868 edition retained the dual dedications.

Naturally, Newman's focus in *The Church of the Fathers* had altered since becoming a Roman Catholic in 1845. Gone was the emphasis on the anti-Erastian High Church principles triggered off by the Irish Church Temporalities Bill of 1833. By this stage, he was more interested in showing how the current Church of England and Bible Christians differed from the early Church. For example, Antony of Egypt,

[76] *March* 25: Feast day of the Annunciation. The actual date was not included in the 1857 edition.

the father of monasticism, now comes across as a latter-day example of an 'enthusiast'. Had he been living in England as a 'Protestant in this Protestant day' and age, he would have been labelled a fanatic. If he wanted to live the life of a monk, he would most probably have been ostracised for unsocial and un-gentlemanlike behaviour. Society, with its strict code of conduct, would have forced the Antonys of this world to bend or break its rules. Apart from hostility and ostracism, English society had no other way of coping with such individuals. It 'provides no occupation for them, does not understand how to turn them to account, lets them run to waste, tempts them to dissent, loses them, is weakened by the loss, and then denounces them'. Contrary to current popular opinion, Antony's lifestyle was not of the 'vulgar, bustling, imbecile, unstable, undutiful' type as most people imagine it was. If the truth be known, it was 'calm and composed, manly, intrepid, magnanimous, full of affectionate loyalty to the Church and to the Truth.'[77]

One of the great achievements of early monasticism was its concern for the truth 'in times and places in which great masses of Catholics had let it slip from them'. Thus, Jerome's cave at Bethlehem and Augustine's monasteries in north Africa became havens of 'holiness' at a time when Christians were becoming more and more secular. And that is why the monastic way of life 'will always be attempted by the more serious and anxious part of the community, whenever Christianity is generally expressed' – in spite of society's disapproving glances. In Protestant

[77] *H.S.* II, pp. 98–9.

countries, where that particular lifestyle is virtually 'unknown', individuals will continue to drop out of the mainstream of religion and join whatever splinter group happens to be in fashion. That is why Methodism continues to attract disillusioned members who were once 'sincerely attached to the Established Church, merely because that Church will admit nothing but what it considers "rational" and "sensible" in religion.'

According to Newman, the average Protestant seems to glory in the fact that *their* Church will never be seduced into adopting monasticism as part of the Christian way of life. If she cannot accept its reality, then 'it is plain that the religious temper of Protestant times is not like that of the primitive Church', for clearly, the early Church '*did*' adopt the monastic way of life.[78] The modern hostility in Protestant circles to monasteries and convents, particularly for women, is a matter of great regret:

> I know not any more distressing development of the cruel temper of Protestantism than the determined, bitter, and scoffing spirit in which it has set itself against institutions which give dignity and independence to the position of women in society. As matters stand, marriage is almost the only shelter which a defenceless portion of the community has against the rude world ... whereas, foundations for single women, under proper precautions, at once hold out protection to those who avail themselves of them, and give dignity to the single state itself,

[78] ibid., pp. 164–5.

> and thus save numbers from the temptation of throwing themselves rashly away upon unworthy objects, thereby transgressing their own sense of propriety, and embittering their future life.[79]

Critical response

The following extracts come from a review of the 1868 edition of *The Church of the Fathers* in an Anglican periodical called *The Church Review*, Saturday, 1 August 1868. Newman kept a copy of it in his room at the Birmingham Oratory:

> The dates, however, which this book carries on its title and dedication pages – 1840, 1857, 1868 – suggest to us a comparison between the relation which it bears to the Newman of the first and that which it bears to the Newman of the two last. How forcibly this sketch of the 'Church of the Fathers' contrasted with Anglicanism even when its writer was still an Anglican, is a fact which we, of all others, are not likely to under-estimate. As we have often shewn in these columns, we consider it of primary importance to press this contrast by every means in our power. But the further question naturally comes to the surface in 1857 or 1868, How does it agree or contrast with the Roman theory of the Church now that its author is a Roman? And here we should mention that in the edition of 1868 we have not the original book as it stood in 1840. We still have the marvellous grace of the translations in which Basil and Gregory, Augustine and

[79] ibid., p. 165.

Antony, speak to us in the inimitable English of Newman, without losing a single characteristic of their age and temper, or scarcely of the language in which they conveyed their thoughts. But the book, otherwise, has been revised. Every turn of thought and expression which looked in an Anglican direction has been chastened, and, so far as was possible in dealing with such an early period of the Church, the tone has been made that of a Roman Catholic. We are, therefore, justified in saying that this is a sketch of some portions of the earlier Church – if not from a Roman point of view, for Newman is too honest to force on a particular point of view, yet, – written by a Roman Catholic. It is, therefore, a curious enquiry how far an historical view of the early Church, taken by an honest Roman Catholic, bears out the theological view which his present position compels him to take? It is a puzzling speculation whether Newman ever asked himself, Where was the supreme and infallible Pope in the days of Basil and Gregory?

... Now if a Roman Catholic addressed himself to consider the circumstances of Basil's time in their relation to his present theory, in all probability his very first step would amount to a sacrifice of his position. What he would do would be to take an outside view of the Churches in Asia Minor, looking at them as from within the 'Catholic and Roman Church.' This is at once an admission that there may be a part of the Catholic Church which is not within the Roman Communion, but which holds to it an external relation. It amounts to a complete justification of the

Anglican position. But then this will scarcely do. We know how a Roman proselytizer attempts to overwhelm the mind of the Anglican waverer, and we must insist that he apply his instrument to the whole history of the Church, as well as to a corner of it. He refuses to admit the conception of any Church save the Holy Roman and Apostolic Church. What really took place at any time within the Church, took place within the Roman Church; consequently, we know what the controversialist has to deal with in the case of St. Basil and the Eastern Churches of his day. He is either dealing with a pretended Bishop and pretended Churches as much outside the Church as Protestants and Anglicans at the present day, or he is dealing with a Roman Catholic Bishop and Roman Catholic portions of the Church. Let him elect which leg to stand upon he likes, and let anyone try to imagine the extraordinary gyrations and figures which, with the weight of the Roman theory on his head, he has in either case to cut. Our complaint is, that Roman controversialists are not over-logical or over-ingenuous. They make very tremendous and straightforward claims, but then they make an equally tremendous assumption beforehand. Question the assumption, and the fabric is immediately in danger of coming down like a house of cards.[80]

Uniform edition: 1873

The Church of the Fathers appeared in its final form as the first section of *Historical Sketches* II in the uniform

[80] Birmingham Oratory Archives A. 43. 1.

edition.[81] It contained an introduction and ten chapters. Two chapters, 'Basil the Great' and 'Trials of Basil', were condensed into one chapter under the title, 'Trials of Basil', and the chapter on Apollinaris was deleted altogether. Apart from these amendments, the text remained virtually unaltered. The final format was as follows:

Introduction
I. Trials of Basil
II. Labours of Basil
III. Basil and Gregory
IV. Rise and Fall of Gregory
V. Antony in Conflict
VI. Antony in Calm
VII. Augustine and the Vandals
VIII. Conversion of Augustine
IX. Demetrias
X. Martin and Maximus

'Primitive Christianity'
As Newman told his publisher, 'Primitive Christianity' was 'just *so much*' of *The Church of the Fathers* 'as I cut off from it in 1857, as being controversial and in a different tone from what I let remain'.[82] Basically, it consisted of the eight chapters deleted from the third edition:

I. Ambrose and Justina

[81] The three volumes of *Historical Sketches* were originally printed out of numerical order.

[82] *Letters and Diaries of John Henry Newman* XXVI, pp. 31–2, letter to B.M. Pickering, 25 February 1872.

II. Ambrose and Valentinian
III. The martyrs Gervasius and Protasius
X Vincentius of Lerins
XI. Apollinaris
XV. Jovinian and his companions
XVI. Canons of the Apostles
XVII. Canons of the Apostles

With the exception of the chapter on Apollinaris, they were dropped from subsequent Catholic editions of *The Church of the Fathers* because of their 'polemical matter', which, he felt, would be of little or 'no interest for Catholic readers'.[83] The one chapter never reprinted in either *The Church of the Fathers* or in 'Primitive Christianity' was 'The penitence of Theodosius'.[84] 'Primitive Christianity' finally appears as part four of *Historical Sketches* I and consists of five chapters:

I. What does St. Ambrose say about it?
II. What says Vincent Of Lerins?
III. What says the History of Apollinaris?
IV. What say Jovinian and his companions?
V. What say the Apostolical Canons?

In the first chapter, 'What does St. Ambrose say about it [Primitive Christianity]?', Newman sets out to defend the supremacy of the Church and to quash claims that the state has any legitimate right to meddle in church affairs. Ambrose's celebrated clash with the imperial court in Milan is an example of the fact that

[83] *H.S.* I, p. 335.
[84] See Appendix 5.

the power of the early Church, throughout these turbulent times, 'was based, not (as Protestants imagine) on governments, or on human law, or on endowments, but on popular enthusiasm, on dogma, on hierarchical power, and on a supernatural Divine Presence.'[85] In the final section, Newman examines the miracles which occurred in Milan after the discovery – a veritable miracle in itself – of the remains of two local martyrs, Gervasius and Protasius, martyred during the reign of the emperor Nero around the year 64. The miracles which were said to have occurred gave enormous boost to Ambrose's position – particularly, 'to his doctrine and life, to his ecclesiastical principles and proceedings', and to the 'Church itself of the fourth century, of which he is one main pillar'. The miracles also gave a 'certain sanction to three things at once, to the Catholic doctrine of the Trinity, to the Church's resistance of the civil power, and to the commemoration of saints and martyrs'.[86]

In the second chapter, 'What says Vincent of Lerins?', Newman suggests that most educated people today cannot fully appreciate the seriousness and 'earnestness' with which early Christians defended their faith. For many members of the present Establishment, the most important aspect of Church unity is its 'quiet and unanimity; as if the Church were not built upon faith, and truth really the first object of the Christian's efforts,' and 'peace' but a secondary consideration. The picture that most people have of your average clergyman is, that he should be, first and foremost, 'a man of peace'. And if he ever steps out of

[85] *H.S.* I, p. 342.
[86] ibid., p. 374.

that role 'to denounce, to resist, or to protest,', they recoil in horror exclaiming, 'O how disgraceful in a minister of peace!' For them, the ideal clergyman should be nothing more than a fairly harmless 'reverend gentleman' with a large family, doling out dollops of 'spiritual consolation' to parishioners. Of course, Newman is not denying that 'confessorship for the Catholic faith' *is* an important consideration of a clergyman's duty and, for that matter, of every Christian. But the Church is much more than a 'promoter of good order and sobriety'.[87] It is also a vigorous defender of the faith.

Yet, in this day and age, if and when differences of opinion do arise in 'matters of doctrine between Christians' – and they inevitably will from time to time – then most well-bred people prefer to turn a blind eye and pretend all's well within the Establishment. For them, doctrinal differences are so irrelevant that they cannot understand what the fuss is about – even when the basic belief in a God or the Trinity may be at stake. These so-called practical people think that, by putting their heads in the sand, problems 'will right themselves' by themselves. Is it not more important, they argue, to present a bold, united front to the real enemy – which is Rome – than to be caught squabbling among ourselves? But, Newman points out, practical people sometimes forget that certain remedies can be 'worse than the disease', and 'that latent heresy may be worse' than direct confrontation. No wonder they do so, since they have been so accustomed to talking of the Church and the State as one entity, and equating Protestantism and

[87] ibid., pp. 375–6.

'true religion' in the one breath. For them, the characteristic hallmark of 'our Church' is its so-called 'tolerance', and that the worst calamity to befall it is to be caught be airing doctrinal differences in public, thus shattering the mythology of harmony and peace. Neither Peter nor Paul ever shied away from confrontation whenever the best interests of the Church was at stake. We must never forget 'that weapons were committed to the Church for use as well as for show.'[88]

Nor must we ever forget Vincent of Lerins' rule which kept Athanasius, Hilary, Basil, Gregory and Ambrose on the straight and narrow against 'the spread of Arianism at the risk of their lives' – namely, to believe only in those things which Christians have been taught 'always, everywhere, and universally'. If we follow this rule faithfully, we shall never stray from the path of orthodoxy. It rescues us 'from the misery of having to find out the truth for ourselves from Scripture on our independent and private judgment'. After all, the God who gave us the Scriptures has also given us an interpreter of those Scriptures.[89]

The next chapter on the history of Apollinaris begins by reminding the reader once again that, in primitive Christianity, the 'path of doctrinal truth' has always been a 'narrow' one. This is in sharp contrast to later times when the path became 'so broad as to be no path at all'; when certain elements of society try to dismiss any vigorous defence of the faith as nothing more than a 'strife of words, perverse disputings, curious questions, and unprofitable technicality', even though the early Church considered such methods as

[88] ibid., pp. 375–7.
[89] ibid., p. 381.

essential tools for salvation. What the Church Fathers called 'heresy', present-day society dubs 'orthodoxy'. It can only be wrong, it would say, as long as the advocates of orthodoxy keep on insisting that something is orthodox in the same crude way that the early Fathers kept on insisting that something in their day was orthodox. If Protestants 'differ from the Church of the Fathers' in these matters, asks Newman, then 'how can they fancy that the early Church was Protestant?'[90] The life of Apollinaris is an excellent example of gauging the connection between modern Protestantism and primitive Christianity.[91]

Apollinaris is one of those characters singled out by Vincent of Lerins in his *Commonitory*.[92] While fellow bishops treat Apollinaris the man kindly and tenderly, they are nevertheless determined to confront Apollinaris the heretic. Most Protestants seem to consider the price of preserving one's faith at any cost as obsessive, trivial and a waste of time. Their opinion of what constitutes heresy and what the Church Fathers consider heresy are poles apart. And is it not a fact, asks Newman, that some Protestants prefer to side with the world in dismissing many doctrines which early Christians fought for, suffered for and died for? If then, 'they thus differ from the Church of the Fathers, how can they fancy that the early Church was Protestant?'[93]

In 'Jovinian and his Companions', Newman mounts

[90] ibid., p. 391.
[91] ibid., p. 392.
[92] Other heresies which Vincent of Lerins examined in the *Commonitory* were those of Nestorius, patriarch of Constantinople, and Photinus, Bishop of Sirmium (Mitrovica in Kosovo in the Balkans).
[93] ibid., p. 391.

a counterattack on a commonly held opinion of his day that the Catholic system, as it existed in the fifth century, was really a corruption of the original Gospel.[94] According to this point of view, virtually every teaching of Christ had, from the beginning, been corrupted by the clergy, pagan philosophy and its jargon. And as this renegade system took over, bishops and clergy began to create an authoritarian system in order to maintain a firm grip on power, ensure survival and extend their sphere of influence into the secular world. In other words, it was a system of 'priestcraft' and 'destructive of Christian liberty.'[95] Even if such a theory fitted the 'facts of the case', Newman suggests, it is still only a theory, and could be countered by an opposite one that was equally satisfactory.

From earliest times, the vast majority of Christians have always believed that the 'Catholic system' has always been apostolic in nature; and that anyone rejecting this claim has to produce compelling evidence to the contrary to prove the charge of corruption. Before making sweeping generalisations, Protestants need to get a birdseye view of the first four centuries of the early Church. 'Is there,' he asks, 'any family likeness' in primitive Christianity to Protestantism? Is not primitive Christianity one and the same everywhere and 'singularly unlike' Protestantism? One has only to look at some of the Church Fathers at the time – 'Hermas with his visions, Ignatius with his dogmatism, Irenæus with his praise of tradition and of the Roman See, Clement with his

[94] Newman's brother, Francis, was of this opinion. See *L.D.* VII, p. 319, letter to Newman, 29 April 1840.

[95] ibid., p. 401.

allegory and mysticism, Cyprian with his "Out of the Church is no salvation", and Methodius with his praise of Virginity.' All these individuals belong to the first four centuries and are the true witnesses of the 'faith of Rome, Africa, Gaul, Asia Minor, Syria, and Egypt.' They certainly do not represent the philosophy of a Martin Luther or a John Calvin:

> They stretch over the whole of Christendom; they are consistent with each other; they coalesce into one religion; but it is not the religion of the Reformation. When we ask, 'Where was your Church before Luther?' Protestants answer, 'Where were you this morning before you washed your face?' But, if Protestants can clean themselves into the likeness of Cyprian or Irenæus, they must scrub very hard, and have well-nigh learned the art of washing the blackamoor white.[96]

In the fifth and final chapter, 'And What do the Apostolical Canons Say?', Newman argues that the customs and practices of the early Church favour Apostolicity rather than Protestantism on virtually every count. What '*positive* evidence' is there, he asks, that the Church has ever believed or taught a Gospel 'substantially different' from what the Apostles taught and from that which is contained in her earliest 'extant documents'? All available evidence, whether that be a lot or a little, he argues, is 'on our side', whether it be the 'consent' of the Church Fathers, the 'protest of heretics' or 'received usage'. An example of 'received usage' would be those ancient eighty-five Canons

[96] ibid., pp. 402–3.

many of which date back to the time of the Apostles.[97] They furnish us with 'large portions ... of the outline of the religion' as practised in the early Church. Not only are they 'definitive in themselves', they enable us to fill in many missing gaps. Which among modern Protestant Churches, he asks, is primitive Christianity like with its Apostolical Canons? Is it like Methodism, the Society of Friends, the Scotch Kirk, or some other Protestant denomination? 'If Protestantism,' he concludes, 'is another name for Christianity, then the Martyrs and Bishops of the early Church, the men who taught the nations, the men who converted the Roman Empire, had themselves to be taught, themselves to be converted. Shall we side with the first age of Christianity, or with the last?'[98]

III. NEWMAN AND THE FATHERS OF THE CHURCH

Newman's conversion in the autumn of 1816 was, arguably, the single most significant event of his life. It resulted in a moderate form of Calvinistic Evangelicalism when he was about fifteen years old and had nearly finished school at Ealing, then a small village about fifteen kilometres (nine miles) west of London. He fell 'under the influence of a definite Creed', such as it was available to him, and discovered that there was such a thing as a dogmatic principle.[99] A family crisis loomed in the background to the event.

[97] ibid., pp. 419–21.
[98] ibid., pp. 441–2.
[99] *Apologia Pro Vita Sua*, p. 4.

In the wake of the Napoleonic wars, the bank, of which his father was a partner, had collapsed and the family was forced to let the house at 17 Southampton Place, London, and move to Alton in Hampshire. It was arranged that he should remain at Ealing School during the summer holidays until the move was completed.[100]

During that summer, he became seriously ill and later recalled that it was accompanied by 'experiences before and after, awful, and known only to God'.[101] He later remembered it as having made him a Christian. With him during the illness was his Evangelical classics master, Walter Mayers, whom he described as the 'human means of this beginning of divine faith' in him. He was even more inspired by the books, mostly from the 'school of Calvin' which Mayers gave him to read. Among them was the *History of the Church of Christ* by the Church historian, Joseph Milner. Milner's history was an Evangelical interpretation of God's elect who were the real Christians and belonged to the great invisible Church of Christ.[102] It really did not matter what visible branch of the Church they actually belonged to as long as they were saved. Since that time, Newman 'never lost' or 'suffered a suspension of the impression,

[100] By the autumn of 1816, the Newman family had resettled in Alton, Hampshire, where his father set about managing a brewery.

[101] *A.W.*, p. 268.

[102] Evangelicals made a distinction between *real* Christians and *nominal* Christians. Real Christians were God's elect (God's chosen few) who belonged to the invisible Church of Christ by the grace of conversion and the energising action of the Holy Spirit. Nominal Christians who had not yet been converted belonged only to the visible Church through baptism.

deep and most pleasurable', which Milner's description of the Church Fathers left on his mind. Thenceforth, he later recalled, the 'vision of the Fathers was always, to my imagination, I may say, a paradise of delight to the contemplation of which I directed my thoughts from time to time, whenever I was free from the engagements proper to my time of life'.[103] But Newman's attitude to the Church Fathers in the 1820s was more ambivalent than this retrospective evaluation. By the time he resigned his curacy at St. Clement's at Oxford and accepted a tutorship at Oriel College, the Evangelical influence was beginning to fade while the influence of his mentor, Richard Whately, a leading liberal Anglican, continued in the ascendant. At the time, this 'Whatelyan' association influenced his attitude to the Church Fathers.

It should be remembered that, by the beginning of the eighteenth century, the Church Fathers commanded limited respect among scholars and thinkers in Great Britain. Even when proved to be 'right', they were considered to be irrelevant to any serious discussion. One has only to read late seventeenth-century theology to realise what occasional weight they carried.[104] And, naturally, Newman himself reflected some of this spirit up to 1827 when he

[103] *Certain Difficulties felt by Anglicans in Catholic Teaching Considered* (*Diff.* I), pp. 370–1.

[104] See G.R. Cragg, *From Puritanism to the Age of Reason*, Cambridge 1950, pp. 149–50; it would be over-simplifying the situation to assume that all Anglican divines thought negatively about the Church Fathers. One has only to recall George Bull (1634–1710), John Pearson (1613–86), James Ussher (1581–1656) and Henry Hammond (1605–60).

began to look at them more sympathetically. He later admitted that he had developed a 'certain disdain for Antiquity which had been growing on me for several years', manifesting itself in 'some flippant language against the Fathers' in his first essay on miracles written for the *Encyclopaedia Metropolitana* in 1825–26.[105] In the essay, he had argued *for* the antecedent probability of miracles in the New Testament, but argued *against* the antecedent probability of miracles in the post-Apostolic Church. At the time, a friend had warned him of the rationalising implications of making such a distinction.[106] In arguing his case, he had relied heavily on the ideas of the anti-patristic writer, Conyers Middleton (1683–1750), fellow of Trinity College, Cambridge.[107] In his *Free Inquiry into the Miraculous Powers*, this scathing controversialist and virtual sceptic argued that there was no compelling reason for believing that any miracles took place in the early Church after the death of the last apostle.[108]

Free Inquiry abounds with many sweeping generalisations. For example:

[105] See the first essay, 'The Miracles of Scripture' in *Two Essays on Biblical and Ecclesiastical Miracles* (*Mir.*), pp. 3–94.

[106] The friend was Edward Bouverie Pusey (1800–82) who was studying in Germany at the time.

[107] *Apo.*, p. 14.

[108] Conyers Middleton, *Free Inquiry into the Miraculous Powers, Which are supposed to have subsisted in the Christian Church, From the Earliest Ages through several successive Centuries*, London 1649. *Free Inquiry* was a 'criticism of the persistence of miraculous powers in the church's second century – an argument not necessarily heterodox given the Protestant agreement that they had ceased at some time or other' (J.G.A. Pocock, 'Gibbon and the primitive church' from *History, Religion, and Culture: British Intellectual History 1750–1950*, S. Collini, R. Whatmore and B Young, eds., Cambridge 2000).

> . . . For I take it to be a maxim, on which we may safely depend, that wherever the Bishops, the Clergy, and the principal Champions of the Christian cause, are found to be tampering with false miracles, and establishing new rites and doctrines by lies and forgeries, it would be vain for us, to look for any true miracle in that age, and that Church. And this was actually the case of the fourth century: in which all its most illustrious Fathers, now Saints of the Catholic Church; St. *Athanasius*, St. *Epiphanius*, St. *Basil*, St. *Gregory* of *Nyssa*, St. *Ambrose*, St. *Jerom* [Jerome], St. *Austin* [Augustine], and St. *Chrysostom* have all recorded and solemnly attested a number of miracles, said to be wrought in confirmation of some favorite institutions of those days, which, in the judgment of all the learned and candid Protestants, are manifestly fictitious, and utterly incredible.[109]

Newman later recalled preaching an Easter sermon in the chapel at Oriel in 1827 and getting into hot water by suggesting that certain clauses of the Athanasian Creed were 'unnecessarily scientific'. He was accused of Arianising.[110]

As he began to move out of the 'shadow of that liberalism which had hung over' these years, Newman's interest in the Fathers resurfaced.[111] It happened in about three stages, with each successive

[109] ibid., pp. lxxv–vi. Both the historian, Edward Gibbon and the scientist, Isaac Newton, thought that many of the Church Fathers had been corrupted by the influence of ancient philosophers, including Aristotle and Plato.

[110] *Apo.*, pp. 13–4.

[111] ibid., p. 25.

attempt yielding more and more insights. In the Long Vacation of 1828, he started reading them chronologically, beginning with Ignatius of Antioch and Justin Martyr. Unfortunately, 'shreds and tatters' of Evangelicalism continued to colour his reading.[112] He was so busy hunting for Protestant doctrines like justification by faith alone, holiness, personal conversion that he ended up being disappointed at not finding them. It was only later that he realised that he was looking for things that were not there and, in the process, 'missed what was there'.[113] He later cautioned anyone studying the Fathers not to read them without some preparatory theological and historical background. At the very least, one should study them in tandem. It was also important to read them thematically rather than chronologically as he first tried to do:[114]

> Whatever then be the true way of interpreting the Fathers, and in particular the Apostolical Fathers, if a man begins by summoning them before him, instead of betaking himself to them, – by seeking to make them evidence for modern dogmas, instead of

[112] *A.W.*, p. 78.

[113] *Certain Difficulties felt by Anglicans in Catholic Teaching* I, p. 371; *Keble Correspondence* (*K.C.*) p. 196. The exercise was not a complete waste of time, however, because it was from his reading of Justin Martyr that Newman derived his notion of a Dispensation of Paganism. See *Arians of the Fourth Century*, pp. 78–89.

[114] *K.C.*, pp. 196–197. Newman's initial reaction to reading Justin at this time was to criticise him for not being more 'explicit' about the subject of the Atonement and the influence of the Holy Spirit. He also criticised Justin for knowing 'mighty little' about Paul (Birmingham Oratory Archives D. 18. 1., Newman's *Theological Commonplace Book*, Justin, columns, 21–4).

> throwing his mind upon their text, and drawing from them their own doctrines, – he will to a certainty miss their sense.[115]

The second attempt began in 1831 when he was invited to write a history of the Council of Nicaea.[116] Because he decided to use ecclesiastical histories and standard commentaries like Bull's *Defensio Fidei Nicaenae* (Defence of the Nicene Creed), he made more headway.[117] Looking back on his efforts at this stage, he was still less than satisfied as he felt that his approach had been somewhat superficial and '*second hand*'.[118] He was happier third time round in 1834, when he decided to throw away the commentaries altogether and tackle the actual writings of the Fathers first hand. Immediately, he found himself launched on to an 'ocean of innumerable currents' and drifting back into the Ante-Nicene Church towards the Church of Alexandria, the 'historical centre of teaching in those times'. Alexandria was the place where the 'battle of Arianism was first fought', and it was the see of Athanasius who, 'in his writings ... refers to the great religious names of an earlier date, to Origen, Dionysius, and others, who were the glory of its see, or of its school'.[119] By this stage, he was now starting to appreciate how the early Church sorted out the various Christological issues of the day.[120]

As the Oxford Movement attracted more and more followers throughout the country, a new generation

[115] *Essays Critical and Historical* I, p. 228.
[116] This would eventually become *Arians of the Fourth Century*.
[117] George Bull, Anglican divine (1634–1710).
[118] *The Letters and Diaries of John Henry Newman* IV, p. 320.
[119] *Apo.*, p. 26.
[120] *L.D.* V, pp. 120; 122; 126.

was being introduced to the Church Fathers for the first time. It was difficult to talk about the early Church without encountering such giants as Augustine of Hippo, John Chrysostom and Athanasius of Alexandria. To really claim continuity with primitive Christianity and know nothing about these individuals was well nigh impossible. Thus it was in August 1836 that a plan was initiated by Pusey, supported by Newman and later by Keble, to translate the Church Fathers into English and publish them in a series to be called the *Library of the Fathers*. The enterprise was extremely successful and became one of the lasting achievements of nineteenth-century Anglo-Catholic scholarship.[121] Although Pusey's original initiative, other people, including Newman, soon came on board. Broadly speaking, Keble took charge of the pastoral and ascetical writings of the Greek Fathers, Pusey the Latin Fathers, and Newman the doctrinal writings of the Eastern Fathers. The first volume in the series was Augustine's *Confessions* in 1838. It was an old translation revised by Pusey who also wrote the preface.

Newman wrote prefaces for *The Catechetical Lectures of Cyril, Archbishop of Jerusalem* (1838), and for the

[121] *A Library of the Fathers of the Holy Catholic Church, anterior to the division of the East and the West*. Translated by members of the English Church. Edited by E.B. Pusey, J.H. Newman, J. Keble, and C. Marriott. Oxford: John Henry Parker; London: J.G.F. & J. Rivington. It was dedicated to 'William [Howley], Lord Archbishop of Canterbury, primate of all England'. It took more than forty-seven years to produce, starting with Augustine's *Confessions* (1838) to S. Cyril on S. John, Volume II in 1885, three years after Pusey's death. All in all, it comprised forty-eight volumes, the work of about thirteen Fathers. It included sixteen volumes of Chrysostom, twelve of Augustine, five of Athanasius, and three of Gregory Nazianzus.

treatises of Cyprian (1839).[122] He also wrote prefaces for *S. Chrysostom on Galatians and Ephesians* (1840) and for *Historical tracts of S. Athanasius, archbishop of Alexandria* (1843).[123] Nor did his involvement end there. In 1839, he began editing the works of Theodoret of Cyrrhus, Leo the Great and Cyril of Alexandria for the *Library of the Fathers*. In addition, he was producing a Latin edition of Dionysius of Alexandria for the university press.[124] He also translated the *Select treatises of S. Athanasius in controversy with the Arians*, the first part being published in 1842, and the second part in 1844. To get some idea of the importance of the Oxford *Library of the Fathers*, one must realise that, up to the 1830s, the traditional method of translating the Fathers into English was to aim at producing strict, literal translations which,

[122] *S. Cyril's Catechetical Lectures* were translated by R.W. Church (1815–90), later Dean of St. Paul's Cathedral in London; *S. Cyprian* was translated by C. Thornton, Tractarian and youngest son of Henry Thornton, the noted Evangelical and member of the Clapham Sect. He died in 1839.

[123] *S. Chrysostom on Galatians and Ephesians* was translated by Tractarian, W.J. Copeland (1804–85); *S. Athanasius' Historical Tracts* was translated by M. Atkinson (1811–89), Tractarian sympathiser and headmaster of St. Bee's School, Cumberland in Cumbria, 1839–54.

[124] *L.D.* VII, pp. 102–3, letters to J.W. Bowden and Miss M.R. Giberne, 11 July 1839. The Dionysius project was never completed because, while working on the Monophysite controversy during the Long Vacation of 1839, he began to see three parties, two extreme parties – Monophysites and Rome – and, situated somewhere in the middle, a third party which he identified as moderate Monophysites. He was struck by the uncanny parallel between the moderate party and the Church of England in its attempt to steer a middle course between Protestantism and Rome. Up till then, he thought that the unique position of the Church of England had 'no exact counterpart in early times'. He was wrong. By the end of August, he had become 'seriously alarmed' at its implications for him as a member of the Church of England (*The Via Media* I, p. 16).

naturally, had very limited public appeal. The new Oxford series broke the mould. Those who participated in the project in the 1830s, Newman later recalled, 'were regarded with much suspicion, both by Catholics and Protestants':

> It was alleged that in truth the only high-church doctrine to be found in the Fathers was Baptismal Regeneration; translators, it was said, who went beyond this were to be watched, and any departure from grammatical and literal accuracy in their renderings was sure to be scored against them as a controversial artifice. It may be added that in some quarters an over-estimation prevailed of the early Christian writers, as if they had an authority so special, and a position so like that of a court of final appeal, that those who had a title to handle their writings were but a few. It was under these conditions and disadvantages of the times that Dr. Pusey's translators, certainly that I myself, began our work. ... Things are much altered since 1836 – 1845.[125]

Newman was also responsible for organising the translation and publication of Aquinas' *Catena aurea* or 'Golden Chain'.[126] The *Catena* was an exposition of the four Gospels with accompanying comments taken from the Church Fathers. Newman organised some of his protegées to translate each of the Gospels. The translation of Matthew, he entrusted to Mark Pattison, soon to be elected fellow of Lincoln College.

125 *Selected Treatises of St. Athanasius* I, p. vi.

126 A new four-volume edition of the *Catena aurea* was republished by Aidan Nichols, OP, Saint Austin Press, Southampton 1997.

Newman himself contributed the preface to the series. Mark's Gospel was entrusted to John Dobrée Dalgairns, Luke to Thomas Dudley Ryder, and John to a person who preferred to remain anonymous.[127] According to the short Advertisement at the beginning of Matthew's Gospel (probably penned by Newman himself) the *Catena* was intended for the 'private study of the Gospels', 'well adapted for family reading' and 'full of thought for those who are engaged in religious instruction'. While it followed the same format as the Oxford *Library of the Fathers*, it was not technically part of the series.[128]

Looking back in 1864 on the influence of the Church Fathers of the Church had on his development, Newman reflected that their 'broad philosophy' fired his imagination:

> Some portions of their teaching, magnificent in themselves, came like music to my inward ear, as if the response to ideas, which, with little external to encourage them, I had cherished so long. These were the mystical or sacramental principle, and spoke of various Economies or Dispensations of the Eternal. I understood these passages to mean that the exterior world, physical and historical, was the

127 Gerard Tracey, librarian and archivist of the Birmingham Oratory thinks that the anonymous contributor was *either* Charles Brook Bridges who became a Catholic in 1845 and then a Jesuit, spending his final years in India, *or* George Hay Forbes, brother of the future Bishop of Brechin in Tayside, Scotland.

128 In the chapter describing the death of Chrysostom, Newman quotes extracts from Chapter XVII of the *Catena aurea* which focuses on Matthew's account of Christ's Transfiguration (Matt. 18: 1–9). He deleted them from the final version in *Historical Sketches* I. See *The Rambler*, September 1860, pp. 341ff.

> manifestation to our senses of realities greater than itself. Nature was a parable: Scripture was an allegory: pagan literature, philosophy, and mythology, properly understood, were but a preparation for the Gospel. The Greek poets and sages were in a certain sense prophets; for 'thoughts beyond their thought to those high bards were given.' There had been a directly divine dispensation granted to the Jews; but there had been in some sense a dispensation carried on in favour of the Gentiles. He who had taken the seed of Jacob for His elect people had not therefore cast the rest of mankind out of His sight.[129]

In 1881, Newman published a considerably revised edition of his Athanasius' treatises on the Arians which was originally part of the *Library of the Fathers* in the early 1840s. They were two volumes, the first containing the text and the second volume containing revised notes, some of which were more like mini-essays. This time round, the translation was much freer. He now saw no difficulty for scholars, provided they were competent enough, to publish a 'free translation' of the writings of the Church Fathers, provided, of course,

> ... he makes an open profession of what he is doing, and has sufficient reasons for doing it; and in the instance of St. Athanasius as little as of any of them, inasmuch as that great theologian, writing, as he did, only when he had a call to write, and some-

[129] ibid., pp. 26–27.

times while he was driven about from place to place, is led to repeat himself, is wanting in methodical exactness, and, with all his lucidity and force, nay even by reason of the Greek idiom, admits or requires explanation. Not as if a translator had any leave to introduce ideas, sentiments, or arguments which are foreign to his original, or may dispense with a watchful caution lest he should be taking liberties with his author; but that it was possible, as I thought, to make a volume unexceptionable in itself, and sufficiently distinct from the one published in Dr. Pusey's series, and with a usefulness of its own, though I did not follow Athanasius's text sentence by sentence, allowing myself in abbreviation where he was diffuse, and in paraphrase where he was obscure.[130]

IV. NEWMAN AS HISTORIAN

In writing 'The Church of the Fathers', 'Primitive Christianity', Newman made no claims to originality or objectivity. From first to last, they are polemical, and unapologetically so. Unlike another contemporary, Sir John Acton (1834–1902), he had received no formal training in the discipline. Nor did he focus on facts as the Scottish historian, Thomas Carlyle, did; nor he get caught up in the sweep and pageantry of history as did the English historian, Thomas Babington Macaulay. Instead of seeing the past as a process of uninterrupted growth, he tended to treat

[130] ibid., pp. vi–vii.

each stage of history as a homogeneous unit, 'with something of the timeless character of philosophical categories'.[131] He approached each one with a mind already made up and tended to interpret it in the light of a particular philosophical worldview which was, in his opinion, clearer, more reliable and more comprehensible than any historical event. Historical time, physical features and environment were of secondary importance. Newman preferred to focus on a person's inner self which motivated him or her to live the life they led. For example, nowhere in any essay, do we get a clear picture of what an Ambrose or an Augustine or a Basil or a Demetrias or a Macrina may have looked like. Such issues were not his primary concern.

V. OTHER NEWMAN SOURCES

In addition to relying extensively on the actual writings of the Church Fathers, Newman also relied on other sources, particularly the Bollandists, the Maurists, the French historian, Louis-Sébastien Le Nain de Tillemont and the Roman historian, Edward Gibbon.

The Bollandists

The Bollandists are known for their *Acta Sanctorum* (Lives of the Saints). They were, and still remain, a group of Jesuits living and working together on a single project under one roof in Antwerp researching

[131] Y. Brilioth, *The Anglican Revival: Studies in the Oxford Movement*, London 1925, p. 224.

the lives of the saints. The group boasts of being the first great endeavour of collaborative scholarship in Europe, and the only seventeenth-century enterprise still successfully operating today.[132] According to the present website of the *Société des Bollandistes*, 'hagiography is not a temporary fashion: it has been a tradition for more than 350 years! It was indeed in 1643 that the first volume of *Acta Sanctorum*, the prestigious collection of ancient and medieval Lives of Saints (68 vol. in folio), was published. ... It is the spirit of a team of specialists, entirely devoted to hagiographical research' – Latin, Greek, Syriac, Arabic, Coptic, Ethiopian, Armenian, Georgian, Slavic, Celtic, as well as other nationalities.[133]

The concept was the brainchild of a young Jesuit called Héribert Rosweyde (1569–1629). A native of Utrecht, Rosweyde realised that, in too many of the lives of saints, the real personality of the individual had been concealed or distorted 'beneath layers of legend and rhetoric, or diluted to insipidity by imagination and error'. So he 'conceived the idea of collecting all the authentic documents' of the saints, and telling their stories 'with the technique of scholarship recently applied so successfully' to other ancient authors such as the Greek dramatist, Sophocles. In 1607, he drew up a prospectus for eighteen volumes and invited critical comments from scholars around Europe. In addition to the prospectus, he laid the groundwork for the *Acta* by producing an edition of the Roman Martyrology in 1613 together with an

[132] ibid., pp. 3–4.

[133] For an overview of its present aims and activities, see <http://www.kbr.be/~socboll/actaSco.html>.

edition of the lives and sayings of the Desert Fathers in 1615 known as *Vitae Patrum*.

His successor, Jean van Bolland (1596–1665), seeing the vast amount of material available, decided to work systematically through the Church's liturgical calendar and deal with each saint commemorated on a day-to-day basis.[134] The January volume of the *Acta Sanctorum*, containing 2,500 folio pages, made its appearance in 1643 and proved an instant success.[135] The Bollandists continued working on the project until their order was suppressed in Belgium in 1773. After the suppression order was lifted in 1837, publication of the *Acta* recommenced and has continued to this day. Newman himself bought a set of the *Acta* with the one hundred pounds left him by his friend, the late John William Bowden (1798–1844). He had his eye on a particularly 'handsome' set owned by the poet and historian, Robert Southey (1774–1843). Unfortunately, the asking price was too high and in the end, he had to settle for an imperfect set still housed in the main library of the Birmingham Oratory.[136]

The Maurists

The famous Congregation of Saint Maur was an offshoot of the Benedictine Order. Saint Maur was a former pupil and disciple of Benedict. According to

[134] This calendar 'therefore was, and is, the Bollandist framework' (D. Knowles, *Great Historical Enterprises: Problems in Monastic History*, pp. 9–10, London 1963).

[135] The February edition, containing three volumes, was published in 1658, again to critical acclaim.

[136] 'Southey's copy was £130.' *Correspondence of John Henry Newman with John Keble and others, 1839–1845* p. 337, letter to E.L. Badeley, Esq. Littlemore, 1 November 1844. The Southey set was purchased by New College, Edinburgh, and added to their library where it remains today.

tradition, Maur introduced the Benedictine order into France in the sixth century and founded the abbey of Glanfeuil which later became known as Saint-Maur-sur-Loire. It was commonly believed in many northern European countries that the writing of the Benedictine rule had been the joint venture of both Benedict and Maur.[137]

In the wake of the Protestant Reformation, the Council of Trent (1545–63) decreed that monastic communities should be established in every region or province under a common rule and presided over by a superior-general.[138] In 1621, a congregation of French Benedictines was formed under the patronage of Saint Maur with their general house at Saint-Germain-des-Prés in Paris.[139] By 1648, the number of abbeys had climbed to eighty. By the end of the century, the number had risen to one hundred and eighty throughout six provinces.[140] The Congregation flourished in France from 1618 until the French Revolution.[141] During that time, it became known

[137] In the *Canterbury Tales*, Geoffrey Chaucer (*c.* 1340–1400) suggests that the Monk described in the prologue was a Benedictine who followed:

'The rule of Saint Maure or of Saint Beneit' (line 173).

[138] Thus, a federation of abbeys rather than an individual abbey became the basic unit to which a monk belonged and within which he could be transferred from one community to another at the discretion of the superior-general.

[139] Saint-Germain-des-Prés was burnt down during the French Revolution. Its great collection of manuscripts was rescued and is now in the Bibliothèque Nationale in Paris.

[140] France, Normandy, Brittany, Burgandy, Chezal-Benoît and Gascony.

[141] On 2 September 1792, the last superior-general (Dom Antoine Chevreux), together with forty members of the abbey, was guillotined. The Congregation itself was dissolved by Pius VII in 1818, having been approved in 1621 by Gregory XV.

throughout Europe for its strict observance of the rule and for its high standards of scholarship in many fields, including patristics.

Under the guidance of their first superior-general, Dom Grégoire Tarrisse (1575–1648), a project was set in motion to publish the history and achievements of the Benedictine Order together with the writings of the Church Fathers, including Basil the Great, Ambrose of Milan, John Chrysostom and Augustine of Hippo. Once a particular project was approved, a monk was put in charge and could enlist the services of other monks from his own community, indeed, from the whole congregation, if necessary, to copy manuscripts, read proofs, compile indexes, and so on. It has been estimated that, in its lifetime, about 220 monks coordinated and supervised various projects, even though personnel were scattered throughout several monasteries in several provinces. All in all, 700 scholarly works were produced on a variety of topics, including the history of the Benedictine Order, patristics, secular history, asceticism, and works on the associated sciences of diplomatics, chronology, numismatics and paleography. In editing ancient documents, particularly those of the Church Fathers, they endeavoured to collect copies of every available manuscript in Europe, carefully noting textual variants and citing as many traditions and opinions as possible. Each edition was provided with instructive introductions, copious notes, and detailed indexes.

Any promising scholar who caught the eye of the superior-general was transferred to the abbey of Saint-Germain-des-Prés which boasted one of the best-equipped libraries in Europe and which, in its heyday, housed such eminent scholars as Dom Jean Mabillon and Dom Bernard Montfaucon. The Mabillon era lasted from 1665 to 1707, concentrating on the Latin Fathers, and the Montfaucon era continued from 1707 to 1741, concentrating on the Greek Fathers. Mabillon's masterpiece was his *De Re Diplomatica* (1681). It was written to a challenge by a Bollandist hagiographer named Daniel Papebroch (1628–1714) who, in an introduction to the second volume of the April saints, proposed a number of guidelines for identifying both genuine and spurious charters. In the process, he cast serious doubt on the authenticity of the Merovingian charters of two Maurist establishments – namely, the abbey of Saint-Denis in the diocese of Paris and the abbey of Corbie in the diocese of Amiens.[142] Mabillon realised that, if scholars were to follow Papebroch's guidelines, the authenticity of a whole range of ancient documents would be thrown into jeopardy. He therefore decided to use his encyclopaedic knowledge of the charters and diplomas in the library of Saint-Germain-des-Prés with the aim of examining the writing, style, form, dates, signatures, seals, signet rings, in order to establish reliable guidelines for authenticating them. Within six years of its publication, scholars, including Papebroch to his credit, had accepted the *De Re Diplomatica* as the definitive work on the subject.[143]

[142] Some of these Merovingian charters would have dated back to about the seventh century.

[143] In spite of weaknesses in, for example, some areas of philology and paleography, *De Re Diplomatica* remained the standard textbook for two centuries. In the third edition of the book, Mabillon's confrères paid the following tribute to his scholarship: 'His [Mabillon's] system is true, and whoever would build on foundations other than his, will build on sand.' (D. Knowles, op. cit., p. 48).

After the death of Mabillon in 1707, Dom Bernard Montfaucon carried on the scholarly tradition. As Mabillon had created the science of diplomatics – that is, the science of critiquing manuscripts, charters, and official letters – Montfaucon created the science of Greek paleography – that is, the science of deciphering and dating ancient documents.[144] In addition, he produced several editions of the writings of Athanasius (3 volumes, 1698), of Origen (2 volumes, 1713) and of John Chrysostom (13 volumes, 1718–38). Newman's own Maurist editions of these Fathers are still housed in the library of the Birmingham Oratory. It also houses the rest of Newman's Maurist editions, including Ambrose of Milan, Augustine of Hippo, Basil the Great, Gregory of Nazianzus, Irenaeus, Justin Martyr, and Cyprian.[145]

Louis-Sébastien Le Nain de Tillemont

In writing *The Church of the Fathers*, Newman relied heavily on the seventeenth-century French historian, Louis-Sébastien Le Nain de Tillemont (1637–1698) as he also did when writing *Arians of the Fourth Century* about the same time.[146] The son of a wealthy lawyer, Tillemont attended the famous school of *Les Petites-Écoles* at Port-Royal, conducted by the Jansenists who advocated a very austere lifestyle which was not

[144] This was the *Paléographie greque* (1708) which complemented Mabillon's *De Re Diplomatica* and, like that masterpiece, remained a standard textbook until quite recently.

[145] see *The Theological Papers of John Henry Newman* II, pp. 162–4.

[146] Louis-Sébastien, the dwarf of Tillemont; see *The Church of the Fathers*, p. 207 and *The Arians of the Fourth Century*, p. 397. Tillemont was one of the first scholars to approach earlier historical writing critically and objectively.

approved of at the French court. In 1667, he took up residence at Port-Royal, and became chaplain shortly afterwards. He then began collaborating in editing the writings of Augustine, Origen and Tertullian. When the Jansenist persecution was renewed during the reign of Louis XIV in 1679, Tillemont retired to the safety of the family estate where he could continue his study of ecclesiastical history without outside interference.

One of his major works was the monumental sixteen-volume *Mémoires pour servir à l'histoire ecclésiatiques des six premiers siècles (Records Useful for the Ecclesiastical History of the First Six Centuries)*. He also wrote a six-volume history of the Roman emperors which he originally planned to publish with the *Mémoires* as one complete work. The plan was to integrate all major sources for the history of the Roman empire and of the early Church, paying strict attention to details of authorship, authenticity, dates, ironing out discrepancies and irregularities along the way. He tried to be as objective as possible and to rely on original sources. As it turned out, both *Mémoires* and *Histoire des Empereurs* were published separately because an official court censor called for changes in the former. As a result, the history of the emperors was published first, between 1690 and 1738, while the volumes of *Mémoires* were delayed and published between 1693 and 1712.[147] It was also delated to Rome but was later given the seal of approval by Clement XI (1700–21). Newman

147 The fifth volume was already in the hands of the publishers at the time of Tillemont's death. Subsequent volumes were published at regular intervals.

himself referred to Tillemont as an 'accurate and cautious' historian.[148]

Like Tillemont (1637–98), Newman took great pains to preserve the integrity of figures like Basil the Great and Gregory of Nazianzus without glossing over personal weaknesses, particularly when they were important to the narrative.[149] In 1833, Frederic Rogers (1811–89), a close friend, former student of Newman and fellow of Oriel College, presented Newman with a set of Tillemont's *Mémoires* from a grateful student.[150] 'You have no notion how useful your Tillemont already is', he wrote to Rogers on 31 August. 'The "Church of the Fathers" is in great measure drawn up from it'.[151]

Edward Gibbon

Newman's own interest in Edward Gibbon (1737–94) began in the Long Vacation of 1818.[152] In spite of 'his faults, his want of simplicity, his affectation', and his occasional 'monotony', few authors could match his brilliance. And when 'I reflect on his happy choice of expressions, his vigorous compression of ideas, and the life and significance of his every word, I am prompted indignantly to exclaim' that there must be very little left in this area for future historians.[153] Because of Gibbon's

[148] *Select Treatises of St. Athanasius* II, p. 239.

[149] See Tillemont, *Mémoires*, XII, p. 2.

[150] 'To J.H. Newman in some small acknowledgement of his kindness to his pupil and very affectionate friend – F. Rogers'

[151] *The Letters and Diaries of John Henry Newman* IV, p. 36. From 1860 to 1871, Rogers was Permanent Under-Secretary of State for the Colonies and was created Lord Blachford in 1876. Towards the end of his life, Newman revealed that, of all his Oxford friendships, 'none approached his intimacy with Lord Blachford'.

[152] *John Henry Newman: Autobiographical Writings*, p. 40.

[153] *L.D.* I, p. 67, letter to J.W. Bowden, October 1819.

well-known hostility to Christianity, Newman, in his Catholic years, preferred to keep references minimal. While not concealing his 'great repugnance' for Gibbon the man, and 'seriously' objecting to his sceptical spirit which is patently obvious on every page of his writings, Gibbon the writer remains an 'integral' part of 'English Literature'. We cannot ignore him, we cannot re-invent him, and we 'cannot expurgate what needs to be exorcised'. In spite of his blatant 'hatred' for Rome and all it stood for, he was, nevertheless, a great writer endowed with unique gifts.[154]

As a matter of interest, in writing *Decline and Fall of the Roman Empire*, Gibbon relied, as Newman was to do in *The Church of the Fathers*, on the work of the Bollandists, particularly the *Acta Sanctorum*. He once described the *Acta* as 'an undertaking which, through the medium of fable and superstition, communicates much historical and philosophical instruction'.[155] He also relied on the Maurists, particularly on Mabillon and Montfaucon. He reserved pride of place, however, for Tillemont whom he referred to as one whose 'inimitable accuracy almost assumes the character of genius' and who helped steer him through the treacherous terrain of Roman politics with the patience and sure-footedness of an Alpine mule which could be trusted even on the 'most slippery paths'.[156]

[154] *Idea of a University*, p. 309.

[155] R. Porter, *Edward Gibbon: Making History*, p. 75, London 1988.

[156] Edward Gibbon, *The Memoirs of the Life of Edward Gibbon with Various Observations and Excursions by Himself*, edited by George Birkbeck Hill, p. 182 and p. 182, 2n, London 1900; see also Edward Gibbon, *The History of the Decline and Fall of the Roman Empire*, III, p. 48, 126n, edited by J.B. Bury, London 1897.

Finally, Newman also relied on, though not to the same extent as any of the above sources, the writings of earlier historians such as Sozomen (early fifth century), Socrates 'Scholasticus' (*c.* 380–450), Sulpicius Severus (*c.* 363–*c.* 420) and Photius (*c.* 810–95).

VI. TEXTUAL VARIANTS

The text of the 1840 edition which Newman published as an Anglican and the text of the uniform edition in *Historical Sketches* which he published as a Roman Catholic in 1873 are considerably different, on several counts. Changes occur on a number of levels and for various reasons. A full critical edition would reveal the extent of the number of minor stylistic changes introduced by Newman to ameliorate the tone and language of the earlier Anglican edition. For example, he deletes stock Protestant statements which he had once used against Rome. The original reference to Basil being wounded by Rome's 'superciliousness' is toned down to his being wounded by Rome's 'reserve'; and the Church's 'calamitous state' becomes the 'Church's internal state'; and that 'noxious Arian "flood"' becomes 'those perilous Arian waters'; 'ultra-Protestants' are now 'Protestants'.

Understandably Newman now substitutes Catholic terms and phrases for the lingua franca of Anglican-Protestant apologetics and controversy, thus making it more accessible to a Catholic audience. For example, in speaking of the Church, Catholics are more at home in talking about the 'divine mission of the Church' rather than about the 'duty of deference to the Church'; about 'convents' and 'monastic bodies' rather than 'religious sisterhoods' and 'religious fraternities'; about 'Augustine' of Hippo rather than 'Austin' of Hippo; and about the 'apostolic *depositum*' rather than the 'apostolic *revelation*'.

More importantly, Newman deletes all pungent Tractarian criticisms of the Anglican Establishment which would have been out of place and unnecessary in the uniform edition. Passages, for example, when he is talking about 'that free-and-easy mode of religion in which ultra-Protestants glory':

> . . . in being independent; they think it a beauty to be all pulling different ways, and to have as many various rites and regimens as there are tastes and likings in the world. They can be quite sentimental and poetical on the subject; expatiate on the excellence of 'agreeing to differ;' descant on the variety of nature, and insist, as philosophers, upon the immateriality of 'differences in Church government,' while what they call 'doctrine' is preserved, or while hearts are one.

He then tells a rather amusing anecdote which, apart from its satire, would have had very little interest for readers:

> There is a popular story of a woman fainting on a Sunday, as the whole town was coming from worship, and an Anabaptist providing the chair, and a Quaker a smelling-bottle, and a Roman Catholic a handkerchief, and a Churchman running for a doctor, and the doctor turning out to be a

> Swedenborgian. It is something of this kind; and then a sagacious father, who seems to have been leading his son round the town instead of taking him to divine service anywhere, points it out to his notice thus: – 'See, my boy, what mankind were made to agree in, and what to differ in!'

He then concludes with the following observation:

> What would the stern old Fathers of Nicæa have said to this? – with their notions of 'the Canon,' what would they have said to a mixed set of religionists, *zonis solutis*, who glory in having nothing external in common, and who prate about 'the superiority of unanimity to uniformity?' Or, as I should rather put it, what do our religionists say to it? or do they get themselves to contemplate the fact, of a vast number of leading men, (to put the matter at the lowest,) from all parts of Christendom, witnessing to the existence of a state of things which they must have known as perfectly as we know what has happened ever since the Reformation, nay, which occupies a less period, and describing circumstances which are quite irreconcilable with modern notions, in the same unhesitating and quiet tone which we should use in speaking of the last three centuries? I believe, when they get themselves to consider it, they are obliged, – they do not scruple, – to say, that an universal corruption, a sudden lapse of the Church, took place *immediately* after the Apostles; though how they can support this hypothesis, when it is narrowly considered, does not appear.

In addition, he plays down, as much as possible, any unnecessary references to the crisis of the Irish Church Temporalities Bill of 1833. For example, any reference to it would have been, apart, that is, from its historical value, of little or no interest to Catholic readers in the 1870s. In referring in the 1840 edition to the incident of Ambrose's celebrated Church-State clash with the emperor Valentinian over the Basilica, he suggests that, if a similar clash were to have occurred between Church and State in England in the sixteenth or nineteenth century, there is no doubt what would have happened and who would have come off second best. Because of the present Church's 'timid policy' on the matter, compromise and gentlemanlike behaviour would have been the order of the day and the 'Basilica would have been surrendered' to the State. There is also no doubt that 'great men' are not made 'more religious by letting them have their own way'.[157]

Finally, in his 'Letters on the Church of the Fathers' in the *British Magazine*, and in the 1840 and 1842 editions, Newman relied for references on patristic editions most easily available to him. In republishing *The Church of the Fathers* in *Historical Sketches*, he standardised all references to the preferred Maurist editions of which he now had a complete collection of his own. So, for example, references in the earlier editions to the works of Gregory of Nazianzus were made to the early Paris edition of J. Billius and F. Morellus. In later editions, page citations were changed to the 1778 Maurist edition of P. Clemencet.

[157] *The Church of the Fathers*, 1840 edition, pp. 306–8; p. 43.

Such changes have been passed over silently in the textual appendix to this edition.

VII. APPENDICES

There are six Appendices. Appendix 1 contains two maps, the first of which provides a bird's-eye view of the places in Asia Minor where Basil the Great and Gregory of Nazianzus lived, worked and died. Many of the places mentioned by Newman in his narrative either no longer exit or have been absorbed into other cities or have had their former names changed or modernised. The second map provides a bird's-eye view of the extent of the Roman Empire around AD 400. Appendix 2 includes the various Advertisements from the 1840 and 1842 editions, as well as those from the 1857 and 1868 editions.

Appendix 3 includes the original 'Chronological Index' from the 1840 edition which is somewhat different from, and more detailed than that of the uniform edition. For the latter edition, it has been re-titled 'Chronology of the Contemporary Events' and commences with the conversion of Justin Martyr in the year 132 and concludes with the year 456 when Demetrias built the basilica of St. Stephen on her property on the Latin road leading out of Rome. The 'Chronological Index', on the other hand, starts with the death of the martyrs Gervasius and Protasius in Milan during the Neronian persecution in the year 64, and concludes with the year 564 when John Scholasticus became patriarch of Constantinople. Appendix 4 contains the textual variants in the 1840 and 1868 editions.

Appendix 5 contains three chapters from the 1840

and 1842 editions one of which was withdrawn from the series altogether while the other two were condensed into one chapter for 'Primitive Christianity'.[158] The withdrawn chapter was 'The penitence of Theodosius' which contains an account of Ambrose's measured response to the massacre of the citizens of Thessalonica on the orders of the hot-headed emperor, Theodosius. The original two chapters of 'Canons of the Apostles' were condensed into one for 'Primitive Christianity'. Rather than insert confusing extracts in the textual appendix, they are reproduced in their entirety for readers to read them in the original 1840 version. Finally, Appendix 6 contains a copy of the original article on the martyrs Gervasius and Protasius which Newman wrote in 1834 for, but withdrew from, the *British Magazine*. After its editor, Hugh James Rose, died in 1840, his widow returned the withdrawn copy to Newman who kept it in his room at the Birmingham Oratory. It consists of three sections, the first on superstition as '*ignorant faith*'; the second devoted to Ambrose's letter to his sister about the discovery of the remains of Gervasius and Protasius; and the final section contains several of Newman's observations on that letter, on the discovery of the relics and on the miracles which followed. It is printed here for the first time.

Francis McGrath FMS
Marist Brothers' Community
Ashgrove
Brisbane
Australia

158 There were variations between the 1840 and 1842 editions, but they were of such a minor nature as to be virtually negligible.

THE CHURCH OF THE FATHERS.

QUÆ EST ISTA, QUÆ PROGREDITUR QUASI AURORA CONSURGENS
TERRIBILIS UT CASTRORUM ACIES ORDINATA.

TO MY DEAR AND MUCH-ADMIRED

ISAAC WILLIAMS, B.D.,

FELLOW OF TRINITY COLLEGE, OXFORD:

THE SIGHT OF WHOM

CARRIES BACK HIS FRIENDS

TO ANCIENT, HOLY, AND HAPPY TIMES.

Feb. 21, 1840.

ADVERTISEMENT.

THE following Sketches, which, with two or three exceptions, appeared in the *British Magazine*, during 1833 and the following years, do not, as the author is very conscious, warrant a title of such high pretension as that which was there prefixed to them and is here preserved. But that title will at least show the object with which they were written, viz. to illustrate, as far as they go, the tone and modes of thought, the habits and manners of the early times of the Church.

The author is aware what numerous imperfections are likely to attach to a work which is made up, in so great a measure as this is, of personal opinions and views, of minute historical details and of translations; nor would he expose himself to the criticisms which it inevitably provokes, did he not think that the chance of bringing out or recommending one or two of the characteristics of primitive Christianity was worth the risk of mistakes, which, after all, would be of a nature to affect himself rather than his readers.

As to the translations, he is very sensible what constant and unflagging attention is requisite in all translation to catch the sense of the original, and what discrimination in the choice of English to do justice to it; and what certainty there is of shortcomings, after all. And further, over and above actual faults, variety of tastes and fluctuation of moods among readers, make it impossible so to translate as to please every-one; and, if a translator be conscious to himself, as he may well be, of viewing either his original or his version differently, according to the season or the feeling in which he takes it up, and finds that he never shall have done with correcting and altering except by an act of self-control, the more easy will it be for him to resign himself to such differences of judgment about his work as he experiences in others.

It should be considered, too, that translation in itself is, after all, but a problem; how, two languages being given, the nearest approximation may be made in the second to the expression of ideas already conveyed through the medium of the first. The problem almost starts with the assumption that something must be sacrificed; and the chief question is, what is the least sacrifice? In a balance of difficulties, one translator will aim at being critically correct, and will become obscure, cumbrous, and foreign; another will aim at being English, and will appear deficient in scholarship. While grammatical particles are followed out, the spirit evaporates; and, while an easy flow of language is secured, new ideas are intruded, or the point of the original is lost, or the drift of the context impaired.

Under these circumstances, perhaps, it is fair to lay down that, while every care must be taken against the introduction of new, or the omission of existing ideas, in translating the original text, yet, in a book intended for general reading, faithfulness may be considered simply to consist in expressing in English the *sense* of the original; the actual words of the latter being viewed mainly as *directions into* its sense, and scholarship being necessary in order to gain the full insight into that sense which they afford; and next, that, where something must be sacrificed, precision or intelligibility, it is better in a popular work to be understood by those who are not critics, than to be applauded by those who are.

This principle has been moreover taken to justify the author in the omission of passages, and now and then in the condensation of sentences, when the extract otherwise would have been too long; a studious endeavour being all along made to preserve the sense from injury.

As to the matter of these Sketches,* it is plain that, though mainly historical, they are in their form and character polemical, as being directed against certain

*Added in Edition of 1857.

Protestant ideas and opinions. This consideration must plead for certain peculiarities which it exhibits, such as its freedom in dealing with saintly persons, the gratuitous character of some of its assertions, and the liberality of many of its concessions. It must be recollected, that, in controversy, a writer grants all that he can afford to grant, and avails himself of all that he can get granted: – in other words, if he seems to admit, it is mainly "for argument's sake;" and if he seems to assert, it is mainly as an "*argumentum ad hominem.*" As to positive statements of his own, he commits himself to as few as he can; just as a soldier on campaign takes no more baggage than is enough, and considers the conveniences of home life as only *impedimenta* in his march.

This being kept in view, it follows that, if the author of this work allows the appearance of infirmity or error in St. Basil or St. Gregory or St. Martin, he allows it because he can afford to pass over allegations, which, even though they were ever so well founded, would not at all interfere with the heroic sanctity of their lives or the doctrinal authority of their words. And if he can bear to entertain the idea of St. Antony being called an enthusiast without protesting, it is because that hypothesis does not even tend to destroy the force of the argument against the religion of Protestants, which is suggested by the contrast existing between their spirit and his.

Nor is this the sole consideration, on which an author may be justified in the use of frankness, after the manner of Scripture, in speaking of the Saints; for their lingering imperfections surely make us love them more, without leading us to reverence them less, and act as a relief to the discouragement and despondency which may come over those, who, in the midst of much error and sin, are striving to imitate them; – according to the saying of St. Gregory on a graver occasion, "Plus nobis Thomæ infidelitas ad fidem, quam fides credentium discipulorum profuit."

And in like manner, the dissatisfaction of Saints, of St. Basil, or again of our own St. Thomas, with the contemporary policy or conduct of the Holy See, while it cannot be taken to justify ordinary men, bishops, clergy, or laity, in feeling the same, is no reflection either on those Saints or on the Vicar of Christ. Nor is his infallibility in dogmatic decisions compromised by any personal and temporary error into which he may have fallen, in his estimate, whether of a heretic such as Pelagius, or of a Doctor of the Church such as Basil. Accidents of this nature are unavoidable in the state of being which we are allotted here below.

INTRODUCTION.

THIS is a world of conflict, and of vicissitude amid the conflict. The Church is ever militant; sometimes she gains, sometimes she loses; and more often she is at once gaining and losing in different parts of her territory. What is ecclesiastical history but a record of the ever-doubtful fortune of the battle, though its issue is not doubtful? Scarcely are we singing *Te Deum*, when we have to turn to our *Misereres:* scarcely are we in peace, when we are in persecution: scarcely have we gained a triumph, when we are visited by a scandal. Nay, we make progress by means of reverses; our griefs are our consolations; we lose Stephen, to gain Paul, and Matthias replaces the traitor Judas.

It is so in every age; it is so in the nineteenth century; it was so in the fourth; and about the fourth I am proposing to write. An eventful century, a drama in three acts, each marvellous in itself, each different from the other two! The first is the history of the Roman Empire becoming Christian; the second, that of the indefectible Church of God seeming to succumb to Arianism; the third, that of countless barbarians pouring in upon both Empire and Christendom together. And, as the great convulsions of the earth involve innumerable commotions in detail and local revolutions, and each district and neighbourhood has its own story of distress and confusion, so, in the events of the social world, what is done in the camp or synod vibrates in every town and in every bishopric. From one end of the century to the other, the most momentous changes and the most startling vicissitudes took place; and the threshold of the Apostles was now darkened by messengers of ill, and now lit up with hope and thanksgiving.

So was it in the fourth century; so will it be to the end:

> Thus bad and good their several warnings give
> Of His approach, whom none may see and live.
> Faith's ear, with awful still delight,
> Counts them like minute bells by night,
> Keeping the heart awake till dawn of morn,
> While to her funeral pile this aged world is borne.

However, I am attempting here, neither the grand outlines, nor the living details of the century, but some scenes or passages which chronologically or morally belong to it. And I preface them with this allusion to the century itself, because they are thereby duly located, and receive their proper colour. And now, without more words, I shall begin my course, travelling after the sun from East to West: beginning with Greece and Asia Minor, and then visiting, in succession, Egypt, Africa, Spain, and Gaul, where I shall come to an end.

CHAPTER I.

TRIALS OF BASIL.

"As a servant longeth for the shade, as the hireling looketh for the end of his work, so I also have had empty months, and wearisome nights have I numbered unto me."

I.

AS Athanasius was the great champion of the Catholic Faith, while the Arians were in the ascendant; so Basil and Gregory in the East, and Ambrose in the West, were the chief instruments of Providence in repairing and strengthening its bulwarks, by word, writing, and deed, when the fury of their assaults was spent. I am not concerned just now with the great Western luminary, Ambrose, but with Basil and Gregory. Of these two saints, one had to contend with an Arian sovereign, the other with an Arian populace; and they gained the victory, each on his own field of battle, the one with the loss of his see, the other at the sacrifice of his life. Premature death, a solitary old age, were the contrary destinies of two great saints and dear friends; the labours of Basil were cut short, and the penances of Gregory were lengthened out. The scene of Gregory's struggle was the imperial city of Constantinople; of Basil's, the length and breadth of Asia Minor and the adjoining provinces. These countries had from the first been overrun by the heretics, and, as far as religion was concerned, were, in the middle of the fourth century, in a deplorable state of confusion. Basil's care of the churches, in that time of trouble, as that of a Missionary or Preacher, extended far beyond the limits of his own jurisdiction ; for by ecclesiastical right he was only priest first, and afterwards bishop, of the church of Cæsarea, and exarch of the remote and barbarous Cappadocia, from A.D. 358 to A.D. 379.

At the former of these dates, Dianius was in possession of the see. He seems to have baptized Basil, who speaks warmly in his praise, expressing the affection and respect he felt for him, and the pleasure he took in his society ; and describing him as a man remarkable for his virtue, as frank, generous, and venerable, while he was amiable and agreeable in his manners. However, he fell in with the fashion of the age, and had for nearly twenty years sided with the court faction against Athanasius and his holy cause. Accordingly, he signed without scruple the heretical formulary of the council of Ariminum, which was presented to him A.D. 360, and in which the test of the Homoüsion, or Consubstantial, contained in the Nicene Creed, was abandoned, and the Catholic doctrine evaded under the pretence of expressing it only in terms of Scripture. Basil felt bitterly this weakness, to give it its mildest name, on the part of one he so much loved ; and though he did not consider that there was a call on him for any public protest, he ceased to hold intercourse with him, nor did he come near him till two years afterwards, when Dianius sent for him to attend his death-bed, and professed solemnly his adherence to the faith of the Church.

Eusebius, the successor of Dianius, was a bishop of orthodox profession, but had little of the theological knowledge or force of character necessary for coping with the formidable heresy by which the Church was assailed. For some reason or other, perhaps from a feeling of jealousy, he manifested a coldness towards the rising theologian, who is to be the subject of this chapter; and Basil, who was now a priest, unwilling to excite the people, or create parties in the Church, retired from the metropolitan city.

2.

His retreat, both now and in the lifetime of Dianius, was the wild region of Pontus, where he had founded a number of monasteries, over one of which he presided He had retired thither first about A.D. 355, (the year in which the Egyptian St. Antony, the first Solitary, died,) for the purposes of study and mortification; and to a mind ardent and sensitive, such as his, nothing was more welcome than such a temporary retreat from the turbulence of ecclesiastical politics. Nor was his life at this time one of inaction or solitude. On occasion of a famine in the neighbouring town and country, he converted his lands into money, to supply the wants of the people; taking upon himself particularly the charge of their children, besides relieving all who applied to him, among whom the Jews are mentioned as receiving a share in his liberality. His monasteries became, in a short time, schools of that holy teaching which had been almost banished from the sees of Asia; and it is said that he was in the practice of making a circuit of the neighbouring towns, from time to time, to preach to them the Nicene doctrine. This indeed was a benefit which was not unfrequently rendered to the Church, in that day of apostasy, by the ascetics, according to the promise that they who have a clean heart shall see God.

"The reason," says Sozomen, "why the doctrines" of the heretics

Eunomius and Apollinaris "had not any extensive success, in addition to the causes above mentioned, is, that the Solitaries of the day took part against them. For those of Syria and Cappadocia, and the neighbouring districts, firmly adhered to the creed of Nicæa. At one time, the oriental provinces, from Cilicia to Phœnicia, were near becoming Apollinarian, while those from Cilicia and the Taurus to the Hellespont and Constantinople were exposed to the heresy of Eunomius; each heresiarch having success in his own neighbourhood. And then the history of Arianism was acted over again; for the populace in those parts had that reverence for the characters and the works of the Solitaries, as to trust their doctrine as orthodox; and they shrank from those who held otherwise, as impure, for their adulterate doctrine; just as the Egyptians followed the Solitaries of Egypt and opposed the Arians."—*Hist.* vi. 27.

Basil had lived in his second retirement about three years, when the attack of the Arians upon the Church of Cæsarea, under the emperor Valens, made his loss felt, and his friend, Gregory of Nazianzus, successfully interposed his mediation between him and Eusebius. Gregory's letters are extant, and I here present them to the reader.

GREGORY TO BASIL.

"This is a time for good counsel and fortitude. We must surpass others in courage, nor suffer all our past toil and labour to be undone in a moment. Why do I write thus? Because our most gracious bishop (for such we ought to think and call Eusebius henceforth) has most amicable and kind feelings towards us, and like steel in the fire, is softened by time. I even expect that you will receive a communication from him, with pleasant words, and a summons, as he himself hinted to me, and many of his confidential friends assure me. Let us then anticipate his advances, either by our presence or by writing, or, what would be better still, by first writing and then making our appearance, lest we be hereafter worsted with disgrace, when we might have conquered by a worsting which was honourable and dignified; which, indeed, most men expect of us. Come, then, according to my entreaty, both on this account, and for the times' sake. In truth, the heretical faction is trampling the Church under foot; some of them are already among us and are at work; others, it is said, will follow soon. Surely there is danger of their sweeping away the word of truth, unless the spirit of our Bezaleel speedily awake, that cunning master-builder of argument and doctrine. If you wish me to be present and to assist in this business, or to be the companion of your journey, I am at your service."—*Ep.* 19.

It is impossible not to be struck with Gregory's delicacy in this letter, in which he speaks as if he himself were estranged from Eusebius, as well as Basil, though he stood at the time high in his favour. His next letter is to the bishop himself, whose intentions he anticipates with equal delicacy.

GREGORY TO EUSEBIUS, BISHOP OF CÆSAREA.

"I know I am addressing one who hates insincerity himself, and is especially keen in detecting it in another, though cloaked in ever so artful and subtle a disguise; and indeed, I may say, if you will pardon the impertinence, I am myself averse to it, both by natural disposition and from Christian education. So I write what is uppermost on my mind, and beg you to excuse my freedom. Indeed it would be an injury to me to restrain me and bid me keep my pain to myself, as a sore festering in my heart. Proud as I am of your notice (for I am a man, as some one says before me), and of your invitations to religious consultations and meetings, yet I cannot bear your holiness's past and present slight of my most honoured brother Basil, whom I selected from the first and still possess as my friend, to live with me and study with me, and search with me into the deepest wisdom. I have no need to be dissatisfied with the opinion I have formed of him, and if I do not say more to his praise, it is lest, in enlarging on his admirable qualities, I should seem to be praising myself. Now, your favour towards me, and discountenance of him, is as if a man should stroke one's head with one hand, and with the other strike one's cheek; or decorate a house with paintings and beautify the outside, while he was undermining its foundations. If there is any thing you will grant me, let it be this; and I trust you will, for really it is equitable. He will certainly defer to you, if you do but pay a reasonable deference to him. For myself, I shall come after him as shadows follow bodies, being small, and a lover of quiet. Miserable indeed should we be, if, while we were desirous of wisdom in other matters, and of choosing the better part, we yet thought little of that grace, which is the end of all our doctrine—charity; especially in the case of one who is our bishop, and so eminent, as we well know, in life, in doctrine, and in the government of his diocese; for the truth must be spoken, whatever be our private feelings."—*Ep.* 20.

Great men love to be courted, and little men must not mind rebuffs. Gregory did not succeed in this first attempt with Eusebius, who seems to have been offended at his freedom; and he himself was disgusted in turn, at the Bishop's stiffness. However, the danger of the Church was too great to allow of the continuance of such feelings on either side, and Gregory had, in a little while, the satisfaction of seeing Basil at Cæsarea.

3.

The vigorous talents of Basil soon put to rights the disorders and variances which had been the scandal of the Church of Cæsarea; and with the assistance of Gregory, he completely vanquished the Eunomian disputants, from whose subtlety the peace of the Church had principally suffered. What was of more consequence to its permanent welfare, he was successful in obliterating all the suspicions which his bishop had entertained of him, and at length gained such influence over him, that he had really the government of the see in his own hands. This was the more desirable, as Eusebius had not been regularly educated for the ministerial office, but had been called by the sudden voice of the people, as sometimes happened, to fill the episcopal chair. At length (A.D. 370) Eusebius died; and Basil, as might be expected, though not without a strong opposition, was elected, at the age of forty, to supply his place. This opposition was excited by the governing powers of the country, who might naturally be supposed to fear a man of Basil's commanding character, and who were joined by some of the bishops of the exarchate, and by an irreligious party in the city itself.

He had not been long in his see when he was brought into open collision with the civil power. The Arian Emperor, Valens, made a progress through the East, from Constantinople to Antioch, in A.D. 371, 372, with the determination of deposing the Catholic bishops in the countries which he traversed; and about the end of the former year he came to Cæsarea. The Prætorian Prefect, Modestus, travelled before him, proposing to the Bishops of the cities, which lay on his road, the alternative of communicating with the Arians, or losing their sees. He summoned Basil into his presence, in his turn, and set before him the arguments which had been already found successful with others,—that it was foolish to resist the times, and to trouble the Church about inconsiderable questions; and he promised him the prince's favour for him and his friends, if he complied. Failing by soft language, he adopted a higher tone; but he found his match. Gregory has preserved the dialogue which passed between them.

"What is the meaning of this, you Basil (said the Prefect, a bitter Arian, not deigning to style him bishop), that you stand out against so great a prince, and are self-willed when others yield?

"BASIL: What would you? and what is my extravagance? I have not yet learned it.

"MODESTUS: Your not worshipping after the emperor's manner, when the rest of your party have given way and been overcome.

"BASIL: I have a Sovereign whose will is otherwise, nor can I bring myself to worship any creature—I a creature of God, and commanded to be a god.

"MODESTUS : For whom do you take me?

"BASIL : For a thing of nought, while such are your commands.

"MODESTUS : Is it, then, a mere nothing for one like you to have rank like myself, and to have my fellowship?

"BASIL : You are Prefect, and in noble place : I own it. Yet God's majesty is greater ; and it is much for me to have your fellowship, for we are both God's creatures. But it is as great a thing to be fellow to any other of my flock, for Christianity lies not in distinction of persons, but in faith.

"The Prefect was angered at this, and rose from his chair, and abruptly asked Basil if he did not fear his power.

"BASIL : Fear what consequences? what sufferings?

"MODESTUS : One of those many pains which a Prefect can inflict.

"BASIL : Let me know them.

"MODESTUS : Confiscation, exile, tortures, death.

"BASIL : Think of some other threat. These have no influence upon me. He runs no risk of confiscation, who has nothing to lose, except these mean garments and a few books. Nor does he care for exile, who is not circumscribed by place, who does not make a home of the spot he dwells in, but everywhere a home whithersoever he be cast, or rather everywhere God's home, whose pilgrim he is and wanderer. Nor can tortures harm a frame so frail as to break under the first blow. You could but strike once, and death would be gain. It would but send me the sooner to Him for whom I live and labour, for whom I am dead rather than alive, to whom I have long been journeying.

"MODESTUS : No one yet ever spoke to Modestus with such freedom.

"BASIL : Peradventure Modestus never yet fell in with a bishop ; or surely in a like trial you would have heard like language. O Prefect, in other things we are gentle, and more humble than all men living, for such is the commandment ; so as not to raise our brow, I say not against 'so great a prince,' but even against one of least account. But when God's honour is at stake, we think of nothing else, looking simply to Him. Fire and the sword, beasts of prey, irons to rend the flesh, are an indulgence rather than a terror to a Christian. Therefore insult, threaten, do your worst, make the most of your power. Let the emperor be informed of my purpose. Me you gain not, you persuade not, to an impious creed, by menaces even more frightful."—*Greg.* Orat. 43.

Modestus parted with him with the respect which firmness necessarily inspires in those who witness it; and, going to the emperor, repeated the failure of his attempt. A second conversation between the bishop and the great officers of the court took place in the presence, as some suppose, of Valens himself, who had generosity enough to admire his high spirit, and to dismiss him without punishment. Indeed, his admiration of Basil occasioned a fresh trial of the archbishop's constancy, more distressing, perhaps, than any which he had hitherto undergone. On the feast of the Epiphany, he attended, with all his court, the church where Basil offered the Holy Sacrifice, and heard his sermon. The collected air of the Bishop, the devotion of the clergy, the numbers and the attention of the congregation, and the power of their voices, fairly overcame him, and he almost fainted away. At the Offertory he made an effort to approach the altar to present his oblation; but none of the ministers of the church presenting themselves to receive it from him, his limbs again gave way, and it was only by the assistance of one of them that he was kept from falling.

It would be a satisfaction to be able to indulge a hope that the good feelings of the emperor were more than the excitement of the moment; but his persevering persecution of the Catholics for years afterwards forbids the favourable supposition. However, for the time Basil gained him. Modestus even became the saint's friend; Cappadocia was secured, in great measure, from the sufferings with which the Catholics elsewhere were visited, and some of the best of the imperial lands in the neighbourhood were made over for the endowment of an hospital which Basil had founded for lepers. He seems in the event to have succeeded in introducing such institutions throughout his province.

4.

Basil, from his multiplied trials, may be called the Jeremiah or Job of the fourth century, though occupying the honoured place of a ruler in the Church at a time when heathen violence was over. He had a sickly constitution, to which he added the rigour of an ascetic life. He was surrounded by jealousies and dissensions at home; he was accused of heterodoxy abroad; he was insulted and roughly treated by great men; and he laboured, apparently without fruit, in the endeavour to restore unity to Christendom and stability to its Churches. If temporal afflictions work out for the saints "an exceeding weight of glory," who is higher in the kingdom of heaven than Basil?

As to his austerities, we know something of them from his own picture what a monk's life should be, and from Gregory's description of them. In a letter to the latter (*Ep.* 2), Basil limits the food of his recluses to bread, water, herbs, with but one meal a day, and allows of sleep only till midnight, when they were to rise for prayer. And he says to the emperor Julian, "Cookery with us is idle; no knife is familiar with blood; our daintiest meal is vegetables with coarsest bread and vapid wine."—*Ep.* 41. Gregory, in like manner, when expecting a visit from Basil, writes to Amphilochius to send him "some fine pot-herbs, if he did not wish to find Basil hungry and cross."—*Ep.* 12. And in his account of him, after his death, he says, that "he had but one inner and one outer garment; his bed was the ground; little sleep, no bath; his food bread and salt, his drink the running stream."—*Orat.* 20. He slept in a hair-shirt, or other rough garment; the sun was his fire; and he braved the severest frosts in the severe climate of Cappadocia. Even when Bishop he was supported by the continual charity of his friends. He kept nothing.

His constitution was naturally weak, or rather sickly. What his principal malady was, is told us in the following passage of his history, which furnishes at the same time another instance of the collisions in which he was involved with the civil power. A widow of rank being importuned with a proposal of marriage from a powerful quarter, fled for refuge to the altar. St. Basil received her. This brought him into trouble with the Vicar of Pontus, whose jurisdiction extended over Cappadocia, and who in extreme indignation summoned him. When he had presented himself, the magistrate gave orders to pull off his outer garment. His inner garment, which remained, did not conceal his emaciated body. The brutal persecutor threatened to tear out his liver. Basil smiled and answered, "Thanks for your intention: where it is at present, it has been no slight annoyance." However, though it is hardly to the point here to mention it, the Vicar got the worst of it. The city rose,—Cæsarea, I suppose; the people swarmed about the Court, says Gregory, as bees smoked out of their home. The armourers, for whom the place was famous, the weavers, nay the women, with any weapon which came to hand, with clubs, stones, firebrands, spindles, besieged the Vicar, who was only saved from immediate death by the interposition of his prisoner.

But to return: on one occasion he gives the following account of his maladies to Eusebius, Bishop of Samosata.

"What was my state of mind, think you, when I received your

piety's letter? When I thought of the feelings which its language expressed, I was eager to fly straight to Syria; but when I thought of the bodily illness, under which I lay bound, I saw myself unequal, not only to flying, but to turning even on my bed. This is the fiftieth day of my illness, on which our beloved and excellent brother and deacon Elpidius has arrived. I am much reduced by the fever, which, failing what it might feed on, lingers in this dry flesh as in an expiring wick, and so has brought on a wasting and tedious illness. Next, my old plague, the liver, coming upon it, has kept me from taking nourishment, prevented sleep, and held me on the confines of life and death, granting just life enough to feel its inflictions. In consequence I have had recourse to the hot springs, and have availed myself of aid from medical men."—*Ep.* 138.

The fever here mentioned seems to have been an epidemic, and so far unusual; but his ordinary state of health will be understood from the following letter, written to the same friend in the beginning of his illness, in which he describes the fever as almost a change for the better.

"In what state the good Isaaces has found me, he himself will best explain to you; though his tongue cannot be tragic enough to describe my sufferings, so great was my illness. Yet any one who knows me ever so little, will be able to conjecture what it was. For, if when I am called well, I am weaker even than persons who are given over, you may fancy what I was when I was thus ill. However, since disease is my natural state, it would follow (let a fever have its jest) that in this change of habit, my health became especially flourishing. But it is the scourge of the Lord which goes on increasing my pain according to my deserts; therefore I have received illness upon illness, so that now even a child may see that this shell of mine must for certain fail, unless perchance God's mercy, vouchsafing to me in His long-suffering time for repentance, now, as often before, extricate me from evils beyond human cure. This shall be as it is pleasing to Him and good for myself."—*Ep.* 136.

Eusebius seems to have been especially the confidant of his bodily sufferings. Five years before, he writes to him a similar description in answer to a similar call. "When," he says, "by God's grace and the aid of your prayers, I seemed to be somewhat recovering from my illness, and had rallied my strength, then the winter came upon me, keeping me in-doors and confining me where I was. It was, indeed, much milder than usual, yet enough to prevent, not only my travelling during it, but even my putting out my head even a little from my room."—*Ep.* 27. And nine years later than this, and three years before his death, he says, that for a time "all remaining hope of life had left him." "I cannot number," he adds, "the various affections which have befallen me, my weakness, the violence of the fever, and the bad state of my constitution."—*Ep.* 198. One especial effect of his complaints was to hinder his travelling, which, as his presence was continually needed, accounts for his frequently insisting on them. To Amphilochius, bishop of Iconium, he writes in the same year: "The remains of my illness are sufficient to keep me from the least motion. I went in a carriage as far as the Martyrs, and had very nearly a relapse; so I am obliged to beg you to excuse me. If the matter could be put off for a few days, then, by God's grace, I will be with you, and share your counsels."—*Ep.* 202. To a friend, whom at an earlier date he was urging to visit him in his retreat, he says, "You must not answer with Diogenes to Alexander, It is no farther from you to me, than from me to you. For my sickness almost makes me like a plant, confined ever to one spot; besides, to pass life in hiding I account among the first of goods."—*Ep.* 9. He elsewhere speaks of his state of health as "bodily weakness, natural to him from childhood to age, and chastening him according to the just judgment of an Allwise Governor."—*Ep.* 203. At forty-five he calls himself an old man; and by the next year he had lost his teeth. He died at the age of fifty.

Yet, in spite of his infirmities, he does not seem at all to have spared himself the fatigue of travelling. He writes to Meletius, bishop of Antioch,—

"Many other journeys from my own country have engaged me. I crossed over to Pisidia, to arrange, in conjunction with the bishops there, the affairs of our Isaurian brethren. The journey to Pontus followed, Eustathius having put Dazimon into sufficient confusion, and persuaded many there to separate from my church. I went as far as my brother Peter's cottage near Neocæsarea. On my return, when I was very ill from the rains and from despondency, letters arrived forthwith from the East," etc.—*Ep.* 216.

5.

Something of St. Basil's tone of mind is seen in the above extracts; it will be seen more fully in three letters of expostulation to friends, written under very different circumstances.

The first is a familiar letter to one who, having congratulated him on his elevation to the see of Cæsarea, was disappointed at not receiving a reply.

BASIL TO PERGAMIUS.

"I am naturally forgetful, and have had a multitude of engagements, which has increased my infirmity. If I do not remember receiving a letter from your nobleness, I still believe you sent it to me; it is impossible you should be incorrect. Yet it is not I that am in fault, but he who did not ask for an answer. However, you now receive from me what will at once account for what is past, and have a claim on you for a reply. So, when you next write, you must not think that you are making a second beginning of our correspondence, but merely paying your debt for my present letter. For though it be an acknowledgment of what has gone before, yet being more than twice as long, it will answer the other office too. Do you observe how sharp leisure makes me? My good friend, let me beg of you not to turn, as you have done, what is a small matter, into a charge so great, that perhaps no greater baseness could be imputed to me. For a forgetfulness of friendships, and insolence engendered by power, contain in them all that is wretched. Whether it is that we do not love, as the Lord has bid us, then we have lost His image; or whether we are puffed up and gorged with vain glory and boasting, we fall into the sure condemnation of the devil. Therefore, if you have accused me advisedly, pray for my escape from the sin which you discern in my conduct; if, on the other hand, from a habit I do not understand, your tongue has fallen into those words, I shall take comfort and shall tax your goodness to adduce facts in proof of it. Be sure of this, that my present annoyance has been the means of humbling me. I am not likely to forget you till I forget myself; so, for the future, do not let my engagements be considered as a proof of a bad disposition."—*Ep.* 56.

Basil's election had been very distasteful to a certain number of the bishops of his province; who, finding they could not prevent it, refused to be present at his consecration, or to hold intercourse with him. Among these was Basil's uncle, Gregory. This was more than usually distressing, inasmuch as Gregory had been more than an ordinary uncle to him. He had been closely connected with Basil's family circle, which was a sort of nursery of bishops and saints. His father, whose name also was Basil, and whose profession was that of rhetoric, was a man of landed property in Pontus and Cappadocia, and of good family, as was his wife Emmelia, Basil's mother. He numbered on the line of both his parents, high functionaries, military and civil. Nor was his descent less illustrious in a Christian aspect. His maternal grandfather was a martyr; his father's parents had been driven to live seven years in the woods and mountains of Pontus, during the Dioclesian persecution. Basil was one of ten children; three of them lived to be bishops; four of them are saints, St. Basil himself, St.

Gregory Nyssen, St. Peter, and St. Macrina, besides his mother, St. Emmelia. Another brother, Naucratius, embraced the life of a solitary, and was drowned while engaged in works of mercy. Such being the character of Basil's paternal home, a difference with Gregory, his paternal uncle, would, under any circumstances, have been painful; but it so happened that the latter had been called to take on him a father's duties towards Basil and his brothers. Their father had died when they were young, and Gregory, who was one of the bishops of Cappadocia, had superintended what remained of Basil's education. As to his mind, it had already been formed by three women, his grandmother Macrina, his mother Emmelia, and another Macrina, his elder sister.

Basil had conceived that his uncle's estrangement from him was removed; but on his saying so, his uncle wrote to him to deny the fact. On this he wrote the following letter, which happily had the desired effect.

BASIL TO HIS UNCLE GREGORY.

"I have kept silence; must there be no end of it? Shall I bear any longer to enforce this most heavy penalty of silence against myself—neither writing nor conversing with you? Indeed, in persisting hitherto in this melancholy determination, I seem to have a right to use the Prophet's words—'I have been still, and refrained myself as a woman in travail'—always anxious to see or hear from you, always for my sins disappointed. No other cause can be assigned for the present state of things, except that my estrangement from your love is certainly an infliction on me for old transgressions. Yet, even though the very naming of estrangement were not a sin, if shown towards you by whomsoever, yet certainly it were, if shown by me, to whom you have been from the first in place of a father. However, the time of my punishment has been long indeed. So I can hold no longer, and am the first to speak; beseeching you to remember both me and yourself, who have treated me, all through my life, with a greater tenderness than relationship could claim, and to love the city which I govern for my sake, instead of alienating yourself from it on my account.

"If, therefore, there is any consolation in Christ, if there is any fellowship of the Spirit, if any bowels of commiseration, fulfil my prayer; put an end at once to this gloom, making a beginning of a more cheerful state of things for the future, becoming yourself the guide of the others towards right, not following another towards wrong. No one's features were ever more strongly marked, than your soul is characterized with peaceableness and mildness. It becomes such an one to draw others to him, and to supply all who approach him, as it were, with the fragrant oil of his own amiableness. There may be obstacles just now; but, in a short time, the blessedness of peace will be recognized. But while our dissension gives opportunity to tale-bearers, our complaints of each other must necessarily be increasing. It is unbecoming in other parties to neglect me, but more than any, in your venerableness. Tell me if I am any where wrong, and I shall be the better in future. But it is impossible to do so without intercourse. If, on the other hand, I have committed no offence, why am I hated? This I say by way of self-defence.

"What those churches will say for themselves, which with so little honour are partners in our dispute, I will not ask, for I have no wish to give offence by this letter, but to remove it. You are too clear-sighted for anything of this kind to escape you; and will take, and lay before others, a much more accurate view than mine can be. Indeed, you were sensible of the existing evils in the churches before I was, and have felt them more keenly, having long ago learnt of the Lord not to despise any of the least of His matters. At present, however, the mischief is not confined to one or two individuals, but whole cities and communities are partners in our misfortune. Comfort me then, either by coming to see me, or by writing, or by sending for me, or in any way you will. My own earnest wish is, that you would make your appearance in my church, so that both I and my people might be benefited by the sight and the words of your grace. This will be best, if possible; but I shall welcome any proposition which you will make. Only, let me beg of you to give me some sure intelligence of your intention."—*Ep.* 59.

6.

This misunderstanding he surmounted: but the following was on a far more painful matter, being not so much a misunderstanding between friends, as a real difference of religious creed, which did not admit of removal.

Eustathius had been one of the pupils of Arius at Alexandria, and was admitted into orders at Antioch by the Arians. After a time, he joined the Semi-Arian, or middle, party in Asia Minor, with whom he continued some years. On the death of the Emperor Constantius, this party lost the patronage of the court; and during the reign of Valens, a purely Arian prince, Eustathius deserted them, and, after a time, professed himself of the new Emperor's religion. Up to this date he had the friendship of Basil, as bearing about him all the marks of a zealous and honest, though erring man. He was austere in his manner of life, professed a most strict adherence to truth, and seemed not destitute of the spirit of Christian love. On occasion of his first lapsing after the death of Constantius, he carried the appearance of sincerity so far as even to betake himself to Rome for the purpose of subscribing the Catholic creed, and to acknowledge publicly his offence. Afterwards he became a bitter enemy of Basil. The following letter was written A.D. 375, about the time of the first rupture between him and Basil, and is interesting as disclosing some particulars of the early life of the latter.

BASIL IN ANSWER TO EUSTATHIUS, BISHOP OF SEBASTE.

"There is a time for silence, and a time for speaking, as the preacher says; so now, after keeping silence a sufficient time, it is seasonable to open my mouth in order to explain what is unknown. For great Job himself endured his afflictions silently a long while, manifesting his fortitude by bearing up against the heaviest afflictions. But after fulfilling that silent conflict, that continued confinement of his grief in the depth of his heart, then he opened his mouth and uttered what all know, and spoke aloud what is told us in Scripture. I too have been near three years silent, and may aspire to the prophet's boast, being as one who heard not, and in whose mouth are no reproofs. Thus I shut up within me the pain that I felt from the calumnies heaped upon me. I expected the evil would cure itself; for I supposed that things were said against me, not from any bad feeling, but from ignorance. Now, however, that I perceive the enmity against me continues, and that the parties who manifest it show no sorrow for what they have said, nor are anxious to heal what is past, but increase their united efforts towards the same end which they originally proposed, to annoy me and injure my reputation with the brethren, silence is no longer safe.

"After long time spent in vanity, and almost the whole of my youth vanishing in the idle toil of studying that wisdom which God has made folly, when at length, roused as from a deep sleep, I gazed upon the marvellous light of Gospel truth, and discerned the unprofitableness of the wisdom taught by the perishing authorities of this world, much did I bewail my wretched life, and pray that guidance would be vouchsafed to me for an entrance into the doctrines of godliness. And above all was it a care to me to reform my heart, which the long society of the corrupt had perverted. So when I read the Gospel, and perceived thence that the best start towards perfection was to sell my goods and share them with my indigent brethren, and altogether to be reckless of this life, and to rid my soul of all sympathy with things on earth, I earnestly desired to find some brother who had made the same choice, and who might make the passage with me over the brief waves of this life. Many did I find in Alexandria, many in the rest of Egypt, and in Palestine, in Cœle-Syria and Mesopotamia, whose abstinence and endurance I admired, and whose constancy in prayer I was amazed at; how they overcame sleep, in spite of the necessity of nature, bearing ever a high and free spirit in hunger and thirst, in cold and nakedness, not regarding the body, nor enduring to spend any thought upon it, but living as if in flesh not their own; how they showed in deed what it is to be sojourners in this world, what it is to have our conversation in heaven. Admiring and extolling the life of these men, who could so in deed carry about with them the dying of the Lord Jesus, I desired that I myself, as far as I could attain, might be an imitator of them."

This expedition was in the year 357, when Basil was

twenty-eight, some years after his stay at Athens, and immediately upon the loss of his brother, Naucratius. He proceeds:

"With this object, finding that there were persons in my own country attempting to rival them, I deemed I had found some aid towards my own salvation, and I made what was seen the token of what was hidden. And since it is difficult to get at the secret heart of a man, I reckoned it was argument enough of humbleness to have an humble clothing; and I gave my faith to the coarse garment, and the girdle, and the untanned sandals. And when many would have dissuaded me from their converse, I would not hear of it, seeing that these men preferred an hardness of living to self-indulgence; and being taken with their extraordinary life, I was zealous in my defence of them. It followed that I would not suffer any attack upon their doctrines, though many contended that they were unsound in creed, and secretly disseminated the doctrines of their master, the founder of the now prevailing heresy. Having never myself heard such from them, I thought the report calumnious. Afterwards, when called to the government of the church, what these chosen guardians and keepers of my life turned out to be, with their pretences to loving aid and intercourse, I say not, lest its seeming incredibility should reflect upon myself, or the belief of it should infect the hearer with misanthropy. And this, indeed, was almost my calamity, had not God's mercies quickly prevented me; for I well nigh fell into a suspicion of every one, thinking truth was nowhere to be found, being wounded in my mind by their deceitful blows. Yet for a while I kept up some sort of intercourse with them; and we had several discussions about points of dogma, and it appeared as if we really agreed. They found in me the same faith which they had heard from me before, for though I have done many things worthy of groans, yet so much I may boast in the Lord, that I never held erroneous doctrine concerning God, nor have had to change my profession. The idea of God which I had from my blessed mother, and her mother Macrina, that has ever grown within me. I did not change about, as reason unfolded, but perfected the rudiments of faith by them delivered to me.

"I am charged of blasphemy towards God, though neither former writing of mine on matters of faith, nor word of mouth uttered publicly by me without book, as usual in the churches of God, can be brought against me. Ask yourself. How often have you visited me at my monastery on the Iris, when my most religious brother, Gregory, was with me, following the same rule of life as myself! Did you then hear from me any such thing? or catch any hint of it, strong or slight? How many days did we pass together as friends, in the village opposite with my mother, and discussed subjects night and day, in which we found each other sympathize?

"A man ought to take much thought—nay, pass many sleepless nights, and seek his duty from God with many tears, ere he ventures to break up a friendship. They ground their conduct altogether on one letter, and that a doubtful one. But in reality this letter is not the cause of their separation. I am ashamed to mention the real reason; and I should not tell it now, nor indeed ever, had not their present behaviour made it necessary for the general good to publish an account of their whole design. These honest persons considered that intimacy with me would stand in the way of their promotion; so, since they had committed themselves by subscription to a creed which I imposed on them (not that I at that time distrusted their views, I own it, but from a wish to obviate the suspicions which most of my brethren who felt with me entertained against them), to prevent their rejection on the part of the now ascendant party, on account of this confession, they then renounced my communion: and this letter was pitched upon as a pretext for the rupture. There cannot be a clearer proof of this than the fact, that, on their disowning me, they circulated their accusations on every side, before acquainting me with them. Their charge was in the hands of others seven days before it reached me: and these persons had received it from others, and intended to send it on. I knew this at the time, from friends who sent me certain intelligence of their measures; but I determined to keep silence, till He, who brings to light the deep secrets, should make manifest their plans by the clearest and most cogent evidence."—*Ep.* 223.

7.

Sensitive, anxious, and affectionate as Basil appears in his letters, he had a reserve and sedateness of manner which his contemporaries sometimes attributed to pride, sometimes to timidity. Gregory Nazianzen notices the former charge, and exclaims:—

"Is it possible for a man to embrace lepers, abasing himself so far, and yet to be supercilious towards those who are in health? to waste his flesh with mortification, yet be swollen in soul with empty elation? to condemn the Pharisee, and to enlarge on his fall through pride, and to know that Christ descended even to a servant's form, and ate with publicans, and washed the disciples' feet, and disdained not the Cross, that He might nail to it *my* sin, and yet to soar beyond the clouds, and count no one his equal; as appears to them who are jealous of him? But I suppose it was the self-possession of his character, and composure and polish, which they named pride."—*Orat.* 43.

This testimony is the stronger, as coming from one whom on one occasion, as we shall see by-and-by, Basil did offend, by behaviour which on the part of some moderns is alleged as the great specimen of his arrogant temper. It is certain, however, from what Gregory says, that the imputation was fastened on him in his day, and the report of it was heard, perhaps believed, by Jerome in his cave at Bethlehem. Words are no safe test of actions; yet most persons, I think, will allow that the following sentences from his Homily on Humility, corroborate what Gregory says in his defence:—

"How," he asks, "shall we attain to saving humility, abandoning the deadly elevation of pride? by practising some act of humility in everything that we do, and by overlooking nothing, from an idea that we shall gain no harm from the neglect. For the soul is influenced by outward observances, and is shaped and fashioned according to its actions. Let, then, thy appearance, and garment, and gait, and sitting, and table, and bedroom, and house, and its furniture, all be directed according to lowliness. And thy speech and singing and conversation, in like manner, look towards meanness and not exaltation. But perhaps thou art awarded the highest seat, and men observe and honour thee? Become equal to those who are in subjection; 'not lording it over the clergy,' saith Scripture; be not like to rulers of this world. For whoso would be first, him our Lord bids be servant of all. In a word, follow after humility, as one enamoured of it. Be in love with it, and it shall glorify thee. So shalt thou nobly journey on to true glory, which is among the Angels; which is with God; and Christ will acknowledge thee as His own disciple, before the Angels, and will glorify thee, if thou learn to copy His humility."—*Hom. de Humil.*

The opposite charge to which his reserve gave rise was that of timidity. It is remarkable that he himself, writing to a friend, playfully notices "the want of spirit" and "the sluggishness" of the Cappadocians, and attributes these qualities to himself.—*Ep.* 48. Accordingly, after his death, the heretic Eunomius accuses the opponent of Valens and Modestus of being "a coward and craven, and skulking from the heavier labours," speaking contemptuously of his "retired cottage and his closely-fastened door, and his fluttered manner on persons entering, and his voice, and look, and expression of countenance, and the other symptoms of fear."—*Greg. Nyss., App.* p. 46. This malicious account may be just so far founded on truth, as to make it worth while noticing a curious difference in a little matter which it brings out between Basil and the great Ambrose of Milan, who was a man of the world; for while the former is here represented as fastening his door, it was the peculiarity of Ambrose never to shut himself into his house, but to be accessible at all times. Philostorgius, the Arian historian, in like manner, speaks of Basil, as "superior to many in the power of discussion; but, from timidity of mind, withdrawing from public disputations." And Gregory makes several remarks on his friend, which serve to illustrate the shyness or refinement of mind complained of by these writers. The following is curious, as bringing Basil before our eyes.

"Such were the virtues of the man, such the fulness of his celebrity, that others, in order to gain reputation, copied many even of his peculiarities, nay, his bodily imperfections; I mean, for instance, his paleness, his beard, the character of his gait, his deliberateness in speaking, as being generally deep in thought, and intent on his subject; which things most of them copying ill, and indeed not understanding, turned into gloom;—moreover, the quality of his garment, and the shape of his bed, and his mode of eating, nothing of which in him was studied, but natural and spontaneous. And you may fall in with many Basils as far as outside goes, figures in shadow; it is too much to say echoes. For echo, at least, repeats the last syllables even more clearly; but these are much farther off from Basil than they desire to be near him. Moreover, it is no longer a common, but the greatest of honours, and with reason, to have ever happened to have been in his company, or to have shown attentions to him, or to carry with one the memory of anything said or done by him, playfully or in earnest, since the by-doings of this man are more precious and illustrious than what others do with labour."—*Orat.* 43.

Reference is made in these last words to Basil's playfulness. This quality his letters abundantly vindicate to him, though it is of a pensive sort. Lest the reader should go away with a more austere notion of him than truth warrants, I will add the following passage from St. Gregory.

"Who made himself more amiable than he to the well-conducted? or more severe when men were in sin? whose very smile was many a time praise, whose silence a reproof, punishing the evil in a man's own conscience. If he was not full of talk, nor a jester, nor a holder forth, nor generally acceptable from being all things to all men, and showing good-nature; what then? Is not this to his praise, not his blame, among sensible men? Yet, if we ask for this, who so pleasant as he in social intercourse, as I know who have had such experience of him? Who could tell a story with more wit? who could jest so playfully? who could give a hint more delicately, so as neither to be overstrong in his rebuke, nor remiss through his gentleness?"—*Orat.* 43.

Basil died on the first of January, A.D. 379, having

been born in 329. He rallied before his death, and his last discourses were delivered with more strength than usual. His closing act was to ordain some of his immediate disciples. He died with the words upon his tongue, "Into Thy hands I commend my spirit."

CHAPTER II.

LABOURS OF BASIL.

"And I said, I have laboured in vain; I have spent my strength without cause, and in vain: therefore my judgment is with the Lord, and my work with my God."

I.

THE instruments raised up by Almighty God for the accomplishment of His purposes are of two kinds, equally gifted with faith and piety, but from natural temper and talent, education, or other circumstances, differing in the means by which they promote their sacred cause. The first of these are men of acute and ready mind, with accurate knowledge of human nature, and large plans, and persuasive and attractive bearing, genial, sociable, and popular, endued with prudence, patience, instinctive tact and decision in conducting matters, as well as boldness and zeal. Such in a measure we may imagine the single-minded, the intrepid, the much-enduring Hildebrand, who, at a time when society was forming itself anew, was the saviour, humanly speaking, of the City of God. Such, in an earlier age, was the majestic Ambrose; such the never-wearied Athanasius. These last-named luminaries of the Church came into public life early, and thus learned how to cope with the various tempers, views, and measures of the men they encountered there. Athanasius was but twenty-seven when he went with Alexander to the Nicene Council, and the year after he was Bishop of Alexandria. Ambrose was consecrated soon after the age of thirty.

Again, there is an instrument in the hand of Providence, of less elaborate and splendid workmanship, less rich in its political endowments, so to call them, yet not less beautiful in its texture, nor less precious in its material. Such is the retired and thoughtful student, who remains years and years in the solitude of a college or a monastery, chastening his soul in secret, raising it to high thought and single-minded purpose, and when at length called into active life, conducting himself with firmness, guilelessness, zeal like a flaming fire, and all the sweetness of purity and integrity. Such an one is often unsuccessful in his own day; he is too artless to persuade, too severe to please; unskilled in the weaknesses of human nature, unfurnished in the resources of ready wit, negligent of men's applause, unsuspicious, open-hearted, he does his work, and so leaves it; and it seems to die; but in the generation after him it lives again, and on the long run it is difficult to say, which of the two classes of men has served the cause of truth the more effectually. Such, perhaps, was Basil, who issued from the solitudes of Pontus to rule like a king, and minister like the lowest in the kingdom; yet to meet little but disappointment, and to quit life prematurely in pain and sorrow. Such was his friend, the accomplished Gregory, however different in other respects from him, who left his father's roof for an heretical city, raised a church there, and was driven back into retirement by his own people, as soon as his triumph over the false creed was secured. Such, perhaps, St. Peter Damiani in the middle age; such St. Anselm, such St. Edmund. No comparison is, of course, attempted here between the religious excellence of the two descriptions of men; each of them serves God according to the peculiar gifts given to him. If we might continue our instances by way of comparison, we should say that St. Paul reminds us of the former, and Jeremiah of the latter.

These remarks are intended as introductory to portions of Basil's letters, on various subjects indeed, but all illustrative of the then distracted state of the Church in his part of Christendom, and of his labours, apparently fruitless at the time, in restoring to it truth and peace.

2.

The disorders of Christendom, and especially of the East, and still more of Asia Minor, were so great in Basil's day, that a heathen spectator might have foretold the total overthrow of the Church. So violent a convulsion never has been experienced in Christendom since, not even in the times of St. Gregory the Seventh and St. Pius the Fifth; it would almost seem as if the powers of evil, foreseeing what the Kingdom of the Saints would be, when once heathen persecutions ceased, were making a final effort to destroy it. In Asia Minor the Church was almost without form, "and void and empty;" religious interests were reduced, as it were, to a state of chaos, and Basil seems to have been the principle of truth and order, divinely formed, divinely raised up, for harmonising the discordant elements, and bringing them to the unity of faith and love. However, the destined result did not show itself in his day. Valens persecuted in behalf of Arianism till the year before the saint's death; the Semi-Arians continued their schism after it: and, trying to lead them towards the truth, Basil exposed himself to calumnies both on the part of his brethren, as if favouring the prevailing heresy, and of the heretics, as if maintaining an opposite one. There were dissensions, too, existing within the Church, as well as without. I have already spoken of Basil's difference with his predecessor Eusebius, and of a party which his uncle joined, which was formed against him on his succeeding to the see. Jealousies or suspicions, of which he was the subject, extended throughout his exarchate. He seems to have had authority, more or less defined, over the whole of the country which the Romans called Pontus, which was more than half of Asia Minor, and comprised in it eleven provinces. Ancyra, Neocæsarea, Tyana, among other principal sees, acknowledged him more or less as their ecclesiastical superior. Now we have records of his being opposed by the bishops of each of these cities. When he passed out of his own district into the neighbouring jurisdiction of Antioch, he found that metropolis distracted by schism; four bishops in the see at once, two heretical, a third acknowledged by Rome and the Alexandrians, a fourth in communion with himself. When he went on to the South and West, and negotiated with Alexandria and Rome for the settlement of these disorders, he met with nothing but disappointment, though saints were upon the ecclesiastical thrones of either city. Such is the history of his episcopate,—for which he exchanged his sweet monastic life.

As to the party of bishops who withstood his election, he overcame most of them in the course of a few years, as he did his uncle, by firmness and kindness, though for a time they gave him trouble. "Our friends," he says to Eusebius of Samosata, shortly after his elevation, "have not shown themselves at all better than we expected. They made their appearance immediately you were gone, and said and did many disagreeable things; and at length departed, confirming their schism with us."—

Ep. 20. Three years afterwards he complains to the same friend of the impediments which their conduct threw in the way of his exertions for the Church.

"That you may not suppose," he says, "that the interests of the Churches are betrayed to our enemies by my negligence, I would have your reverence know, that the bishops in communion with me, whether from disinclination, or from continued suspicion of me and want of frankness, or from that opposition to right measures, which the devil engenders, refuse to act with me. In profession, indeed, the greater number of us are all together, including the excellent Bosporius; but in truth in not one even of the most important matters do they act with me. The despondency which this occasions is the principal cause why I do not get well, indisposition returning to me continually from excessive grief. What can I do by myself? the canons, as you yourself know, do not permit one man to put them in force. Yet what remedy have I not tried? What rule is there to which I have not called their attention, by letter or in conversation? For they came up into town on the news of my death; and, when it pleased God that they found me alive, I represented to them what was reasonable. And they defer to me when present, and promise all that is reasonable; but when they have gone away, they recur to their own opinion."—*Ep.* 141.

Among the injuries which Eustathius inflicted upon Basil, was his spreading a report that Basil was a follower of the heresiarch Apollinaris. This calumny, which is alluded to in the letter written in his own defence in answer to Eustathius, which I have quoted in the foregoing chapter, seems to have reached and been believed by the bishop of Ancyra, by name Athanasius; who, having been once an Arian, had since conformed, and shown a good deal of zeal for the true faith. This bishop said some very harsh things of Basil in consequence; which led the latter, who had an esteem for him, to write him the following letter:—

BASIL TO ATHANASIUS, BISHOP OF ANCYRA.

"I am told by persons who come to me from Ancyra, and that by many more than I can number, and all saying the same thing, that you, dear friend (how may I use mild terms?) have not the kindest recollections of me, nor feel in the way natural to you. For myself, nothing that can happen astonishes me, be sure of that; there is no one at all whose change would contradict my expectation, since I have long learned the weakness of human nature and its proneness to turn right round. Hence I think it no great matter, though my cause has fallen back, and for the honour which I had, calumny and slight are my present portion. But this is what seems to me so very strange and preternatural, that you should be the man to be angry or incensed with me; nay, and to use threats against me, as those say who heard them. Now, as to the threats, I must speak frankly, I plainly laughed at them. Indeed, I should be a very child to fear such bugbears. But what is a real cause of apprehension to me, and of much anxiety, is, that an accurate judgment, such as yours,—which I believed was preserved for the comfort of the Churches, both as a rare foundation of orthodoxy and a seed of ancient and genuine love,—that it should so far yield to the existing state of things, as to trust the calumnies of chance-comers more than your long experience of myself, and to be carried away without evidence, to such extravagant suspicions. Yet why do I say suspicions? for a person who was indignant, and who threatened, as they report of you, seems to have manifested the anger, not of suspicion, but of clear and unanswerable conviction.

"But as I have said, I ascribe it all to the times; for what was the trouble, excellent man, in your (as it were) talking with me confidentially in a short letter, on the matters you wished to speak about? or, if you did not like to trust such things to writing, why not send for me? But if it was altogether necessary to speak out, and the impetuosity of anger left no time for delay, at any rate you might have made use of some intimate friend, who could keep a secret, to convey your message to us. But, as the case stands, who has come to you on any business, whose ears have not been filled with the charge, that I am writing and putting together certain mischievous things? For this was your very word, as accurate reporters say. I have thought a good deal on the subject, but am in as great difficulty as ever. It has come into my mind to think whether some heretic, maliciously giving my name to his own writing, has not distressed your orthodoxy, and led you to utter that speech. You yourself may free me from my perplexity, if you would kindly state, without reserve, what has induced you to take such offence at me"—*Ep.* 25.

3.

Another achievement of the same Eustathius was the separation of a portion of the coast of Pontus from the Church of Cæsarea, on the pretence that its Bishops were in heresy, which for a time caused Basil great despondency, as if he were being left solitary in all Christendom, without communion with other places. With the advice of the bishops of Cappadocia, he addressed an expostulation to these separatists; a portion of which runs as follows:—

"Up to this day I live in much affliction and grief, having the feeling present before me, that you are wanting to me. For when God tells me—who took on Him His sojourn in the flesh for the very purpose that, by patterns of duty, He might regulate our life, and might by His own voice announce to us the Gospel of the kingdom—when He says, 'By this shall all men know that you are My disciples, if you love one another,' and whereas the Lord left His own peace to His disciples as a farewell gift, when about to complete the dispensation in the flesh, saying, 'Peace I leave with you, My peace I give you,' I cannot persuade myself that without love to others, and without, as far as rests with me, peaceableness towards all, I can be called a worthy servant of Jesus Christ. I have waited a long while for the chance of your love paying us a visit. For ye are not ignorant that we, being exposed on all sides, as rocks running out into the sea, sustain the fury of the heretical waves, which, because they break around us, fail to cover the district behind us. I say 'we,' in order to refer it, not to human power, but to the grace of God, who, by the weakness of men shows His power, as says the prophet, in the person of the Lord, 'Will ye not fear me, who have placed the sand as a boundary to the sea?'—for by the weakest and most contemptible of all things, the sand, the Mighty One has bounded the great and full sea

Since, then, this is our position, it became your love to be frequent in sending true brothers to visit us who labour with the storm, and more frequently letters of love, partly to confirm our courage, partly to correct any mistake of ours. For we confess that we are liable to numberless mistakes, being men, and living in the flesh.

"Let not this consideration influence you—'We dwell on the sea, we are exempt from the sufferings of the generality, we need no succour from others; so what is the good to us of foreign communion?' For the same Lord who divided the islands from the continent by the sea, bound the island Christians to the continental by love. Nothing, brethren, separates us from each other, but deliberate estrangement. We have one Lord, one faith, the same hope. The hands need each other; the feet steady each other. The eyes possess their clear apprehension from agreement. We, for our part, confess our own weakness, and we seek your fellow-feeling. For we are assured, that though ye are not present in body, yet by the aid of prayer, ye will do us much benefit in these most critical times. It is neither decorous before men, nor pleasing to God, that you should make avowals which not even the Gentiles adopt, which know not God. Even they, as we hear though the country they live in be sufficient for all things, yet, on account of the uncertainty of the future, make much of alliances with each other, and seek mutual intercourse as being advantageous to them. Yet we,—the sons of fathers, who have decreed, that by brief notes the proofs of communion should be carried about from one end of the earth to the other, and that all should be citizens and familiars with all,—we now sever ourselves from the whole world, and are neither ashamed at our solitariness, nor shudder that on us is fallen the fearful prophecy of the Lord, 'Because of lawlessness abounding, the love of the many shall wax cold.'"—*Ep.* 203.

It does not appear what success attended this appeal; difficulties of a similar but more painful nature, which occurred at the same time, hide from us the sequel of the history. I allude to the alienation from him of the Church of Neocæsarea, a place dear to Basil, as having been his residence in youth, the home of many of his relations, and the see of St. Gregory, the Wonder-worker, in the third century, from whom, through his father's family, Basil had especially received his traditions of Christian truth. There seems to have been in high quarters there a lurking attachment to Sabellian doctrine. Sabellianism is the opposite extreme to Arianism; and its upholders would call Basil Arian, first because he was Catholic, and not Sabellian, as is the way with the partisans of extremes; and next because he had Semi-Arian friends. This was one chief cause of the opposition shown to him; but there were other causes unknown. It is remarkable that the coolness began during the episcopate of Musonius, though he was a man whom Basil mentions with much respect and gratitude. He thus speaks of him, on his death, in a letter of condolement addressed to the Neocæsareans. This was before Basil became Bishop.

"A man is gone, undeniably preëminent among his contemporaries for all earthly endowments, the bulwark of his country, the ornament of the Churches, a pillar and ground of the truth, the firm stay of faith in Christ, a protection to his friends, invincible by his adversaries, a guardian of the rules of the Fathers, a foe to innovation; exemplifying in himself the Church's primitive fashion, moulding the form of the Church, committed to him, after its ancient constitution, as after some sacred image, so that those who lived with him seemed to have lived with those who have been luminaries in it for two hundred years and more." He adds, "I would have you aware, that if this blessed man did not concur with me in the pacification of the Churches, on account of certain previous views, as he avowed to me, yet (as God knows, and men know who have had experience of me) at least I omitted no opportunity of fellowship of sentiment with him, and of inviting his assistance in the struggle against heretics."—*Ep.* 28.

4.

But to return: if Basil's Semi-Arian acquaintances brought suspicion upon himself in the eyes of Catholic believers, much more, I say, would they be obnoxious to persons attached, as certain Neocæsareans were, to the Sabellian party, who were in the opposite extreme to the Semi-Arians, and their especial enemies in those times. It is not wonderful, then, that, some years after, he had to write to the Church in question in a strain like the following:—

"There has been a long silence on both sides, revered and well-beloved brethren, just as if there were angry feelings between us. Yet who is there so sullen and implacable towards the party which has injured him, as to lengthen out the resentment which has begun in disgust, through almost a whole life of man? This is happening in our case, though no just occasion of estrangement exists, as far as I myself know, but on the contrary, there being, from the first, many strong reasons for the closest friendship and unity. The greatest and first is this, our Lord's command, who pointedly says: 'By this shall all men know that ye are My disciples, if ye have love one to another.' Next, if it tend much towards intimacy to have the same teachers, there are to you and to me the same teachers of God's mysteries and spiritual Fathers, who from the beginning were the founders of your Church. I mean the great Gregory, and all who, succeeding in order to the throne of your episcopate, like stars rising one after another, have tracked the same course, so as to leave the tokens of the heavenly polity most clear to all who have desire for them. Why is it, then, O venerable among cities, for through you I address the whole city, that no courteous writing comes from you, no welcome voice, but your ears are open to those who aim at slander? What say I, brethren? not that I am a sinless man; not that my life is not full of numberless faults. I know myself; and indeed I cease not my tears by reason of my sins, if by any means I may be able to appease my God, and to escape the punishment threatened against them: But this I say: let him who judges me, search for motes in my eye, if he can say that his own is clear: And in a word, brethren, if my offences admit of cure, why does not such a one obey the Doctor of the Churches, saying, 'Reprove, rebuke, exhort?' If, on the other hand, my iniquity be past cure, why does he not withstand me to the face, and by publishing my transgressions, deliver the

Churches from the mischief which I bring on them? There are bishops; let appeal be made to them. There is a clergy in each of God's dioceses; let the most eminent be assembled. Let whoso will, speak freely, that I may have to deal with a charge, not a slander. If the fault be in a point of faith, let the document be pointed out to me. Again let a fair and impartial inquiry be appointed. Let the accusation be read; let it be brought to the test, whether it does not arise from ignorance in the accuser, not from blame in the matter of the writing. For right things often seem otherwise to those who are deficient in accurate judgment. Equal weights seem unequal, when the arms of the balance are of different sizes."

I interrupt the thread of his self-defence to call attention to this happy illustration. The weights in a balance are the antagonist arguments for and against a point; and its arms represent the opposing assumptions and presumptions on either side, which, varying with each individual judging, modify and alter the motive force of the weights. He continues:—

"Let no one suppose I am making excuses to evade the charge. It is put into your hands, dearest brethren, to investigate for yourselves the points alleged against me. If there be anything you do not understand, put questions to me through persons of your appointment, who will do justice to me; or ask of me explanations in writing. And take all kinds of pains, that nothing may be left unsifted.

"What clearer evidence can there be of my faith, than that I was brought up by my grandmother, blessed woman! who came from you? I mean the celebrated Macrina, who taught me the words of the most blessed Gregory; which, as far as memory had preserved down to her day, she cherished herself, while she fashioned and formed me, while yet a child, upon the doctrines of piety. And when I gained the capacity of thought, my reason being matured by full age, I travelled over much sea and land, and whomever I found walking in the rule of religious faith as delivered to us, those I set down as fathers.

"The fair thing would be to judge of me, not from one or two who do not walk uprightly in the truth, but from the multitude of bishops throughout the world, united with me through the grace of the Lord. Make inquiry of Pisidians, Lycaonians, Isaurians, Phrygians of both provinces, Armenians your neighbours, Macedonians, Achæans, Illyrians, Gauls, Spaniards, the whole of Italy, Sicilians, Africans, the healthy part of Egypt, whatever is left of Syria ; all of whom send letters to me, and in turn receive them from me. Whoso shuns communion with me, he, it cannot escape your accuracy, cuts himself off from the whole Church. Look round about, brethren, with whom do *you* hold communion? if you will not receive it from me, who remains to acknowledge you? Do not reduce me to the necessity of counselling anything unpleasant concerning a Church so dear to me. Ask your fathers, and they will tell you that, though our districts were divided in position, yet in mind they were one, and were governed by one sentiment. Intercourse of the people was frequent ; frequent the visits of the clergy ; the pastors, too, had such mutual affection, that each used the other as teacher and guide in things pertaining to the Lord."—*Ep.* 204.

5.

No good could come of these expostulations, however sincere and affectionate, when there was an heretical spirit at work at bottom. But now let us turn from the North to the South, from Basil's own neighbourhood to foreign Churches, from the small Sabellian party at home, to the extended Arian confederation abroad. We shall find fresh trials befalling Basil. Arianism, indeed, itself, in spite of the patronage of Valens, languished and gave tokens of dying a natural death; but its disputants had raised questions which perplexed numbers whom they did not draw over; till at length the sacred subject in controversy was so clouded and confused by explanations, refinements, and distinctions, that there seemed no chance of Christians ever becoming unanimous in the orthodox creed. The particular party labouring under this mistiness of theological opinions at that day were called Semi-Arians, or Macedonians, for reasons it is not necessary here to detail. They were zealous opponents of the Arians, though originating from among them; and, after the death of Constantius (A.D. 361), they showed a disposition to come back to the Catholics. A union was partially effected, but matters were still in an unsatisfactory state on Basil's elevation (A.D. 371), when he wrote the following letter concerning them to the great Athanasius, then on the point of removal from the Church below:—

BASIL TO ATHANASIUS, BISHOP OF ALEXANDRIA.

"I suppose there is no one feels such pain at the present condition, or rather want of condition of the Churches, as your Grace; comparing, as you naturally must, the present with the past, and considering the difference between the two, and the certainty there is, if the evil proceeds at its present pace, that in a short time the Churches will altogether lose their existing constitution. I have often thought with myself, if the corruption of the Churches seems so sad to me, what must be the feelings of one who has witnessed their former stability and unanimity in the faith. And as your Perfectness has more abundant grief, so one must suppose you have greater anxiety for their welfare. For myself, I have been long of opinion, according to my imperfect understanding of ecclesiastical matters, that there was one way of succouring our Churches—viz., the coöperation of the bishops of the West. If they would but show, as regards our part of Christendom, the zeal which they manifested in the case of one or two heretics among themselves, there would be some chance of benefit to our common interests; the civil power would be persuaded by the argument derived from numbers, and the people in each place would follow their lead without hesitation. Now there is no one more able to accomplish this than yourself, from sagacity in counsel, and energy in action, and sympathy for the troubles of the brethren, and the reverence felt by the West for your hoary head. Most Reverend Father, leave the world some memorial worthy of your former deeds. Crown your former numberless combats for religion with this one additional achievement. Send to the bishops of the West, from your Holy Church, men powerful in sound doctrine: relate to them our present calamities; suggest to them the mode of relieving us. Be a Samuel to the Churches; condole with flocks harassed by war; offer prayers of peace; ask grace of the Lord, that He may give some token of peace to the Churches. I know letters are but feeble instruments to persuade so great a thing; but while you have no need to be urged on by others, any more than generous combatants by the acclamation of boys, I, on the other hand, am not as if lecturing the ignorant, but adding speed to the earnest.

"As to the remaining matters of the East, you will perhaps wish the assistance of others, and think it necessary to wait for the arrival of the Western bishops. However, there is one Church, the prosperity of which depends entirely on yourself—Antioch. It is in your power so to manage the one party, and to moderate the other, as at length to restore strength to the Church by their union. You know, better than anyone can tell you, that, as is seen in the prescriptions of wise physicians, it is necessary to begin with treating the more vital matters. Now what can be more vital to Christendom than the welfare of Antioch? If we could but settle the differences there, the head being restored, the whole body would regain health."—*Ep.* 66.

I have already observed, that there were two orthodox bishops at Antioch, one of the original succession, the other of the Arian, who had conformed. At the period under review, the Eastern bishops, and Basil among them, had bound themselves in communion with the bishop of the Arian stock; whereas Athanasius, as well as the Western Churches, were, from the very first, on terms of friendship and intercourse with the representative of the original line. In this letter, then, Basil invites Athanasius to what was, in fact, impossible, even to the influence and talents of the great primate of Egypt; for, having recognised one side in dispute, he could not mediate between them. Nothing, then, came of the application.

6.

Basil next addressed himself to the Western Churches. A letter is extant, which is seemingly written to the then Pope, Damasus, on the affairs of the East.

"What," he says, "can be more pleasant than to see persons who are so far disjoined by place, yet, by the union of love, connected into harmony of membership in the body of Christ? Nearly the whole East, most reverend Father, by which I mean the country from Illyricum to Egypt, labours under a heavy storm and surge. We have been in expectation of a visitation from your tender compassion, as the one remedy of these evils. Your extraordinary love has in past time ever charmed our souls, and they were encouraged for a while by the glad report that we were to have some visitation on your part. Send persons like-minded with us, either to reconcile the parties at variance, or to bring the Churches of God to unity, or at least to give you a clearer understanding of the authors of the confusion: so that you may be clear in future with whom it is fitting to hold communion. We are pressing for nothing at all new, but what was customary with the other blessed and divinely-favoured men of old time, and especially with you: We know, from the memory of former times, as we learn on questioning our fathers, and from documents which we still preserve, that Dionysius,* that most blessed bishop, who was eminent with you for orthodoxy and other virtues, visited by letter our Church of Cæsarea, and consoled by letter our fathers, and sent persons to ransom the brotherhood from captivity."—*Ep.* 70.

He next addressed the Western bishops generally, in two letters, which give a most painful account of the state of the East.

BASIL TO HIS HOLY BRETHREN, THE BISHOPS OF THE WEST:

"The merciful God, who ever joins comfort to affliction, has lately given me some consolation amid my sorrows, in the letters which our most reverend Father, Athanasius, has transmitted to us from

* Pope, about A.D. 260.

your Holinesses. Our afflictions are well known without my telling; the sound of them has now gone forth over all Christendom. The dogmas of the fathers are despised; apostolical traditions are set at nought; the discoveries of innovators hold sway in the Churches. Men have learned to be speculatists instead of theologians. The wisdom of the world has the place of honour, having dispossessed the glorying in the Cross. The pastors are driven away, grievous wolves are brought in instead, and plunder the flock of Christ. Houses of prayer are destitute of preachers; the deserts are full of mourners: the aged sorrow, comparing what is with what was; more pitiable the young, as not knowing what they are deprived of. What has been said is sufficient to kindle the sympathy of those who are taught in the love of Christ, yet, compared with the facts, it is far from reaching their gravity."—*Ep.* 90.

In the second letter, addressed to the bishops of Italy and Gaul, he says:—

"The danger is not confined to one Church; not two or three only have fallen in with this heavy tempest. Almost from the borders of Illyricum down to the Thebais, this evil of heresy spreads itself. The doctrines of godliness are overturned; the rules of the Church are in confusion; the ambition of the unprincipled seizes upon places of authority; and the chief seat is now openly proposed as a reward for impiety; so that he whose blasphemies are the more shocking, is more eligible for the oversight of the people. Priestly gravity has perished; there are none left to feed the Lord's flock with knowledge; ambitious men are ever spending, in purposes of self-indulgence and bribery, possessions which they hold in trust for the poor. The accurate observance of the canons is no more; there is no restraint upon sin. Unbelievers laugh at what they see, and the weak are unsettled; faith is doubtful, ignorance is poured over their souls, because the adulterators of the word in wickedness imitate the truth. Religious people keep silence; but every blaspheming tongue is let loose. Sacred things are profaned; those of the laity who are sound in faith avoid the places of worship, as schools of impiety, and raise their hands in solitude with groans and tears to the Lord in heaven.

"While, then, any Christians seem yet to be standing, hasten to us; hasten then to us, our own brothers; yea, we beseech you. Stretch out your hands, and raise us from our knees, suffer not the half of the world to be swallowed up by error ; nor faith to be extinguished in the countries whence it first shone forth. What is most melancholy of all, even the portion among us which seems to be sound, is divided in itself, so that calamities beset us like those which came upon Jerusalem when it was besieged."—*Ep.* 92.

Elsewhere Basil says: "The name of the episcopate has at length belonged to wretched men, the slaves of slaves, none of the servants of God choosing to make himself their rivals, none but the abandoned."—*Ep.* 239. His friend Gregory gives us, in various parts of his works, the very same account of the Eastern Church in his day.

"At this time," he says, "the most holy Order is like to become the most contemptible portion of all that is ours. For the chief seat is gained by evil-doing more than by virtue ; and the sees belong not to the more worthy, but to the more powerful. A ruler is easily found, without effort, who is but recent in point of reputation, sown and sprung up all at once, as fable speaks of giants. We make saints in a day, and we bid men have wisdom who have not learned it, nor have brought beforehand anything to their Order, over and above the will to rise to it."—*Orat.* 43.

7.

The letters addressed to the bishops of the West, which have already been reviewed, were written in 372. In the course of three years, Basil's tone changes about his brethren there : he had cause to be dissatisfied with them, and above all with Pope Damasus, who, as he thought, showed little zeal for the welfare of the East. Basil's discontent is expressed in various letters. For instance, a fresh envoy was needed for the Roman mission ; and he had thoughts of engaging in it his brother Gregory, bishop of Nyssa.

"But," he says, "I see no persons who can go with him, and I feel that he is altogether inexperienced in ecclesiastical matters; and that, though a candid person would both value and improve his acquaintance, yet when a man is high and haughty, and sits aloft, and is, in consequence, unable to hear such as speak truth to him from the earth, what good can come for the common weal, from his intercourse with one who is not of the temper to give in to low flattery?"—*Ep.* 215.

It is observable and curious, that he who was unjustly accused by saints of pride, falls into a like injustice of accusing another saint of pride himself. In another letter, he says to his friend Eusebius:—

"The saying of Diomede suggests itself as applicable, 'I would thou hadst not begged, for haughty is that man.' For, in truth, an elated mind, if courted, is sure to become only still more contemptuous. Besides, if the Lord be entreated, what need we more? but if God's wrath remain, what succour lies for us in Western superciliousness?* They neither know nor bear to learn the true state of things, but, preoccupied by false suspicions, they are now doing just what they did before in the case of Marcellus, when they quarrelled with those who told them the truth, and by their measures strengthened the heresy. As to myself, I had in mind to write to their chief, putting aside form—nothing, indeed, ecclesiastical, but just so much as to insinuate, that they do not know our real state, nor go the way to learn it; and to write generally, concerning the impropriety of pressing hard upon those who are humbled by temptations, or of considering haughtiness as dignity, a sin which is, by itself, sufficient to make God our enemy."—*Ep.* 239.

Though he began to despair of aid from the West, he did not less need it. By the year 376 matters had got worse in the East, and, in spite of his dissatisfaction, he was induced to make a fresh application to his distant brethren. His main object was to reconcile the East and West together, whereas the latter, so far from supporting the Catholics of Asia against the Arians, had

* τῆς δυτικῆς ὀφρύος.

been led to acknowledge a separate communion at Antioch,—almost to introduce a fresh succession,—and had thereby indirectly thrown suspicion upon the orthodoxy of Basil and his friends.

"Why," he expostulates, "has no writing of consolation been sent to us, no invitation of the brethren, nor any other of those attentions which are due to us from the law of love? This is the thirteenth year since the heretical war arose against us, during which more afflictions have come on the Churches than are remembered since Christ's Gospel was preached. Matters have come to this:—the people have left their houses of prayer, and assemble in deserts; a pitiable sight, women and children, old men and others infirm, wretchedly faring in the open air amid the most profuse rains, and snow-storms, and winds, and frost of winter; and again in summer under a scorching sun. To this they submit, because they will not have part in the wicked Arian leaven."—*Ep.* 342.

He repeats this miserable description in another letter, addressed about the same time specially to the bishops of Italy and Gaul.

"Only one offence is now vigorously punished, an accurate observance of our fathers' traditions. For this cause the pious are driven from their countries and transported into the deserts. The iniquitous judges have no reverence for the hoary head, nor for pious abstinence, nor for a Gospel life continued from youth to age. The people are in lamentation; in continual tears at home and abroad; condoling in each other's sufferings. Not a heart so stony but at a father's loss must feel bereavement. There is a cry in the city, a cry in the country, in the roads, in the deserts; one pitiable voice of all, uttering melancholy things. Joy and spiritual cheerfulness are no more; our feasts, are turned into mourning; our houses of prayer are shut up; our altars deprived of the spiritual worship. No longer are there Christians assembling, teachers presiding, saving instructions, celebrations, hymns by night, or that blessed exultation of souls, which arises from communion and fellowship of spiritual gifts. Lament for us; that the Only-begotten is blasphemed, and there is no one to protest; the Holy Spirit is set at nought, and he who could refute, is an exile. Polytheism has got possession. They have among them a great God and a lesser; 'Son' is considered not to denote nature, but to be a title of honour. The Holy Spirit does not complete the Trinity, nor partake in the Divine and Blessed Nature, but, as if one among creatures, is carelessly and idly added to Father and Son. The ears of the simple are led astray, and have become accustomed to heretical profaneness. The infants of the Church are fed on the words of impiety. For what can they do? Baptisms are in Arian hands; the care of travellers; visitation of the sick; consolation of mourners; succour of the distressed; helps of all sorts; administration of the mysteries; which all, being performed by them, become a bond to the people to be on a good understanding with them; so that in a little while, even though liberty be granted to us, no hope will remain that they, who are encompassed by so lasting a deceit, should be brought back again to the acknowledgment of the truth."—*Ep.* 243.

8.

I will add one letter more; written several years before these last; and addressed to Evagrius, a priest of Antioch, who had taken part in Basil's negotiations with Rome, and had expressed an intention, which he did not fulfil, of communicating with Meletius, the bishop of Antioch, whom Basil and the East acknowledged. The letter insinuates the same charges against the Western bishops, which we have seen him afterwards expressing with freedom.

BASIL TO EVAGRIUS, PRESBYTER.

"So far from being impatient at the length of your letter, I assure you I thought it even short, from the pleasure it gave me in reading it. For is there anything more pleasing than the idea of peace? Or, is anything more suitable to the sacred office, or more acceptable to the Lord, than to take measures for effecting it? May you have the reward of the peacemaker, since so blessed an office has been the object of your good desires and efforts. At the same time, believe me, my revered friend, I will yield to none in my earnest wish and prayer to see the day when those who are one in sentiment shall all fill the same assembly. Indeed, it would be monstrous to feel pleasure in the schisms and divisions of the Churches, and not to consider that the greatest of goods consists in the knitting together the members of Christ's body. But, alas! my inability is as real as my desire. No one knows better than yourself, that time alone is the remedy of ills that time has matured. Besides, a strong and vigorous treatment is necessary to get at the root of the complaint. You will understand this hint, though there is no reason why I should not speak out.

"Self-importance, when rooted by habit in the mind, yields to the exertions of no one man, nor one letter, nor a short time; unless there be some arbiter in whom all parties have confidence, suspicions and collisions will never altogether cease. If indeed the influence of divine grace were shed upon me, and gave me power in word and deed and spiritual gifts to prevail with these rival parties, then this daring experiment might be demanded of me; though, perhaps, even then you would not advise me to attempt this adjustment of things by myself, without the coöperation of the bishop [Meletius of Antioch] on whom principally falls the care of the church. But he cannot come hither, nor can I easily undertake a long journey while the winter lasts, or rather I cannot any how, for the Armenian mountains will be soon impassable even to the young and vigorous, to say nothing of my continued bodily ailments. I have no objection to write to tell him all this; but I have no expectation that writing will lead to anything, for I know his cautious character, and after all, written words have little power to convince the mind. There are so many things to urge, and to hear, and to answer, and to object, and to all this a letter is unequal, as having no soul, and being in fact only so much waste paper. However, as I have said, I will write. Only give me credit, most religious and dear brother, for having no private feeling in the matter. Thank God, I have such towards no one. I have not busied myself in the investigation of the supposed or real complaints which are brought against this or that man; so my opinion has a claim on your attention as that of one who really cannot act from partiality or prejudice. I only desire, through the Lord's good-will, that all things may be done with ecclesiastical propriety,

"I was vexed to find from my dear son, Dorotheus, our associate in the ministry, that you had been unwilling to communicate with him. This was not the kind of conversation which you had with me, as well as I recollect. As to my sending to the West, it is quite out of the question. I have no one fit for the service. Indeed, when I look round, I seem to have no one on my side. I can but pray I may be found in the number of those seven thousand who have not bent the knee to Baal. I know the present persecutors of all of us seek my life; yet that shall not diminish aught of the zeal which I owe to the Churches of God."—*Ep.* 156.

The reader cannot have failed to remark the studiously courteous tone in which the foregoing letters are written. The truth is, Basil had to deal on all hands with most untoward materials, which one single harsh or heedless word addressed to his correspondents would have served to set in a blaze. Thus he, the Exarch of Cæsarea, made himself the servant of all.

"My brother Dorotheus," he writes to Peter of Alexandria, the successor of Athanasius, in 377, "distressed me by failing, as you report, in gentleness and mildness in his conversations with your excellency. I attribute this to the times. For I seem, for my sins, to prosper in nothing, since the worthiest brethren are found deficient in gentleness and fitness for their office, from not acting according to my wishes."—*Ep.* 266.

Basil did not live to see the Churches, for which he laboured, in a more Catholic condition. The notes of the Church were impaired and obscured in his part of Christendom, and he had to fare on as he best might,—admiring, courting, yet coldly treated by the Latin world, desiring the friendship of Rome, yet wounded by her reserve,—suspected of heresy by Damasus, and accused by Jerome of pride.

CHAPTER III.

BASIL AND GREGORY.

"What are these discourses that you hold one with another, as you walk and are sad?"

I.

IT often happens that men of very dissimilar talents and tastes are attracted together by their very dissimilitude. They live in intimacy for a time, perhaps a long time, till their circumstances alter, or some sudden event comes to try them. Then the peculiarities of their respective minds are brought out into action; and puarrels ensue, which end in coolness or separation. It would not be right or true to say that this is exemplified in the instance of the two blessed Apostles, whose "sharp contention" is related in the Book of Acts; for they had been united in spirit once for all by a divine gift; and yet their strife reminds us of what takes place in life continually. And it so far resembled the everyday quarrels of friends, in that it arose from difference of temper and character in those favoured servants of God. The zealous heart of the Apostle of the Gentiles endured not the presence of one who had swerved in his course; the indulgent spirit of Barnabas felt that a first fault ought not to be a last trial. Such are the two main characters which are found in the Church,—high energy, and sweetness of temper; far from incompatible, of course, united in Apostles, though in different relative proportions, yet only partially combined in ordinary Christians, and often altogether parted from each other.

This contrast of character, leading, first, to intimacy, then to differences, is interestingly displayed, though painfully, in one passage of the history of Basil and Gregory;—Gregory the affectionate, the tender-hearted, the man of quick feelings, the accomplished, the eloquent preacher,—and Basil, the man of firm resolve and hard deeds, the high-minded ruler of Christ's flock, the diligent labourer in the field of ecclesiastical politics. Thus they differed; yet not as if they had not much in common still; both had the blessing and the discomfort of a sensitive mind; both were devoted to an ascetic life; both were men of classical tastes; both were special champions of the Catholic creed; both were skilled in argument, and successful in their use of it; both were in highest place in the Church, the one Exarch of Cæsarea, the other Patriarch of Constantinople. I will now attempt to sketch the history of their intimacy.

2.

Basil and Gregory were both natives of Cappadocia, but here, again, under different circumstances; Basil was born of a good family, and with Christian ancestors; Gregory was the son of the bishop of Nazianzus, who had been brought up an idolater, or rather an Hypsistarian, a mongrel sort of religionist, part Jew, part Pagan. He was brought over to Christianity by the efforts of his wife Nonna, and at Nazianzus admitted by baptism into the Church. In process of time he was made bishop of that city; but not having a very firm hold of the faith, he was betrayed in 360 into signing the Ariminian creed, which caused him much trouble, and from which at length his son recovered him. Cæsarea being at no unsurmountable distance from Nazianzus, the two friends had known each other in their own country; but their intimacy began at Athens, whither they separately repaired for the purposes of education. This was about A.D. 350, when each of them was twenty-one years of age. Gregory came to the seat of learning shortly before Basil, and thus was able to be his host and guide on his arrival; but fame had reported Basil's merits before he came, and he seems to have made his way, in a place of all others most difficult to a stranger, with a facility peculiar to himself. He soon found himself admired and respected by his fellow-students; but Gregory was his only friend, and shared with him the reputation of talents and attainments. They remained at Athens four or five years; and, at the end of the time, made the acquaintance of Julian, since of evil name in history as the Apostate. Gregory thus describes in after life his early intimacy with Basil:—

"Athens and letters followed on my stage;
Others may tell how I encountered them;—
How in the fear of God, and foremost found
Of those who knew a more than mortal lore;—
And how, amid the venture and the rush
Of maddened youth with youth in rivalry,
My tranquil course ran like some fabled spring,
Which bubbles fresh beneath the turbid brine;
Not drawn away by those who lure to ill,
But drawing dear ones to the better part.
There, too, I gained a further gift of God,
Who made me friends with one of wisdom high,
Without compeer in learning and in life.
Ask ye his name?—in sooth, 'twas Basil, since
My life's great gain,—and then my fellow dear
In home, and studious search, and knowledge earned.

May I not boast how in our day we moved
A truest pair, not without name in Greece;
Had all things common, and one only soul
In lodgment of a double outward frame?
Our special bond, the thought of God above,
And the high longing after holy things.
And each of us was bold to trust in each,
Unto the emptying of our deepest hearts;
And then we loved the more, for sympathy
Pleaded in each, and knit the twain in one."

The friends had been educated for rhetoricians, and their oratorical powers were such, that they seemed to have every prize in prospect which a secular ambition could desire. Their names were known far and wide, their attainments acknowledged by enemies, and they themselves personally popular in their circle of acquaintance. It was under these circumstances that they took the extraordinary resolution of quitting the world together,—extraordinary the world calls it, utterly perplexed to find that any conceivable objects can, by any sane person, be accounted better than its own gifts and favours. They resolved to seek baptism of the Church. and to consecrate their gifts to the service of the Giver. With characters of mind very different,—the one grave, the other lively; the one desponding, the other sanguine; the one with deep feelings, the other with feelings acute and warm;—they agreed together in holding, that the things that are seen are not to be compared to the things that are not seen. They quitted the world, while it entreated them to stay.

What passed when they were about to leave Athens represents as in a figure the parting which they and the world took of each other. When the day of valediction arrived, their companions and equals, nay, some of their tutors, came about them, and resisted their departure by entreaties, arguments, and even by violence. This occasion showed, also, their respective dispositions; for the firm Basil persevered, and went; the tender-hearted Gregory was softened, and stayed a while longer. Basil, indeed, in spite of the reputation which attended him, had, from the first, felt disappointment with the celebrated abode of philosophy and literature; and seems to have given up the world from a simple conviction of its emptiness.

"He," says Gregory, "according to the way of human nature, when, on suddenly falling in with what we hoped to be greater, we find it less than its fame, experienced some such feeling, began to be sad, grew impatient, and could not congratulate himself on his place of residence. He sought an object which hope had drawn for him; and he called Athens 'hollow blessedness.'"

Gregory himself, on the contrary, looked at things more cheerfully; as the succeeding sentences show.

"Thus Basil; but I removed the greater part of his sorrow, meeting it with reason, and smoothing it with reflections, and saying (what was most true) that character is not at once understood, nor except by long time and perfect intimacy; nor are studies estimated, by those who are submitted to them, on a brief trial and by slight evidence. Thus I reassured him, and by continual trials of each other, I bound myself to him."—*Orat.* 43.

3.

Yet Gregory had inducements of his own to leave the world, not to insist on his love of Basil's company. His mother had devoted him to God, both before and after his birth; and when he was a child he had a remarkable dream, which made a great impression upon him.

"While I was asleep," he says in one of his poems, which runs thus in prose, "a dream came to me, which drew me readily to the desire of chastity. Two virgin forms, in white garments, seemed to shine close to me. Both were fair and of one age, and their ornament lay in their want of ornament, which is a woman's beauty. No gold adorned their neck, nor jacinth ; nor had they the delicate spinning of the silkworm. Their fair robe was bound with a girdle, and it reached down to their ankles. Their head and face were concealed by a veil, and their eyes were fixed on the ground. The fair glow of modesty was on both of them, as far as could be seen under their thick covering. Their lips were closed in silence, as the rose in its dewy leaves. When I saw them, I rejoiced much ; for I said that they were far more than mortals. And they in turn kept kissing me, while I drew light from their lips, fondling me as a dear son. And when I asked who and whence the women were, the one answered, 'Purity,' the other, 'Sobriety ;' 'We stand by Christ, the King, and delight in the beauty of the celestial virgins. Come, then, child, unite thy mind to our mind, thy light to our light ; so shall we carry thee aloft in all brightness through the air, and place thee by the radiance of the immortal Trinity.'"—*Carm.* p. 930.

He goes on to say, that he never lost the impression this made upon him, as "a spark of heavenly fire," or "a taste of divine milk and honey."

As far, then, as these descriptions go, one might say that Gregory's abandonment of the world arose from an early passion, as it may be called, for a purity higher than his own nature ; and Basil's, from a profound sense of the world's nothingness and the world's defilements. Both seem to have viewed it as a sort of penitential exercise, as well as a means towards perfection.

When they had once resolved to devote themselves to the service of religion, the question arose, how they might best improve and employ the talents committed to them. Somehow, the idea of marrying and taking orders, or taking orders and marrying, building or improving their parsonages, and showing forth the charities, the humanities, and the gentilities of a family man, did not suggest itself to their minds. They fancied that they must give up wife, children, property, if they would be perfect; and, this being taken for granted, that their choice lay between two modes of life, both of which they regarded as extremes. Here, then, for a time, they were in some perplexity. Gregory speaks of two ascetic disciplines, that of the solitary or hermit, and that of the secular;* one of which, he says, profits a man's self, the other his neighbour. Midway, however, between these lay the Cœnobite, or what we commonly call the monastic; removed from the world, yet acting in a certain select circle. And this was the rule which the friends at length determined to adopt, withdrawing from mixed society in order to be of the greater service to it.

The following is the passage in which Gregory describes the life which was the common choice of both of them:—

"Fierce was the whirlwind of my storm-toss'd mind,
Searching, 'mid holiest ways, a holier still.
Long had I nerved me, in the depths to sink
Thoughts of the flesh, and then more strenuously.
Yet, while I gazed upon diviner aims,
I had not wit to single out the best:
For, as is aye the wont in things of earth,
Each had its evil, each its nobleness.
I was the pilgrim of a toilsome course,
Who had o'erpast the waves, and now look'd round.
With anxious eye, to track his road by land.
Then did the awful Thesbite's image rise,
His highest Carmel, and his food uncouth:
The Baptist wealthy in his solitude;
And the unencumbered sons of Jonadab.
But soon I felt the love of holy books,
The spirit beaming bright in learned lore,
Which deserts could not hear, nor silence tell.

* *ἄζυγες* and *μιγάδες*.

Long was the inward strife, till ended thus :—
I saw, when men lived in the fretful world,
They vantaged other men, but risked the while
The calmness and the pureness of their hearts.
They who retired held an uprighter port,
And raised their eyes with quiet strength towards heaven ;
Yet served self only, unfraternally.
And so, 'twixt these and those, I struck my path,
To meditate with the free solitary,
Yet to live secular, and serve mankind."

4.

Not many years passed after their leaving Athens, when Basil put his resolution into practice ; and, having fixed upon Pontus for his retirement, wrote to Gregory to remind him of his promise. On Gregory's hesitating, he wrote to expostulate with him Gregory's answer was as follows :—

"I have not stood to my word, I own it ; having protested, ever since Athens and our friendship and union of heart there, that I would be your companion, and follow a strict life with you. Yet I act against my wish, duty annulled by duty, the duty of friendship by the duty of filial reverence. . . . . However, I still shall be able to perform my promise in a measure, if you will accept thus much. I will come to you for a time, if, in turn, you will give me your company here : thus we shall be quits in friendly service, while we have all things common. And thus I shall avoid distressing my parents, without losing you."—*Ep.* I.

When we bear in mind what has been already mentioned about Gregory's father, we may well believe that there really were very urgent reasons against the son's leaving him, when it came to the point, over and above the ties which would keep him with a father and mother both advanced in years. Basil, however, was disappointed; and instead of retiring to Pontus, devoted a year to visiting the monastic institutions of Syria and Egypt. On his return, his thoughts again settled on his friend Gregory; and he attempted to overcome the obstacle in the way of their old project, by placing himself in a district called Tiberina, near Gregory's own home. Finding, however, the spot cold and damp, he gave up the idea of it. On one occasion, while he was yet living in Cæsarea, where for a time he had taught rhetoric, Gregory wrote to him the following familiar letter, as from a countryman to an inhabitant of a town, not without a glance at Basil's peculiarities:—

"You shall not charge Tiberina upon me, with its ice and bad weather, O clean-footed, tip-toeing, capering man! O feathered, flighty man, mounted on Abaris's arrow, who, Cappadocian though you be, shun Cappadocia! A vast injury it is, when you townspeople are sallow, and have not your breath full, and dole out the sun; and we are plump and in plenty, and have elbow-room! However, such is your condition; you are gentlemanlike, and wealthy, and a man of the world; I cannot praise it. Say not a word more, then, against our mud (you did not make the town, nor I the winter); if you do, I will match our wading with your trading,* and all the wretched things which are found in cities."—*Ep.* 2.

Meanwhile Basil had chosen for his retreat a spot near Neocæsarea, in Pontus, close by the village where lay his father's property, where he had been brought up in childhood by his grandmother, Macrina, and whither his mother and sister had retired for a monastic life after his father's death. The river Iris ran between the two places. Within a mile of their monastery was the Church of the Forty Martyrs, where father, mother, and sister were successively buried. These Martyrs were a number of the victims of the persecution of Licinius, at Sebaste; Emmelia, Basil's mother, had collected their relics, and

* ἀντὶ πηλῶν τοὺς καπήλους.

he himself and his brother Gregory of Nyssa have left us homilies in celebration of them. Here, then, it was that St. Basil dwelt in holy retirement for five or six years. On settling there, he again wrote to Gregory :—

"My brother Gregory writes me word that he has long been wishing to be with me, and adds, that you are of the same mind : however, I could not wait, partly as being hard of belief, considering I have been so often disappointed, and partly because I find myself pulled all ways with business. I must at once make for Pontus, where, perhaps, God willing, I may make an end of wandering. After renouncing, with trouble, the idle hopes which I once had, or rather the dreams (for it is well said, that hopes are waking dreams), I departed into Pontus in quest of a place to live in. There God has opened on me a spot exactly answering to my taste, so that I actually see before my eyes what I have often pictured to my mind in idle fancy.

"There is a lofty mountain, covered with thick woods, watered towards the north with cool and transparent streams. A plain lies beneath, enriched by the waters which are ever draining off upon it ; and skirted by a spontaneous profusion of trees almost thick enough to be a fence ; so as even to surpass Calypso's Island, which Homer seems to have considered the most beautiful spot on earth. Indeed, it is like an island, enclosed as it is on all sides ; for deep hollows cut it off in two directions ; the river, which has lately fallen down a precipice, runs all along one side, and is impassable as a wall ; while the mountain, extending itself behind, and meeting the hollows in a crescent, stops up the path at its roots. There is but one pass, and I am master of it. Behind my abode there is another gorge, rising to a ledge up above, so as to command the extent of the plain and the stream which bounds it, which is not less beautiful to my taste than the Strymon, as seen from Amphipolis. For while the latter flows leisurely, and swells into a lake almost, and is too still to be a river, the former is the most rapid stream I know, and somewhat turbid, too, by reason of the rock which closes on it above ; from which, shooting down, and eddying in a deep pool, it forms a most pleasant scene for myself or anyone else ; and is an inexhaustible resource to the country people, in the countless fish which its depths contain. What need to tell of the exhalations from the earth, or the breezes from the river? Another might admire the multitude of flowers, and singing-birds; but leisure I have none for such thoughts. However, the chief praise of the place is, that being happily disposed for produce of every kind, it nurtures what to me is the sweetest produce of all, quietness; indeed, it is not only rid of the bustle of the city, but is even unfrequented by travellers, except a chance hunter. It abounds indeed in game, as well as other things, but not, I am glad to say, in bears or wolves, such as you have, but in deer, and wild goats, and hares, and the like. Does it not strike you what a foolish mistake I was near making when I was eager to change this spot for your Tiberina, the very pit of the whole earth? Pardon me, then, if I am now set upon it; for not Alcmæon himself, I suppose, would endure to wander further when he had found the Echinades."—*Ep*. 14.

Gregory answered this letter by one which is still extant, in which he satirises, point by point, the picture of the Pontic solitude which Basil had drawn to allure him, perhaps from distaste for it, perhaps in the temper of one who studiously disparages what, if he had admitted the thought, might prove too great a temptation to him. He ends thus:—

"This is longer perhaps than a letter, but shorter than a comedy. For yourself, it will be good of you to take this castigation well; but if you do not, I will give you some more of it."—*Ep*. 7.

5.

Basil *did* take it well; but this did not save him from the infliction of the concluding threat; for Gregory, after paying him a visit, continues in the same bantering strain in a later epistle.

GREGORY TO BASIL.

"Since you take my castigation in good part, I will now give you some more of it; and, to set off with Homer, let us

'Pass on, and sing thy garniture within,'

to wit, the dwelling without roof and without door,—the hearth without fire and smoke,—walls, however, baked enough, lest the mud should trickle on us, while we suffer Tantalus's penalty, thirst in the midst of wet ;—that sad and hungry banquet, for which you called me from Cappadocia, not as for the frugal fare of the Lotophagi, but as if for Alcinous's board for one lately shipwrecked and wretched. I have remembrance of the bread and of the broth —so they were named—and shall remember them : how my teeth got stuck in your hunches, and next lifted and heaved themselves as out of paste. You, indeed, will set it out in tragic style yourself, taking a sublime tone from your own sufferings. But for me, unless that true Lady Bountiful, your mother, had rescued me quickly, showing herself in need, like a haven to the tempest-tossed, I had been dead long ago, getting myself little honour, though much pity, from Pontic hospitality. How shall I omit those ungardenlike gardens, void of pot-herbs? or the Augean store, which we cleared out and spread over them ; what time we worked the hillside plough, vine-dresser I, and dainty you, with this neck and hands, which still bear the marks of the toil (O earth and sun, air and virtue! for I will rant a bit), not the Hellespont to yoke, but to level the steep. If you are not annoyed at this description, nor am I; but if you are, much more I at the reality. Yet I pass over the greater part, from tender remembrance of those other many things which I have shared with you."—*Ep.* 5.

This certainly is not a picture of comfort; and curiously contrasts with Basil's romantic view of the same things. But for the following letter, one could fancy that it was too much even for Gregory; but on Basil seeming to be hurt, he wrote thus :—

GREGORY TO BASIL.

"What I wrote before, concerning your Pontic abode, was in jest, not in earnest; but now I write very much in earnest. 'Who shall make me as in months past, as in the days' when I had the luxury of suffering hardship with you? since voluntary pain is a higher thing than involuntary comfort. Who shall restore me to those psalmodies, and vigils, and departures to God through prayer, and that (as it were) immaterial and incorporeal life? or to that union of brethren, in nature and soul, who are made gods by you, and carried on high? or to that rivalry in virtue and sharpening of heart, which we consigned to written decrees and canons? or to that loving study of divine oracles, and the light we found in them, with the guidance of the Spirit? or, to speak of lesser and lower things, to the bodily labours of the day, the wood-drawing and the stone-hewing, the planting and the draining? or to that golden plane, more honourable than that of Xerxes, under which, not a jaded king, but a weary monk did sit?—planted by me, watered by Apollos (that is, your honourable self), increased by God, unto my honour; that there should be preserved with you a memorial of my loving toil, as Aaron's rod that budded (as Scripture says and we believe) was kept in the ark. It is very easy to wish all this, not easy to gain it. Do you, however, come to me, and revive my virtue, and work with me; and whatever benefit we once gained together, preserve for me by your prayers, lest otherwise I fade away by little and little, as a shadow, while the day declines. For you are my breath, more than the air, and so far only do I live, as I am in your company, either present, or, if absent, by your image." —*Ep.* 6.

From this letter it appears that Basil had made up for Gregory's absence by collecting a brotherhood around him; in which indeed he had such success that he is considered the founder of the monastic or cœnobitic discipline in Pontus,—a discipline to which the Church gave her sanction, as soon as her establishment by the temporal power had increased the reasons for asceticism, and, increasing its professors, had created the necessity of order and method among them. The following letter, written by Basil at the time of the foregoing letters of Gregory, gives us some insight into the nature of his rule, and the motives and feelings which influenced him: it is too long to do more than extract portions of it.

BASIL TO GREGORY.

"Your letter brought you before me, just as one recognizes a friend in his children. It is just like you, to tell me it was but little to describe the place, without mentioning my habits and method of life, if I wished to make you desirous to join me ; it was worthy of a soul which counts all things of earth as nothing, compared with that blessedness which the promises reserve for us. Yet really I am ashamed to tell you how I pass night and day in this lonely nook. Though I have left the city's haunts, as the source of innumerable ills, yet I have not yet learned to leave myself. I am like a man who, on account of sea-sickness, is angry with the size of his vessel as tossing overmuch, and leaves it for the pinnace or boat, and is sea-sick and miserable still, as carrying his delicacy of stomach along with him. So I have got no great good from this retirement. However, what follows is an account of what I proposed to do, with a view of tracking the footsteps of Him who is our guide unto salvation, and who has said : 'If any one will come after Me, let him deny himself, and take up his cross, and follow Me.'

"We must strive after a quiet mind. As well might the eye ascertain an object put before it, while it is wandering restless up and down, and sideways, without fixing a steady gaze upon it, as a mind, distracted by a thousand worldly cares, be able clearly to apprehend the truth. He who is not yet yoked in the bonds of matrimony, is harassed by frenzied cravings, and rebellious impulses, and hopeless attachments ; he who has found his mate is encompassed with his own tumult of cares : if he is childless, there is desire of children ; has he children, anxiety about their education ; attention to his wife, care of his house, oversight of his servants, misfortunes in trade, quarrels with his neighbours, lawsuits, the risks of the merchant, the toil of the farmer. Each day, as it comes, darkens the soul in its own way ; and night after night takes up the day's anxieties, and cheats the mind with corresponding illusions. Now, one way of escaping all this is separation from the whole world ; that is, not bodily separation, but the severance of the soul's sympathy with the body, and so to live without city, home, goods, society, possessions, means of life, business, engagements, human learning, that the heart may readily receive every impress of divine teaching. Preparation of heart is the unlearning the prejudices of evil converse. It is the smoothing the waxen tablet before attempting to write on it. Now, solitude is of the greatest use for this purpose, inasmuch as it stills our passions, and gives opportunity to our reason to cut them out of the soul."

This then is the meaning and drift of monasteries and monastic life, to serve God without distraction :—

"Pious exercises nourish the soul with divine thoughts. What state can be more blessed than to imitate on earth the choruses of Angels ?—to begin the day with prayer, and honour our Maker with hymns and songs ?—as the day brightens, to betake ourselves, with prayer attending on it throughout, to our labours, and to sweeten our work with hymns, as if with salt? Soothing hymns compose the mind to a cheerful and calm state. Quiet, then, as I have said, is the first step in our sanctification ; the tongue purified from the gossip of the world ; the eyes unexcited by fair colour or comely shape ; the ear not relaxing the tone of the mind by voluptuous songs, nor by that especial mischief, the talk of light men and jesters. Thus the mind, saved from dissipation from without, nor, through the senses, thrown upon the world, falls back upon itself, and thereby ascends to the contemplation of God.

"The study of inspired Scripture is the chief way of finding our duty ; for in it we find both instruction about conduct, and the lives of blessed men delivered in writing, as some breathing images of godly living, for the imitation of their good works. Hence, in whatever respect each one feels himself deficient, devoting himself to this imitation, he finds, as from some dispensary, the due medicine for his ailment. He who is enamoured of chastity, dwells upon the history of Joseph, and from him learns chaste actions finding him not only able to master the assaults of pleasure, but virtuous by habit. He is taught endurance from Job. Or, should he be inquiring how to be at once meek and great-hearted, hearty against sin, meek towards men, he will find David noble in warlike exploits, meek and unruffled as regards revenge on enemies. Such, too, was Moses, rising up with great heart upon sinners against God, but with meek soul bearing their evil-speaking against himself."

He would make the monk to be the true gentleman, for he continues :—

"This, too, is a very principal point to attend to,—knowledge how to converse; to interrogate without over-earnestness; to answer without desire of display ; not to interrupt a profitable speaker, nor to desire ambitiously to put in a word of one's own ; to be measured in speaking and hearing; not to be ashamed of receiving, or to be grudging in giving, information, nor to disown what one has learned from others, as depraved women practise with their children, but to refer it candidly to the true parent. The middle tone of voice is best, neither so low as to be inaudible, nor ill-bred from its high pitch. One should reflect first what one is going to say, and then give it utterance; be courteous when addressed, amiable in social intercourse; not aiming to be pleasant by smartness, but cultivating gentleness in kind admonitions. Harshness is ever to be put aside, even in censuring."—*Ep.* 2.

These last remarks are curious, considering the account which, as we have seen, Gregory has left us of Basil's own manner. In another epistle, of an apologetic character, he thus speaks of the devotional exercises of his monastery:—

"Our people rise, while it is yet night, for the house of prayer; and after confessing to God, in distress and affliction and continued tears, they rise up and turn to psalm-singing. And now, being divided into two, they respond to each other, thereby deepening their study of the holy oracles, and securing withal attention of heart without wandering. Next, letting one lead the chant, the rest follow him; and thus, with variety of psalmody, they spend the night, with prayers interspersed; when day begins to dawn, all in common, as from one mouth and one heart, lift up to the Lord the psalm of confession, each making the words of repentance his own."—*Ep.* 207.

Such was Basil's life till he was called to the priesthood, which led to his leaving his retirement for Cæsarea: by night, prayer; by day, manual labour, theological study, and mercy to the poor.

6.

The next kindly intercourse between Basil and Gregory took place on occasion of the difference between Basil and his bishop, Eusebius; when, as has been already related, Gregory interfered successfully to reconcile them. And the next arose out of circumstances which followed the death of Gregory's brother, Cæsarius. On his death-bed he had left all his goods to the poor; a bequest which was thwarted, first, by servants and others about him, who carried off at once all the valuables on which they could lay hands; and, after Gregory had come into possession of the residue, by the fraud of certain pretended creditors, who appealed to the law on his refusing to satisfy them. Basil, on this occasion, seconded his application to the Prefect of Constantinople, who was from Cæsarea, and had known the friends intimately there, as well as at Athens.

We now come to the election of Basil to the Exarchate of Cappadocia, which was owing in no small degree to the exertions of Gregory and his father in his favour. This event, which was attended with considerable hazard of defeat, from the strength of the civil party, and an episcopal faction opposed to Basil, doubtless was at the moment a cause of increased affection between the friends, though it was soon the occasion of the difference and coolness which I spoke of in the beginning of this chapter. Gregory, as I have said, was of an amiable temper, fond of retirement and literary pursuits, and of cultivating Christianity in its domestic and social aspect, rather than amid the toils of ecclesiastical warfare. I have also said enough to show that I have no thought whatever of accusing so great a Saint of any approach to selfishness; and his subsequent conduct at Constantinople made it clear how well he could undergo and fight up against persecution in the quarrel of the Gospel. But such scenes of commotion were real sufferings to him, even independently of the personal risks which they involved; he was unequal to the task of ruling, and Basil in vain endeavoured to engage him as his assistant and comrade in the government of his exarchate. Let the following letter of Gregory explain his feelings :—

GREGORY TO BASIL.

'I own I was delighted to find you seated on the high throne, and to see the victory of the Spirit, in lifting up a light upon its candlestick, which even before did not shine dimly. Could I be otherwise, seeing the general interests of the Church so depressed, and so in need of a guiding hand like yours? However, I did not hasten to you at once, nor will I; you must not ask it of me. First, I did not, from delicacy towards your own character, that you might not seem to be collecting your partisans about you with indecency and heat, as objectors would say; next, for my own peace and reputation. Perhaps you will say, 'When, then, will you come, and till when will you delay?' Till God bids, till the shadows of opposition and jealousy are passed. And I am confident it cannot be long before the blind and the lame give way, who are shutting out David from Jerusalem."—*Ep.* 45.

At length Gregory came to Cæsarea, where Basil showed him all marks of affection and respect: and when Gregory declined any public attentions, from a fear of the jealousy it might occasion, his friend let him do as he would, regardless, as Gregory observes, of the charge which might fall on himself, of neglecting Gregory, from those who were ignorant of the circumstances. However, Basil could not detain him long in the metropolitan city, as the following letter shows, written on occasion of a charge of heterodoxy, which a monk of Nazianzus advanced against Basil, and which Gregory had publicly and indignantly opposed, sending, however, to Basil to gain a clearer explanation from himself. Basil was much hurt to find he had anything to explain to Gregory. He answers in the following letter :—

BASIL TO GREGORY.

"I have received the letter of your religiousness, by the most reverend brother Hellenius; and what you have intimated, he has told me in plain terms. How I felt on hearing it, you cannot doubt at all. However, since I have determined that my affection for you shall outweigh my pain, whatever it is, I have accepted it as I ought to do, and I pray the Holy God, that my remaining days or hours may be as carefully conducted in their disposition towards you as they have been in past time, during which, my conscience tells me, I have been wanting to you in nothing, small or great."

After saying that his life was a practical refutation of the calumny, that a brief letter would not do what years had failed in doing, and hinting that the matter ought never to have been brought before him, and that they who listen to tales against others will have tales told of themselves, he continues:—

"I know what has led to all this, and have urged every topic to hinder it; but now I am sick of the subject, and will say no more about it;—I mean, our little intercourse. For had we kept our old promise to each other, and had we had due regard to the claims which the churches have on us, we should have been the greater part of the year together; and then there would have been no opening for these calumniators. Pray have nothing to say to them; let me persuade you to come here and assist me in my labours, particularly in my contest with the individual who is now assailing me. Your very appearance would have the effect of stopping him; as soon as you show these disturbers of our country that you will, by God's blessing, place yourself at the head of our friends, you will break up their cabal, and you will 'shut every unjust mouth that speaketh lawlessly against God.' And thus facts will show who are your followers in good, and who it is that halts and betrays through cowardice the word of truth. If, however, the Church be betrayed, why then I shall care little to set men right about myself by means of words, who account of me as men would naturally account who have not yet learned to measure themselves. Perhaps, in a short time, by God's grace, I shall be able to refute their slanders by very deed, for it seems likely that I shall have soon to suffer somewhat for the truth's sake more than usual; the best I can expect is banishment. Or, if this hope fails, after all, Christ's judgment-seat is not far distant."—*Ep.* 71

7.

The allusion in the last sentences is to the attempts upon him of the Emperor Valens, which were then impending. We have seen in a former chapter how they were encountered and baffled by Basil's intrepidity; Valens appeared to be reconciled to him; but his jealousy of him led him to a measure which involved consequences to Basil, worse than any worldly loss, the loss of Gregory. To lessen Basil's power, Valens divided Cappadocia into two parts. This was about two years after Basil's elevation. In consequence, a dispute arose between him and Anthimus, Bishop of Tyana. Anthimus contended that an ecclesiastical division must necessarily follow the civil, and that, in consequence, he himself, as holding the chief see in the second Cappadocia, was now the rightful metropolitan of that province. The justice of the case was with Basil, but he was opposed by the party of bishops who were secretly Arianizers, and had already opposed themselves to his election. Accordingly, having might on his side, Anthimus began to alienate the monks from Basil, to appropriate those revenues of the Church of Cæsarea which lay in his province, and to expel or gain over the presbyters, giving, as an excuse, that respect and offerings ought not to be paid to heterodox persons.

Gregory at once offered his assistance to his friend, hinting to him, at the same time, that some of those about him had some share of blame in the dispute. It happened unfortunately for their friendship that they were respectively connected with distinct parties in the Church. Basil knew and valued, and gained over many of the Semi-Arians, who dissented from the Catholic doctrine more from over-subtlety, or want of clearness of mind, than from unbelief. Gregory was in habits of intimacy with the monks of Nazianzus, his father's see, and these were eager for the Nicene formula, almost as a badge of party. In the letter last cited, Basil reflects upon these monks; and, on this occasion, Gregory warned him in turn against Eustathius and his friends, whose orthodoxy was suspicious, and who, being ill-disposed towards Anthimus, were likely to increase the difference between the latter and Basil. It may be observed that it was this connexion between Basil and Eustathius to which Anthimus alluded, when he spoke against paying offerings to the heterodox.

Gregory's offer of assistance to Basil was frankly made, and seems to have been as frankly accepted. "I will come, if you wish me," he had said, "if so be, to advise with you, if the sea wants water, or you a counsellor; at all events, to gain benefit, and to act the philosopher, by bearing ill usage in your company."—*Ep.* 47. Accordingly, they set out together for a district of Mount Taurus, in the second Cappadocia, where there was an estate or Church dedicated to St. Orestes, the property of the see of Cæsarea. On their return with the produce of the farm, they were encountered by the retainers of Anthimus, who blocked up the pass, and attacked their company. This warfare between Christian bishops was obviously a great scandal in the Church, and Basil adopted a measure which he considered would put an end to it. He increased the number of bishoprics in that district, considering that residents might be able to secure the produce of the estate without disturbance, and moreover to quiet and gain over the minds of those who had encouraged Anthimus in his opposition. Sasima was a village in this neighbourhood, and here he determined to place his friend Gregory, doubtless considering that he could not show him a greater mark of confidence than to commit to him the management of the quarrel, or could confer on him a post, to his own high spirit more desirable, than the place of risk and responsibility.

Gregory had been unwilling even to be made a priest; but he shrank with fear from the office of a bishop. He had upon him that overpowering sense of the awfulness of the ministerial commission which then commonly prevailed in more serious minds. "I feel myself to be unequal to this warfare," he had said on his ordination, "and therefore have hid my face, and slunk away. And I sought to sit down in solitude, being filled with bitterness, and to keep silence from a conviction that the days were evil, since God's beloved have kicked against the truth, and we have become revolting children. And besides this, there is the eternal warfare with one's passions, which my body of humiliation wages with me night and day, part hidden, part open;—and the tossing to and fro and whirling, through the senses and the delights of life; and the deep mire in which I stick fast; and the law of sin warring against the law of the spirit, and striving to efface the royal image in us, and whatever of a divine effluence has been vested in us. Before we have subdued with all our might the principle which drags us down, and have cleansed the mind duly, and have surpassed others much in approach to God, I consider it unsafe either to undertake cure of souls, or mediatorship between God and man, for some such thing is a priest." —*Or.* 2.

With these admirable feelings the weakness of the man mingled itself: at the urgent command of his father he had submitted to be consecrated; but the reluctance which he felt to undertake the office was now transferred to his occupying the see to which he had been appointed.

There seems something indeed conceited in my arbitrating between Saints, and deciding how far each was right and wrong. But I do not really mean to do so: I am but reviewing their external conduct in its historical development. With this explanation I say, that an ascetic, like Gregory, ought not to have complained of the country where his see lay, as deficient in beauty and interest, even though he might be allowed to feel the responsibility of a situation which made him a neighbour of Anthimus. Yet such was his infirmity; and he repelled the accusations of his mind against himself, by charging Basil with unkindness in placing him at Sasima. On the other hand, it is possible that Basil, in his eagerness for the settlement of his exarchate, too little consulted the character and taste of Gregory; and, above all, the feelings of duty which bound him to Nazianzus. This is the account which Gregory gives of the matter, in a letter which displays much heat, and even resentment, against Basil:—

"Give me," he says, "peace and quiet above all things. Why should I be fighting for sucklings and birds, which are not mine, as if in a matter of souls and canons? Well, play the man, be strong, turn everything to your own glory, as rivers suck up the mountain torrent, thinking little of friendship or intimacy, compared with high aims and piety, and disregarding what the world will think of you for all this, being the property of the Spirit alone; while, on my part, so much shall I gain from this your friendship, not to trust in friends, nor to put anything above God."—*Ep.* 48.

In the beginning of the same letter, he throws the blame upon Basil's episcopal throne, which suddenly made him higher than Gregory. Elsewhere he accuses him of ambition, and desire of aggrandizing himself. Basil, on the other hand, seems to have accused him of indolence, slowness, and want of spirit.

8.

Such was the melancholy crisis of an estrangement which had been for some time in preparation. Henceforth no letters, which are preserved, passed between the two friends; and but one act of intercourse is discoverable in their history. That exception indeed is one of much interest: Basil went to see Gregory at Nazianzus in A.D. 374, on the death of Gregory's father. But this was only like a sudden gleam, as if to remind us that charity still was burning within them; and scarcely mitigates the sorrowful catastrophe, from the point of view in which history presents it. Anthimus appointed a rival bishop to the see of Sasima; and Gregory, refusing to contest the see with him, returned to Nazianzus. Basil laboured by himself. Gregory retained his feeling of Basil's unkindness even after his death; though he revered and admired him not less, or even more, than before, and attributed his conduct to a sense of duty. In his commemorative oration, after praising his erection of new sees, he says:—

"To this measure I myself was brought in by the way. I do not seem bound to use a soft phrase. For admiring as I do all he did, more than I can say, this one thing I cannot praise,—for I will confess my feeling, which is in other ways not unknown to the world, —his extraordinary and unfriendly conduct towards me, of which time has not removed the pain. For to this I trace all the irregularity and confusion of my life, and my not being able, or not seeming, to command my feelings, though the latter of the two is a small matter; unless, indeed, I may be suffered to make this excuse for him, that, having views beyond this earth, and having departed hence even before life was over, he viewed everything as the Spirit's; and knowing how to reverence friendship, then only slighted it, when it was a duty to prefer God, and to make more account of the things hoped for than of things perishable."—*Orat.* 43.

These lamentable occurrences took place before two years of Basil's episcopate had run out, and eight or nine years before his death; he had before and after them many trials, many sorrows; but this loss of Gregory probably was the greatest of all.

CHAPTER IV.

RISE AND FALL OF GREGORY.

"Who will give me in the wilderness a lodging-place of wayfaring men, and I will leave my people and depart from them. Because they are all adulterers, an assembly of transgressors; and they have bent their tongue, as a bow, for lies, and not for truth."

I.

"THIS, O Basil, to thee, from me,"—thus Gregory winds up his sermon upon Basil,—"this offering to thee from a tongue once most dear to thee! thy fellow in honour and in age! If it approaches to be worthy of thee, the praise is thine; for, relying upon thee, I have set about this oration concerning thee. But if it be beneath and much beside my hope, what is to be expected from one worn down with years, sickness, and regret for thee? However, the best we can is acceptable to God. But O that thou, divine and sacred heart, mayest watch over me from above, and that thorn of my flesh, which God has given for my discipline, either end it by thy intercessions, or persuade me to bear it bravely! and mayest thou direct my whole life towards that which is most convenient! and when I depart hence, then mayest thou receive me into thy tabernacles!"—*Orat.* 43.

Gregory delivered this discourse on his return to Cæsarea from Constantinople, three years after St. Basil's death; a busy, turbulent, eventful three years, in which he had been quite a different man from what he was before, though it was all past and over now, and was about to be succeeded by the same solitude in which Basil's death found him.

Gregory disliked the routine intercourse of society; he disliked ecclesiastical business, he disliked publicity, he disliked strife, he felt his own manifold imperfections, he feared to disgrace his profession, and to lose his hope; he loved the independence of solitude, the tranquillity of private life; leisure for meditation, reflection, self-government, study, and literature. He admired, yet he playfully satirized, Basil's lofty thoughts and heroic efforts. Yet, upon Basil's death, Basil's spirit, as it were, came into him; and within four months of it, he had become a preacher of the Catholic faith in an heretical metropolis, had formed a congregation, had set apart a place for orthodox worship, and had been stoned by the populace. Was it Gregory, or was it Basil, that blew the trumpet in Constantinople, and waged a successful war in the very seat of the enemy, in despite of all his fluctuations of mind, misgivings, fastidiousness, disgust with self, and love of quiet? Such was the power of the great Basil, triumphing in his death, though failing throughout his life. Within four or five years of his departure to his reward, all the objects were either realized, or in the way to be realized, which he had so vainly attempted, and so sadly waited for. His eyes had failed in longing; they waited for the morning, and death closed them ere it came. He died on the 1st of January, 379; on the 19th of the same month the glorious Emperor Theodosius was invested with the imperial purple; by the 20th of April, Gregory had formed a Church in Constantinople; in February, in the following year, Theodosius declared for the Creed of Nicæa;

in November he restored the Churches of Constantinople to the Catholics. In the next May he convoked, in that city, the second General Council, which issued in the pacification of the Eastern Church, in the overthrow of the great heresy which troubled it, and (in a measure, and in prospect) in its union with the West. "Pretiosa in conspectu Domini mors sanctorum ejus."

It was under such circumstances, when our Saint had passed through many trials, and done a great work, when he, a recluse hitherto, had all at once been preacher, confessor, metropolitan, president of a General Council, and now was come back again to Asia as plain Gregory—to be what he had been before, to meditate and to do penance, and to read, and to write poems, and to be silent as in former years, except that he was now lonely,* —his friend dead, his father dead, mother dead, brother Cæsarius, sister Gorgonia dead, and himself dead to this world, though still to live in the flesh for some eight dreary years,—in such a time and in such a place, at Cæsarea, the scene of Basil's labours, he made the oration to which I have referred above, and invoked Basil's glorified spirit; and his invocation ends thus:—"And when I depart hence, mayest thou receive me into thy tabernacles, so that, living together with one another, and beholding together more clearly and more perfectly the Holy and Blessed Trinity, whose vision we now receive in poor glimpses, we may there come to the end of all our desires, and receive the reward of the warfare which we have waged, which we have endured! To thee, then, these words from me; but me who will there be to praise, leaving life after thee? even should I do aught praiseworthy, in Christ Jesus our Lord, to whom be glory for ever.—Amen."

* Vid. Greg. Ep. 80, and Carm. p. 990.

2.

The circumstances which brought Gregory to Constantinople were the following:—It was now about forty years since the Church of Constantinople had lost the blessing of orthodox teaching and worship. Paul, who had been elected bishop at the beginning of this period, had been visited with four successive banishments from the Arian party, and at length with martyrdom. He had been superseded in his see, first by Eusebius, the leader of the Arians, who denied our Lord's divinity; then by Macedonius, the head of those who denied the divinity of the Holy Spirit; and then by Eudoxius, the Arianizer of the Gothic tribes. On the death of the last-mentioned, A.D. 370, the remnant of the Catholics elected for their bishop, Evagrius, who was immediately banished by the Emperor Valens; and, when they petitioned him to reverse his decision, eighty of their ecclesiastics, who were the bearers of their complaints, were subjected to an atrocious punishment for their Christian zeal, being burned at sea in the ship in which they had embarked. In the year 379, the orthodox Theodosius succeeded to the empire of the East; but this event did not at once alter the fortunes of the Church in his metropolis. The body of the people, nay, the populace itself, and, what is stranger, numbers of the female population, were eagerly attached to Arianism, and menaced violence to any one who was bold enough to preach the true doctrine. Such was the internal state of the Church; in addition to which must be added, the attitude of its external enemies:—the Novatians, who, orthodox themselves in doctrine, yet possessed a schismatical episcopacy, and a number of places of worship in the city;—the Eunomians, professors of the Arian heresy in its most undisguised blasphemy, who also had established a bishop there;—and the Semi-Arians and Apollinarists, whose heretical sentiments have been referred to in my foregoing pages. This was the condition of Constantinople when the orthodox members of its Church, under the sanction and with the coöperation of the neighbouring bishops, invited Gregory, whose gifts, religious and intellectual, were well known to them, to preside over it, instead of the heretical Demophilus, whom Valens, three years before, had placed there.

The history of Gregory's doings and fortunes at Constantinople may be told in a few words. A place of worship was prepared for him by the kindness of a relative. There he began to preach the true doctrine,—first, amid the contempt, then amid the rage and violence, of the Arian population. His congregation increased; he was stoned by the multitude, and brought before the civil authorities on the charge of creating a riot. At length, however, on Theodosius visiting the capital, he was recognized by him as bishop, and established in the temporalities of the see. However, upon the continued opposition of the people, and the vexatious combinations against him of his brother bishops, he resigned his see during the session of the second General Council, and retired to Asia Minor.

I do not intend to say more upon St. Gregory's public career; but, before leaving the subject, I am tempted to make two reflections.

First, he was fifty years old when he was called to Constantinople; a consolatory thought for those who see their span of life crumbling away under their feet, and they apparently doing nothing. Gregory was nothing till he was almost an old man; had he died at Basil's age, he would have done nothing. He seems to have been exactly the same age as Basil; but Basil had done his work and was taken away before Gregory had begun his.

The second reflection that suggests itself is this: in what a little time men move through the work which is, as it were, the end for which they are born, and which is to give a character to their names with posterity. They are known in history as the prime movers in this work, or as the instruments of that; as rulers, or politicians, or philosophers, or warriors; and when we examine dates, we often find that the exploits, or discoveries, or sway, which make them famous, lasted but a few years out of a long life, like plants that bloom once, and never again. Their ethical character, talents, acquirements, actions seem concentrated on a crisis, and give no sign of their existence as far as the world's annals are concerned, whether before or after. Gregory lived sixty years; his ecclesiastical life was barely three.

3

When, turning from that ecclesiastical life, we view Gregory in his personal character, we have before us the picture of a man of warm affections, amiable disposition, and innocent life. As a son, full of piety, tenderness, and watchful solicitude; as a friend or companion, lively, cheerful, and open-hearted; overflowing with natural feelings, and easy in the expression of them; simple, good, humble, primitive. His aspirations were high, as became a saint, his life ascetic in the extreme, and his conscience still more sensitive of sin and infirmity. At the same time, he was subject to alternations of feeling; was deficient all along in strength of mind and self-control; and was harassed, even in his old age, by irritability, fear, and other passions, which one might think that even years, not to say self-discipline, would have brought into subjection. Such mere temptations and infirmities in no way interfere with his being a Saint, and, since they do not, it is consolatory to our weak hearts and feeble wills to find from the precedent of Gregory, that, being what we are, we nevertheless may be in God's favour. These then are some of the conspicuous points in Gregory's character; and the following extracts from his writings, in verse and prose, are intended in some measure to illustrate them.

At first sight, many persons may feel surprised at the rhetorical style of his sermons, or orations, as they are more fitly called: the following passage accounts for this characteristic of them. He considered he had gained at Athens, while yet in the world, a rare talent, the science of thought and speech; and next he considered that what had cost him so much, should not be renounced, but consecrated to religious uses.

"This I offer to God," he says, "this I dedicate, which alone I have left myself, in which only I am rich. For all other things I have surrendered to the commandment and the Spirit; and I have exchanged for the all-precious pearl whatever I had; and I have become, or rather long to become, a great merchant, buying things great and imperishable with what is small and will certainly decay. Discourse alone I retain, as being the servant of the Word, nor should I ever willingly neglect this possession; rather I honour and embrace and take more pleasure in it than in all other things in which the many take pleasure; and I make it my life's companion, and good counsellor, and associate, and guide heavenward, and ready comrade. I have said to Wisdom, 'Thou art my sister.' With this I bridle my impetuous anger, with this I appease wasting envy, with this I lull to rest sorrow, the chain of the heart; with this I sober the flood of pleasure, with this I put a measure, not on friendship, but on dislike. This makes me temperate in good fortune, and high-souled in poverty; this encourages me to run with the prosperous traveller, to stretch a hand to the falling, to be weak with the weak, and to be merry with the strong. With this, home and foreign land are all one to me, and change of places, which are foreign to me equally, and not mine own. This makes me see the difference between two worlds, withdraws me from one joins me to the other."—*Orat.* 6. 6.

When he was ordained priest, he betook himself in haste to Pontus, and only after a time returned to Nazianzus. He thus speaks of this proceeding :—

"The chief cause was my surprise at the unexpected event ; as they who are astounded by sudden noises, I did not retain my power of reflection, and therefore I offended against propriety, which I had cherished my whole time. Next, a certain love insinuated itself, of the moral beauty of quiet, and of retirement ; for of this I had been enamoured from the beginning, more perhaps than any who have studied letters, and in the greatest and most severe of dangers, I had vowed to pursue it, nay, had even reached so far as to be on its threshold. Accordingly, I did not endure being tyrannized over, and being thrust into the midst of tumult, and dragged forcibly away from this mode of life, as if from some sacred asylum. For nothing seemed to me so great, as by closing up the senses, and being rid of flesh and world, and retiring upon one's self, and touching nothing human, except when absolutely necessary, and conversing with one's self and God, to live above things visible, and to bear within one the divine vision always clear, pure from the shifting impressions of earth,—a true mirror unsullied of God and the things of God, now and ever, adding light to light, the brighter to the dimmer, gathering even now in hope the blessedness of the world to come,—and to associate with Angels, while still on earth, leaving the earth and raised aloft by the spirit. Whoso of you is smitten with this love, knows what I say, and will be indulgent to my feeling at that time."—*Orat.* 2.

He professes that he could not bring himself to make a great risk, and to venture ambitiously, but preferred to be safe and sure.

"Who is there, when he has not yet devoted himself and learned to receive God's hidden wisdom in mystery, being as yet a babe, yet fed on milk, yet unnumbered in Israel, yet unenlisted in God's army, yet unable to take up Christ's Cross as a man, not yet an honoured member of Him at all, who would, in spite of this, submit with joy and readiness to be placed at the head of the fulness of Christ ?* No one, if I am to be the counsellor ; for this is the greatest of alarms, this the extremest of dangers, to every one who understands how great a thing it is to succeed, and how ruinous to fail. Let another sail for traffic, so I said, and cross the expanse of ocean, and keep constant company with winds and waves, to gain much, if so be, and to risk much. This may suit a man apt in sailing, apt in trafficking ; but what I prefer is to remain on land, to plough a small glebe and a dear one, to pay distant compliments to lucre and the sea, and thus to live, as I may be able, with a small and scanty loaf, and to linger along a life safe and surgeless, not to hazard a vast and mighty danger for mighty gains. To a lofty mind, indeed, it is a penalty not to attempt great things, not to exercise its powers upon many persons, but to abide in what is small, as if lighting a small house with a great light, or covering a child's body with a youth's armour ; but to the small it is safety to carry a small burden, nor, by undertaking things beyond his powers, to incur both ridicule and a risk ; just as to build a tower becomes him only who has wherewith to finish."—*Orat.* 2.

4.

It is plain that the gentle and humble-minded Gregory was unequal to the government of the Church and province of Constantinople, which were as unworthy, as they were impatient, of him. Charges of his incompetency formed part of the ground on which a successful opposition was made to him in the second General Council. What notions, however, his enemies had of fitness, is plain from the following extract. The truth is, Gregory was in no sense what is called, rightly or wrongly, a party man ; and while he was deficient, perhaps, in the sagacity, keenness, vigour, and decision for which a public man too often incurs the reproach of that name, he also had that kindness of heart, dispassionate-

* Vide Eph. i. 23.

ness, and placability, which more justly avail to rescue a person from it. It was imputed to him that he was not severe enough with his fallen persecutors. He thus replies:—

> "Consider what is charged against me. 'So much time is passed,' they say, 'of your governing the Church, at the critical moment, with the emperor's favour, which is of such importance. What symptom of the change is there? How many persecutors had we before! what misery did we not suffer! what insults, what threats, what exiles, what plunderings, what confiscations, what burnings of our clergy at sea, what temples profaned with blood of saints, and instead of temples made charnel-houses! What has followed? We have become stronger than our persecutors, and they have escaped!' So it is. For me it is enough of vengeance upon our injurers to have the power of retaliation. But these objectors think otherwise; for they are very precise and righteous in the matter of reprisals, and therefore they expect the advantage of the opportunity. 'What prefect,' they ask, 'has been punished? or populace brought to its senses? or what incendiaries? what fear of ourselves have we secured to us for the time to come?'"—*Orat.* 42.

Gregory had by far too little pomp and pretence to satisfy a luxurious and fastidious city. They wanted "a king like the nations;" a man who had a presence, who would figure and parade and rustle in silk, some Lord Mayor's preacher or West-end divine, who could hold forth and lay down the law, and be what is thought dignified and grand; whereas they had no one but poor, dear, good Gregory, a monk of Nazianzus, a personage who, in spite of his acknowledged learning and eloquence, was but a child, had no knowledge of the world, no manners, no conversation, and no address; who was flurried and put out in high society, and who would have been a bad hand at a platform speech, and helpless in the attempt to keep a modern vestry in order.

"Perhaps, too," he continues, "they may cast this slur upon me, as indeed they have, that I do not keep a good table, nor dress richly; and that there is a want of style when I go abroad, and a want of pomp when people address me. Certainly, I forgot that I had to rival consuls and prefects and illustrious commanders, who have more wealth than they know what to do with. If all this is heinous, it has slipped my mind; forgive me this wrong; choose a ruler instead of me, who will please the many; restore me to solitude, to rusticity, and to God, whom I shall please, though I be parsimonious."

And shortly before,—

"This is my character: I do not concur in many points with the many; I cannot persuade myself to walk their pace; this may be rudeness and awkwardness, but still it is my character. What to others are pleasures, annoy me; and what I am pleased with, annoys others. Indeed, it would not surprise me, even were I put into confinement as a nuisance, and were I considered to be without common wits by the multitude, as is said to have happened to a Greek philosopher, whose good sense was accused of being derangement, because he made jest of all things, seeing that the serious objects of the many were really ridiculous; or if I were accounted full of new wine, as Christ's disciples, from their speaking with tongues, the power of the Spirit being mistaken in them for excitement of mind."—*Ibid.*

He has a similar passage, written, after his resignation, in verse, which must here be unworthily exhibited in prose.

"This good," he says, "alone will be free and secure from restraint or capture,—a mind raised up to Christ. No more shall I be entertained at table by mortal prince, as heretofore,—I, Gregory, to pack a few comforts into me, placed in the midst of them, bashful and speechless, not breathing freely, feasting like a slave. No magistrate shall punish me with a seat, either near him, or below him, giving its due place to a grovelling spirit. No more shall I clasp blood-stained hands, or take hold of beard, to gain some small favour. Nor, hurrying with a crowd to some sacred feast of birthday, burial, or marriage, shall I seize on all that I can, some things for my jaws, and some for attendants with their greedy palms, like Briareus's ; and then carrying myself off, a breathing grave, late in the evening, drag along homeward my ailing carcass, worn out, panting with satiety, yet hastening to another fat feast, before I have shaken off the former infliction."—*Carm.* ii. 17.

One who is used to bread and water is overset by even a family dinner ; much less could Gregory bear a city feast or conservative banquet.

5.

On his return to Asia, first he had stayed for a time at Nazianzus ; thence he went to Arianzus, the place of his birth. Here he passed the whole of Lent without speaking, with a view of gaining command over his tongue, in which, as in other respects, he painfully felt or fancied his deficiency. He writes the following notes to a friend :—"You ask what my silence means? it means measurement of speaking, and not speaking. For he who can do it in whole, will more easily do it in part. Besides, it allays anger, when it is not brought out into words, but is extinguished in itself."—*Ep.* 96. Again : "I do not forbid your coming to me ; though my tongue be still, my ears shall be gladly open to your conversation ; since to hear what is fitting is not less precious than to speak it."—97. And again : "I am silent in conversation, as learning to speak what I ought to speak ; moreover, I am exercising myself in mastery of the passions. If this satisfies the inquirer, it is well ; if not, at least silence brings this gain, that I have not to enter into explanations."—98.

Gregory was now fifty-two or three ; there is something remarkable in a man so advanced in life taking such vigorous measures to overcome himself.

The following passages from his poems allude to the same, or similar infirmities :—

I lost, O Lord, the use of yesterday ;
Anger came on, and stole my heart away.
O may this morning's light until the evening stay !

Again :

The serpent comes anew ! I hold Thy feet.
Help, David ! help, and strike thy harp-strings sweet !
Hence ! choking spirit, hence ! to thine own hell retreat.

Some temptation or other is alluded to in the following poems ; though perhaps it is not fair to make a poet responsible, in his own person, for all he speaks as if from himself.

Here are his thoughts for the

MORNING.

I rise, and raise my claspèd hands to Thee.
Henceforth the darkness hath no part in me,
    Thy sacrifice this day ;
Abiding firm, and with a freeman's might
Stemming the waves of passion in the fight.
    Ah ! should I from Thee stray,
My hoary head, Thy table where I bow,
Will be my shame, which are mine honour now.
Thus I set out ;—Lord, lead me on my way !

And then, after "the burden of the day, and the heat,' we find him looking back when he comes to the

EVENING.

O Holiest Truth, how have I lied to Thee !
I vowed this day Thy festival should be ;
    Yet I am dim ere night.
Surely I made my prayer, and I did deem
That I could keep in me Thy morning beam
    Immaculate and bright.

But my foot slipped, and, as I lay, he came,
My gloomy foe, and robbed me of heaven's flame.
Help Thou my darkness, Lord, till I am light.

In the verses on Morning an allusion may be observed to his priesthood. The following lines bear a more express reference to it, and perhaps to Penance also :—

In service o'er the mystic feast I stand,
I cleanse Thy victim-flock, and bring them near
In holiest wise, and by a bloodless rite.
O Fire of Love ! O gushing Fount of Light !
(As best I know, who need Thy cleansing hand),
Dread office this, bemirèd souls to clear
Of their defilement, and again make bright.

These lines may have an allusion which introduces us to the following :—

As viewing sin, e'en in its faintest trace,
Murder in wrath, and in the wanton oath
The perjured tongue, and therefore shunning them,
So deem'd I safe a strict virginity.
And hence our ample choir of holiest souls
Are followers of the unfleshly seraphim,
And Him who 'mid them reigns in lonely light.
These, one and all, rush towards the thought of death,
And hope of second life, with single heart,
Loosed from the law and chain of marriage vow.
For I was but a captive at my birth,
Sin my first life, till its base discipline
Revolted me towards a nobler path.
Then Christ drew near me, and the Virgin-born
Spoke the new call to join His virgin-train.
So now towards highest heaven my innocent brow
I raise exultingly, sans let or bond,
Leaving no heir of this poor tabernacle
To ape me when my proper frame is broke ;
But solitary with my only God,
And truest souls to bear me company.

6.

It so happens that we have a vast deal of Gregory's poetry, which he doubtless never intended for publication, but which formed the recreation of his retirement. From one of these compositions the following playful extract, on the same subject, is selected :—

As when the hand some mimic form would paint,
It marks its purpose first in shadows faint,
And next its store of varied hues applies,
Till outlines fade, and the full limbs arise ;
So in the earlier school of sacred lore
The virgin life no claim of honour bore,
While in Religion's youth the Law held sway
And traced in symbols dim that better way.
But, when the Christ came by a virgin-birth,—
His radiant passage from high heaven to earth,—
And, spurning father for His mortal state,
Did Eve and all her daughters consecrate ;
Solved fleshly laws, and in the letter's place
Gave us the spirit and the word of grace ;—
Then shone the glorious Celibate at length,
Robed in the dazzling lightnings of its strength,
Surpassing spells of earth and marriage vow,
As soul the body, heaven this world below,
The eternal peace of saints life's troubled span,
And the high throne of God the haunts of man.
So now there circles round the King of Light
A heaven on earth, a blameless court and bright,
Aiming as emblems of their God to shine,
Christ in their heart, and on their brow His sign,
Soft funeral lights in the world's twilight dim,
Seeing their God, and ever one with Him.

Ye countless multitude, content to bow
To the soft thraldom of the marriage vow !
I mark your haughty step, your froward gaze,
Gems deck your hair, and silk your limbs arrays ;

Come, tell the gain which wedlock has conferred
On man; and then the single shall be heard.

The married many thus might plead, I ween;
Full glib their tongue, right confident their mien:—
"Hear, all who live! to whom the nuptial rite
Has brought the privilege of life and light,
We, who are wedded, but the law obey,
Stamped at creation on our blood and clay,
What time the Demiurge our line began,
Oped Adam's side, and out of man drew man.
Thenceforth let children of a mortal sod
Honour the law of earth, the primal law of God.

"List, you shall hear the gifts of price that lie
Gathered and bound within the marriage tie.
What taught the arts of life, the truths that sleep
In earth, or highest heaven, or vasty deep?
What filled the mart, and urged the vessel brave
To link in one far countries o'er the wave?
What raised the town?—what gave the type and germ
Of social union, and of sceptre firm?
Who the first husbandman, the glebe to plough,
And rear the garden, but the marriage vow?

"Nay, list again! who seek its kindly chain,
A second self, a double presence gain;
Hands, eyes, and ears, to act or suffer here,
Till e'en the weak inspire both love and fear—
A comrade's sigh, to soothe when cares annoy—
A comrade's smile, to elevate his joy.

"Nor say it weds us to a carnal life;
When want is urgent, fears and vows are rife.
Light heart is his, who has no yoke at home,
Scant prayer for blessings as the seasons come.
But wife, and offspring, goods which go or stay,
Teach us our need, and make us trust and pray.
Take love away, and life would be defaced,
A ghastly vision on a howling waste,
Stern, heartless, reft of the sweet spells, which swage
The throes of passion, and which gladden age.

No child's sweet pranks, once more to make us young;
No ties of place about our heart-strings flung;
No public haunts to cheer; no festive tide,
Where harmless mirth and smiling wit preside;
A life, which scorns the gifts which Heaven assign'd,
Nor knows the sympathy of human kind.

"Prophets and teachers, priests and victor kings,
Decked with each grace which heaven-taught nature brings,
These were no giant offspring of the earth,
But to the marriage-promise owe their birth:—
Moses and Samuel, David, David's son,
The blessed Thesbite, and more blessed John,
The sacred twelve in apostolic choir,
Strong-hearted Paul, instinct with seraph-fire,
And others, now or erst, who to high heaven aspire.
Bethink ye; should the single state be best,
Yet who the single, but my offspring blest?
My sons, be still, nor with your parents strive,
They coupled in their day, and so ye live."

Thus Marriage pleads. Now let her rival speak;
Dim is her downcast eye, and pale her cheek;
Untrimmed her gear; no sandals on her feet;
A sparest form for austere tenant meet.
She drops her veil her modest face around,
And her lips open, but we hear no sound.
I will address her:—"Hail! O child of heaven,
Glorious within! to whom a post is given
Hard by the throne, where Angels bow and fear,
E'en while thou hast a name and mission here,
O deign thy voice, unveil thy brow, and see
Thy ready guard and minister in me.
Oft hast thou come heaven-wafted to my breast,
Bright Spirit! so come again, and give me rest!"

. . . "Ah! who has hither drawn my backward feet,
Changing for worldly strife my lone retreat?
Where, in the silent chant of holy deeds,
I praise my God, and tend the sick soul's needs;
By toils of day, and vigils of the night,
By gushing tears, and blessed lustral rite,

I have no sway amid the crowd, no art
In speech, no place in council or in mart;
Nor human law, nor judges throned on high,
Smile on my face, and to my words reply.
Let others seek earth's honours; be it mine
One law to cherish, and to track one line;
Straight on towards heaven to press with single bent,
To know and love my God, and then to die content."
etc., etc.

It would take up too much time to continue the poem, of which I have attempted the above rude and free translation (or rather paraphrase, as indeed are all the foregoing); or to introduce any other specimens of the poetical talents of this accomplished Father of the Church.

I end with one or two stanzas, which give an account of the place and circumstances of his retirement. I am obliged again to warn the reader, that he must not fancy he has gained an idea of Gregory's poetry from my attempts at translation; and should it be objected that this is not treating Gregory well, I answer, that at least I am as true to the original as if I exhibited it in plain prose.

Some one whispered yesterday
  Of the rich and fashionable,
"Gregory, in his own small way,
  Easy was, and comfortable.

Had he not of wealth his fill,
  Whom a garden gay did bless,
And a gently trickling rill,
  And the sweets of idleness?"

I made answer: "Is it ease
  Fasts to keep, and tears to shed?
Vigil hours and wounded knees,
  Call you these a pleasant bed?

Thus a veritable monk
  Does to death his fleshly frame;
Be there who in sloth are sunk,
  They have forfeited the name."

And thus I take leave of St. Gregory, a man who is as great theologically as he is personally winning.

CHAPTER V.

ANTONY IN CONFLICT.

"He found him in a desert land, in a place of horror and of wilderness He led him about, and taught him; and He kept him as the apple of His eye."

I.

IT would be a great mistake for us to suppose that we need quit our temporal calling, and go into retirement, in order to serve God acceptably. Christianity is a religion for this world, for the busy and influential, for the rich and powerful, as well as for the poor. A writer of the age of Justin Martyr expresses this clearly and elegantly :—"Christians differ not," he says, "from other men, in country, or language, or customs. They do not live in any certain cities, or employ any particular dialect, or cultivate peculiar habits of life. They dwell in cities, Greek and barbarian, each where he finds himself placed; and while they submit to the fashion of their country in dress and food, and the general conduct of life, still they maintain a system of interior polity, which, beyond all controversy, is admirable and strange. The countries they inhabit are their own, but they dwell like aliens. They marry, like other men, and do not exclude their children from their affections; their table is open to all around them; they live in the flesh, but not according to the flesh; they walk on earth, but their conversation is in heaven."—*Ad Diogn.* 5.

Yet, undeniable as it is, that there is never an obligation upon Christians in general to leave, and often an obligation against leaving, their worldly engagements and possessions, still it is as undeniable that such an abandonment is often praiseworthy, and in particular cases a duty. Our Saviour expressly told one, who was rich and young, "to sell all, and give to the poor;" and surely He does not speak in order to immortalize exceptions or extreme cases, or fugitive forms of argument, refutation, or censure. Even looking at the subject in a merely human light, one may pronounce it to be a narrow and shallow system, that Protestant philosophy, which forbids all the higher and more noble impulses of the mind, and forces men to eat, drink, and be merry, whether they will or no. But the mind of true Christianity is expansive enough to admit high and low, rich and poor, one with another.

If the primitive Christians are to be trusted as witnesses of the genius of the Gospel system, certainly it is of that elastic and comprehensive character which removes the more powerful temptations to extravagance, by giving, as far as possible, a sort of indulgence to the feelings and motives which lead to it, correcting them the while, purifying them, and reining them in, ere they get excessive. Thus, whereas our reason naturally loves to expatiate at will to and fro through all subjects known and unknown, Catholicism does not oppress us with an irrational bigotry, prescribing to us the very minutest details of thought, so that a man can never have an opinion of his own; on the contrary, its creed is ever what it was, and never moves out of the ground which it originally occupied, and it is cautious and precise in its decisions, and distinguishes between things necessary and things pious to believe, between wilfulness and ignorance. At the same time, it asserts the supremacy of faith, the guilt of unbelief, and the divine mission of the Church; so that reason is brought round again and subdued to the obedience of Christ, at the very time when it seems to be launching forth without chart upon the ocean of speculation. And it pursues the same course in matters of conduct. It opposes the intolerance of what are called "*sensible* Protestants." It is shocked at the tyranny of those who will not let a man do anything out of the way without stamping him with the name of fanatic. It deals softly with the ardent and impetuous, saying, in effect—"My child, you may do as many great things as you will; but I have already made a list for you to select from. You are too docile to pursue ends merely because they are of your own choosing; you seek them because they are *great.* You wish to live above the common course of a Christian;—I can teach you to do this, yet without arrogance." Meanwhile the sensible Protestant divine keeps to his point, hammering away on his own ideas, urging every one to be as every one else, and moulding all minds upon his one small model; and when he has made his ground good to his own admiration, he finds that half his flock have after all turned Wesleyans or Independents, by way of searching for something divine and transcendental.

2.

These remarks are intended as introductory to some notice of the life of St. Antony, the first monk, who finished his work in Egypt just about the time that St. Basil was renewing that work in Asia Minor. The words "monk," "monastic," mean "solitary," and, if taken literally, certainly denote a mode of life which is so far contrary to nature as to require some special direction or inspiration for its adoption. Christ sent His Apostles by two and two; and surely He knew what was in man from the day that He said—"It is not good for him to be alone." So far, then, Antony's manner of life may be ill-fitted to be a rule for others; but his pattern in this respect was not adopted by his followers, who by their numbers were soon led to the formation of monastic societies, nay, who, after a while, entangled even Antony himself in the tie of becoming in a certain sense their religious head and teacher. Monachism consisting, not in solitariness, but in austerities, prayers, retirement, and obedience, had nothing in it, surely, but what was perfectly Christian, and, under circumstances, exemplary; especially when viewed in its connexion with the relative duties, which were soon afterwards appropriated to it, of being almoner of the poor, of educating the clergy, and of defending the faith. In short, Monachism became, in a little while, nothing else than a peculiar department of the Christian ministry—a ministry not of the sacraments, but especially of the word and doctrine; not indeed by any formal ordination to it, for it was as yet a lay profession, but by the common right, or rather duty, which attaches to all of us to avow, propagate, and defend the truth, especially when such zeal for it has received the countenance and encouragement of our spiritual rulers.

St. Antony's life, written by his friend, the great Athanasius, has come down to us. Some critics, indeed, doubt its genuineness, or consider it interpolated. Rivetus and others reject it; Du Pin decides, on the whole, that it is his, but with additions; the Benedictines and Tillemont ascribe it to him unhesitatingly. I conceive no question can be raised with justice about its *substantial* integrity; and on rising from the perusal of it, all candid readers will pronounce Antony a wonderful man. Enthusiastic he certainly must be accounted, according to English views of things; and had he lived a Protestant in this Protestant day, he would have been exposed to a serious temptation of becoming a fanatic. Longing for some higher rule of life than any which the ordinary forms of society admit, and finding our present lines too rigidly drawn to include any character of mind that is much out of the way, any rule that is not "gentleman-like," "comfortable," and "established," and hearing nothing of the Catholic Church, he might possibly have broken what he could not bend. The question is not, whether such impatience is not open to the charge of wilfulness and self-conceit; but whether, on the contrary, such special resignation to worldly comforts as we see around us, is not often the characteristic of nothing else than selfishness and sloth;—whether there are not minds with ardent feelings, keen imaginations, and undisciplined tempers, who are under a strong irritation prompting them to run wild,—whether it is not our duty (so to speak) to play with such, carefully letting out line enough lest they snap it,—and whether the Protestant Establishment is as indulgent and as wise as might be desired in its treatment of such persons, inasmuch as it provides no occupation for them, does not understand how to turn them to account, lets them run to waste, tempts them to dissent, loses them, is weakened by the loss, and then denounces them.

But to return to Antony. Did I see him before me, I might be tempted, with my cut and dried opinions, and my matter-of-fact ways, and my selfishness and pusillanimity, to consider him somewhat of an enthusiast; but what I desire to point out to the reader, and especially to the Protestant, is the subdued and Christian form which was taken by his enthusiasm, if it must be so called. It was not vulgar, bustling, imbecile, unstable, undutiful; it was calm and composed, manly, intrepid, magnanimous, full of affectionate loyalty to the Church and to the Truth.

3.

Antony was born A.D. 251, while Origen was still alive, while Cyprian was bishop of Carthage, Dionysius bishop of Alexandria, and Gregory Thaumaturgus of Neocæsarea; he lived till A.D. 356, to the age of 105, when Athanasius was battling with the Emperor Constantius, nine years after the birth of St. Chrysostom, and two years after that of St. Augustine. He was an Egyptian by birth, and the son of noble, opulent, and Christian parents. He was brought up as a Christian, and, from his boyhood, showed a strong disposition towards a solitary life. Shrinking from the society of his equals, and despising the external world in comparison of the world within him, he set himself against what is considered a liberal education—that is, the study of philosophy and of foreign languages. At the same time, he was very dutiful to his parents, simple and self-denying in his habits, and attentive to the sacred services and readings of the Church.

Before he arrived at man's estate he had lost both his parents, and was left with a sister, who was a child, and an ample inheritance. His mind at this time was earnestly set upon imitating the Apostles and their converts, who gave up their possessions and followed Christ. One day, about six months after his parents' death, as he went to church, as usual, the subject pressed seriously upon him. The Gospel of the day happened to contain the text—"If thou wilt be perfect, go sell all that thou hast." Antony applied it to himself, and acted upon it. He had three hundred acres,* of especial fertility, even for Egypt; these he at once made over to the use of the poor of his own neighbourhood. Next, he turned into money all his personal property, and reserving a portion for his sister's use, gave the rest to the poor. After a while he was struck by hearing in church the text—"Be not solicitous for to-morrow;" and considering he had not yet fully satisfied the Evangelical counsel, he gave away what he had reserved, placing his sister in the care of some women, who had devoted themselves to the single state.

He commenced his ascetic life, according to the custom then observed, by retiring to a place not far from his own home. Here he remained for a while to steady and fix his mind in his new habits, and to gain what advice he could towards the perfect formation of them, from such as had already engaged in the like object. This is a remarkable trait, as Athanasius records it, as showing how little he was influenced by self-will or a sectarian spirit in what he was doing, how ardently he pursued an ascetic life as in itself good, and how willing he was to become the servant of any who might give him directions in pursuing it. But this will be best shown by an extract:—

"There was, in the next village, an aged man who had lived a solitary life from his youth. Antony, seeing him, 'was zealous in a good thing,' and first of all adopted a similar retirement in the neighbourhood of the village. And did he hear of any zealous person anywhere, he would go and seek him out, like a wise man; not returning home till he had seen him, and gained from him some stock, as it were, for his journey towards holiness. He

* *Arura*—Three quarters of an English acre.—*Gibbon.*

laboured with his hands, according to the words—'If anyone will not work, neither let him eat;' laying out part of his produce in bread, part on the poor. He prayed continually, having learned that it is a duty to pray in private without ceasing. So attentive, indeed, was he to sacred reading, that he let no part of the Scripture fall from him to the ground, but retained all, memory serving in place of book. In this way he gained the affections of all; he, in turn, subjecting himself sincerely to the zealous men whom he visited, and marking down, in his own thoughts, the special attainment of each in zeal and ascetic life—the refined manners of one, another's continuance in prayer, the meekness of a third, the kindness of a fourth, the long vigils of a fifth, the studiousness of a sixth. This one had a marvellous gift of endurance, that of fasting and sleeping on the ground; this was gentle, that long-suffering; and in one and all he noted the devotion towards Christ, and love one towards another. Thus furnished, he returned to his own ascetic retreat, henceforth combining in himself their separate exercises, and zealously minded to exemplify them all. This, indeed, was his only point of emulation with those of his own age, viz. that he might not come off second to them in good things; and this he so pursued as to annoy no one, rather to make all take delight in him. Accordingly, all the villagers of the place, and religious persons who were acquainted with him, seeing him such, called him God's beloved, and cherished him as a son or as a brother."—§ 4.

Of course this account is the mere relation of a fact; but, over and above its historical character, it evidently is meant as the description of a type of character which both the writer and those for whom he wrote thought eminently Christian. Taking it then as being, in a certain line, the *beau ideal* of what Protestants would call the enthusiasm of the time, I would request of them to compare it with the sort of religion into which the unhappy enthusiast of the present day is precipitated by the high and dry system of the Establishment; and he will see how much was gained to Christianity, in purity, as well as unity, by that monastic system, the place of which in this country is filled by methodism and dissent.

After a while, our youth's enthusiasm began to take its usual course. His spirits fell, his courage flagged; a reaction followed, and the temptations of the world which he had left assaulted him with a violence which showed that as yet he had not mastered the full meaning of his profession. Had he been nothing more than an enthusiast, he would have gone back to the world. The property he had abandoned, the guardianship of his sister, his family connexions, the conveniences of wealth, worldly reputation, disgust of the sameness and coarseness of his food, bodily infirmity, the tediousness of his mode of living, and the absence of occupation, presented themselves before his imagination, and became instruments of temptation. Other and fiercer assaults succeeded. However, his faith rose above them all, or rather, as Athanasius says, "not himself, but the grace of God that was in him." His biographer proceeds:—

"Such was Antony's first victory over the devil, or rather the Saviour's glorious achievement in him, 'who hath condemned sin in the flesh, that the justification of the law may be fulfilled in us, who walk not according to the flesh, but according to the Spirit.' Not, however, as if Antony, fancying the devil was subdued, was neglectful afterwards, and secure; knowing from the Scriptures that there are many devices of the enemy, he was persevering in his ascetic life. He was the more earnest in chastising his body, and bringing it into subjection, lest, triumphing in some things, in others he might be brought low. His vigils were often through the whole night. He ate but once in the day, after sunset; sometimes after two days, often after four: his food was bread and salt,—his drink, water only. He never had more than a mat to sleep on, but generally lay down on the ground. He put aside oil for anointing, saying that the youthful ought to be forward in their asceticism, and, instead of seeking what might relax the body, to accustom it to hardships, remembering the Apostle's words—'When I am weak, then am I powerful.' He thought it unsuitable to measure either holy living, or retirement for the sake of it, by length of time; but by the earnest desire and deliberate resolve of being holy. Accordingly, he never himself used to take any account of the time gone by; but, day by day, as if ever fresh beginning his exercise, he made still greater efforts to advance, repeating to himself continually the saying of the Apostle, 'forgetting the things that are behind, and stretching forth myself to those that are before.'"—§ 7.

4.

Such was his life for about fifteen years. At the end of this time, being now thirty-five, he betook himself to the desert, having first spent some days in prayers and holy exercises in the tombs. Here, however, I am compelled to introduce another subject, which has already entered into Athanasius's text, though it has not been necessary to notice it,—his alleged conflicts with the evil spirits; to it, then, let us proceed.

It is quite certain, then, that Antony believed himself to be subjected to sensible and visible conflicts with evil spirits. It would not be consistent with our present argument to rescue him from the imputation of enthusiasm: he must be here considered an enthusiast, else I cannot make use of him; the very drift of my account of him being to show how enthusiasm is sobered and refined by being submitted to the discipline of the Church, instead of being allowed to run wild externally to it. I say, if he were not an enthusiast, or at least in danger of being such, we should lose one chief instruction which his life conveys. To maintain, however, that he was an enthusiast, is far from settling the question to which the narrative of his spiritual conflicts gives rise; so I shall first make some extracts descriptive of them, and then comment upon them.

The following is the account of his visit to the tombs:—

"Thus bracing himself after the pattern of Elias, he set off to the tombs, which were some distance from his village; and giving directions to an acquaintance to bring him bread after some days' interval, he entered into one of them, suffered himself to be shut in, and remained there by himself. This the enemy not enduring, yea, rather dreading, lest before long he should engross the desert also with his holy exercise, assaulted him one night with a host of spirits, and so lashed him, that he lay speechless on the ground from the torture, which, he declared, was far more severe than from strokes which man could inflict. But, by God's Providence, who does not overlook those who hope in Him, on the next day his acquaintance came with the bread; and, on opening the door, saw him lying on the ground as if dead. Whereupon he carried him to the village church, and laid him on the ground; and many of his relations and the villagers took their places by the body, as if he were already dead. However, about midnight his senses returned, and collecting himself, he observed that they were all asleep except his aforesaid acquaintance; whereupon he beckoned him to his side, and asked of him, without waking any of them, to carry him back again to the tombs.

"The man took him back: and when he was shut in, as before, by himself, being unable to stand from his wounds, he lay down, and began to pray. Then he cried out loudly, 'Here am I, Antony; I do not shun your blows. Though ye add to them, yet nothing shall separate me from the love of Christ.' And then he began to sing, 'If armies in camp should stand together against me, my heart shall not fear.' The devil has no trouble in devising diverse shapes of evil. During the night, therefore, the evil ones made so great a tumult, that the whole place seemed to be shaken, and, as if they broke down the four walls of the building, they seemed to rush in in the form of wild beasts and reptiles. . . . But Antony, though scourged and pierced, felt indeed his bodily pain, but the rather kept vigil in his soul. So, as he lay groaning in body, yet a watcher in his mind, he spoke in taunt—'Had ye any power, one of you would be enough to assail me; you try, if possible, to frighten me with your number, because the Lord has spoiled you of your strength. Those pretended forms are the proofs of your impotence. Our seal and wall of defence is faith in our Lord.' After many attempts, then, they gnashed their teeth at him, because they were rather making themselves a sport than him. But the Lord a second time remembered the conflict of Antony, and came to his help.

Raising his eyes, he saw the roof as if opening, and a beam of light descending towards him; suddenly the devils vanished, his pain ceased, and the building was whole again. Upon this Antony said, 'Where art Thou, Lord? why didst Thou not appear at the first, to ease my pain?' A voice answered, 'Antony, I was here, but waited to see thy bearing in the contest; since, therefore, thou hast sustained and not been worsted, I will be to thee an aid for ever, and I will make thy name famous in every place.'"—§§ 9, 10.

After this preliminary vigil, Antony made for the desert, where he spent the next twenty years in solitude. Athanasius gives the following account of his life there:—

"The following day he left the tombs, and his piety becoming still more eager, he went to the old man before mentioned, and prayed him to accompany him into the desert. When he declined by reason of his age and the novelty of the proposal, he set off for the mountain by himself . . . . and finding beyond the river a strong place, deserted so long a while that venomous reptiles abounded there, he went thither, and took possession of it, they farther retreating, as if one pursued them. Blocking up the entrance, and laying in bread for six months (as the Thebans are wont, often keeping their bread a whole year), and having a well of water indoors, he remained, as if in a shrine, neither going abroad himself, nor seeing any of those who came to him. . . . He did not allow his acquaintance to enter; so, while they remained often days and nights without, they used to hear noises within; blows, pitiable cries, such as 'Depart from our realm! what part hast thou in the desert? thou shalt perforce yield to our devices.' At first they thought he was in dispute with some men who had entered by means of ladders; but when they had contrived to peep in through a chink, and saw no one, then they reckoned it was devils that they heard, and, in terror, called Antony. He cared for them more than for the spirits, and coming at once near the door, bade them go away and not fear; 'for,' he said, 'the devils make all this feint to alarm the timid. Ye, then, sign yourselves, and depart in confidence, and let them make game of themselves.'" —§§ 12, 13

5.

To enter into the state of opinion and feeling which

such accounts imply, it is necessary to observe, that, as regards the Church's warfare with the devil, the primitive Christians, as Catholics since, considered themselves to be similarly circumstanced with the Apostles. They did not draw a line, as is the fashion with Protestants, between the condition of the Church in their day and in the first age, but believed that what she had been, such she was still in her trials and in her powers; that the open assaults of Satan, and their own means of repelling them, were such as they are described in the Gospels. Exorcism was a sacred function with them, and the energumen took his place with catechumens and penitents, as in the number of those who had the especial prayers, and were allowed some of the privileges, of the Christian body. Our Saviour speaks of the power of exorcising as depending on fasting and prayer, in certain special cases, and thus distinctly countenances the notion of a direct conflict between the Christian athlete and the powers of evil,—a conflict, carried on, on the side of the former, by definite weapons, for definite ends, and not that indirect warfare merely which an ordinary religious course of life implies. "This kind can go out by nothing but by prayer and fasting." Surely none of Christ's words are chance words; He spoke *with a purpose*, and the Holy Spirit guided the Evangelists in their selection of them *with a purpose;* and if so, this text is a rule and an admonition, and was acted upon as such by the primitive Christians, whether from their received principles of interpretation or the traditionary practice of the Church.

In like manner, whether from their mode of interpreting Scripture, or from the opinions and practices which came down to them, they conceived the devil to be allowed that power over certain brute animals which

Scripture sometimes assigns to him. He is known on one memorable occasion to have taken the form of a serpent; at another time, a legion of devils possessed a herd of swine. These instances may, for what we know, be revealed *specimens* of a whole side of the Divine Dispensation, viz., the interference of spiritual agencies, good and bad, with the course of the world, under which, perhaps, the speaking of Balaam's ass falls; and the early Christians, whether so understanding Scripture, or from their traditionary system, acted as if they really were such specimens. They considered that brute nature was widely subjected to the power of spirits; as, on the other hand, there had been a time when even the Creator Spirit had condescended to manifest Himself in the bodily form of a dove. Their notions concerning local demoniacal influences as existing in oracles and idols, in which they were sanctioned by Scripture, confirmed this belief. Accordingly, they took passages like the following literally, and used them as a corroborative proof: "Behold, I have given you power to tread upon *serpents* and *scorpions*, and upon all the power of the enemy." "They shall take up *serpents*, and if they drink any deadly thing, it shall not hurt them." "Your adversary, the devil, as a roaring *lion*, goeth about, seeking whom he may devour." "I saw three unclean spirits, like *frogs* . . . they are the spirits of devils, working signs." Add to these, Daniel's vision of the four beasts; and the description of leviathan, in the book of Job, which was interpreted of the evil spirit.

Moreover, there is a ground of deep philosophy on which such notions may be based, and which appears to have been held by these primitive Christians; viz., that visible things are types and earnests of things invisible. The elements are, in some sense, symbols and tokens of spiritual agents, good and bad. Satan is called the prince of the air. Still more mysterious than inanimate nature is the family of brute animals, whose limbs and organs are governed by some motive principle unknown. Surely there is nothing abstractedly absurd in considering certain hideous developments of nature as tokens of the presence of the unseen author of evil, as soon as we once admit that he exists. Certainly the sight of a beast of prey, with his malevolent passions, savage cruelty, implacable rage, malice, cunning, sullenness, restlessness, brute hunger, irresistible strength, though there cannot be sin in any of these qualities themselves, awakens very awful and complicated musings in a religious mind. Thus a philosophical view of nature would be considered, in the times I speak of, to corroborate the method of Scripture interpretation which those same times adopted.

But, moreover, Scripture itself seemed, in the parallel case of demoniacs, to become its own interpreter. It was notorious that in the Apostolic age devils made human beings their organs; why, then, much more, should not brute beasts be such? The simple question was, whether the state of things in the third century was substantially the same as it was in the first; and this, I say, the early Christians *assumed* in the affirmative, and certainly, whether they were judges of this question or not, I suppose they were as good judges as Protestants are. The case of demoniacs should be carefully considered, since their sufferings often seem to have been neither more nor less than what would now be hastily attributed to natural diseases, and would be treated by medical rules. The demoniac whom the Apostles could not cure had certain symptoms which in another would have been called epileptic. Again, the woman who was bowed together for eighteen years, and was cured by Christ, is expressly said to have had "a spirit of infirmity," to have been "bound by Satan." If, then, what looks like disease may sometimes be the token of demoniacal presence and power, though ordinarily admitting of medical treatment, why is it an objection to the connexion of the material or animal world with spirits, that the laws of mineral agents, or the peculiarities of brute natures, can also be drawn out into system on paper, and can be anticipated and reckoned on by our knowledge of that system? The same objection lies, nay, avails, against the one and the other. The very same scoffing temper which rejects the teaching of the Church, primitive and modern, concerning Satan's power, as "Pagan," "Oriental," and the like, does actually assail the inspired statements respecting it also, explains away demoniacal possessions as unreal, and maintains that Christ and His Apostles spoke by way of accommodation, and in the language of their day, when they said that Satan bound us with diseases and plagues, and was "prince of the power of the air."

Dreams are another department of our present state of being, through which, as Scripture informs us, the Supernatural sometimes acts; and in the same general way; *i.e.* not always, and by ascertainable rules, but by the virtue of occasional, though real, connexion with them.

6.

On the whole, then, I am led to conclude that, supposing I found a narrative, such as Antony's, of *the Apostles' age*, it would be sufficiently agreeable to the narratives of Scripture to make me dismiss from my mind all *antecedent* difficulties in believing it. On the other hand, did the miracle of the swine occur in the life of St. Antony, I venture to maintain that men of this scientific day would not merely suspend their judgment, or pronounce it improbable (which they might have a right to do), but would at once, and peremptorily, pronounce it altogether incredible and false: so as to make it appear that

> "There are more things in heaven and earth, Horatio,
> Than are dreamt of in your philosophy."

I have no wish to trifle, or argue with subtlety upon a very deep subject. This earth had become Satan's kingdom; our Lord came to end his usurpation; but Satan retreated only inch by inch. The Church of Christ is hallowed ground, but external to it is the kingdom of darkness. Many serious persons think that the evil spirits have, even now, extraordinary powers in heathen lands, to say nothing of the remains of their ancient dominion in countries now Christian. There are strange stories told in heathen populations of sorcerers and the like. Nay, how strange are the stories which only in half-heathen, or even Christian places, have come perhaps to our own knowledge! How unaccountable to him who has met with them are the sudden sounds, the footsteps, and the noises which he has heard in solitary places, or when in company with others!

These things being considered, were I a candid Protestant, I would judge of Antony's life thus:—I should say: "There may be enthusiasm here; there may be, at times, exaggerations and misconceptions of what, as they really happened, meant nothing. And still, it may be true also that that conflict, begun by our Lord when He was interrogated and assaulted by Satan, was continued in the experience of Antony, who lived not so very long after Him. How far the evil spirit acted, how far he was really present in material forms, how far on the other hand was dream, how far imagination, is little to the purpose. I see, anyhow, the root of a great truth here, and think that those are wiser who admit something than those who deny everything. I see Satan frightened at the invasions of the Church upon his kingdom ; I see him dispossessed by fasting and prayer, as was predicted ; I see him retreating step by step ; and I see him doing his utmost in whatever way to resist. Nor is there anything uncongenial to the Gospel system, that so direct a war, with such definite weapons, should be waged upon him ; a war which has not the ordinary duties of life and of society for its subject-matter and instruments. That text about fasting and prayer is a canon in sanction of it : our Saviour too Himself was forty days in the wilderness ; and St. Peter at Joppa, and St. John at Patmos, show us that duties of this world may be providentially suspended under the Gospel, and a direct intercourse with the next world may be opened upon the Christian."

And if so much be allowed, certainly there is nothing in Antony's life to make us suspicious of him personally. His doctrine surely was pure and unimpeachable ; and his temper is high and heavenly,—without cowardice, without gloom, without formality, and without self-complacency. Superstition is abject and crouching, it is full of thoughts of guilt ; it distrusts God, and dreads the powers of evil. Antony at least has nothing of this. being full of holy confidence, divine peace, cheerfulness, and valorousness, be he (as some men may judge) ever so much an enthusiast. But on this subject I shall say something in the next chapter.

CHAPTER VI.

ANTONY IN CALM.

"The land that was desolate and impassable shall be glad, and the wilderness shall rejoice and shall flourish like the lily. And that which was dry land shall become a pool, and the thirsty land springs of water."

1.

I HAVE said enough about St. Antony's history; let me now introduce the reader to his character, which I shall best do by setting before him some unconnected passages, as they occur in the narrative of his life.

It is remarkable that his attempts at curing diseases were not always successful; his prayers being *experimental*, not, as in the case of the Apostles, immediately suggested by the same Power which was about miraculously to manifest Itself. Of course there were then in the Church, as at all times, extraordinary and heavenly gifts; but still they were distinct from those peculiar powers which we ascribe to the Apostles, as immediate ministers of the Revelation.

"He united in sympathy and prayer with those who were in suffering," says Athanasius, "and *often*, and in many cases, the Lord heard him. When heard, he did not boast; *when unsuccessful*, he did not murmur; but, under all circumstances, he gave thanks himself to the Lord, and exhorted the sufferers to be patient, and to be assured that their cure was out of the power of himself, and indeed of any man, and lay with God only, *who wrought when He would, and towards whom He chose.* The patients in consequence accepted *even the words* of the old man as a medicine, learning themselves not to despise the means, but rather to be patient, while those who were healed were instructed not to give thanks to Antony but to God only."—§ 56.

This passage deserves notice also, as showing the unvarnished character of the narrative. Superstitious and fabulous histories are not candid enough to admit such failures as are implied in it. The following is to the same purpose. He was asked to allow a paralytic woman and her parents to visit him, with the hope of a cure, and he refused, on the ground that, if her life was to be preserved, her own prayers might be efficacious without him.

"'Go,' he humbly answered, 'and, *unless she be dead already,* you will find her cured. This happy event is not my doing, that she should come to me, a miserable man, to secure it; but the cure is from the Saviour, who shows mercy *in every place,* on those who call upon Him. *To her prayers,* then, the Lord has been gracious; to me is but revealed, by His loving-kindness, that He means to cure her where she is.'"—§ 58.

Antony held that faith had power with God for any work: and he took delight in contrasting with this privilege of exercising faith that poor measure of knowledge which is all that sight and reason open on us at the utmost. He seems to have felt there was a divine spirit and power in Christianity such as irresistibly to commend it to religious and honest minds, coming home to the heart with the same conviction which any high moral precept carries with it, and leaving argumentation behind as comparatively useless, except by way of curiously investigating motives and reasons for the satisfaction of the philosophical analyst. And then, when faith was once in operation, it was the instrument of gaining the knowledge of truths which reason could but feebly presage, or could not even have imagined.

Some philosophers came to discourse with him; he says to them:

"'Since you prefer to insist on demonstrative argument, and, being skilled in the science of it, would have us also refrain from worshipping God without a demonstrative argument, tell me first, how is the knowledge of things in general, and especially of religion, absolutely ascertained? Is it by a demonstration of argument, or through an operative power of faith? And which of the two will you put first?' They said, Faith, owning that it was absolute knowledge. Then Antony rejoined, 'Well said, for faith results from a disposition of the soul; but dialectics are from the science of the disputant. They, then, who possess the operative power of faith can supersede, nay, are but cumbered with demonstration in argument; for what we apprehend by faith, you are merely endeavouring to arrive at by argument, and sometimes cannot even express what we apprehend. Faith, then, which operates, is better and surer than your subtle syllogisms.'"—§ 77.

Again:

"'Instead of demonstrating in the persuasive arguments of Gentile wisdom, as our Teacher says, we persuade by faith, which vividly anticipates a process of argument.'"—§ 80.

After curing some demoniacs with the sign of the cross, he adds:

"'Why wonder ye at this? It is not we who do it, but Christ, by means of those who believe on Him. Do ye too believe, and ye shall see that our religion lies not in some science of argument, but in faith, which operates through love towards Jesus Christ; which if ye attained, ye too would no longer seek for demonstrations drawn from argument, but would account faith in Christ all-sufficient.'"—*Ibid.*

Antony, as we have already seen, is far from boasting of his spiritual attainments:

"It is not right to glory in casting out devils, nor in curing diseases, nor to make much of him only who casts out devils, and to undervalue him who does not. On the contrary, study the ascetic life of this man and that, and either imitate and emulate or improve it. For to do miracles is not ours, but the Saviour's; wherefore He said to His disciples, 'Rejoice not that spirits are subject unto you,' etc. To those who take confidence, not in holiness but in miracles, and say, 'Lord, did we not cast out devils in Thy name?' He makes answer, 'I never knew you,' for the Lord does not acknowledge the ways of the ungodly. On the whole, then, we must pray for the gift of discerning spirits, that, as it is written, we may not believe every spirit."—§ 38.

In like manner he dissuades his hearers from seeking the gift of prophecy; in which he remarkably differs from heathen ascetics, such as the Neo-platonists, who considered a knowledge of the secret principles of nature the great reward of their austerities.

"What is the use of hearing beforehand from the evil ones what is to happen? Or, why be desirous of such knowledge, even though it be true? It does not make us better men; nor is it a token of religious excellence at all. None of us is judged for what he does not know, nor accounted happy for his learning and acquirements; but in each case the question is this, whether or not he has kept the faith, and honestly obeyed the commandments? Wherefore we must not account these as great matters, nor live ascetically for the sake of them—viz. in order to know the future; but to please God by a good conversation. But if we are anxious at all to foresee what is to be, it is necessary to be pure in mind. Certainly I believe that that soul which is clean on every side, and established in its highest nature, becomes keen-sighted, and is able to see things more and further than the devils, having the Lord to reveal them to it. Such was the soul of Eliseus, which witnessed Giezi's conduct, and discerned the heavenly hosts which were present with it."—§ 34.

2.

These extracts have incidentally furnished some

evidence of the calmness, and I may say coolness of Antony's judgment—*i.e.* waiving the question of the truth of the principles and facts from which he starts. I am aware that an objector would urge that this is the very peculiarity of aberrations of the intellect, to reason correctly upon false premisses; and that Antony in no way differs from many men nowadays, whom we consider unable to take care of themselves. Yet surely, when we are examining the evidence for the divine mission of the Apostles, we do think it allowable to point out their good sense and composure of mind, though they assume premisses as Antony does. And, considering how extravagant and capricious the conduct of enthusiasts commonly is, how rude their manners, how inconstant their resolutions, how variable their principles, it is certainly a recommendation to our solitary to find him so grave, manly, considerate, and refined,—or, to speak familiarly, so gentlemanlike, in the true sense of that word. We see something of this in the account which Athanasius gives us of his personal appearance after his twenty years' seclusion, which has nothing of the gaunt character, or the uncouth expression, of one who had thrown himself out of the society of his fellow-men. I shall be obliged to make a long extract, if I begin; and yet I cannot help hoping that the reader will be pleased to have it.

"He had now spent nearly twenty years exercising himself thus by himself, neither going abroad nor being seen for any time by any one. But at this date, many longing to copy his ascetic life, and acquaintances coming and forcibly breaking down and driving in the door, Antony came forth as from some shrine, fully perfect in its mysteries, and instinct with God. This was his first appearance outside the enclosure, and those who had come to see him were struck with surprise at the little change his person had undergone, having neither a full habit, as being without exercise, nor the shrivelled character which betokens fasts and conflicts with the evil ones. He was the same as they had known him before his retreat. His mind also was serene, neither narrowed by sadness nor relaxed by indulgence, neither over-merry nor melancholy. He showed no confusion at the sight of the multitude, no elation at their respectful greetings. The Lord gave him grace in speech, so that he comforted many who were in sorrow, and reconciled those who were at variance, adding in every case, that they ought to set nothing of this world before love towards Christ. And while he conversed with the people, and exhorted them to remember the bliss to come, and God's loving-kindness to us men in not sparing His own Son, but giving Him up for us all, he persuaded many to choose the monastic life. And from that time monasteries have been raised among the mountains, and the desert is made a city by monks leaving their all and enrolling themselves in the heavenly citizenship."

His biographer then goes on to record one of his discourses. It was spoken in the Egyptian language, and ran as follows:

"Holy Scripture is sufficient for teaching, yet it is good to exhort one another in the faith, and refresh one another with our discourses. You then, as children, bring hither to your father whatever you have learned; and I in turn, as being your elder, will now impart to you what I have experienced. Let this preëminently be the common purpose of every one of you, not to give in when once you have begun, not to faint in your toil, not to say, 'We have been long enough at these exercises.' Rather as though, day after day, we were beginning for the first time, let our zeal grow stronger; for even the whole of human life is very short compared with eternity, or rather nothing. And every thing in this world has its price, and you get no more than an equivalent; yet the promise of everlasting life is bought at a trifling purchase. 'The days of our years are three score and ten years,' as Scripture says, 'and if, in the strong, they be four score;' yet, did we persist in our exercises for the whole four score, or for a hundred, this would not be the measure of our reign in glory. Instead of a hundred years, we shall reign for ages upon ages; not upon this poor earth upon which is our struggle, but our promised inheritance is in heaven. We lose a corruptible body to receive it back incorruptible.

"Wherefore, my children, let us not weary, nor think we have been a long while toiling, or that we are doing any great thing; for our present sufferings are not to be compared to the glory that shall be revealed in us. Let us not look at the world, or reckon we have made great sacrifices, for even the whole earth is but a small spot compared to the expanse of heaven. Though we had possessed it all, and had given it all up, it is nothing to the kingdom of heaven. It is no more than a man's making little of one copper coin in order to gain a hundred gold ones; thus he who is lord of the whole earth, and bids it farewell, does but give up little and gains a hundredfold. But if the whole earth be so little, what is it to leave a few acres? or a house? or a store of gold? Surely we should not boast or be dejected upon such a sacrifice. If we do not let these things go for virtue's sake, at death at length we shall leave them, and often to whom we would not, as says Ecclesiastes. What gain is it to acquire what we cannot carry away with us? Far different are prudence, justice, temperance, fortitude, understanding, charity, love of the poor, faith towards Christ, gentleness, hospitality; obtain we these, and we shall find them there before us, making ready a dwelling for us in the country of the meek."

After reminding his brethren that they have the Lord to work with them, and that they must fulfil the Apostles' rule of dying daily,—by rising as though they should not last till evening, and going to rest as though they should never rise, "life being of an uncertain nature, doled out by Providence from day to day," he continues:

"Therefore, having now set out upon the path of virtue, let us rather stretch forward to what is before. Be not alarmed when you hear speak of virtue, nor feel towards the name as if you were strangers to it; for it is not far from us, it is not external to us; the work is in us, and the thing is easy, if we have but the will. Greeks travel beyond the sea to learn letters,—we need not travel for the kingdom of heaven, or cross the sea for virtue. Christ anticipates us, 'The kingdom of heaven (He says) is within you; virtue needs but the will.

"We have able and subtle enemies, the evil spirits; with these we must wrestle, as the Apostle says. There is need of much prayer and self-discipline to gain, through the Holy Spirit, the gift of discerning of spirits, to detect their nature, viz. which of them are the less abandoned, which the more, what is the aim of each, what each affects, and how each is overthrown and ejected. When the Lord came on earth, the enemy fell, and his power waxed weak; therefore, as being a tyrant, though powerless, he keeps not quiet even in his fall, but threats, for he can do no more. Let each of you consider this, and he may scorn the evil spirits. Behold, we are here met together and speak against them, and they know that, as we make progress, they will grow feebler. Had they then leave, they would suffer none of us Christians to live; had they power, they would not come on with a noise, or put forth phantoms, or change their shapes to further their plans; one of them would be enough, did he come, to do what he could and wished to do. Such as have power do not make a display in order to kill another, nor alarm by noises, but use their power to effect at once what they wish. But evil spirits, since they can do nothing, are but as actors in a play, changing their shapes and frightening children by their tumult and their make-belief; whereas the true Angel of the Lord, sent by Him against the Assyrians, needed not tumult, appearance, noise, or clatter, but, in that quiet exercise of his power, he slew at once a hundred four score and five thousand. But the devils have not power even over the swine: much less over man made in God's image."—§§ 14—29.

3.

What can be more calm, more fearless, more noble than his bearing in this passage? Call his life a romance, if you think fit; still, I say, at least, we have in the narrative the ideal of a monk, according to the teaching of the fourth century. You cannot say that Antony was a savage self-tormentor, an ostentatious dervise; that he had aught of pomposity or affectation, aught of cunning and hypocrisy. According to Athanasius's description —who was personally acquainted with him—

"His countenance had a great and extraordinary beauty in it.

This was a gift from the Saviour; for, if he was in company with a number of monks, and any stranger wished to have a sight of him, directly that he came to them, he would pass by the rest, and run to Antony, as being attracted by his appearance. Not that he was taller or larger than others; but there was a peculiar composure of manner and purity of soul in him. For, being unruffled in soul, all his outward expressions of feeling were free from perturbation also; so that the joy of his soul made his very face cheerful, and from the gestures of the body might be understood the composure of his soul, according to the text, 'A glad heart maketh a cheerful countenance; but by grief of mind the spirit is cast down.' Thus Jacob detected Laban's treachery, and said to his wives, 'I see your father's countenance, that it is not towards me as yesterday.' Thus Samuel, too, discovered David; for he had beaming eyes, and teeth white as milk. In like manner one might recognise Antony; for he was never agitated, his soul being in a deep calm,—never changed countenance, from his inward joyfulness."—§ 67.

His own words assign one of the causes of this tranquillity. He says:

"The vision granted us of the holy ones is not tumultuous; for 'He shall not contend, nor cry out,' nor shall any one hear their voice. So quietly and gently does it come, that the soul is straightway filled with joy, exultation, and confidence, knowing that the Lord is with them, who is our joy, and God the Father's power. And its thoughts are preserved from tumult and tempest; so that, being itself illuminated fully, it is able of itself to contemplate the beings that appear before it. A longing after divine and future things takes possession of it, till it desires altogether to be joined unto them, and to depart with them. Nay, and if there be some who, from the infirmity of man, dread the sight of these good ones, such apparitions remove their alarm at once by their love, as Gabriel did to Zacharias, and the Angel at the divine tomb to the women, and that other who said to the shepherds in the Gospel, 'Fear not.'"—§ 35.

Such sentiments, beautiful as they are, might in another be ascribed to mere mysticism; but not so in the case of Antony, considering his constant profession and practice of self-denying and active virtue, and the plain practical sense of his exhortations. He took a vigorous part in the religious controversies of his day, reverencing the authorities of the Church, and strenuously opposing both the Meletian schismatics and the Arians. The following is an account of another of his interviews with heathen philosophers. They came with the hope of jeering at his ignorance of literature:

"Antony said to them, 'What do you say? which is prior, the mind or letters? And which gives rise to which, mind to letters, or letters to mind?' When they answered that mind was prior, and invented letters, Antony replied, 'He, then, whose mind is in health, does not need letters.' This answer struck all who were present, as well as the philosophers. They went away surprised that an uneducated man should show such understanding. For, indeed, he had nothing of the wildness of one who had lived and grown old on a mountain; but was polished in his manners, and a man of the world."—§ 73.

It has sometimes been objected, that hagiographists commonly fail in point of dignity, in the miracles which they introduce into their histories. I am not called here to consider the force of this objection; but Antony at least is clear of the defect; had his miracles and visions been ascribed to St. Peter or St. Paul, I conceive they would not have been questioned, evidence being supposed. For instance:

"Once, when he was going to take food, having stood up to pray, about the ninth hour, he felt himself carried away in spirit, and, strange to say, he saw himself, as if out of himself, while he stood looking on, and borne into the air by certain beings. Next, he saw some hateful and terrible shapes, stationed in the air, and stopping the way to prevent his passing on. His conductors resisted, but they asked whether he was not impeachable. But on their beginning to reckon up from his birth, his conductors interrupted them, saying, 'The Lord has wiped out all his earlier sins; but a reckoning may lawfully be made from the time he became a monk, and promised himself to God.' His accusers hereupon began ; but, when they could prove nothing, the way became clear and open ; and immediately he found himself returned, as it were, to himself, and forming with himself one Antony as before. Then forgetting his meal, he remained the rest of that day, and the whole of the following night, groaning and praying ; for he was astonished at finding against how many we have to wrestle, and by what an effort we must pass through the air heavenward. He remembered that this is what the Apostle said, 'the prince of the power of this air,'—and his special exhortation in consequence, 'Put on the panoply of God, that ye may be able to resist in the evil day.' When we heard it, we called to mind the Apostle's words, 'Whether in the body, or out of the body, I know not ; God knoweth.' "—§ 65.

Again :

" He had had a discussion with some persons, who had come to him, concerning the passage of the soul, and the abode which was allotted to it. On the following night, some one calls him from above in these words, 'Antony, rise, go forth, and behold.' Accordingly he went forth, knowing whom he should obey, and, looking up, he saw a huge something, unsightly and horrid, standing and reaching up to the clouds, and beings were ascending as if with wings, and it was catching at them with its hands. Of these, it brought some to a stand ; while others, flying past it, went upwards without further trouble. In such cases, that huge monster would gnash its teeth ; rejoicing, on the other hand, over those whom it cast down. Immediately Antony heard a voice, saying, 'Look, and understand.' And his mind was opened, and he comprehended that he saw the passage of souls, and the enemy, envious of the faithful, seizing and stopping those whom he had an advantage over, but foiled in his attempts upon those who had not obeyed him. After this vision, taking it as a warning, he made still more strenuous efforts to advance forward daily."—§ 66.

Once more :

"Once, when he was sitting and working, he fell into a trance, and groaned much at the sight he saw. After a while, he turned to those who were with him groaning, and prayed with much trembling, remaining a long time on his knees. When, at length, he rose, the old man began to weep. His friends, trembling and in great alarm themselves, begged to know what it was, and urged him till he was forced to tell. 'O, my children,' he said at length, with a deep sigh, 'it were better to die before that vision is fulfilled.' On their pressing him, he continued with tears, 'Wrath is about to overtake the Church, which is to be given over to men like irrational brutes. For I saw the table of the Lord's house hemmed in by mules, who were striking about with their hoofs at everything within, as is the way with unmannered beasts. You see, now, why I groaned so much; for I heard a voice, saying, My altar shall be polluted.' This the old man saw; two years after, the assaults of the Arians took place, when they plundered the churches, and gave the sacred vessels to heathens to carry, and compelled the heathens from the workshops to attend their religious meetings with them, and in their presence wanton insults offered to the Lord's table."—§ 82.

4.

At length the hour came for him to die; and Antony and his monks made their respective preparations for it. The narrative runs thus:

"The brethren urging him to remain with them, and there finish his course, he would not hear of it, as for other reasons, which were evident, even though he did not mention them, so especially because of the custom of the Egyptians in respect to the dead. For the bodies of good men, especially of the holy martyrs, they used to enfold in linen cloths; and, instead of burying, to place them upon biers, and keep them within their houses, thinking thus to honour the departed. Antony had applied even to bishops on this subject, begging them to admonish their people; and had urged it upon laymen, and had rebuked women, saying, that the practice was consistent neither with received rule, nor at all with religion. 'The bodies of patriarchs and prophets are preserved to this day in sepulchres; and the Lord's body itself was laid in a tomb, and a stone at the entrance kept it hidden till He rose the third day.' By such arguments he showed the irregularity of not burying the dead, however holy; 'for what can be more precious or holy than the Lord's body?' And he persuaded many to bury for the future, giving thanks to the Lord for such good instruction."

This was a matter of discipline and of discretion, as to which the custom of the Church may vary at different times; but with that we are not concerned here; to proceed:

"Antony, then, being aware of this, and fearing lest the same should be done to his own body, bidding farewell to the monks in the outer mountain, made hastily for the inner mountain, where he commonly dwelt, and after a few months, fell ill. Then calling to him two who lived with him, as ascetics, for fifteen years past, and ministered to him on account of his age, he said to them, 'I, as it is written, go the way of my fathers; for I perceive I am called by the Lord. You, then, be sober, and forfeit not the reward of your long asceticism; but, as those who have made a beginning, be diligent to hold fast your earnestness. Ye know the assaults of the evil spirit, how fierce they are, yet how powerless. Fear them not; rather breathe the spirit of Christ, and believe in Him always. Live as if dying daily; take heed to yourselves, and remember the admonitions you have heard from me. Have no fellowship with the schismatics, nor at all with the heretical Arians. Be diligent the rather to join yourselves, first of all, to the Lord, next to the Saints, that after death they may receive you as friends and intimates into the eternal habitations. Such be your thoughts, such your spirit; and if you have any care for me, remember me as a father. Do not let them carry my body into Egypt, lest they store it in their houses. One of my reasons for coming to this mountain was to hinder this. You know I have ever reproved those who have done this, and charged them to cease from the custom. Bury, then, my body in the earth, in obedience to my word, so that no one may know the place, except yourselves. In the resurrection of the dead it will be restored to me incorruptible by the Saviour. Distribute my garments as follows:—let Athanasius, the bishop, have the one sheep-skin and the garment I sleep on, which he gave me new, and which has grown old with me. Let Serapion, the bishop, have the other sheep-skin. As to the hair-shirt, keep it for yourselves. And now, my children, farewell; Antony is going, and is no longer with you.'

"After these words, they kissed him. Then he stretched himself out, and seemed to see friends come to him, and to be very joyful at the sight (to judge from the cheerfulness of his countenance as he lay), and so he breathed his last, and was gathered to his fathers

His attendants, as he had bidden them, wrapped his body up, and buried it: and no one knows yet where it lies, except these two. As to the two friends who were bequeathed a sheep-skin a-piece of the blessed Antony, and his tattered garment, each of them preserves it as a great possession. For when he looks at it, he thinks he sees Antony; and when he puts it on, he is, as it were, carrying about him his instructions with joy."—§§ 90, 92.

Such was in life and death the first founder of the monastic system; and his example, both as seen, and far more in the narrative of his biographer, was like a fire kindled in Christendom, which "many waters could not quench." Not that I would defend the details of any popular form of religion, considering that its popularity implies some condescension to the weaknesses of human nature; yet, if I must choose between the fashionable doctrines of one age and of another, certainly I shall prefer that which requires self-denial, and creates hardihood and contempt of the world, to some of the religions now in esteem, which rob faith of all its substance, its grace, its nobleness, and its strength, and excuse self-indulgence by the arguments of spiritual pride, self-confidence, and security;—which, in short, make it their boast that they are more *comfortable* than that ancient creed which, together with joy, leads men to continual smiting on the breast, and prayers for pardon, and looking forward to the judgment-day, as to an event really to happen to themselves individually.

The following is Athanasius's account of the effect produced by Antony in Egypt, even in his lifetime; and perhaps in his lifetime it was not only in its beginning, but in its prime. For all things human tend not to be, and the first fervour of zeal and love is the most wonderful. Yet even when its original glory had faded, the monastic home was ever, as now, the refuge of the penitent and the school of the saint. But let us hear Athanasius:

"Among the mountains there were monasteries, as if tabernacles filled with divine choirs, singing, studying, fasting, praying, exulting in the hope of things to come, and working for almsdeeds, having love and harmony one towards another. And truly it was given one there to see a peculiar country of piety and righteousness. Neither injurer nor injured was there, nor chiding of the tax-collector; but a multitude of ascetics, whose one feeling was towards holiness. So that a stranger, seeing the monasteries and their order, would be led to cry out, 'How beauteous are thy homes, O Jacob, and thy tabernacles, O Israel; as shady groves, as a garden on a river, as tents which the Lord has pitched, and as cedars by the waters.'"– § 44.

CHAPTER VII.

AUGUSTINE AND THE VANDALS

"The just perisheth, and no man layeth it to heart; and men of mercy are taken away, for there is none to understand; for the just man is taken away from before the face of evil."

I.

I BEGAN by directing the reader's attention to the labours of two great bishops, who restored the faith of Christianity where it had long been obscured. Now, I will put before him, by way of contrast, a scene of the overthrow of religion,—the extinction of a candlestick,—effected, too, by champions of the same heretical creed which Basil and Gregory successfully resisted. It will be found in the history of the last days of the great Augustine, bishop of Hippo, in Africa. The truth triumphed in the East by the power of preaching; it was extirpated in the South by the edge of the sword.

Though it may not be given us to appropriate the prophecies of the Apocalypse to the real events to which they belong, yet it is impossible to read its inspired pages, and then to turn to the dissolution of the Roman empire, without seeing a remarkable agreement, on the whole, between the calamities of that period and the sacred prediction. There is a plain announcement in the inspired page, of "Woe, woe, woe, to the inhabitants of the earth;" an announcement of "hail and fire mingled with blood," the conflagration of "trees and green grass," the destruction of ships, the darkening of the sun, and the poisoning of the rivers over a third of their course. There is a clear prophecy of revolutions on the face of the earth and in the structure of society. And, on the other hand, let us observe how fully such general foretokenings are borne out, among other passages of history, in the Vandalic conquest of Africa.

The coast of Africa, between the great desert and the Mediterranean, was one of the most fruitful and opulent portions of the Roman world. The eastern extremity of it was more especially connected with the empire, containing in it Carthage, Hippo, and other towns, celebrated as being sees of the Christian Church, as well as places of civil importance. In the spring of the year 428, the Vandals, Arians by creed, and barbarians by birth and disposition, crossed the Straits of Gibraltar, and proceeded along this fertile district, bringing with them devastation and captivity on every side. They abandoned themselves to the most savage cruelties and excesses. They pillaged, ravaged, burned, massacred all that came in their way, sparing not even the fruit-trees, which might have afforded some poor food to the remnant of the population, who had escaped from them into caves, the recesses of the mountains, or into vaults. Twice did this desolating pestilence sweep over the face of the country.

The fury of the Vandals was especially exercised towards the memorials of religion. Churches, cemeteries, monasteries, were objects of their fiercest hatred and most violent assaults. They broke into the places of worship, cut to pieces all internal decorations, and then set fire to them. They tortured bishops and clergy with the hope of obtaining treasure. The names of some of the victims of their ferocity are preserved. Mansuetus, bishop of Utica, was burnt alive ; Papinianus, bishop of Vite, was laid upon red-hot plates of iron. This was near upon the time when the third General Council was assembling at Ephesus, which, from the insecure state of the roads, and the universal misery which reigned among them, the African bishops were prevented from attending. The Clergy, the religious brotherhoods, the holy virgins, were scattered all over the country. The daily sacrifice was stopped, the sacraments could not be obtained, the festivals of the Church passed unnoticed. At length, only three cities remained unvisited by the general desolation,—Carthage, Hippo, and Cirtha.

2.

Hippo was the see of St. Austin, then seventy-four years of age (forty almost of which had been passed in ministerial labours), and warned, by the law of nature, of the approach of dissolution. It was as if the light of prosperity and peace were fading away from the African Church, as sank the bodily powers of its great earthly ornament and stay. At this time, when the terrors of the barbaric invasion spread on all sides, a bishop wrote to him to ask whether it was allowable for the ruler of a Church to leave the scene of his pastoral duties in order to save his life. Different opinions had heretofore been expressed on this question. In Augustine's own country Tertullian had maintained that flight was unlawful, but he was a Montanist when he so wrote. On the other hand, Cyprian had actually fled, and had defended his conduct when questioned by the clergy of Rome. His contemporaries, Dionysius of Alexandria, and Gregory of Neocæsarea, had fled also; as had Polycarp before them, and Athanasius after them.

Athanasius also had to defend his flight, and he defended it, in a work still extant, thus:—First, he observes, it has the sanction of numerous Scripture precedents. Thus, in the instance of confessors under the old covenant, Jacob fled from Esau, Moses from Pharao, David from Saul; Elias concealed himself from Achab three years, and the sons of the prophets were hid by Abdias in a cave from Jezebel. In like manner under the Gospel, the disciples hid themselves for fear of the Jews, and St. Paul was let down in a basket over the wall at Damascus. On the other hand, no instance can be adduced of over-boldness and headstrong daring in the saints of Scripture. But our Lord Himself is the chief exemplar of fleeing from persecution. As a child in arms He had to flee into Egypt. When He returned, He still shunned Judea, and retired to Nazareth. After raising Lazarus, on the Jews seeking His life, "He walked no more openly among them," but retreated to the neighbourhood of the desert. When they took up stones to cast at Him, He hid Himself; when they attempted to cast Him down headlong, He made His way through them; when He heard of the Baptist's death, He retired across the lake into a desert place, apart. If it be said that He did so, because His time was not yet come, and that when it was come, He delivered up Himself, we must ask, in reply, how a man can know that his time is come, so as to have a right to act as Christ acted? And since we do not know, we must have patience; and, till God by His own act determines the time, we must "wander in sheep-skins and goat-skins," rather than take the matter into our own hands; as even Saul, the persecutor, was left by David in the hands of God, whether He would "strike him, or his day should come to die, or he should go down to battle and perish."

If God's servants, proceeds Athanasius, have at any time presented themselves before their persecutors, it was at God's command: thus Elias showed himself to Achab; so did the prophet from Juda, to Jeroboam; and St. Paul appealed to Cæsar. Flight, so far from implying cowardice, requires often greater courage than not to flee. It is a greater trial of heart. Death is an end of all trouble; he who flees is ever expecting death, and dies daily. Job's life was not to be touched by Satan, yet was not his fortitude shown in what he suffered? Exile is full of miseries. The after-conduct of the saints showed they had not fled for fear. Jacob, on his death-bed, contemned death, and blessed each of the twelve Patriarchs; Moses returned, and presented himself before Pharao; David was a valiant warrior; Elias rebuked Achab and Ochazias; Peter and Paul, who had once hid themselves, offered themselves to martyrdom at Rome. And so acceptable was the previous flight of these men to Almighty God, that we read of His showing them some special favour during it. Then it was that Jacob had the vision of Angels; Moses saw the burning bush; David wrote his prophetic Psalms; Elias raised the dead, and gathered the people on Mount Carmel. How would the Gospel ever have been preached throughout the world, if the Apostles had not fled? And, since their time, those, too, who have become martyrs, at first fled; or, if they advanced to meet their persecutors, it was by some secret suggestion of the Divine Spirit. But, above all, while these instances abundantly illustrate the rule of duty in persecution, and the temper of mind necessary in those who observe it, we have that duty itself declared in a plain precept by no other than our Lord: "When they shall persecute you in this city," He says, "flee into another;" and "let them that are in Judea flee unto the mountains."

Thus argues the great Athanasius, living in spirit with the saints departed, while full of labour and care here on earth. For the arguments on the other side, let us turn to a writer, not less vigorous in mind, but less subdued in temper. Thus writes Tertullian on the same subject, then a Montanist, a century and a half earlier:—Nothing happens, he says, without God's will. Persecution is sent by Him, to put His servants to the test; to divide between good and bad: it is a trial; what man has any right to interfere? He who gives the prize, alone can assign the combat. Persecution is more than permitted, it is actually appointed by Almighty God. It does the Church much good, as leading Christians to increased seriousness while it lasts. It comes and goes at God's ordering. Satan could not touch Job, except so far as God gave permission. He could not touch the Apostles, except as far as an opening was allowed in the words, "Satan hath desired to have you, but I have prayed for thee," Peter, "and thou, being once converted, confirm thy brethren." We pray, "Lead us not into temptation, but deliver us from evil;" why, if we may deliver ourselves? Satan is permitted access to us, either for punishment, as in Saul's case, or for our chastisement. Since the persecution comes from God, we may not lawfully avoid it, nor can we avoid it. We cannot, because He is all powerful; we must not, because He is all good. We should leave the matter entirely to God. As to the command of fleeing from city to city, this was temporary. It was intended to secure the preaching of the Gospel to the nations. While the Apostles preached to the Jews,—till they had preached to the Gentiles,—they were to flee;

but one might as well argue, that we now are not to go "into the way of the Gentiles," but to confine ourselves to "the lost sheep of the house of Israel," as that we are now to "flee from city to city." Nor, indeed, was going from city to city a flight; it was a continued preaching; not an accident, but a rule: whether persecuted or not, they were to go about; and before they had gone through the cities of Israel, the Lord was to come. The command contemplated only those very cities. If St. Paul escaped out of Damascus by night, yet afterwards, against the prayers of the disciples and the prophecy of Agabus, he went up to Jerusalem. Thus the command to flee did not last even through the lifetime of the Apostles; and, indeed, why should God introduce persecution, if He bids us retire from it? This is imputing inconsistency to His acts. If we want texts to justify our not fleeing, He says, "Whoso shall confess Me before men, I will confess him before My Father." "Blessed are they that suffer persecution;" "He that shall persevere to the end, he shall be saved;" "Be not afraid of them that kill the body;" "Whosoever does not carry his cross and come after Me, cannot be My disciple." How are these texts fulfilled when a man flees? Christ, who is our pattern, did not more than pray, "If it be possible, let this chalice pass:" we, too, should both stay and pray as He did. And it is expressly told us, that "We also ought to lay down our lives for the brethren." Again, it is said, "Perfect charity casteth out fear;" he who flees, fears; he who fears, "is not perfected in charity." The Greek proverb is sometimes urged, "He who flees, will fight another day;" yes, and he may flee another day, also. Again, if bishops, priests, and deacons flee, why must the laity stay? or must they flee also? "The good shepherd," on the contrary, "layeth down his life for his sheep;" whereas, the bad shepherd "seeth the wolf coming, and leaveth the sheep, and fleeth." At no time, as Jeremiah, Ezekiel, and Zechariah tell us, is the flock in greater danger of being scattered than when it loses its shepherd. Tertullian ends thus:—"This doctrine, my brother, perhaps appears to you hard; nay, intolerable. But recollect that God has said, 'He that can take, let him take it;' that is, he who receives it not, let him depart. He who fears to suffer cannot belong to Him who has suffered. He who does not fear to suffer is perfect in love, that is, of God. Many are called, few are chosen. Not he who would walk the broad way is sought out by God, but he who walks the narrow." Thus the ingenious and vehement Tertullian.

3.

With these remarks for and against flight in persecution, we shall be prepared to listen to Augustine on the subject;—I have said, it was brought under his notice by a brother bishop, with reference to the impending visitation of the barbarians. His answer happily is preserved to us, and extracts from it shall now be set before the reader.

"TO HIS HOLY BROTHER AND FELLOW-BISHOP HONORATUS, AUGUSTINE SENDS HEALTH IN THE LORD.

"I thought the copy of my letter to our brother Quodvultdeus, which I sent to you, would have been sufficient, dear brother, without the task you put on me of counselling you on the proper course to pursue under our existing dangers. It was certainly a short letter; yet I included every question which it was necessary to ask and answer, when I said that no persons were hindered from retiring to such fortified places as they were able and desirous to secure; while, on the other hand, we might not break the bonds of our ministry, by which the love of Christ has engaged us not to desert the Church, where we are bound to serve. The following is what I laid down in the letter I refer to :—'It remains, then,' I say, 'that, though God's people in the place where we are be ever so few, yet, if it does stay, we, whose ministration is necessary to its staying, must say to the Lord, Thou art our strong rock and place of defence.'

"But you tell me that this view is not sufficient for you, from an apprehension lest we should be running counter to our Lord's command and example, to flee from city to city. Yet is it conceivable that He meant that our flocks, whom He bought with His own blood, should be deprived of that necessary ministration without which they cannot live? Is He a precedent for this, who was carried in flight into Egypt by His parents when but a child, before He had formed Churches which we can talk of His leaving? Or, when St. Paul was let down in a basket through a window, lest the enemy should seize him, and so escaped his hands, was the Church of that place bereft of its necessary ministration, seeing there were other brethren stationed there to fulfil what was necessary? Evidently it was their wish that he, who was the direct object of the persecutors' search, should preserve himself for the sake of the Church. Let, then, the servants of Christ, the ministers of His word and sacraments, do in such cases as He enjoined or permitted. Let such of them, by all means, flee from city to city, as are special objects of persecution; so that they who are not thus attacked desert not the Church, but give meat to those their fellow-servants, who they know cannot live without it. But in a case when all classes—I mean bishops, clergy, and people—are in some common danger, let not those who need the aid of others be deserted by those whom they need. Either let one and all remove into some fortified place, or, if any are obliged to remain, let them not be abandoned by those who have to supply their ecclesiastical necessity, so that they may survive in common, or suffer in common what their Father decrees they should undergo."

Then he makes mention of the argument of a certain bishop, that "if our Lord has enjoined upon us flight, in persecutions which may ripen into martyrdom, much more is it necessary to flee from barren sufferings in a barbarian and hostile invasion," and he says, "this is true and reasonable, in the case of such as have no ecclesiastical office to tie them;" but he continues:

"Why should men make no question about obeying the precept of fleeing from city to city, and yet have no dread of 'the hireling who seeth the wolf coming, and fleeth, because he careth not for the sheep?' Why do they not try to reconcile (as they assuredly can) these two incontrovertible declarations of our Lord, one of which suffers and commands flight, the other arraigns and condemns it? And what other mode is there of reconciling them than that which I have above laid down? viz., that we, the ministers of Christ, who are under the pressure of persecution, are *then* at liberty to leave our posts, when no flock is left for us to serve; or again, when, though there be a flock, yet there are others to supply our necessary ministry, who have not the same reason for fleeing,—as in the case of St. Paul; or, again, of the holy Athanasius, bishop of Alexandria, who was especially sought after by the emperor Constantius, while the Catholic people, who remained together in Alexandria, were in no measure deserted by the other ministers. But when the people remain, and the ministers flee, and the ministration is suspended, what is that but the guilty flight of hirelings, who care not for the sheep? For then the wolf will come,—not man, but the devil, who is accustomed to persuade such believers to apostasy, who are bereft of the daily ministration of the Lord's Body; and by your, not knowledge, but ignorance of duty, the weak brother will perish, for whom Christ died.

"Let us only consider, when matters come to an extremity of danger, and there is no longer any means of escape, how persons flock together to the Church, of both sexes, and all ages, begging for baptism, or reconciliation, or even for works of penance, and one and all of them for consolation, and the consecration and application of the sacraments. Now, if ministers are wanting, what ruin awaits those, who depart from this life unregenerate or unabsolved! Consider the grief of their believing relatives, who will not have them as partakers with themselves in the rest of eternal life; consider the anguish of the whole multitude, nay, the cursings of some of them, at the absence of ministration and ministers.

"It may be said, however, that the ministers of God ought to avoid such imminent perils, in order to preserve themselves for the profit of the Church for more tranquil times. I grant it where others are present to supply the ecclesiastical ministry, as in the case of Athanasius. How necessary it was to the Church, how beneficial, that such a man should remain in the flesh, the Catholic faith bears witness, which was maintained against the Arians by his voice and his love. But when there is a common danger, and when there is rather reason to apprehend lest a man should be thought to flee, not from purpose of prudence, but from dread of dying, and when the example of flight does more harm than the service of living does good, it is by no means to be done. To be brief, holy David withdrew himself from the hazard of war, lest perchance he should 'quench the light of Israel,' at the instance of his people, not on his own motion. Otherwise, he would have occasioned many imitators of an inactivity which they had in that case ascribed, not to regard for the welfare of others, but to cowardice."

Then he goes on to a further question, what is to be done in a case where all ministers are likely to perish, unless some of them take to flight? or when persecution is set on foot only with the view of reaching the ministers of the Church? This leads him to exclaim:

"O, that there may be then a quarrel between God's ministers, *who* are to remain, and *who* to flee, lest the Church should be deserted, whether by all fleeing or all dying! Surely there will ever be such a quarrel, where each party burns in its own charity, yet indulges the charity of the other. In such a difficulty, the lot seems the fairest decision, in default of others. God judges better than man in perplexities of this sort; whether it be His will to reward the holier among them with the crown of martyrdom, and to spare the weak, or again, to strengthen the latter to endure evil, removing those from life whom the Church of God can spare the better. Should it, however, seem inexpedient to cast lots,—a measure for which I cannot bring precedent,—at least, let no one's flight be the cause of the Church's losing those ministrations which, in such dangers, are so necessary and so imperative. Let no one make himself an exception, on the plea of having some particular grace, which gives him a claim to life, and therefore to flight.

"It is sometimes supposed that bishops and clergy, remaining at their posts in dangers of this kind, mislead their flocks into staying, by their example. But it is easy for us to remove this objection or imputation, by frankly telling them not to be misled by our remaining. 'We are remaining for your sake,' we must say, 'lest you should fail to obtain such ministration, as we know to be necessary to your salvation in Christ. Make your escape, and you will then set us free.' The occasion for saying this is when there seems some real advantage in retiring to a safer position. Should all or some make answer, 'We are in His hands from whose anger no one can flee anywhere; whose mercy every one may find everywhere, though he stir not, whether some necessary tie detains him, or the uncertainty of safe escape deters him;' most undoubtedly such persons are not to be left destitute of Christian ministrations.

"I have written these lines, dearest brother, in truth, as I think, and in sure charity, by way of reply, since you have consulted me; but not as dictating, if, perchance, you may find some better view to guide you. However, better we cannot do in these perils than pray the Lord our God to have mercy upon us."—*Ep.* 228.

4.

The luminous judgment, the calm faith, and the single-minded devotion which this letter exhibits, were fully maintained in the conduct of the far-famed writer, in the events which followed. It was written on the first entrance of the Vandals into Africa, about two years before they laid siege to Hippo; and during this interval of dreadful suspense and excitement, as well as of actual suffering, amid the desolation of the Church around him, with the prospect of his own personal trials, we find this unwearied teacher carrying on his works of love by pen, and word of mouth,—eagerly, as knowing his time was short, but tranquilly, as if it were a season of prosperity. He commenced a fresh work against the opinions of Julian, a friend of his, who, beginning to run well, had unhappily taken up a bold profession of Pelagianism; he wrote a treatise on Predestination, at the suggestion of his friends, to meet the objections urged against former works of his on the same subject; sustained a controversy with the Arians; and began a history of heresies. What makes Augustine's diligence in the duties of his episcopate, at this season, the more remarkable, is, that he was actually engaged at the same time in political affairs, as a confidential friend and counsellor of Boniface, the governor of Africa (who had first invited and then opposed the entrance of the Vandals), and accordingly was in circumstances especially likely to unsettle and agitate the mind of an aged man.

At length events hastened on to a close. Fugitive multitudes betook themselves to Hippo. Boniface threw himself into it. The Vandals appeared before it, and laid siege to it. Meanwhile, Augustine fell ill. He had about him many of the African bishops, and among other friends, Possidius, whose account of his last hours is preserved to us. "We used continually to converse together," says Possidius, "about the misfortunes in which we were involved, and contemplated God's tremendous judgments which were before our eyes, saying, 'Thou art just, O Lord, and Thy judgment is right.' One day, at meal time, as we talked together, he said, 'Know ye that in this our present calamity, I pray God to vouchsafe to rescue this besieged city, or (if otherwise) to give His servants strength to bear His will, or, at least, to take me to Himself out of this world.' We followed his advice, and both ourselves, and our friends' and the whole city offered up the same prayer with him. On the third month of the siege he was seized with a fever, and took to his bed, and was reduced to the extreme of sickness."

Thus, the latter part of his prayer was put in train for accomplishment, as the former part was subsequently granted by the retreat of the enemy from Hippo. But to continue the narrative of Possidius:—"He had been used to say, in his familiar conversation, that after receiving baptism, even approved Christians and priests ought not to depart from the body without a fitting and sufficient course of penance. Accordingly, in the last illness, of which he died, he set himself to write out the special penitential psalms of David, and to place them four by four against the wall, so that, as he lay in bed, in the days of his sickness, he could see them. And so he used to read and weep abundantly. And lest his attention should be distracted by any one, about ten days before his death, he begged us who were with him to hinder persons entering his room except at the times when his medical attendants came to see him, or his meals were brought to him. This was strictly attended to, and all his time given to prayer. Till this last illness, he had been able to preach the word of God in the church without intermission with energy and boldness, with healthy mind and judgment. He slept with his fathers in a good old age, sound in limb, unimpaired in sight and hearing, and, as it is written, while we stood by, beheld, and prayed with him. We took part in the sacrifice to God at his funeral, and so buried him."

Though the Vandals failed in their first attack upon Hippo, during Augustine's last illness, they renewed it shortly after his death, under more favourable circumstances. Boniface was defeated in the field, and retired to Italy; and the inhabitants of Hippo left their city. The Vandals entered and burned it, excepting the library of Augustine, which was providentially preserved.

The desolation which, at that era, swept over the face of Africa, was completed by the subsequent invasion of the Saracens. Its five hundred churches are no more. The voyager gazes on the sullen rocks which line its coast, and discovers no token of Christianity to cheer the gloom. Hippo* has ceased to be an episcopal city; but its great Teacher, though dead, yet speaks; his voice is gone out into all lands, and his words unto the ends of the world. He needs no dwelling-place, whose home is the Catholic Church; he fears no barbarian or heretical desolation, whose creed is destined to last unto the end.

* Since this was written, the French have reinstated the see.

CHAPTER VIII.

CONVERSION OF AUGUSTINE.

"Thou hast chastised me and I was instructed, as a steer unaccustomed to the yoke. Convert me, and I shall be converted, for Thou art the Lord my God. For after Thou didst convert me, I did penance, and after Thou didst show unto me, I struck my thigh. I am confounded and ashamed, because I have borne the reproach of my youth."

I.

A CHANCE reader may ask, What was the history of that celebrated Father, whose last days were the subject of my last chapter? What had his life been, what his early years, what his labours? Surely he was no ordinary man, whose end, in all its circumstances, is so impressive. We may answer in a few words, that Augustine was the son of a pious mother, who had the pain of witnessing, for many years, his wanderings in doubt and unbelief, who prayed incessantly for his conversion, and at length was blessed with the sight of it. From early youth he had given himself up to a course of life quite inconsistent with the profession of a catechumen, into which he had been admitted in infancy. How far he had fallen into any great excesses is doubtful. He uses language of himself which may have the worst of meanings, but may, on the other hand, be but the expression of deep repentance and spiritual sensitiveness.

In his twentieth year he embraced the Manichæan heresy, in which he continued nine years. Towards the end of that time, leaving Africa, his native country, first for Rome, then for Milan, he fell in with St. Ambrose; and his conversion and baptism followed in the course of his thirty-fourth year. This memorable event, his conversion, has been celebrated in the Western Church from early times, being the only event of the kind thus distinguished, excepting the conversion of St. Paul.

His life had been for many years one of great anxiety and discomfort, the life of one dissatisfied with himself, and despairing of finding the truth. Men of ordinary minds are not so circumstanced as to feel the misery of irreligion. That misery consists in the perverted and discordant action of the various faculties and functions of the soul, which have lost their legitimate governing power, and are unable to regain it, except at the hands of their Maker. Now the run of irreligious men do not suffer in any great degree from this disorder, and are not miserable; they have neither great talents nor strong passions; they have not within them the materials of rebellion in such measure as to threaten their peace. They follow their own wishes, they yield to the bent of the moment, they act on inclination, not on principle, but their motive powers are neither strong nor various enough to be troublesome. Their minds are in no sense under rule; but anarchy is not in their case a state of confusion, but of deadness; not unlike the internal condition as it is reported of eastern cities and provinces at present, in which, though the government is weak or null, the body politic goes on without any great embarrassment or collision of its members one with another, by the force of inveterate habit. It is very different when the moral and intellectual principles are vigorous, active, and developed. Then, if the governing power be feeble, all the subordinates are in the position of rebels in arms; and what the state of a mind is under such circumstances, the analogy of a civil community will suggest to us. Then we have before us the melancholy spectacle of high aspirations without an aim, a hunger of the soul unsatisfied, and a never-ending restlessness and inward warfare of its various faculties. Gifted minds, if not submitted to the rightful authority of religion, become the most unhappy and the most mischievous. They need both an object to feed upon, and the power of self-mastery; and the love of their Maker, and nothing but it, supplies both the one and the other. We have seen in our own day, in the case of a popular poet, an impressive instance of a great genius throwing off the fear of God, seeking for happiness in the creature, roaming unsatisfied from one object to another, breaking his soul upon itself, and bitterly confessing and imparting his wretchedness to all around him. I have no wish at all to compare him to St. Augustine; indeed, if we may say it without presumption, the very different termination of their trial seems to indicate some great difference in their respective modes of encountering it. The one dies of premature decay, to all appearance, a hardened infidel; and if he is still to have a name, will live in the mouths of men by writings at once blasphemous and immoral: the other is a Saint and Doctor of the Church. Each makes confessions, the one to the saints, the other to the powers of evil. And does not the difference of the two discover itself in some measure, even to our eyes, in the very history of their wanderings and pinings? At least, there is no appearance in St. Augustine's case of that dreadful haughtiness, sullenness, love of singularity, vanity, irritability, and misanthropy, which were too certainly the characteristics of our own countryman. Augustine was, as his early history shows, a man of affectionate and tender feelings, and open and amiable temper; and, above all, he sought for some excellence external to his own mind, instead of concentrating all his contemplations on himself.

2.

But let us consider what his misery was;—it was that of a mind imprisoned, solitary, and wild with spiritual thirst; and forced to betake itself to the strongest excitements, by way of relieving itself of the rush and violence of feelings, of which the knowledge of the Divine Perfections was the true and sole sustenance. He ran into excess, not from love of it, but from this fierce fever of mind. "I sought what I might love,"* he says in his Confessions, "in love with loving, and safety I hated, and a way without snares. For within me was a famine of that inward food, Thyself, my God; yet throughout that famine I was not hungered, but was without any longing for incorruptible sustenance, not because filled therewith, but the more empty, the more I loathed it. For this cause my soul was sickly and full of sores; it miserably cast itself forth, desiring to be scraped by the touch of objects of sense."—iii. 1.

"O foolish man that I then was," he says elsewhere, "enduring impatiently the lot of man! So I fretted, sighed, wept, was distracted; had neither rest nor counsel. For I bore about a shattered and bleeding soul, impatient of being borne by me, yet where to repose it I found not; not in calm groves, nor in games and music, nor in fragrant spots, nor in curious banquetings, nor in indulgence of the bed and the couch, nor, finally, in books or poetry found it repose. All things looked ghastly, yea, the very light. In groaning

* Most of these translations are from the Oxford edition of 1838.

and tears alone found I a little refreshment. But when my soul was withdrawn from them, a huge load of misery weighed me down. To Thee, O Lord, it ought to have been raised, for Thee to lighten; I knew it, but neither could nor would; the more, since when I thought of Thee, Thou wast not to me any solid or substantial thing. For Thou wert not Thyself, but a mere phantom, and my error was my God. If I offered to discharge my load thereon, that it might rest, it glided through the void, and came rushing down against me; and I had remained to myself a hapless spot, where I could neither be, nor be from thence. For whither should my heart flee from my heart? whither should I flee from myself? whither not follow myself? And yet I fled out of my country; for so should mine eyes look less for *him*, where they were not wont to see him."—iv. 12.

He is speaking in this last sentence of a friend he had lost, whose death-bed was very remarkable, and whose dear familiar name he apparently has not courage to mention. "He had grown up from a child with me," he says, "and we had been both schoolfellows and play-fellows." Augustine had misled him into the heresy which he had adopted himself, and when he grew to have more and more sympathy in Augustine's pursuits, the latter united himself to him in a closer intimacy. Scarcely had he thus given him his heart, when God took him.

"Thou tookest him," he says, "out of this life, when he had scarce completed one whole year of my friendship, sweet to me above all sweetness in that life of mine. A long while, sore sick of a fever, he lay senseless in the dews of death, and being given over, he was baptized unwitting; I, meanwhile little regarding, or presuming that his soul would retain rather what it had received of me than what was wrought on his unconscious body."

The Manichees, it should be observed, rejected baptism. He proceeds:

"But it proved far otherwise; for he was refreshed and restored.

Forthwith, as soon as I could speak with him (and I could as soon as he was able, for I never left him, and we hung but too much upon each other), I essayed to jest with him, as though he would jest with me at that baptism, which he had received, when utterly absent in mind and feeling, but had now understood that he had received. But he shrunk from me, as from an enemy; and with a wonderful and sudden freedom bade me, if I would continue his friend, forbear such language to him. I, all astonished and amazed, suppressed all my emotions till he should grow well, and his health were strong enough for me to deal with him as I would. But he was taken away from my madness, that with Thee he might be preserved for my comfort: a few days after, in my absence, he was attacked again by fever, and so departed."—iv. 8.

3.

From distress of mind Augustine left his native place, Thagaste, and came to Carthage, where he became a teacher in rhetoric. Here he fell in with Faustus, an eminent Manichean bishop and disputant, in whom, however, he was disappointed; and the disappointment abated his attachment to his sect, and disposed him to look for truth elsewhere. Disgusted with the licence which prevailed among the students at Carthage, he determined to proceed to Rome, and disregarding and eluding the entreaties of his mother, Monica, who dreaded his removal from his own country, he went thither. At Rome he resumed his profession; but inconveniences as great, though of another kind, encountered him in that city; and upon the people of Milan sending for a rhetoric reader, he made application for the appointment, and obtained it. To Milan then he came, the city of St. Ambrose, in the year of our Lord 385.

Ambrose, though weak in voice, had the reputation of eloquence; and Augustine, who seems to have gone with introductions to him, and was won by his kindness of manner, attended his sermons with curiosity and interest. "I listened," he says, "not in the frame of mind which became me, but in order to see whether his eloquence answered what was reported of it: I hung on his words attentively, but of the matter I was but an unconcerned and contemptuous hearer."—v. 23. His impression of his style of preaching is worth noticing: "I was delighted with the sweetness of his discourse, more full of knowledge, yet in manner less pleasurable and soothing, than that of Faustus." Augustine was insensibly moved: he determined on leaving the Manichees, and returning to the state of a catechumen in the Catholic Church, into which he had been admitted by his parents. He began to eye and muse upon the great bishop of Milan more and more, and tried in vain to penetrate his secret heart, and to ascertain the thoughts and feelings which swayed him. He felt he did not understand him. If the respect and intimacy of the great could make a man happy, these advantages he perceived Ambrose to possess; yet he was not satisfied that he was a happy man. His celibacy seemed a drawback: what constituted his hidden life? or was he cold at heart? or was he of a famished and restless spirit? He felt his own malady, and longed to ask him some questions about it. But Ambrose could not easily be spoken with. Though accessible to all, yet that very circumstance made it difficult for an individual, especially one who was not of his flock, to get a private interview with him. When he was not taken up with the Christian people who surrounded him, he was either at his meals or engaged in private reading. Augustine used to enter, as all persons might, without being announced; but after staying awhile, afraid of interrupting him, he departed again. However, he heard his expositions of Scripture every Sunday, and gradually made progress.

He was now in his thirtieth year, and since he was a youth of eighteen had been searching after truth; yet he was still "in the same mire, greedy of things present," but finding nothing stable.

"To-morrow," he said to himself, "I shall find it; it will appear manifestly, and I shall grasp it: lo, Faustus the Manichee will come and clear every thing! O you great men, ye academics, is it true, then, that no certainty can be attained for the ordering of life? Nay, let us search diligently, and despair not. Lo, things in the ecclesiastical books are not absurd to us now, which sometime seemed absurd, and may be otherwise taken and in a good sense. I will take my stand where, as a child, my parents placed me, until the clear truth be found out. But where shall it be sought, or when? Ambrose has no leisure; we have no leisure to read; where shal we find even the books? where, or when, procure them? Let set times be appointed, and certain hours be ordered for the health of our soul. Great hope has dawned; the Catholic faith teaches not what we thought; and do we doubt to knock, that the rest may be opened? The forenoons, indeed, our scholars take up; what do we during the rest of our time? why not this? But if so, when pay we court to our great friend, whose favours we need? when compose what we may sell to scholars? when refresh ourselves, unbending our minds from this intenseness of care?

"Perish every thing: dismiss we these empty vanities; and betake ourselves to the one search for truth! Life is a poor thing, death is uncertain; if it surprises us, in what state shall we depart hence? and when shall we learn what here we have neglected? and shall we not rather suffer the punishment of this negligence? What if death itself cut off and end all care and feeling? Then must this be ascertained. But God forbid this! It is no vain and empty thing, that the excellent dignity of the Christian faith has overspread the whole world. Never would such and so great things be wrought for us by God, if with the body the soul also came to an end. Wherefore delay then to abandon worldly hopes, and give ourselves wholly to seek after God and the blessed life? But wait: even those things are pleasant; they have some and no small sweetness. We must not lightly abandon them, for it were a shame to return again to them. See, how great a matter it is now to obtain some station, and then what should we wish for more? We have store of powerful friends ; if nothing else offers, and we be in much haste, at least a presidency may be given us ; and a wife with some fortune, that she increase not our charges ; and this shall be the bound of desire. Many great men, and most worthy of imitation, have given themselves to the study of wisdom in the state of marriage."—vi. 18, 19,

4.

In spite of this reluctance to give up a secular life, yet in proportion as the light of Christian truth opened on Augustine's mind, so was he drawn on to that higher Christian state on which our Lord and His Apostle have bestowed special praise. So it was, and not unnaturally in those times, that high and earnest minds, when they had found the truth, were not content to embrace it by halves ; they would take all or none, they would go all lengths, they would covet the better gifts, or else they would remain as they were. It seemed to them absurd to take so much trouble to find the truth, and to submit to such a revolution in their opinions and motives as its reception involved ; and yet, after all, to content themselves with a second-best profession, unless there was some plain duty obliging them to live the secular life they had hitherto led. The cares of this world, and the deceitfulness of riches, the pomp of life, the pride of station, and the indulgence of sense, would be tolerated by the Christian, then only, when it would be a sin to renounce them. The pursuit of gain may be an act of submission to the will of parents ; a married life is the performance of a solemn and voluntary vow ; but it may often happen, and did happen in Augustine's day especially, that there are no religious reasons against a man's giving up the world, as our Lord and His Apostles renounced it. When his parents were heathen, or were Christians of his own high temper, when he had no fixed engagement or position in life, when the State itself was either infidel or but partially emerging out of its old pollutions, and when grace was given to desire and strive after, if not fully to reach, the sanctity of the Lamb's virginal company, duty would often lie, not in shunning, but in embracing an ascetic life. Besides, the Church in the fourth century had had no experience yet of temporal prosperity; she knew religion only amid the storms of persecution, or the uncertain lull between them, in the desert or the catacomb, in insult, contempt, and calumny. She had not yet seen how opulence, and luxury, and splendour, and pomp, and polite refinement, and fashion, were compatible with the Christian name; and her more serious children imagined, with a simplicity or narrowness of mind which will in this day provoke a smile that they ought to imitate Cyprian and Dionysius in their mode of living and their habits, as well as in their feelings, professions, and spiritual knowledge. They thought that religion consisted in deeds, not words. Riches, power, rank, and literary eminence, were then thought misfortunes, when viewed apart from the service they might render to the cause of truth; the atmosphere of the world was thought unhealthy:—Augustine then, in proportion as he approached the Church, ascended towards heaven.

Time went on; he was in his thirty-second year; he still was gaining light; he renounced his belief in fatalism; he addressed himself to St. Paul's Epistles. He began to give up the desire of distinction in his profession: this was a great step; however, still his spirit mounted higher than his heart as yet could follow.

"I was displeased," he says, "that I led a secular life; yea, now that my desires no longer inflamed me, as of old, with hopes of honour and profit, a very grievous burden it was to undergo so heavy a bondage. For in comparison of Thy sweetness, and 'the beauty of Thy honour, which I loved,' these things delighted me no longer. But I still was enthralled with the love of woman : nor did the Apostle forbid me to marry, although he advised me to something better, chiefly wishing that all men were as he himself. But I, being weak, chose the more indulgent place ; and, because of this alone, was tossed up and down in all beside, faint and wasted with withering cares, because in other matters I was constrained, against my will, to conform myself to a married life, to which I was given up and enthralled. I had now found the goodly pearl, which, selling all that I had, I ought to have bought ; and I hesitated."—viii. 2.

Finding Ambrose, though kind and accessible, yet reserved, he went to an aged man named Simplician, who, as some say, baptized St. Ambrose, and eventually succeeded him in his see. He opened his mind to him, and happening in the course of his communications to mention Victorinus's translation of some Platonic works, Simplician asked him if he knew that person's history. It seems he was a professor of rhetoric at Rome, was well versed in literature and philosophy, had been tutor to many of the senators, and had received the high honour of a statue in the Forum. Up to his old age he had professed, and defended with his eloquence, the old pagan worship. He was led to read the Holy Scriptures, and was brought, in consequence, to a belief in their divinity. For a while he did not feel the necessity of changing his profession ; he looked upon Christianity as a philosophy, he embraced it as such, but did not propose to join what he considered the Christian sect, or, as Christians would call it, the Catholic Church. He let Simplician into his secret ; but whenever the latter pressed him to take the step, he was accustomed to ask, "whether walls made a Christian." However, such a state could not continue with a man of earnest mind : the leaven worked ; at length he unexpectedly called upon Simplician to lead him to church. He was admitted a catechumen, and in due time baptized, "Rome wondering, the Church rejoicing." It was customary at Rome for the candidates for baptism to profess their faith from a raised place in the church, in a set form of words. An offer was made to Victorinus, which was not unusual in the case of bashful and timid persons, to make his profession in private. But he preferred to make it in the ordinary way. "I was public enough," he made answer, "in my profession of rhetoric, and ought not to be frightened when professing salvation." He continued the school which he had before he became a Christian, till the edict of Julian forced him to close it. This story went to Augustine's heart, but it did not melt it. There was still the struggle of two wills, the high aspiration and the habitual inertness.

"I was weighed down with the encumbrance of this world, pleasantly, as one is used to be with sleep; and my meditations upon Thee were like the efforts of men who would awake, yet are steeped again under the depth of their slumber. And as no one would wish always to be asleep, and, in the sane judgment of all, waking is better, yet a man commonly delays to shake off sleep, when a heavy torpor is on his limbs, and though it is time to rise, he enjoys it the more heartily while he ceases to approve it: so, in spite of my conviction that Thy love was to be obeyed rather than my own lusts, yet I both yielded to the approval, and was taken prisoner by the enjoyment. When Thou saidst to me, 'Rise, thou that sleepest, and arise from the dead, and Christ will enlighten thee,' and showedst the plain reasonableness of Thy word, convinced by its truth, I could but give the slow and sleepy answer, 'Presently;' 'yes, presently;' 'wait awhile;' though that presently was never present, and that awhile became long. It was in vain that I delighted in Thy law in the inner man, while another law in my members fought against the law of my mind, and led me captive to the law of sin, which was in my members."—viii. 12.

5.

One day, when he and his friend Alypius were together at home, a countryman, named Pontitian, who held an office in the imperial court, called on him on some matter of business. As they sat talking, he observed a book upon the table, and on opening it found it was St. Paul's Epistles. A strict Christian himself, he was agreeably surprised to find an Apostle, where he expected to meet with some work bearing upon Augustine's profession. The discourse fell upon St. Antony, the celebrated Egyptian solitary, and while it added to Pontitian's surprise to find that they did not even know his name, they, on the other hand, were still more struck with wonder at the relation of his Life, and the recent date of it. Thence the conversation passed to the subject of monasteries, the purity and sweetness of their discipline, and the treasures of grace which through them had been manifested in the desert. It turned out that Augustine and his friend did not even know of the monastery, of which Ambrose had been the patron, outside the walls of Milan. Pontitian went on to give an account of the conversion of two among his fellow-officers under the following circumstances. When he was at Treves, one afternoon, while the emperor was in the circus, he happened to stroll out, with three companions, into the gardens close upon the city wall. After a time they split into two parties, and while he and another went their own way, the other two came upon a cottage, which they were induced to enter. It was the abode of certain recluses, "poor in spirit," as Augustine says, "of whom is the kingdom of heaven;" and here they found the life of St. Antony, which Athanasius had written about twenty years before (A.D. 364—366). One of them began to peruse it; and, moved by the narrative, they both of them resolved on adopting the monastic life.

The effect produced by this relation on Augustine was not less than was caused by the history of Antony itself upon the imperial officers, and almost as immediately productive of a religious issue. He felt that they did but represent to him, in their obedience, what was wanting in his own, and suggest a remedy for his disordered and troubled state of mind. He says:

"The more ardently I loved these men, whose healthful state of soul was shown in surrendering themselves to Thee for healing, so much the more execrable and hateful did I seem to myself in comparison of them. For now many years had passed with me, as many perhaps as twelve, since my nineteenth, when, upon reading Cicero's 'Hortensius,' I was first incited to seek for wisdom; and still I was putting off renunciation of earthly happiness, and simple search after a treasure which, even in the search, not to speak of the discovery, was better than the actual possession of heathen wealth and power, and than the pleasures of sense poured around me at my will. But I, wretched, wretched youth, in that springtime of my life, had asked indeed of Thee the gift of chastity, but had said, 'Give me chastity and continence, but not at once.' I feared, alas, lest Thou shouldst hear me too soon, and cure a thirst at once, which I would fain have had satisfied, not extinguished . . . But now . . . disturbed in countenance as well as mind, I turn upon Alypius, 'What ails us?' say I, 'what is this? what is this story? See; the unlearned rise and take heaven by violence, while we, with all our learning, all our want of heart, see where we wallow in flesh and blood! Shall I feel shame to follow their lead, and not rather to let alone what alone is left to me?' Something of this kind I said to him, and while he eyed me in silent wonder, I rushed from him in the ferment of my feelings."—viii. 17—19.

He betook himself to the garden of the house where he lodged, Alypius following him, and sat for awhile in bitter meditation on the impotence and slavery of the human will. The thought of giving up his old habits of life once for all pressed upon him with overpowering force, and, on the other hand, the beauty of religious obedience pierced and troubled him. He says:

"The very toys of toys, and vanities of vanities, my old mistresses, kept hold of me; they plucked my garment of flesh, and whispered softly, 'Are you indeed giving us up? What! from this moment are we to be strangers to you *for ever?* This and that, shall it be allowed you from this moment *never again?*' Yet, what a view began to open on the other side, whither I had set my face and was in a flutter to go; the chaste majesty of Continency, serene, cheerful, yet without excess, winning me in a holy way to come without doubting, and ready to embrace me with religious hands full stored with honourable patterns! So many boys and young maidens, a multitude of youth and every age, grave widows and aged virgins, and Continence herself in all, not barren, but a fruitful mother of children, of joys by Thee, O Lord, her Husband. She seemed to mock me into emulation, saying, 'Canst not thou what these have done, youths and maidens? Can they in their own strength or in the strength of their Lord God? The Lord their God gave me unto them. Why rely on thyself and fall? Cast thyself upon His arm. Be not afraid. He will not let you slip. Cast thyself in confidence, He will receive thee and heal thee.' Meanwhile Alypius kept close to my side, silently waiting for the end of my unwonted agitation."

He then proceeds to give an account of the termination of this struggle:

"At length burst forth a mighty storm, bringing a mighty flood of tears; and to indulge it to the full, even unto cries, in solitude, I rose up from Alypius, . . . who perceived from my choked voice how it was with me. He remained where we had been sitting, in deep astonishment. I threw myself down under a fig-tree, I know not how, and allowing my tears full vent, offered up to Thee the acceptable sacrifice of my streaming eyes. And I cried out to this effect:—'And Thou, O Lord, how long, how long, Lord, wilt Thou be angry? For ever? Remember not our old sins!' for I felt that they were my tyrants. I cried out, piteously, 'How long?

how long? to-morrow and to-morrow? why not *now?* why not in this very hour put an end to this my vileness?' While I thus spoke, with tears, in the bitter contrition of my heart, suddenly I heard a voice, as if from a house near me, of a boy or girl chanting forth again and again, 'TAKE UP AND READ, TAKE UP AND READ!' Changing countenance at these words, I began intently to think whether boys used them in any game, but could not recollect that I had ever heard them. I left weeping and rose up, considering it a divine intimation to open the Scriptures and read what first presented itself. I had heard that Antony had come in during the reading of the Gospel, and had taken to himself the admonition, 'Go, sell all that thou hast,' etc., and had turned to Thee at once, in consequence of that oracle. I had left St. Paul's volume where Alypius was sitting, when I rose thence. I returned thither, seized it, opened, and read in silence the following passage, which first met my eyes, '*Not in rioting and drunkenness, not in chambering and impurities, not in contention and envy, but put ye on the Lord Jesus Christ, and make not provision for the flesh in its concupiscences.*' I had neither desire nor need to read farther. As I finished the sentence, as though the light of peace had been poured into my heart, all the shadows of doubt dispersed. Thus hast Thou converted me to Thee, so as no longer to seek either for wife or other hope of this world, standing fast in that rule of faith in which Thou so many years before hadst revealed me to my mother."—viii. 26—30.

The last words of this extract relate to a dream which his mother had had some years before, concerning his conversion. On his first turning Manichee, abhorring his opinions, she would not for a while even eat with him, when she had this dream, in which she had an intimation that where she stood, there Augustine should one day be with her. At another time she derived great comfort from the casual words of a bishop, who, when importuned by her to converse with her son, said at length with some impatience, "Go thy ways, and God bless thee, for it is not possible that the son of these tears should perish!" It would be out of place, and is perhaps unnecessary, to enter here into the affecting and well-known history of her tender anxieties and persevering prayers for Augustine. Suffice it to say, she saw the accomplishment of them; she lived till Augustine became a Catholic; and she died in her way back to Africa with him. Her last words were, "Lay this body anywhere; let not the care of it in any way distress you; this only I ask, that wherever you be, you remember me at the Altar of the Lord."

"May she," says her son, in dutiful remembrance of her words, "rest in peace with her husband, before and after whom she never had any; whom she obeyed, with patience bringing forth fruit unto Thee, that she might win him also unto Thee. And inspire, O Lord my God, inspire Thy servants, my brethren,—Thy sons, my masters,—whom, in heart, voice, and writing I serve, that so many as read these confessions, may at Thy altar remember Monica, Thy handmaid, with Patricius, her sometime husband, from whom Thou broughtest me into this life; how, I know not. May they with pious affection remember those who were my parents in this transitory light,—my brethren under Thee, our Father, in our Catholic Mother, —my fellow-citizens in the eternal Jerusalem, after which Thy pilgrim people sigh from their going forth unto their return: that so, her last request of me may in the prayers of many receive a fulfilment, through my confessions, more abundant than through my prayers."—ix. 37.

6.

But to return to St. Augustine himself. His conversion took place in the summer of 386 (as seems most probable), and about three weeks after it, taking advantage of the vintage holidays, he gave up his school, assigning as a reason a pulmonary attack which had given him already much uneasiness. He retired to a friend's villa in the country for the rest of the year, with a view of preparing himself for baptism at the Easter following. His religious notions were still very imperfect and vague.

He had no settled notion concerning the nature of the soul, and was ignorant of the mission of the Holy Ghost. And still more, as might be expected, he needed correction and reformation in his conduct. During this time he broke himself of a habit of profane swearing, and, in various ways, disciplined himself for the sacred rite for which he was a candidate. It need scarcely be said that he was constant in devotional and penitential exercises.

In due time the sacrament of baptism was administered to him by St. Ambrose, who had been the principal instrument of his conversion; and he resolved on ridding himself of his worldly possessions, except what might be necessary for his bare subsistence, and retiring to Africa, with the purpose of following the rule of life which it had cost him so severe a struggle to adopt. Thagaste, his native place, was his first abode, and he stationed himself in the suburbs, so as to be at once in retirement and in the way for usefulness, if any opening should offer in the city. His conversion had been followed by that of some of his friends, who, together with certain of his fellow-citizens, whom he succeeded in persuading, joined him, and who naturally looked up to him as the head of their religious community. Their property was cast into a common stock, whence distribution was made according to the need of each. Fasting and prayer, almsgiving and Scripture-reading, were their stated occupations; and Augustine took upon himself the task of instructing them and variously aiding them. The consequence naturally was, that while he busied himself in assisting others in devotional habits, his own leisure was taken from him. His fame spread, and serious engagements were pressed upon him of a nature little congenial with the life to which he had hoped to dedicate himself. Indeed, his talents were of too active and influential a character to allow of his secluding himself from the world, however he might wish it.

Thus he passed the first three years of his return to Africa, at the end of which time, A.D. 389, he was admitted into holy orders. The circumstances under which this change of state took place are curious, and, as in the instance of other Fathers, characteristic of the early times. His reputation having become considerable, he was afraid to approach any place where a bishop was wanted, lest he should be forcibly consecrated to the see. He seems to have set his heart on remaining for a time a layman, from a feeling of the responsibility of the ministerial commission. He considered he had not yet mastered the nature and the duties of it. But it so happened, that at the time in question, an imperial agent or commissioner, living at Hippo, a Christian and a serious man, signified his desire to have some conversation with him, as to a design he had of quitting secular pursuits and devoting himself to a religious life. This brought Augustine to Hippo, whither he went with the less anxiety, because that city had at that time a bishop in the person of Valerius. However, it so happened that a presbyter was wanted there, though a bishop was not; and Augustine, little suspicious of what was to happen, joined the congregation in which the election was to take place. When Valerius addressed the people and demanded whom they desired for their pastor, they at once named the stranger, whose reputation had already spread among them. Augustine burst into tears, and some of the people, mistaking the cause of his agitation, observed to him that though the presbyterate was lower than his desert, yet, notwithstanding, it stood next to the episcopate. His ordination followed, as to which Valerius himself, being a Greek, and unable to speak Latin fluently, was chiefly influenced by a wish to secure an able preacher in his own place. It may be remarked, as a singular custom in the African Church hitherto, that presbyters either never preached, or never in the presence of a bishop. Valerius was the first to break through the rule in favour of Augustine.

On his coming to Hippo, Valerius gave him a garden belonging to the Church to build a monastery upon ; and shortly afterwards we find him thanking Aurelius, bishop of Carthage, for bestowing an estate either on the brotherhood of Hippo or of Thagaste. Soon after we hear of monasteries at Carthage, and other places, besides two additional ones at Hippo. Others branched off from his own community, which he took care to make also a school or seminary of the Church. It became an object with the African Churches to obtain clergy from him. Possidius, his pupil and friend, mentions as many as ten bishops out of his own acquaintance, who had been supplied from the school of Augustine.

7.

Little more need be said to conclude this sketch of an eventful history. Many years had not passed before Valerius, feeling the infirmities of age, appointed Augustine as his coadjutor in the see of Hippo, and in this way secured his succeeding him on his death ; an object which he had much at heart, but which he feared might be frustrated by Augustine's being called to the government of some other church. This elevation necessarily produced some change in the accidents of his life, but his personal habits remained the same. He left his monastery, as being too secluded for an office which especially obliges its holder to the duties of hospitality ; and he formed a religious and clerical community in the episcopal house. This community consisted chiefly of presbyters, deacons, and sub-deacons, who gave up all personal property, and were supported upon a common fund. He himself strictly conformed to the rule he imposed on others. Far from appropriating to any private purpose any portion of his ecclesiastical income, he placed the whole charge of it in the hands of his clergy, who took by turns the yearly management of it, he being auditor of their accounts. He never indulged himself in house or land, considering the property of the see as little his own as those private possessions, which he had formerly given up. He employed it, in one way or other, directly or indirectly, as if it were the property of the poor, the ignorant, and the sinful. He had "counted the cost," and he acted like a man whose slowness to begin a course was a pledge of zeal when he had once begun it.

CHAPTER IX.

DEMETRIAS.

"He that glorieth, let him glory in the Lord; for not he that commendeth himself is approved, but whom the Lord commendeth."

I.

AUGUSTINE was the founder of the monastic system in Africa; a system which, with all its possible perversions, and its historical fortunes, has a distinct doctrinal place in the evangelical dispensation. Even viewed as a mere human addition to the institutions of that dispensation, Monachism has as fair a claim on us for a respectful treatment as the traditionary usages of the Rechabites had upon the Jews, which are implicitly sanctioned in the reward divinely accorded to the filial piety which occasioned them. If a Protestant says, that it may be abused, this is only what I might object with at least equal force against many of his own doctrines, such as justification by faith only, which he considers true and important nevertheless. But even if it could be convicted of superstition, fanaticism, priestcraft, and the other charges which he brings against it, still anyhow he surely must acknowledge it to be, not a simple self-originated error, but merely a corruption of what *is* in itself *good*—the result of a *misunderstanding* of primitive faith and strictness; nothing more. However, perhaps he will go on to ask what is the force of "merely" and "nothing more," as if a corruption were not an evil great enough in itself. But let me ask him in turn, *could* his *present* system, in which he glories so much, by any possibility be corrupted, to use his word, into monasticism? is there any sort of tendency in it towards—rather, are not all its tendencies from—such a result? If so, it is plain that the religious temper of Protestant times is not like that of the primitive Church, the existing liability in systems to certain degeneracies respectively being a sort of index of the tone and temper of each. As the corruptions, so are the respective originals. If his system never could become superstitious, it is not primitive. Clearly, then, whether or not Monachism is right, he at least is wrong, as differing in mind and spirit from that first Christian system, which *did* become monastic.

One great purpose answered by Monachism in the early ages was the maintenance of the Truth in times and places in which great masses of Catholics had let it slip from them. Under such sad circumstances, the spouse of Christ "fled into the wilderness, where she hath a place prepared of God." Thus in those perilous Arian waters, which "the serpent cast out after the woman,"

> When withering blasts of error swept the sky,
> And Love's last flowers seemed fain to droop and die,
> How sweet, how lone the ray benign
> On sheltered nooks of Palestine!
> Then to his early home did Love repair,
> And cheered his sickening heart with his own native air.

That was the cave of Bethlehem, to which St. Jerome retired; but Augustine's monasteries were not intended for this purpose. They were intended as the refuge of piety and holiness, when the increasing spread of religion made Christians more secular. And we may confidently pronounce that such provisions, in one shape or other, will always be attempted by the more serious and anxious part of the community, whenever Christianity is generally professed. In Protestant countries, where monastic orders are unknown, men run into separatism with this object. Methodism has carried off many a man who was sincerely attached to the Established Church, merely because that Church will admit nothing but what it considers "rational" and "sensible" in religion.

2.

There is another reason for such establishments, which applies particularly to women; convents are as much demanded, in the model of a perfect Church, by Christian charity, as monastic bodies can be by Christian zeal. I know not any more distressing development of the cruel temper of Protestantism than the determined, bitter, and scoffing spirit in which it has set itself against institutions which give dignity and independence to the position of women in society. As matters stand, marriage is almost the only shelter which a defenceless portion of the community has against the rude world; —a maiden life, that holy estate, is not only left in desolateness, but oppressed with heartless ridicule and insult;—whereas, foundations for single women, under proper precautions, at once hold out protection to those who avail themselves of them, and give dignity to the single state itself, and thus save numbers from the temptation of throwing themselves rashly away upon unworthy objects, thereby transgressing their own sense of propriety, and embittering their future life.

And if women have themselves lost so much by the

established state of things, what has been the loss of the poor, sick, and aged, to whose service they might consecrate that life which they refuse to shackle by the marriage vow? what has been the loss of the ignorant, sinful, and miserable, among whom those only can move without indignity who bear a religious character upon them; for whom they only can intercede or exert themselves, who have taken leave of earthly hopes and fears; who are secured by their holy resolve, from the admiring eye or the persuasive tongue, and can address themselves to the one heavenly duty to which they have set themselves with singleness of mind? Those who are unmarried, and who know, and know that others know, that they are likely one day to marry, who are exposed to the thousand subtle and fitful feelings of propriety, which, under such circumstances, are ever springing up in the modest breast, with a keen sensitiveness ever awake, and the chance of indefinable sympathies with others any moment arising, such persons surely may be beautiful in mind, and noble and admirable in conduct, but they cannot take on them the high office of Sisters of Mercy.

However, this chapter is to have nothing to do with monasteries or communities, if this be any relief to the Protestant reader, but is to furnish a specimen of what to some persons may seem as bad, yet has been undeniably a practice of Christians, not from the fourth century, but from the time of St. Philip's daughters in the Acts, viz.: the private and domestic observance of an ascetic life for religion's sake, and to the honour of Christ.

"There were always ascetics in the Church," says the learned Bingham, "but not always monks retiring to the deserts and mountains, or living in monasteries and cells, as in after ages. Such were all those that inured themselves to greater degrees of abstinence and fasting than other men. In like manner, they who were more than ordinarily intent upon the exercise of prayer, and spent their time in devotion, were justly thought to deserve the name of ascetics. The exercise of charity and contempt of the world in any extraordinary degree, as when men gave up their whole estate to the service of God or use of the poor, was another thing that gave men the denomination and title of ascetics. The widows and virgins of the Church, and all such as confined themselves to a single life, were reckoned among the number of ascetics, though there was neither cloister nor vow to keep them under this obligation. Origen alludes to this name, when he says the number of those who exercised themselves in perpetual virginity among the Christians was great in comparison of those few who did it among the Gentiles. Lastly, all such as exercised themselves with uncommon hardships or austerities, for the greater promotion of piety and religion, as in frequent watchings, humicubations, and the like, had the name ascetics also."—*Antiqu.* vii. 1, §§ 1—3.

At present the only representatives among Protestants of these ancient solitaries are found in those persons whom they commonly taunt and ridicule under the name of "old maids" and "single gentlemen;" and it sometimes is seriously objected to the primitive doctrine of celibacy, that "bachelors are just the most selfish, unaccommodating, particular, and arbitrary persons in the community;" while "ancient spinsters are the most disagreeable, cross, gossiping, and miserable of their sex." Dreariness unmitigated, a shivering and hungry spirit, a soul preying on itself, a heart without an object, affections unemployed, life wasted, self-indulgence in prosperous circumstances, envy and malice in straitened; deadness of feeling in the male specimen, and impotence of feeling in the female, concentrated selfishness in both; such are the only attributes with which the imagination of modern times can invest St. Ambrose, bishop and confessor, or St. Macrina, sister of the great Basil. Now it may seem an unaccountable waywardness in one who has been brought up in the pure light of the nineteenth century, but I really am going to say a few words about such an old maid, or holy virgin, as we please to call her. In the year 413, the rich and noble Demetrias, a descendant of some of the most illustrious Roman houses, and moving in the highest circles, as we now speak, of the metropolis of the world, devoted herself at Carthage to a single life. It will be worth while to relate some particulars of her history.

3.

She was the daughter of Anicius Hermogenianus Olybrius, who was consul A.D. 395, and Anicia Juliana, his relation. Her father, who died young, was son of the well-known Sextus Probus, prefect of Italy from 368 to 375, who addressed St. Ambrose, while yet a catechumen, and appointed to a civil post in Liguria, in the celebrated and almost prophetic words, "Act not as magistrate, but as bishop." The riches of this prefect were so abundant, that some Persian noblemen, who in the year 390 came to Milan to St. Ambrose, went, as the second object of curiosity, to Rome, to see the grandeur of Probus, His wife, that is, the paternal grandmother of Demetrias, Anicia Faltonia Proba, belonged, as her first name shows, to one of the most noble families in Rome. The consulate seemed hereditary in it; its riches and influence were unbounded; while its members appear to have been Christians from the time of Constantine, or, as some suppose, from the time of the persecutions. Of the same illustrious house was Juliana, the mother of Demetrias.

Rome was taken by Alaric in 410; and on this most awful visitation, among other heirs of grace, three women were found in the devoted city,—Faltonia Proba, Juliana, and Demetrias,—grandmother, mother, and daughter,—

two widows and a girl. Faltonia, and Juliana, her daughter-in-law, had, in the days of their prosperity, exerted themselves at Rome in favour of St. Chrysostom, then under persecution, and now, in their own troubles, they found a comforter and guide in St. Augustine. So closely was Christendom united then, that ladies in Rome ministered to one bishop at Constantinople, and took refuge with another in Africa. At first they seem all to have fallen into the hands of the barbarians, and many of the holy virgins of the city, who had sought protection with Proba, were torn from her house. At length, obtaining liberty to leave Rome, she embarked for Africa with her daughter-in-law and grand-daughter, and a number of widows and virgins who availed themselves of her departure to escape likewise. Our history shall be continued in the following letter, written by St. Augustine to this high-born and well-connected lady:—

"AUGUSTINE, BISHOP, SERVANT OF CHRIST AND OF CHRIST'S SERVANTS, TO THAT RELIGIOUS HANDMAID OF GOD, PROBA, HEALTH IN THE LORD OF LORDS.

"Bearing in mind your request and my promise, that I would write to you on the subject of prayer, when He to whom we pray had given me time and power, I ought, without delay, to discharge my engagement, and in the love of Christ consult your pious desire. How much that request of yours delighted me, as showing your high sense of a high duty, words cannot express. Indeed, how should you rather employ your widowhood than in continued prayer, night and day, according to the admonition of the Apostle? For he says, 'Let her that is a widow indeed, and desolate, hope in God, and continue in supplications and prayers night and day;' although it is at first sight strange, that one who is noble according to this world, like you, rich, and mother of such a family, and therefore, though a widow, not desolate, should have her heart engaged and supremely possessed by the care to pray, save that you have the wisdom to perceive that in this world and in this life no soul can be beyond care.

"Therefore, He who has given you that thought, is in truth doing therein what He promised so wonderfully and pitifully to His disciples, when saddened, not for themselves, but for the race of man, and despairing that any could be saved, on His saying, that it was easier for a camel to enter a needle's eye than for a rich man the kingdom of heaven; He answered them, 'With God is easy what with man is impossible.' He, even while He was yet here in the flesh, sent the rich Zacchæus into the kingdom of heaven; and after that He was glorified by His resurrection and ascension, imparting His Holy Spirit, He made many rich persons to contemn this world, and to increase in riches by losing the desire of them. For why should *you*, for instance, be thus anxious to pray to God, but that you trusted in Him? and why should you trust in Him, did you trust in uncertain riches, and despise that most wholesome precept of the Apostle, 'Charge the rich of this world not to be high-minded, nor to hope in uncertain riches, but in the living God, that they may obtain true life'?

"And so, for love of that true life, you ought to think yourself, even in this world, desolate, whatever be your outward prosperity. In this life's darkness, in which we are pilgrims from the Lord, and walk by faith, not by sight, the Christian soul ought to esteem itself desolate, lest it cease from prayer; and to learn to fix the eye of faith on the words of divine and holy Scriptures, as a lamp in a dark place, until the day dawn, and the morning star arise in our hearts. This is the true life, which the rich are bid lay hold of by good works; and this is true consolation, for which the widow now has desolation, and though she have sons and grandsons, and order her household piously, urging it on all of hers that they put their trust in God, yet she says in prayer, 'For Thee my soul, for Thee my flesh, O how many ways, hath thirsted, in a desert land, where there is no way and no water."

Then he refers to our Lord's own precept of prayer, and to the reasons of His giving it:

"To obtain this blessed life, we are taught by the true blessed Life Himself to pray not much speaking, as though the more wordy we were, the surer we were heard; since we pray to Him, who, as the Lord Himself says, knows our necessities before we ask of Him. But if so, it may seen strange, why, though He has forbidden much speaking, yet, while knowing our necessities before we ask of Him, He has encouraged us to pray, in the words, 'One ought always to pray, and not to faint.' It may surprise us, until we understand, that our Lord and God does not wish our will to be made clear to Him, which He cannot but know, but that, our desire being exercised in prayers, we may be able to receive what He prepares to give. In faith indeed, and hope, and charity, we are always praying, with uninterrupted desire ; but we ask God in words also, at certain intervals of hours and times, that by those outward signs we may admonish ourselves, and may see into ourselves, what progress we have made in this desire, and may stimulate ourselves the more to heighten it. We recall our minds at certain hours to the business of prayer, from those other cares and businesses, by which that desire itself is, in a measure, chilled ; admonishing ourselves, by the words of prayer, to reach forward to that which we desire, lest what is already chilling may altogether cool, and may be altogether quenched, unless now and then rekindled.

"This being the case, even prolonged prayer, when one has time for it,—that is, when other good and necessary actions are not superseded, though even in the midst of them, we ought in desire ever to be praying,—such long prayer is neither wrong nor useless. Nor is this continued prayer, as some think, much speaking : many words is one thing, a continued affection another. For it is written of the Lord Himself, that He 'passed the night in prayer,' and that He prayed 'more largely ;' in which what did He but set us an example?—in this world making supplications in season, with the Father hearing them for evermore.

"The brethren in Egypt are said to make frequent prayers, but those as short as possible, and somehow darted forward rapidly, lest lively attention, which is so necessary in praying, should become faint and dull by a slow performance ; and thus they themselves show plainly that this attention, as it should not be wearied out if it cannot be sustained, so it is not prematurely to be broken if it can. To speak much, is to urge our necessities in prayer with superfluous words ; but to pray much, is to knock for Him to whom we pray, with prolonged and pious exercise of the heart. This is often done more by groans than speeches, by weeping than by addresses. For He sets our tears in His sight, and our groaning is not hid from Him, who, having made all things by His Word, does not ask for words of man.

"Pray, then, as a widow of Christ, who have not yet the sight of

Him whose aid you entreat. And though you be most opulent, pray as one of the poor; for you have not yet the true riches of the world to come, where there is no dread of loss. Though you have children and grandchildren, and a numerous household, yet pray as one desolate; for all temporal things are uncertain, though they are to remain even to the end of this life for our consolation. And surely, remember to pray with earnestness for me. For I am unwilling that you should render to me my dangerous honour, yet should withhold that my necessary support. Christ's household prayed for Peter and for Paul; and, while it is my joy that you are of His household, it is my need incomparably more than that of Peter or Paul that brotherly prayers should be my succour. Strive ye in prayer, in a peaceable and holy strife; not striving against each other, but against the devil, the enemy of all saints. By fastings, and watchings, and all chastisement of the body, prayer is especially aided. Let each of you do what she can; what one cannot, she does in her who can; if so be, in her who can, she loves that, which she therefore does not do herself because she cannot. Accordingly, she who has less strength must not hinder her who has more, and she who has more must not be hard with her who has less. For your conscience is owed to God; to none of yourselves owe ye anything, but to love one another. May God hear you, who is able to do above what we ask or understand."—*Ep.* 130.

4.

The exiled ladies seem to have settled down in Carthage, and we hear nothing of them for several years. At the end of that time, a remarkable event happened; Demetrias, who now had arrived at woman's estate, declared her resolve of devoting herself to a single life; as it would seem, at her own instance, though Augustine and Alypius, by this time bishop of Thagaste, were unconscious instruments in her determination. Her mother and grandmother appear to have been backward in the matter, or rather to have destined her, as a matter of course, to a married life, and to have provided her with a husband. Fame was not slow in spreading the news of her singular resolve far and wide. The rank and prospects of the party making it, and the intercommunion of the Catholic Church, afforded reason and means for its dissemination. It reached the East, where Proba had possessions, and it penetrated into the monastery at Bethlehem, which was the home of St. Jerome. This celebrated Father was then in his eighty-third year; but "his eye was not dim, neither were his teeth moved." Old age neither hindered nor disinclined him from taking an interest in the general concerns of the Church. At the instance of Proba and Juliana, he addressed to Demetrias a letter, or rather tract, in order to encourage her in her determination; and as it happens to relate some of the circumstances under which that determination was made, it may suitably here be introduced to the reader's notice.

Before entering into them, a word or two about St. Jerome. I do not scruple then to say, that, were he not a saint, there are words and ideas in his writings from which I should shrink; but as he *is* a saint, I shrink with greater reason from putting myself in opposition, even in minor matters and points of detail, to one who has the *magisterium* of the Church pledged to his saintly perfection. I cannot, indeed, force myself to approve or like these particulars on my private judgment or feeling; but I can receive things on faith against both the one and the other. And I readily and heartily do take on faith these characteristics, words or acts, of this great Doctor of the Universal Church; and think it is not less acceptable to God or to him to give him my religious homage than my human praise.

"It is the rule of rhetoricians," says he, "to adduce grandfathers, and forefathers, and every past distinction of the line, for the glory of him who is the subject of their praise; that fertile root may spake up for barren branches, and what is wanting in the fruit may show to advantage in the stem. I ought to recount the famous names of the Probi or Olybrii, and the illustrious line of Anician blood, in which none, or next to none, has failed of the consulate; or I ought to bring forward Olybrius, our maiden's father, who, to the grief of all Rome, was unmaturely carried off. I dare not say more, lest I deal ungently with the holy matron's wound, and the recounting of his virtues be a renewing of her grief. A pious son, a dear husband, a kind lord, a courteous citizen, a consul when a boy, but a senator more illustrious in the amiableness of his life. Happy in his death, who saw not his country's ruin; still happier in his offspring, who has added to the nobility of his ancestress Demetrias, by the perpetual chastity of Demetrias his daughter.

"But what am I about? In forgetfulness of my purpose, while I advise this young maiden, I have been praising the world's goods, whereas rather it is the very praise of our virgin, that she has despised them all, regarding herself not as noble, not as surpassing rich, but as a child of man. An incredible fortitude, amid jewels and silk, troops of slaves and waiting-women, the obsequiousness and attentions of a thronging household, and the refined dainties of a lordly establishment, to have longed for painful fastings, coarse garments, spare diet! In truth, she had read the Lord's words, 'They who are clothed in soft garments are in the houses of kings.' She gazed in wonder at the life of Elias and John Baptist, both of them with their loins girt and mortified with a leathern belt; and one of them appearing in the spirit and power of Elias, the Lord's forerunner, prophesying in his parent's womb, and even before the day of judgment praised by the Judge's voice. She admired the ardour of Anna, daughter of Phanuel, who, up to the extreme of age, served the Lord in His temple with prayer and fastings. She longed for the choir of Philip's four virgin daughters, and wished herself one of these, who, by virginal chastity, had gained the gift of prophecy. By these and like meditations, she nourished her mind, fearing nothing more than to grieve grandmother and mother, whose pattern encouraged her, whose intention frightened her,—not that the holy resolve displeased them, but, for the greatness of the thing, they durst not wish it. A trouble came upon that recruit of Christ, and, like Esther, a hatred of her apparel. They say who saw her and know (holy and noble ladies, whom the fierce tempest of enemies drove from the Gallic coast to inhabit these holy places, by way of Africa), that at nights, when no one knew, except the virgins in her mother's and grandmother's company, she was never clad in linen, never reposed on soft down; but on the bare earth, with her tiny hair-cloth for bedding, and her face bedewed with continual tears, there was she, prostrate in heart at her Saviour's knees, that He would accept her resolve, fulfil her longing, and soften grandmother and mother."

5.

The time came, as with so many also in this day, when the struggle between nature and grace must have its issue; St. Jerome proceeds:

"When now the day of her marriage was at hand, and the wedding apartment was preparing, secretly, and without witnesses, and with the night for her comforter, it is said she armed herself by counsels such as these: 'What doest thou, Demetrias? why such fright in defending thy honour? thou must be free and bold. If such thy fear in peace, what had been thy deed in martyrdom? If thou canst not brook the look of relatives, how couldst thou brook the tribunal of persecutors? If man's pattern does not stir thee, let Agnes, blessed martyr, encourage and quiet thee, who overcame her age and her tyrant, and consecrated by martyrdom her profession of chastity. Thou knowest not, poor maid, thou knowest not, it seems to whom thou owest thy virginity. It is a while since thou didst tremble amid barbarian hands, and didst hide thyself in the bosom and the robe of grandmother and mother. Thou didst see thyself a captive, and thy honour not thine own. Thou didst shudder at the savage faces of the foe; didst see with silent groan God's virgins carried off. Thy city, once the head of the world, is the Roman people's grave; and wilt thou on the Libyan shore, an exile, accept an exile spouse? Who shall be thy bridemaid? What train shall conduct thee? Shall the harsh Punic sing thy liberal Fescennine? Away with all delay. God's perfect charity casteth out fear. Take the shield of faith, the breastplate of justice, the helmet of salvation; go out to battle. Honour rescued has its own martyrdom. Why apprehensive of thy grandmother? why in fear of thy parent? Perhaps they have a will, because they deem that thou hast none.' On fire with these incentives, and many more, she cast from her the ornaments of her person and secular dress, as if they were encumbrances to her resolve. Costly necklaces, precious pearls, brilliant jewels, she replaces in their cabinet; she puts on a common tunic, and over it a more common cloak; and, without notice, suddenly throws herself at her grandmother's knees, showing who she was only by weeping and lamentation. Aghast was that holy and venerable lady, seeing the altered dress of her grandchild; while her mother stood astounded with delight. What they wished, they could not believe. Their voice was gone; their cheeks flushed and paled, they feared, they rejoiced; their thronging thoughts went to and fro. Grandchild and grandmother, daughter and mother, rush tumultuously upon each other's lips. They weep abundantly for joy, they raise the sinking maid with their hands, they clasp her trembling form. They acknowledge in her resolve their own mind, and they express their joy that the virgin was making a noble family more noble by her virginity. She had found a deed which she might offer to her race,—a deed to slake the ashes of the Roman city.

"Gracious Jesu! what exultation then in the whole household. As if from a fruitful root many virgins budded out at once, and a crowd of dependents and handmaidens followed the example of their patroness and mistress. The profession of virginity became rife in every house; their rank in the flesh various, their reward of chastity the same. I say too little. All the Churches through Africa almost danced for joy. Not cities alone, but towns, villages, even cottages, were pervaded by the manifold fame of it. All the islands between Africa and Italy were filled with this news; it tripped not in its course, and the rejoicing ran forward. Then Italy put off her mourning garb, and the shattered walls of Rome in part recovered their pristine splendour, thinking that God was propitious to themselves in the perfect conversion of their nursling. The report penetrated to the shores of the East, and even in the inland cities the triumph of Christian glory was heard. Who of Christ's virgins but boasted in her fellowship with Demetrias? what mother but cried blessing upon thy womb, O Juliana? I never praised in Proba the antiquity of her race, the greatness of her wealth and influence, either as a wife or a widow, as others, perhaps, in a mercenary strain. My object is, in ecclesiastical style, to praise the grandmother of my maiden, and to render thanks that she has strengthened her grandchild's will by her own. Else my monastic cell, common food, mean dress, and age upon the eve of death, and store for a brief span, rid me of all reproach of flattery. And now, what remains of my treatise shall be directed to the virgin herself; a noble virgin: noble not less by sanctity than by birth, who is in the more danger of a lapse, the higher she has ascended."

6.

Then he proceeds to give her some good practical advice:

"One thing especially, child of God, will I admonish you, to possess your mind with a love of sacred reading. When you were in the world, you loved the things of the world; to rouge and whiten your complexion, to deck your hair, and rear a tower of borrowed locks. Now, since you have left the world, and by a second step after baptism have made engagement with your adversary, saying to him, 'I renounce thee, devil, with thy words, thy pomp, and thy works:' keep the covenant thou hast pledged. I speak this, not from any misgiving about you, but according to the duty of a fearful and cautious monitor, dreading in you even what is so safe.

"The arms of fasting are also to be taken up, and David's words to be sung, 'I humbled my soul in fasting;' and 'I ate ashes as it were bread;' and, 'When they were sick, I put on sackcloth.' For a meal, Eve was cast out of Paradise; Elias, exercised by a fast of forty days, is carried off to heaven in a chariot of fire. Moses is fed forty days and nights by intercourse and converse with God; proving, in his own instance, the exact truth of the saying, 'Man liveth not by bread alone, but by every word which proceedeth out of the mouth of God.' The Saviour of man, who left us the pattern of His perfection and life, after baptism, is forthwith taken in the Spirit to fight against the devil, and after beating down and crushing him, to give him over to His own disciples to trample on. Against the young of either sex our enemy uses the ardour of their time of life; these are the fiery darts of the devil, which both wound and inflame, and are prepared by the king of Babylon for the three children. And as at that time a Fourth, having the form as of the Son of Man, mitigated the infinite heat, and amid the conflagration of a raging furnace, taught the flame to lose its virtue, and to threaten to the eye what to the touch it did not fulfil; so, also, in a virginal mind, by celestial dew and strict fasts, the fire of youth is quenched, and the life of Angels is compassed in a human frame.

"Nor yet do we enjoin on you unmeasured fastings, or an extravagant abstinence from food, which at once breaks delicate frames, and makes them sickly, ere the foundation of holy conversation is yet laid. Even philosophers have held that 'virtues are a mean, vices extreme;' and hence one of the seven sages says, 'Nothing too much.' You should fast short of panting and failing in breath, and of being carried or led by your companions; but so far as to subdue your appetite, yet to be able to attend to sacred reading, psalms, and watching as usual. Fasting is not an absolute virtue, but the foundation of other virtues; and 'sanctification and honour,' 'without which no man shall see God,' is a step for such as are mounting to the highest, nor will it crown the virgin, if it be alone."

Lastly, he speaks of the great virtue of obedience, the special characteristic of a spouse of Christ:

"Imitate your heavenly Spouse; 'be subject' to your grandmother and mother. See no man, youths especially, except with them. It is their pattern, it is the holy conduct of their house, which has taught you to seek virginity, to know Christ's precepts, to know what is expedient for you, what you ought to choose. Therefore, do not think that what you are belongs to yourself alone; it is theirs who have brought out in you their own virtue, and budded forth in you, as the most costly flower of 'honourable marriage and the bed undefiled;' a flower which will not bear its perfect fruit till you humble yourself under the mighty hand of God, and ever remember what is written, 'God resisteth the proud, and giveth grace to the humble.' Now where grace is in question, there is not recompensing of works, but bounty of a giver, according to the Apostle's saying, 'Not of him that willeth, nor of him that runneth, but of God that showeth mercy.' And yet to will and not to will is ours; yet not ours, what is even ours, without God's showing mercy.

"I end as I began, not content with one admonition. Love Holy Scriptures, and Wisdom will love thee; love her, and she will keep thee; honour her, and she will embrace thee. Let these be the ornaments abiding on thy neck and in thine ears. Let thy tongue know nought but Christ; let it have power to utter nought but what is holy. Let the sweetness of thy grandmother and mother ever be in thy mouth, whose following is the very form of holiness."—*Ep.* 130.

7.

Sage and sobering as is the advice here given (and I wish I had room to extract more of it), yet, I suppose, under the circumstances, a calm looker-on might have thought it not uncalled for,—might have apprehended, as perhaps St. Jerome did himself, that when a young lady was brought out as a pattern to the whole Catholic world, written to and about by bishops and doctors of the Church, by grave and aged men, the most remarkable personages of their time,—under such circumstances, without some special and almost miraculous gift of grace, the said maiden's head stood in danger of being turned by the compliment. And holy and admirable as Demetrias was, she was, in fact, for awhile in hazard, and that from the influence of the particular heresy of the day, which was a temptation especially adapted to her case. When sinners repent and turn to God, and, by way of showing sorrow and amendment, subject themselves to voluntary mortifications, the memory of what they were, and the prospect of judgment to come, are likely, it is to be hoped, to keep them from spiritual pride. But when a young and innocent girl, whose baptismal robe the world has not sullied, takes up a self-denying life in order to be nearer to God, and to please Him more entirely, who does not see the danger she is in of self-importance and self-conceit,—the danger of forgetting that she is by nature a sinner, as others, and that whatever she has of spiritual excellence, and whatever she does praiseworthy, is entirely of God's supernatural grace? And to a person so disposed, Pelagius was at that day at hand a ready tempter, prepared to sanctify all these evil feelings, and to seal and fix them as if on the basis of religious principle. The heresiarch was on the earth in person, when Demetrias renounced the world, and he did not neglect the occasion. By this time the noble exiles had apparently returned to Rome; and Pelagius despatched a letter, or rather treatise, still extant, with a view of instructing and guiding the daughter of the Olybrii and Anicii. He professes to write it at the instance of Juliana; nor is it surprising that the latter should not have been able to detect the doctrinal errors of a man of unblemished life, who, three years after, contrived to baffle the Apostolic see,—the very see which St. Jerome, in a part of the foregoing letter which I have not found room to translate, recommends to Demetrias as the guide of her faith.

It is not to my purpose here to make extracts from Pelagius's treatise, which is full of good advice, and does no more than imply, though it does imply, his uncatholic opinions of the power and perfectibility of unaided human nature. These opinions one would almost suspect that Jerome was indirectly opposing in some portions of the foregoing letter, as if the aged saint, now near his end, had a forecast of the temptation which was coming on mother and daughter. But however this may be, we have, in the year 417, a direct remonstrance, addressed by Augustine and Alypius to Juliana, on the subject of Pelagius's treatise, the author of which, however, they did not know for certain at the time. Proba, at this date, seems to have been dead.

"It was a great satisfaction to us, lady,—honoured for services of Christian duty, and our deservedly illustrious daughter,—that your letter happened to find us together at Hippo, and able to convey to you our joint gratulations at the news of your welfare, and lovingly assure you of ours, which we trust is dear to you.

For we are sure you understand the debt of religious affection we owe you, and the care we have for you in the sight of God and man. So highly, indeed, has our ministry been blessed in your house, by our Saviour's grace and pity, that when a human marriage had already been arranged, the holy Demetrias preferred the spiritual embrace of that Spouse who is beautiful above the children of men, and whom she has wedded in order that the spirit may be more fruitful while the flesh remains inviolate. Yet this influence of our exhortations on that believing and noble virgin would have been unknown to us, had not your own letters most happily and authentically informed us, after our departure, when in a little while she had made profession of virginal chastity, that this great gift of God, which He plants and waters by His servants, Himself giving the increase, had been the produce of our husbandry.

"No one, under these circumstances, can call it intrusion, if, with a most affectionate interest, we are solicitous in warning you against doctrines contrary to the grace of God. For, though the Apostle bids us be instant in preaching the word, not in season only, but out of season, we do not reckon you among such as would deem our word or writing out of season, when we speak to warn you seriously against unsound doctrine. Accordingly you accepted our former admonition with gratitude in the letter to which we now reply, saying, 'I am full of thanks for your reverence's pious advice, bidding me deny my ears to these men, who often corrupt our venerable faith with their erroneous writing.'

"Your following words, in which you say that 'you and your small household are far removed from such men; and that your whole family so strictly follows the Catholic faith as never to have deviated, never been betrayed into any heresy, not only fatal, but even small,' give us still greater ground for speaking to you concerning those who are trying to corrupt what hitherto has been sound. How can we forbear to warn those whom we are so bound to love, after reading a treatise which some one has written . . . in which the holy Demetrias may learn, if so be, that her virginal sanctity and all her spiritual riches are her own work; and, as a perfection of her blessedness, may be taught (if we may say the words) to be ungrateful to her God? So it is; these are the words, 'You are possessed of that for which you are deservedly preferred to others; nay, the more, in that your personal nobility and opulence belong to your friends, not to you; but spiritual riches none but yourself can provide for you. In that is your right praise, your deserved preference, which cannot be except of thee and in thee.' Forbid it, that a virgin of Christ should take pleasure in such words, who has a religious understanding of the innate poverty of the human heart, and therefore wears no ornaments there but the gifts of her Bridegroom! Who was it that separated you from the mass of death and perdition which is in Adam? He surely, who came to seek and to save that which was lost. When, then, a man hears the Apostle ask, 'Who made thee to differ?' shall he answer, 'My religious will, my faith, my justice,' and not rather go on to hear what follows, 'What hast thou which thou hast not received?'

"We have that opinion of the Christian conduct and humility in which this pious maiden has been trained, that we feel assured, that on reading the words in question, if she read them, she sighed deeply, and humbly struck her breast, perhaps wept, and earnestly prayed the Lord, to whom she is dedicated, and by whom she is sanctified, that as the words were not hers, but another's, so her faith may not be of such a temper as to admit of the thought that she has what may give her title to glory in herself, not in the Lord. For her glory is indeed in herself, not in the words of others, according to the Apostle's saying, 'Let every one prove his own work, and so he shall have glory in himself, and not in another.' But forbid it that *she* should be her own glory, and not He, to whom it is said, 'My glory, and the lifter up of my head.' For then is her glory religiously in her, when God, who is in her, is Himself her glory; from whom she has all the goods which make her good, and will have all which will make her better, as far as in this life she can be better; and which will make her perfect, when she is perfected by divine grace, not by human praise.

"However, we had rather have your assurance in writing, that, we are not deceived in this view of her feelings. We know full well that you and all yours are, and ever have been, worshippers of the undivided Trinity. But there are fatal heresies on other points of doctrine. Such is that which has been the subject of this letter, on which, perhaps, we have said more than is sufficient to a judgment so faithful and conscientious as yours is."—*Ep.* 188.

8.

That this letter produced the result intended, cannot be doubted. What became of Juliana after this does not appear, though it is supposed she died at Rome.

As to Demetrias, it is interesting to find extant a treatise of a later date addressed to her on the subject of humility. It has been ascribed by some to St. Prosper, by others to St. Leo, and introduces the subject of Pelagianism. A sentence or two will show us the style of the work. "Enter," says the author, "into the chamber of thy mind, and in the secret place of that thy most pure conscience look round on what ornaments are there stored up for thee; and, whatever splendid, whatever beautiful and costly, thou shalt there find, doubt not it is of divine workmanship and a gift, and so in all the goods of thy opulence acknowledge both the grace of the Giver, and His right of ownership. For thou hast received what thou hast; and whatever has accrued to thee by the diligence of thy efforts, through Him has it been increased by whom it was begun. Therefore, thou must use what God has bestowed; and must even beg of Him that thou mayst use His gifts faithfully and wisely."—*c.* 22. It may be observed that this author, whoever he is, seems not to have seen St. Austine's letter to Juliana on the same subject. It is pleasant to find that, while the ancient bishops and teachers exhorted the rich to renunciation of the world, they did not flatter them on their complying, but kept a vigilant eye on them, from youth to age, lest they should find a temptation where they looked for a blessing.

This work was written about A. D. 430; the last notice which history has preserved to us of this holy and interesting lady is after the sack of Rome by Genseric, when she might be about sixty years of age. She ends as she began. The sacred edifices had suffered in various ways from the fury and cupidity of the barbarians; St. Leo, who had dissuaded Genseric from burning the city, exerted his influence in various directions after their retiring, to add to the number of churches. Under his advice, Demetrias built the Basilica of St. Stephen, on property of her own, situated on the Latin road, three miles from Rome. With mention of this good deed, of which there is yearly memory in the Roman breviary on the 11th of April, the festival of St. Leo, we may suitably take our leave of one who preferred giving her wealth to the Church to spending it in the aggrandizement of some patrician house,

CHAPTER X.

MARTIN AND MAXIMUS.

" He lieth in ambush, that he may catch the poor man; he will crouch and fall, when he shall have power over the poor."

I.

WHO has not heard of St. Martin, Bishop of Tours, and Confessor? In our part of the world at least he is well known, as far as name goes, by the churches dedicated to him. Even from British times a church has existed under his tutelage in the afterwards metropolitan city of Canterbury; though we know little or nothing of churches to St. Ambrose, St. Augustine, St. Jerome, St. Basil, or St. Athanasius. Considering how many of our temples are called after the Apostles, and how many of them piously preserve the earthly name of those who may be said to "have no memorial," and are "as if they had never been," as St. George, or St. Nicolas; it is a peculiarity in St. Martin's history that he should be at once so well known and so widely venerated; renowned in this life, yet honoured after it. And such honour has been paid him from the first. He died in the last years of the fourth century; his successor at Tours built a chapel over his tomb in that city; St. Perpetuus, also of Tours, about seventy years afterwards built a church and conveyed his relics thither. In the course of another seventy years his name had taken up its abode in Canterbury, where it remains. Soon after a church was dedicated to him at Rome, and soon after in Spain. He alone of the Confessors had a service of his own in the more ancient breviaries; he is named, too, in the mass of Pope Gregory, which commemorates, after our Lady and the Apostles, "Linus, Cletus, Clement, Sextus, Cornelius, Cyprian, Laurence, Chrysostom, John and Paul, Cosmas and Damian, Hilary, *Martin*, Augustine, Gregory, Jerome, Benedict, and all Saints."

I am not going to present the reader with more than a slight sketch of his history, which we have received on very authentic testimony, as in St. Antony's case, though St. Martin, like St. Antony, has left no writings behind him. Nay, the biographer of St. Martin is not merely a friend (such as St. Athanasius), who saw him only now and then, but he was a disciple, an intimate, an eye-witness, as well as a man of cultivated mind and classical attainments,—Sulpicius Severus, who wrote his memoir even while the subject of it was alive, and while his memory was fresh.

2.

Martin was born about the year 316, in Pannonia, in a town which now forms part of Hungary; his father was a pagan, and had risen from the ranks to the command of a cohort. A soldier has no home, and his son was brought up at Pavia in North Italy with very little education. What influenced Martin is not known; but at the age of ten he fled to the Church against the wish of his parents, and enrolled himself as a catechumen. Under these first impressions of religion, he formed the desire of retiring to the desert as a solitary; however, things do not happen here below after our wishes ; so at fifteen he was seized, upon his father's instance, and enlisted in the army. In consequence, he remained a soldier five years, and, in the course of them, was sent into Gaul. It is recorded of him, that at a time when he was stationed at Amiens, being then eighteen, he encountered at the gate of the city a poor man without clothes. It was mid-winter, and the weather more than ordinarily severe ; he had nothing on him but his single military cloak and his arms. The youth took his sword, cut the cloak in two, and gave half to the beggar. The bystanders jeered or admired, according to their turn of mind ; and he went away. Next night he had a dream : he saw our Lord clad in the half cloak which he had bestowed on the poor man. The Divine Vision commanded the youth's attention, and then said to the Angels who stood around, "Martin, yet a catechumen, hath wrapped Me in this garment." On this Martin proceeded forthwith to baptism, and two years afterwards left the army.

Of the next fourteen years we know nothing ; then, he had recourse to the celebrated St. Hilary, who was afterwards bishop of Poictiers, and an illustrious confessor in the Arian troubles. Martin, however, was destined to precede him in suffering, and that in the same holy cause. He undertook a visit to his parents, who now seem to have retired into Pannonia, with a view to their conversion. When he was in the passes of the Alps he fell in with bandits. Sulpicius gives this account of what happened :

"One of them raised an axe and aimed it at his head, but another intercepted the blow. However, his hands were bound behind him, and he was given in custody to one of them for plunder. This man took him aside, and began to ask him who he was. He answered, 'A Christian.' He then inquired whether he felt afraid. He avowed, without wavering, that he never felt so much at ease, being confident that the Lord's mercy would be specially with him in temptations; rather he felt sorry for him, who, living by robbery, was unworthy of the mercy of Christ. Entering, then, on the subject of the Gospel, he preached the Word of God to him. To be brief, the robber believed, attended on him, and set him on his way, begging his prayers. This man afterwards was seen in the profession of religion; so that the above narrative is given as he was heard to state it."—*Vit. M.* c. 4.

Martin gained his mother, but his father persisted in paganism. At this time Illyricum was almost given over to Arianism. He did not scruple to confess the Catholic doctrine there, was seized, beaten with rods publicly, and cast out of the city. Little, again, is known of these years of his life. Driven from Illyricum, he betook himself to Milan, A.D. 356, when he was about forty years old. Here he lived several years in solitude, till he was again driven out by the Arian bishop Auxentius. On leaving Hilary, he had promised to return to him; and now Hilary being restored from exile, he kept his word, after a separation of about nine or ten years. He came to Poictiers, and formed in its neighbourhood the first monastic establishment which is known to have existed in France.

He was made bishop of Tours in the year 372, about the time that Ambrose and Basil were raised to their respective sees, and that Athanasius died. There were parties who opposed Martin's election, alleging, as Sulpicius tells us, that "he was a contemptible person, unworthy of the episcopate, despicable in countenance, mean in dress, uncouth in his hair." Such were the outward signs of a monk; and a monk he did not cease to be, after that he had become a bishop. Indeed, as far as was possible, he wished to be still just what he had been, and looked back to the period of his life when he was a private man, as a time when he was more sensibly favoured with divine power than afterwards. Sulpicius thus speaks of him in his episcopate:

"He remained just what he was before; with the same humbleness of heart, the same meanness of dress, and with a fulness of authority and grace which responded to the dignity of a bishop without infringing on the rule and the virtue of a monk. For a while he lived in a cell built on to the church; but, unable to bear the interruptions of visitors, he made himself a monastery about two miles out of the city. So secret and retired was the place, that he did not miss the solitude of the desert. On one side it was bounded by the high and precipitous rock of a mountain, on the other the level was shut in by the river Loire, which makes a gentle bend. There was but one way into it, and that very narrow. His own cell was of wood. Many of the brethren made themselves dwellings of the same kind, but most of them hollowed out the stone of the mountain which was above them. There were eighty scholars who were under training after the pattern of their saintly master. No one had aught his own; all things were thrown into a common stock. It was not lawful, as to most monks, to buy or sell any thing. They had no art except that of transcribing, which was assigned to the younger: the older gave themselves up to prayer. They seldom left their cell, except to attend the place of prayer. They took their meal together after the time of fasting. No one tasted wine, except compelled by bodily weakness. Most of them were clad in camel's hair; a softer garment was a crime; and what of course makes it more remarkable is, that many of them were accounted noble, who, after a very different education, had forced themselves to this humility and patience; and we have lived to see a great many of them bishops. For what is that city or church which did not covet priests from the monastery of Martin?"—*Vit. M.* c. 7.

Once on a time, a person whom he had benefited by his prayers sent him a hundred pounds of silver. Martin put it aside for redeeming captives. Some of the brothers suggested that their own fare was scanty and their clothing deficient. "We," he made answer, "are fed and clad by the Church, provided we seem to appropriate nothing to ourselves."—*Dial.* iii. 19.

It will be seen from the passage quoted overleaf, that St. Martin, though not himself a man of learning, made his monastic institution subservient to theological purposes. This monastery became afterwards famous under the name of the Abbey of Marmoutier; eventually it conformed to the Benedictine rule.

3.

St. Martin was a man of action as well as of meditation; and his episcopate is marked with strenuous deeds sufficient to convince all readers of his history, that, whatever blame this age may be disposed to throw on him, it cannot be imputed on the side of mysticism or indolence. Gaul was, even at this time, almost pagan: its cities, indeed, had long enjoyed the light of Christianity, and had had the singular privilege of contributing both Greek and Latin Fathers to the Catholic Church. Marseilles, Lyons, Vienne, Toulouse, Tours, Arles, Narbonne, Orleans, Paris, Clermont, and Limoges, seem to have been episcopal sees; but the country people had never been evangelized, and still frequented their idol temples. It is difficult to assign the limits of Martin's diocese, and perhaps they were not very accurately determined. On the east of Tours, we hear of his evangelical prowess in Burgundy and the neighbourhood of Autun, and on the north towards Chartres; the nearest sees round about were Poictiers, Limoges, Clermont, and Orleans; and his presence is mentioned, though perhaps only on political or synodal business, at Paris, Treves, and Vienne.

In the first years of Martin's episcopate, heathen

sacrifices were forbidden by law; and the resignation with which the pagans submitted to the edict, at least showed, what the history of the times so often shows otherwise, that their religion had no great hold on their hearts. Martin took upon him to enter and destroy the kingdom of Satan with his own hands. He went, unarmed, among the temples, the altars, the statues, the groves, and the processions of the false worship, attended by his monastic brethren: he presented himself to the barbarian multitude, converted them, and made them join with him in the destruction of their time-honoured establishment of error. What were his weapons of success does not appear, unless we are willing to accept his contemporary biographer's statement, that he was attended by a divine influence manifesting itself in distinct and emphatic miracles. In consequence of his triumphant exertions, he is considered the Apostle of Gaul; and this high mission is sufficient to account for his miraculous power. It is on this ground that even Protestants have admitted a similar gift in St. Augustine, Apostle of England.

Nor had Martin only to do with barbarians and idolators; he came across a powerful sovereign. This had been the lot of St. Basil a few years before, but with a very different kind of warfare. Basil was assailed by persecution; Martin was attempted by flattery and blandishment. It is harder to resist the world's smiles than the world's frowns. We began with the combat between Basil and Valens; let us end with a tale of temptation, which a crafty monarch practised upon a simple monk.

4.

The sovereign with whom Martin came into collision

was Maximus, the usurper of Britain, Gaul, and Spain, with whom we are made familiar in the history of St. Ambrose. Gratian becoming unpopular, Maximus had been proclaimed emperor by the soldiers in Britain, had landed on the opposite coast with a great portion of the British nation (who emigrated on the occasion, and settled afterwards in Bretagne), and had been joined by the armies of Gaul. Gratian had fled from Paris to Lyons, attended by only 300 horse; the governor of the Lyonese had played the traitor, and Maximus's general of horse, who was in pursuit of the emperor, had come up and murdered him. The usurper incurred, not unjustly, the stigma of the crime by which he profited, though he protested, whether truly or not, that he was not privy to the intentions of his subordinate. He was equally earnest, and perhaps sincere, in maintaining that he had been proclaimed by the legions of Britain against his will. So much Sulpicius confirms, speaking of him as "a man to be named for every excellence of life, if it had been allowed him either to refuse a diadem placed upon him, not legitimately, by a mutinous soldiery, or to abstain from civil war;" "but," he continues, "a great sway could neither be refused without hazard, nor be held without arms."—*Dial.* ii. 7.

Maximus established his court at Treves, and thither proceeded a number of bishops to intercede, as in duty bound, for criminals, captives, exiles, proscribed persons, and others whom the civil commotion had compromised. Martin went up with the rest, and it soon became obvious to the world that there was some vast difference between him and them; that they allowed themselves in flattery and subserviency towards the usurper, but that Martin recollected that he had the authority of an Apostle, and was bound to treat the fortunate soldier, not according to his success, but according to his conduct.

Maximus asked him, again and again, to the imperial table, but in vain; he declined, "alleging," according to Sulpicius, "that he could not partake in the hospitality of one who had deprived one emperor of his dominions, another of his life." "However," continues our biographer, "when Maximus declared that he had not of his own will assumed the imperial power; that he had but defended in arms that compulsory sovereignty which the troops had, by a Divine Providence, imposed on him; that God's favour did not seem estranged from one who had gained such incredible success; and that he had killed no enemy, except in the field,—at length, overcome either by his arguments or his prayers, he came to supper, the emperor rejoicing wonderfully that he had prevailed with him."—*Vit. M.* c. 23.

Martin seems to have been not quite satisfied with his concession, and Maximus seemed determined to make the most of it. The day of entertainment was made quite a gala day; the first personages about the court were invited; the monk Martin was placed on a couch close to the usurper, and near him was his attendant presbyter, seated between two counts of the highest rank, the brother and uncle of Maximus. In the middle of the banquet, according to custom, the wine-cup was handed to Maximus; he transferred it to Martin, wishing him first to taste, and then to pass it to himself with the blessing and good auspice which a bishop could convey. Martin took it, and drank; but he saw through the artifice; and, instead of handing it to the emperor, passed it to his own presbyter, as being higher in true rank, as Sulpicius says, than any others, even the most noble, who were there assembled.

Maximus was a crafty man ; and perhaps he thought he had discovered a weak point in Martin. He broke out into admiration of his conduct, and his guests did the like. Martin gained more by loftiness than others by servility. The feast ended ; not so the emperor's assaults upon a saintly personage. He presented him with a vase of porphyry, and it was accepted.

Maximus now became a penitent, with what sincerity it is impossible to say. And at length, it would appear, he obtained absolution from Martin for his crimes ; he sent for him often, and communed with him on the present and the future, on the glory of the faithful and the immortality of saints. Meanwhile the empress took her part in humbling herself before one who indeed, of all men alive, had certainly, in his miraculous power, the clearest credentials of his commission from the Author of all grace. She attended the exhortations of the aged bishop, and wept at his feet : but let us hear Sulpicius's account of what happened. "Martin," he says, "who never had been touched by any woman, could not escape this lady's assiduous, or rather servile attentions. Neither the power of dominion, nor the dignity of empire, nor the diadem, nor the purple did she regard. Prostrate on the ground, they could not tear her from Martin's feet. At length she begged her husband, and then both begged Martin, to allow her, by herself, without assistance of attendants, to serve him up a repast ; nor could the blessed man hold out any longer. The hands of the empress go through the chaste service ; she spreads a seat ; she places a table by it ; water she offers for his hands ; food, which she herself had cooked, she sets before him ; she at a distance, as servants are taught, stands motionless, as if fixed to the ground, while he sits ; showing in all things the reverence of an attendant, and the humbleness of a handmaid. She mixes his draught, she presents it to him. When the small meal is ended, she sweeps up with all carefulness the broken bits and crumbs of bread, preferring such relics to imperial dainties. Blessed woman, in such devotion willing to be compared to her who came from the ends of the earth to hear Solomon!" —*Dial.* ii. 7. Yes, blessed the princess who performs such humble service; but "a more blessed thing is it to give rather than to receive." Let us see what came of it.

5.

Maximus was not only a penitent, but he was a champion of the orthodox faith, nay, even to enforcing it with the sword. And Martin, while at court, had not only to intercede for the partisans of Gratian, but also, if possible, to rescue from the said imperial sword, and from the zeal of some brother bishops, certain heretics who had been treated with extreme severity, both by the local hierarchy and the civil power. These were the Priscillianists of Spain, and their principal persecutor was Ithacius, a bishop of the same country. Their history was as follows: Priscillian, a man of birth, ability, and character, undertook in Spain the dissemination of an Egyptian form of the Gnostic or the Manichæan heresy, and formed a party. The new opinion spread through all parts of the country, and was embraced by some of its bishops. A Council condemned them; they retaliated by consecrating Priscillian to the see of Avila. On this the Council called in the civil power against the heretics, and the heretical bishops on their part made for Pope Damasus at Rome. Failing to circumvent the see of St. Peter, they betook themselves to Milan. Failing with St. Ambrose, they bribed the officers of the court; and thus, whereas the Council had gained an imperial rescript, exterminating them from the whole Roman Empire, they obtained another restoring them to their own churches in Spain. This was the state of things when Gratian lost his life by the revolt of Maximus, who was in consequence naturally disposed to take part against the heretics whom Gratian's government had been at that moment supporting.

Ithacius, the acting Bishop of the Council, had been obliged to fly to Gaul; and in A.D. 384, when the civil troubles were over, he went up to Treves, had an interview with Maximus, and obtained from him a summons of the heretics to a Council to be held at Bourdeaux. Priscillian was obliged to attend; but being put on his defence, instead of answering, he appealed to the new emperor, and the orthodox bishops committed the scandalous fault of allowing his appeal.

Such an appeal, in a matter of faith or internal discipline, was contrary at once to principle and to precedent. It was inconsistent with the due maintenance of our Lord's canon, "Cæsar's to Cæsar, and God's to God;" and with the rule contained in St. Paul's charge to Timothy to "keep the deposit;" and it had been already condemned in the case of the Donatists, who, on appealing to Constantine against the Church, had encountered both the protest of the Catholic Fathers and the indignant refusal of the emperor. However, the Ithacians had united themselves too closely to the State to be able to resist its encroachments. This is the point of time in which Martin enters into the history of the dispute; Priscillian was brought to Treves; Ithacius, his accuser, followed; and there they found Martin, come thither, as we have seen, on matters of his own.

Martin naturally viewed the Ithacian faction with displeasure; he condemned the appeals which in a matter of faith had been made to the civil power, and he looked forward with horror to the sort of punishment which that power was likely to inflict. Accordingly, he remonstrated incessantly with Ithacius on the course he was pursuing; and Ithacius, a man of loud speech, and luxurious and prodigal habits, did not scruple to retort upon the devout and ascetic Martin, that the monk was nothing short of a Gnostic himself, and therefore naturally took the part of the Priscillianists.

Unable to persuade his brother bishops, Martin addressed himself to Maximus, representing to him, to use the words of Sulpicius, "that it was more than enough that, after the heretics had been condemned by an episcopal decision, they should be removed from their churches; but that it was a new and unheard-of impiety for a temporal judge to take cognizance of an ecclesiastical cause."—*Hist.* ii. The interposition of one, to whom emperor and empress were paying such extraordinary court, of course was of no slight weight. It was effectual for protecting the Priscillianists all the time he continued at Treves; but the time came when he must take his departure for his own home; and before doing so, he exacted a promise of the usurper that nothing sanguinary should be perpetrated against them.

He went; Ithacius did *not* go; the promise was forgotten; matters went on as if Martin had never been at Treves; the heretics were tried by the judge of the palace, and were found guilty of witchcraft and various immoralities. Priscillian and others were beheaded, and others afterwards were either killed or banished: Ithacius sheltered himself under the protection of Maximus, and Maximus wrote to the see of St. Peter, not to justify, but to take credit for his conduct.

What return he, or rather his ecclesiastical advisers,

received from Siricius, the Pope of the day, and from the body of the Church, need not here be mentioned in detail. Suffice it to say, that a solemn protest was entered against their proceedings, in the course of the following years, by St. Siricius, St. Ambrose, and Councils held at Milan and Turin. Ithacius was deposed, excommunicated, and banished. Felix, bishop of Treves, though a man of irreproachable character, and not bishop at the time of the crime, yet, as a partisan of the guilty bishops, was excommunicated with all who supported him; and when St. Ambrose came to Treves on his second embassy, he separated himself not only from the adherents of Maximus, but of Ithacius too. This, however, is to digress upon subsequent and general history, with which we have nothing to do; let us go back to St. Martin.

6.

On the year that followed the execution of Priscillian, Martin had again to visit Treves, as a mediator for certain civil governors, Narses and Leucadius, whose loyalty to Gratian had gained for them the resentment of his conqueror. A Council of bishops was just then assembled in the imperial city, with the double purpose of formally acquitting Ithacius, and of consecrating Felix, who has just now been mentioned, to the vacant see of Treves. The news arrived that Martin was coming, and spread great dismay among the assembled Fathers. They betook themselves to Maximus, and gained his consent to forbid Martin's entrance into the city except on a promise of communicating with themselves. Martin eluded their vigilance, and entered at night. He had come, as I have said, only on political business, though such as became a bishop to undertake; but when he got to Treves, he was met with news which more intimately concerned every Catholic, and needed his more prompt and urgent intercession. A day or two before he came, the Ithacian party had prevailed on the emperor to send military commissioners into Spain to detect, arrest, pillage, and kill all heretics; a mission which, considering that the broad test of heresy adopted by the soldiers was paleness of face and peculiarity of dress, was likely to terminate in a great accession doubtless, of wealth to the imperial treasury, but in as great a destruction of innocent persons and orthodox believers. The prospect of such outrages affected Martin still more than the severity directed against the Priscillianists; though "he was piously solicitous," says Sulpicius, "to rescue the heretics themselves, as well as the Christians, who were to be troubled under this pretence."—*Dial.* iii. 16. Accordingly, he was urgent in his intervention at court, but Maximus had by this time forgotten the lesson of humility which, two years since, he and the empress had so dutifully learned; or perhaps he thought, for one reason or another, that he had got an advantage over Martin, and understood him. Anyhow, he put off from day to day his answer to Martin's request, whether in behalf of the Spanish Catholics, or of the two friends of Gratian, who had been the cause of his journey.

Meanwhile Martin refused to communicate with the party of Ithacius; a vigorous step, to which only one bishop, Theognistus, out of all there assembled, had found himself equal. The Ithacians betook themselves in haste to Maximus, "complaining," says Sulpicius, "that they were prejudged, predisposed of, if the pertinacity of Theognostus was armed by the authority of Martin; that the latter ought never to have been allowed to enter the city; that he was no longer engaged in the mere defence, but in the rescue of the heretics; that nothing was gained by the death of Priscillian if Martin exacted reprisals for it. And lastly, they threw themselves on the ground, and with tears and lamentations implored the imperial power to show its vigour in its dealings with, after all, but one man."—*Dial.* iii. 16. Maximus began to believe that Martin really was a Priscillianist.

However, he both felt a reverence for him, whatever were the grounds of it, and he understood perfectly well that Martin was not to be prevailed on by threats of personal violence. He pursued a way with him which perhaps he thought successful on the former visit of Martin. He gave the Saint a private interview, and addressed him in a complimentary manner. He alleged, that the heretics had been punished, not at the instance of the bishops, but by the secular courts in a regular way for their evil deserts; that such a procedure formed no reason for blaming and separating from Ithacius and the rest; that Theognistus, the only outstanding bishop, had been influenced by personal feelings; and that a Council had acquitted Ithacius. Finding, however, he made no way with Martin, the emperor burst out into anger, quitted him hastily, and gave orders for the execution of Narses and Leucadius, the partisans of Gratian, on whose behalf Martin had come to Treves. The news of this determination came to the Saint during the following night: no time was to be lost; his kindness of heart was too much for him; he gave way; he entered the palace; he promised to communicate with the Ithacians, on condition that Narses and Leucadius should be spared, and that the military inquisitors which had been sent into Spain should be recalled. The emperor readily granted his terms in full; and the next day Felix was consecrated, Martin assisting and communicating with the persecutors of Priscillian. They urged him with much earnestness to sign an instrument in attestation of his concession, but this he refused.

7.

Writers of great seriousness have not been unwilling to suggest that, extraordinary as was St. Martin's habitual humility, yet he might have experienced some elation of mind from the remarkable honours which he had received from the court on his first visit to Treves; but, whatever was the cause of his change of purpose, that he might have acted better, was soon confessed by himself. Thus ended his intercourse with the great world. He had gained the object which had brought him to Treves; Maximus, too, had gained his: there was nothing more to detain him in the imperial city, and the day after his act of concession he set off on his return to Tours.

He went on his way with downcast mind, sighing, as his biographer tells us, to think that he had even for an hour shared in a communion so unhealthy to the soul; when now an occurrence took place, which, it seems, he ever studiously concealed, though his intimate friends got acquainted with it. About ten miles from Treves his journey lay through deep and lonely woods; he let his companions go forward, and remained by himself, examining his conscience, and first blaming, and then again defending what he had done. While he was thus engaged, he was favoured with a supernatural vision: an Angel appeared to him, and said, "Martin, thou art pricked in heart with reason; but no other escape opened to thee. Retrieve thy virtue; resume thy firmness; lest thou risk, not thy renown, but thy salvation."

Martin lived eleven years after this, but, somewhat in the spirit of Gregory Nazianzen, he never went to council or meeting of bishops again. And afterwards, when he was engaged with the *energumeni*, or demoniacs,

"He used from time to time to confess to us," says Sulpicius, "with tears, that from the mischief of that communion, which he joined for a moment, and that not in heart, but on compulsion, he was sensible of a diminution of his supernatural gift."

Sulpicius also happens to mention in another connection, that in the last years of his life—

"when the prefect Vincentius, a person of singular worth, and as excellent a man in every respect as was to be found in any part of Gaul, passed through Tours, he often begged of Martin to entertain him in his monastery, alleging the example of blessed Ambrose the bishop, who at that time was said now and then to receive consuls and prefects at dinner; but that the man of high mind would not grant his request, lest it should give secret entrance to vanity and elation of spirit."—*Dial.* i. 17.

Such self-imposed penances were quite in the spirit of those ages of sanctity. Notice has been taken of Gregory's silence during Lent in a former chapter; and Sulpicius in his old age, on being betrayed for an instant into an advocacy of Pelagian doctrine, punished himself with silence to the end of his life.

8.

Martin's end was delayed till he was past the common age of man. With the weight of eighty years upon him, he had betaken himself to a place, at the extremity of his charge, to settle a quarrel existing between the clergy there. When he set out to return, his strength suddenly failed him, and he felt his end was approaching. A fever had already got possession of him. He assembled his disciples, and announced to them that he was going: they, with passionate laments, deprecated such a calamity, as involving the exposure of his flock to the wolves. The Saint was moved, and used words which have become famous in the Church, "Lord, if I be yet necessary to Thy people, I decline not the labour; Thy will be done!" His wish was heard, not his prayer. His fever lay upon him; during the trial he continued his devotions as usual, causing himself to be laid in sackcloth and ashes. On his disciples asking to be allowed to place straw under him instead, he made answer, "Sons, it becomes a Christian to die in ashes. Did I set any other example I should sin myself." They wished to turn him on his side, to ease his position; but he expressed a wish to see heaven rather than earth, that his spirit might, as it were, be setting out on its journey. It is said that on this he saw the evil spirit at his side. "Beast of blood," he exclaimed, "why standest thou here? Deadly one, thou shalt find nothing in me; Abraham's bosom is receiving me." With these words he died.

At this time, Sulpicius, his biographer, was away, apparently at Toulouse. One morning, a friend had just departed from him; he was sitting alone in his cell, thinking of the future and the past, of his sins, and the last judgment.

"My limbs," he writes to the friend who had thus left him, "being wearied by the anguish of my mind, I laid them down on my bed, and, as is customary in sorrow, fell into a sleep,—the sleep of the morning hours, light and broken, and taking but wavering and doubtful possession of the limbs, when one seems, contrary to the nature of deep slumber, to be almost awake in one's sleep.

Then suddenly I seem to myself to see holy Martin, the bishop, clad in a white robe, with face like a flame, eyes like stars, and glittering hair; and, while his person was what I had known it to be, yet, what can hardly be expressed, I could not look at him, though I could recognize him. He slightly smiled on me, and bore in his right hand the book which I had written of his life. I embrace his sacred knees, and ask his blessing as usual; and I feel the soft touch of his hand on my head, while, together with the usual words of blessing, he repeats the name of the cross, familiar in his mouth: next, while I gaze upon him, and cannot take my fill of his face and look, suddenly he is caught aloft, till, after completing the immense spaces of the air, I following with my eyes the swift cloud that carried him, he is received into the open heaven, and can be seen no more. Not long after, I see the holy presbyter Clare, his disciple, who had lately died, ascending after his master. I, shameless one, desire to follow; while I set about it, and strain after lofty steps, I wake up, and, shaking off my sleep, begin to rejoice in the vision, when a boy, who was with me, enters sadder than usual, with a speaking and sorrowful countenance: 'Why so sad and eager to speak?' say I. 'Two monks,' he answers, 'are just come from Tours; they bring the news that Martin is departed.' I was overcome, I confess; my tears burst forth, I wept abundantly. Even now while I write, my brother, my tears are flowing, nor is any comfort adequate to this most unruly grief. However, when the news came, I felt a wish that you should be partner in my grief, who were companion in my love. Come, then, to me at once, that we may mourn him together, whom we love together; although I am aware that such a man is not really to be mourned, who, after conquering and triumphing over the world, has at length received the crown of justice."—*Ep.* 2.

This letter is written to a private friend, at the time of St. Martin's death, as appears on the face of it; the memoirs of the Saint are written with equal earnestness and simplicity. They were circulated throughout Christendom with astonishing rapidity: but the miraculous accounts they contained were a difficulty with great numbers. Accordingly, in the last of his publications, Sulpicius gave the names of living witnesses in corroboration of his own statements. "Far be such suspicion," he adds, "from any one who lives under God's eye; for Martin does not need support from fictions; however, I open before Thee, O Christ, the fidelity of my whole narrative, that I have neither said, nor will say, aught but what I have either seen myself, or have ascertained from plain authorities, or for the most part from his own mouth."—*Dial.* iii. 5.

Martin was buried at Tours, and two thousand of his monks attended the funeral. As has been said, he was more than eighty years old at the time of his death, out of which he had been bishop twenty-five. Some say that he died on a Sunday, at midnight. His festival is placed in the calendar on the 11th of November, the day either of his death or of his burial. His relics were preserved in his episcopal city till these latter days, when the Huguenots seized and burned them. Some portions, however, are said still to remain.

9.

St. Martin, as I have several times said, is famous for his miraculous powers. He is even said to have raised the dead. He was persecuted by the Evil One, as St. Antony had been before him. One of these assaults has so deep an instruction in it, and is so apposite both to the foregoing narrative and to this age, that I shall take leave of the reader with relating it:—

"While Martin was praying in his cell, the evil spirit stood before him, environed in a glittering radiance, by such pretence more easily to deceive him; clad also in royal robes, crowned with a golden and jewelled diadem, with shoes covered with gold, with serene face, and bright looks, so as to seem nothing so little as what he was. Martin at first was dazzled at the sight; and for a long while both parties kept silence. At length the Evil One began:—

'Acknowledge,' he says, 'O Martin, whom thou seest. I am Christ; I am now descending upon earth, and I wished first to manifest myself to thee.' Martin still kept silent, and returned no answer. The devil ventured to repeat his bold pretence. 'Martin, why hesitate in believing, when thou seest I am Christ?' Then he, understanding by revelation of the Spirit that it was the Evil One and not God, answered, 'Jesus, the Lord, announced not that He should come in glittering clothing, and radiant with a diadem. I will not believe that Christ is come, save in that state and form in which He suffered, *save with the show of the wounds of the Cross.*' At these words the other vanished forthwith as smoke, and filled the cell with so horrible an odour as to leave indubitable proofs who he was. That this so took place, I know from the mouth of Martin himself lest any one should think it fabulous."—*Vit. B. M.* 25.

The application of this vision to Martin's age is obvious; I suppose it means in this day, that Christ comes not in pride of intellect, or reputation for philosophy. These are the glittering robes in which Satan is now arraying. Many spirits are abroad, more are issuing from the pit; the credentials which they display are the precious gifts of mind, beauty, richness, depth, originality. Christian, look hard at them with Martin in silence, and ask them for the print of the nails.

CHRONOLOGY OF THE CONTEMPORARY EVENTS.

(The dates are, for the most part, according to Tillemont.)

A.D.

132. St. Justin converted, p. 94.
166. Flight of St. Polycarp from persecution, p. 130.
211. Tertullian writes his treatise against flight in persecution, p. 132.
250. Flight of St. Cyprian, St. Gregory of Neocæsarea, and St. Dionysius, in the Dacian persecution, pp. 129, 130.
251. St. Antony born, pp. 99, 154; Novatian, schismatic, p. 78.
253. Origen dies, p. 99.
255. Manichæus, heretic, p. 143.
260. St. Dionysius, Pope, p. 42.
270. St. Antony adopts the solitary life, p. 103.
285. St. Antony retires into the desert, p. 103.
304. St. Macrina and her husband in the woods in Pontus, in the Dioclesian persecution, p. 17.
305. St. Antony begins to have disciples, p. 117.
306. Meletian schism in Egypt, p. 121.
316. St. Martin born in Pannonia, p. 186.
320. The forty Martyrs of Sebaste in the Licinian persecution, p. 58.
325. The first General Council at Nicæa; Arius condemned, pp. 4, 76.
326. St. Athanasius Bishop of Alexandria, pp. 4, 40, 97, 154
329. St. Gregory and St. Basil born, pp. 27, 51; Gregory, the father, made Bishop of Nazianzus, p. 51.
331. St. Martin enlists in the army, p. 187.
336. St. Martin leaves the army, p. 187.
338. Eusebius of Nicomedia usurps the see of Constantinople, p. 78.
340. St. Macrina, grandmother to St. Basil, dies, pp. 22, 38.
341. Macedonius usurps the see of Constantinople, p. 78.
347. St. Chrysostom born, p. 99.
349. Basil, St. Basil's father, dies, p. 18; St. Emmelia and St. Macrina (junior) retire from the world, p. 18.
350. St. Basil and St. Gregory at Athens, p. 52; St. Martin goes to St. Hi-

A. D.

lary, pp. 187, 8; St. Paul of Constantinople martyred by the Arians, p. 78.

354. St. Augustine born, p. 99; Eustathius, Bishop of Sebaste, p. 20.

355. St. Antony supports St. Athanasius, pp. 6, 121; St. Basil leaves Athens, p. 54.

356. St. Gregory leaves Athens, p. 54; St. Antony dies, pp. 5, 99; St. Martin retires to Milan, p. 188; St. Hilary is banished to the East, p. 188; St. Basil teaches rhetoric at Cæsarea, p. 58; alludes to Apollinaris, p. 32; retires from the world, pp. 5, 56.

357. Naucratius, St. Basil's brother, drowned, p. 18; St. Basil goes into Syria, etc., pp. 21, 38, 58; St. Athanasius writes in defence of his flight, p. 130.

358. St. Basil retires into Pontus, pp. 5, 57; his chants, pp. 61, 64, 65.

359. Council of Ariminum, pp. 4, 51.

360. St. Martin establishes his monastery at Poictiers, p. 188; Eudoxius usurps the see of Constantinople, p. 78; St. Basil separates from Dianius, p. 4; the monks of Nazianzus separate from St. Gregory's father, pp. 51, 2.

361. St. Meletius, Bishop of Antioch, pp. 16, 31, 41, 47; Constantius dies, p. 40.

362. St. Gregory ordained priest, pp. 71, 82; St. Basil returns to Cæsarea, and is ordained priest, p. 5; Macedonius, heresiarch, pp. 40, 78.

363. Athanasius of Ancyra conforms, p. 32; Julian shuts up the Christian schools, p. 153.

364. St. Athanasius writes the life of St. Antony, pp. 97, 154; St. Gregory reconciles the monks of Nazianzus to his father, pp. 52, 70.

366. St. Damasus made Pope, p. 42; St. Gregory reconciles St. Basil to his bishop, pp. 6, 65; the Eunomians, pp. 6, 78.

367. Persecution under Valens, pp. 9, 30, 78.

369. Cæsarius dies, and St. Basil assists St. Gregory in securing his property, p. 66.

370. Eudoxius, Arian Bishop of Constantinople, dies, p. 78; eighty Catholic clergy burnt at sea, pp. 78, 84; St. Basil raised to the see of Cæsarea, pp. 9, 66.

371. St. Basil writes to St. Athanasius, p. 40; he resists Valens and Modestus, p. 9, etc.; slandered by a monk of Nazianzus, p. 67; Patricius, Augustine's father, dies a Christian, p. 158.

372. St. Martin elected Bishop of Tours, p. 188; St. Gregory, Bishop of Nyssa, p. 18; dispute between St. Basil and Anthimus, p. 69; St. Gregory made Bishop of Sasima, p. 70; complains of St. Basil, p. 72.

373. Augustine joins the Manichees, p. 143; St. Basil falls ill, p. 14; proposes to send St. Gregory of Nyssa to Rome, p. 44; St. Athanasius dies [al. A.D. 371], p. 40.

A.D.

374. St. Gregory's father dies, p. 73 ; St. Amphilochius, Bishop of Iconium, pp. 12, 15 ; Probus makes his speech to St. Ambrose, pp. 168 ; St. Ambrose elected Bishop of Milan, p. 188 ; Marcellus, accused of Sabellianism, dies, p. 79.

375. St. Basil goes into Pisidia and Pontus, p. 16 ; enters a protest against Eustathius, p. 20 ; complains of St. Damasus, p. 45.

376. Demophilus, Arian Bishop of Constantinople, p. 79 ; Augustine teaches rhetoric at Carthage, p. 147.

377. St. Meletius and St. Eusebius pp. 14, 31 ; in ill-esteem at Rome, pp. 45, 47 ; Apollinaris, heretic, p. 32.

379. Death of St. Basil, pp. 26, 75 ; accession of Theodosius, p. 76 ; St. Gregory goes to Constantinople, p. 79.

380. Theodosius declares for the Church, p. 78 ; St. Peter, Bishop of Sebaste, p. 18.

381. Priscillian made Bishop of Avila, p. 195 ; Second General Council held at Constantinople, pp. 79, 83.

382. St. Gregory retires to Asia, pp. 75, 79 ; pronounces oration in praise of St. Basil, pp. 73, 75 ; passes Lent without speaking, p. 86.

383. Maximus assumes the purple ; Gratian killed, p. 192 ; Augustine goes to Rome, p. 147.

384. St. Martin, at Treves, is courted by Maximus and his empress, p. 194, Augustine goes to Milan, pp. 147 ; Council of Bordeaux, p. 196 ; Priscillian, heretic, executed, p. 197.

386. St. Martin's second visit to Treves ; he communicates with the Ithacians, p. 198 ; etc. ; Augustine converted, p. 157, etc.

387. Augustine baptized by St. Ambrose, p. 159 ; St. Monica dies, p. 158.

388. St. Augustine settles at Thagaste, p. 159.

389. St. Gregory Nazianzen dies, p. 93 ; Ithacius deposed and banished, p. 198 ; St. Augustine ordained priest at Hippo, p. 160.

390. Council of Milan against the Ithacians, p. 198.

392. Sulpicius Severus introduced to St. Martin, p. 186.

395. St. Augustine consecrated coadjutor to Valerius, p. 161.

396. Sulpicius writes the life of St. Martin, p. 186.

397. St. Martin dies, p. 203.

398. St. Augustine writes his Confessions, p. 145. etc. ; Council of Turin, p. 198.

403. St. Chrysostom in persecution, p. 169.

405. Sulpicius writes his Dialogues, p. 204, etc. ; Pelagius commences his heresy, p. 179.

410. Rome taken by Alaric, August 24th, p. 168.

411. St. Augustine writes to Proba, p. 169.

413. Demetrias devotes herself to religion, p. 172, etc.

414. St. Jerome writes to Demetrias, p. 179 Pelagius writes to Demetrias, p. 180.

A.D.

417. St. Augustine and St. Alypius write to Juliana, p. 180; Pope Zozimus for a while baffled by Pelagius, p. 180.

418. Sulpicius deceived by the Pelagians, p. 202.

420. St. Jerome dies, p. 173.

428. The Vandals cross to Africa, p. 128; St. Augustine writes to Honoratus, p. 134.

430. Treatise of unknown author addressed to Demetrias, p. 183; the Vandals besiege Hippo, p. 139; death of St. Augustine, p. 140.

431. Third General Council, held at Ephesus, p. 129.

440. St. Leo elected Pope, p. 184.

455. Sack of Rome by Genseric, p. 183.

456 Demetrias builds the church of St. Stephen, p. 184.

IV.

PRIMITIVE CHRISTIANITY.

(*From the* British Magazine, 1833—1836.)

PREFATORY NOTICE.

THE following Papers originally belonged to the "Church of the Fathers," as it appeared in the *British Magazine*, in the years 1833-1836, and as it was published afterwards in one volume, with additions and omissions, in 1840. They were removed from the subsequent Catholic editions, except the chapter on Apollinaris, as containing polemical matter, which had no interest for Catholic readers. Now they are republished under a separate title.

The date of their composition is a sufficient indication of the character of the theology which they contain. They are written under the assumption that the Anglican Church has a place, as such, in Catholic communion and Apostolic Christianity. This is a question of fact, which the Author would now of course answer in the negative, retaining still, and claiming as his own, the positive principles and doctrines which that fact is, in these Papers, taken to involve.

PRIMITIVE CHRISTIANITY.

PRIMITIVE CHRISTIANITY.

CHAPTER I.

WHAT DOES ST. AMBROSE SAY ABOUT IT?

§ 1. *Ambrose and Justina.*

NO considerate person will deny that there is much in the spirit of the times, and in the actual changes which the British Constitution has lately undergone, which makes it probable, or not improbable, that a material alteration will soon take place in the relations of the Church towards the State, to which it has been hitherto united. I do not say that it is out of the question that things may return to their former quiet and pleasant course, as in the good old time of King George III; but the very chance that they will not makes it a practical concern for every churchman to prepare himself for a change, and a practical question for the clergy, by what instruments the authority of Religion is to be supported, should the protection and patronage of the Government be withdrawn. Truth, indeed, will always support itself in the world by its native vigour; it will never die while heaven and earth last, but be handed down from saint to saint until the end of all things. But this was the case before our Lord came, and is still the case, as we may humbly trust, in heathen countries. My puestion concerns *the*

Church, that peculiar institution which Christ set up as a visible home and memorial of Truth; and which, as being in this world, must be manifested by means of this world. I know it is common to make light of this solicitude about the Church, under the notion that the Gospel may be propagated without it,—or that men are about the same under every Dispensation, their hearts being in fault, and not their circumstances,—or for other reasons, better or worse as it may be; to all which I am accustomed to answer (and I do not see how I can be in error), that, if Christ had not meant His Church to answer a purpose, He would not have set it up, and that our business is not to speculate about possible Dispensations of Religion, but to resign and devote ourselves to that in which we are actually placed.

Hitherto the English Church has depended on the State, *i. e.* on the ruling powers in the country—the king and the aristocracy; and this is so natural and religious a position of things when viewed in the abstract, and in its actual working has been productive of such excellent fruits in the Church, such quietness, such sobriety, such external propriety of conduct, and such freedom from doctrinal excesses, that we must ever look back upon the period of ecclesiastical history so characterized with affectionate thoughts; particularly on the reigns of our blessed martyr St. Charles, and King George the Good. But these recollections of the past must not engross our minds, or hinder us from looking at things as they are, and as they will be soon, and from inquiring what is intended by Providence to take the place of the time-honoured instrument, which He has broken (if it be yet broken), the regal and aristocratical power. I shall offend many men when I say, we must *look to the people;* but let them give me a hearing.

Well can I understand their feelings. Who at first sight does not dislike the thoughts of gentlemen and clergymen depending for their maintenance and their reputation on their flocks? of their strength, as a visible power, lying not in their birth, the patronage of the great, and the endowment of the Church (as hitherto), but in the homage of a multitude? I confess I have before now had a great repugnance to the notion myself; and if I have overcome it, and turned from the Government to the People, it has been simply because I was forced to do so. It is not we who desert the Government, but the Government that has left us; we are forced back upon those below us, because those above us will not honour us; there is no help for it, I say. But, in truth, the prospect is not so bad as it seems at first sight. The chief and obvious objection to the clergy being thrown on the People, lies in the probable lowering of Christian views, and the adulation of the vulgar, which would be its consequence; and the state of Dissenters is appealed to as an evidence of the danger. But let us recollect that we are an apostolical body; we were not made, nor can be unmade by our flocks; and if our influence is to depend on *them*, yet the Sacraments reside with *us*. We have that with us, which none but ourselves possess, the mantle of the Apostles; and this, properly understood and cherished, will ever keep us from being the creatures of a populace.

And what may become necessary in time to come, is a more religious state of things also. It will not be denied that, according to the Scripture view of the Church, though all are admitted into her pale, and the rich inclusively, yet, the poor are her members with a peculiar suitableness, and by a special right. Scripture is ever casting slurs upon wealth, and making much of poverty. "To the poor the Gospel is preached." "God hath chosen the poor of this world, rich in faith and heirs of the kingdom." "If thou wilt be perfect, sell all that thou hast, and give to the poor." To this must be added the undeniable fact that the Church, when purest and when most powerful, *has* depended for its influence on its consideration with the many. Becket's letters, lately published,[1] have struck me not a little; but of course I now refer, not to such dark ages as most Englishmen consider these, but to the primitive Church —the Church of St. Athanasius and St. Ambrose. With a view of showing the power of the Church at that time, and on what it was based, not (as Protestants imagine) on governments, or on human law, or on endowments, but on popular enthusiasm, on dogma, on hierarchical power, and on a supernatural Divine Presence, I will now give some account of certain ecclesiastical proceedings in the city of Milan in the years 385, 386,—Ambrose being bishop, and Justina and her son, the younger Valentinian, the reigning powers.

I.

Ambrose was eminently a popular bishop, as every one knows who has read ever so little of his history. His very promotion to the sacred office was owing to an unexpected movement of the populace. Auxentius, his Arian predecessor in the see of Milan, died, A.D. 374, upon which the bishops of the province wrote to the then Emperor, Valentinian the First, who was in Gaul, requesting him to name the person who was to succeed him. This was a prudent step on their part, Arianism having introduced such matter for discord and faction

[1] Vid. *British Magazine*, 1832, etc. And Froude's Remains, part II. vol. ii.

among the Milanese, that it was dangerous to submit the election to the people at large, though the majority of them were orthodox. Valentinian, however, declined to avail himself of the permission thus given him ; the choice was thrown upon the voices of the people, and the cathedral, which was the place of assembling, was soon a scene of disgraceful uproar, as the bishops had anticipated. Ambrose was at that time civil governor of the province of which Milan was the capital : and, the tumult increasing, he was obliged to interfere in person, with a view of preventing its ending in open sedition. He was a man of grave character, and had been in youth brought up with a sister, who had devoted herself to the service of God in a single life ; but as yet was only a catechumen, though he was half way between thirty and forty. Arrived at the scene of tumult, he addressed the assembled crowds, exhorting them to peace and order. While he was speaking, a child's voice, as is reported, was heard in the midst of the crowd to say, "Ambrose is bishop ;" the populace took up the cry, and both parties in the Church, Catholic and Arian, whether influenced by a sudden enthusiasm, or willing to take a man who was unconnected with party, voted unanimously for the election of Ambrose.

It is not wonderful that the subject of this sudden decision should have been unwilling to quit his civil office for a station of such high responsibility; for many days he fought against the popular voice, and that by the most extravagant expedients. He absconded, and was not recovered till the Emperor, confirming the act of the people of Milan, published an edict against all who should conceal him. Under these strange circumstances, Ambrose was at length consecrated bishop. His ordination was canonical only on the supposition that it came under those rare exceptions, for which the rules of the Church allow, when they speak of election "by divine grace," by the immediate suggestion of God; and if ever a bishop's character and works might be appealed to as evidence of the divine purpose, surely Ambrose was the subject of that singular and extraordinary favour. From the time of his call he devoted his life and abilities to the service of Christ. He bestowed his personal property on the poor: his lands on the Church; making his sister tenant for life. Next he gave himself up to the peculiar studies necessary for the due execution of his high duties, till he gained that deep insight into Catholic truth, which is evidenced in his writings, and in no common measure in relation to Arianism, which had been the dominant creed in Milan for the twenty years preceding his elevation. Basil of Cæsarea, in Cappadocia, was at this time the main pillar of Catholic truth in the East, having succeeded Athanasius of Alexandria, who died about the time that both Basil and Ambrose were advanced to their respective sees. He, from his see in the far East, addresses the new bishop in these words in an extant Epistle:—

> "Proceed in thy work, thou man of God; and since thou hast not received the Gospel of Christ of men, neither wast taught it, but the Lord himself translated thee from among the world's judges to the chair of the Apostles, fight the good fight, set right the infirmities of the people, wherever the Arian madness has affected them; renew the old foot-prints of the Fathers, and by frequent correspondence build up thy love towards us, of which thou hast already laid the foundation."—*Ep.* 197.

I just now mentioned St. Thomas Becket. There is at once a similarity and a contrast between his history and that of Ambrose. Each of the two was by education and society what would now be called a gentleman.

Each was in high civil station when he was raised to a great ecclesiastical position; each was in middle age. Each had led an upright, virtuous life before his elevation; and each, on being elevated, changed it for a life of extraordinary penance and saintly devotion. Each was promoted to his high place by the act, direct or concurrent, of his sovereign; and each showed to that sovereign in the most emphatic way that a bishop was the servant, not of man, but of the Lord of heaven and earth. Each boldly confronted his sovereign in a great religious quarrel, and staked his life on its issue;—but then comes the contrast, for Becket's earthly master was as resolute in his opposition to the Church as Becket was in its behalf, and made him a martyr; whereas the Imperial Power of Rome quailed and gave way before the dauntless bearing and the grave and gracious presence of the great prelate of Milan. Indeed, the whole Pontificate of Ambrose is a history of successive victories of the Church over the State; but I shall limit myself to a bare outline of one of them.

2.

Ambrose had presided in his see about eleven years at the time when the events took place which are here to be related. Valentinian was dead, as well as his eldest son Gratian. His second son, who bore his own name, was Emperor of the West, under the tutelage of Justina, his second wife.

Justina was an Arian, and brought up her son in her own heretical views. This was about the time when the heresy was finally subdued in the Eastern Churches; the Ecumenical Council of Constantinople had lately been held, many Arian bishops had conformed, and laws had been passed by Theodosius against those who held out. It was natural under such circumstances that a number of the latter should flock to the court of Milan for protection and patronage. The Gothic officers of the palace were Arians also, as might be supposed, after the creed of their nation. At length they obtained a bishop of their persuasion from the East; and having now the form of an ecclesiastical body, they used the influence of Valentinian, or rather of his mother, to extort from Ambrose one of the churches of Milan for their worship.

The bishop was summoned to the palace before the assembled Court, and was formally asked to relinquish St. Victor's Church, then called the Portian Basilica, which was without the walls, for the Arian worship. His duty was plain; the churches were the property of Christ; he was the representative of Christ, and was therefore bound not to cede what was committed to him in trust. This is the account of the matter given by himself in the course of the dispute:—

> "Do not," he says, "O Emperor, embarrass yourself with the thought that you have an Emperor's right over sacred things. Exalt not yourself, but, as you would enjoy a continuance of power, be God's subject. It is written, God's to God, and Cæsar's to Cæsar. The palace is the Emperor's, the churches are the bishop's."—*Ep.* 20.

This argument, which is true at all times, was much more convincing in an age like the primitive, before men had begun to deny that Christ had left a visible representative of Himself in His Church. If there was a body to whom the concerns of religion were intrusted, there could be no doubt it was that over which Ambrose presided. It had been there planted ever since Milan became Christian, its ministers were descended from the Apostles, and it was the legitimate trustee of the sacred property. But in our day men have been taught to doubt whether there *is* one Apostolic Church, though it is mentioned in the Creed: nay, it is grievous to say, clergymen have sometimes forgotten, sometimes made light of their own privileges. Accordingly, when a question arises now about the spoliation of the Church, we are obliged to betake ourselves to the rules of *national* law; we appeal to precedents, or we urge the civil consequences of the measure, or we use other arguments, which, good as they may be, are too refined to be very popular. Ambrose rested his resistance on grounds which the people understood at once, and recognized as irrefragable. They felt that he was only refusing to surrender a trust. They rose in a body, and thronged the palace gates. A company of soldiers was sent to disperse them; and a riot was on the point of ensuing, when the ministers of the Court became alarmed, and despatched Ambrose to appease the tumult, with the pledge that no further attempt should be made on the possessions of the Church.

Now some reader will here interrupt the narrative, perhaps, with something of an indignant burst about connecting the cause of religion with mobs and outbreaks To whom I would reply, that the multitude of men is always rude and intemperate, and needs restraint, —religion does not make them so. But being so, it is better they should be zealous about religion, and repressed by religion, as in this case, than flow and ebb again under the irrational influences of this world. A mob, indeed, is always wayward and faithless; but it is a good sign when it is susceptible of the hopes and fears of the world to come. Is it not probable that, when religion is thus a popular subject, it may penetrate, soften, or stimulate hearts which otherwise would know nothing of its power? However, this is not, properly speaking my present point, which is to show how a Church may be in "favour with all the people" without any subserviency to them. To return to our history.

3.

Justina, failing to intimidate, made various underhand attempts to remove the champion of orthodoxy. She endeavoured to raise the people against him. Failing in this object, next, by scattering promises of place and promotion, she set on foot various projects to seize him in church, and carry him off into banishment. One man went so far as to take lodgings near the church, and had a carriage in readiness, in order to avail himself of any opportunity which offered to convey him away. But none of these attempts succeeded.

This was in the month of March; as Easter drew on, more vigorous steps were taken by the Court. On April 4th, the Friday before Palm Sunday, the demand of a church for the Arians was renewed; the pledges which the government had given, that no further steps should be taken in the matter, being perhaps evaded by changing the church which was demanded. Ambrose was now asked for the New or Roman Basilica, which was within the walls, and larger than the Portian. It was dedicated to the Apostles, and (I may add, for the sake of the antiquarian,) was built in the form of a cross. When the bishop refused in the same language as before, the imperial minister returned to the demand of the Portian Church; but the people interfering, and being clamorous against the proposal, he was obliged to retire to the palace to report how matters stood.

On Palm Sunday, after the lessons and sermon were over in the Basilica, in which he officiated, Ambrose was engaged in teaching the creed to the candidates for baptism, who, as was customary, had been catechized during Lent, and were to be admitted into the Church on the night before Easter-day. News was brought him that the officers of the Court had taken possession of the Portian Church, and were arranging the imperial hangings in token of its being confiscated to the Emperor; on the other hand, that the people were flocking thither. Ambrose continued the service of the day; but, when he was in the midst of the celebration of the Eucharistical rite, a second message came that one of the Arian priests was in the hands of the populace.

> "On this news (he says, writing to his sister,) I could not keep from shedding many bitter tears, and, while I made oblation, I prayed God's protection that no blood might be shed in the Church's quarrel: or if so, that it might be mine, and that not for my people only, but for those heretics."—*Ep.* 20.

At the same time he despatched some of his clergy to the spot, who had influence enough to rescue the unfortunate man from the mob.

Though Ambrose so far seems to have been supported only by a popular movement, yet the proceedings of the following week showed that he had also the great mass of respectable citizens on his side. The imprudent measures of the Court, in punishing those whom it considered its enemies, disclosed to the world their number and importance. The tradesmen of the city were fined two hundred pounds of gold, and many were thrown into prison. All the officers, moreover, and place-men of the courts of justice, were ordered to keep in-doors during the continuance of the disorders; and men of higher rank were menaced with severe consequences, unless the Basilica were surrendered.

Such were the acts by which the Imperial Court solemnized Passion week. At length a fresh interview was sought with Ambrose, which shall be described in his own words :—

"I had a meeting with the counts and tribunes, who urged me to give up the Basilica without delay, on the ground that the Emperor was but acting on his undoubted rights, as possessing sovereign power over all things. I made answer, that if he asked me for what was my own—for instance, my estate, my money, or the like—I would make no opposition : though, to tell the truth, all that was mine was the property of the poor ; but that he had no sovereignty over things sacred. If my patrimony is demanded, seize upon it ; my person, here I am. Would you take to prison or to death ? I go with pleasure. Far be it from me to entrench myself within the circle of a multitude, or to clasp the altar in supplication for my life ; rather I will be a sacrifice for the altar's sake.

"In good truth, when I heard that soldiers were sent to take possession of the Basilica, I was horrified at the prospect of bloodshed, which might issue in ruin to the whole city. I prayed God that I might not survive the destruction, which might ensue, of such a place, nay, of Italy itself. I shrank from the odium of having occasioned slaughter, and would sooner have given my own throat to the knife. . . . I was ordered to calm the people. I replied, that all I could do was not to inflame them ; but God alone could appease them. For myself, if I appeared to have instigated them, it was the duty of the government to proceed against me, or to banish me. Upon this they left me."

Ambrose spent the rest of Palm Sunday in the same Basilica in which he had been officiating in the morning : at night he went to his own house, that the civil power might have the opportunity of arresting him, if it was thought advisable.

4.

The attempt to gain the Portian seems now to have been dropped ; but on the Wednesday troops were marched before day-break to take possession of the New Church, which was within the walls. Ambrose, upon the news of this fresh movement, used the weapons of an apostle. He did not seek to disturb them in their possession ; but, attending service at his own church, he was content with threatening the soldiers with a sentence of excommunication. Meanwhile the New Church, where the soldiers were posted, began to fill with a larger congregation than it ever contained before the persecution. Ambrose was requested to go thither, but, desirous of drawing the people away from the scene of imperial tyranny, lest a riot should ensue, he remained where he was, and began a comment on the lesson of the day, which was from the book of Job. First, he commended them for the Christian patience and resignation with which they had hitherto borne their trial, which indeed was, on the whole, surprising, if we consider the inflammable nature of a multitude. "We petition your Majesty," they said to the Emperor ; "we use no force, we feel no fear, but we petition." It is common in the leader of a multitude to profess peaceableness, but very unusual for the multitude itself to persevere in doing so. Ambrose went on to observe, that both they and he had in their way been tempted, as Job was, by the powers of evil. For himself, his peculiar trial had lain in the reflection that the extraordinary measures of the government, the movements of the Gothic guards, the fines of the tradesmen, the various sufferings of the faithful, all arose from, as it might be called, his obstinacy in not yielding to what seemed an overwhelming necessity, and giving the Basilica to the Arians. Yet he felt that to do so would be to peril his soul ; so that the request was but the voice of the tempter, as he spoke in Job's wife, to make him "say a word against God, and die," to betray his trust, and incur the sentence of spiritual death.

Before this time the soldiers who had been sent to the New Church, from dread of the threat of excommunication, had declared against the sacrilege, and joined his own congregation; and now the news came that the royal hangings had been taken down. Soon after, as he was continuing his address to the people, a fresh message came to him from the Court to ask him whether he had an intention of domineering over his sovereign? Ambrose, in answer, showed the pains he had taken to be obedient to the Emperor's will, and to hinder disturbance: then he added:—

"Priests have by old right bestowed sovereignty, never assumed it; and it is a common saying, that sovereigns have coveted the priesthood more than priests the sovereignty. Christ hid Himself, lest He should be made a king. Yes! we have a dominion of our own. The dominion of the priest lies in his helplessness, as it is said, 'When I am weak, then am I strong.'"

And so ended the dispute for a time. On Good Friday the Court gave way; the guards were ordered from the Basilica, and the fines were remitted. I end for the present with the view which Ambrose took of the prospect before him:—

"Thus the matter rests; I wish I could say, has ended: but the Emperor's words are of that angry sort which shows that a more severe contest is in store. He says I domineer, or worse than domineer. He implied this when his ministers were entreating him, on the petition of the soldiers, to attend church. 'Should Ambrose bid you,' he made answer, 'doubtless you would give me to him in chains.' I leave you to judge what these words promise. Persons present were all shocked at hearing them; but there are parties who exasperate him."

§ 2. *Ambrose and Valentinian.*

I.

IN the opposition which Ambrose made to the Arians, as already related, there is no appearance of his appealing to any law of the Empire in justification of his refusal to surrender the Basilica to them. He rested it upon the simple basis of the Divine Law, a common-sense argument which there was no evading. "The Basilica has been made over to Christ; the Church is His trustee; I am its ruler. I dare not alienate the Lord's property. He who does so, does it at his peril." Indeed, he elsewhere expressly repudiates the principle of dependence in this matter on human law. "Law," he says, "has not brought the Church together, but the faith of Christ." However, Justina determined to have human law on her side. She persuaded her son to make it a capital offence in any one, either publicly or privately, even by petition, to interfere with the assemblies of the Arians; a provision which admitted a fair, and might also bear, and did in fact receive, a most tyrannical interpretation. Benevolus, the Secretary of State, from whose office the edict was to proceed, refused to draw it up, and resigned his place; but of course others less scrupulous were easily found to succeed him. At length it was promulgated on the 21st of January of the next year, A.D. 386, and a fresh attempt soon followed on the part of the Court to get possession of the Portian Basilica, which was without the walls.

The line of conduct which Ambrose had adopted

remained equally clear and straight, whether before or after the promulgation of this edict. It was his duty to use all the means which Christ has given the Church to prevent the profanation of the Basilica. But soon a new question arose for his determination. An imperial message was brought to him to retire from the city at once, with any friends who chose to attend him. It is not certain whether this was intended as an absolute command, or (as his words rather imply) a recommendation on the part of government to save themselves the odium, and him the suffering, of public and more severe proceedings. Even if it were the former, it does not appear that a Christian bishop, so circumstanced, need obey it; for what was it but in other words to say, "Depart from the Basilica, and leave it to us?"—the very order which he had already withstood. The words of Scripture, which bid Christians, if persecuted in one city, flee to another, are evidently, from the form of them, a discretionary rule, grounded on the expediency of each occasion, as it arises. A mere threat is not a persecution, nor is a command; and though we are bound to obey our civil rulers, the welfare of the Church has a prior claim upon our obedience. Other bishops took the same view of the case with Ambrose; and, accordingly, he determined to stay in Milan till removed by main force, or cut off by violence.

2.

The reader shall hear his own words in a sermon which he delivered upon the occasion:—

"I see that you are under a sudden and unusual excitement," he said, "and are turning your eyes on me. What can be the reason of this? Is it that you saw or heard that an imperial message had been brought to me by the tribunes desiring me to depart hence whither I would, and to take with me all who would follow me?

What! did you fear that I would desert the Church, and, for fear of my life, abandon you? Yet you might have attended to my answer. I said that I could not, for an instant, entertain the thought of deserting the Church, in that I feared the Lord of all more than the Emperor of the day: in truth that, should force hurry me off, it would be my body, not my mind, that was got rid of; that, should he act in the way of kingly power, I was prepared to suffer after the manner of a priest.

"Why, then, are you thus disturbed? I will never leave you of my own will; but if compelled, I may not resist. I shall still have the power of sorrowing, of weeping, of uttering laments: when weapons, soldiers, Goths, too, assail me, tears are my weapons, for such are the defences of a priest. In any other way I neither ought to resist, nor can; but as to retiring and deserting the Church, this is not like me; and for this reason, lest I seem to do so from dread of some heavier punishment. Ye yourselves know that it is my wont to submit to our rulers, but not to make concessions to them; to present myself readily to legal punishment, and not to fear what is in preparation.

"A proposal was made to me to deliver up at once the Church plate. I made answer, that I was ready to give anything that was my own, farm or house, gold or silver; but that I could withdraw no property from God's temple, nor surrender what was put into my hands, not to surrender, but to keep safely. Besides, that I had a care for the Emperor's well-being; since it was as little safe for him to receive as for me to surrender: let him bear with the words of a free-spoken priest, for his own good, and shrink from doing wrong to his Lord.

"You recollect to-day's lesson about holy Naboth and his vineyard. The king asked him to make it over to him, as a ground, not for vines, but for common pot-herbs. What was his answer? 'God forbid I should give to thee the inheritance of my fathers!' The king was saddened when another's property was justly denied him; but he was beguiled by a woman's counsel. Naboth shed his blood rather than give up his vines. Shall he refuse his own vineyard, and we surrender the Church of Christ?

"What contumacy, then, was there in my answer? I did but say at the interview, 'God forbid I should surrender Christ's heritage!' I added, 'the heritage of our fathers;' yes, of our Dionysius, who died in exile for the faith's sake, of Eustorgius the Confessor, of Myrocles, and of all the other faithful bishops back. I answered as a priest: let the Emperor act as an Emperor; he shall rob me of my life sooner than of my fidelity.

"In what respect was my answer other than respectful? Does the Emperor wish to tax us? I make no opposition. The Church lands pay taxes. Does he require our lands? He has power to claim them; we will not prevent him. The contributions of the people will suffice for the poor. Let not our enemies take offence at our lands; they may away with them, if it please the Emperor; not that I give them, but I make no opposition. Do they seek my gold? I can truly say, silver and gold I seek not. But they take offence at my raising contributions. Nor have I any great fear of the charge. I confess I have stipendiaries; they are the poor of Christ's flock; a treasure which I am well used in amassing. May this at all times be my offence, to exact contributions for the poor. And if they accuse me of defending myself by means of them, I am far from denying, I court the charge. The poor *are* my defenders, but it is by their prayers. Blind though they be, lame, feeble, and aged, yet they have a strength greater than that of the stoutest warriors. In a word, gifts made to them are a claim upon the Lord; as it is written, 'He who giveth to the poor, lendeth to God;' but a military guard oftentimes has no title to divine grace.

"They say, too, that the people are misled by the verses of my hymns. I frankly confess this also. Truly those hymns have in them a high strain above all other influence. For can any strain have more of influence than the confession of the Holy Trinity, which is proclaimed day by day by the voice of the whole people? Each is eager to rival his fellows in confessing, as he well knows how, in sacred verses, his faith in Father, Son, and Holy Spirit. Thus all are made teachers, who else were scarce equal to being scholars.

"No one can deny that in what we say we pay to our sovereign due honour. What indeed can do him higher honour than to style him a son of the Church? In saying this, we are loyal to him without sinning against God. For the Emperor is within the Church, but not over the Church; and a religious sovereign seeks, not rejects, the Church's aid. This is our doctrine, modestly avowed, but insisted on without wavering. Though they threaten fire, or the sword, or transportation, we, Christ's poor servants, have learned not to fear. And to the fearless nothing is frightful; as Scripture says, 'Their blows are like the arrows of a child.'"—*Serm. contr Auxent.*

3.

Mention is made in this extract of the Psalmody which Ambrose adopted about this time. The history of its introduction is curiously connected with the subject before us, and interesting, inasmuch as this was the beginning of a change in the style of Church music, which spread over the West, and continues even among ourselves to this day; it is as follows:—

Soldiers had been sent, as in the former year, to surround his church, in order to prevent the Catholic service there; but being themselves Christians, and afraid of excommunication, they went so far as to allow the people to enter, but would not let them leave the building. This was not so great an inconvenience to them as might appear at first sight: for the early Basilicas were not unlike the heathen temples, or our own collegiate chapels, that is, part of a range of buildings, which contained the lodgings of the ecclesiastics, and formed a fortress in themselves, which could easily be fortified from within or blockaded from without. Accordingly, the people remained shut up within the sacred precincts for some days, and the bishop with them. There seems to have been a notion, too, that he was to be seized for exile, or put to death; and they naturally kept about him to "see the end," to suffer with him or for him, according as their tempers and principles led them. Some went so far as to barricade the doors of the Basilica;[1] nor could Ambrose prevent this proceeding, unnecessary as it was, because of the good feelings of the soldiery towards them, and indeed impracticable in such completeness as might be sufficient for security.

Some persons may think that Ambrose ought to

[1] Vid. 2 [4] Kings vi. 32.

have used his utmost influence against it, whereas in his sermon to the people he merely insists on its uselessness, and urges the propriety of looking simply to God, and not at all to such expedients, for deliverance. It must be recollected, however, that he and his people in no sense drew the sword from its sheath; he confined himself to passive resistance. He had violated no law; the Church's property was sought by a tyrant: without using any violence, he took possession of that which he was bound to defend with his life. He placed himself upon the sacred territory, and bade them take it and him together, after St. Laurence's pattern, who submitted to be burned rather than deliver up the goods with which he had been intrusted for the sake of the poor. However, it was evidently a very uncomfortable state of things for a Christian bishop, who might seem to be responsible for all the consequences, yet was without control over them. A riot might commence any moment, which it would not be in his power to arrest. Under these circumstances, with admirable presence of mind, he contrived to keep the people quiet, and to direct their minds to higher objects than those around them, by Psalmody. Sacred chanting had been one especial way in which the Catholics of Antioch had kept alive, in Arian times, the spirit of orthodoxy. And from the first a peculiar kind of singing—the antiphonal or responsorial, answering to our cathedral chanting—had been used in honour of the sacred doctrine which heresy assailed. Ignatius, the disciple of St. Peter, was reported to have introduced the practice into the Church of Antioch, in the doxology to the Trinity. Flavian, afterwards bishop of that see, revived it during the Arian usurpation, to the great edification and encouragement of the oppressed Catholics. Chrysostom used it in the vigils at Constantinople, in opposition to the same heretical party; and similar vigils had been established by Basil in the monasteries of Cappadocia. The assembled multitude, confined day and night within the gates of the Basilica, were in the situation of a monastic body without its discipline, and Ambrose rightly considered that the novelty and solemnity of the oriental chants, in praise of the Blessed Trinity, would both interest and sober them during the dangerous temptation to which they were now exposed. The expedient had even more successful results than the bishop anticipated; the soldiers were affected by the music, and took part in it; and, as we hear nothing more of the blockade, we must suppose that it thus ended, the government being obliged to overlook what it could not prevent.

It may be interesting to the reader to see Augustine's notice of this occurrence, and the effect of the Psalmody upon himself, at the time of his baptism.

> "The pious populace (he says in his Confessions) was keeping vigils in the church prepared to die, O Lord, with their bishop, Thy servant. There was my mother, Thy handmaid, surpassing others in anxiety and watching, and making prayers her life.
>
> "I, uninfluenced as yet by the fire of Thy Spirit, was roused however by the terror and agitation of the city. Then it was that hymns and psalms, after the oriental rite, were introduced, lest the spirits of the flock should fail under the wearisome delay."—*Confess.* ix. 15.

In the same passage, speaking of his baptism, he says:—

> "How many tears I shed during the performance of Thy hymns and chants, keenly affected by the notes of Thy melodious Church! My ears drank up those sounds, and they distilled into my heart as sacred truths, and overflowed thence again in pious emotion, and gushed forth into tears, and I was happy in them."—*Ibid.* 14.

Elsewhere he says :—

"Sometimes, from over-jealousy, I would entirely put from me and from the Church the melodies of the sweet chants which we use in the Psalter, lest our ears seduce us ; and the way of Athanasius, Bishop of Alexandria, seems the safer, who, as I have often heard, made the reader chant with so slight a change of note, that it was more like speaking than singing. And yet when I call to mind the tears I shed when I heard the chants of Thy Church in the infancy of my recovered faith, and reflect that at this time I am affected, not by the mere music, but by the subject, brought out, as it is, by clear voices and appropriate tune, then, in turn, I confess how useful is the practice."—*Confess.* x. 50.

Such was the influence of the Ambrosian chants when first introduced at Milan by the great bishop whose name they bear; there they are in use still, in all the majestic austerity which gave them their original power, and a great part of the Western Church uses that modification of them which Pope Gregory introduced at Rome in the beginning of the seventh century.

4.

Ambrose implies, in the sermon from which extracts were given above, that a persecution, reaching even to the infliction of bodily sufferings, was at this time exercised upon the bishops of the Exarchate. Certainly he himself was all along in imminent peril of his life, or of sudden removal from Milan. However, he made it a point to frequent the public places and religious meetings as usual; and indeed it appears that he was as safe there as at home, for he narrowly escaped assassination from a hired ruffian of the Empress's, who made his way to his bed-chamber for the purpose. Magical arts were also practised against him, as a more secret and certain method of ensuring his destruction.

I ought to have mentioned, before this, the challenge sent to him by the Arian bishop to dispute publicly with him on the sacred doctrine in controversy; but was unwilling to interrupt the narrative of the contest about the Basilica. I will here translate portions of a letter sent by him, on the occasion, to the Emperor.

"To the most gracious Emperor and most happy Augustus "Valentinian, Ambrosius Bishop,—

"Dalmatius, tribune and notary, has come to me, at your Majesty's desire, as he assures me, to require me to choose umpires, as Auxentius[1] has done on his part. Not that he informed me who they were that had already been named; but merely said that the dispute was to take place in the consistory, in your Majesty's presence, as final arbitrator of it.

"I trust my answer will prove sufficient. No one should call me contumacious, if I insist on what your father, of blessed memory, not only sanctioned by word of mouth, but even by a law: —That in cases of faith, or of ecclesiastics, the judges should be neither inferior in function nor separate in jurisdiction—thus the rescript runs; in other words, he would have priests decide about priests. And this extended even to the case of allegations of wrong conduct.

"When was it you ever heard, most gracious Emperor, that in a question of faith laymen should be judges of a bishop? What! have courtly manners so bent our backs, that we have forgotten the rights of the priesthood, that I should of myself put into another's hands what God has bestowed upon me? Once grant that a layman may set a bishop right, and see what will follow. The layman in consequence discusses, while the bishop listens; and the bishop is the pupil of the layman. Yet, whether we turn to Scripture or to history, who will venture to deny that in a question of faith, in a question, I say, of faith, it has ever been the bishop's business to judge the Christian Emperor, not the Emperor's to judge the bishop?

"When, through God's blessing, you live to be old, then you will

[1] The Arian bishop, who had lately come from the East to Milan, had taken the name of Auxentius, the heretical predecessor of Ambrose.

know what to think of the fidelity of that bishop who places the rights of the priesthood at the mercy of laymen. Your father, who arrived, through God's blessing, at maturer years, was in the habit of saying 'I have no right to judge between bishops;' but now your Majesty says, 'I ought to judge.' He, even though baptized into Christ's body, thought himself unequal to the burden of such a judgment; your Majesty, who still have to earn a title to the sacrament, claims to judge in a matter of faith, though you are a stranger to the sacrament to which that faith belongs.

"But Ambrose is not of such value, that he must degrade the priesthood for his own well-being. One man's life is not so precious as the dignity of all those bishops who have advised me thus to write; and who suggested that Auxentius might be choosing some heathen perhaps or Jew, whose permission to decide about Christ would be a permission to triumph over Him. What would pleasure them but blasphemies against Him? What would satisfy them but the impious denial of His divinity—agreeing, as they do, full well with the Arian, who pronounces Christ to be a creature with the ready concurrence of Jews and heathens?

"I would have come to your Majesty's Court, to offer these remarks in your presence; but neither my bishops nor my people would let me; for they said that, when matters of faith were discussed in the Church, this should be in the presence of the people.

"I could have wished your Majesty had not told me to betake myself to exile somewhere. I was abroad every day; no one guarded me. I was at the mercy of all the world; you should have secured my departure to a place of your own choosing. Now the priests say to me, 'There is little difference between voluntarily leaving and betraying the altar of Christ; for when you leave, you betray it.'

"May it please your Majesty graciously to accept this my declining to appear in the Imperial Court. I am not practised in attending it, except in your behalf; nor have I the skill to strive for victory within the palace, as neither knowing, nor caring to know, its secrets."—*Ep.* 21.

The reader will observe an allusion in the last sentence of this defence to a service Ambrose had rendered the Emperor and his mother, upon the murder of Gratian; when, at the request of Justina, he undertook the difficult embassy to the usurper Maximus, and was the means of preserving the peace of Italy. This Maximus now interfered to defend him against the parties whom he had on a former occasion defended against Maximus; but other and more remarkable occurrences interposed in his behalf, which shall be mentioned in the next section.

§ 3. *Ambrose and the Martyrs.*

I.

A TERMINATION was at length put to the persecution of the Church of Milan by an occurrence of a very different nature from any which take place in these days. And since such events as I am to mention do not occur now, we are apt to argue, not very logically, that they did not occur then. I conceive this to be the main objection which will be felt against the following narrative. Miracles never took place then, because we do not see reason to believe that they take place now. But it should be recollected, that if there are no miracles at present, neither are there at present any martyrs. Might we not as cogently argue that no martyrdoms took place then, because no martyrdoms take place now? And might not St. Ambrose and his brethren have as reasonably disbelieved the possible existence of parsonages and pony carriages in the nineteenth century, as we the existence of martyrs and miracles in the primitive age? Perhaps miracles and martyrs go together. Now the account which is to follow does indeed relate to miracles, but then it relates to martyrs also.

Another objection which may be more reasonably urged against the narrative is this: that in the fourth century there were many miraculous tales which even Fathers of the Church believed, but which no one of any way of thinking believes now. It will be argued, that because some miracles are alleged which did not really take place, that therefore none which are alleged took place either. But I am disposed to reason just the contrary way. Pretences to revelation make it probable that there is a true Revelation; pretences to miracles make it probable that there are real ones; falsehood is the mockery of truth; false Christs argue a true Christ; a shadow implies a substance. If it be replied that the Scripture miracles are these true miracles, and that it is they, and none other but they, none after them, which suggested the counterfeit; I ask in turn, if so, what becomes of the original objection, that *no* miracles are true, because some are false? If this be so, the Scripture miracles are to be believed as little as those after them; and this is the very plea which infidels have urged. No; it is not reasonable to limit the scope of an argument according to the exigency of our particular conclusions; we have no leave to apply the argument *for* miracles only to the first century, and that *against* miracles only to the fourth. If forgery in some miracles proves forgery in all, this tells against the first as well as against the fourth century; if forgery in some argues truth in others, this avails for the fourth as well as for the first.

And I will add, that even credulousness on other occasions does not necessarily disqualify a person's evidence for a particular alleged miracle; for the sight of one true miracle could not but dispose a man to believe others readily, nay, too readily, that is, would make him what is called credulous.

Now let these remarks be kept in mind while I go on to describe the alleged occurrence which has led to them. I know of no direct objection to it in particular, viewed in itself; the main objections are such antecedent considerations as I have been noticing But if Elisha's bones restored a dead man to life, I know of no antecedent reason why the relics of Gervasius and Protasius should not, as in the instance to be considered, have given sight to the blind.

2.

The circumstances were these:—St. Ambrose, at the juncture of affairs which I have described in the foregoing pages, was proceeding to the dedication of a certain church at Milan, which remains there to this day, with the name of "St. Ambrose the Greater;" and was urged by the people to bury relics of martyrs under the altar, as he had lately done in the case of the Basilica of the Apostles. This was according to the usage of those times, desirous thereby both of honouring those who had braved death for Christ's sake, and of hallowing religious places with the mortal instruments of their triumph. Ambrose in consequence gave orders to open the ground in the church of St. Nabor, as a spot likely to have been the burying-place of martyrs during the heathen persecutions.

Augustine, who was in Milan at the time, alleges that Ambrose was directed in his search by a dream. Ambrose himself is evidently reserved on the subject in his letter to his sister, though he was accustomed to make her his confidant in his ecclesiastical proceedings; he only speaks of his heart having burnt within him in presage of what was to happen. The digging commenced, and in due time two skeletons were discovered, of great size, perfect, and disposed in an orderly way; the head of each, however, separated from the body, and a quantity of blood about. That they were the remains of martyrs, none could reasonably doubt; and their names were ascertained to be Gervasius and Protasius; how, it does not appear, but certainly it was not so alleged on any traditionary information or for any popular object, since they proved to be quite new names to the Church of the day, though some elderly men at length recollected hearing them in former years. Nor is it wonderful that these saints should have been forgotten, considering the number of the Apostolic martyrs, among whom Gervasius and Protasius appear to have a place.

It seems to have been usual in that day to verify the genuineness of relics by bringing some of the *energumeni*, or possessed with devils, to them. Such afflicted persons were present with St. Ambrose during the search; and, before the service for exorcism commenced, one of them gave the well-known signs of horror and distress which were customarily excited by the presence of what had been the tabernacle of divine grace.

The skeletons were raised and transported to the neighbouring church of St. Fausta. The next day, June 18th, on which they were to be conveyed to their destination, a vast concourse of people attended the procession. This was the moment chosen by Divine Providence to give, as it were, signal to His Church, that, though years passed on, He was still what He had been from the beginning, a living and a faithful God, wonder-working as in the lifetime of the Apostles, and true to His word as spoken by His prophets unto a thousand generations. There was in Milan a man of middle age, well known in the place, by name Severus, who, having become blind, had given up his trade, and was now supported by charitable persons. Being told the cause of the shoutings in the streets, he persuaded his guide to lead him to the sacred relics. He came near; he touched the cloth which covered them: and he regained his sight immediately.

This relation deserves our special notice from its distinct miraculousness and its circumstantial character; but numerous other miracles are stated to have followed. Various diseases were cured and demoniacs dispossessed by the touch of the holy bodies or their envelopments.

3.

Now for the evidence on which the whole matter rests. Our witnesses are three: St. Augustine, St. Ambrose, and Paulinus, the secretary of the latter, who after his death addressed a short memoir of his life to the former.

1. St. Augustine, in three separate passages in his works, two of which shall here be quoted, gives his testimony. First, in his City of God, in an enumeration of miracles which had taken place since the Apostles' time. He begins with that which he himself had witnessed in the city of St. Ambrose:—

"The miracle," he says, "which occurred at Milan, while I was there, when a blind man gained sight, was of a kind to come to the knowledge of many, because the city is large, and the Emperor was there at the time, and it was wrought with the witness of a vast multitude, who had come together to the bodies of the martyrs Protasius and Gervasius; which, being at the time concealed and altogether unknown, were discovered on the revelation of a dream to Ambrose the bishop; upon which that blind man was released from his former darkness, and saw the day."—xxii. 8.

And next in his sermon upon the feast-day of the two martyrs:—

"We are celebrating, my brethren, the day on which, by Ambrose the bishop, that man of God, there was discovered, precious in the sight of the Lord, the death of His Saints; of which so great glory of the martyrs, then accruing, even I was a witness. I was there, I was at Milan, I know the miracles which were done, God attesting to the precious death of His Saints; that by those miracles henceforth, not in the Lord's sight only, but in the sight of men also, that death might be precious. A blind man, perfectly well known to the whole city, was restored to sight ; he ran, he caused himself to be brought near, he returned without a guide. We have not yet heard of his death ; perhaps he is still alive. In the very church where their bodies are, he has vowed his whole life to religious service. We rejoiced in his restoration, we left him in service."—*Serm.* 286. *vid.* also 318.

The third passage will be found in the ninth book of St. Augustine's Confessions, and adds to the foregoing extracts the important fact that the miracle was the cause of Justina's relinquishing her persecution of the Catholics.

2. Now let us proceed to the evidence of St. Ambrose, as contained in the sermons which he preached upon the occasion. In the former of the two he speaks as follows of the miracles wrought by the relics :—

"Ye know, nay, ye have yourselves seen, many cleansed from evil spirits, and numbers loosed from their infirmities, on laying their hands on the garment of the saints. Ye see renewed the miracles of the old time, when, through the advent of the Lord Jesus, a fuller grace poured itself upon the earth ; ye see most men healed by the very shadow of the sacred bodies. How many are the napkins which pass to and fro ! what anxiety for garments which are laid upon the most holy relics, and made salutary by their very touch ! It is an object with all to reach even to the extreme border, and he who reaches it will be made whole. Thanks be to Thee, Lord Jesus, for awakening for us at this time the spirits of the holy martyrs, when Thy Church needs greater guardianship. Let all understand the sort of champions I ask for—those who may act as champions, not as assailants. And such have I gained for you, my religious people, such as benefit all, and harm none. Such defenders I solicit, such soldiers I possess, not the world's soldiers, but soldiers of Christ. I fear not that such will give offence ; because the higher is their guardianship, the less exceptionable is it also. Nay, for them even who grudge me the martyrs, do I desire the martyrs' protection. So let them come and see my body-guard ; I own I have such arms about me. 'These put their trust in chariots and these in horses; but we will glory in the name of the Lord our God.'

"Elisæus, as the course of Holy Scripture tells us, when hemmed in by the Syrian army, said to his frightened servant, by way of calming him, 'There are more that are for us than are against us.' And to prove this, he begged that Gehazi's eyes might be opened; upon which the latter saw innumerable hosts of Angels present to the prophet. We, though we cannot see them, yet are sensible of them. Our eyes were held as long as the bodies of the saints lay hid in their graves. The Lord has opened our eyes: we have seen those aids by which we have often been defended. We had not the sight of these, yet we had the possession. And so, as though the Lord said to us in our alarm, 'Behold what martyrs I have given you!' in like manner our eyes are unclosed, and we see the glory of the Lord, manifested, as once in their passion, so now in their power. We have got clear, my brethren, of no slight disgrace; we had patrons, yet we knew it not. We have found this one thing, in which we have the advantage of our forefathers—they lost the knowledge of these holy martyrs, and we have obtained it.

"Bring the victorious victims to the spot where is Christ the sacrifice. But He upon the altar, who suffered for all; they under it, who were redeemed by His passion. I had intended this spot for myself, for it is fitting that where the priest had been used to offer, there he should repose; but I yield the right side to the sacred victims; that spot was due to the martyrs. Therefore let us bury the hallowed relics, and introduce them into a fitting home; and celebrate the whole day with sincere devotion."—*Ep.* 22.

In his latter sermon, preached the following day, he pursues the subject:—

"This your celebration they are jealous of, who are wont to be; and, being jealous of it, they hate the cause of it, and are extravagant enough to deny the merits of those martyrs, whose works the very devils confess. Nor is it wonderful; it commonly happens that unbelievers who deny are less bearable than the devil who confesses. For the devil said, 'Jesus, Son of the living Son, why hast Thou come to torment us before the time?' And, whereas the Jews heard this, yet they were the very men to deny the Son of God. And now ye have heard the evil spirits crying out, and confessing to the martyrs, that they cannot bear their pains, and saying, 'Why are ye come to torment us so heavily?' And the Arians say, 'They are not martyrs, nor can they torment the devil, nor dispossess any one;' while the torments of the evil spirits are evidenced by their own voice, and the benefits of the martyrs by the recovery of the healed, and the tokens of the dispossessed.

"The Arians say, 'These are not real torments of evil spirits, but they are pretended and counterfeit.' I have heard of many things pretended, but no one ever could succeed in feigning himself a devil. How is it we see them in such distress when the hand is laid on them? What room is here for fraud? what suspicion of imposture?

"They deny that the blind received sight; but he does not deny that he was cured. He says, 'I see, who afore saw not.' He says, 'I ceased to be blind,' and he evidences it by the fact. They deny the benefit, who cannot deny the fact. The man is well known; employed as he was, before his affliction, in a public trade, Severus his name, a butcher his business: he had given it up when this misfortune befell him. He refers to the testimony of men whose charities were supporting him; he summons them as evidence of his present visitation, who were witnesses and judges of his blindness. He cries out that, on his touching the hem of the martyrs' garment, which covered the relics, his sight was restored to him. We read in the Gospel, that when the Jews saw the cure of the blind man, they sought the testimony of the parents. Ask others, if you distrust me; ask persons unconnected with him, if you think that his parents would take a side. The obstinacy of these Arians is more hateful than that of the Jews. When the latter doubted, at least they inquired of the parents; these inquire secretly, deny openly, as giving credit to the fact, but denying the author."—*Ibid.*

3. We may corroborate the evidence of those two Fathers with that of Paulinus, who was secretary to St. Ambrose, and wrote his life, about A.D. 411.

"About the same time," he says, "the holy martyrs Protasius and Gervasius revealed themselves to God's priest. They lay in the Basilica, where, at present, are the bodies of the martyrs Nabor and Felix; while, however, the holy martyrs Nabor and Felix had crowds to visit them, as well the names as the graves of the martyrs

Protasius and Gervasius were unknown ; so that all who wished to come to the rails which protected the graves of the martyrs Nabor and Felix, were used to walk on the graves of the others. But when the bodies of the holy martyrs were raised and placed on litters, thereupon many possessions of the devil were detected. Moreover, a blind man, by name Severus, who up to this day performs religious service in the Basilica called Ambrosian, into which the bodies of the martyrs have been translated, when he had touched the garment of the martyrs, forthwith received sight. Moreover, bodies possessed by unclean spirits were restored, and with all blessedness returned home. And by means of these benefits of the martyrs, while the faith of the Catholic Church made increase, by so much did Arian misbelief decline."—§ 14.

4.

Now I want to know what reason is there for stumbling at the above narrative, which will not throw uncertainty upon the very fact that there was such a Bishop as Ambrose, or such an Empress as Justina, or such a heresy as the Arian, or any Church at all in Milan. Let us consider some of the circumstances under which it comes to us.

1. We have the concordant evidence of three distinct witnesses, of whom at least two were on the spot when the alleged miracles were wrought, one writing at the time, another some years afterwards in a distant country. And the third, writing after an interval of twenty-six years, agrees minutely with the evidence of the two former, not adding to the miraculous narrative, as is the manner of those who lose their delicate care for exactness in their admiration of the things and persons of whom they speak.

2. The miracle was wrought in public, on a person well known, on one who continued to live in the place where it was professedly wrought, and who, by devoting himself to the service of the martyrs who were the instru-

ments of his cure, was a continual memorial of the mercy which he professed to have received, and challenged inquiry into it, and refutation if that were possible.

3. Ambrose, one of our informants, publicly appealed, at the time when the occurrence took place, to the general belief, claimed it for the miracle, and that in a sermon which is still extant.

4. He made his statement in the presence of bitter and most powerful enemies, who were much concerned, and very able to expose the fraud, if there was one; who did, as might be expected, deny the hand of God in the matter; but who, for all that appears, did nothing but deny what they could not consistently confess, without ceasing to be what they were.

5. A great and practical impression was made upon the popular mind in consequence of the alleged miracles: or, in the words of an historian, whose very vocation it is to disbelieve them, "Their effect on the minds of the people was rapid and irresistible; and the feeble sovereign of Italy found himself unable to contend with the favourite of heaven."[1]

6. And so powerfully did all this press upon the Court, that, as the last words of this extract intimate, the persecution was given up, and the Catholics left in quiet possession of the churches.

On the whole, then, are we not in the following dilemma? If the miracle did not take place, then St. Ambrose and St. Augustine, men of name, said they had ascertained a fact which they did not ascertain, and said it in the face of enemies, with an appeal to a whole city, and that continued during a quarter of a century. What instrument of refutation shall we devise against a case like this, neither so violently *à priori* as to supersede the testimony

[1] Gibbon, Hist. ch. 27.

of Evangelists, nor so fastidious of evidence as to imperil Tacitus or Cæsar? On the other hand, if the miracle did take place, a certain measure of authority, more or less, surely must thereby attach to St. Ambrose—to his doctrine and his life, to his ecclesiastical principles and proceedings, to the Church itself of the fourth century, of which he is one main pillar. The miracle gives a certain sanction to three things at once, to the Catholic doctrine of the Trinity, to the Church's resistance of the civil power, and to the commemoration of saints and martyrs.

Does it give any sanction to Protestantism and its adherents? shall we accept it or not? shall we retreat, or shall we advance? shall we relapse into scepticism upon all subjects, or sacrifice our deep-rooted prejudices? shall we give up our knowledge of times past altogether, or endure to gain a knowledge which we think we have already—the knowledge of divine truth?

CHAPTER II.

WHAT SAYS VINCENT OF LERINS?

I.

IT is pretty clear that most persons of this day will be disposed to wonder at the earnestness shown by the early bishops of the Church in their defence of the Catholic faith. Athanasius, Hilary, Basil, Gregory, and Ambrose resisted the spread of Arianism at the risk of their lives. Yet their repeated protests and efforts were all about what? The man of the world will answer, "strifes of words, perverse disputings, curious questions, which do not tend to advance what ought to be the one end of all religion, peace and love. This is what comes of insisting on orthodoxy; putting the whole world into a fever!" *Tantum religio potuit*, etc., as the Epicurean poet says.

Such certainly is the phenomenon which we have to contemplate: theirs was a state of mind seldom experienced, and little understood, in this day; however, for that reason, it is at least interesting to the antiquarian, even were it not a sound and Christian state also. The highest end of Church union, to which the mass of educated men now look, is quiet and unanimity; as if the Church were not built upon faith, and truth really the first object of the Christian's efforts, peace but the second. The one idea which statesmen, and lawyers, and journalists, and men of letters have of a clergyman is, that he is by profession "a man of peace:" and if he has occasion to denounce, or to resist, or to protest, a cry is raised, "O how disgraceful in a minister of peace!" The Church is thought invaluable as a promoter of good order and sobriety; but is regarded as nothing more. Far be it from me to seem to disparage what is really one of her high functions; but still a part of her duty will never be tantamount to the whole of it. At present the *beau idéal* of a clergyman in the eyes of many is a "reverend gentleman," who has a large family, and "administers spiritual consolation." Now I make bold to say, that confessorship for the Catholic faith is one part of the duty of Christian ministers, nay, and Christian laymen too. Yet, in this day, if at any time there is any difference in matters of doctrine between Christians, the first and last wish—the one sovereign object—of so-called judicious men, is to hush it up. No matter what the difference is about; *that* is thought so little to the purpose, that your well-judging men will not even take the trouble to inquire what it is. It may be, for what they know, a question of theism or atheism; but they will not admit, whatever it is, that it can be more than secondary to the preservation of a good understanding between Christians. They think, whatever it is, it may safely be postponed for future consideration—that things will right themselves—the one pressing object being to present a bold and extended front to our external enemies, to prevent the outward fabric of the Church from being weakened by dissensions, and insulted by those who witness them. Surely the Church exists, in an especial way, for the sake of the faith committed to her keeping. But our practical men forget there may be remedies worse than the disease; that latent heresy may be worse than a contest of "party;" and, in their treatment of the Church, they fulfil the satirist's well-known line:—

"Propter vitam vivendi perdere causas."

No wonder they do so, when they have been so long accustomed to merge the Church in the nation, and to talk of "Protestantism" in the abstract as synonymous with true religion; to consider that the characteristic merit of our Church is its "tolerance," as they call it, and that its greatest misfortune is the exposure to the world of those antagonistic principles and views which are really at work within it. But talking of exposure, what a scandal it was in St. Peter to exert his apostolical powers on Ananias; and in St. John, to threaten Diotrephes! What an exposure in St. Paul to tell the Corinthians he had "a rod" for them, were they disobedient! One should have thought, indeed, that weapons were committed to the Church for use as well as for show; but the present age apparently holds otherwise, considering that the Church is then most primitive, when it neither cares for the faith itself, nor uses the divinely ordained means by which it is to be guarded. Now, to people who acquiesce in this view, I know well that Ambrose or Augustine has not more of authority than an English non-juror; still, to those who do not acquiesce in it, it may be some little comfort, some encouragement, some satisfaction, to see that they themselves are not the first persons in the world who have felt and judged of religion in that particular way which is now in disrepute.

2.

However, some persons will allow, perhaps, that doctrinal truth ought to be maintained, and that the clergy ought to maintain it; but then they will urge that we should not make the path of truth too narrow; that it is a royal and a broad highway by which we travel heavenward, whereas it has been the one object of theologians, in every age, to encroach upon it, till at length it has become scarcely broad enough for two to walk abreast in. And moreover, it will be objected, that over-exactness was the very fault of the fourth and fifth centuries in particular, which refined upon the doctrines of the Holy Trinity and our Lord's Incarnation, till the way of life became like that razor's edge, which is said in the Koran to be drawn high over the place of punishment, and must be traversed by every one at the end of the world.

Now I cannot possibly deny, however disadvantageous it may be to their reputation, that the Fathers do represent the way of faith as narrow, nay, even as being the more excellent and the more royal for that very narrowness. Such is orthodoxy certainly; but here it is obvious to ask whether this very characteristic of it may not possibly be rather an argument for, than against, its divine origin. Certain it is, that such nicety, as it is called, is not unknown to other religious dispensations, creeds, and covenants, besides that which the primitive Church identified with Christianity. Nor is it a paradox to maintain that the whole system of religion, natural as well as revealed, is full of similar appointments. As to the subject of ethics, even a heathen philosopher tells us, that virtue consists in a mean—that is, in a point between indefinitely-extending extremes; "men being in one way good, and many ways bad." The same principle, again, is seen in the revealed system of spiritual communications; the grant of grace and privilege depending on positive ordinances, simple and definite—on the use of a little water, the utterance of a few words, the imposition of hands, and the like; which, it will perhaps be granted, are really essential to the conveyance of spiritual blessings, yet are confessedly as formal and technical as any creed can be represented to be. In a word, such technicality is involved in the very idea of a *means*, which may even be defined to be a something appointed, at God's inscrutable pleasure, as the necessary condition of something else; and the simple question before us is, merely the *matter of fact*, viz., whether any doctrine *is* set forth by Revelation as necessary to be believed *in order* to salvation? Antecedent difficulty in the question there is none; or rather, the probability is in favour of there being some necessary doctrine, from the analogy of the other parts of religion. The question is simply about the matter of fact.

This analogy is perspicuously expressed in one of the sermons of St. Leo:—"Not only," he says, "in the exercise of virtue and the observance of the commandments, but also in the path of faith, strait and difficult is the way which leads to life; and it requires great pains, and involves great risks, to walk without stumbling along the one footway of sound doctrine, amid the uncertain opinions and the plausible untruths of the unskilful, and to escape all peril of mistake when the toils of error are on every side."—*Serm.* 25.

St. Gregory Nazianzen says the same thing:—"We have bid farewell to contentious deviations of doctrine, and compensations on either side, neither Sabellianizing nor Arianizing. These are the sports of the evil one, who is a bad arbiter of our matters. But we, pacing along the middle and royal way, *in which also the essence of the virtues lies*, in the judgment of the learned, believe in Father, Son, and Holy Ghost."—*Orat.* 32.

On the whole, then, I see nothing very strange either in

orthodoxy lying in what at first sight appears like subtle and minute exactness of doctrine, or in its being our duty to contend even to confessorship for such exactness. Whether it be thus exact, and whether the exactness of Ambrose, Leo, or Gregory be the true and revealed exactness, is quite another question: all I say is, that it is no great difficulty to believe that it may be what they say it is, both as to its truth and as to its importance.

3.

But now supposing the question is asked, are Ambrose, Leo, and Gregory right? and is our Church right in maintaining with them the Athanasian doctrine on those sacred points to which it relates, and condemning those who hold otherwise? what answer is to be given? I answer by asking in turn, supposing any one inquired how we know that Ambrose, Leo, or Gregory was right, and our Church right, in receiving St. Paul's Epistles, what answer we should make? The answer would be, that it is a matter of history that the Apostle wrote those letters which are ascribed to him. And what is meant by its being a matter of history? why, that it has ever been so believed, so declared, so recorded, so acted on, from the first down to this day; that there is no assignable point of time when it was not believed, no assignable point at which the belief was introduced; that the records of past ages fade away and vanish *in* the belief; that in proportion as past ages speak at all, they speak in one way, and only fail to bear a witness, when they fail to have a voice. What stronger testimony can we have of a past fact?

Now evidence such as this have we for the Catholic doctrines which Ambrose, Leo, or Gregory maintained; they have never and nowhere *not* been maintained; or in other words, wherever we know anything positive of ancient times and places, there we are told of these doctrines also. As far as the records of history extend, they include these doctrines as avowed always, everywhere, and by all. This is the great canon of the *Quod semper, quod ubique, quod ab omnibus*, which saves us from the misery of having to find out the truth for ourselves from Scripture on our independent and private judgment. He who gave Scripture, also gave us the interpretation of Scripture; and He gave the one and the other gift in the same way, by the testimony of past ages, as matter of historical knowledge, or as it is sometimes called, by Tradition. We receive the Catholic doctrines as we receive the canon of Scripture, because, as our Article expresses it, "*of their authority*" *there* "*was never any doubt in the Church.*"

We receive them on Catholic Tradition, and therefore they are called Catholic doctrines. And that they are Catholic, is a proof that they are Apostolic; they never could have been universally received in the Church, unless they had had their origin in the origin of the Church, unless they had been made the foundation of the Church by its founders. As the separate successions of bishops in various countries have but one common origin, the Apostles, so what has been handed down through these separate successions comes from that one origin. The Apostolic College is the only point in which all the lines converge, and from which they spring. Private traditions, wandering unconnected traditions, are of no authority, but permanent, recognised, public, definite, intelligible, multiplied, concordant testimonies to one and the same doctrine, bring with them an overwhelming evidence of apostolical origin. We ground the claims of orthodoxy on no powers of reasoning, however great, on the credit of no names, however imposing, but on an external fact on an argument the same as that by which we prove the genuineness and authority of the four gospels. The unanimous tradition of all the churches to certain articles of faith is surely an irresistible evidence, more trustworthy far than that of witnesses to certain facts in a court of law, by how much the testimony of a number is more cogent than the testimony of two or three. That this really is the ground on which the narrow line of orthodoxy was maintained in ancient times, is plain from an inspection of the writings of the very men who maintained it, Ambrose, Leo, and Gregory, or Athanasius and Hilary, and the rest, who set forth its Catholic character in more ways than it is possible here to instance or even explain.

4.

However, in order to give the general reader some idea of the state of the case, I will make some copious extracts from the famous tract of Vincent of Lerins on Heresy, written in A.D. 434, immediately after the third Ecumenical Council, held against Nestorius. The author was originally a layman, and by profession a soldier. In after life he became a monk and took orders. Lerins, the site of his monastery, is one of the small islands off the south coast of France. He first states what the principle is he would maintain, and the circumstances under which he maintains it; and if his principle is reasonable and valuable in itself, so does it come to us with great weight under the circumstances which he tells us led him to his exposition of it:[1]

"Inquiring often," he says, "with great desire and attention, of very many excellent, holy, and learned men, how and by what means I might assuredly, and as it were by some general and ordi-

[1] The Oxford translation of 1837 is used in the following extracts.

nary way, discern the true Catholic faith from false and wicked heresy; to this question I had usually this answer from them all, that whether I or any other desired to find out the fraud of heretics, daily springing up, and to escape their snares, and to continue in a sound faith himself safe and sound, that he ought, by two ways, by God's assistance, to defend and preserve his faith; that is, first, by the authority of the law of God; secondly, by the tradition of the Catholic Church."—*Ch.* 2.

It will be observed he is speaking of the *mode* in which an *individual* is to seek and attain the truth; and it will be observed also, as the revered Bishop Jebb has pointed out, that he is allowing[1] and sanctioning the use of personal inquiry. He proceeds:—

"Here some man, perhaps, may ask, seeing the canon of the Scripture is perfect, and most abundantly of itself sufficient for all things, what need we join unto it the authority of the Church's understanding and interpretation? The reason is this, because the Scripture being of itself so deep and profound, all men do not understand it in one and the same sense, but divers men diversely, this man and that man, this way and that way, expound and interpret the sayings thereof, so that to one's thinking, 'so many men, so many opinions' almost may be gathered out of them: for Novatian expoundeth it one way, Photinus another; Sabellius after this sort, Donatus after that; Arius, Eunomius, Macedonius will have this exposition, Apollinaris and Priscilian will have that; Jovinian, Pelagius, Celestius, gather this sense, and, to conclude, Nestorius findeth out that; and therefore very necessary it is for the avoiding of so great windings and turnings, of errors so various, that the line of expounding the Prophets and Apostles be directed and drawn, according to the rule of the Ecclesiastical and Catholic sense.

"Again, within the Catholic Church itself we are greatly to consider that we hold that which hath been believed *everywhere*,

[1] [He allows of it in the *Absence* at the time of the Church's authoritative declaration concerning the particular question in debate. He would say, "There was no need of any Ecumenical Council to condemn Nestorius; he was condemned by Scripture and tradition already."—1872.]

always, and *of all men :* for that is truly and properly *Catholic* (as the very force and nature of the word doth declare) which comprehendeth all things in general after an universal manner, and that shall we do if we follow *universality*, *antiquity*, *consent.* Universality shall we follow thus, if we profess that one faith to be true which the whole Church throughout the world acknowledgeth and confesseth. Antiquity shall we follow, if we depart not any whit from those senses which it is plain that our holy elders and fathers generally held. Consent shall we likewise follow, if in this very Antiquity itself we hold the definitions and opinions of all, or at any rate almost all, the priests and doctors together."—*Ch.* 2, 3.

It is sometimes said, that what is called orthodoxy or Catholicism is only the opinion of one or two Fathers—fallible men, however able they might be, or persuasive—who created a theology, and imposed it on their generation, and thereby superseded Scriptural truth and the real gospel. Let us see how Vincent treats such individual teachers, however highly gifted. He is speaking in the opening sentence of the Judaizers of the time of St. Paul :—

"When, therefore, such kind of men, wandering up and down through provinces and cities to set their errors to sale, came also unto the Galatians, and these, after they had heard them, were delighted with the filthy drugs of heretical novelty, loathing the truth, and casting up again the heavenly manna of the Apostolic and Catholic doctrine : the authority of his Apostolic office so puts itself forth as to decree very severely in this sort. 'But although (quoth he) we or an Angel from heaven evangelize unto you beside that which we have evangelized, be he Anathema.'[1] What meaneth this that he saith, 'But although we ?' why did he not rather say, 'But although I ?' that is to say, Although Peter, although Andrew, although John, yea, finally, although the whole company of the Apostles, evangelize unto you otherwise than we have evangelized, be he accursed. A terrible censure, in that for maintaining the possession of the first faith, he spared not himself, nor any other of the Apostles ! But this is a small matter : 'Although an Angel from

[1] Gal. i. 8.

heaven (quoth he) evangelize unto you, beside that which I have evangelized, be he Anathema,' he was not contented for keeping the faith once delivered to make mention of man's weak nature, unless also he included those excellent creatures the Angels. . . But peradventure he uttered those words slightly, and cast them forth rather of human affection than decreed them by divine direction. God forbid : for it followeth, and that urged with great earnestness of repeated inculcation, 'As I have foretold you (quoth he), and now again I tell you, If anybody evangelize unto you beside that which you have received, be he Anathema.' He said not, If any man preach unto you beside that which you have received, let him be blessed, let him be commended, let him be received, but let him be *Anathema*, that is, separated, thrust out, excluded, lest the cruel infection of one sheep with his poisoned company corrupt the sound flock of Christ."—*Ch.* 12 and 13.

5.

Here, then, is a point of doctrine which must be carefully insisted on. The Fathers are primarily to be considered as *witnesses*, not as *authorities*. They are witnesses of an existing state of things, and their treatises are, as it were, *histories*,—teaching us, in the first instance, matters of fact, not of opinion. Whatever they themselves might be, whether deeply or poorly taught in Christian faith and love, they speak, not their own thoughts, but the received views of their respective ages. The especial value of their works lies in their opening upon us a state of the Church which else we should have no notion of. We read in their writings a great number of high and glorious principles and acts, and our first thought thereupon is, "All this must have had an existence somewhere or other in those times. These very men, indeed, may be merely speaking by rote, and not understand what they say; but it matters not to the profit of their writings what they were themselves." It matters not to the profit of their writings, nor again to the authority resulting from them; for the *times* in which they wrote of course *are* of authority, though the Fathers themselves may have none. Tertullian or Eusebius may be nothing more than bare witnesses; yet so much as this they have a claim to be considered.

This is even the strict Protestant view. We are not obliged to take the Fathers as *authorities*, only as *witnesses*. Charity, I suppose, and piety will prompt the Christian student to go further, and to believe that men who laboured so unremittingly, and suffered so severely in the cause of the Gospel, really did possess some little portion of that earnest love of the truth which they professed, and were enlightened by that influence for which they prayed; but I am stating the strict Protestant doctrine, the great polemical principle ever to be borne in mind, that the Fathers are to be adduced in controversy merely as testimonies to an existing state of things, not as authorities. At the same time, no candid Protestant will be loth to admit, that the state of things to which they bear witness, *is*, as I have already said, a most grave and conclusive authority in guiding us in those particulars of our duty about which Scripture is silent; succeeding, as it does, so very close upon the age of the Apostles.

Thus much I claim of consistent Protestants, and thus much I grant to them. Gregory and the rest may have been but nominal Christians. Athanasius himself may have been very dark in all points of doctrine, in spite of his twenty years' exile and his innumerable perils by sea and land; the noble Ambrose, a high and dry churchman; and Basil, a mere monk. I do not dispute these points; though I claim "the right of private judgment," so far as to have my own very definite opinion in the matter, which I keep to myself.

6.

Such being the plain teaching of the Fathers, and such the duty of following it, Vincentius proceeds to speak of the misery of doubting and change:—

"Which being so, he is a true and genuine Catholic that loveth the truth of God, the Church, the body of Christ; that preferreth nothing before the religion of God; nothing before the Catholic faith; not any man's authority, not love, not wit, not eloquence, not philosophy; but contemning all these things, and in faith abiding fixed and stable, whatsoever he knoweth the Catholic Church universally in old times to have holden, that only he purposeth with himself to hold and believe; but whatsoever doctrine, new and not before heard of, such an one shall perceive to be afterwards brought in of some one man, beside all or contrary to all the saints, let him know that doctrine doth not pertain to religion, but rather to temptation, especially being instructed with the sayings of the blessed Apostle St. Paul. For this is that which he writeth in his first Epistle to the Corinthians: 'There must (quoth he) be heresies also, that they which are approved may be made manifest among you.' . . .

"O the miserable state of [waverers]! with what seas of cares, with what storms, are they tossed! for now at one time, as the wind driveth them, they are carried away headlong in error; at another time, coming again to themselves, they are beaten back like contrary waves; sometime with rash presumption they allow such things as seem uncertain, at another time of pusillanimity they are in fear even about those things which are certain; doubtful which way to take, which way to return, what to desire, what to avoid, what to hold, what to let go; which misery and affliction of a wavering and unsettled heart, were they wise, is as a medicine of God's mercy towards them.

"Which being so, oftentimes calling to mind and remembering the selfsame thing, I cannot sufficiently marvel at the great madness of some men, at so great impiety of their blinded hearts, lastly, at so great a licentious desire of error, that they be not content with the rule of faith once delivered us, and received from our ancestors, but do every day search and seek for new doctrine, ever desirous to add to, to change, and to take away something from, religion; as though that were not the doctrine of God, which it is enough to have once revealed, but rather man's institution, which cannot but by continual amendment (or rather correction) be perfected."—*Ch.* 25, 26.

7.

Then he takes a text, and handles it as a modern preacher might do. His text is this:—

"O Timothy, keep the *depositum*, avoiding the profane novelties of words, and oppositions of falsely-called knowledge, which certain professing have erred about the faith."

He dwells successively upon *Timothy*, on the *deposit*, on *avoiding*, on *profane*, and on *novelties*.

First, *Timothy* and the "*deposit:*"—

"Who at this day is Timothy, but either generally the whole Church, or especially the whole body of prelates, who ought either themselves to have a sound knowledge of divine religion, or who ought to infuse it into others? What is meant by *keep the deposit?* Keep it (quoth he) for fear of thieves, for danger of enemies, lest when men be asleep, they oversow cockle among that good seed of wheat, which the Son of man hath sowed in His field. 'Keep (quoth he) the deposit.' What is meant by this deposit? that is, that which is committed to thee, not that which is invented of thee; that which thou hast received, not that which thou hast devised; a thing not of wit, but of learning; not of private assumption, but of public tradition; a thing brought to thee, not brought forth of thee; wherein thou must not be an author, but a keeper; not a beginner, but a follower; not a leader, but an observer. Keep the deposit. Preserve the talent of the Catholic faith safe and undiminished; that which is committed to thee, let that remain with thee, and that deliver. Thou hast received gold, render then gold; I will not have one thing for another; do not for gold render either impudently lead, or craftily brass; I will, not the show, but the very nature of gold itself. O Timothy, O priest, O teacher, O doctor, if God's gift hath made thee meet and sufficient by thy wit, exercise, and learning, be the Beseleel of the spiritual tabernacle, engrave the precious stones of God's doctrine, faithfully set them, wisely adorn them, give them brightness, give them grace, give them beauty. That which men before believed obscurely, let them by thy exposition understand more clearly. Let posterity rejoice for coming to the understanding of that by thy means, which antiquity without that understanding had in veneration. Yet for all this, in such sort deliver the same things which thou hast learned, that albeit thou teachest after a new manner yet thou never teach new things."

Next, "*avoiding*:"—

"'O Timothy (quoth he), keep the deposit, avoid profane novelties of words.' Avoid (quoth he) as a viper, as a scorpion, as a basilisk, lest they infect thee not only by touching, but also with their very eyes and breath. What is meant by *avoid?*[1] that is, not so much as to eat with any such. What importeth this *avoid?* 'If any man (quoth he) come unto you, and bring not this doctrine,'[2] what doctrine but the Catholic and universal, and that which, with incorrupt tradition of the truth, hath continued one and the selfsame, through all successions of times, and that which shall continue for ever and ever? What then? 'Receive him not (quoth he) into the house, nor say God speed; for he that saith unto him God speed, communicateth with his wicked works.'"

Then, "*profane*:"—

"'Profane novelties of words' (quoth he); what is *profane?* Those which have no holiness in them, nought of religion, wholly external to the sanctuary of the Church, which is the temple of God. 'Profane novelties of words (quoth he), of words, that is, novelties of doctrines, novelties of things, novelties of opinions, contrary to old usage, contrary to antiquity, which if we receive, of necessity the faith of our blessed ancestors, either all, or a great part of it, must be overthrown; the faithful people of all ages and times, all holy saints, all the chaste, all the continent, all the virgins, all the clergy, the deacons, the priests, so many thousands of confessors, so great armies of martyrs, so many famous and populous cities and commonwealths, so many islands, provinces, kings, tribes, kingdoms, nations; to conclude, almost now the whole world, incorporated by the Catholic faith to Christ their Head, must needs

1 1 Cor. v. 11. 2 2 John 10, 11.

be said, so many hundreds of years, to have been ignorant, to have erred, to have blasphemed, to have believed they knew not what."

Lastly, "*novelties*:"—

"'Avoid (quoth he) profane *novelties* of words,' to receive and follow which was never the custom of Catholics, but always of heretics. And, to say truth, what heresy hath ever burst forth, but under the name of some certain man, in some certain place, and at some certain time? Who ever set up any heresy, but first divided himself from the consent of the universality and antiquity of the Catholic Church? Which to be true, examples do plainly prove. For who ever before that profane Pelagius presumed so much of man's free will, that he thought not the grace of God necessary to aid it in every particular good act? Who ever before his monstrous disciple Celestius denied all mankind to be bound with the guilt of Adam's transgression? Who ever before sacrilegious Arius durst rend in pieces the Unity of Trinity? Who ever before wicked Sabellius durst confound the Trinity of Unity? Who ever before cruel Novatian affirmed God to be merciless, in that He had rather the death of a sinner than that he should return and live? Who ever before Simon Magus, durst affirm that God our Creator was the Author of evil, that is, of our wickedness, impieties, and crimes; because God (as he said) so with His own hands made man's very nature, that by a certain proper motion and impulse of an enforced will, it can do nothing else, desire nothing else, but to sin. Such examples are infinite, which for brevity-sake I omit, by all which, notwithstanding, it appeareth plainly and clearly enough, that it is, as it were, a custom and law in all heresies, ever to take great pleasure in profane novelties, to loath the decrees of our forefathers, and to make shipwreck of faith, by oppositions of falsely-called knowledge; contrariwise that this is usually proper to all Catholics, to keep those things which the holy Fathers have left, and committed to their charge, to condemn profane novelties, and, as the Apostle hath said, and again forewarned, 'if any man shall preach otherwise than that which is received,' to anathematize him."—*Ch.* 27—34.

From these extracts, which are but specimens of the whole Tract, I come to the conclusion that Vincent was a very sorry Protestant.

CHAPTER III.

WHAT SAYS THE HISTORY OF APOLLINARIS?

IN the judgment of the early Church, the path of doctrinal truth is narrow; but, in the judgment of the world in all ages, it is so broad as to be no path at all. This I have said above; also, that the maintenance of the faith is considered by the world to be a strife of words, perverse disputings, curious questionings, and unprofitable technicality, though by the Fathers it is considered necessary to salvation. What they call heresy, the man of the world thinks just as true as what they call orthodoxy, and only then wrong when pertinaciously insisted on by its advocates, as the early Fathers insisted on orthodoxy. Now do, or do not, Protestants here take part with the world in disliking, in abjuring doctrinal propositions and articles, such as the early Church fought for? Certainly they do. Well, then, if they thus differ from the Church of the Fathers, how can they fancy that the early Church was Protestant?

In the Treatise I have been quoting, Vincent gives us various instances of heresiarchs, and tells us what he thinks about them. Among others, he speaks of Apollinaris and his fall; nor can we have a better instance than that of Apollinaris of the grave distress and deep commiseration with which the early Fathers regarded those whom the present Protestant world thinks very good kind of men, only fanciful and speculative, with some twist or hobby of their own. Apollinaris, better than any one else, will make us understand what was thought of the guilt of heresy in times which came next to the Apostolic, because the man was so great, and his characteristic heresy was so small. The charges against Origen have a manifest breadth and width to support them; Nestorius, on the other hand, had no high personal merits to speak for him; but Apollinaris, after a life of laborious service in the cause of religion, did but suffer himself to teach that the Divine Intelligence in our Lord superseded the necessity of His having any other, any human intellect; and for this apparently small error, he was condemned. Of course it was not small really; for one error leads to another, and did eventually in his case; but to all appearance it was small, yet it was promptly and sternly denounced and branded by East and West; would it be so ruthlessly smitten by Protestants now?

A brief sketch of his history, and of the conduct of the Church towards him, may not be out of place in the experiments I am making with a view of determining the relation in which modern Protestantism stands towards primitive Christianity.

I.

His father, who bore the same name, was a native of Alexandria, by profession a grammarian or schoolmaster; who, passing from Berytus to the Syrian Laodicea, married and settled there, and eventually rose to the presbyterate in the Church of that city. Apollinaris, the son, had been born there in the early part of the fourth century, and was educated for the profession of rhetoric. After a season of suspense, as to the ultimate destination of his talents, he resolved on dedicating them to the service of the Church; and, after being admitted into reader's orders, he began to distinguish himself by his opposition to philosophical infidelity. His work against Porphyry, the most valuable and elaborate of his writings, was extended to as many as thirty books. During the reign of Julian, when the Christian schools were shut up, and the Christian youth were debarred from the use of the classics, the two Apollinares, father and son, exerted themselves to supply the inconvenience thence resulting from their own resources. They wrote heroical pieces, odes, tragedies, and dialogues, after the style of Homer and Plato, and other standard authors, upon Christian subjects; and the younger, who is the subject of this Chapter, wrote and dedicated to Julian a refutation of Paganism, on grounds of reason.

Nor did he confine himself to the mere external defence of the Gospel, or the preparatory training of its disciples. His expositions on Scripture were the most numerous of his works; he especially excelled in eliciting and illustrating its sacred meaning, and he had sufficient acquaintance with the Hebrew to enable him to translate or comment on the original text. There was scarcely a controversy of the age, prolific as it was in heresies, into which he did not enter. He wrote against the Arians, Eunomians, Macedonians, and Manichees; against Origen and Marcellus; and in defence of the Millenarians. Portions of these doctrinal writings are still extant, and display a vigour and elegance of style not inferior to any writer of his day.

Such a man seemed to be raised up providentially for the Church's defence in an evil day; and for awhile he might be said resolutely and nobly to fulfil his divinely appointed destiny. The Church of Laodicea, with the other cities of Syria, was at the time in Arian possession; when the great Athanasius passed through on his return to Egypt, after his second exile (A.D. 348), Apollinaris communicated with him, and was in consequence put out of the Church by the bishop in possession. On the death of Constantius (A.D. 361), the Catholic cause prevailed; and Apollinaris was consecrated to that see, or to that in Asia Minor which bears the same name.

2.

Such was the station, such the reputation of Apollinaris, at the date of the Council thereupon held at Alexandria, A.D. 362, for settling the disorders of the Church; and yet, in the proceedings of this celebrated assembly, the first intimation occurs of the existence of that doctrinal error by which he has been since known in history, though it is not there connected with his name. The troubles under Julian succeeded, and diverted the minds of all parties to other objects. The infant heresy slept till about the year 369; when it gives us evidence of its existence in the appearance of a number of persons, scattered about Syria and Greece, who professed it in one form or other, and by the solemn meeting of a Council in the former country, in which its distinctive tenets were condemned. We find that even at this date it had run into those logical consequences which make even a little error a great one; still the name of Apollinaris is not connected with them.

The Council, as I have said, was held in Syria, but the heresy which occasioned it had already, it seems, extended into Greece; for a communication, which the there assembled bishops addressed to Athanasius on the subject, elicited from him a letter, still extant, addressed to Epictetus, bishop of Corinth, who had also written to him upon it. This letter, whether from tenderness to Apollinaris, or from difficulty in bringing the heresy home to him, still does not mention his name. Another work written by Athanasius against the heresy, at the very end of his life, with the keenness and richness of thought which distinguish his writings generally, is equally silent; as are two letters to friends about the same date, which touch more or less on the theological points in question. All these treatises seem to be forced from the writer, and are characterized by considerable energy of expression: as if the Catholics addressed were really perplexed with the novel statements of doctrine, and doubtful how Athanasius would meet them, or at least required his authority before pronouncing upon them; and, on the other hand, as if Athanasius himself were fearful of conniving at them, whatever private reasons he might have for wishing to pass them over. Yet there is nothing in the history or documents of the times to lead one to suppose that more than a general suspicion attached to Apollinaris; and, if we may believe his own statement, Athanasius died in persuasion of his orthodoxy. A letter is extant, written by Apollinaris on this subject, in which he speaks of the kind intercourse he had with the Patriarch of Alexandria, and of their agreement in faith, as acknowledged by Athanasius himself. He claims him as his master, and at the same time slightly hints that there had been points to settle between them, in which he himself had given way. In another, written to an Egyptian bishop, he seems to refer to the very epistle to Epictetus noticed above, expressing his approbation of it. It is known, moreover, that Athanasius gave the usual letters of introduction to Timotheus, Apollinaris's intimate friend, and afterwards the most extravagant teacher of his sect, on his going to the Western Bishops, and that, on the ground of his controversial talents against the Arians.

Athanasius died in A.D. 371 or 373; and that bereavement of the Church was followed, among its calamities, by the open avowal of heresy on the part of Apollinaris. In a letter already referred to, he claims Athanasius as agreeing with him, and then proceeds to profess one of the very tenets against which Athanasius had written. In saying this, I have no intention of accusing so considerable a man of that disingenuousness which is almost the characteristic mark of heresy. It was natural that Athanasius should have exercised an influence over his mind; and it was as natural that, when his fellow-champion was taken to his rest, he should have found himself able to breathe more freely, yet have been unwilling to own it. While indulging in the speculations of a private judgment, he might still endeavour to persuade himself that he was not outstepping the teaching of the Catholic Church. On the other hand, it appears that the ecclesiastical authorities of the day, even when he professed his heresy, were for awhile incredulous about the fact, from their recollection of his former services and his tried orthodoxy, and from the hope that he was but carried on into verbal extravagances by his opposition to Arianism. Thus they were as unwilling to impute to him heresy, as he to confess it. Nay, even when he had lost shame, attacked the Catholics with violence, and formed his disciples into a sect, not even then was he himself publicly animadverted on, though his creed was anathematized. His first condemnation was at Rome, several years after Athanasius's death, in company with Timotheus, his disciple. In the records of the General Council of Constantinople, several years later, his sect is mentioned as existing, with directions how to receive back into the Church those who applied for reconciliation. He outlived this Council about ten years; his sect lasted only twenty years beyond him; but in that short time it had split into three distinct denominations, of various degrees of heterodoxy, and is said to have fallen more or less into the errors of Judaism.

3.

If this is a faithful account of the conduct of the Church towards Apollinaris, no one can accuse its rulers of treating him with haste or harshness; still they accompanied their tenderness towards him personally with a conscientious observance of their duties to the Catholic Faith, to which our Protestants are simply dead. Who now in England, except very high churchmen, would dream of putting a man out of the Church for what would be called a mere speculative or metaphysical opinion? Why could not Apollinaris be a "spiritual man," have "a justifying faith," "apprehend" our Lord's merits, have "a personal interest in redemption," be in possession of "experimental religion," and be able to recount his "experiences," though he had some vagaries of his own about the nature of our Lord's soul? But such ideas did not approve themselves to Christians of the fourth century, who followed up the anathemas of Holy Church with their own hearty adhesion to them. Epiphanius speaks thus mournfully:—

"That aged and venerable man, who was ever so singularly dear to us, and to the holy Father, Athanasius, of blessed memory, and to all orthodox men, Apollinaris, of Laodicea, he it was who originated and propagated this doctrine. And at first, when we were assured of it by some of his disciples, we disbelieved that such a man could admit such an error into his path, and patiently waited in hope, till we might ascertain the state of the case. For we argued that his youths, who came to us, not entering into the profound views of so learned and clear-minded a master, had invented these statements of themselves, not gained them from him. For there were many points in which those who came to us were at variance with each other : some of them ventured to say that Christ had brought down His body from above (and this strange theory, admitted into the mind, developed itself into worse notions) ; others of them denied that Christ had taken a soul ; and some ventured to say that Christ's body was consubstantial with the Godhead, and thereby caused great confusion in the East." *Hær.* lxxvii. 2.

He proceeds afterwards :—

"Full of distress became our life at that time, that between brethren so exemplary as the forementioned, a quarrel should at all have arisen, that the enemy of man might work divisions among us. And great, my brethren, is the mischief done to the mind from such a cause. For were no question ever raised on the subject, the matter would be most simple (for what gain has accrued to the world from such novel doctrine, or what benefit to the Church? rather has it not been an injury, as causing hatred and dissension?) : but when the question was raised, it became formidable ; it did not tend to good ; for whether a man disallows this particular point, or even the slightest, still it is a denial. For we must not, even in a trivial matter, turn aside from the path of truth. No one of the ancients ever maintained it—prophet, or apostle, or evangelist, or commentator—down to these our times, when this so perplexing doctrine proceeded from that most learned man aforesaid. His was a mind of no common cultivation ; first in the preliminaries of literature in Greek education, then as a master of dialectics and argumentation. Moreover, he was most grave in his whole life, and reckoned among the very first of those who ever deserved the love of the orthodox, and so continued till his maintenance of this doctrine. Nay, he had undergone banishment for not submitting to the Arians ;—but why enlarge on it? It afflicted us much, and gave us a sorrowful time, as is the wont of our enemy."—*Ibid.* 24.

St. Basil once got into trouble from a supposed intimacy with Apollinaris. He had written one letter to him on an indifferent matter, in 356, when he himself was as yet a layman, and Apollinaris orthodox and scarcely in orders. This was magnified by his opponent Eustathius into a correspondence and intercommunion between the archbishop and heresiarch. As in reality Basil knew very little even of his works, the description which the following passages give is valuable, as being, in fact, a sort of popular opinion about Apollinaris, more than an individual judgment. Basil wrote the former of the two in defence of himself; in the latter, other errors of Apollinaris are mentioned, besides those to which I have had occasion to allude, for, as I have said, errors seldom are found single.

"For myself," says Basil, "I never indeed considered Apollinaris as an enemy; nay, there are respects in which I reverence him; however, I did not so connect myself with him as to make myself answerable for his alleged faults, considering, too, that I have a complaint of my own against him, on reading some of his compositions. I hear, indeed, that he is become the most copious of all writers; yet I have fallen in with but few of his works, for I have not leisure to search into such, and besides, I do not easily form the acquaintance of recent writers, being hindered by bodily health from continuing even the study of inspired Scripture laboriously, and as is fitting."—*Ep.* 244, § 3.

The other passage runs thus:—

"After Eustathius comes Apollinaris; he, too, no slight disturber of the Church; for, having a facility in writing and a tongue which served him on every subject, he has filled the world with his compositions, despising the warning, 'Beware of making many books,' because in the many are many faults. For how is it possible, in much speaking, to escape sin?"—*Ep.* 263, § 4.

And then he goes on to mention some of the various gross errors, to which by that time he seemed to be committed.

Lastly, let us hear Vincent of Lerins about him :—

"Great was the heat and great the perplexity which Apollinaris created in the minds of his auditory, when the authority of the Church drew them one way, and the influence of their teacher drew them the other, so that, wavering and hesitating between the two, they could not decide which was to be chosen. You will say, he ought at once to have been put aside ; yes, but he was so great a man, that his word carried with it an extraordinary credence. Who indeed was his superior in acumen, in long practice, in view of doctrine? As to the number of his volumes against heresies, I will but mention as a specimen of them that great and noble work of his against Porphyry, in not less than thirty books, with its vast collection of arguments. He would have been among the master-builders of the Church, had not the profane lust of heretical curiosity incited him to strike out something new, to pollute withal his labours throughout with the taint of leprosy, so that his teaching was rather a temptation to the Church than an edification."—*Ch.* 16.

It is a solemn and pregnant fact, that two of the most zealous and forward of Athanasius's companions in the good fight against Arianism, Marcellus and Apollinaris, fell away into heresies of their own ; nor did the Church spare them, for all their past services. "Let him that thinketh he standeth, take heed lest he fall"

"Alas, my brother ! round thy tomb,
In sorrow kneeling, and in fear,
We read the pastor's doom,
Who speaks and will not hear.

"The gray-haired saint may fail at last,
The surest guide a wanderer prove ;
Death only binds us fast
To the bright shore of love."

CHAPTER IV.

AND WHAT SAY JOVINIAN AND HIS COMPANIONS?

I.

VINCENTIUS wrote in the early part of the fifth century, that is, three good centuries and more after the death of St. John; accordingly, we sometimes hear it said that, true though it be, that the Catholic system, as we Anglicans maintain it, existed at that time, nevertheless it was a system quite foreign to the pure Gospel, though introduced at a very early age; a system of Pagan or Jewish origin, which crept in unawares, and was established on the ruins of the Apostolic faith by the episcopal confederation, which mainly depended on it for its own maintenance. In other words, it is considered by some persons to be a system of priestcraft, destructive of Christian liberty.

Now, it is no paradox to say that *this* would be a sufficient answer to such a speculation, were there no other, viz., that no answer *can* be made to it. I say, supposing it could not be answered at all, that fact would be a fair answer. All discussion must have data to go upon; without data, neither one party can dispute nor the other. If I maintained there were negroes in the moon, I should like to know how these same philosophers would answer me. Of course they would not attempt it: they would confess they had no grounds for denying it, only they would add, that I had no grounds for asserting it. They would not prove that I was wrong, but call upon me to prove that I was right. They would consider such a mode of talking idle and childish, and unworthy the consideration of a serious man ; else, there would be no end of speculation, no hope of certainty and unanimity in anything. Is a man to be allowed to say what he will, and bring no reasons for it ? Even if his hypothesis fitted into the facts of the case, still it would be but an hypothesis, and might be met, perhaps, in the course of time, by another hypothesis, presenting as satisfactory a solution of them. But if it would not be necessarily true, though it were adequate, much less is it entitled to consideration before it is proved to be adequate—before it is actually reconciled with the facts of the case ; and when another hypothesis has, from the beginning, been in the possession of the field. From the first it has been believed that the Catholic system is Apostolic ; convincing reasons must be brought against this belief, and in favour of another, before that other is to be preferred to it.

Now the new and gratuitous hypothesis in question does not appear, when examined, even to harmonize with the facts of the case. One mode of dealing with it is this :—Take a large view of the faith of Christians during the centuries before Constantine established their religion. Is there any family likeness in it to Protestantism ? Look at it, as existing during that period in different countries, and is it not one and the same, and a reiteration of itself, as well as singularly unlike Reformed Christianity? Hermas with his visions, Ignatius with his dogmatism, Irenæus with his praise of tradition and of the Roman See, Clement with his allegory and mysticism, Cyprian with his "Out of the Church is no salvation," and Methodius wlth his praise of Virginity, all of thsm writers between the first and fourth centuries, and witnesses of the faith of Rome, Africa, Gaul, Asia Minor, Syria, and Egypt, certainly do not represent the opinions of Luther and Calvin. They stretch over the whole of Christendom; they are consistent with each other; they coalesce into one religion; but it is not the religion of the Reformation. When we ask, "Where was your Church before Luther?" Protestants answer, "Where were you this morning before you washed your face?" But, if Protestants can clean themselves into the likeness of Cyprian or Irenæus, they must scrub very hard, and have well-nigh learned the art of washing the blackamoor white.

2

If the Church system be not Apostolic, it must, some time or other, have been introduced, and then comes the question, when? We maintain that the known circumstances of the previous history are such as to preclude the possibility of any time being assigned, ever so close upon the Apostles, at which the Church system did not exist. Not only cannot a time be shown when the free-and-easy system now in fashion did generally exist, but no time can be shown in which it can be colourably maintained that the Church system was brought in. It will be said, of course, that the Church system was gradually introduced. I do not say there have never been introductions of any kind; but let us see what they amount to here. Select for yourself your doctrine, or your ordinance, which you say was introduced, and try to give the history of its introduction. Hypothetical that history will be, of course; but we will not scruple at that;—we will only ask one thing, that it should cut clean between the real facts of the case, though it bring none in its favour; but it will not be able to do even this. The rise of the doctrine of the Holy Trinity, of the usage of baptizing infants, of the eucharistic offering, of the episcopal prerogatives, do what one will, can hardly be made short of Apostolical times. This is not the place to prove all this; but so fully is it felt to be so, by those who are determined not to admit these portions of Catholicism, that in their despair of drawing the line between the first and following centuries, they make up their minds to intrude into the first, and boldly pursue their supposed error into the very presence of some Apostle or Evangelist. Thus St. John is sometimes made the voluntary or involuntary originator of some portions of our creed. Dr. Priestley, I believe, conjectures that his amanuensis played him false, as regards his teaching upon the sacred doctrine which that philosopher opposed. Others take exceptions to St. Luke, because he tells us of the "handkerchiefs, or aprons," which "were brought from St. Paul's body" for the cure of diseases. Others have gone a step further, and have said, "Not Paul, but Jesus." Infidel, Socinian, and Protestant, agree in assailing the Apostles, rather than submitting to the Church.

3.

Let our Protestant friends go to what quarter of Christendom they will, let them hunt among heretics or schismatics, into Gnosticism outside the Church, or Arianism within it, still they will find no hint or vestige anywhere of that system which they are now pleased to call Scriptural. Granting that Catholicism be a corruption, is it possible that it should be a corruption springing up everywhere at once? Is it conceivable that at least no opponent should have retained any remnant of the system it supplanted?—that no tradition of primitive purity should remain in any part of Christendom ?—that no protest, or controversy, should have been raised, as a monument against the victorious error? This argument, conclusive against modern Socinianism, is still more cogent and striking when directed against Puritanism. At least, there *were* divines in those early days who denied the sacred doctrine which Socinianism also disowns, though commonly they did not profess to do so on authority of tradition ; but who ever heard of Erastians, Supralapsarians, Independents, Sacramentarians, and the like, before the sixteenth and seventeenth centuries ? It would be too bold to go to prove a negative : I can only say that I do not know in what quarter to search for the representatives, in the early Church, of that "Bible religion," as it is called, which is now so much in favour. At first sight, one is tempted to say that all errors come over and over again ; that this and that notion now in vogue has been refuted in times past. This is indeed a general truth—nay, for what I know, these same bold speculatists will bring it even as an argument for their not being in error, that Antiquity says nothing at all, good or bad, about their opinions. I cannot answer for the extent to which they will throw the *onus probandi* on us ; but I protest—be it for us, or be it against us—I cannot find this very religion of theirs in ancient times, whether in friend or foe, Jew or Pagan, Montanist or Novatian ; though I find surely enough, and in plenty, the general characteristics, which are conspicuous in their philosophy, of self-will, eccentricity, and love of paradox.

So far from it, that if we wish to find the rudiments of the Catholic system clearly laid down in writing, those who are accounted least orthodox will prove as liberal in their information about it as the strictest Churchman

We can endure even the heretics better than our opponents can endure the Apostles. Tertullian, though a Montanist, gives no sort of encouragement to the so-called Bible Christians of this day; rather he would be the object of their decided abhorrence and disgust. Origen is not a whit more of a Protestant, though he, if any, ought, from the circumstances of his history, to be a witness against us. It is averred that the alleged revolution of doctrine and ritual was introduced by the influence of the episcopal system; well, here is a victim of episcopacy, brought forward by our opponents as such. Here is a man who was persecuted by his bishop, and driven out of his country; and whose name after his death has been dishonourably mentioned, both by Councils and Fathers. He surely was not in the episcopal conspiracy, at least; and perchance may give the latitudinarian, the anabaptist, the Erastian, and the utilitarian, some countenance. Far from it; he is as high and as keen, as removed from softness and mawkishness, as ascetic and as reverential, as any bishop among them. He is as superstitious (as men now talk), as fanatical, as formal, as Athanasius or Augustine. Certainly, there seems something providential in the place which Origen holds in the early Church, considering the direction which theories about it are now taking; and much might be said on that subject.

Take another instance:—There was, in the fourth century, a party of divines who were ecclesiastically opposed to the line of theologians, whose principles had been, and were afterwards, dominant in the Church, such as Athanasius, Jerome, and Epiphanius; I mean, for instance, Eusebius, Cyril of Jerusalem, and others who were more or less connected with the Semi-Arians. If, then, we see that in all points, as regards the sacraments and sacramentals, the Church and its ministers, the form of worship, and other religious duties of Christians, Eusebius and Cyril agree entirely with the most orthodox of their contemporaries, with those by party and country most separated from them, we have a proof that that system, whatever it turns out to be, was received before their time—*i.e.* before the establishment of Christianity under Constantine; in other words, that we must look for the gradual corruption of the Church, if it is to be found, not when wealth pampered it, and power and peace brought its distant portions together, but while it was yet poor, humble, and persecuted, in those times which are commonly considered pure and primitive. Again, the genius of Arianism, as a party and a doctrine, was to discard antiquity and mystery; that is, to resist and expose what is commonly called priestcraft. In proportion, then, as Cyril and Eusebius partook of that spirit, so far would they be in their own cast of mind indisposed to the Catholic system, both considered in itself and as being imposed on them.

Now, have the writers in question any leaning or tenderness for the theology of Luther and Calvin? rather they are as unconscious of its existence as of modern chemistry or astronomy. That faith is a closing with divine mercy, not a submission to a divine announcement, that justification and sanctification are distinct, that good works do not benefit the Christian, that the Church is not Christ's ordinance and instrument, and that heresy and dissent are not necessarily and intrinsically evil: notions such as these they do not oppose, simply because to all appearance they never heard of them. To take a single passage, which first occurs, in which Eusebius, one of the theologians in question, gives us his notion of the Catholic Church:—

"These attempts," he says, speaking of the arts of the enemy, "did not long avail him, Truth ever consolidating itself, and, as time went on, shining into broader day. For while the devices of adversaries were extinguished at once, confuted by their very activity,—one heresy after another presenting its own novelty, the former specimens ever dissolving and wasting variously in manifold and multiform shapes,—the brightness of the Catholic and only true Church went forward increasing and enlarging, yet ever in the same things and in the same way, beaming on the whole race of Greeks and barbarians with the awfulness, and simplicity, and nobleness, and sobriety, and purity of its divine polity and philosophy. Thus the calumny against our whole creed died with its day, and there continued alone our discipline, sovereign among all, and acknowledged to be pre-eminent in awfulness and sobriety, in its divine and philosophical doctrines; so that no one of this day dares to cast any base reproach upon our faith, nor any such calumny such as it was once customary for our enemies to use."—*Hist.* iv. 7.

Or to take a passage on a different subject, which almost comes first to hand, from St. Cyril, another of this school of divines:—

"Only be of good cheer, only work, only strive cheerfully; for nothing is lost. Every prayer of thine, every psalm thou singest is recorded; every alms-deed, every fast is recorded; every marriage duly observed is recorded; continence kept for God's sake is recorded; but the first crowns in record are those of virginity and purity; and thou shalt shine as an Angel. But as thou hast gladly listened to the good things, listen without shrinking to the contrary. Every covetous deed of thine is recorded; every fleshly deed, every perjury, every blasphemy, every sorcery, every theft, every murder. All these things are henceforth recorded, if thou do these after baptism; for thy former deeds are blotted out."—*Cat.* xv. 23.

Cyril and Eusebius, I conceive, do not serve at all better than Origen to show that faith is a feeling, that it makes a man independent of the Church, and is efficacious apart from baptism or works. I do not know any ancient divines of whom more can be made.

4.

Where, then, is primitive Protestantism to be found? There is one chance for it, not in the second and third centuries, but in the fourth; I mean in the history of Aerius, Jovinian, and Vigilantius,—men who may be called, by some sort of analogy, the Luther, Calvin, and Zwingle, of the fourth century. And they have been so considered both by Protestants and by their opponents; so covetous, after all, of precedent are innovators, so prepared are Catholics to believe that there is nothing new under the sun. Let me, then, briefly state the history and tenets of these three religionists.

1. Aerius was an intimate friend of Eustathius, bishop of Sebaste, in Armenia, whose name has already occurred above. Both had embraced a monastic life; and both were Arians in creed. Eustathius, being raised to the episcopate, ordained his friend presbyter, and set him over the almshouse or hospital of the see. A quarrel followed, from whatever cause; Aerius left his post, and accused Eustathius of covetousness, as it would appear, unjustly. Next he collected a large number of persons of both sexes in the open country, where they braved the severe weather of that climate. A congregation implies a creed, and Aerius founded or formed his own on the following points: 1. That there was no difference between bishop and presbyter. 2. That it was judaical to observe Easter, because Christ is our Passover. 3. That it was useless, or rather mischievous, to name the dead in prayer, or to give alms for them. 4. That fasting was judaical, and a yoke of bondage. If it be right to fast, he added, each should choose his own day; for instance, Sunday rather than Wednesday and Friday: while Passion Week he spent in feasting and merriment,

And this is pretty nearly all we know of Aerius, who flourished between A.D. 360 and 370.

2. Jovinian was a Roman monk, and was condemned, first by Siricius at Rome, then by St. Ambrose and other bishops at Milan, about A.D. 390. He taught, 1. That eating with thanksgiving was just as good as fasting. 2. That, *cæteris paribus*, celibacy, widowhood, and marriage, were on a level in the baptized. 3. That there was no difference of rewards hereafter for those who had preserved their baptism; and, 4. That those who had been baptized with full faith could not fall; if they did, they had been baptized, like Simon Magus, only with water. He persuaded persons of both sexes at Rome, who had for years led a single life, to desert it. The Emperor Honorius had him transported to an island on the coast of Dalmatia; he died in the beginning of the fifth century.

3. Vigilantius was a priest of Gaul or Spain, and flourished just at the time Jovinian died: he taught, 1. That those who reverenced relics were idolaters; 2. That continence and celibacy were wrong, as leading to the worst scandals; 3. That lighting candles in churches during the day, in honour of the martyrs, was wrong, as being a heathen rite; 4. That Apostles and Martyrs had no presence at their tombs; 5. That it was useless to pray for the dead; 6. That it was better to keep wealth and practice habitual charity, than to strip one's-self of one's property once for all; and 7. That it was wrong to retire into the desert. This is what we learn of these three (so-called) reformers, from the writings of Epiphanius and Jerome.

Now you may say, "What can we require more than this? Here we have, at the time of a great catastrophe, Scriptural truth come down to us in the burning matter which melted and preserved it, in the persecuting language of Epiphanius and Jerome. When corruptions began to press themselves on the notice of Christians, here you find three witnesses raising their distinct and solemn protest in different parts of the Church, independently of each other, in Gaul, in Italy, and in Asia Minor, against prayers for the dead, veneration of relics, candles in the day-time, the merit of celibacy, the need of fasting, the observance of days, difference in future rewards, the defectibility of the regenerate, and the divine origin of episcopacy. Here is pure and scriptural Protestantism." Such is the phenomenon on which a few remarks are now to be offered.

5.

1. I observe then, first, that this case so presented to us, does not answer the purpose required. The doctrine of these three Protestants, if I am to be forced into calling them so, is, after all, but negative. We know what they protested *against*, not what they protested *for*. We do not know what the system of doctrine and ritual was which they substituted for the Catholic, or whether they had any such. Though they differed from the ancients, there is no proof that they agreed with the moderns. Parties which differ from a common third, do not necessarily agree with each other; from two negative propositions nothing is inferred. For instance, the moral temper and doctrinal character of the sixteenth century is best symbolized by its views about faith and justification, to which I have already referred, and upon the duty of each individual man drawing his own creed from the Scriptures. This is its positive shape, as far as it may be considered positive at all. Now does any one mean to maintain that Aerius, Jovinian, or Vigilantius, held justification by faith only in the sense of John Wesley, or of John

Newton? Did they consider that baptism was a thing of nought; that faith did everything; that faith was trust, and the perfection of faith assurance; that it consisted in believing that "I am pardoned;" and that works might be left to themselves, to come as they might, as being *necessary* fruits of faith, without our trouble? Did they know anything of the "apprehensive" power of faith, or of man's proneness to consider his imperfect services, done in and by grace, as adequate to purchase eternal life? There is no proof they did. Let then these three protesters be ever so cogent an argument against the Catholic creed, this does not bring them a whit nearer to the Protestant; though in fact there is nothing to show that their protest was founded on historical grounds, or on any argument deeper than such existing instances of superstition and scandal in detail as are sure to accumulate round revelation.

Further, even if a modern wished, he would not be able to put up with even the negative creed of these primitive protesters, whatever his particular persuasion might be. Their protest suits no sect whatever of this day. It is either too narrow or too liberal. The Episcopalian, as he is styled, will not go along with Aerius's notions about bishops; nor will the Lutheran subscribe to the final perseverance of the saints; nor will the strict Calvinist allow that all fasting is judaical; nor will the Baptist admit the efficacy of baptism: one man will wonder why none of the three protested against the existence of the Church itself; another that none of them denied the received doctrine of penance; a third that all three let pass the received doctrine of the Eucharist. Their protestations are either too much or too little for any one of their present admirers. There is no one of any of the denominations of this day but will think them wrong in some points or other; that is all we know about them; but if we all think them wrong on some points, is that a good reason why we should take them as an authority on others?

Or, again, do we wish to fix upon what *can* be detected in their creed of a positive character, and distinct from their protests? We happen to be told what it was in the case of one of them. Aerius was an Arian; does this mend matters? Is there any agreement at all between him and Luther here? If Aerius is an authority against bishops, or against set fasts, why is he not an authority against the Creed of St. Athanasius?

2. What has been last said leads to a further remark. I observe, then, that if two or three men in the fourth century are sufficient, against the general voice of the Church, to disprove one doctrine, then still more are two or three of an earlier century able to disprove another. Why should protesters in century four be more entitled to a hearing than protesters in century three? Now it so happens, that as Aerius, Jovinian, and Vigilantius in the fourth protested against austerities, so did Praxeas, Noetus, and Sabellius in the third protest against the Catholic or Athanasian doctrine of the Holy Trinity. A much stronger case surely could be made out in favour of the latter protest than of the former. Noetus was of Asia Minor, Praxeas taught in Rome, Sabellius in Africa. Nay, we read that in the latter country their doctrine prevailed among the common people, then and at an earlier date, to a very great extent, and that the true faith was hardly preached in the churches.

3. Again, the only value of the protest of these three men would be, of course, that they *represented* others; that they were exponents of a state of opinion which

prevailed either in their day or before them, and which was in the way to be overpowered by the popular corruptions. What are Aerius and Jovinian to me as individuals? They are worth nothing, unless they can be considered as organs and witnesses of an expiring cause. Now, it does not appear that they themselves had any notion that they were speaking in behalf of any one, living or dead, besides themselves. They argued against prayers for the departed from reason, and against celibacy, hopeless as the case might seem, from Scripture. They ridiculed one usage, and showed the ill consequence of another. All this might be very cogent in itself, but it was the conduct of men who stood by themselves and were conscious of it. If Jovinian had known of writers of the second and third centuries holding the same views, Jovinian would have been as prompt to quote them as Lutherans are to quote Jovinian. The protest of these men shows that certain usages undeniably existed in the fourth century; it does not prove that they did not exist also in the first, second, and third. And how does the fact of their living in the fourth century prove there were Protestants in the first? What we are looking for is a Church of primitive heretics, of baptists and independents of the Apostolic age, and we must not be put off with the dark and fallible protests of the Nicene era.

Far different is the tone of Epiphanius in his answer to Aerius:—

"If one need refer," he says, speaking of fasting, "to the constitution of the Apostles, why did they there determine the fourth and sixth day to be ever a fast, except Pentecost? and concerning the six days of the Pascha, why do they order us to take nothing at all but bread, salt, and water? . . Which of these parties is the rather correct? this deceived man, who is now among us, and is still alive, or they who were witnesses before us, possessing before our time the tradition in the Church, and they having received it from their fathers, and those very fathers again having learned it from those who lived before them? . . The Church has received it, and it is unanimously confessed in the whole world, before Aerius and Aerians were born."—*Hær.* 75, § 6.

4. Once more, there is this very observable fact in the case of each of the three, that their respective protests seem to have arisen from some personal motive. Certainly what happens to a man's self often brings a thing home to his mind more forcibly, makes him contemplate it steadily, and leads to a successful investigation into its merits. Yet still, where we know personal feelings to exist in the maintenance of any doctrine, we look more narrowly at the proof for ourselves; thinking it not impossible that the parties may have made up their minds on grounds short of reason. It is natural to feel distrust of controversialists, who, to all appearance, would not have been earnest against a doctrine or practice, except that it galled themselves. Now it so happens that each of these three Reformers lies open to this imputation. Aerius is expressly declared by Epiphanius to have been Eustathius's competitor for the see of Sebaste, and to have been disgusted at failing. *He* is the preacher against bishops. Jovinian was bound by a monastic vow, and *he* protests against fasting and coarse raiment. Vigilantius was a priest; and, therefore, *he* disapproves the celibacy of the clergy. No opinion at all is here ventured in favour of clerical celibacy; still it is remarkable that in the latter, as in the two former cases, private feeling and public protest should have gone together.

6.

These distinct considerations are surely quite sufficient to take away our interest in these three Reformers.

These men are not an historical clue to a lost primitive creed, more than Origen or Tertullian ; and much less do they afford any support to the creed of those moderns who would fain shelter themselves behind them. That there were abuses in the Church then, as at all times, no one, I suppose, will deny. There may have been extreme opinions and extreme acts, pride and pomp in certain bishops, over-honour paid to saints, fraud in the production of relics, extravagance in praising celibacy, formality in fasting ; and such errors would justify a protest, which the Catholic Fathers themselves are not slow to make ; but they would not justify that utter reprobation of relics, of celibacy, and of fasting, of episcopacy, of prayers for the dead, and of the doctrine of defectibility, which these men avowed—avowed without the warrant of the first ages—on grounds of private reason, under the influence of personal feeling, and with the accompaniment of but a suspicious orthodoxy. It does certainly look as if our search after Protestantism in Antiquity would turn out a simple failure ;—whatever Primitive Christianity was or was not, it was not the religion of Luther. I shall think so, until I find Ignatius and Aerius, in spite of their differences about bishops, agreeing in his doctrine of justification ; until Irenæus and Jovinian, though at daggers drawn about baptism, shall yet declare Scripture to be the sole rule of faith ; until Cyprian and Vigilantius, however at variance about the merit of virginity, uphold in common the sacred right and duty of private judgment.

CHAPTER V.

AND WHAT DO THE APOSTOLICAL CANONS SAY?

1.

SUCH, then, is the testimony borne in various ways by Origen, Eusebius, and Cyril, by Aerius, Jovinian, and Vigilantius, to the immemorial reception among Christians of those doctrines and practices which the private judgment of this age considers to be unscriptural. I have been going about from one page to another of the records of those early times, prying and extravagating beyond the beaten paths of orthodoxy, for the chance of detecting some sort of testimony in favour of our opponents. With this object I have fallen upon the writers aforesaid; and, since they have been more or less accused of heterodoxy, I thought there was at least a chance of their subserving the cause of Protestantism, which the Catholic Fathers certainly do not subserve; but they, though differing from each other most materially, and some of them differing from the Church, do not any one of them approximate to the tone or language of the movement of 1517. Every additional instance of this kind does but go indirectly to corroborate the testimony of the Catholic Church.

It is natural and becoming in all of us to make a brave struggle for life; but I do not think it will avail the Protestant who attempts it in the medium of ecclesiastical history. He will find himself in an element in which he cannot breathe. The problem before him is to draw a line between the periods of purity and alleged corruption, such, as to have all the Apostles on one side, and all the Fathers on the other; which may insinuate and meander through the dove-tailings and inosculations of historical facts, and cut clean between St. John and St. Ignatius, St. Paul and St. Clement; to take up a position within the shelter of the book of Acts, yet safe from the range of all other extant documents besides. And at any rate, whether he succeeds or not, so much he must grant, that if such a system of doctrine as he would now introduce ever existed in early times, it has been clean swept away as if by a deluge, suddenly, silently, and without memorial; by a deluge coming in a night, and utterly soaking, rotting, heaving up, and hurrying off every vestige of what it found in the Church; before cock-crowing; so that "when they rose in the morning" her true seed "were all dead corpses"—nay, dead and buried—and without grave-stone. "The waters went over them; there was not one of them left; they sunk like lead in the mighty waters." Strange antitype, indeed, to the early fortunes of Israel!—then the enemy was drowned, and "Israel saw them dead upon the sea-shore." But now, it would seem, water proceeded as a flood "out of the serpent's mouth," and covered all the witnesses, so that not even their dead bodies "lay in the streets of the great city." Let him take which of his doctrines he will,—his peculiar view of self-righteousness, of formality, of superstition; his notion of faith, or of spirituality in religious worship; his denial of the virtue of the sacraments, or of the ministerial commission, or of the visible Church; or his doctrine of the divine efficacy of the Scriptures as the one appointed instrument of religious teaching; and let him consider how far

Antiquity, as it has come down to us, will countenance him in it. No; he must allow that the alleged deluge has done its work; yes, and has in turn disappeared itself; it has been swallowed up in the earth, mercilessly as itself was merciless.

2.

Representations such as these have been met by saying that the extant records of Primitive Christianity are scanty, and that, *for what we know,* what is not extant, had it survived, would have told a different tale. But the hypothesis that history *might* contain facts which it does *not* contain, is no positive evidence for the truth of those facts; and this is the present question, what is the *positive* evidence that the Church ever believed or taught a Gospel substantially different from that which her extant documents contain? All the evidence that is extant, be it much or be it little, is on our side: Protestants have none. Is none better than some? Scarcity of records—granting for argument's sake there is scarcity—may be taken to account for Protestants having no evidence; it will not account for our having some, for our having all that is to be had; it cannot become a positive evidence in their behalf. That records are few, does not show that they are of none account.

Accordingly, Protestants had better let alone facts; they are wisest when they maintain that the Apostolic system of the Church was certainly lost;—lost, when they know not, how they know not, without assignable instruments, but by a great revolution lost—of *that* there can be no doubt; and then challenge us to prove it was not so. "Prove," they seem to say, "if you can, that the real and very truth is not so entirely hid in primitive history as to leave not a particle of evidence betraying it. This is the very thing which misleads you, that all the arguments are in your favour. Is it not possible that an error has got the place of the truth, and has destroyed all the evidence but what witnesses on its side? Is it not possible that all the Churches should everywhere have given up and stifled the scheme of doctrine they received from the Apostles, and have substituted another for it? Of course it is; it is plain to common sense it may be so. Well, we say, what *may be, is;* this is our great principle: we say that the Apostles considered episcopacy an indifferent matter, though Ignatius says it is essential. We say that the table is not an altar, though Ignatius says it is. We say there is no priest's office under the Gospel, though Clement affirms it. We say that baptism is not an enlightening, though Justin takes it for granted. We say that heresy is scarcely a misfortune, though Ignatius accounts it a deadly sin; and all this, because it is our right, and our duty, to interpret Scripture in our own way. We uphold the pure unmutilated Scripture; the Bible, and the Bible only, is the religion of Protestants; the Bible and our own sense of the Bible. We claim a sort of parliamentary privilege to interpret laws in our own way, and not to suffer an appeal to any court beyond ourselves. We know, and we view it with consternation, that all Antiquity runs counter to our interpretation; and therefore, alas, the Church was corrupt from *very* early times indeed. But mind, we hold all this in a truly Catholic spirit, not in bigotry. We allow in others the right of private judgment, and confess that we, as others, are fallible men. We confess facts are against us; we do but claim the liberty of theorizing in spite of them. Far be it from us to say that we are certainly right; we only say that the whole early Church was certainly wrong. We do not impose our belief on any one; we only say that those who take the contrary side are Papists, firebrands, persecutors, madmen, zealots, bigots, and an insult to the nineteenth century."

To such an argument, I am aware, it avails little to oppose historical evidence, of whatever kind. It sets out by protesting against all evidence, however early and consistent, as the testimony of fallible men; yet at least, the imagination is affected by an array of facts; and I am not unwilling to appeal to the imagination of those who refuse to let me address their reason. With this view I have been inquiring into certain early works, which, or the authors of which, were held in suspicion, or even condemned by the ruling authorities of the day, to see if any vestige of an hypothetical Protestantism could be discovered in them; and, since they make no sign, I will now interrogate a very different class of witnesses. The consent of Fathers is one kind of testimony to Apostolical Truth; the protest of heretics is another; now I will come, thirdly, to received usage. To give an instance of the last mentioned argument, I shall appeal to the Apostolical Canons, though a reference to them will involve me in an inquiry, interesting indeed to the student, but somewhat dry to the general reader.

3.

These Canons, well known to Antiquity, were at one time supposed to be, strictly speaking, Apostolical, and published before A.D. 50. On the other hand, it has been contended that they are later than A.D. 450, and the work of some heretics. Our own divines take a middle course, considering them as published before A.D. 325, having been digested by Catholic authorities in the course of the two preceding centuries, or at the end of the second, and received and used in most parts of Christendom. This judgment has since been acquiesced in by the theological world, so far as this—to suppose the matter and the enactments of the Canons to be of the highest antiquity, even though the edition which we possess was not published so early as Bishop Beveridge, for instance, supposes. At the same time it is acknowledged by all parties, that they, as well as some other early documents, have suffered from interpolation, and perhaps by an heretical hand.

They are in number eighty-five,[1] of which the first fifty are considered of superior authority to the remaining thirty-five. What has been conjectured to be their origin will explain the distinction. It was the custom of the early Church, as is well known, to settle in Council such points in her discipline, ordinances, and worship, as the Apostles had not prescribed in Scripture, as the occasion arose, after the pattern of their own proceedings in the fifteenth chapter of the Acts; and this, as far as might be, after their unwritten directions, or after their practice, or at least, after their mind, or as it is called in Scripture, their "minding" or "spirit." Thus she decided upon the question of Easter, upon that of heretical baptism, and the like. And, after that same precedent in the Acts, she recorded her decisions in formal decrees, and "delivered them for to keep" through the cities in which her members were found. The Canons in question are supposed to be some of these decrees, of which, first and nearest to the Apostles' times, or in the time of their immediate successors, were published fifty; and in the following age, thirty-five more, which had been enacted in the interval. They claim, then, to be, first,

[1] This account is for the most part taken from Bishops Beveridge and Pearson.

the recorded judgment of great portions of the Ante-Nicene Church, chiefly in the eastern provinces, upon certain matters in dispute, and to be of authority so far as that Church may be considered a representative of the mind of the Apostles; next, they profess to embody in themselves positive decisions and injunctions of the Apostles, though without clearly discriminating how much is thus directly Apostolical, and how much not. I will here attempt to state some of the considerations which show both their antiquity and their authority, and will afterwards use them for the purpose which has led me to mention them.

4.

1. In the first place, it would seem quite certain that, as, on the one hand, Councils were held in the primitive Church, so, on the other, those Councils enacted certain Canons. When, then, a Collection presents itself professing to consist of the Ante-Nicene Canons, there is nothing at all to startle us; it only professes to set before us that which we know anyhow must have existed. We may conjecture, if we please, that the fact that there were Canons may have suggested and encouraged a counterfeit. Certainly; but though the fact that there were Canons will account for a counterfeit, it will not account for those original Canons being lost; on the contrary, what is known to have once existed as a rule of conduct, is likely to continue in existence, except under particular circumstances. Which of the two this existing Collection is, the genuine or the counterfeit, must depend on other considerations; but if these considerations be in favour of its genuineness, then this antecedent probability will be an important confirmation.

Canons, I say, must have existed, whether these be

the real ones or no; and the circumstance that there were real ones existing must have tended to make it difficult to substitute others. It would be no easy thing in our own Church to pass off another set of Articles for the Thirty-nine, and to obliterate the genuine. Canons are public property, and have to be acted upon by large bodies. Accordingly, as might be expected, the Nicene Council, when enacting Canons of its own, refers to certain Canons as already existing, and speaks of them in that familiar and indirect way which would be natural under the circumstances, just as we speak of our Rubrics or Articles. The Fathers of that Council mention certain descriptions of persons whom "*the Canon* admits into holy orders;" they determine that a certain rule shall be in force, "according to the Canon which says so and so;" they speak of a transgression of the Canon, and proceed to explain and enforce it. Nor is the Nicene the only Council which recognizes the existence of certain Canons, or rules, by which the Church was at that time bound. The Councils of Antioch, Gangra, Constantinople, and Carthage, in the same century, do so likewise; so do individual Fathers, Alexander, Athanasius, Basil, Julius, and others.

Now here we have lighted upon an important circumstance, whatever becomes of the particular Collection of Canons before us. It seems that at the Nicene Council, only two centuries and a quarter after St. John's death, about the distance of time at which we live from the Hampton Court Conference, all Christendom confessed that from time immemorial it had been guided by certain ecclesiastical rules, which it considered of authority, which it did not ascribe to any particular persons or synods (a sign of great antiquity), and which writers of the day assigned to the Apostles. I suppose we know pretty well, at this day, what the customs of our Church have been since James the First's time, or since the Reformation; and if respectable writers at present were to state some of them,—for instance, that it is and has been the rule of our Church that the king should name the bishops, that Convocation should not sit without his leave, or that Easter should be kept according to the Roman rule,—we should think foreigners very unreasonable who doubted their word. Now, in the case before us, we find the Church Catholic, the first time it had ever met together since the Apostles' days, speaking as a matter of course of the rules to which it had ever been accustomed to defer.

If we knew no more than this, and did not know what the rules were; or if, knowing what they were, we yet decided, as we well might, that the particular rules are not of continual obligation; still, the very circumstance that there *were* rules from time immemorial would be a great fact in the history of Christianity. But we do know, from the works of the Fathers, the *subjects* of these Canons, and that to the number of thirty or forty of them; so that we might form a code, as far as it goes, of primitive discipline, quite independent of the particular Collection which is under discussion. However, it is remarkable that all of these thirty or forty are found in this Collection, being altogether nearly half the whole number, so that the only question is, whether the rest are of that value which we know belongs to a great proportion of them. It is worth noticing, that *no* Ecclesiastical Canon is mentioned in the historical documents of the primitive era which is not found in this Collection, for it shows that, whoever compiled it, the work was done with considerable care. The opponents to its genuineness bring, indeed, several exceptions, as they wish to consider them; but these admit of so satisfactory an explanation as to illustrate the proverb, that *exceptio probat regulam.*

Before going on to consider the whole Collection, let us see in what terms the ancient writers speak of those particular Canons to which they actually refer.

(1.) Athanasius speaks as follows:—"Canons and forms," he says, when describing the extraordinary violences of the Arians, "were not given to the Churches in this day, but were *handed down* from our fathers well and securely. Nor, again, has the faith had its beginning in this day, but has passed on even to us from the Lord through His disciples. Rouse yourselves, then, my brethren, to prevent that from perishing unawares in the present day *which has been observed in the Churches from ancient times down to us*, and ourselves from incurring a responsibility in what has been intrusted to us."—*Ep. Encycl.* 1. It is remarkable, in this extract, that St. Athanasius accurately distinguishes between the Faith which came from Christ, and the Canons received from the Fathers of old time: which is just the distinction which our divines are accustomed to make.

(2) Again: the Arians, by simoniacal dealings with the civil power, had placed Gregory in the see of Alexandria. Athanasius observes upon this:—"Such conduct is both *a violation of the Ecclesiastical Canons*, and forces the heathen to blaspheme, as if appointments were made, not by Divine ordinance, but by merchandise and secular influence."—*Ibid.* 2.

(3) Arsenius, bishop of Hypsela, who had been involved in the Meletian[1] schism, and had acted in a hostile way towards Athanasius, at length reconciled himself to the Church. In his letter to Athanasius he promises "to be

[1] The Egyptian Meletius, from which this schism has its name, must not be confounded with Meletius of Antioch.

obedient to *the Ecclesiastical Canon*, according to ancient usage, and never to put forth any regulation, whether about bishops or any other public ecclesiastical matter, without the sanction of his metropolitan, but to *submit to all the established Canons*."—*Apol. contr. Arian.* 69.

(4) In like manner, St. Basil, after speaking of certain crimes for which a deacon should be reduced to lay communion, proceeds, "for *it is an ancient Canon*, that they who lose their degree should be subjected to this kind of punishment only."—*Ep.* 188. Again: "*The Canon* altogether excludes from the ministry those who have been twice married."

(5) When Arius and his abettors were excommunicated by Alexander of Alexandria, they betook themselves to Palestine, and were re-admitted into the Church by the bishops of that country. On this, Alexander observes as follows:—"A very heavy imputation, doubtless, lies upon such of my brethren as have ventured on this act, in that it is *a violation of the Apostolical Canon*." —*Theod. Hist.* i. 4.

(6) When Eusebius declined being translated from the see of Cæsarea to Antioch, Constantine complimented him on his "observance of the commandments of God, *the Apostolical Canon*, and the rule of the Church,"—*Vit. Constant.* iii. 61,—which last seems to mean the regulation passed at Nicæa.

(7) In like manner, Julius, bishop of Rome, speaks of a violation of "*the Apostles' Canons;*" and a Council held at Constantinople, A.D. 394, which was attended by Gregory Nyssen, Amphilochius, and Flavian, of a determination of "*the Apostolical Canons.*"

It will be observed that in some of these instances the Canons are spoken of in the plural, when the particular infraction which occasions their mention relates only to one of them. This shows they were collected into a code, if, indeed, that need be proved; for, in truth, that various Canons should exist, and be in force, and yet not be put together, is just as unlikely as that no collection should be made of the statutes passed in a session of Parliament.

With this historical information about the existence, authority, and subject-matter of certain Canons in the Church from time immemorial, we should come to many anti-Protestant conclusions, even if the particular code we possess turned out to have no intrinsic authority. And now let us see how the matter stands on this point as regards this code of eighty-five Canons.

5.

2. If this Collection existed *as* a Collection in the time of the above writers and Councils, then, considering they allude to nearly half its Canons, and that no Canons are anywhere producible which are not in it, and that they do seem to allude to a Collection, and that no other Collection is producible, we certainly could not avoid the conclusion that they referred to *it*, and that, therefore, in quoting parts of it they sanction the whole. If no book is to be accounted genuine except such parts of it as happen to be expressly cited by other writers,—if it may not be regarded as a whole, and what is actually cited made to bear up and carry with it what is not cited,—no ancient book extant can be proved to be genuine. We believe Virgil's Æneid to be Virgil's, because we know he wrote an Æneid, and because particular passages which we find in it, and in no other book, are contained, under the name of Virgil, in subsequent writers or in criticisms, or in accounts of it. We do not divide it into rhapsodies, *because* it only exists in fragments in the testimony of later literature. For the same

reason, if the Canons before us can be shown to have existed as one book in Athanasius's time, it is natural to conceive that they are the very book to which he and others refer. All depends on this. If the Collection was made after his time, of course he referred to some other; but if it existed in his time, it is more natural to suppose that there was one Collection than two distinct ones, so similar, especially since history is silent about there being two.

However, I conceive it is not worth while to insist upon so early a formation of the existing Collection. Whether it existed in Athanasius's time, or was formed afterwards, and formed by friend or foe, heretic or Catholic, seems to me immaterial, as I shall by-and-by show. First, however, I will state, as candidly as I can, the arguments for and against its antiquity *as* a Collection.

Now there can be no doubt that the early Canons were formed into one body; moreover, certain early writers speak of them under the name of "the Apostles' Canons," and "Apostolical Canons." So far I have already said. Now, certain collectors of Canons, of A.D. (more or less) 550, and they no common authorities, also speak of "the Apostolical Canons," and incorporate them into their own larger collections; and these which they speak of are the very body of Canons which we now possess under the name. We know it, for the digest of these collectors is preserved. No reason can be assigned why they should not be speaking of the *same* Collection which Gregory Nyssen and Amphilochius speak of, who lived a century and a half before them; no reason, again, why Nyssen and Amphilochius should not mean the same as Athanasius and Julius, who lived fifty to seventy years earlier than themselves. The writers of A.D. 550 might be just as certain that they and St. Athanasius quoted the same work, as we, at this day, that our copy of it is the same as Beveridge's, Pearson's, or Ussher's.

The authorities at the specified date (A.D. 550) are three—Dionysius Exiguus, John of Antioch, patriarch of Constantinople, and the Emperor Justinian. The learning of Justinian is well known, not to mention that he speaks the opinion of the ecclesiastical lawyers of his age. As to John of Antioch and Dionysius, since their names are not so familiar to most of us, it may be advisable to say thus much—that John had been a lawyer, and was well versed both in civil and ecclesiastical matters,—hence he has the title of Scholasticus; while Dionysius is the framer of the Christian era, as we still reckon it. They both made Collections of the Canons of the Church, the latter in Latin, and they both include the Apostolical Canons, as we have them, in their editions; with this difference, however (which does not at present concern us), that Dionysius published but the first fifty, while John of Antioch enumerates the whole eighty-five.

Such is the main argument for the existence of our Collection at the end of the third century; viz., that, whereas *a* Collection of Apostolic Canons is acknowledged at that date, *this* Collection is acknowledged by competent authorities to be that Apostolic record at the end of the fifth. However, when we inspect the language which Dionysius uses concerning them, in his prefatory epistle, we shall find something which requires explanation. His words are these, addressed to Stephen, bishop of Salona:—"We have, in the first place, translated from the Greek what are called the Canons of the Apostles; *which, as we wish to apprise your holiness, have not gained an easy credit from very many persons.* At the same time, some of the decrees of the [Roman] pontiffs, at a later date, seem to be taken from these very Canons." Here Dionysius must only mean, that they were not received *as* Apostolic; for that they were received, or at least nearly half of them, is, as I have said, an historical fact, whatever becomes of the Collection as a Collection. He must mean that a claim had been advanced that they were to be received as part of the apostolic *depositum;* and he must be denying that they had more than *ecclesiastical* authority. The distinction between divine and ecclesiastical injunctions requires little explanation: the latter are imposed by the Church for the sake of decency and order, as a matter of expedience, safety, propriety, or piety. Such is the rule among ourselves, that dissenting teachers conforming must remain silent three years before they can be ordained; or that a certain form of prayer should be prescribed for universal use in public service. On the other hand, the appointment of the Sacraments is apostolic and divine. So, again, that no one can be a bishop unless consecrated by a bishop, is apostolic; that three bishops are necessary in consecration, is ecclesiastical; and, though ordinarily an imperative rule, yet, under circumstances, admits of dispensation. Or again, it has, for instance, in this day been debated whether the sanctification of the Lord's-day is a divine or an ecclesiastical appointment. Dionysius, then, in the above extract, means nothing more than to deny that the Apostles enacted these Canons; or, again, that they enacted them *as* Apostles; and he goes on to say that the Popes had acknowledged the *ecclesiastical* authority of some of them by embodying them in their decrees. At the same time, his language certainly seems to show as much as this, and it is confirmed by that of other writers, that the Latin Church, though using them separately as authority, did not receive them as a Collection with the implicit deference which they met with in the East; indeed, the last thirty-five, though two of them were cited at Nicæa, and one at Constantinople, A.D. 394, seem to have been in inferior account. The Canons of the General Councils took their place, and the Decrees of the Popes.

6.

This, then, seems to be the state of the case as regards the Collection or Edition of Canons, whether fifty or eighty-five, which is under consideration. Speaking, not of the Canons themselves, but of this particular edition of them, I thus conclude about it—that, whether it was made at the end of the third century, or later, there is no sufficient proof that it was strictly of authority; but that it is not very material that it should be proved to be of authority, nay, or even to have been made in early times. Give us the Canons themselves, and we shall be able to prove the point for which I am adducing them, even though they were not at first formed into a collection. They are, one by one, witnesses to us of a state of things.

Indeed, it must be confessed, that probability is against this Collection having ever been regarded as an authority by the ancient Church. It was an *anonymous* Collection; and, as being anonymous, seemed to have no claim upon Christians. They would consider that a collection or body of Canons could only be imposed by a *Council;* and since the Council could not be produced which imposed this in particular, they had no reason to admit it. They might have been in the practice of acting upon this Canon, and that, and the third, and so on to the eighty-fifth, from time immemorial, and that as Canons, not as mere customs, and might confess the obligation of each: and yet might say, "We never looked upon them as a *code*," which should be something complete and limited to itself. The true sanction of each was the immemorial observance of each, not its place in the Collection, which implied a competent framer. Moreover, in proportion as General Councils were held, and enacted Canons, so did the vague title of mere usage, without definite sanction, become less influential, and the ancient Canons fell into disregard. And what made this still more natural was the circumstance that the Nicene Council did re-enact a considerable number of those which it found existing. It substituted then a definite authority, which, in after ages, would be much more intelligible than what would have by that time become a mere matter of obscure antiquity. Nor did it tend to restore their authority, when their advocates, feeling the difficulty of their case, referred the Collection to the Apostles themselves: first, because this assertion could not be maintained; next, because, if it could, it would have seemingly deprived the Church of the privilege of making Canons. It would have made those usages divine which had ever been accounted only ecclesiastical. It would have raised the question whether, under such circumstances, the Church had more right to add to the code of really Apostolic Canons than to Scripture; discipline, as well as doctrine, would have been given by direct revelation, and have been included in the fundamentals of religion.

If, however, all this be so, it follows that we are not at liberty to argue, from one part of this Collection having been received, that therefore every other was also; as if it were one authoritative work. No number of individual Canons being proved to be of the first age will tend to prove that the remainder are of the same. It is true;

and I do not think it worth while to contest the point. For argument-sake I will grant that the bond, which ties them into one, is not of the most trustworthy and authoritative description, and will proceed to show that even those Canons which are not formally quoted by early writers ought to be received as the rules of the Ante-Nicene Church, independently of their being found in one compilation.

7.

3. I have already said that nearly half of the Canons, as they stand in the Collection, are quoted as Canons by early writers, and thus placed beyond all question, as remains of the Ante-Nicene period: the following arguments may be offered in behalf of the rest:—

(1) They are otherwise known to express *usages* or *opinions* of the Ante-Nicene centuries. The simple question is, whether they had been reflected on, recognized, converted into principles, enacted, obeyed; whether they were the unconscious and unanimous result of the one Christian spirit[1] in every place, or were formal determinations from authority claiming obedience. This being the case, there is very little worth disputing about; for (whether we regard them as being religious practices or as religious antiquities) if uniform custom was in favour of them, it does not matter whether they were enacted or not. If they were not, their universal observance is a still greater evidence of their extreme antiquity, which, in that case, can be hardly short of the Apostolic age; and we shall refer to them in the existing Collection, merely for the sake of convenience, as being brought together in a short compass.

Nay, a still more serious conclusion will follow, from

[1] The ἐκκλησιαστικὸν φρόνημα.

supposing them not to be enactments—much more serious than any I am disposed to draw. If it be maintained that these observances, though such, did not arise from injunctions on the part of the Church, then, it might be argued, the Church has no power over them. As not having imposed, she cannot abrogate, suspend, or modify them. They must be referred to a higher source, even to the inspired Apostles; and their authority is not ecclesiastical, but divine. We are almost forced, then, to consider them as enactments, even when they are not recognized by ancient writers as such, lest we should increase the authority of some of them more than seems consistent with their subject-matter.

Again, if such Canons as are not appealed to by ancient writers are nevertheless allowed to have been really enacted, on the ground of our finding historically that usage corresponds to them; it may so be that others, about which the usage is not so clearly known, are real Canons also. There is a *chance* of their being genuine; for why, in drawing the line, should we decide by the mere accident of the usage admitting or not admitting of clear historical proof?

(2) Again, all these Canons, or at least the first fifty, are composed in uniform style; there is no reason, as far as the internal evidence goes, why one should be more primitive than another, and many, we know, were certainly in force as Canons from the earliest times.

(3) This argument becomes much more cogent when we consider *what* that style is. It carries with it evident marks of primitive simplicity, some of which I shall instance. The first remark which would be made on reading them relates to their brevity, the breadth of the rules which they lay down, and their plain and unartificial mode of stating them. An instance of this, among

others which might be taken, is supplied by a comparison of the 7th of them with one of a number of Canons passed at Antioch by a Council held A. D. 341, and apparently using the Apostolical Canons as a basis for its own. The following, read with the words in brackets, agrees, with but slight exceptions, with the Antiochene Canon, and, without them, with the Apostolical :—

"All who come [to church] and hear the [holy] Scriptures read, but do not remain to prayer [with the people,] and [refuse] the holy communion [of the Eucharist, these] must be put out of the Church, as disorderly, [until, by confession, and by showing fruits of penitence, and by entreaty, they are able to gain forgiveness."]

(4) Now this contrast, if pursued, will serve to illustrate the antiquity of the Apostolical Canons in several ways, besides the evidence deducible from the simplicity of their structure. Thus the word "metropolitan" is introduced into the thirty-fifth Canon of Antioch; no such word occurs in the Ap. stolical Canon from which it is apparently formed. There it is simply said, "the principal bishop;" or, literally, the primus. This accords with the historical fact, that the word metropolitan was not introduced till the fourth century. The same remark might be made on the word "province," which occurs in the Canon of Antioch, not in the other. This contrast is strikingly brought out in two other Canons, which correspond in the two Collections. Both treat of the possessions of the Church; but the Apostolical Canon says simply, "the interests of the Church," "the goods of the Church;" but the Antiochene, composed after Christianity had been acknowledged by the civil power, speaks of "the revenue of the Church," and "the produce of the land."

Again, when attempts have been made to show that certain words are contained in the Canons before us which were not in use in the Ante-Nicene times, they have in every case failed in the result, which surely may be considered as a positive evidence in favour of their genuineness. For instance, the word "clergy," for the ministerial body, which is found in the Apostolical Canons, is also used by Origen, Tertullian, and Cyprian. The word "reader," for an inferior order in the clergy, is used by Cornelius, bishop of Rome; nay, by Justin Martyr. "Altar," which is used in the Canons, is the only word used for the Lord's table by St. Cyprian, and, before him, by Tertullian and Ignatius. "Sacrifice" and "oblation," for the consecrated elements, found in the Canons, are also found in Clement of Rome, Justin Irenæus, and Tertullian.

This negative evidence of genuineness extends to other points, and surely is of no inconsiderable weight. We know how difficult it is so to word a forgery as to avoid all detection from incongruities of time, place, and the like. A forgery, indeed, it is hardly possible to suppose this Collection to be, both because great part of it is known to be genuine, and because no assignable object would be answered by it; but let us imagine the compiler hastily took up with erroneous traditions, or recent enactments, and joined them to the rest. Is it possible to conceive, under such circumstances, that there would be no anachronisms or other means of detection? And if there are none such, and much more if the compiler, who lived perhaps as early as the fourth century, found none such (supposing we may assume him willing and qualified to judge of them), nay, if Dionysius Exiguus found none such, what reasons have we for denying that they are the produce of those early times to which they claim to belong? Yet so it is; neither rite, nor heresy, nor observance, nor phrase, is found in them which is foreign to the Ante-Nicene period. Indeed, the only reason one or two persons have thrown suspicion on them has been an unwillingness on their part to admit episcopacy, which the Canons assert ; a necessity which led the same parties to deny the genuineness of St. Ignatius' epistles.[1]

(5) I will make one more remark:—First, these Canons come to us, not from Rome, but from the East, and were in a great measure neglected, or at least superseded in the Church, after Constantine's day, especially in the West, where Rome had sway ; these do not embody what are called "Romish corruptions." Next, there is ground for suspecting that the Collection or Edition which we have was made by heretics, probably Arians, though they have not meddled with the main contents of them. Thus, while the neglect of them in later times separates them from Romanism, the assent of the Arians is a second witness, in addition to their recognition by the first centuries, in evidence of their Apostolical origin. Those first centuries observe them; contemporary heretics respect them ; only later and corrupt times pass them by. May they not be taken as a fair portrait, as far as they go, of the doctrines and customs of Primitive Christianity ?

8.

I do wish out-and-out Protestants would seriously lay to heart where they stand when they would write a history of Christianity. Are there any traces of Luther before Luther ? Is there anything to show that what they call the religion of the Bible was ever professed by any persons, Christians, Jews, or heathen ? Again, are there any traces

[1] Vid. the parallel case of the Ignatian Epistles in the Author's Essays, vol. i., p. 266.

in history of a process of change in Christian belief and practice, so serious, or so violent, as to answer to the notion of a great corruption or perversion of the Primitive Religion? Was there ever a time, what was the time, when Christianity was not that which Protestants protest against, as if formal, unspiritual, self-righteous, superstitious, and unevangelic? If that time cannot be pointed out, is not "the Religion of Protestants" a matter, not of past historical fact, but of modern private judgment? Have they anything to say in defence of their idea of the Christianity of the first centuries, except that that view of it is necessary to their being Protestants. "Christians," they seem to say, "*must* have been in those early times different from what the record of those times shows them to have been, and they must, as time went on, have fallen from that faith and that worship which they had at first, though history is quite silent on the subject, *or else* Protestantism, which is the apple of our eye, is not true. We are driven to hypothetical facts, or else we cannot reconcile with each other phenomena so discordant as those which are presented by ancient times and our own. We claim to substitute *à priori* reasoning for historical investigation, by the right of self-defence and the duty of self-preservation."

I have urged this point in various ways, and now I am showing the light which the Canons of the Apostles throw upon it. There is no reasonable doubt that they represent to us, on the whole, and as far as they go, the outward face of Christianity in the first centuries;—now will the Protestant venture to say that he recognizes in it any likeness of his own Religion? First, let him consider what is conveyed in the very idea of Ecclesiastical Canons? This: that Christians could not worship according to their fancy, but must think and pray by rule, by a set of rules issuing from a body of men, the Bishops, over whom the laity had no power whatever. If any men at any time have been priest-ridden, such was the condition of those early Christians. And then again, what becomes of the Protestant's watchword, "the Bible, the whole Bible, and nothing but the Bible," if a set of Canons might lawfully be placed upon their shoulders, as if a second rule of faith, to the utter exclusion of all free-and-easy religion? and what room was there for private judgment, if they had to obey the bidding of certain fallible men? and what is to be done with the great principle, "Unity, not Uniformity," if Canons are to be recognized, which command uniformity as well as unity?

So much at first sight; but when we go on to examine what these Canons actually contain, their incompatibility with the fundamental principles of Protestantism becomes still more patent. I will set down some instances in proof of this. Thus, we gather from the Canons the following facts about Primitive Christianity:—viz., that,

1. There was a hierarchy of ordained ministers, consisting of the three orders of Bishops, Priests, and Deacons.

2. Their names were entered on a formal roll or catalogue.

3. There were inferior orders, such as readers and chanters.

4. Those who had entered into the sacred orders might not afterwards marry.

5. There were local dioceses, each ruled by a Bishop.

6. To him and him only was committed the care of souls in his diocese.

7. Each Bishop confined himself to his own diocese.

8. No secular influence was allowed to interfere with the appointment of Bishops.

9. The Bishops formed one legislative body, and met in Council twice a year, for the consideration of dogmatic questions and points in controversy.

10. One of them had the precedence over the rest, and took the lead; and, as the priests and people in each diocese obeyed their Bishop, so in more general matters the Bishops deferred to their Primus.

11. Easter and Pentecost were great feasts, and certain other days feasts also. There was a Lent Fast; also a Fast on Easter Eve; and on Wednesdays and Fridays.

12. The state of celibacy was recognized

13. Places of worship were holy.

14. There was in their churches an altar, and an altar service.

15. There was a sacrifice in their worship, of which the materials were bread and wine.

16. There were oblations also of fruits of the earth, in connection with the sacrifice.

17. There were gold and silver vessels in the rite, and these were consecrated.

18. There were sacred lamps, fed with olive oil, and incense during the holy rite.

19. Baptism was administered in the name of Father, Son, and Holy Ghost.

20. Excommunication was inflicted on Christians who disgraced their profession.

21. No one might pray, even in private, with excommunicated persons, except at the cost of being excommunicated himself.

22. No one might pray with heretics, or enter their churches, or acknowledge their baptism, or priesthood.

9

These rules furnish us with large portions, and the

more important, of the outline of the religion of their times; and are not only definitive in themselves, but give us the means of completing those parts of it which are not found in them. Considered, then, as a living body, the primitive Christian community was distinguished by its high sacerdotal, ceremonial, mystical character. Which among modern religious bodies was it like? Was it like the Wesleyans? was it like the Society of Friends? was it like the Scotch Kirk? was it like any Protestant denomination at all? Fancy any model Protestant of this day in a state of things so different from his own! With his religious societies for the Church, with his committees, boards, and platforms instead of Bishops, his *Record* and *Patriot* newspapers instead of Councils, his concerts for prayer instead of anathemas on heresy and schism, his spoutings at public meetings for exorcisms, his fourths of October for festivals of the Martyrs, his glorious memories for commemorations of the dead, his niggard vestry allowances for gold and silver vessels, his gas and stoves for wax and oil, his denunciations of self-righteousness for fasting and celibacy, and his exercise of private judgment for submission to authority—would he have a chance of finding himself at home in a Christianity such as this? is it his own Christianity?

I end, then, as I began:—If Protestantism is another name for Christianity, then the Martyrs and Bishops of the early Church, the men who taught the nations, the men who converted the Roman Empire, had themselves to be taught, themselves to be converted. Shall we side with the first age of Christianity, or with the last?

NOTE ON P. 366.

Lately the relics of St. Ambrose have been discovered in his Church at Milan, as were the relics of St. Gervasius and St. Protasius several years since. On this subject I received a month since a letter from a friend, who passed through Milan, and saw the sacred remains. I will quote a portion of his letter to me :—

"*Sept.* 17, 1872.

"I am amazed at the favour which was shown me yesterday at the Church of St. Ambrogio. I was accidentally allowed to be present at a private exposition of the relics of St. Ambrose and the Saints Gervasius and Protasius. I have seen complete every bone in St. Ambrose's body. There were present a great many of the clergy, three *medici*, and Father Secchi, who was there on account of his great knowledge of the Catacombs, to testify to the age, etc., of the remains. It was not quite in chance, for I wanted to go to Milan, solely to venerate St. Ambrose once more, and to thank him for all the blessings I have had as a Catholic and a Priest, since the day that I said Mass over his body. The churches were shut when I arrived ; so I got up early next morning and went off to the Ambrosian. I knelt down before the high altar, and thought of all that had happened since you and I were there, twenty-six years ago. As I was kneeling, a cleric came out ; so I asked him to let me into the *scurolo*, which was boarded up all round for repairs. He took me there, but he said : 'St. Ambrose is not here ; he is above ; do you wish to see him?' He took me round through the corretti into a large room, where, on a large table, surrounded by ecclesiastics and medical men, were three skeletons. The two were of immense size, and very much alike, and bore the marks of a violent death ; their age was determined to be about twenty-six years. When I entered the room, Father Secchi was examining the marks of martyrdom on them. Their throats had been cut with great violence, and the neck vertebræ were injured on the inside. The *pomum Adami* had been broken, or was not there; I forget which. This bone was quite perfect in St. Ambrose ; his body was wholly uninjured ; the lower jaw (which was broken in one of the two martyrs) was wholly uninjured in him, beautifully formed, and every tooth, but one molar in the lower jaw, quite perfect and white and regular. His face had been long, thin, and oval, with a high arched forehead. His bones were nearly white; those of the other two were very dark. His fingers long and very delicate; his bones were a marked contrast to those of the two martyrs.

"The finding, I was told, was thus :—In the ninth century the Bishop of Milan translated the relics of St. Ambrose, which till then had laid side by side with the martyrs in one great stone coffin of two compartments, St. Gervase being, according to the account, nearest to St. Ambrose. He removed St. Ambrose from this coffin into the great porphyry urn which we both saw in the *scurolo;* leaving the martyrs where they were. In 1864 the martyrs' coffin was opened, and one compartment was found empty, except a single bone, the right-ankle bone, which lay by itself in that empty compartment. This was sent to the Pope as all that remained of St. Ambrose ; in the other compartment were the two skeletons complete. St. Ambrose's urn was not opened till the other day, when it was removed from its place for the alterations. The bones were found perfect all but the ankle bone. They then sent for it to Rome, and the President of the Seminary showed me how it fitted exactly in its place, having been separated from it for nine centuries.

"The Government seems very desirous to make a handsome restoration of the whole chapel, and the new shrine will be completed by May next."

Thus far my friend's letter.

I have not been able in such historical works as are at my command to find notice of Archbishop Angelbert's transferring St. Ambrose's body from the large coffin of the martyrs to the porphyry urn which has been traditionally pointed out as the receptacle of the Saint, and in which he was recently found. That the body, however, recently disinterred actually was once in the coffin of the martyrs is evidenced by its right-ankle bone being found there. Another curious confirmation arises from my friend's remark about the missing tooth, when compared with the following passage from Ughelli, Ital. Sacr. t. iv. col. 82 :—

"Archbishop Angelbert was most devout to the Church of St. Ambrose, and erected a golden altar in it, at the cost of 30,000 gold pieces. The occasion of this gift is told us by Galvaneus, among others, in his Catalogue, when he is speaking of Angelbert. His words are these:— 'Angelbert was Archbishop for thirty-five years, from A.D. 826, and out of devotion he extracted a tooth from the mouth of St. Ambrose, and placed it in his [episcopal] ring. One day the tooth fell out from the ring; and, on the Archbishop causing a thorough search to be made for it, an old woman appeared to him, saying, "You will find the tooth in the place from which you took it." On hearing this, the Archbishop betook himself to the body of St. Ambrose, and found it in the mouth of the blessed Ambrose. Then, to make it impossible for anything in future [or anything else, de cætero] to be taken from his body, he hid it under ground, and caused to be made the golden altar of St. Ambrose, etc.

Castellionæus in his Antiquities of Milan (apud Burman. Antiqu. Ital. t. 3, part 1. col. 487) tells us that the Archbishop lost his relic "as he was going in his pontifical vestments to the Church of St. Lawrence on Palm Sunday. He found he had lost it in the way thither, for, on taking off his gloves, he saw it was gone

It would seem from my friend's letter that either the Archbishop took away the tooth a second time, or the miracle of its restoration did not take place.

It should be added that the place in which Angelbert hid the sacred relics was so well known, that in the twelfth century Cardinal Bernard, Bishop of Parma, was allowed to see and venerate them,—Vid. Puricelli's Ambros. Basil. Descriptio. c. 58 and c. 352, ap. Burman. Thesaur. Antiqu. Ital. t. 4, part 1.

That St. Ambrose was buried in his own church, called even from the time of his death the "Ambrosian," and the church where he had placed the bones of the two martyrs, Gervasius and Protasius, by the side of whom he proposed to have his own body placed, is plain from his own words and those of Paulinus his Secretary.

For the controversy on the subject vid. Castellion. *ubi supra.*

THE END

EDITOR'S NOTES

(Scripture references are from the Douay-Rheims translation which, as a Roman Catholic, Newman uses after 1845 though he still sometimes quotes the King James' or Authorised Version, or sometimes a paraphrased version of them. Where the name of a particular book differs from the Douay-Rheims version, the Authorised Version is also given in brackets.)

The Church of the Fathers

p. i. QUÆ EST ISTA ... ACIES ORDINATA: Canticle of Canticles 6: 9; for the 1840 edition, Newman inserted a quote from the King James' Version (Song of Solomon 6: 10): 'Who is she that looketh forth as the morning, fair as the moon, clear as the sun, and terrible as an army with banners?' In later editions as a Roman Catholic, he inserted an abbreviated quote from the Vulgate, the Latin version of which is: 'quae est ista quae progreditur quasi aurora consurgens pulchra ut luna electa ut sol terribilis ut acies ordinata'.

p. iii. *Isaac Williams*: (1802–65), Newman's great Oxford friend, his curate at St. Mary the University Church, Oxford, and a fellow of Trinity College. Williams published several volumes of poetry, including *The Cathedral or the Catholic and Apostolic Church in England* in 1838. That same year, he became the centre of controversy with his *Tract* 80, 'On Reserve in Communicating Religious Knowledge'. His failure in 1842 to get the Oxford Chair of Poetry vacated by fellow Tractarian, John Keble, dealt a severe blow to the Oxford Movement. For the 1857 edition, Newman added a further dedication, this time to a friend, Robert Isaac Wilberforce (1802–57), who was the second son of the emancipator of slavery, became a Catholic in 1854 and died a few weeks before ordination in Rome.

pp. v–ix. *ADVERTISEMENT*: with the exception of the final paragraph, this advertisement is the original 1840 advertisement, together with most of the 1857 advertisement.

p. v. *British Magazine*: founded in 1832 by High Churchman, Hugh James Rose (1795–1838) as a vehicle for High Church views. Its full title was *The British Magazine, and Monthly Register of Religious and Ecclesiastical Information, Parochial History, and Documents Respecting the State of the Poor, Progress of the Poor, etc.* Rose remained editor until his untimely death (see *Apologia pro Vita Sua (Apo.)*, pp. 37–39).

p. viii. "*argumentum ad hominem*": 'argument designed to focus on the person rather than the argument'.

p. viii. *impedimenta*: 'baggage'.

p. viii. *St. Basil*: (*c.* 330–79), Basil the Great, Bishop of Cæsarea and exarch of Cappadocia (central Asia Minor) and one of the three celebrated Cappadocian Fathers.

p. viii. *St. Gregory*: (*c.* 329–90), native of Nazianzus (south-west of Caeasarea, Cappadocia) and one of the celebrated three Cappadocian Fathers.

p. viii. *St. Martin*: (*c.* 320–97), Bishop of Tours in the Loire valley in Roman Gaul.

p. ix. *St. Gregory on a graver occasion*: Gregory the Great was consecrated pope on 3 September, 590. At the time, Italy was in the midst of plague, famine and floods. The Tiber had burst its banks, causing enormous damage to Rome. Lombards were on the move burning and slaughtering. The Church of Milan was divided and a split with the eastern Church was looming on the horizon. Gregory was all too aware that he was taking charge of an 'old and grievously shattered ship (for on all sides the waves enter, and the planks, battered by a daily and violent storm, sound of shipwreck)' (*Register of the Epistles of Gregory the Great*, Book 1, Epistle IV, to John, Bishop of Constantinople).

p. ix. "*Plus nobis Thomae infidelitas . . . credentium discipulorum profuit*": 'Rather, the infidelity of Thomas served our faith more than the faith of the apostles who believed' (Gregory the Great, *Homily on John the Evangelist*, XXVI, 7).

p. ix. *St Thomas*: as Chancellor of England, Thomas Becket (*c.* 1118–70) supported Henry II in his claim that clergy must be tried in civil court. He reversed his position on becoming Archbishop of Canterbury in 1162. He also opposed Henry's scheme to tax the Church. As a result, he was murdered by four of Henry's henchmen in Canterbury Cathedral late in the afternoon of 29 December 1170. Pope Alexander III canonised him three years later. Henry performed public penance at the tomb of Thomas the following year.

p. ix. *Doctor of the Church*: individuals whom the Church considers to have spiritual and theological insights of universal value. The Church officially recognises thirty-three doctors, including Basil the Great, Gregory of Nazianzus, Augustine of Hippo, Thomas Aquinas. So far the Church has recognised three women as Doctors of the Church, Teresa of Avila (1515–82), Catherine of Siena (1347–80) and Teresa of Lisieux (1873–97).

p. ix. *Pelagius*: (*c.* 354–*c.* 420), monk from Britain who acted as a spiritual director to certain wealthy families of Rome and who denied the doctrine of divine grace and original sin. After the sack of Rome in 410, he fled to Roman north Africa and from there to Palestine where Jerome accused him of heresy. He believed that individuals could avoid sin and be saved without the help of God's grace; that forgiveness of sin means forgiveness from punishment, not necessarily renewal of grace; and that people can live sinless lives by exercising free will. Pope Innocent I (401–17) excommunicated him in 417 and the Council of Carthage condemned his teachings in 418. Except for a few extracts in the writings of Jerome and Augustine, his most outspoken critic, nothing survives of his writings.

Introduction

p. 1. *The Church is ever militant*: the phrase, 'Church Militant' refers to members of the Church living on earth at any one time and engaged in the perennial battle against the forces of evil. 'Now, considering that at that very time our Lord did appear as a teacher, and founded not merely a religion, but . . . a system of religious warfare, an aggressive and militant body, a dominant Catholic Church, which aimed at the benefit of all nations, by the spiritual conquest of all; and that this warfare, then begun by it, has gone on without cessation down to this day, and now is as living and real as ever it was; that that militant body has from the first filled the world, that it . . .has abolished great social anomalies and miseries, has elevated the female sex to its proper dignity, has protected the poorer classes, has destroyed slavery, encouraged literature and philosophy, and had a principal part in that civilization of human kind' (*An Essay in Aid of a Grammar of Assent (G.A.)*, pp. 444–445; see also *Sermons bearing on Subjects of the Day (S.D.)*, Sermons VIII, XVI–XVIII).

p. 1. *sometimes she gains, sometimes she loses*: on 30 April 1877, Newman commented to an old friend, Lord Emly, William Monsell (1812–94): 'As to your question, the Church has ever seemed dying, and has been especially bad (to appearance) every 300 years. Think of it when the whole force of the Roman Empire was against it. Well, they triumphed, against all human calculation. Hardly had things got into shape, when down came the barbarians and all was undone and they had to begin again. Would not the prospect of the future look as terrible to St. Augustine and St. Leo (humanly) as it does to our generation? It is impossible to forecast the future, when you have no precedents – and the history of Christianity is a succession of fresh and fresh trials – never the same twice. We can only say, "The Lord that delivered me from the lion and the bear, He will deliver me from the Philistine" (1 Kings (1 Samuel) 17: 37). But we cannot anticipate the exact shape the conflict will take' (*The Letters and Diaries of John Henry Newman (L.D.)* XXVIII, p. 196).

p. 1. *Te Deum*: traditional hymn of praise and thanksgiving to God the Father and Son sung at the conclusion of special occasions; traditionally attributed to Ambrose of Milan (*c.* 339–97) to celebrate, it is said, the baptism of St. Augustine of Hippo (354–430). It has often been set to music by composers like Johann Sebastian Bach (1685–1750), Franz Josef Haydn (1732–1806), Guiseppi Verdi (1813–1901), and, more recently, by Arvo Part (b. 1935) and John Rutter (b. 1945).

p. 1. *Misereres*: Miserere, the first word in the Vulgate translation of Psalm 50, meaning 'Have mercy', expressing grief and sorrow chiefly for the sinful human condition; historically associated with David's adultery with Bathsheba (2 Kings (2 Samuel) 11–12). It is one of seven penitential psalms, the others being psalms 6, 31, 37, 101, 129, and 142.

p. 1. *Stephen*: one of seven deacons selected by the apostles to administer to the pastoral needs of the poor in the church of Jerusalem. He was the first Christian martyr, around 35 (Acts 8: 2).

p. 1. *Paul*: before his own conversion, Paul was present at Stephen's martyrdom (Acts 7: 57) and was himself executed in Rome during the Neronian persecution around AD 65.

p. 1. *Matthias*: apostle and evangelist who replaced Judas Iscariot after the Ascension (Acts 1: 15–26).

p. 1. *Arianism*: name of a fourth-century heresy which rejected the divinity of Jesus Christ and focused on the *differences* rather than the *similarities* between the Father and the Son. Because the Son was a created being, Arians argued, he must have had a beginning and was therefore a subordinate being to the Father who had always existed from eternity. This teaching had its origins in the teachings of Arius (*c.* 260–336) a priest from Alexandria who came into open conflict with his bishop, the orthodox Alexander. The emperor Constantine ordered them to stop squabbling over such an 'insignificant and worthless' issue. 'Is it right for brothers to oppose brothers, for the sake of trifles?', he wrote. 'Such conduct might be expected from the multitude, or from the recklessness of boyhood; but is little in keeping with your sacred profession, and with your personal wisdom' (*The Arians of the Fourth Century (Ari.)*, pp. 248–249). According to the Church historian, Socrates (*c.* 380–450), Arius argued that '(1) If the Father gave birth to the Son, He who was born has an origin of existence; (2) therefore once the Son was not; (3) therefore He is created out of nothing' (Socrates, *Ecclesiastical History from AD 305–438*, Book I, Chapter 5; *The Arians of the Fourth Century (Ari.)*, p. 205). Athanasius believed that Arianism was 'the forerunner of Antichrist' (*Select Treatises of St. Athanasius (Ath.)* II, p. 13).

p. 2. *synod*: regular meeting of local bishops at which matters necessary for the welfare of the diocese are discussed.

p. 2. *the fourth century*: 'Arianism of the fourth century was not a popular heresy. The laity, as a whole, revolted from it in every part of Christendom. It was an epidemic of the schools and of theologians, and to them it was mainly confined. It did not spread among the parish priests and their flocks, or the great body of the monks; though, as time went on, it gained a certain portion of some of the larger towns, and some monastic communities. The classes which had furnished martyrs in the persecutions were in no sense the seat of the heresy' (*Trials of Theodoret, (T.T.)*, p. 144).

p. 2. *Thus bad and good . . . world is borne*: from *The Christian Year: Thoughts in Verse for the Sundays and Holy days Throughout the Year* by John Keble (1792–1868), Oxford, 1827, Advent Sunday, p. 11.

Chapter I: Trials of Basil

Synopsis: Eusebius, Bishop of Caesarea and Exarch of Cappadocia, cannot cope with the formidable heresy of Arianism assailing the local Church. He therefore enlists the services of a brilliant, young, orthodox priest called Basil who has been living as a monk on the family estate at Annesi north-east of Neocaesarea near the junction of the Iris and Lycus rivers. Basil performs the task so well that Eusebius becomes jealous, forcing Basil back to his retreat at Annesi. When Eusebius dies, Basil succeeds him, though not without stiff opposition from the local Arian party. In spite of constant illness and harassment, Basil throws himself into the job. While critics accuse him of arrogance and cowardice, his letters reveal another side of him, affectionate, compassionate and sensitive. When he dies, Basil is just fifty years old.

p. 3. *Basil*: (*c.* 330–79), Basil the Great, Bishop of Caesarea and Exarch of

Cappadocia from 370 and one of three Cappadocian Fathers alongside Gregory of Nyssa and Gregory of Nazianzus. After a first-class education at Constantinople and Athens, he taught rhetoric at Caesarea for a while before visiting monasteries in Syria, Mesopotamia, Palestine and Egypt. On return, he was baptised and established a small monastic community on the family estate at Annesi near the junction of the Iris and Lycus rivers. Basil wrote a rule of life for monks which is still widely used in the east. In 360, he was ordained reader by Dianus, Bishop of Caesarea and Exarch of Cappadocia. Two years later, he was ordained priest by the next incumbent, Eusebius, whom he succeeded in 370. In his 'Letter to the Duke of Norfolk' in 1874, Newman asked: 'Does any Anglican Bishop for the last 300 years recall to our minds the image of St. Basil?' (*Certain Difficulties felt by Anglicans in Catholic Teaching (Diff.)* II, p. 207).

p. 3. "*As a servant longeth . . . have I numbered unto me*": Job 7: 2–3.

p. 3. *Athanasius*: (*c.* 300–73), orthodox Bishop of Alexandria (328–73) at the age of thirty-three, one of the most important Church figures of the fourth century, prolific writer, astute politician, 'illustrious champion' of the Nicene creed (*The Via Media (V.M.)* I, p. 228) and Doctor of the Church. He waged war against Arianism first in his capacity as adviser to his predecessor, Alexander of Alexandria, and later as Bishop of Alexandria. Throughout his long episcopate, he was exiled five times, and managed to return to his see each time when a new emperor ascended the throne or when the political climate was favourable. His determined opposition to Arianism was a crucial factor in its eventual downfall. 'This renowned Father', wrote Newman, 'is in ecclesiastical history the special doctor of the sacred truth which Arius denied, bringing it out into shape and system so fully and luminously that he may be said to have exhausted his subject, as far as it lies open to the human intellect' (*Ath.* II, p. 51). Newman described Athanasius as 'the foremost doctor of the Divine Sonship, being the most modest as well as the most authoritative of teachers' (ibid., pp. 56–57). He is also 'the first and the great teacher' of the Incarnation. 'He collected together the inspired notices scattered through David, Isaias, St. Paul, and St. John, and he engraved indelibly upon the imaginations of the faithful, as had never been before, that man is God, and God is man, that in Mary they meet, and that in this sense Mary is the centre of all things' *(Diff.* II, 87).

p. 3. *Arians were in the ascendant*: in effect, Arians denied the full divinity of Jesus Christ, considering him a secondary or subordinate deity, having existed since before creation, but not co-eternally with God the Father. 'Arians said that they believed in our Lord's divinity, but when they were pressed to confess His eternity, they denied it: thereby showing in fact that they never had believed in His divinity at all' (*G.A.*, p. 151). Although the Council of Nicaea (325) formally condemned Arianism, it subsequently 'ran its course, through various modifications of opinion, and with various success, till the date of the second General Council, held AD 381, at Constantinople, when the resources of heretical subtilty being at length exhausted, the Arian party was ejected from the Catholic body, and formed into a distinct sect, exterior to it' (*The Arians of the Fourth Century*, p. 1). Initially, the emperor Constantine thought the dispute was nothing more than a 'question of words'. 'On finding, however, both before and at the Council [Nicaea], the general opinion to be against Arius, the originator of the disturbance, he changed his course in favour of orthodoxy, at the cost of abandoning thereby his personal friends, and zealously defended the side professed by the majority. After a few years he changed back again, and exposed the bishops and populations of the Church to the revenge of an exasperated faction. (*Essays Critical and Historical* I, pp. 123–4). From the first, there were three parties among the Arians. The 'Arians proper, afterwards called Anomœans; the Semi-Arian reaction from them; and the Court party, called Eusebians or Acacians, from their leaders, Eusebius of Nicomedia and Acacius of Cæsarea, which sometimes sided with the Semi-Arians, sometimes with the Arians proper, sometimes attempted a compromise of Scripture terms' (*Ath.* II, p. 28).

p. 3. *Gregory*: Bishop of Nazianzus (*c.* 329–89); see note to p. 50 (*The Church of the Fathers* (*C.F.*)).

p. 3. *Ambrose*: Bishop of Milan (*c.* 339–97); see note to p. 339 (*P.C.*).

p. 3. *an Arian sovereign*: Valens, emperor of the east (364–78); see note to p. 6 (*C.F.*).

p. 3. *Constantinople*: site of ancient Byzantium, situated at the tip of a promontory on the European side of the Bosporus; founded by Constantine the Great (306–37) as the 'New Rome'. It became the empire's new economic and military headquarters. Rather than rule from a city with pagan associations like Rome, Constantine wanted a new capital that would be Christian from the beginning. It was at Constantinople where tensions first surfaced between the imperial court and the Church over Arianism; modern Istanbul since 1930.

p.3. *Asia Minor*: very large peninsula roughly corresponding to modern Asian Turkey (also known as Anatolia) surrounded by the Black Sea in the north, the Mediterranean Sea in the south and the Aegean Sea in the west. It covers an area of almost 650,000 square kilometres (250,000 square miles). Along its southern coastline runs the Taurus and Antitaurus

Mountains while the rest of the peninsula forms the Anatolian plateau, crisscrossed by several mountain ranges and dotted with numerous lakes. In the fourth century of the early Church, the principal Roman provinces included Pontus, Cappadocia, Bithynia, Galatia, Cilicia, Lycia and Asia (the western province).

pp. 3–4. *These countries had . . . deplorable state of confusion*: for the next forty years or so, Arianism was virtually the state religion of the east. The emperor Constantius II (337–61) was Arian. So too subsequently were Valens (364–78) and Valentinian II (375–92), although Valentinian renounced it after the death of his mother, Justina. Those who refused to go along with Arianism were tortured or exiled and their churches desecrated (see Socrates, *Ecclesiastical History*, Book II, Chapter 27; see also *Ari.*, pp. 446–468).

p. 4. *Cæsarea*: ancient city originally named Mazaca, situated high on the north-west slopes of Mount Argaeus, the highest mountain in Cappadocia (4,000 metres or 13,000 feet) and an extinct volcano, located on the Halys river. In AD 17, the emperor Tiberius created Cappadocia a province and renamed it Caesarea. In Basil's day, it was the capital of Cappadocia with a population of almost 200,000 people and situated on the main highway from Mesopotamia to Constantinople. It was the see of Basil the Great. There were several other cities throughout the empire with the name of Caesarea; for example, the port of Caesarea Maritima, Herod's chief port in Roman Palestine, south of modern Haifa; Caesarea Philippi at the foot of Mount Hermon in Israel; Caesarea Libani north-east of Tripoli; Caesarea Germanicia in south-east Asia Minor; and Caesarea in Mauretania, Roman north Africa.

p. 4. *exarch*: title used both civilly and ecclesiastically; civilly, an exarch was governor or viceroy of any important province such as the exarchs of Italy, who ruled from Ravenna in the name of the emperor at Constantinople from 552 to 751. Ecclesiastically, an exarch was initially a metropolitan bishop who had jurisdiction over local or rural bishops ('chorepiscopi') in his diocese or province. Even as late as the Council of Chalcedon (451), patriarchs were still called exarchs. In fact, early ecclesiastical writers used the terms 'metropolitan', 'archbishop', 'exarch' and 'patriarch' indiscriminately. When 'patriarch' became the official title for the bishops of Rome, Alexandria, Antioch, Constantinople and Jerusalem, the title 'exarch' was reserved for those who ruled the three remaining political dioceses of the eastern prefecture, namely, Asia (from Ephesus), Cappadocia-Pontus (from Caesarea), and Thrace (from Heraclea). As exarch of Cappadocia, Basil had jurisdiction over more than fifty chorepiscopi.

p. 4. *Cappadocia*: region in central Anatolia surrounded by Pontus to the north, Cilicia to the south, Armenia and the Euphrates river to the west (Acts 2: 9; 1 Pet. 1: 1). In the fourth century, it was an important centre of Christianity, the scene of the labours of Basil the Great, Gregory of Nazianzus and Gregory of Nyssa. It is mostly composed of a high plateau and rich in mineral resources, particularly copper and iron. Its capital was Caesarea. Cappadocia was annexed as a Roman province around AD 17. The violent eruptions of Mount Argaeus, a now-extinct volcano, once covered the region with a thick layer of mud and ash which, when hardened and after many ages of wind erosion, created a bizarre landscape dotted with chimney-like rock formations which locals hollowed out and used as dwellings or churches. They are known as 'fairy chimneys'.

p. 4. *Dianius*: (d. *c.* 362), Bishop of Caesarea and Exarch of Cappadocia for more than twenty years. He seems to be have been a weak, vacillating individual without any strong theological convictions. He generally sided with the strongest party, even to the extent of voting against Athanasius and voting at the Council of Ariminum (359) to replace the Nicene creed with a vaguely worded creed that was susceptible of an Arian interpretation.

p. 4. *council of Ariminum*: convened by the Arian emperor, Constantius II in 359 to settle the Arian issue in favour of the Arian party; of the 400 bishops from the west who attended, eighty were Arian. Due to the politicking of at least two Arian bishops from the Balkans, Valens and Ursacius, plus pressure from Taurus, the emperor's representative, the assembled bishops, 'worn out by the artifice of long delay on the part of the Arians' agreed to an 'ambiguous formula' susceptible of an Arian interpretation. Constantius gave orders that no one was to 'stir out of the city, till they should agree upon a confession of faith'. The other council took place at Seleucia in Cilicia (south-east Asia Minor) and consisted of 150 bishops from the east, only a handful 'from Egypt were champions' of the Nicene formula (*Ari.*, pp. 348; 449).

p. 4. *Ariminum*: modern Rimini in the region of Emilia Romagna on the Adriatic coast of north-central Italy, situated close to the mouth of the Ariminus river and about 15 kilometres (9 miles) from the Rubicon which formed the southern boundary of Cisalpine Gaul. It was founded as a Roman colony in about the middle of the third century and strategically located at the junction of the Via Flaminiana and Via Aemiliana.

p. 4. *Homoüsion, or Consubstantial*: homoüsion, Greek term meaning 'of one substance'; translates in Latin as 'consubstantial'; central to the orthodox argument against Arianism and to the solution of the Trinitarian problem offered at Nicaea in 325. According to Athanasius of Alexandria, Hosius of Cordova (Spain) had a major hand in drawing it up but, according to Hilary of Poitiers (France), so too did Athanasius (see *G.A.*, pp. 142ff.). 'The question of the homoüsion ... was a party question between Antioch and Alexandria. Its adoption at Nicaea was the reversal of an act of the forefathers of the Asiatics in the great Council of Antioch sixty years before' when it was considered 'dangerous' (*T.T.*, p. 146). 'Though above three hundred Bishops had accepted it at Nicaea, the great body of the Episcopate in the next generation considered it inexpedient' (*Ari.*, p. 434).

p. 4. *Eusebius*. important civil servant who, much to the emperor's displeasure, succeeded Dianius as orthodox Bishop of Caesarea in 362; not to be confused with another Eusebius (*c.* 260–*c.* 339), Bishop of Caesarea in Palestine and first major Church historian.

p. 5. *formidable heresy by which the Church was assailed*: 'From a little spark a great fire was kindled. The quarrel began in the Alexandrian Church, then it spread through the whole of Egypt, Lybia, and the farther Thebais; then it ravaged the other provinces and cities, till the war of words enlisted not only the prelates of the churches, but the people too. At length the exposure was so extraordinary, that even in the heathen theatres, the divine doctrine became the subject of the vilest ridicule' (*Ari.*, p. 140).

p. 5. *wild region of Pontus*: long, narrow, strip of land in north-east Asia Minor, running along the southern coastline of the Black Sea ('Pontus Euxinus'). It was also known as 'Cappadocia on the Pontus'. The region was enclosed by high, wild mountain ranges, but extremely fertile on the coast, inland and on its many plateaux. People from Pontus were among those in Jerusalem who listened to Peter on the day of Pentecost (Acts 2:9).

p. 5. *St. Antony*: (*c.* 251–356), father of early monasticism in Egypt. See note to p. 94 (*C.F.*).

p. 5. *apostasy*: act of a baptised person who rejects Christianity and incurs excommunication. To people such as the Donatists of Roman north Africa, apostasy was unforgivable and irredeemable. The emperor Julian (361–63) was nicknamed 'the Apostate' for rejecting Christianity and reviving paganism. In 2 Thessalonians 2–3, Paul the Apostle warns of a great apostasy as a prelude to the second coming of Jesus. It is not the same as heresy or schism. Heresy involves rejection of certain aspects of official Church teaching, whereas schism is refusal to recognise the Church's authority in certain matters.

p. 5. *ascetics*: individuals practising a strict, penitential lifestyle.

p. 5. *that they who have a clean heart shall see God*: Matthew 5: 8.

p. 5. *Sozomen*: fifth-century Church historian about whom little is known except that he was a native of Palestine and practised as a lawyer in Constantinople. He wrote a history of the Church from the Council of Nicaea (325) down to the year 425. Though orthodox himself, he displayed little appreciation of what was actually at stake in Christological debates of the period. He died sometime after 450.

p. 6. *Cilicia*: maritime province on the south-east coastline of Asia Minor whose principal city was Tarsus, birthplace of Paul the Apostle and the place where he carried on his apostolate for a period (Galatians 1: 21).

p. 6. *Phoenicia*: generally refers to that region roughly corresponding to present-day Lebanon together with parts of Syria, Israel and Turkey; the word itself may be derived from the Greek word meaning 'purple' and referred to its citizens who traded in purple cloth and dye with the Greeks; it may also be derived from Phoenix, son of Agenor, King of Tyre. The Phoenician community were among the first Gentiles visited by Jesus. After leaving Jerusalem, Matthew tells us that Jesus retired into the districts of Tyre and Sidon. 'And, behold, a Canaanite woman came out of that territory and cried to him, saying, "Have pity on me, O Lord, Son of David! My daughter is sorely beset by a devil" ' (Matthew 15: 21–27). Even today, the bishops of major Lebanon cities carry the honorary title of 'Metropolitan of Phoenicia Maritima'.

p. 6. *Hellespont*: see note to p. 61 (*C.F.*).

p. 6. *Constantinople*: see note to p. 3 (*C.F.*).

p. 6. *Apollinarian*: disciple of Apollinaris of Laodicea (*c.* 310–*c.* 390) in Syria who argued that a divine nature and a human nature could not be reconciled in the person of Jesus Christ and that Jesus possessed a divine consciousness but not a human one.

p. 6. *Eunomius*: (*c.* 325–*c.* 395), leader of a radical form of Arianism known as *Anomoeanism* which claimed that God the Father cannot be divided and that Jesus and the Father were unlike in essence. For a short period of time when *Anomoeanism* was in the ascendant, he became Bishop of Cyzicus (modern Bal Kiz on the Asiatic coast of the Propontis) but resigned after a few months. He died in exile around 395. Eunomius possessed 'a faculty of subtle disputation and hard mathematical reasoning' and had 'a fierce, and in one sense an honest, disdain of compromise and dissimulation' (*Ari.*, p. 339).

p. 6. *heresiarch*: instigator or founder of a heresy such as Arius and Eutyches.

p. 6. *Valens*: (364–78), last Arian emperor of the east who failed to win over Basil the Great. Valens was the brother of Valentinian I. His death in a disastrous battle against the Goths at Hadrianople (north-west of Constantinople) preceded 'the final downfall of Arianism in the Eastern Church'. (*Ari.*, p. 379).

p. 7. *Bezaleel*: son of Uri from the tribe of Juda; a talented artist especially in metal work, employed by Moses to construct the tabernacle in the wilderness, including the ark of the covenant (Exodus 31: 1–11; 35: 30ff.; 36: 1, 37–39). Gregory compares Basil to him.

p. 7. *for I am a man*: Matthew 8: 9; Luke 7: 8.

p. 9. *Antioch*: capital of Syria, situated on the Orontes river; until the rise of Constantinople, Antioch was the capital of Coele-Syria (Greater Syria) ranking alongside Rome, Alexandria, and Constantinople as one of the great cities of the Roman Empire; founded in 300 BC by Seleucus I, King of Syria. It was once host to figures such as Julius Caesar, Diocletian, Constantine the Great, and John Chrysostom. Its location as a strategic important trade route brought it prosperity and a sophisticated culture. 'During the interval between the Nicene Council and the death of Constantius (325–61), Antioch was the metropolis of the heretical, as Alexandria of the orthodox party. At Antioch, the heresy recommenced its attack upon the Church after the decision of Nicaea. In a council held at Antioch [345], it first showed itself in the shape of Semi-Arianism ... '(*Ari.*, p. 9); not to be confused with Antioch in Pisidia which Paul visited on his first missionary journey (Acts 14: 14–15). Peter the Apostle was its first bishop, Evodius its second, and Ignatius its third. By the fourth century, Antioch was a cosmopolitan city of Syrians, Greeks, Jews and Romans, approximately half of whom were Christian.

p. 9. *Prætorian Prefect*: originally, title given to the commander of the imperial bodyguard (praetorian guard), formed by the emperor Augustus to protect the emperor from assassins as Brutus and his fellow conspirators had murdered his uncle Julius Caesar. In the sweeping political changes that ensued in the wake of the emperors Diocletian and Constantine the Great, the Praetorian Prefect lost his military status and become a powerful civilian minister. The Empire was divided into four prefectures each under the control of a prefect. The Praetorian prefects were thus the most powerful civilian government ministers. There were Praetorian prefects of the East, of Gaul, of Italy and Africa, and of Greece and the central Balkans. Each prefecture was then sub-divided into several dioceses and each diocese was further sub-divided into provinces.

p. 9. *Modestus*: pragmatic Praetorian Prefect of the eastern prefecture; who practised Christianity under the orthodox Constans I (joint emperor, 337–50), who sacrificed to pagan idols under Julian the Apostate (361–63) and who sided with the Arian party under Valens (364–78). In his *Ecclesiastical History*, Theodoret of Cyrrhus (*c.* 393–*c.* 468) described him as a 'wolf' (Book IV, Chapter XV).

p. 10. *Peradventure Modestus … a bishop*: at that time, Roman civil law considered bishops to have the same legal status as local magistrates.

p. 11. *his persevering persecution …the favourable supposition*: a very determined Arian, Valens (364–78) executed orthodox members of the Church and exiled bishops, including Athanasius of Alexandria. When he fell in battle, many orthodox Christians believed that his death was a sign of divine retribution. His body was never recovered.

p. 12. *heterodoxy*: unorthodoxy.

p. 12. "*an exceeding weight of glory*": 2 Corinthians 4: 17.

p. 12. *Julian*: (332–363), Roman emperor of the east from 361 and the son of Constantine I's half-brother, Julius Constantius, who was massacred along with most of Constantine's relatives in 337 on the orders of the three brother-emperors, Constantine II, Constantius II and Constans who wanted to eliminate potential rivals. Julian and his half-brother were the only two survivors. As a result, Julian rejected Christianity and everything it stood for. On becoming emperor in 361, he publicly declared himself a pagan and re-instated pagan cults and provided them with an infrastructure designed to rival Christianity. He proclaimed religious toleration in the vain hope of undermining Christianity, but the plan backfired. He recalled all banished bishops, knowing them to be a smorgasbord of 'Semi-Arians, Macedonians, Anomœans, as well as orthodox'. His object was the 'renewal of those dissensions, by means of toleration, which Constantius had endeavoured to terminate by means of force … being persuaded, that Christianity could not withstand the shock of parties, not less discordant, and far more zealous, than the sects of philosophy' (*Ari.*, p. 354). According to the historian, Edward Gibbon, Julian 'invited to his palace the leaders of the hostile sects, that he might enjoy the agreeable spectacle of their furious encounters' (*Decline and Fall of the Roman Empire*, Chapter XXIII). Newman once described Julian as the 'foe of Christian education. He, in whom every Catholic sees the shadow of the future Antichrist, was all but the pattern-man of philosophical virtue' (*The Idea of a University defined and illustrated (Idea)*, p. 194 ; *An Essay on the Development of Christian Doctrine*, p. 403). He was killed in battle by a Persian spear, buried, according to his wishes, outside Tarsus in Cilicia, but was eventually brought back to Constantinople. Among his surviving writings are eighty letters, eight speeches, the satirical *Misopogon* ('Beard-Hater'), and the humorous *Caesars*.

p. 12. *Amphilochius*: (*c*. 340–95), orthodox Bishop of Iconium (south-west of Nazianzus,) from 373 and the scene of Paul's early missionary activities (Acts 14). He was the cousin of Gregory Nazianzus (south-west of Caesarea) and a friend of Basil 'the Great' and Gregory of Nyssa (west of Caesarea).

p. 13. *Eusebius*: orthodox Bishop of Samosata on the Euphrates in northern Syria from 361 and a strong opponent of Arianism. A close friend of Basil the Great and Gregory of Nazianzus, he was exiled in 374 by Valens, last Arian emperor in the east, (364–378), but recalled by Gratian, the anti-Arian emperor in the west in 378. He was accidentally killed by a brick thrown at his head by an Arian woman in 380; not to be confused with the political pro-Arian Eusebius of Nicomedia (d. *c*. 342) or the historian Eusebius of Caesarea (d. *c*. 340) in Syria. This Eusebius died in 380.

p. 14. *Elpidius*: one of Basil's couriers, friend and advocate of Christian who was imprisoned for three years in 406.

p. 14. *Isaaces*: friend who visited Basil around 373 and reported to Eusebius of Samosata that Basil was in poor health and burdened with a host of problems.

p. 15. *as far as the Martyrs*: it is not certain which spot Basil is referring to; Tillemont thinks it was the tomb of St. Eupsychius, a young man, who, according to the historian, Sozomen, was executed for his part in demolishing the pagan Temple of Fortune at Caesarea during the reign of Julian the Apostate (*Ecclesiastical History from* AD *323–425*, Book V, Chapter 11).

p. 15. *Diogenes*: (*c*. 412–*c*. 323 BC), philosopher from the port of Sinope in Paphlagonia on the Black Sea, and probably the most famous cynic of them all. He practised a life of the utmost simplicity, relying on the barest basics and refusing to have anything to do with the comforts of civilization. He lived in a barrel. By day, he walked the streets of Athens carrying a lantern searching for an honest citizen, but never found one. When Alexander the Great met him in Corinth and inquired what he could do for him, Diogenes told him to get out of the way as he was blocking the sunshine.

p. 16. *Meletius*: (360–81), orthodox Bishop of Antioch in Syria who was expelled by the Arian emperor, Constantius II, for preaching an orthodox sermon during his inauguration ceremony. He once belonged to the Semi-Arian party, but later joined the orthodox ranks. Julian the Apostate restored him in 362 but he was banished again in 365 and 371 by Valens, the last Arian emperor in the east. He presided over the Council of Constantinople (381) during which he died. He was a friend of Basil the Great and 'his funeral oration was preached by St. Gregory Nyssen; he is spoken of as a saint by St. [John] Chrysostom, and has a place in the Roman calendar; yet, on the other hand, he was not acknowledged by the Pope of his day ... he was not in communion with Alexandria; he refused to communicate with Athanasius, and he is severely spoken of by Jerome' (*Essays Critical and Historical II (Ess.)* pp. 62–4; see note to p. 121).

p. 16. *Pisidia*: district in southern Asia Minor, south of Phrygia and north of Pamphylia. It is a mountainous country, traversed by the Taurus mountains and inhabited by a warlike people who maintained a fierce independence until the country was annexed by the Romans in the first century AD. Paul preached at Antioch in Pisidia (Acts 13: 14; 14: 23). Although outside Basil's jurisdiction, his intervention there is best explained by the fact that his friend, Amphilocius was Bishop of Iconium, a place often mentioned in the journeys of Paul and Barnabas (Acts 13: 51; 14: 1–6, 20).

p. 16. *Isaurian brethren*: warlike inhabitants from the wild and rugged region of Isauria located on the borders of Pisidia and Lycaonia, on the northern side of the Taurus mountains, in southern Asia Minor. They were brigands who launched raids into the surrounding districts carrying off whatever they could pillage and plunder. When their capital, Isaura, a strongly fortified city at the foot of the Taurus mountains, was besieged by the Macedonians in the fourth century BC, Isaurians torched the town rather than capitulate. Although partially brought under control by the Romans in the first century BC, they were never completely subdued until the arrival of the Seljuk Turks in the eleventh century AD.

p. 16. *Eustathius*: Bishop of Sebaste (354–*c.* 380) south of Neocaesarea and on the Halys river; see *Primitive Christianity (P.C.)*, p. 399.

p. 16. *Dazimon*: ancient fortress overlooking the town of Comana Pontica in Pontus, south-west of Neocaesarea on the Iris river.

p. 16. *my brother Peter's cottage*: settlement on the Iris river in Pontus; Peter succeeded Basil as Bishop of Caesarea.

p. 16. *Pergamius*: prominent citizen to whom Basil wrote a good-humoured reply and about whom very little is known.

p. 17. *Basil's uncle*: Gregory the Elder, father of Gregory of Nazianzus (south-west of Caesarea); he became a second father when Basil's own father died in 374. He supervised his education and was present at his consecration as bishop. For some reason or other, a misunderstanding arose between them. It was never fully resolved.

p. 17. *Diocletian persecution*: last and most savage Roman persecution of the early Church beginning in 303 and ending in 311. Towards the end of his reign, Diocletian (284–305) unleashed the most extensive and systematic persecution of Christians. His aim was nothing less than the annihilation of Christianity. It was a life-and-death struggle between the old Roman way of life and the new. He issued four imperial decrees. The first prohibited all Christian assemblies and ordered the destruction of churches and their sacred books. The next two ordered the arrest of the clergy if they did not sacrifice to the Roman gods. In 304, a final decree included all Christians. In 305, Diocletian abdicated and retired to his palace in Salona; modern Split in Croatia.

p. 18. *St. Gregory Nyssen*: (*c.* 335–95), youngest of the Cappadocian Fathers alongside Basil the Great and Gregory of Nazianzus. On the division of Cappadocia and to minimise the influence of Anthimus, Basil made him Bishop of Nyssa (west of Caesarea) in 372. He had little taste for administration and was sacked in 376 for alleged mismanagement by the local Arian party, but returned two years later. He took an active role in the first Council of Constantinople (381) before fading into obscurity. He was a highly original thinker and a prolific writer. He placed a great deal of emphasis on the unity of the Trinity and on Christ's two natures.

p. 18. *St. Peter*: (*c.* 349–*c.* 393), youngest brother of Basil the Great and Gregory of Nyssa. Basil the Great employed him on delicate missions; after the death of Eustathius around 380, he was ordained Bishop of Sebaste (south of Neocaesarea).

p. 18. *St. Macrina*: (*c.* 325–79), Macrina the Younger, eldest sister of Basil the Great and Gregory of Nyssa; called 'the Younger' to distinguish her from Macrina the Elder, her grandmother. She encouraged Basil to take up an ecclesiastical career. After their father's death, Basil took her and his mother Emmelia to the family estate at Annesi on the Iris river which they developed into a monastery and of which she became its leader after the death of Emmelia. Newman described her life as 'one of the most beautiful in the early history of the Church' (*Birmingham Oratory Archives (BOA)*, C. 2. 10, from an evening talk given by Newman at the Birmingham Oratory, 31 August 1857). After her death, Gregory wrote the *Life of Macrina.*

p. 18. *Naucratius*: (b. *c.* 330), only brother of Basil the Great who did not become a priest. He left his property and retired at the age of twenty-two to a wood above the Iris in Pontus where he died in a tragic hunting accident.

p. 18. *his uncle's estrangement*: it is uncertain what actually triggered it off.

p. 18. '*I have been still, and refrained myself as a woman in travail*': Isaiah 42: 14.

p. 20. *Arius*: (*c.* 260–336), presbyter and theologian from Alexandria whose denial of Christ's divinity sparked off deep division within the early Church. 'His heresy, thus founded in a syllogism, spread itself by instruments of a kindred character. First, we read of the excitement which his readings produced in Egypt and Lybia; then of his letters addressed to Eusebius and to Alexander, which display a like pugnacious and almost satirical spirit; and then of his verses composed for the use of the populace in ridicule of the orthodox doctrine. But afterwards, when the heresy was arraigned before the Nicene Council [325], and placed on the defensive, and later still, when its successes reduced it to the necessity of occupying the chairs of theology, it suffered the fate of other dogmatic heresies before it; split, in spite of court favour, into at least four different creeds, in less than twenty years; and at length gave way to the despised but indestructible truth which it had for a time obscured' (*Ari.*, pp. 28–9). Fragments of verses and other writings known as *Thalia* popularising his teaching plus three of his letters survive.

p. 20. *Eustathius*: (*c.* 300–*c.* 378), Bishop of Sebaste south of Neocaesarea in Pontus from 354. See (*P.C.*), p. 399.

p. 20. *Semi-Arian, or middle, party*: name used to describe bishops and theologians who refused to accept the orthodox decrees of the Nicene Council (325) about the Son being of the *same* substance (*homoousios*) as the Father. Nor would they accept the extreme Arian position that Jesus was a mere man. They adopted a middle position preferring to say that the Son was *similar* in substance to the Father. Their symbol was *homoiouios* (of like substance). Their creed involved contradictory terms, 'parallel to those of which the orthodox were accused; – that the Son was born before all times, yet not eternal; not a creature, yet not God; of His substance, yet not the same in substance; and His exact and perfect resemblance in all things, yet not a second Deity' (*Ari.*, p. 299). This via-media position was embraced by the emperor Constantius II (337–361) and was in the 'ascendancy for about thirty years, till the death of the generation by whom it had been formed and protected; – with quarrels and defections among themselves, restless attempts at stability in faith, violent efforts after a definite creed, fruitless projects of comprehension' (*Diff.* I, 385; see also *Ari.,* pp. 293–306). According to Newman, one special test of an heretical party is its 'constant effort to make alliance with other heresies and schisms, though differing itself from them. Thus the Semiarians attempted the Donatists, and the Arians the Meletians, and the Nestorians (I think) the Pelagians.' (Letter to Robert Isaac Wilberforce, 26 January 1842, *L.D.* VIII, p. 441).

p. 20. *Constantius*: Constantius II, joint emperor of the east (337–50) and sole emperor (350–361). He was the second son of Constantine 'the Great'. He sided with the Arian party 'far more decidedly' than his father. 'He fiercely persecuted the orthodox, assembled Council after Council to destroy the authority of the Nicene [creed], and at the end of his reign dragooned 400 bishops in the West [at Ariminum in 359] and 150 in the East [at Seleucia in Cilicia in 359] into giving an indirect denial to the doctrine witnessed to and solemnly professed in 325. Thus political influences told strongly against, not for, the triumph throughout Christendom of the tradition of orthodoxy. The creed of Nicaea was not the imposition of secular power' (*Ess.* I, p. 124). By the time of his death, the Church was virtually Arian. Athanasius used to refer to Constantius as Antichrist. 'Let Christ be expected', he said, 'for antichrist is in possession' (*Ath.* II, pp. 13–14).

p. 20. "*There is a time . . . for speaking*": Ecclesiastes 3: 7.

p. 20. *great Job*: Job 3: 1ff.

p. 21. *in whose mouth are no reproofs*: Psalm 37: 15 (Psalm 38: 14).

p. 21. *Cœle-Syria*: Greater Syria with Antioch as its capital (1 Machabees 10: 69).

p. 21. *Mesopotamia*: region watered by the Euphrates, Tigris and tributaries, roughly covering modern Iraq and part of Syria; the word itself means 'land between the rivers' and comes from the Greek *mesos* meaning 'middle' and *potamos* 'river'.

p. 23. *Iris*: though not as long a river as the Halys, the Iris rises in southern Pontus near Neocaesarea, flows north past Comana Pontica (west of Neocaesarea) and into the Black Sea. It is about 420 kilometres (260 miles) long. Basil spent his childhood on the banks of the Iris near the village of Annesi in northern Pontus.

p. 23. *one letter*: according to Basil, it was a twenty-year old letter written to Apollinaris.

p. 24. *Jerome in his cave at Bethlehem*: (*c.* 342–*c.* 420), scholar and ascetic who was born at Stridon in north-west Illyricum (Balkans); he became secretary to Pope Damasus I between 382 and 385. Jerome made many enemies by his acid tongue and hard-line views. He was forced out of Rome after the death of Damasus in 384, lived in Bethelem from 386. His greatest achievement was the translation of the Bible into Latin. The finished product became known as the Vulgate ('in common use'). In 1526, the Council of Trent stipulated that it must be used for public readings and worship. The committee which translated the Bible into English in 1611 (the King James or Authorised Version) relied heavily on it. His study, it was said, was a cave close by the cave of the Nativity in Bethelem. It was here that he stored, at great expense, his library containing classical and sacred works, including Origen, Irenaeus and Eusebius of Caesarea. According to tradition, he was buried in that cave.

p. 24. '*not lording it over the clergy*': 1 Peter 5: 3.

p. 25. *Philostorgius*: (*c.* 368–*c.* 439), radical Arian historian from Cappadocia who wrote a church history in twelve books after visiting Arian communities throughout the east. It covered the period from 300 to 425 and was intended to continue Eusebius of Caesarea's *Ecclesiastical History*. The reality was that it was really a defence of the radical Arian school of thought.

p. 27. "*Into Thy hands I commend my spirit*": Psalm 30: 6 (Psalm 31: 5).

Chapter II: Labours of Basil

Synopsis: Basil does not live to savour the fruits of victory over Arianism on whose behalf the emperor Valens campaigns vigorously until his death in battle against the Visigoths at Hadrianople (Edirne) in 378, one year before Basil's. His efforts to entice the Semi-Arian party back to orthodoxy make him a target of jealousy and suspicion. A group of local bishops refuse to cooperate. One particular thorn in his side is Eustathius, Bishop of Sebaste, who proceeds to separate a portion of Pontus from the Church of Caesarea on the pretence that some of its bishops, including Basil, are in heresy. A despondent Basil makes appeals for help to the bishops of the west, but they turn their backs on him.

p. 28. "*And I said, . . . with my God.*": Isaiah 49: 4.

p. 28. *Hildebrand*: Pope Gregory VII (1073–85) who made Church reform the cornerstone of his pontificate. He denounced clerical marriages, forbade the buying and selling of Church offices and abolished the investiture of bishops and abbots by lay princes. He shaped the course of the western Church for centuries (see *Ess.* II, p. 254 ff.; *Discussions and Arguments on Various Subjects (D.A.)*, pp. 25; 33–36).

p. 29. *Alexander*: orthodox Bishop of Alexandria from around 312 to 328 and one of the earliest opponents of the presbyter Arius whom he excommunicated at a local synod of Egyptian bishops around 319 along with several of his followers. With Hosius of Cordova and his soon-to-be successor Athanasius, he took a leading role in the Council of Nicaea (325) which supported his stand against Arius. He died in 328.

p. 29. *Nicene Council*: the 'first Ecumenical Council met at Nicæa in Bithynia, in the summer of AD 325. It was attended by about 300 bishops, chiefly from the eastern provinces of the empire, besides a multitude of priests, deacons, and other functionaries of the Church. Hosius, one of the most eminent men of an age of saints, was president. The Fathers who took the principal share in its proceedings were Alexander of Alexandria, attended by his deacon Athanasius, then about twenty-seven years of age, and soon afterwards his successor in the see; Eustathius, patriarch of Antioch, Macarius of Jerusalem, Cæcilian of Carthage, the object of the hostility of the Donatists, Leontius of Cæsarea in Cappadocia, and Marcellus of Ancyra, whose name was afterwards unhappily notorious in the Church. The number of Arian Bishops is variously stated at thirteen, seventeen, or twenty-two; the most conspicuous of these being the well-known prelates of Nicomedia and Cæsarea, both of whom bore the name of Eusebius' (*Ari.*, pp. 250–251). The Council condemned Arius and drafted the Nicene Creed in its original form. It lasted two months and twelve days. At that time and subsequently, Ecumenical Councils were a 'novelty in the Church; and that their sovereign authority and immutability of their decisions were points not familiar to the apprehension of every bishop. This shows itself in the subsequent events of the fourth century' (*T.T.*, p. 147).

p. 29. *Such, perhaps was Basil*: 'One of the more striking points of Basil's character,' wrote Newman in his original essay for the *British Magazine*, 'was his utter disregard of mere human feelings when the interests of religion were concerned. This admirable trait, which is so great a desideratum in our present ecclesiastical temper, appears in his history with a clearness and determinateness which is called harshness by weaker minds' (*British Magazine*, 'Letters on the Church of the Fathers', No. VIII, Volume VI, August 1834, p. 153).

p. 29. *heretical city*: reference to that brief period in the life of Gregory of Nazianzus (south-west of Caesarea) from the beginning of 379 to the middle of 381 when he left his solitude to go to Constantinople to champion the orthodox cause. According to the historian, Socrates, those who remained loyal to the Nicene formula were not only excommunicated they were also exiled. Not only that, the Arian party then 'resorted to all kinds of scourgings, a variety of tortures, and confiscation of property. Many were punished with exile, some died under the torture, and others were put to death while being driven from their country. These atrocities were exercised throughout all the eastern cities, but especially at Constantinople' (Socrates, *Ecclesiastical History*, Book II, Chapter 27; quoted in *Ari.*, pp. 460–461).

p. 29. *St. Peter Damiani*: (1007–72), Benedictine monk who was an uncompromising preacher against clerical abuses particularly when it came to administering the Sacraments. Leo XII declared him a Doctor of the Church in 1828.

p. 29. *St. Anselm*: (*c.* 1033–1109), philosopher and Archbishop of Canterbury whose strong Church-State principles brought him into conflict with William II (1087–1100) and Henry I (1100–35). His stubborn insistence on independence of the Church led to a serious rift with the two monarchs both of whom sent him into exile. Clement XI declared him a Doctor of the Church in 1720.

p. 29. *St. Edmund*: (*c.* 1170–1240), Edmund Rich, Archbishop of Canterbury in 1233, appointed by Henry III (1216–72) who forced him out of Canterbury in 1240. He died at Soissy, north-east of Paris, on 16 November, that same year.

p. 30. *St. Gregory the Seventh*: see (*C.F.*) Hildebrand, p. 28.

p. 30. *St. Pius the Fifth*: pope between 1566 and 1572 who worked hard to implement the recommendations of the Council of Trent in the wake of the Protestant Reformation. He completed the Roman Catechism

(1566), had it translated into several languages, reformed the breviary (1568) and missal (1570), ordered a new edition of the works of Thomas Aquinas (1570) whom he made a Doctor of the Church in 1567. He excommunicated Elizabeth I in 1570.

p. 30. *Semi-Arians*: see (*C.F.*) note to p. 20.

p. 30. "*and void and empty*": Genesis 1: 2.

p. 31. *Ancyra*: ancient trading city whose location made it an ideal trading centre because of its location on the main highways from Constantinople (via Nicaea) to Syria, Mesopotamia, Armenia and the Black Sea. In the first century BC, it became the capital of Galatia, and flourished under Augustus. It was famous for a marble temple built and dedicated to Augustus (31 BC–AD 14) during his lifetime; modern Ankara, capital of Turkey.

p. 31. *Neocæsarea*: civil and religious capital of Pontus Polemoniacus, situated on the eastern bank of the Lycus river, east of Comana Pontica; celebrated for its size, layout and beauty; Gregory the Wonder-worker was born there.

p. 31. *Tyana*: city situated in southern Cappadocia at the northern foot of the Antitaurus mountains south-east of Nazianzus and on the main highway to Cilicia, Syria and Mesopotamia. It was both a powerful military fortress and a prosperous commercial centre. It was the birthplace of the charismatic Apollonius of Tyana, a contemporary of Christ.

p. 31. *schism*: split in the Church, generally over authority and disciplinary issues; heresy, on the other hand, involves matters of doctrine, not simply authority. The word itself dates from the second century and was used to refer to such movements as Donatism and Montanism.

p. 31. *four bishops in the see at once*: Eudoxius, Aetius, Paulinus and Meletius. Eudoxius, and Aetius were radical Arians. Paulinus was recognised by the orthodox Athanasius and the Bishop of Rome. Meletius in turn was recognised by the orthodox Basil.

p. 31. *Eusebius of Samosata*: see (*C.F.*) note to p. 13.

p. 32. *Bosporius*: confidential friend of Basil the Great, Bishop of Colonia near Nazianzus for almost forty years and attended the Council of Constantinople (381).

p. 32. *heresiarch*: see (*C.F.*) note to p. 6.

p. 32. *Apollinaris*: Bishop of Laodicea in Syria; see (*P.C.*) note to p. 391.

p. 32. *Athanasius*: pro-Arian Bishop of Ancyra (Ankara). Despite his theological leanings and the harsh things he said about Basil, the latter still described him as a real 'pillar and foundation of the Church' (Letter xxix).

p. 34. '*By this shall all ... love one another*': John 13: 35.

p. 34. '*Peace I leave ... I give you*': John 14: 27.

p. 34. '*Will ye not fear ... a boundary to the sea?*': Jeremiah 5: 22.

p. 35. '*Because of lawlessness ... many shall wax cold*': Matthew 24: 12.

p. 35. *St. Gregory, the Wonder-worker*: (*c.* 213–*c.* 260), orthodox Bishop of Neocaesarea, the civil and religious capital of Pontus around 243. Gregory's reputation depended very much on stories about his miraculous powers. These are said to have ranged from moving mountains to drying up swamps. Hence his name 'Thaumaturgus' – Wonder-worker (see *Dev.*, pp. 417–418; *Diff.* II, pp. 74–75).

p. 36. *Sabellianism*: facilitated rather than originated the 'disturbances occasioned by the Arian heresy'. Its followers regarded God the Father and God the Son as one person and later maintained that the Trinity was one God in God's relationship with humanity as creator, incarnate redeemer and sanctifier. 'Its peculiar tenet is the denial of the distinction of Persons in the Divine Nature; or the doctrine of the *Monarchia* ... like that which has led to the term "Unitarianism" at the present day. It was first maintained as a characteristic of party by a school established ... in Proconsular Asia, towards the end of the second century'. It was named after Sabellius, a 'bishop or presbyter in Pentapolis, a district of Cyrenaica, included within ... the Alexandrian Patriarchate' (*Ari.*, pp. 116–118). In order to preserve the unity of the Godhead, Sabellius denied the independence of each person of the Trinity. It was condemned by Pope Callistus I (217–22). 'It is difficult to decide what Sabellius's doctrine really was; nor is this wonderful, considering the perplexity and vacillation which is the ordinary consequence of abandoning Catholic truth' (*Ath.* II, pp. 254–256).

p. 36. *Musonius*: Gregory the Wonder-worker's successor to the see of Neocaesarea. Even though orthodox, he objected to Basil's elevation to the see of Caesarea. When he died, in 368, Basil charitably declared that sound doctrine prevailed in the see of Neocaesarea up to the time of 'the blessed Musonius whose teaching still rings in your ears' (Letter CCX).

p. 37. '*By this shall . . . love one to another*': John 13: 35.

p. 37. '*Reprove, rebuke, exhort ?*': 2 Timothy 4: 2.

p. 38. *Macrina*: Basil's paternal grandmother who brought him up at her country estate at Annesi on the banks of the Iris in northern Pontus. She had a lasting influence on the intellectual and spiritual development of her grandchildren. She died around 440.

p. 40. *Macedonians*: members of a sect who questioned the divinity of the Holy Spirit; for one reason or another, they were associated with Macedonius, Bishop of Constantinople who fell out of favour with Arian emperor, Constantius II, and was deposed around 360. They were also known as 'pneumatomachi' meaning 'fighters against the spirit'. 'Whether or not the Macedonians explicitly denied the divinity of the Holy Spirit, is uncertain; but they viewed Him as essentially separate from, and external to, the One Indivisible Godhead' (*Ari.*, p. 392, 5n).

p. 41. *two orthodox bishops at Antioch*: Paulinus who was supported by Damasus, Bishop of Rome, and by Athanasius, Bishop of Alexandria; and Meletius who was supported by Basil the Great and the eastern bishops.

p. 42. *Damasus*: (*c.* 305–84), Bishop of Rome from 366 in favour of Roman primacy and the first pope to refer to Rome as the *Apostolic See.* He helped stop the spread of Arianism and Macedonianism in the west and made Rome the ultimate court of appeal for western bishops. Nevertheless, he was unable to get rid of Auxentius, Arian Bishop of Milan. In spite of protestations from the east, he supported Paulinus in the Meletian schism at Antioch in Syria.

p. 42. *Illyricum*: the names, Illyricum, Illyria, Pannonia and Dalmatia cover roughly the same area of what we know today as the Balkans. Before the arrival of the Romans, it was known as Illyria, and inhabited by tribes of warlike people. After being conquered by Rome, it became known as Illyricum and Pannonia. Many of its warriors enlisted in the Roman army and became some of its finest soldiers, including a batch of outstanding generals. During the late third and early fourth centuries, some of these commanders went on to become Roman emperors, including the ruthless Trajanus Decius (249–51) and Diocletian (284–305). Martin of Tours (*c.* 320–97) was also a native of the region. Paul the Apostle preached in the principal cities of that vast region from Jerusalem to Illyricum (Romans 15: 19).

p. 43. *Thebais*: in Upper (southern) Egypt; Egypt was divided into three regions: Upper (southern) Egypt (Thebais); central Egypt (Heptanomis); and Lower (northern) Egypt (Nile Delta).

p. 44. *Ep. 92.*: immediately following Basil's letters to the Bishops of the West in his original essay for the *British Magazine*, Newman went on to explain that these were 'portions of two letters written to the West, and afford us some consolation at the present day, by shewing us that the present miserable disarrangement of the church is no new thing in its history. We cannot be more tyrannized over without, and divided within, than the Christian communities in behalf of which Basil was exerting himself. It is remarkable, too, that he had few, if any, assistants in his labours of love. St. Paul himself, in the brightest age of the gospel, lamented the scantiness of those who were single-hearted in its defence. The same has been the lot of the true cause in modern times' (*British Magazine*, 'Letters on the Church of the Fathers, No. VI, Volume V, June 1834, p. 682). Newman deleted all of this for the 1840 and subsequent editions.

p. 45. *Diomede*: a remarkable Greek warrior of the Trojan war who comes across as one of the most attractive characters in Homer's *Iliad*. He even fights the gods and inflicts wounds on them. At one stage of the epic, he attacks Aeneas by hurling a boulder and steals his magic horses (Book V). His name means 'god-like cunning'.

p. 45. *I would that hadst not begged, for haughty is that man*: more of a paraphrase than the actual quote itself which is as follows: 'Your majesty,' he [Diomede] said, 'Agamemnon, son of Atreus, King of Men; it is a thousand pities that you brought yourself to plead with my lord Achilles and make such a princely offer. He is a proud man at the best of times; and now you have given him an even better conceit of himself' (Homer, *Iliad*, Book IX, p. 179, Penguin Classics).

p. 45. *Marcellus*: (*c.* 280–374), orthodox Bishop of Ancyra (Ankara) who initially supported Athanasius at the Council of Nicaea (325) against the scheming Eusebius of Nicomedia. According to Basil the Great, his support of the *homoousion* formula led to a 'heresy diametrically opposite to that of Arius' (Letter LXIX). He was subsequently deposed in 336 for suggesting that the Son and the Holy Spirit were mere manifestations of the Godhead for the purposes of creation and redemption. Although restored in 337, he was deposed again in 339 and posthumously condemned by the first Council of Constantinople (381). He died *c.* 374.

p. 47. *Polytheism*: belief in a number of gods, not necessarily of equal importance and dignity, each identified by performing certain duties; for example in Greek mythology, the god Neptune looked after the ocean, while the goddess Cybele looked after wild animals and the earth.

p. 47. *Evagrius*: referred to as Evagrius of Antioch to distinguish him from Evagrius the historian (*c.* 536–600). He travelled to Italy with Eusebius of Vercellae. His feedback to Basil from the Western bishops seems to have been unsatisfactory. His consecration by the dying Paulinus whom Rome recognised as the legitimate Bishop of Antioch in 388 prolonged the Meletian schism (Theodoret, *Ecclesiastical History*, Book V, Chapter 23). In the original essay in the *British Magazine*, Newman prefaced Basil's letter to Evagrius thus: 'The following letter relates principally to the schism at Antioch. Evagrius, to whom it was written, was inclined to the Latin party in that church – i.e., the party which Basil discountenanced' (*British Magazine*, 'Letters on the Church of the Fathers', No. VI, Volume V, June 1834, p. 683).

p. 47. *Meletius*: orthodox Bishop of Antioch in Syria; see (*C.F.*) note to p. 16.

p. 49. *Dorotheus*: confidant of Basil and go-between with Pope Damasus I. At one meeting, with Damasus and Peter of Alexandria, Dorotheus uncharacteristically lost his temper when Meletius of Antioch and Eusebius of Samosata were wrongly accused of Arianism.

p. 49. *those seven thousand who . . . knee to Baal*: 3 Kings (1 Kings) 19: 18.

p. 49. *Peter of Alexandria*: Bishop of Alexandria from 300 who survived the persecution of Diocletian in 303, went into hiding in another wave of persecution in 306. In his absence, Melitius of Lycopolis (modern Asyut, east-central Egypt on the Nile) took over his see and so began the Melitian schism in Egypt. When Peter returned to Alexandria to deal with it, he was captured and beheaded by the emperor, Maximinus Daia in 311.

Chapter III: Basil and Gregory

Synopsis: Basil the Great and Gregory of Nazianzus are diametrically opposite characters, the former an extrovert, the latter an introvert. This chapter focuses on their student friendship in Athens where they decide to consecrate their lives to God. Basil retires to Pontus but Gregory remains in Athens. Basil makes up for his absence by gathering a community of like-minded individuals around him. He remains in retirement for five or six years until he returns to Caesarea as secretary to the Exarch Bishop, Eusebius. When Eusebius becomes jealous of his abilities and talents,

Gregory helps to patch up personal differences. Gregory and his father are instrumental in bringing about Basil's election as Exarch Bishop of Cappadocia when Eusebius dies. He then assists Basil in a quarrel with Anthimus, Bishop of Tyana when the pro-Arian emperor Valens decides to partition Cappadocia in order to reduce Basil's influence. As part of his strategy to out-manoeuvre Valens and Anthimus, Basil pressurises Gregory into becoming bishop of an out-of-the-way, but politically strategic village called Sasima. A reluctant and angry Gregory is consecrated, but returns home to Nazianzus without ever setting foot in Sasima. And so begins the famous alienation between Basil and Gregory. Losing Gregory's friendship becomes Basil's greatest trial.

p. 50. *Gregory*: (*c.* 329–90), native of Nazianzus who was one of the three Cappadocian Fathers alongside Basil the Great and Gregory of Nyssa (south-west of Caesarea). Of the trio, Gregory was probably the best preacher. When he was about thirty, Gregory elected to live an ascetic way of life, but affection for his family kept him from living a completely solitary life. Like Basil and Augustine, he reluctantly submitted to ordination in 362. His friendship with Basil suffered a serious setback in 371 when the latter, for political purposes, made him a bishop of an out-of-the-way place called Sasima to thwart the ambitions of a rival bishop. While giving in to Basil's pressure, he never went there. When his father died in 374, Gregory became Bishop of Nazianzus, but retired from public life the following year to Seleucia in Cilicia. In 379, the orthodox party, then a minority party in Arian Constantinople, pressured him into becoming their bishop. That was also short-lived because the politicking and bickering at the Council of Constantinople (381) so demoralised him that he retired to his native Nazianzus, this time for good. 'In such a time as this, did the great Doctor, St. Gregory Nazianzen, he too an old man, a timid man, a retiring man, fond of solitude and books, and unpractised in the struggles of the world, suddenly appear in the Arian city of Constantinople; and, in despite of a fanatical populace, and an heretical clergy, preach the truth, and prevail, – to his own wonder, and to the glory of that grace which is strong in weakness, and is ever nearest to its triumph when it is most despised' (*Mix.*, p. 243).

p. 50. "*What are these discourses . . . and are sad*": Luke 24: 17.

p. 50. *It often happens*: in the original essay for the *British Magazine*, Newman began it with a quote from John Keble's *Christian Year* for St. Mark's feast day (p. 292):

> "Oh! Who shall dare, in this frail scene,
> On holiest, happiest thoughts to lean –

On friendship, kindred, or on love?
Since not apostles' hands can clasp
Each other in so firm a grasp,
But they shall change and variance prove."

(*British Magazine*, 'Letters on the Church of the Fathers', No. VII, Volume VI, July 1834, p. 42; deleted in the 1840 and subsequent editions).

p. 50. *two blessed Apostles*: after the Council of Jerusalem (49), Paul suggested to Barnabas that they re-visit the various cities in Asia Minor where they had already preached the Good News. Barnabas wanted John Mark to accompany them, but Paul refused to work with someone 'who had deserted them in Pamphylia and had not accompanied them in the work'. The disagreement became so heated that they parted company (Acts 15: 35–39; 13:13).

p. 50. "*sharp contention*": Acts 15: 39.

p. 51. *Exarch of Cæsarea*: Basil the Great, Bishop of Caesarea and exarch of Cappadocia (370–79).

p. 51. *Patriarch*: bishop; from the Greek 'patriarches' meaning 'head of a family'. Initially, patriarchs included the Bishops of Antioch, Alexandria and Rome who had primacy over local bishops. It was later extended to include Constantinople and Jerusalem. Patriarchs were independent of and equal to one another in authority.

p. 51. *Patriarch of Constantinople*: Gregory of Nazianzus (379–81).

p. 51. *Cappadocia*: see *(C.F.)* note to p. 4.

p. 51. *Hypsistarian*: member of a fourth-century sect in Cappadocia who refused to recognise God as 'Father'. They preferred the title of 'All Ruler and Highest' and incorporated many Jewish and oriental features into their worship.

p. 51. *Ariminian creed*: in 359, the Council of Ariminum (modern Rimini in Italy) replaced the Nicene Creed with a creed susceptible of an Arian interpretation. 'Four hundred Bishops were collected at Ariminum, of whom eighty were Arians; and the civil officer [Taurus], to whom Constantius had committed the superintendence of their proceedings, had orders not to let them stir, till they should agree upon a confession of faith.... Thus ended this celebrated Council; the result of which is well characterized in the lively statement of Jerome: "The whole world groaned in astonishment to find itself Arian"' (*Ari.*, p. 350).

p. 52. *Nazianzus*: small town south-east of Caesarea and north-west of Tyana; now the modern village of Nenizi. Initially, it was under the control of the exarch of Cappadocia, at that time Basil the Great. When the Arian emperor Valens decided to partition Cappadocia into Upper (Prima) and Lower (Secunda) Cappadocia to minimise Basil's influence, Nazianzus fell under the jurisdiction of Anthimus, Bishop of Tyana.

p. 52. *Julian . . . the Apostate*: Roman emperor from 361 to 363; see (*C.F.*) note to p. 12.

p. 52. *Athens*: '. . . where all archetypes of the great and the fair were found in substantial being, and all departments of truth explored, where taste and philosophy were majestically enthroned as in a royal court, where there was no sovereignty but that of the human mind, and no nobility but that of genius, where professors were rulers, and princes did homage, hither flocked continually from the very corners of the orbis terrarum, the many-tongued generation, just rising, or just risen into manhood, in order to gain wisdom' (*Historical Sketches (H.S.)* III, 18- 23; see also *D.A.*, pp. 327–331). Paul the Apostle preached at Athens (Acts 17: 15–33) and complimented the citizens on their religious spirit.

p. 53. *rhetoricians*: individuals who practised the art of oratory; rhetoric, the art of persuasion, involved presenting an argument according to established rules and conventions and associated with the study of grammar, literature and formal logic. 'Most of the young men at Athens in their folly are mad after rhetorical', wrote Gregory of Nazianzus, "not only those who are ignobly born and unknown, but even the noble and illustrious, in the general mass of young men difficult to keep under control. They are just like men devoted to horses and exhibitions, as we see, at the horse-races . . .' (Gregory of Nazianzus, Oration XLIII, para. 15).

p. 53. *They resolved to seek baptism*: Basil and Gregory made their decision to be baptised in the middle of a violent storm off the coast of Cyprus en route to Athens. In those days, adult baptism was more common than infant baptism. Most parents, including the mothers of Augustine of Hippo and John Chrysostom, delayed their child's baptism, because of a deep reverence for the sacrament and from a superstition that infant baptism may mean forfeiting the grace of baptism in later life.

p. 53. *that the things . . . are not seen*: 2 Corinthians 4: 18.

p. 54. *a dream*: dreams played an important part in the spirituality of the times as they did in the spirituality of Monica, mother of St. Augustine. In a sermon preached on 29 May 1836, on 'The Mysterious of our

Present Being' Newman asked his congregation to 'consider what a strange state we are in when we dream, and how difficult it would be to convey to a person who had never dreamed what was meant by dreaming. *His* vocabulary would contain no words to express any middle idea between perfect possession and entire suspension of the mind's powers. He would understand what it was to be awake, what it was to be insensible; but a state between the two he would neither have words to describe, nor ... inclination to believe.... I do not say there is no conceivable accumulation of evidence that would subdue a man's reason, ... but I mean, that this earthly mystery *might* be brought before a man with about that degree of evidence in its favour which the Gospel has, not ordinarily overpowering, but constituting a *trial* of his heart, a trial ... whether the mysteries contained in it do or do not arouse his pride. Dreaming is not a fiction, but a real state of the mind, though only one or two in the whole world ever dreamed; and if these one or two or a dozen men, spoke to the rest of the world, and unanimously witnessed to the existence of that mysterious state, many doubtless would resist their report, as they do the mysteries of the Gospel, ... yet in that case they would doubtless be resisting a truth (*Parochial and Plain Sermons (P.S.)*, IV, xix, p. 288). For striking instances of the impact which dreams had on Newman particularly in his early life, see *John Henry Newman: Autobiographical Writings (A.W.)*, pp. 161; 166–7 where he wrote: 'Dreams address themselves so immediately to the mind, that to express in any form of words the feelings produced by ... my mysterious visitant were a fruitless endeavour.... It is not idle to make a memorandum of this, for out of dreams often much good can be extracted.' On dreams as a mode of communication with the after-life, see *John Henry Newman: the Philosophical Notebook (P.N.)* II, 181–7.

p. 55. *jacinth*: name given by ancients to a blue-coloured precious stone similar to or possibly the same as sapphire.

p. 56. *Cœnobite*: person in vows and living in community as opposed to a hermit who lived alone; derived from Greek *koinobios*, meaning 'living in community'.

p. 56. *Thesbite*: surname of Elijah, the prophet (3 Kings (I Kings) 17: 1; 21:17, 28; 4 Kings (2 Kings) 1: 3, 8; 9: 36).

p. 56. *Carmel*: mountain located high above the modern port of Haifa in Israel and the traditional site of Elijah's triumph over the priests of Baal (3 Kings (I Kings) 18).

p. 56. *Jonadab*: son of Recab and chieftain of an Israelite clan called the

Rechabites. He accompanied Jehu, King of Israel in his chariot to slaughter members of Ahab's household and the worshippers of Baal (4 Kings (2 Kings) 10: 15ff.). He forbade his followers to drink wine, plant vineyards or build houses (Jeremiah 35: 6ff.).

p. 56. ἄζυγες: Greek word meaning 'solitary'.

p. 56. μιγάδες: Greek word meaning 'secular'.

p. 57. *a strict life*: what Newman translates as 'a strict life' may also be translated as 'a life of philosophy', a term used by the Cappadocian Fathers to describe a life devoted to Scripture, asceticism and theology.

p. 58. *Gregory's own home*: Arianzus.

p. 58. *Abaris's arrow*: legendary servant of the god Apollo who fled from Scythia (in the Caucusus) to Greece to avoid a plague. His master gave him a golden arrow which made him invisible and by means of which he could fly round the world without having to eat. It could also cure sickness and speak oracles. Herodotus mentions it in his *History* (Book IV, para. 36).

p. 58. *spot near Neocaesarea in Pontus*: Basil spent his childhood on the banks of the Iris, near the small settlement of Annesi north-west of Neocaesarea, near the junction of the Iris and Lycus rivers.

p. 58. *Neocæsarea*: largest town in northern Pontus situated on the eastern bank of the Lycus river. It was the capital of the district and celebrated for its size, layout and beauty. Gregory the Wonder-worker was born there.

p. 58. *Church of the Forty Martyrs*: church built at Annesi by Basil's mother Emmelia in honour of the Forty Martyrs of Sebaste to which their relics were translated. Around 320, forty Christian soldiers of the twelfth legion (the Thundering Legion) were martyred at Sebaste, (south of Neocaesarea) during the reign of the emperor Licinius (308–324) for refusing to sacrifice to the state gods. The story goes that they were left naked on a frozen lake with tubs of hot water on the bank to entice them to sacrifice. One soldier who could not resist the temptation had his place taken by a heathen legionnaire who declared himself a Christian on the spot.

p. 58. *Licinius*: emperor of the east (308–24), defeated and executed by Constantine the Great. Of all the tyrants of his age, Licinius was one of the cruellest – selfish, ambitious, cold, calculating and unimaginative. In 313, he and Constantine issued the Edict of Milan which granted religious freedom to all religions, including Christianity. Persecution in any shape or form was supposed to come to a halt. But when tensions later rose between the two emperors, Licinius renewed the persecution of Christians in the east. He prohibited synods of bishops to meet; expelled high-ranking Christians from court; deprived them of office and titles and forced Christian soldiers to sacrifice to the state gods. Constantine finally defeated him at the battle of Chrysopolis in 323 on the Asiatic side of the Bosphorus. He was eventually executed.

p. 59. *My brother Gregory writes me* . . .: 'Basil had, at this time,' wrote Newman in the original essay for the *British Magazine*, 'rid himself of his private property, rightly considering that an unmarried man wanted little for *support*, and a cleric needed nothing to give him *rank*. "He had but one tunic," says his friend, after his death, " and one outer garment; a bed on the ground, little sleep, no luxurious bath, [such the decorations of his rank;] and his pleasantest meal, bread and salt. [novel dainties]; and his drink, that sober liqor of which there is no stint, which is elaborated in the gushing spring." ' (*British Magazine*, 'Letters on the Church of the Fathers', No. VII, Volume VI, July 1834, p. 46; deleted in the 1840 and subsequent editions).

p. 59. *Calypso's Island*: in Greek mythology, Calypso was daughter of the god Atlas. She lived on the mythical island of Ogygia in the Ionian sea, somewhere between Greece and southern Italy. This 'bewitching nymph' welcomed a shipwrecked Ulysses and kept him captive for seven years 'deep in her arching caverns, craving him for a husband' (Homer *Odyssey*, I).

p. 59. *Strymon*: river rising in southern Bulgaria and flowing south marking the boundary between Greek Macedonia to the west and Thrace to the east before emptying into the Aegean Sea; it is about 420 kilometres (260 miles) in length; modern Struma river.

p. 59. *Amphipolis*: Athenian colony near the mouth of the Strymon river founded around 437 BC; about 100 kilometres (60 miles) east of Thessalonica, and stragetically situated on the western half of a hill with commanding views of the countryside from the Aegean Sea to the great Macedonian plains. Paul the Apostle passed through there after being delivered from prison at Philippi (Acts 17: 1).

p. 60. *Alcmæon*: in Greek mythology, Alcmæon murdered his mother to avenge his father's death. As a result, he was hounded from place to place by the Furies. He found temporary refuge on a small group of islands known as the Echinades (see next note) until his own brothers murdered him.

p. 60. *Echinades*: small group of islands off the west coast of the Gulf of Corinth in the Ionian Sea. Because of their jagged coastline, they were named after the 'echinus' (sea-urchin). Alcæmon found temporary refuge there from the Furies (see above note). The famous battle of Lepanto was fought nearby in 1571.

p. 60. '*Pass on, and sing thy garniture within,*': spoken by Alcinous, King of Phaeacia (modern Corfu), celebrated for his legendary generosity (Homer, *Odyssey*, VIII).

p. 61. *Tantalus's penalty*: in Greek mythology, the gods despatched him to the underworld either for feeding his son's flesh to the gods (or for stealing their nectar or for revealing divine secrets) by forcing him to stand in a pool of water which came up to his chin but which receded each time he bent down to drink. At the same time, the branches of a fruit-laden tree above his head tantalisingly drew back whenever he reached up to pluck fruit.

p. 61. *Lotophagi*: 'lotus-eaters' who, according to Homer, lived on the coast of north Africa and fed on a diet of lotus fruit. Those who ate it became very lethargic, losing all desire to return home. When Odysseus landed there, some of his crew ate the fruit, forgot about home and had to be dragged back to the ships (Homer, *Odyssey*, IX).

p. 61. *Alcinous's board*: Alcinous was a generous and prosperous king of Phaeacia (modern Corfu) who entertained Ulysses after he had been washed up on the island while escaping from Lotus-land. In this particular letter, Gregory is contrasting the abundance of Alcinous's table to the meagre diet of the lotus-eaters (Homer, *Odyssey*, VIII).

p. 61. *Augean store*: as one of his labours, Hercules had to clean the filthy stables of Augeas, King of Elis (north-west of the Peloponnese) who kept enormous herds of cattle. To clear the piled-up waste of years from the stables in a single day, he diverted the course of the river Alpheus through them.

p. 61. *Hellespont*: narrow stretch of water dividing Europe from Asia and uniting the Propontis (Sea of Mamara) in the north with the Aegean Sea in the south. It is about 64 kilometres (40 miles) long and ranging from1.6 to 6.4 kilometres (1 to 4 miles) wide. It forms an important commercial link between the Mediterranean and Black seas. It is now known as the Dardanelles with the town of Gallipoli on the European side and Çanakkale on Asian side.

p. 62. *that golden plane*: reference to a golden plane-tree given to Darius I

(521–486 BC), King of ancient Persia, by a certain Pythius, the son of Atys from Lydia in Asia Minor and one of the wealthiest men in the world; mentioned in the *History* of Herodotus (Book VII, para. 27).

p. 62. *Xerxes*: King of ancient Persia (486–465 BC) and son of Darius I; he is the same Assuerus mentioned in the Book of Daniel (Daniel 11: 2; 1 Esdras 4: 6).

p. 62. *Apollos*: Gregory's affectionate nickname for Basil; in the New Testament, Apollos was a Jew from Alexandria who became a successful missionary, preaching at Ephesus and Corinth (1 Corinthians 1: 12; Acts 18: 24–26).

p. 62. *Aaron's rod*: Numbers 17: 16–26.

p. 62. *the nature of his rule*: Basil is generally looked upon as the founder of eastern monasticism. In fact, all eastern orthodox monks follow a variation of his monastic rule. It is sometimes forgotten that Basil's concept of monasticism was preceded and inspired by a community of nuns organised by his sister, Macrina. Though strict, it avoids the extreme austerities of the desert hermits. For example, private fasting could not be practised without permission of the local community leader.

pp. 62–3. *Basil to Gregory*: in his original essay for the *British Magazine*, Newman added: 'Basil advocates a state of life, of all others the most desirable, which, in the early ages, the clergy scarcely could attain except in monastic institutions; but which, in our favoured country, where Christianity has long been established, is in substance the privilege of ten thousand parsonages up and down the land' (*British Magazine*, 'Letters on the Church of the Fathers', No. VII, Volume VI, July 1834, p. 45; deleted in the 1840 and subsequent editions).

p. 63. '*If any one . . . and follow Me*': Matthew 16: 24; Luke 9: 23; Mark 8: 34.

p. 64. "*The study of inspired Scripture*": both Basil and Gregory encouraged the study of Scripture following the example of Origen (*c.* 185–*c.* 254). During their time together, they complied an anthology of Origen's writings entitled *Philocalia* ('goodly sayings'), showing Origen's approach to the study of Scripture.

p. 64. "*He who is enamoured . . . evil-speaking against himself*": in their preaching, both Basil and Gregory took every opportunity to point out the valuable lessons to be learnt from Old Testament characters like Joseph, Job, David and Moses.

pp. 64–65. *the true gentleman*: in the eighth discourse of *Idea of a University*, Newman made similar sorts of remarks: 'Hence, it is that it is almost a definition of a gentleman to say he is one who never inflicts pain.' A gentleman is 'mainly occupied in merely removing the obstacles which hinder the free and unembarrassed action of those about him ... The true gentleman ... carefully avoids whatever may cause a jar or a jolt in the minds of those with whom he is cast; – all clashing of opinion, or collision of feeling, all restraint, or suspicion, or gloom, or resentment; his great concern being to make every one at their ease and at home. He has eyes on all his company; he is tender towards the bashful, gentle towards the distant, and merciful towards the absurd; he can recollect to whom he is speaking; he guards against unseasonable allusions, or topics which may irritate; he is seldom prominent in conversation, and never wearisome. He makes light of favours while he does them, and seems to be receiving when he is conferring ... He never speaks of himself except when compelled, never defends himself by a mere retort, he has no ears for slander or gossip, is scrupulous in imputing motives to those who interfere with him, and interprets every thing for the best. He is never mean or little in his disputes, never takes unfair advantage, never mistakes personalities or sharp sayings for arguments, or insinuates evil which he dare not say out' (*Idea*, pp. 208–9).

p. 65. *Ep. 2.*: in the original *British Magazine* essay, Newman inserted the following observation following Basil's letter to Gregory: ' It is unnecessary to quote more from this letter, in which Basil advocates a state of life, of all others the most desirable, which, in the early ages, the clergy scarcely could attain except in monastic institutions; but which, in our favoured country, where Christianity has long been established, is in its substance the privilege of ten thousand parsonages up and down the land' (*British Magazine*, 'Letters on the Church of the Fathers', No. VII, Volume VI, July 1834, p. 45; deleted for the 1840 and subsequent editions).

p. 65. *called to the priesthood*: Basil was ordained by Eusebius, Bishop of Caesarea and exarch of Cappadocia around 362. His subsequent success in handling diocesan affairs became the cause of friction and alienation between the two men.

p. 66. *Cæsarius*: he was forty years old.

p. 66. *Prefect of Constantinople*: Sophronius, a native of Caesarea in Cappadocia and an early friend and fellow-student of Basil the Great and Gregory of Nazianzus; he entered the civil service and was appointed Prefect of Constantinople by the emperor Valens in 365.

p. 67. *Gregory to Basil*: in the original *British Magazine* essay, Newman included a second letter with more playful banter. It gives an insight into the intimacy of their friendship at the time. 'What can you mean by saying that I treat your interests as so much trash, my beloved Basil? ... what induced you to venture on so strong an assertion? – that I might venture on a counter assertion? – how could your mind conceive it, or ink write, or paper take it? O Athens, truth, and literary toil! I declare your letter has almost made my style tragic. Is it that you do not know me, or do not know one who is the light of his age, the sonorous trumpet, the royal home of eloquence? What, Gregory take little account of your concerns! Whom else on earth does he look up to? ... I know you may, if you please, justly accuse me of not making as much of you as I ought; but this is the fault of the whole world, for yourself and your own glorious voice alone can do you justice ... Call me a madman rather than an undervaluer of you. But perhaps you blame me for loving this tranquil retirement. Pardon me; but I must confess that this, and this alone, is a higher gift than the learning and eloquence of Basil' (*British Magazine*, 'Letters on the Church of the Fathers', No. VII, Volume VI, July 1834; deleted in the 1840 and subsequent editions).

p. 67. *before the blind ... David from Jerusalem*: 2 Kings (2 Samuel) 5: 6.

p. 68. *Hellenius*: confidential friend of Basil the Great and Gregory of Nazianzus; native of Armenia and inspector of customs.

p. 68. '*shut every unjust ... lawlessly against God*': Psalm 62: 12 (Psalm 63: 11).

p. 69. *Valens divided Cappadocia*: to minimise Basil's authority and influence, Valens proceeded to partition Cappadocia into Cappadocia Prima (Upper) in the north with Caesarea as capital, and Cappadocia Secunda (Lower) in the south with Tyana as its capital. This led to Anthimus, Bishop of Tyana, becoming the de facto exarch of Cappadocia Secunda in spite of Basil's objection that it was an ecclesiastical, not a civil matter. Basil decided to establish new sees to make up for those lost from the division. Thus it was that he made his brother Gregory bishop of Nyssa, in the north-western part of Cappadocia Prima. Basil then pressurised Gregory of Nazianzus into becoming Bishop of Sasima which was hardly worthy of being an episcopal see. It was little more than a crossroads on the way from Caesarea to Tyana. Basil hoped that Gregory's presence there would thwart the influence of Anthimus, but Gregory, although reluctantly accepting episcopal consecration, refused to go to Sasima – since there was good reason to fear for his life if he did. Basil, however, could never understand his reluctance.

p. 69. *Anthimus*: ambitious and quarrelsome Bishop of Tyana, south of Caesarea and south-east of Nazianzus. Originally, Anthimus was on friendly terms with Basil. When Valens partitioned Cappadocia into Upper and Lower Cappadocia, Anthimus 'thought it right that the ecclesiastical boundaries should be settled by the civil ones: and therefore claimed those newly added, as belonging to him, and severed from their former metropolitan'. Basil, on the other hand, 'clung to the ancient custom, and to the division which had come down from our fathers. Many painful results either actually followed, or were struggling in the womb of the future. Synods were wrongly gathered by the new metropolitan, and revenues seized upon. Some of the presbyters of the churches refused obedience, others were won over. In consequence the affairs of the churches fell into a sad state of dissension and division' (Gregory's funeral oration on Basil the Great, XLIII, para. 58).

p. 69. *Tyana*: capital city of Lower Cappadocia south of Sasima and situated at the foot of the Antitaurus mountains on the highway to Cilicia, Syria and Mesopotamia. Its strategic position rendered it important commercially and militarily.

p. 69. *Semi-Arians*: see (*C.F.*) note to p. 20.

p. 70. *St. Orestes*: monastery situated at the foot of Taurus mountain range in Lower Cappadocia. What enraged Anthimus most was 'that the revenues of the Taurus, which passed along before his eyes, accrued to his rival [Basil], as also the offerings at St. Orestes, of which he was greatly desirous to reap the fruits' (Oration XLIII, para. 58).

p. 70. *gain over the minds ... Anthimus in his opposition*: according to Gregory, 'three most desirable consequences' ensued the division: 'a greater care for souls, the management of each city of its own affairs, and the cessation of the war in this quarter' (Orations XLIII, para. 59).

p. 70. *Sasima*: insignificant, out-of-the-way hamlet approximately 37 kilometres (23 miles) south-east of Nazianzus and standing at the fork of a road heading north-east to Caesarea and north-west to Nazianzus. Gregory speaks of the place with contempt and disgust. It is highly probable that he never set foot in the place; present village of Zamzama.

p. 71. *Gregory had been unwilling ... of a bishop*: if Gregory considered the priesthood too exalted for him, the office of bishop was even more so.

p. 71. *at the urgent command ... to be consecrated*: in gaining another bishop, Basil lost a best friend; even in his famous oration at Basil's funeral, Gregory was still smarting at being used so callously as a political pawn.

p. 73. *death of Gregory's father*: Gregory the Elder was almost one hundred years old when he died in 374. He had been Bishop of Nazianzus for about forty-five years.

p. 74. *loss of Gregory . . . greatest of all*: in his original essay for the *British Magazine*, Newman wrote: 'One of the more striking points of Basil's character was his utter disregard of mere human feelings when the interests of religion were concerned. This admirable trait, which is so great a desideratum in our present ecclesiastical temper, appears in his history with a clearness and determinateness which is called harshness by weaker minds. Not only his private substance, but his episcopal revenues, were given up to the service of the poor and the church. He wore the coarsest apparel, and lived on the cheapest food, that he might erect colleges and almhouses. In the midst of his dispute with Anthimus, he was engaged at home in building the cathedral of Cæsarea, which he surrounded with other structures for the bishop's dwelling and the inferior ecclesiastics. To these were added apartments for the reception of foreigners, whether passing through the country or afflicted with sickness; and schools for the education of the young' (*British Magazine*, 'Letters on the Church of the Fathers', No. VIII, Volume VI, August 1834, pp. 153–4).

Chapter IV: Rise and Fall of Gregory

Synopsis: It is as if Basil's fighting spirit enters into Gregory after his death. It is now forty years since the Arian party seized control of the Church of Constantinople. On the death of Eudoxius, Arian Bishop of Constantinople in 370, orthodox Christians try to elect an orthodox successor named Evagrius, but the Arian emperor Valens banishes him. In 379, the staunchly orthodox Theodosius I, becomes emperor of the east. For a while, very little changes, and the Church of Constantinople continues to remain under the firm control of the Arians. When Valens dies (379), the orthodox party invites Gregory of Nazianzus to become their bishop instead of Demophilus, the present Arian incumbent, whom Valens had appointed three years previously. Gregory accepts the invitation and opens a Church at a relative's house and begins evangelising the local population with considerable success, much to the contempt and rage of the Arian population. His congregation increases. He is stoned by a mob and hauled before civil authorities for allegedly inciting a riot. Eventually, Theodosius visits the capital and officially recognises Gregory as the legitimate Bishop of Constantinople. Because of the bickering and politicking of his fellow bishops, he becomes so demoralised that he resigns during the first Council of Constantinople

(381) and retires to his beloved Nazianzus. All in all, his public life lasts barely three years.

p. 75. "*Who will give . . . and not for truth*": Jeremiah 9: 2–3.

p. 75. *Orat. 43*: at this point, Newman inserted the following comment in both the 1840 and 1842 editions, but omitted it in later editions: 'The English Church has removed such addresses from her services, on account of the abuses to which they have led; and she pointedly condemns what she calls, the Roman doctrine concerning Invocation of Saints, as "a fond thing:" however Gregory, not knowing what would come after his day, thus expressed the yearnings of his heart, and, as we may almost suppose, at the time he thus made them public, had already received an answer to them. He delivered the above-mentioned discourse on his return to Cæsarea from Constantinople, three years after St. Basil's death . . .' (*The Church of the Fathers*, 1840 edition, pp. 145–6). As long as Newman remained an Anglican, he continued to oppose direct invocations of the saints. As far he was concerned, it was a practice that could be abused, even in private prayer.

p. 76. *Gregory disliked the routine intercourse of society*: While on holiday in Palermo, Sicily in 1833, Newman wrote a poem about Gregory of Nazianzus in which he describes him as a 'Peace-loving man, of humble heart and true'. He begins the final stanza with these words:

> Thou couldst a people raise, but couldst not rule:–
> So, gentle one,
> Heaven set thee free, – for, ere thy years were full,
> Thy work was done . . . (Palermo, June 12, 1833).

p. 76. *he disliked ecclesiastical business . . . study, and literature*: 'And yet,' Newman wrote in his original essay for the *British Magazine*, 'in spite of his deficiency in moral force and stability, and the hastiness of his temper, there is in Gregory a beauty of character, an affectionateness, an amiableness, and an ardent zeal, which must ever recommend him to the love and reverence of the apostolical Christian. His was not that amiableness which is the outward garb of idleness, insipidity, and lukewarmness about great and stirring purposes; nor that, again, which dishonours itself with the embrace of the heretic, the schismatic, and the unbeliever. Bear witness, Constantinople, the imperial city, and the church of Anastasia, which he founded, to the strictness and ardour of his orthodoxy!' (*British Magazine*, 'Letters on the Church of the Fathers', No. VIII, Volume VI, August 1834, p. 154; deleted in the 1840 and subsequent editions).

p. 76. *so vainly attempted, and so sadly waited for*: Newman may have had Gregory in mind when he preached the sermon, 'Jeremiah, a Lesson for the Disappointed' on 12 September, 1830: 'Look through the Bible, and you will find God's servants, even though they began with success, end with disappointment; not that God's purposes or His instruments fail, but that the time for reaping what we have sown is hereafter, not here; and that here there is no great visible fruit in any one man's lifetime' (*P.S.* VIII, p. 130).

p. 76. *glorious Emperor Theodosius was invested with the imperial purple*: Theodosius I (379–95); the death of the emperor Valens in battle and the destruction of his army at Hadrianopolis in August 378 left the east vulnerable and defenceless. Thus it was that Valens' nephew, the young emperor, Gratian, enticed Theodosius out of retirement in Spain, because of his military background, to step into his uncle's shoes. During the winter of 379–80, he became dangerously ill and was baptised by Ascolius, orthodox Bishop of Thessalonica in Greece, just before his campaign against the Goths. He was a ruthless general but religious and orthodox. He ruled with absolute authority except where his authority came into conflict with the Catholic Church. Immediately on his arrival in Constantinople, he expelled Demophilus, the Arian bishop and installed Gregory of Nazianzus. He then declared that the faith professed by the Bishop of Rome was the only true religion, ordered all churches to be handed over to the orthodox party, expelled dissenting clergy and convened a council at Constantinople to put an end to Arianism once and for all. Throughout his reign, Theodosius issued about fifteen edicts against heretics and heresies, most of them against those rejecting the Trinity. For the last two years of his life, he was sole emperor and the last to rule an undivided empire.

p. 77. *Pretiosa in conspectu Domini mors sanctorum ejus*: 'Precious in the sight of the Lord is the death of his saints' (Psalm 115:15).

p. 77. *come back to Asia as plain Gregory*: in the year (382) following his resignation as patriarch of Constantinople, Gregory made the following observation about episcopal synods: 'If I must speak the truth ... I feel disposed to shun every conference of Bishops; because I never saw Synod brought to a happy issue, nor remedying, but rather increasing, existing evils. For ever there is rivalry and ambition, and these have the mastery of reason; – do not think me extravagant for saying so, – and a mediator is more likely to be attacked himself, than to succeed in his pacification. Accordingly, I have fallen back upon myself, and consider quiet the only security of life'. As for Church synods and councils, 'I salute from afar, since I have experienced that most of them (to speak moderately) are but sorry affairs.' (*Ari.*, p. 388).

p. 77. *his friend dead . . . sister Gorgonia dead*: Basil died in 379; his father, Gregory the Elder and Nonna, his mother, died in 374; Caesarius, the physician, died about 369 and Gorgonia shortly afterwards.

p. 78. *Paul*: (d. *c.* 350), orthodox Bishop of Constantinople who succeeded the ageing Alexander in 340. He was, however, quickly replaced by the 'unprincipled' and politically ambitious Eusebius of Nicomedia (341–42) and then by Macedonius (342–48, 350–60), both of whom had the support of the Arian emperor, Constantius II (337–61). Sozomen suggests that he may have been strangled while in exile by the followers of Macedonius (*Ecclesiastical History*, Book III, Chapter 3).

p. 78. *Eusebius*: (d. *c.* 342), Arian Bishop of Berytus (modern Beirut), and then Bishop of Nicomedia (317); at the Council of Nicaea (325), he signed the orthodox creed, but argued against the condemnation of Arius, for which he was deposed by Constantine the Great. A consummate politician, he was recalled in 328, continued working against the Nicene Creed, and succeeded in having many orthodox supporters exiled, including Athanasius in 335. In 337, he baptised Constantine the Great on his deathbed and was appointed to the see of Constantinople in 338. He was the brains behind the Arian party. His 'influence is quickly discernible in the change which ensued in its language and conduct. While a courteous tone was assumed towards the defenders of the orthodox doctrine, the subtleties of dialectics, in which the sect excelled, were used, not in attacking, but in deceiving its opponents, in making unbelief plausible, and obliterating the distinctive marks of the true creed. It must not be forgotten that it was from Nicomedia, the see of Eusebius, that Constantine wrote his epistle to Alexander and Arius' describing the dispute as 'insignificant and worthless' (*Ari.*, pp. 261; 248).

p. 78. *Macedonius*: (d. *c.* 362), following the death of Eusebius of Nicomedia (*c.* 342), Macedonius was appointed Bishop of Constantinople. He supported the Semi-Arian cause at the Council of Seleucia (359) and occupied the see on two occasions (342–48, 350–60). He was deposed in 360 and died shortly afterwards; see (*P.C.*) note to p. 383.

p. 78. *Eudoxius*: Bishop of Constantinople from 360 to 369, succeeding Macedonius; he was leader of a radical Arian faction which claimed that the Father could not be divided and that Jesus Christ was therefore a creature who was unlike the Father in substance. It was at the dedication of the great cathedral of St. Sophia at Constantinople, 'that he uttered the wanton impiety, which has characterised him with a distinctness, which supersedes all historical notice of his conduct, or discussion of his religious opinions. "When Eudoxius," says Socrates, "had taken his seat on the episcopal throne, his first words were these celebrated ones, 'The Father is . . .irreligious; the Son . . . religious.' When a noise and confusion ensued, he added, 'Be not distressed at what I say; for the Father is irreligious, as worshipping none; but the Son is religious towards the Father'. On this the tumult ceased, and in its place an intemperate laughter seized the congregation; and it remains as a good saying even to this time"' (*Ari.*, p. 277; Socrates, *Ecclesiastical History*, II, Chapter 43).

p. 78. *Evagrius*: pro-Arian Bishop of Constantinople from 369 to 370, succeeding Eudoxius.

p. 78. *atrocious punishment*: the year was 370; according to Socrates the historian, the pro-Arian Valens was 'filled with wrath; but dissembled his displeasure in their presence, and gave Modestus the prefect a secret order to apprehend these persons, and put them to death. . . . The prefect fearing that he should excite the populace to a seditious movement against himself, if he attempted the public execution of so many, pretended to send the men away into exile. Accordingly as they received the intelligence of their destiny with great firmness of mind the prefect ordered that they should be embarked as if to be conveyed to their several places of banishment, having meanwhile enjoined on the sailors to set the vessel on fire, as soon as they reached the mid sea, that their victims being so destroyed, might even be deprived of burial. This injunction was obeyed; for when they arrived at the middle of the Astacian Gulf [Gulf of Aztaca], the crew set fire to the ship, and then took refuge in a small barque which followed them, and so escaped. Meanwhile it came to pass that a strong easterly wind blew, and the burning ship was roughly driven but moved faster and was preserved until it reached a port named Dacidizus, where it was utterly consumed together with the men who were shut up in it' (Socrates, *Ecclesiastical History*, Book IV, Chapters 14–16; Sozomen, *Ecclesiastical History*, Book VI, Chapters 13–14).

p. 78. *Novatians*: disciples of Novatian, a second-century Roman priest and rival Bishop of Rome; a hardliner and author of a 'harsh and arrogant discipline' (*Ari.*, p. 16). Novatian objected to the re-admission of those who had apostatised during the Decian persecution (250–51). In fact, he and his followers argued that the Church did not have the power to grant forgiveness to anyone guilty of murder, adultery or apostasy. 'Once fallen, always fallen' was their motto. Novatians built up their own network of Churches which survived for hundreds of years. It is probable that Novatian himself died a martyr's death around 258.

p. 78. *Eunomians*: small band of radical Arians living in and around Constantinople towards the end of the fourth century; followers of Arius who accepted that the Father and the Son were united in will, but refused to accept the Nicene formula that Jesus is 'of one substance' with the Father on the one hand and the teaching of Basil of Ancrya that Jesus was 'of similar substance' with the Father on the other. They were called after Eunomius, Bishop of Cyzicus (*c.* 325–*c.* 395) who was run out of town for his long-winded speeches. They believed that only God the Father was 'ungenerated', all other beings were generated, including Jesus Christ who was adopted. According to Newman, 'Arius asserted that the Second Person of the Blessed Trinity was not able to comprehend the First, whereas Eunomius's characteristic tenet was in an opposite direction, viz. that not only the Son, but that all men could comprehend God; yet no one can doubt that Eunomianism was a true development, not a corruption of Arianism' (*Dev.*, p. 174; see also *Ari.*, pp. 337–40).

p. 79. *Demophilus*: after the massacre of the eighty clerics in the Gulf of Aztaca west of Nicomedia in 370, Valens replaced Evagrius with Demophilus as the new Bishop of Constantinople. 'At Constantinople Demophilus the successor of Eudoxius presided over the Arian faction, and was in possession of the churches; but those who were averse to communion with him held their assemblies apart' (Socrates, *Ecclesiastical History*, Book V, Chapter 3). He was expelled in 380 by Theodosius I for refusing to endorse the Nicene Creed and died around 386.

p. 79. *kindness of a relative*: when Gregory first arrived in Constantinople round Easter 379, the churches of the city were in the hands of Semi-Arians. He 'had no more suitable place of worship than his own lodgings'. So he erected an altar in a private home where 'he preached the Catholic doctrine to the dwindled communion over which he presided.... His congregation increased; the house, in which they assembled, was converted into a church by the pious liberality of its owner, with the name of Anastasia [the resurrection], in the hope of that resurrection which now awaited the long-buried truths of the Gospel' (*Ari.*, p. 381). Gregory later spoke of that Church as 'the new Shiloh, where the ark was fixed after its forty years of wandering in the desert' (Orations XLII, para. 26).

p. 79. *he resigned his see*: unlike many confrères, Gregory had no stomach for the bickering and politicking he encountered at Constantinople. As a result, he resigned and retired to his farm at Arianzus near Nazianzus. The staunchly orthodox Theodosius I (379–395) reluctantly 'accepted his resignation; but at length allowed him to depart from Constantinople, Nectarius being placed on the patriarchal throne in his stead' (*Ari.*, p. 391). By comparison, Nectarius' period of office was relatively uneventful.

p. 79. *the second General Council*: Council of Constantinople (381) convened by the orthodox emperor Theodosius I to put an end to Arianism; the western Church 'enjoyed at this time an almost perfect peace, and sent no deputies to Constantinople'. But the eastern Church, 'besides the distractions caused by the various heretical off-shoots of Arianism, its indirect effects existed in the dissensions of the Catholics themselves; in the schism at Antioch; in the claims of Maximus to the see of Constantinople; and in the recent disturbances at Alexandria, where the loss of Athanasius was already painfully visible. Added to these, was the ambiguous position of the Macedonians; who resisted the orthodox doctrine, yet were only by implication heretical, or at least some of them far less than others. Thirty-six of their Bishops attended the Council, principally from the neighbourhood of the Hellespont; of the orthodox there were 150, Meletius, of Antioch, being the president' (*Ari.*, pp. 388–389). 'From the date of this Council, Arianism was formed into a sect exterior to the Catholic Church; and, taking refuge among the Barbarian Invaders of the Empire, is merged among those external enemies of Christianity, whose history cannot be regarded as strictly ecclesiastical' (ibid., pp. 392–393).

p. 81. '*Thou art my sister*': Proverbs 7: 4.

p. 83. *just as to build a tower . . . who has wherewith to finish*: Luke 14: 28.

p. 84. "*a king like the nations*": 1 Kings (1 Samuel) 8: 5.

p. 84. *Lord Mayor's preacher*: in 1831, Newman warned a friend about the pitfalls of accepting such positions. 'As to Town-preacherships, they seem to me dangerous to the holder, as corrupting the minister into the orator . . . a pulpit makes one *un*real, rhetorical – conceited – it hardens the heart, while it effeminates it. . . . One out of many dilemmas in which a London-preacher finds himself, is the following – let *him withstand* the popular love of novelty and desire of excitement, he must preach (what will be called) *dully* and if so, he will *empty his chapel* – let him try to keep his congregation together, he will be pampering their bad tempers and habits' (*L.D.* II. pp. 337–8, letter to Simeon Lloyd Pope, 21 June 1831).

p. 84. *West-end divine*: reference to popular preachers of the day who would address packed houses in Exeter Hall, the Freemason's Hall and the Hanover Square Rooms, London. Newman thought that the object of these performances was to entertain rather than instruct. They were not meant to be 'an act of thanks or praise where it is due, not a contemplation of religious subjects, not even the spread of information on religious subjects, but an exhibition of persons and oratory'. In fact, he suggested, that 'little as we like the playhouse, if we were compelled to go to one or the other, we would as lieve go thither to this celebrated Hall on a show-day' ('Exeter Hall', *British Critic*, July 1838, pp. 190–211).

p. 85. *parsimonious*: frugal.

p. 86. *Briareus*: according to Greek mythology, Briareus was one of the Hecatonchires each with a hundred hands and fifty heads. His father, Uranus, threw him into Tartarus, that region of the underworld reserved for punishment of the worst criminals of the ancient world such as Sisyphus and Tantalus. Briareus was eventually rescued by Zeus who enlisted his help in fighting the Titans.

p. 86. *Nazianzus . . . Arianzus*: finding the administration even of a small place like Nazianzus too much for him, Gregory eventually retired in 383 to nearby Arianzus where he had a small farm, writing and devoting himself to a quiet ascetical life until his death around 389.

p. 88. *As viewing sin . . . bear me company*: in his original essay for the *British Magazine*, Newman preceded this poem with the following observation: 'Though Gregory did not retire into the solitudes of Pontus with his friend [Basil], and had perhaps more of what is now called a domestic character, yet he was not less devoted than Basil to that state of life, which, in the primitive church, was considered the highest, though not imperative on any one. There is frequent evidence of this in his poems; and it is necessary to be aware of it in order fully to enter into the child-like and heavenly simplicity of his mind.' (*British Magazine*, 'Letters on the Church of the Fathers', No. VIII, Volume VI, August 1834, p. 156; deleted in 1840 and subsequent editions).

p. 89. *Gregory's poetry*: Gregory wrote most of his poetry during his final years at Arianzus. Though by no means a first-class poet, some of his verses nevertheless show genuine feeling and beauty. About 400 poems are extant. Newman translated several and included them in *Verses on Various Occasions*, pp. 193–202.

p. 90. *Demiurge*: name given by Plato in his dialogue the *Timaeus* to a subordinate creator God who fashioned the physical world into conformity with some eternal ideal world; derived from the Greek 'demiourgis' meaning 'craftsman'. Gnostics used the idea of a Demiurge to explain the origin and existence of evil in the world by introducing aeons or angels who had sprung from, but were independent of the one supreme God. One of these angels was the Demiurge who had created the world, without God's knowledge. As this Demiurge was an imperfect being, his defects were reflected in his handiwork. It was he who gave the Jews their imperfect law, Gnostics tending to identify him with Jehovah of the Hebrew Scriptures. Not only was he responsible for the blemishes of the Old Testament dispensation, he also tried to conceal from the human race knowledge of the one supreme God and covet for himself the homage and worship due to God alone. For this purpose, God chose Jesus as the vehicle by which God might convey this knowledge to the human race.

pp. 92–93. *Some one whispered yesterday . . . They have forfeited the name*: the original conclusion for the *British Magazine* was as follows: 'It would take up too much time to continue the poem, of which I have attempted the above rude translation; nor is it to the purpose to set before the reader of the present day a formal defence and recommendation of celibacy, though there is no reason why Gregory should not have his own opinion about it as well as another. I end with the following specimen, which is of a different character: –

> THE DEATH OF A YOUNG MAIDEN.
> Painful to lose; but twice our pain, bereft
> Of what is dear; and thrice, of maiden young;
> More hardly still the mourner's heart is wrung,
> Should she be fair; and it is thoroughly cleft,
> If she have promised love, and then her pledge have left.

(*British Magazine*, 'Letters on the Church of the Fathers', No. VIII, Volume VI, August 1834, p. 158; deleted in the 1840 and subsequent editions).

The poem must have stuck a chord with Newman since he had lost his youngest sister, Mary, suddenly and unexpectedly, at Brighton on the eve of the Epiphany 1828, probably of peritonitis. She was just nineteen. Newman was devastated.

p. 93. *great theologically*: his rhetorical skills and unerring defence of the Nicene creed, as revealed in his five *Theological Orations*, earned him the title of *The Theologian* ('Theologus'). He preached them in a small household church known as the Anastasia in Constantinople, between 379 and 381. It is a title shared only with John the Evangelist. At the time, Gregory 'held his assemblies within the city in a small oratory, adjoining to which the emperors afterwards built a magnificent church, and named it *Anastasia* meaning the Church of the Resurrection (Sozamen, *Ecclesiastical History*, Book V, Chapter 7).

p. 93. *personally winning*: in 1869, Newman wrote to a close friend about wanting no official role in the forthcoming first Vatican Council. He compared himself to Gregory of Nazianzus because 'I like going my own way, and having my time my own, living without pomp or state, or pressing engagements. Put me into official garb, and I am worth nothing; leave me to myself, and every now and then I shall do something. Dress me up and you shall soon have to make my shroud – leave me alone, and I shall live the appointed time' (*L.D.* XXIV, p. 213, to Maria Rosina Giberne, Ash Wednesday, 10 February 1869).

Chapter V: Antony in Conflict

Synopsis: Antony of Egypt is the father of Christian monasticism. While still a young man, he loses both parents and is left to care for his young sister. After making provision for her, he distributes the rest of his inheritance to the poor and retires into the desert to live as a hermit. He soon attracts a following of like-minded individuals and becomes their leader. He is tempted to return to the pleasures of the world, but refuses to capitulate. Even though he lives the life of a hermit, he keeps in touch with what is going on in Church affairs and supports Athanasius in his fight against Arianism. He remains a loyal son of the Church and his practice of the ascetic life is balanced and mature to the end.

p. 94. *Antony*: (*c.* 251–*c.* 356), Anthony of Egypt was the father of Christian monasticism. He was born to well-to-do parents in Coma, near Memphis in Middle Egypt, and lost them at the age of eighteen. After making provision for his younger sister, he gave the rest of his inheritance to the poor, joined a nearby monastery and became a disciple of Paul of Thebes (d. *c.* 340) who taught him the basics of the ascetic life. He later lived alone for about twelve years in some empty tombs where, it seemed, he had his encounters with the devil. He then moved further into the desert where he lived in an abandoned mountain fortress where he attracted many visitors. He once left his mountain retreat to support Athanasius in his fight against Arianism. When he was dying, he took two companions and retired for the last time into solitude. He was about 105 years old. Athanasius wrote his biography which helped popularise desert monasticism. It did not focus on historical details as such, rather on his influence on people and his celebrated epic battles with the devil.

p. 94. "*He found him in a desert land . . . apple of his eye*": Deuteronomy 32: 10.

p. 94. *Christianity is a religion . . . for the poor*: in 1 Timothy 4: 8, Paul reminds us that 'godliness is valuable in every way, holding promise for both the present life, and the life to come.'

p. 95. "*to sell all, and give to the poor*": Luke 18: 22.

p. 95. *Protestant philosophy*: in *Grammar of Assent*, Newman summarised Protestant philosophy thus: '... the fundamental dogma of Protestantism is the exclusive authority of Holy Scripture; but in holding this a Protestant holds a host of propositions, explicitly or implicitly, and holds them with assents of various character. Among these propositions, he holds that Scripture is the Divine Revelation itself, that it is inspired, that nothing is known in doctrine but what is there, that the Church has no authority in matters of doctrine, that, as claiming it, it was condemned long ago in the Apocalypse, that St. John wrote the Apocalypse, that justification is by faith only, that our Lord is God, that there are seventy-two generations between Adam and our Lord' (*G.A.*, pp. 243–4).

p. 96. "*'sensible' Protestants*": in the original essay for the *British Magazine*, Newman added the phrase: 'as much as that of papists' (*British Magazine*, 'Letters on the Church of the Fathers', No. XIII, Volume VIII, July 1835, p. 41); he altered it in the 1840 edition to 'as much as that as Romanists', but deleted the phrase for subsequent Catholic editions.

p. 96. *Wesleyans*: followers of John Wesley (1703–91) and Charles Wesley (1707–88), the founders of Methodism.

p. 96. *Independents*: alternative name for Congregationalists and Presbyterians.

p. 97. *two by two*: Luke 10: 1.

p. 97. "*It is not good for him to be alone*": Genesis 2: 18.

p. 97. *Monachism*: alternative name for monasticism; the words 'monk' and 'monasticism' are derived from the Greek word 'monos' meaning 'alone'. 'In no aspect of the Divine system do we see more striking developments than in the successive fortunes of Monachism. Little did the youth Antony foresee, when he set off to fight the evil one in the wilderness, what a sublime and various history he was opening, a history which had its first developments even in his own lifetime' (*Dev.*, p. 393).

p. 97. *St. Antony's life ... by Athanasius*: most of our knowledge about Antony comes from the writings of Athanasius' *Life of Saint Antony* written about a year after his death in 357. More than anything else, it popularised desert monasticism and its values in both the east and the west. Athanasius modelled it on the Greek model of writing biography which tended to idealise important public figures. While light on historical detail, it focused on Antony's personal influence on people and on his epic battles with Satan. Athanasius portrayed Antony as the ideal monk by his discernment of spirits and miraculous powers – gifts which he always attributed to God and never to himself.

p. 97. *Rivetus*: Andreas Rivetus (1572–1651), strict Calvinist, scripture scholar and implacable enemy of the Roman Catholic Church.

p. 97. *Du Pin*: Louis-Ellies Du Pin (1657–1719), teacher of theology at the Sorbonne and philosophy at the Royal College, author of *Bibliothèque universelle de tous les auteurs ecclèsiastiques* (58 volumes) between 1686 and 1704. The work was censured by the Archbishop of Paris in 1691, and suppressed in 1696.

p. 97. *Benedictines*: congregation of French Benedictine monks of St. Maur who were famous for their scholarship and whose history extended from 1618 to 1818. Throughout its distinguished career, the congregation included many great patristic scholars including Mabillon (1632–1707) and Montfacon (1655–1741). Newman's personal copy of the works of Athanasius, including the *Life of Saint Antony*, was a Maurist edition.

p. 97. *Tillemont*: see *Mémoires*, Volume VII, pp. 101–44.

p. 99. *affectionate loyalty to the Church and to the Truth*: like Athanasius, Antony was an active champion of the Nicene Creed. Once, when certain Arians suggested that his opinions coincided with their own, Antony journeyed to Alexandria to support him, declaring that their ideas were a 'forerunner of Antichrist' (Athanasius, *Life of Saint Antony*, para. 69).

p. 99. *AD 251*: most scholars agree that Antony was born some time shortly after 250 and died at the impressive age of 105.

p. 99. *Egyptian by birth*: according to Sozomen, Antony's 'fame was so widely spread throughout the deserts of Egypt, that the emperor Constantine, for the reputation of the man's virtue, sought his friendship, honoured him with correspondence, and urged him to write about what he might need. He was an Egyptian by race, and belonged to an illustrious family of Coma, which was situated near the Heraclea which is on the Egyptian borders' (Sozomen, *Ecclesiastical History*, Book I: Chapter 13).

p. 99. *a strong disposition towards a solitary life*: the French Oratorian, Louis Bouyer, suggests that Antony's family was brought up at a time when Christians were being persecuted and when fidelity to Christ showed itself by isolating oneself from the world. That Antony did not attend school is a detail which witnesses not so much to supernatural wisdom, but to the Christian character of his upbringing and to his making early connections between Christianity and the solitary life (Louis Bouyer, *La Vie de S. Antoine*, Éditions Fontenelle, 1950, pp. 42–3).

p. 100. "*If thou wilt be perfect, go sell all that thou hast*": Matthew 19: 21.

p. 100. "*Be not solicitous for tomorrow*": Matthew 6: 34.

p. 100. *placing his sister in the care of some women*: Antony entrusted his sister, Dious, to a 'house of virgins' to complete her education. It was a family-run concern under the care of the local bishop, and one where individuals retained their independence (see Louis Bouyer, *La Vie de S. Antoine*, Éditions Fontenelle, 1950, p. 52).

p. 100. *He commenced his ascetic life*: Antony commenced his religious life near Coma (Middle Egypt), apprenticing himself to an old hermit (Paul of Thebes) who taught him the basics of the ascetic life. He later lived for twelve or fifteen years in some tombs further away from the village. When 'others followed his example, he was obliged to give them guidance, and thus he found himself, by degrees, at the head of a large family of solitaries, five thousand of whom were scattered in the district of Nitria alone. He lived to see a second stage in the development; the huts in which they lived were brought together, sometimes round a church, and a sort of subordinate community, or college, formed among certain individuals of their number. St. Pachomius was the first who imposed a general rule of discipline upon the brethren, gave them a common dress, and set before them the objects to which the religious life was dedicated. Manual labour, study, devotion, bodily mortification, were now their peculiarities; and the institution, thus defined, spread and established itself through Eastern and Western Christendom' (*Dev.*, p. 394).

p. 101. '*If anyone will not work, neither let him eat*': 2 Thessalonians 3: 10.

p. 101. *pray in private without ceasing*: Luke 18: 1; 1 Thessalonians 5: 17.

p. 101. *the high and dry system of the Establishment*: according to Newman, the Established Church of his day had many layers, including 'ecclesiastics who enjoy great revenues and have not much to do (such as the members of Cathedral chapters), many have long since deteriorated in the pursuit of their personal advantage. Those who held high positions in great towns have been led to adopt the habits of a great position and of external display, and have boasted a formal orthodoxy which was cold and almost entirely devoid of interior life. These self-indulgent pastors have for a long time been nick-named "two-bottle orthodox", as though their greatest religious zeal manifested itself in the drinking of port wine to the health of "the Church and King". The pompous dignitaries of great town parishes have also been surnamed the "high and dry" school or Church' (quoted in Wilfrid Ward's *Kingsley versus Newman 1864–5*, pp. xxvi–xxvii).

p. 102. *methodism*: see (*C.F.*) note to p. 165.

p. 102. *dissent*: see (*P.C.*) note to p. 341.

p. 102. *instruments of temptation*: Athanasius tells us that the devil 'tried to lead him [Antony] away from the discipline, whispering to him the remembrance of his wealth, care for his sister, claims of kindred, love of money, love of glory, the various pleasures of the table and the other relaxations of life, and at last the difficulty of virtue and the labour of it; he suggested also the infirmity of the body and the length of the time. In a word he raised in his mind a great dust of debate, wishing to debar him from his settled purpose' (Athanasius, *Life of Saint Antony*, para. 5).

p. 102. '*who hath condemned ... according to the Spirit*': Romans 8: 3–4.

p. 102. *many devices of the enemy*: Ephesians 6: 11.

p. 102. *bringing it into subjection*: 1 Corinthians 9: 27.

pp. 102–103. '*When I am weak, then am I powerful*': 2 Corinthians 12: 10.

p. 103. '*forgetting the things that are behind ... those that are before*': Philippians 3: 13.

p. 104. *Elias*: reference to that incident when the prophet Elias spent the night in a cave on Mount Horeb – the mountain of God (3 Kings (1 Kings) 19: 9–10).

p. 104. *yet nothing shall separate me from the love of Christ*: Romans 8: 35.

p. 104. '*If armies in camp should stand ... my heart shall not fear*': Psalm 26: 3 (Psalm 27: 3).

p. 105. *a strong place*: Antony eventually died in his cliff-side cave in 356 on Mount Kolzim on the north-west corner of the Red Sea, aged 105.

p. 106. *energumen*: in the early Church, 'energumen' was a term used of demoniacs and others possessed of abnormal mental and physical behaviour. Following Christ's example, they were treated with care and an exorcist had to be called in.

p. 106. "*This kind can go out by nothing but by prayer and fasting*": Mark 9: 28.

p. 107. *a legion of devils*: Newman later referred to Antony's celebrated battles with demons in his poem, the *Dream of Gerontius* (1865):

> But, when some child of grace, Angel or Saint,
> Pure and upright in his integrity
> Of nature, meets the demons on their raid,
> They scud away as cowards from the fight.
> Nay, oft hath the holy hermit in his cell,
> Not yet disburden'd of mortality,
> Mock'd at their threats and warlike overtures
> (*Verses on Various Occasions (V.V.)*, p. 347).

p. 107. *Balaam's ass*: Numbers 22: 21–34.

p. 107. *Creator Spirit had ... in the bodily form of a dove*: see Luke 3: 22; Matthew 3: 16.

p. 107. "*Behold, I have given you power ... of the enemy*": Luke 10: 19.

p. 107. "*They shall take up ... shall not hurt them*": Mark 16: 18.

p. 107. "*Your adversary, the devil ... seeking whom he may devour*": 1 Peter 5: 8.

p. 107. "*I saw three unclean spirits ... working signs*": Apocalypse (Revelation) 16: 13–14.

p. 107. *Daniel's vision of the four beasts*: Daniel 7: 1–28.

p. 107. *leviathan*: some huge monster; according to scripture, some sort of animal (Psalm 103: 26; perhaps a crocodile as described in Job 40–41; or a sea serpent as in Isaiah 27: 1).

p. 107. *that visible things ... of things invisible*: Romans 1: 20.

p. 108. *The demoniac whom the Apostles could not cure*: Mathew 17: 16–20.

p. 108. *the woman who was bowed together for eighteen years*: Luke 13: 10–13.

p. 109. "*a spirit of infirmity,*" ... "*bound by Satan*": Luke 13: 11–16.

p. 109. "*prince of the power of the air*": Ephesians 2: 2.

p. 109. *Dreams are another department*: see Genesis 28: 11–16; Job 7: 14; 33: 15; Matthew 1: 20–25; 2: 12, 13–15.

p. 110. "*There are more things . . . in your philosophy*": *Hamlet*, Act 1, scene 5, lines 166–167.

p. 111. *Joppa*: seaport of Palestine on the eastern Mediterranean; Hiram, King of Tyre, sent rafts laden with timber there for Solomon (2 Paralipomenon 2: 16); Jonah boarded ship here when trying to escape Yahweh (Jonas 1: 3); Peter the Apostle restored Dorcas to life here (Acts 9: 36–42); and it was here that Peter 'saw heaven opened, and a certain vessel descending unto him, as it had been a great sheet at the four corners, and let down to the earth. Wherein were all manner of four-footed beasts of the earth, and wild beasts, and creeping things, and fowls of the air' (Acts 10: 11–12).

p. 111. *Patmos*: northernmost island of the Dodecanese group in the Aegean Sea about 60 kilometres (37 miles) south-west of Ephesus where John the Apostle was banished towards the end of the reign of the emperor Domitian (51–96) and where he is said to have had a vision and to have written the Apocalypse (Revelation 1: 9).

Chapter VI: Antony in Calm

Synopsis: In this chapter, Newman focuses on certain aspects of Antony's character by examining extracts from Athanasius' *Life of Saint Antony* which highlight his faith, his cool judgement and personal dignity. According to Athanasius, the source of his faith is his personal relationship with God. Right to the end of his life Antony remains invariably cheerful, sociable and well-balanced.

p. 112. "*The land that was desolate . . . springs of water*": Isaiah 35: 1, 7.

p. 112. *extraordinary and heavenly gifts*: reference to those particular divine gifts singled out by Paul the Apostle which regularly surfaced in early Christian communities: 'When you come together, each one has a hymn, a lesson, a revelation, a tongue, or an interpretation. Let all things be done for building up' (1 Corinthians 14: 26).

p. 113. *philosophical analyst*: in his original essay for the *British Magazine*, Newman added the following statement: 'Probably he [the philosophical analyst] would not have been at all disconcerted, even could it have been proved to him that his [Antony's] cures were the *natural* effect of imagination in the patient; accounting them as rewards to faith, any how, not as evidence to the reason. Perhaps this consideration will tend to solve Paley's difficulty, better than he does himself, why the early Fathers appeal so faintly and scantily to the argument from miracles. That argument is not ordinarily the actual mode by which the mind is subdued to the obedience of Christ' (*British Magazine*, 'Letters on the Church of the Fathers', No. XV, Volume VIII, September 1835, p. 278). In 1839, we find Newman returning to this idea in his tenth University Sermon, 'Faith and Reason, contrasted as Habits of Mind': 'Miracles, though they contravene the physical laws of the universe, tend to the due fulfilment of its moral laws. And in matter of fact, when they were wrought, they addressed persons who were already believers, not in the mere probability, but even in the truth of supernatural revelations' (*Fifteen Sermons preached before the University of Oxford (U.S.)* X, p. 196).

pp. 113–14. *And then, when faith was once . . . could not even have imagined*: in his original essay for the *British Magazine*, Newman wrote: 'He [Antony] considered, contrariwise to present notions, that the *consciousness of being* rational, was no necessary condition of being rational. I mean, it is the present opinion, that no one can be acting according to reason, unless he reflects on himself and recognises his own rationality. A peasant, who cannot tell *why* he believes, is supposed to have no reason for believing. This is worth noticing, for it is parallel to many other dogmas into which a civilized age will be sure to fall. Antony, on the other hand, considered there was something great and noble in believing and acting on the Gospel, without asking for proof; making experiment of it, and being rewarded by the success of it. He put arguments for belief, to speak paradoxically, *after*, not *before* believing . . .' (*British Magazine*, 'Letters on the Church of the Fathers', No. XV, Volume VIII, September 1835, pp. 277–8). We find Newman returning to this idea in his thirteenth University Sermon, 'Implicit and Explicit Reason' in 1840: 'All men reason, for to reason is nothing more than to gain truth from former truth, without the intervention of sense, to which brutes are limited; but all men do not reflect upon their own reasonings, much less reflect truly and accurately, so as to do justice to their own meaning; but only in proportion to their abilities and attainments. In other words, all men have a reason, but not all men can give a reason' (*U.S.* XIII, pp. 258–9).

p. 114. "'*Instead of demonstrating . . . process of argument.*'": 'I would rather be bound to defend the reasonableness of assuming that Christianity is true, than to demonstrate a moral governance from the physical world. Life is for action. If we insist on proofs for every thing, we shall never come to action: to act you must assume, and that assumption is faith.' (*G.A.*, p. 95).

p. 114. "'*Why wonder ye at this . . . in Christ sufficient*'": in his original essay for the *British Magazine*, Newman added the following paragraph: 'As Antony would not be startled at his cures being set down to the power of imagination, so I conceive, in like manner, he would have admitted his gift of prescience to be, not miraculous, but the result of deep and continued meditation, acute reflection, and that calmness and dispassionateness of mind which self-denying habits naturally create, aided, of course, by the special evangelical influences of the Spirit, which, in his age, were manifested far more fully than in our own' (*British Magazine*, 'Letters on the Church of the Fathers', No. XV, Volume VIII, September 1835, p. 278).

p. 115. '*Rejoice not that spirits are not subject unto you*': Luke 10: 20.

p. 115. '*Lord, did we not cast out devils in Thy name?*': Matthew 7: 22.

p. 115. *we may not believe every spirit*: 1 John 4: 1.

p. 115. *Neo-platonists*: Neoplatonism was the last great pagan philosophy; its teaching, derived from Plato and his disciples, emphasised mysticism, ecstasy and prophecy as legitimate sources of knowledge. Although its leading figure was Plotinus (*c.* 205–70), his teacher, Ammonius Saccus (175–242), a self-educated labourer from Alexandria, was more likely its founder. When Plotinus settled in Rome around 244, he founded a school of Neoplatonism. Plotinus rejected Plato's ideas of two disparate and distinct orders of being such as good and evil, universal and particular, material and transcendent. He believed in one order of being containing all levels of existence. At the centre was a mysterious unity which revealed a divine logos (word). Neoplatonism had an enormous impact on the theology of the early Church, particularly on figures like Clement of Alexandria (*c.* 150–*c.* 220), Origen (*c.* 185–*c.* 253), Hypatia (*c.* 375–415) and Augustine of Hippo (354–430) who was already a Neoplatonist before his conversion in 386. Christian Neoplatonists wanted to lay a solid intellectual foundation for theology.

p. 115. *Such was the soul of Eliseus, which witnessed Giezi's conduct*: Giezi was the servant of Eliseus who employed him on several missions to the Sunamite woman whose son was miraculously restored to life (4 Kings (2 Kings) 4). This was the same Giezi who was struck with leprosy for his greed in seeking a reward of two talents from Naaman the Syrian commander in (4 Kings (2 Kings) 5).

p. 116. *Yet surely . . . assume premisses as Antony does*: according to the Acts of the Apostles, outsiders assumed that the apostles were 'filled with new wine' on the first Pentecost (Acts 2: 6–13).

p. 117. *not sparing his own Son, but giving Him up for us all*: Romans 8: 32.

p. 117. *Holy Scripture is sufficient for teaching*: Antony is simply reflecting fourth-century Christianity which did not separate theology from Scripture.

p. 117. '*The days of our years . . . they be four score*': Psalm 89: 10 (Psalm 90: 10).

p. 117. *our reign in glory*: see Romans 8: 18.

p. 118. *We lose a corruptible body to receive it back incorruptible*: 1 Corinthians 15: 53.

p. 118. *our present sufferings . . . revealed in us*: Romans 8: 18.

p. 118. *If we do not let these things . . . as says Ecclesiastes*: see Ecclesiastes 5–6; Psalm 48: 11–12.

p. 118. '*The kingdom of heaven . . . within you*': Luke 17: 21.

p. 119. *whereas the true Angel . . . a hundred four score and five thousand*: 4 Kings (2 Kings) 19: 35.

p. 119. *What can be more calm . . . the teaching of the fourth century*: what strikes the reader in Athanasius' *Life of Saint Antony* is the psychological balance in Antony's battles with demons and his overall approach to the spiritual life. In his original essay for the *British Magazine*, Newman described Antony as 'grave, manly, considerate, and refined – in a word, to speak familiarly, so gentlemanlike' (*British Magazine*, 'Letters on the Church of the Fathers', No. XV, Volume VIII, September 1835, p. 279).

p. 119. *You cannot say that Antony . . . cunning and hypocrisy*: the original sentence in the *British Magazine* runs thus: 'Antony was no savage saint, no ostentatious dervise; he had no pomposity or affectation, nothing of cunning and hypocrisy' (*British Magazine*, 'Letters on the Church of the Fathers', No. XV, Volume VIII, September 1835, p. 279). He included it in the first three editions, changing to its present form for subsequent editions.

p. 119. *dervise*: one of several variants of a Persian word 'dervish', meaning a poor, Mohammedan mendicant who has taken a vow of poverty and lives a quite austere life. Among dervishes there are various orders, some of whom are famous for their fantastic dancing, whirling and howling.

p. 120. '*A glad heart maketh . . . the spirit is cast down*': Proverbs 15: 13.

p. 120. *Thus Jacob detected. . . to his wives*: Jacob was the son of Isaac and Rebecca and Laban was his uncle; to escape his brother Esau's anger, Jacob sought refuge with Laban who had two daughters, Rachel and Leah. There he worked seven years for Rachel's hand in marriage, but Laban deceived him into marrying Leah. He then worked another seven years before marrying Rachel as well. After a further six years, he managed to obtain most of Laban's flocks before returning home to his father Isaac with his wives and children (Genesis 29–31).

p. 120. '*I see your father's countenance . . . towards me as yesterday*': Genesis 31: 5.

p. 120. *Thus Samuel, too, discovered David*: Samuel was the last and one of the greatest judges of Israel; he discovered the future king of Israel working as a shepherd tending his father's flocks (1 Kings (1 Samuel) 16: 1–13).

p. 120. *beaming eyes*: see1 Kings (1 Samuel) 16: 12.

p. 120. *teeth white as milk*: this phrase does not refer to David but to Judah, son of Jacob (Genesis 49 in Scripture, 12).

p. 120. '*He shall not contend . . .hear their voice*': Isaiah 42: 2; Matthew 12: 19.

p. 120. *as Gabriel did to Zacharias*: Luke 1: 11–20.

p. 120. *and the Angel at the divine tomb*: Matthew 28: 2–7; Mark 16: 2–7.

p. 120. '*Fear not*': Luke 2: 10; Matthew 28: 5.

p. 121. *Meletian schismatics and the Arians*: there was a schism in Egypt named after a certain Meletius, who was Bishop of Lycopolis, modern Asyut on the Nile in Upper (southern) Egypt in the early years of the fourth century. Meletius took the opportunity of seizing the see of Alexandria while Peter the legitimate incumbent was absent. 'He was convicted of sacrificing to idols in the persecution, and deposed by a Council under Peter, Bishop of Alexandria and (subsequently) a martyr. Meletius separated from the communion of the Church and commenced a schism; at the time of the Nicene Council it included as many as twenty-eight or thirty Bishops; in the time of Theodoret [of Cyrrhus], a century and a quarter later, it included a number of monks. Though not hetero-dox, they supported the Arians on their first appearance, in their contest with the Catholics. The Council of Nicaea [325], instead of deposing their Bishops, allowed them on their return a titular rank in their sees, but forbade them to exercise their functions. … The Meletian schismatics of Egypt formed an alliance with the Arians from the first. … There was another Meletius, Bishop of Antioch, in the latter part of the same century. At one time, he belonged to the Semi-Arian party, but joined the orthodox, and was the first president of the second Ecumenical Council [Constantinople (381)]' (*Ath.* II, p. 222; see also *Ari.*, pp. 238–239; 281; *H.S.* I, pp. 426–427; see also note *C.F.*, p. 16).

p. 121. *hagiographists*: traditional writers of saints' lives; from the Greek *hagios* meaning 'sacred' or 'holy' and *graphos* meaning 'something written'.

p. 122. '*the prince of the power of this air*': Ephesians 2: 2–3.

p. 122. '*Put on the panoply … resist the evil day*': Ephesians 6: 11.

p. 122. '*Whether in the body … I know not; God knoweth*': 2 Corinthians 12: 2.

pp. 122–3. *Once, when he was sitting … to the Lord's table*: immediately after this quote, Newman inserted the following paragraph in his original essay for the *British Magazine*: 'It is satisfactory to find in Antony clear marks of his *protestantism*, in a good sense of that ambiguous word – I mean, of his adherence to scripture as the rule of faith, and his freedom from those superstitions with which Popery has overlaid its sacred contents. The appeal to scripture in the narrative of Athanasius, is so frequent and reverential as to be a virtual proof of his holding the protestant doctrine of its exclusive authority as the record of necessary truth' (*British Magazine*, 'Letters on the Church of the Fathers', No. XV, Volume VIII, September 1835, p. 281; included in the 1840 and subsequent editions but deleted from the 1868 edition).

p. 123. '*The bodies of patriarchs … the third day*': see John 19: 41; Matthew 27: 60.

p. 124. *two who lived with him*: Antony died in the presence of Amathas and Macarius who had looked after him for the last fifteen years of his life. He was over one hundred years old.

p. 124. '*I, as it is written, go the way of my fathers*': Genesis 49: 29.

p. 124. *Bury, then, my body in the earth*: Antony's body, it seems, was discovered by a 'revelation' in 561 and transferred to Alexandria. When the Saracens overran Egypt, it was transferred to Constantinople and, finally, to Vienne (near Lyons on the Rhone) in the tenth century.

p. 124. *Serapion*: (d. *c.* 362), a monk from Egypt, friend of Antony and Athanasius, head of the Catechetical School of Alexandria and Bishop of Thmuis on the Nile delta from around 340. He attended a council at Sardica (Sophia, capital of Bulgaria) where he opposed attempts to depose Athanasius. Athanasius and he had similar theological views which is why the former used him as his intermediary with the pro-Arian, Constantius II who eventually banished him around 358. At his request, Athanasius wrote several treatises against Arianism and held Serapion in such high regard as to allow him to alter them as he saw fit.

p. 125. "*many waters could not quench*": Canticle of Canticles 8: 7 [The Song of Solomon].

p. 126. *Among the mountains . . . cedars by the waters*: In his original essay for the *British Magazine*, Newman rounded it off with the following paragraph which contained an extract from a poem by the English metaphysical poet George Herbert (1593–1633): 'I cannot conclude more appropriately than by Herbert's lines on the subject. (Church Militant, v, 37–48)

> 'To Egypt first she [Religion] came; where they did prove
> Wonders of anger once, but now of love.
> The Ten Commandments there did flourish, more
> Than the ten bitter plagues had done before
> *Holy Macarius and great Antony*
> Made Pharoah, Moses; changing the history.
> Goshen was darkness; Egypt, full of lights;
> Nilus, for monsters, brought forth Israelites.
> Such power hath mighty baptism to produce,
> For things mishapen, things of highest use.
> How dear to me, O God, thy counsels are!
> Who may with thee compare?'
> (*British Magazine*, 'Letters on the Church of the Fathers', No. XV, Volume VIII, September 1835, p. 284).

p. 126. '*How beauteous are . . . and thy tabernacles, O Israel*': Numbers 24: 5–6.

Chapter VII: Augustine and the Vandals

Synopsis: In 429, Vandals, under their king, Genseric, land in Roman north Africa and begin devastating everything in their path. Being Arians, they replace orthodox bishops with Arian ones. Although seventy-four years old, Augustine carries on his pastoral duties. When a fellow bishop asks him whether a priest is free to leave the scene of his pastoral duties to save his life, Augustine's answer is as follows. Firstly, a priest is free to flee provided there is no one left to look after. Secondly, any priest who is not a victim of persecution should remain at his post. Thirdly, if every priest is likely to be targeted, then lots should be drawn to decide who stays and who goes. With Vandals at the gates of Hippo, Augustine dies of fever on 28 August, 430. He was the last Bishop of Hippo.

p. 127. *Augustine:* (354–430), Bishop of Regius Hippo (modern Annaba, Algeria) in Roman north Africa, and one of the four traditional Fathers of the Latin (Western) Church, alongside Ambrose, Jerome and Gregory the Great. Augustine was born of a pagan father and a Christian mother in Thagaste (modern Souk Ahras, Algeria), about 100 kilometres (60 miles) south of Hippo. As a young man, he formed a relationship with a concubine by whom he had a son named Adeodatus ('gift of God') in 372. Cicero's *Hortensius* inspired him to devote himself to the pursuit of truth. (373). He began this lifelong search by becoming a teacher of rhetoric, then a Manichaean, then a Neoplatonist, finally a Christian. In 385, he was appointed to the prestigious chair of rhetoric at the imperial court in Milan where he soon fell under the spell of Ambrose, Bishop of Milan, who baptised him in 386. His Neoplatonism gave him an intellectual foundation for his theological and spiritual writings. Except for this short five-year stint in Italy, Augustine spent his entire life in Roman north Africa. On return, he was ordained priest against his will in 391 and, soon after, consecrated Bishop of Hippo. He died in 430, the city's last bishop. Among his many treatises were his celebrated *Confessions*, *The City of God* and *On the Trinity*. At the heart of his theology was a tireless defence of the faith against heresy, including Manichaeism, Donatism and Pelagianism. Augustine's teaching against Donatism was to play a surprising role in Newman's own theological development (see *Apo.*, pp. 109–111; 237).

p. 127. "*The just perisheth . . . the face of evil*": Isaiah 57: 1.

pp. 127–128. "*Woe, woe, woe, to the inhabitants of the earth*": Apocalypse (Revelation) 8: 13.

p. 128. *hail and fire . . . trees and green grass*: Apocalypse (Revelation) 8: 7.

p. 128. *coast of Africa*: the Roman province of Africa was that region of land round Carthage and Hippo Regius, modern Tunisia and Algeria; it was virtually surrounded by Numidia which was much larger.

p. 128. *Vandals*: general term applied to eastern Germans who crossed an ice-bound Rhine river in December, AD 406, invaded Gaul and entered Spain in 409, leaving a trail of devastation in their wake. In 429, they invaded Roman north Africa where they overran a number of Roman provinces and established a powerful kingdom from where they dominated the western Mediterranean. Their religion was Arian with the result that they persecuted orthodox clergy and confiscated Church property.

p. 128. *Carthage*: ancient city in Roman north Africa occupying a key position on a peninsula in the Bay of Tunis near modern Tunis, about 280 kilometres (175 miles) east of Hippo; on the coast of northern Africa, and about 160 kilometres (100 miles) west of Sicily (Ezechiel 27: 12).

p. 129. *Hippo*: ancient city of Hippo Regius (modern Annaba, Algeria) on the Mediterranean coast in Roman north Africa, so named because of its popularity with the ancient kings of Numidia (Algeria and Tunisia). It was about 280 kilometres (175 miles) west of Carthage and one of the most flourishing cities in Roman north Africa. Although a busy seaport, it also owed its wealth to food, particularly corn. Compared with Tagaste, Augustine's birthplace in the hinterland, it was a fairly cosmopolitan city. Nothing remains today of Hippo except a few ruins near the mouth of the Seybouse river.

p. 129. *Mansuetus, bishop of Utica*: martyred with Papinianus of Vite under the Arian king, Geiseric. The city of Utica was about 40 kilometres (25 miles) north of Carthage.

p. 129. *Papinianus, bishop of Vite*: martyred with Mansuetus of Utica (north of Carthage) under the Arian king, Geiseric. The exact location of Vite is uncertain. It was probably south of Carthage. It was also the home of Victor Vitensis, Bishop of Vite (*c.* 430) and chronicler of Vandal Christianity.

p. 129. *third General Council . . . at Ephesus*: met from 22 June to the end of October, 431. Ephesus (modern Selçuk) was a major port on the western coast of Asia Minor. The purpose of the council was to deliver an ultimatum to Nestorius, Bishop of Constantinople, whom Cyril of Alexandria had accused of heretical views. Pope Celestine instructed Cyril to tell Nestorius that, unless he recanted within ten days of receiving the ultimatum, he was to consider himself excommunicated and deposed.

p. 129. *Cirtha*: important trading centre in north-east Algeria, on the Rhumel river, major intersection for Roman roads throughout Numidia, and about 140 kilometres (87 miles) south-west of Hippo. Having been destroyed in AD 311, it was rebuilt by Constantine the Great and renamed in his honour. The city was eventually pillaged by invading Vandals in the fifth century.

p. 129. *Austin*: anglicised form of 'Augustine'.

p. 129. *a bishop*: Honoratus, Bishop of Thiaba, located west of Tagaste.

p. 129. *Tertullian*: see (*C.F.*) note to p. 132.

p. 129. *Montanist*: follower of a popular, second-century, hardline apocalyptic movement founded by Montanus, a priest from Phrygia (western Asia Minor). Montanists were critical of the growing authority of bishops and of the New Testament canon. They believed that the end of the world was imminent. They disapproved of re-marriage, of any relaxation to fasting customs and of flight during times of persecution. Tertullian was its most celebrated convert.

p. 129. *Cyprian*: (*c.* 205–58), rhetorician and lawyer who became a Christian around 246 and Bishop of Carthage shortly afterwards. During the Decian persecution (249–51), Cyprian fled and continued to administer his diocese from a distance. On return, he had to deal first with what to do with the 'lapsi', that is, with those who had apostatised during the persecution, and, secondly, to fight for his see for which there were three contenders, Fortunatus who was in favour of general forgiveness of the 'lapsi'; Maximus who was in favour of general punishment, and Cyprian who steered a middle course, readmitting the 'lapsi' after an appropriate period of penance. Cyprian was at odds with Pope Stephen I over the validity of baptism by heretics. Because he maintained that such baptisms were invalid, the pope threatened to excommunicate him. When another round of persecution erupted in 258, Cyprian was arrested, and when he refused to sacrifice to the Roman gods, he was beheaded. Many consider him to be a model bishop. He also had an exalted view of the Church outside of which there was no salvation.

p. 129. *Dionysius of Alexandria*: (active *c.* 233–64), pupil of Origen, head of the Catechetical School of Alexandria (*c.* 233–48) and orthodox Bishop of Alexandria (*c.* 248–*c.* 64). During the Decian persecution (249–51), he fled Alexandria and was later banished to Libya during the Valerian persecution (257–60). Like Cyprian, he too returned to find his local church in disarray. In 1834, Newman undertook an edition of Dionysius for the University Press at Oxford. This was his *third* serious attempt at studying the Church Fathers. His earlier treatments of 'facts and Fathers' had been superficial and '*second hand*' (*L.D.* IV, p. 320). He was happier third time round using primary sources without the aid of second-hand commentaries. The result was that he was carried 'forward into a very large field of reading' and he began to get some clue into how the early Church dealt with Christological issues of the day (*L.D.* V, p. 120; p. 122; p. 126). During preparatory work, he also began to see more clearly the pitfalls of rationalism and the need to respond positively.

p. 130. *Gregory of Neocaesarea*: (*c.* 213–60), Bishop of Neocaesarea (east of Comana Pontica); he studied with Origen at Caesarea Maritima in Palestine and became bishop around 243. 'It is said of this primitive Father, who was the Apostle of a large district in Asia Minor, that he found in it only seventeen Christians, and on his death left in it only seventeen pagans' (*V.M.* I, p. lxxvii). He is also known as Gregory the Wonder-worker (Thaumaturgus). During the Decian persecutions (249–51), he advised his flock to flee, and he himself fled to the mountains.

p. 130. *Polycarp*: (*c.* 69–155), one of the Apostolic Fathers who was said to have been converted by the apostles and to have been a disciple of John the Evangelist. Polycarp forms an important link between the apostles and the apologists of the second century. He was Bishop of Smyrna (north of Ephesus) and was martyred round 156 during the reign of Antoninus Pius (138–61). His major writing was his *Letter to the Philippians* and is generally associated with the epistles and martyrdom of Ignatius of Antioch. He himself was martyred at Smyrna at the age of 86.

p. 130. *Athanasius also had to defend ... work still extant*: around 357, Athanasius wrote a *Defence of His Flight* in reply to his critics, 'Leontius, now at Antioch, and Narcissus of the city of Nero, and George, now at Laodicea, and the Arians' who charged him with cowardice because 'when I myself was sought by them [persecutors], I did not surrender myself into their hands' (*Defence of His Flight*, para. 1).

p. 130. *Jacob fled from Esau*: Genesis 27: 43.

p. 130. *Moses from Pharao*: Exodus 2: 15.

p. 130. *David from Saul*: 1 Kings (1 Samuel) 19: 18.

p. 130. *Elias concealed himself from Achab three years*: 3 Kings (1 Kings) 17–18.

p. 130. *the sons of the prophets were hid ... from Jezebel*: 3 Kings (1 Kings) 18: 4.

p. 130. *In like manner . . . fear of the Jews*: John 20: 19.

p. 130. *St. Paul was let down . . . wall at Damascus*: 2 Corinthians 11: 33.

p. 130. "*He walked no more openly among them*": John 11: 54.

p. 130. *He hid Himself*: John 18: 4.

p. 130. "*wander in sheep-skins and goat-skins*": Hebrews 11: 37.

pp. 130–131. "*strike him . . . battle and perish*": 1 Kings (1 Samuel) 26: 10.

p. 131. *thus Elias showed himself to Achab*: 3 Kings (1 Kings) 18: 2.

p. 131. *St. Paul appealed to Caesar*: Acts 25: 8–12.

p. 131. *Jacob, on his deathbed . . . the twelve Patriarchs*: Genesis 49; the twelve Patriarchs were Jacob's sons: Reuben; Simeon; Levi; Judah; Issachar; Zebulun; Dan; Joseph; Benjamin; Naphtali; Gad; Asher (1 Chronicles 2: 1–2).

p. 131. *Moses returned . . . before Pharao*: Exodus 10: 3.

p. 131. *David was a valiant warrior*: 1 Kings (1 Samuel) 17: 42–58; 2 Kings (2 Samuel) 8.

p. 131. *Elias rebuked Achab and Ochazias*: 1 Kings (1 Samuel) 18–9; 4 Kings (2 Kings) 1: 16.

p. 131. *Then it was that Jacob had the vision of Angels*: Genesis 28: 12.

p. 131. *Moses saw the burning bush*: Exodus 3: 2.

p. 131. *David wrote his prophetic Psalms*: 2 Kings (2 Samuel) 23: 1.

p. 131. *Elias raised the dead... on Mount Carmel*: 3 Kings (1 Kings) 17: 17–24; 18: 20–40.

pp. 131–132. "*When they shall persecute . . . flee unto the mountains*": Matthew 10: 23; 24: 16.

p. 132. *Tertullian*: (*c*. 160–*c*. 220), apologist and writer from Carthage, and one of the first theologians to write extensively in Latin. He was the first to borrow the term *trinitas* (trinity) to describe the Godhead. He paved the way for orthodox Trinitarian and Christological doctrines. Around 206, he joined a popular, apocalyptic sect within Christianity known as Montanism whose strict asceticism, he thought, better suited his personality. Because of his hawkish, tough-minded, legalistic approach to theology, he made many enemies. He was sceptical of the value of Greek philosophy in articulating Christian truths. 'What has Athens to do with Jerusalem?', he once asked. His writings were mainly polemical, against heresies, against Marcion who taught that the God of the New Testament was different from the God of the Old Testament, and against Praxeas who taught that the three persons of the Trinity were different modes or aspects of God. Because Montanism was not strict enough for him, he eventually founded his own group which came to be known as Tertullianists.

p. 132. *Satan could not . . . God gave permission*: Job 2: 6.

p. 132. "*Satan hath desired . . . confirm thy brethren*": Luke 22: 31–32.

p. 132. "*Lead us not . . . but deliver us from evil*": Matthew 6: 13; Luke 11: 4.

p. 133. "*into the way of the Gentiles*": Matthew 10: 5.

p. 133. "*the lost sheep of the house of Israel*": Matthew 15: 24.

p. 133. *Agabus*: Jewish-Christian prophet in Antioch (Syria) thought to have been among the seventy-two disciples appointed by Jesus. He visited Antioch and predicted a great famine during the reign of the emperor Claudius (Acts 11: 27–30). This was the same Agabus who also predicted the Paul's imprisonment in Jerusalem (Acts 21: 10–13).

p. 133. "*Whoso shall confess Me . . . before my Father*": Matthew 10: 32.

p. 133. "*Blessed are they that suffer persecution*": Matthew 5: 10.

p. 133. "*He that shall persevere to the end, he shall be saved*": Matthew 10: 22; 24: 13.

p. 133. "*Be not afraid of them that kill the body*": Matthew 10: 28.

p. 133. "*Whosoever does not carry . . . cannot be My disciple*": Luke 14: 27.

p. 133. '*If it be possible, let this chalice pass*': Matthew 26: 39.

p. 133. "*We also ought to lay down our lives for the brethren*": 1 John 3: 16.

p. 133. "*Perfect charity casteth out fear*": 1 John 4: 18.

p. 133. "*is not perfected in charity*": 1 John 4: 18.

p. 133. "*He who flees, will fight another day*": attributed to the Greek orator, Demosthenes, when he was accused of running away from the battle of Chaeronea north-west of Thebes in Greece in 338 BC. It was Alexander the Great's first battle.

pp. 133–134. "*The good shepherd . . . for his sheep*": John 10: 11.

p. 134. "*seeth the wolf . . . and fleeth*": John 10: 12.

p. 134. "*He that can take, let him take it*": Matthew 19: 12.

p. 134. *Honoratus*: Bishop of Thiaba west of Tagaste.

p. 134. *Quodvultdeus*: Bishop of Carthage who fled from the marauding Vandals; before doing so, he asked Augustine what a bishop should do when harassed by the enemy. Augustine replied there were two kinds of circumstances under which the flight of a bishop was justifiable. Firstly, as in the case of Athanasius and Cyprian, when only the bishop was being attacked and his duties could be carried out by someone not being persecuted. Secondly, when the whole flock had fled and there was no one left to administer to.

p. 135. *Thou art our strong rock and place of defence*: Psalm 31: 3.

p. 135. *flee from city to city*: Matthew 10: 23.

p. 135. *when St. Paul . . . escaped his hands*: 2 Corinthians 9: 33.

p. 136. '*the hireling who seeth not . . . for the sheep*': John 10: 12–13.

p. 136. *and by your, not knowledge, . . . whom Christ died*: 2 Corinthians 8: 9; 11.

p. 137. *quench the light of Israel*: 2 Kings (2 Samuel) 21:17.

p. 138. *Julian*: (*c.* 380–455), Pelagian Bishop of Eclanum in Apulia (southern Italy) who carried on an acrimonious debate with Augustine, criticising the latter's views on sexuality and predestination. It preoccupied the last decade of Augustine's life.

p. 138. *Pelagianism*: named after the teaching of Pelagius, a fifth-century monk who believed that human beings can do good and achieve salvation independently of God's saving grace. He denied the doctrine of original sin. The Pelagian controversy drove Augustine to adopt positions which critics, both then and later, thought regrettable.

p. 138. *Predestination*: the act of predestining or predetermining by which God from the beginning decrees who goes to heaven and who goes to hell (see Romans 8: 29–30; Ephesians 1: 4–5). Augustine wrote about it in *De Praedestinatione* between 428 and 429. In one form or another, his ideas have continued to surface time and time again, as, for example, in the writings of John Calvin (1509–64) and Cornelius Otto Jansen (1585–1638).

p. 138. *sustained a controversy with the Arians*: 'Conference with the Arian Maximin'; 'Against the Arians'; 'Against Maximin'; all written around 428.

pp. 138–139. *history of heresies*: 'On Heresies, to Quodvultdeus'; written around 429.

p. 139. *Boniface*: (d. *c.* 432), ambitious Roman general who supported Aelia Gallia Placidia and her son, Valentinian III, against the usurper John following the death of the emperor Honorius in 423. As a result, he was rewarded with the title 'Count of Africa' and became governor of Roman north Africa. He refused to return to Rome when ordered home in 427. The civil war which broke out between Rome and himself prepared the way for the Vandal invasion two years later. After a truce was arranged between Rome and himself, Boniface turned on the Vandals, but was himself besieged and finally defeated at Hippo in 430. I t was during that siege that his friend Augustine died. The Byzantine historian, Procopius (d. *c.* 565) maintained that Boniface was responsible for letting Vandals into Roman north Africa. He was finally killed in battle against a rival commander (see Edward Gibbon, *History of the Decline and Fall of the Roman Empire*, Chapter XXXIII).

p. 139. *Possidius*: (*c.* 365–*c.* 440), Augustine's earliest biographer who joined Augustine's community at Hippo and became Bishop of Calama, about 65 kilometres (40 miles) south-west of Hippo on his recommendation. When Vandals invaded Roman north Africa in 428, Possidius fled to Hippo where he was present at Augustine's death on 28 August 430, in the third month of the siege of Hippo.

p. 139. '*Thou art just, O Lord, and Thy judgment is right*': Psalm 118: 137.

p. 140. *He slept with his fathers in a good old age*: according to his first biographer, Possidius, Augustine was seventy-six years old when he died on 28

August 430, in the thirty-fifth year of his episcopate (*Life of Augustine*, p. 31).

p. 140. *Though the Vandals ... more favourable circumstances*: at the time, Vandals were besieging Hippo as Augustine lay dying within its walls. Shortly afterwards, they captured the city and burnt it to the ground. They then overran Carthage and established a kingdom that would last for a hundred years.

p. 140. *Saracens*: Muslims who invaded and occupied parts of the Christian world in Asia, Africa and Europe between the seventh and eleventh centuries. It was a collective term used by Europeans in the Middle Ages to refer to Arabs and Muslims.

p. 141. *his words unto the ends of the world*: 'Anselm, Aquinas, Petrarch (never without a pocket copy of the *Confessions*), Luther, Bellarmine, Pascal, and Kierkegaard all stand in the shade of his [Augustine's] broad oak. His writings were among the favourite books of Wittgenstein. He was the *bete noire* of Nietszche. His psychological analysis anticipated parts of Freud; he first discovered the existence of the "sub-conscious". He was *the first modern man* in the sense that with him the reader feels himself addressed at a level of extraordinary psychological depth and confronted by a coherent system of thought, large parts of which still make potent claims to attention and respect. He affected the way in which the West has subsequently thought about the nature of man and what we mean by the word "God"' (Henry Chadwick, *Augustine*, Oxford 1991, p. 3).

p. 141. *to last unto the end*: in the original essay for the *British Magazine*, Newman added one final sentence: 'Still he is the guide of the church in such matters, teaching us the details of our duty, and encouraging us in perplexity, doubt, and sorrow' (*British Magazine*, 'Letters on the Church of the Fathers', No. 10, Volume VI, October 1834, p. 402).

p. 141n. *Since this was written, the French have reinstated the see*: France re-occupied the area in 1832.

Chapter VIII: Conversion of Augustine

Synopsis: Augustine's mother enrols him as a catechumen while still a child. As a teenager, he rebels against everything Christianity stands for. When he is twenty, he becomes a Manichean and remains one for the next ten years. After the death of a friend who is a baptised Christian, Augustine leaves his native Tagaste, and travels to Carthage where he becomes a teacher of rhetoric. While there, he meets Faustus, a famous Manichean bishop, whom, he thinks, is the answer to all his prayers. Unfortunately, he discovers that Faustus is a fraud and, apart from mouthing a few clichés, is incapable of original thought. Augustine then departs for Italy where he is appointed to the prestigious chair of rhetoric in Milan where Ambrose is bishop. Ambrose's sermons impress him so much that he re-enrols in the catechumenate. The story of Antony of Egypt has a tremendous impact on him. When he reads Romans 13: 13–14, it is as though 'the light of confidence flooded into my heart and all the darkness of doubt was dispelled' (*Confessions*, Book VIII, Chapter 12). He resigns his chair of rhetoric, is baptised on Holy Saturday in 387 and returns to his native Tagaste where he sets up a monastery. During a visit to nearby Hippo, he is conscripted by the local community to become a priest, sets up another monastery and eventually becomes Bishop of Hippo where he dies in 430.

p. 142. "*Thou has chastised me . . . the reproach of my youth.*": Jeremiah 31: 18–19.

p. 142. *He uses language . . . repentance and spiritual sensitiveness.*: Augustine wrote his celebrated *Confessions* shortly after becoming Bishop of Hippo around 397. The thirteen books are a series of prose poems in conversation with God and are the product of someone 'who had come to regard his past as a training for his present career'. It is a deeply personal story and 'owes its lasting appeal to the way in which Augustine, in his middle-age, has dared to open himself up to the feelings of youth' which he analyses with 'ferocious honesty' (Peter Brown, *Augustine of Hippo*, London, 1967, pp. 162; 169; 170; 171). Augustine's elevation to see of Hippo was not without its critics. There were suspicions of his Manichean past, rumors of a mistress and an illegitimate son, plus jealousy toward this well-educated outsider who was rising rapidly through the ranks. Augustine himself was troubled by his new responsibilities. *Confessions* was a timely opportunity to examine his personal relationship with God.

p. 143. *Manichæan heresy*: not of Christian origin, but an imported religious cult from Persia that was becoming popular in Roman society as an alternative to Christianity, similar, in some ways, to Zoroastrianism; named after Mani (*c.* 216–*c.* 276) who was born at Seleucia-Ctesiphon, capital of the Persian empire. It manifested itself in a 'revulsion of the material world, and became the rationale for an ultra-ascetic morality'. Its followers regarded '"the lower half of the body" as the disgusting work of the devil, the very prince of darkness. Sex and the dark were intimately associated in Mani's mind, and the Dark was with the very essence of evil'. Evil was the result of a primeval, ongoing cosmic struggle between light and darkness. They denied the authority of the Old Testament and deleted any New Testament text connected with the Old Testament. Baptism was not for everyone (Henry Chadwick, *Augustine*, Oxford 1986, pp. 11–13).

p. 143. *nine years*: Manichees had two classes of followers, the Elect and Hearers. 'Absolute celibacy was required only of the higher grade, the Elect. Mere Hearers, of whom Augustine became one, were allowed sexual relations at "safe" periods of the month, and were expected to take steps to avoid conceiving a child; but if a child arrived, that was not a ground for expulsion from the society. Hearers therefore were allowed to live with wives or, as in Augustine's case, concubines, but were not encouraged to think about of sexuality in any positive light. It was the devil's invention' (Henry Chadwick, *Augustine*, Oxford 1986, pp. 11–12).

p. 143. *thirty-fourth year*: except for the years in Italy between 382 and 388, Augustine spent his entire life in Roman north Africa.

p. 144. *popular poet*: George Gordon Noel Byron (1788–1824), sixth Baron Byron of Rochdale who was an immensely popular, unconventional, English romantic poet whose life was as colourful and as outrageous as his poetry. The idea that people were free to choose their own lifestyle was a recurring theme in his poetry. The publication of *Childe Harold's Pilgrimage* brought him public acclaim. He left England in 1816, never to return.

p. 145. "*I sought what I might love,*": the 1838 translation of Augustine's *Confessions* from which Newman quotes extensively throughout this essay was based on an earlier translation recently updated by fellow Tractarian, Edward Bouverie Pusey (1800–82) for Oxford *The Library of the Fathers.*

pp. 145–158. *his Confessions*: Augustine wrote *Confessions* 'in the last three years of the fourth century AD by a man in his mid-forties, recently made a bishop, needing to come to terms with a past in which numerous enemies and critics showed an unhealthy interest', especially in his past life. The word 'confession' means the dual act of praising God and of acknowledging one's weaknesses (*Saint Augustine Confessions*, translated with an introduction and notes by Henry Chadwick, Oxford 1991, pp. xiii; x).

p. 146. *a friend he had lost*: Augustine does not disclose the name of his friend (*Confessions,* Book IV, Chapter 4).

p. 146. *Manichees . . . rejected baptism.*: in the Manichee scheme of things, baptism was reserved for the elect only. Hearers were regarded as catechumens (Augustine, *In Answer to the Letter of Petilian, the Donatist, Bishop of Cirta*, Book III, Chapter 20).

p. 147. *Thagaste*: or Tagaste; a small country town about 80 kilometres (50 miles) south-east of Hippo Regius; modern Souk Ahras.

p. 147. *Faustus*: Manichean Bishop of Milevis about 180 kilometres (112 miles) south-east of Hippo. He had a reputation as a teacher. When Augustine met him in Carthage, he soon discovered that Faustus was a charlatan who relied on a handful of clichés. 'As soon as it became clear to me that Faustus was quite uninformed about the subjects in which I had expected him to be an expert, I began to lose hope that he could lift the veil and resolve the questions which perplexed me' (*Confessions*, Book V, Chapter 7).

p. 147. *Disgusted with the licence ... among the students at Carthage,*: some students were nicknamed *wreckers*, a title, Augustine tells us, of 'ferocious devilry which the fashionable set chose for themselves'. While living among them, he felt a 'perverse sense of shame' because he was not like them. 'Without provocation they would set upon some timid newcomer, gratuitously affronting his sense of decency for their own amusement and using it as fodder for their spiteful jests. This was the devil's own behaviour or not far different. *Wreckers* was a fit name for them, for they were already adrift and total wrecks themselves. The mockery and trickery which they loved to practice on others was a secret snare of the devil, by which they were mocked and tricked themselves' (*Confessions*, Book III, Chapter 3).

p. 147. *Monica*: (*c.* 331–87), mother of Augustine; she was a Berber from Roman north Africa and a deeply committed Christian married to Patricius who remained a pagan until just before his death. She followed Augustine to Rome and then to Milan where she supported Ambrose in his struggle against the Arians and was present at her son's baptism. When she died at the port of Ostia Antica, harbour of ancient Rome, en route to north Africa, she was fifty-six years old. 'After her husband's death all her thoughts centered on this her beloved son, and it was now that her bitterest trial commenced, and that the saintly character was formed within her, and she comes out as the model of patient persevering prayer' (BOA, C. 2. 10, address delivered by Newman at the Birmingham Oratory, 12 October 1857).

p. 147. *To Milan then he came*: some friends had heard that the newly appointed prefect of Rome, Quintus Aurelius Symmachus, was looking for a competent professor of rhetoric for the imperial court at Milan, at that time the most prestigious academic post in the Latin world. So they arranged for Augustine to be interviewed by Symmachus who offered him the post. Thus it was that Augustine headed north to Milan and took up his new appointment towards the end of 384.

p. 149. *knock ... may be opened*: Matthew 7: 7.

p. 150. *Many great men ... in the state of marriage.*: Socrates, Plato and

Cicero were married men. Augustine decided to remain single. 'However much thou please to portray her [a wife] and adorn her with all manner of gifts, I have determined,' he wrote, 'that nothing is so much to be avoided by me as such a bed-fellow: I perceive that nothing more saps the citadel of manly strength, whether of mind or body, than female blandishments and familiarities.... Wherefore, I believe I am contradicting neither justice nor utility in providing for the liberty of my mind by neither desiring, nor seeking, nor taking a wife' (Augustine, *Soliloquies*, Book I, para. 17).

p. 150. *which our Lord and His Apostle have bestowed special praise*: see Matthew 5: 48; 19: 21; 1 Corinthians 7.

p. 151. *he addressed himself to St. Pauls's Epistles*: 'Most eagerly, then, did I seize that venerable writing of Thy Spirit, but more especially the Apostle Paul; and those difficulties vanished away, in which he at one time appeared to me to contradict himself, and the text of his discourse not to agree with the testimonies of the Law and the Prophets. And the face of that pure speech appeared to me one and the same; and I learned to "rejoice with trembling". So I commenced, and found that whatsoever truth I had there read was declared here with the recommendation of Thy grace; that he who sees may not so glory as if he had not received not only that which he sees, but also that he can see (for what hath he which he hath not received?); and that he may not only be admonished to see Thee, who art ever the same, but also may be healed, to hold Thee; and that he who from afar off is not able to see, may still walk on the way by which he may reach, behold, and possess Thee' (*Confessions* Book VII, Chapter 21).

p. 152. '*the beauty of Thy honour, which I loved*': Psalm 26: 8.

p. 152. *that all men were as he himself*: 1 Corinthians 7: 7.

p. 152. *goodly pearl*: Matthew 13: 16.

p. 152. *Simplician*: (d. *c.* 400), Platonist and acquainted with Marius Victorinus, the translator of Plotinus, who became a Christian because of Simplician's example. Simplician may have been the one to show Augustine how to harmonise Platonism and Christianity. He succeeded Ambrose as Bishop of Milan in 397.

p. 152. *Victorinus's translation of some Platonic works*: Augustine himself 'was never greatly influenced by the obscure theological writings of Victorinus. But his readings in Plotinus and Porphory, translated into Latin by Victorinus, set his mind on fire' (Henry Chadwick, *Augustine*, Oxford 1986, p. 16; *Confessions*, Book VIII, Chapter 5).

p.152. *Forum*: open-air meeting place for all sorts of activities in a Roman town. In Rome, for example, there was the Forum Boarium (meat market), the Forum Holitorium (vegetable market), the Forum Piscinum (fish market) and the Forum Frumentarium (grain market). The particular forum referred to here is the Forum Romanum, the political, legal and religious hub of Rome.

p. 153. *from a raised place in the church*: in early Christian basilicas, a rostrum (known as an ambo) was placed in the nave surrounded by a low wall and used for the reading of the Gospels and Epistles. Important church notices were also read from it. It was also used for preaching and issuing edicts and excommunications; it was from this spot that heretics came to recant. Sometimes the bishop preached from it, as indeed did John Chrysostom, who, according to the historian Socrates, used the ambo to address the people, in order to be better heard (*Ecclesiastical History*, Book VI, Chapter 5). It was later replaced by the modern pulpit.

p. 153. *edict of Julian*: on becoming emperor, Julian (361–63) tried to restore paganism to its former glory. He filled the court with pagan philosophers and sacrificed daily to the gods. Among his decrees was one excluding Christians from teaching literature and rhetoric. That included Victorinus himself who elected to 'give up his own school of words rather than desert your Word, by which you make *the lips of infants vocal with praise*' (*Confessions*, Book VIII, Chapter 5).

p. 154. *Alypius*: Augustine's lifelong friend who was a highly competent lawyer and magistrate who was baptised alongside Augustine on Easter Saturday in Milan, 387. After residing with Augustine in the monastery in Hippo, he was made bishop of Augustine's native town, Tagaste, in 394. (see *Confessions*, Books VI–VIII; XI–XII).

p. 154. *Pontitian*: a fellow African; see *Confessions*, Book VIII, Chapter 6.

p. 154. *Monastery . . . outside the walls of Milan*: it has been suggested that this particular monastery was the first one established in Europe; some suggest that Rome may have been the first, while others suggest Aquileia in northern Italy, near Venice.

p. 154. *Treves*: modern Trier, one of Germany's oldest cities and a port situated on the Moselle river in western Germany, near the border of Luxembourg and about 200 kilometres (125 miles) west of Frankfurt. It was a natural jumping-off point to northern Gaul and the Rhineland. It was founded by Caesar Augustus around 15 BC, became capital of the Roman province of Belgica in the first century and capital of the prefecture of Gaul in the third century. It was named after the Treveri, people from eastern Gaul. It was referred to as the 'second Rome'. The English knew it as Trier; and the French as Trèves. At the end of the third century, the emperor Diocletian set up his imperial court there and made it the capital of the western empire.

p. 154. *life of St. Antony*: originally written in Greek and later translated into Latin by Evagrius of Antioch around 388.

p. 155. *Cicero's 'Hortentius'*: 'In the ordinary course of study, I lighted upon a certain book of Cicero, whose language, though not his heart, almost all admire. This book of his contains an exhortation to philosophy, and is called *Hortentius*. This book, in truth, changed my affections, and turned my prayers to Thyself, O Lord, and made me have other hopes and desires'. 'All my empty dreams suddenly lost their charm and my heart began to throb with a bewildering passion for the wisdom of eternal truth' (*Confessions*, Book III, Chapter 4).

p. 155. *take heaven by violence*: Matthew 11: 12.

p. 156. *acceptable sacrifice*: 1 Peter 2: 5.

p. 156. '*And Thou, O Lord, how long ...*': Psalm 79: 5, 8.

p. 157. *Antony*: Athanasius' *Life of Saint Antony*, paras. 2, 3.

p. 157. '*Go, sell all that thou hast,*': Matthew 19: 21.

p. 157. '*Not in rioting and drunkenness ... in its concupiscences.*': Roman 13: 13–14.

p. 157. *dream*: Monica once dreamt that she was standing on a wooden rule when an angel asked why she was weeping. She replied that she was grieving over the loss of her son's faith. He told her to 'take heart for, if she looked carefully, she would see that where she was', there also was her son. 'And when she looked, she saw me [Augustine] standing beside her on the same rule'. When Monica related the dream to Augustine, he said it merely showed that she would eventually come over to his point of view, and not vice versa. 'No!', she insisted without hesitation, 'He did not say "Where he is, you are", but "Where *you* are, he is" ' (*Confessions*, Book III, Chapter 11).

p. 157. "*Go thy ways ... tears should perish*!": traditionally attributed to Ambrose himself.

p. 158. *on her way back to Africa*: Monica died at Ostia Antica, then a prosperous port at the mouth of the Tiber, situated about 35 kilometres (22 miles) from Rome on the Via Ostiensis. 'And so on the ninth day of her illness, when she was fifty-six and I was thirty-three, her pious and devoted soul was set free from the body' (*Confessions*, Book IX, Chapter 11).

p. 158. *Patricius*: Augustine's father who was baptised on his deathbed.

p. 158. *assigning as a reason a pulmonary attack*: during the summer of 326, Augustine developed a chest infection which affected his voice, making it impossible for him to teach. Some scholars suggest that the illness was psychosomatic and that, throughout these tense months, he was showing signs of a nervous breakdown (*Confessions*, Book IX, Chapter 2).

p. 158. *a friend's villa in the country*: in the summer of 386, Augustine resigned his academic post because of ill health and retired for the winter to a nearby country villa loaned by Verecundus, a colleague from Milan. It was situated at a place called Cassiciacum, near the very scenic Lake Como in northern Italy. With him were his son, mother, brother, cousins, friends, plus a couple of students. They spent each day studying, debating and reading together.

p. 159. *constant in devotional and penitential exercises*: throughout these months, Augustine would rise at dawn, read the Psalms, work on the estate, write letters, do some tutoring and join in philosophical discussions. Part of each night was given over to prayer and meditation. He also wrote several books, including *Soliloquies* which is both a self-portrait and a dialogue between his *reason* and his *soul* (see Peter Brown, *Augustine of Hippo*, London 1967, pp. 115–27).

p. 159. *sacrament of baptism*: after spending the winter of 386–87 at Cassiacum, Augustine and his party returned to Milan for the forty days of preparation for baptism leading up to Easter. Then, at the Easter vigil service on Holy Saturday night, Augustine was baptised by Ambrose in the baptistery next to the main basilica of Milan. 'Passing behind curtains, Augustine would descend, alone, stark naked, into a deep pool of water. Three times, Ambrose would hold his shoulders beneath the gushing fountain. Later, dressed in a pure white robe, he would enter the main basilica ablaze with candles; and, amid the acclamations of the congregation, he and his fellow neophytes would take their place on a slightly raised floor, by the altar, for a first participation in the mysteries of the Risen Christ' (see Peter Brown, *Augustine of Hippo*, p. 124).

p. 159. *Thagaste, his native place*: on return to North Africa, Augustine settled in his native Tagaste in 389 and set up a community, very similar, probably, to the daily routine of Cassiciacum. Augustine spent more than two years there before being 'grabbed' and 'made a priest' at Hippo in 389 (see Peter Brown, *Augustine of Hippo*, p. 138).

p. 160. *Valerius*: Bishop of Hippo Regius who quickly recognised Augustine's talents. It was not long before Augustine was being invited to preach in place of Valerius who was Greek. When he died in 395, Augustine succeeded him.

p. 160. *and unable to speak Latin fluently*: though not ignorant of Greek, Augustine who was more at home with Latin. The result was that Augustine rarely used Greek Christian authors in the same way he used his Latin translations of Greek pagan philosophers. This was the 'great lacuna of Augustine's middle age' (Peter Brown, *Augustine of Hippo*, p. 271).

p. 161. *Soon after we hear . . . besides two additional ones at Hippo.*: according to Possidius, his biographer, Augustine left behind several monasteries for men and women (Possidius *Life of Augustine*, Chapter 31).

p. 161. *ten bishops . . . supplied from the school of Augustine*: among them were Alypius who became Bishop of Tagaste, Aurelius, Bishop of Carthage, Evodius who became Bishop of Uzalis, about 60 kilometres (37 miles) north of Carthage), and Severus who became Bishop of Milevis, about 180 kilometres (112 miles) south-west of Hippo.

Chapter IX: Demetrias

Synopsis: The story of the lady Demetrias is an example of a life of virginity dedicated to Jesus Christ. There is indisputable evidence that this way of life was widely practised in the early Church. Demetrias comes from one of the most illustrious families in Rome. With her grandmother, her mother and several companions, she sets sail for Carthage where they set up a community under the guidance of Augustine. News of her decision spreads throughout the Mediterranean world. Jerome from Bethlehem offers practical advice. So too does the heretic Pelagius, but Augustine warns Demetrias to be wary of anything the latter says. The last details we learn of her is that she is helping to build the basilica of St. Stephen on her property about 5 kilometres (3 miles) from Rome on the Latin road, sometime after the sack of Rome by the Vandal king, Gaiseric, in 455.

p. 163. "*He that glorieth . . . whom the Lord commandeth*": 2 Corinthians 10: 17–18.

p. 163. *Monachism*: see note to p. 97 (*C.F.*).

p. 163. *Rechabites*: religious clan in Israel, whose chieftain was Jonadab, son of Rechab. They abstained from wine because Jonadab commanded them to forego this pleasure. They were tempted but refused, for which God rewarded them (Jeremiah 35: 2–6; 19).

p. 163. *justification by faith only*: difference of belief in the way which sinners are justified before God. It formed the main stumbling block between Catholics and Protestants at the time of the Reformation and since. Protestant theology maintains that justification was that act by which a merciful God, by virtue of Christ's sacrifice on Calvary, acquits us of any punishment due to sin and treats us as though we are righteous. Luther maintained that justification was granted to us by the disposition of faith *alone* (*sola fides*) and that it brings with it the imputation of the merits of Christ to sinners (Romans 3: 24). Rome maintained that justification was a matter of faith *and* good works.

p. 163. *priestcraft*: term first coined by John Dryden (1631–1700) in the opening lines of his satirical, pro-Protestant poem *Absolom and Achitophel* (1681) during an attempt to prevent the Catholic Duke of York (later James II) from succeeding his Protestant brother, Charles II to the throne:

> 'In pious times, e'r priestcraft did begin,
> Before polygamy was made a sin.'

The term became a catch-cry for anticlerical writers like Richard Baron in *The Follies of Priestcraft and Orthodoxy shaken* (1767, 4 volumes) giving 'everlasting reasons for opposing all priests' (Roy Porter, *Enlightenment: Britain and the Creation of the Modern World*, London 2000, pp. 110–11). Thomas Arnold (1795–1842), the celebrated headmaster of Rugby, maintained that the idea of a 'human priesthood' was invented midst the turmoils of the second century. The early Church 'pretended that the clergy were not simply rulers and teachers . . . but that they were essentially mediators between God and the church'. Thus was the laity 'virtually disfranchised' and the 'character of the institution was utterly corrupted' (Thomas Arnold, *Christian Life, its Course, its Hindrances, and its Helps*, London 1845, pp. li–lii).

p. 164. *Clearly, then, whether or not . . . which did become monastic.*: in his original essay for the *British Magazine*, Newman confessed that 'I regard the monastic life as holding a real place in the dispensation of the gospel, at least providentially. To say there is nothing about it in Scripture, even were it true, is about as sensible as to say there is nothing about deans and chapters, rich rectors, bishops in parliament; nothing (much more) about the lawfulness of commerce, the rights of man, &c. Certainly it is as accordant with Scripture that a Christian should live in prayer and fasting, poverty and almsgiving, as that he should pass all his best days in making money, gain a patent of peerage, and found a family. It is not more culpable, *in the nature of things*, for a given individual to take a vow of celibacy, than to take a vow in marriage; though of course it is as sinful in a father to force a daughter into a convent as it is to force her to a marriage she dislikes, and as inexpedient to take a monastic vow hastily, as to marry before one has come to years of discretion. And if people lift up their hands and eyes and cry out this is Popery, I beg to ask them in which of the Articles monasticism is condemned? and, since I do not force them to agree with me, I claim that liberty of "private judgment" in indifferentials which I accord to them. I beg to remind them that St. Paul, as far as the letter of his epistle goes, does prefer and recommend celibacy; and, if they explain his language otherwise, I hope in very charity they will explain away mine too, and, instead of censuring it, maintain that it does not mean what it seems to mean, any more than St. Paul's, that I have reservations, expectations, limitations, provisos, &c. &c., which, as in St. Paul's case, turn my "yea, yea" into "nay, nay" ' (*British Magazine*, 'Letter on the Fathers of the Church', No. XII, Volume VII, June 1835, p. 663). Except for the first sentence of the paragraph, Newman deleted the rest in the 1840, 1842 and 1858 editions.

p. 164. "*fled into the wilderness . . . place prepared of God*": Revelation 12: 16.

p. 164. "*the serpent cast out after the woman*": Genesis 4.

p. 164. *When withering blasts . . . own native air.*: extract from *The Christian Year* by John Keble, number 3, first Sunday of Advent, p. 10.

p. 165. *Methodism*: popular, lower middle-class religious movement that rose out of the teachings of John Wesley (1703–91). Emphasis was on reading the Bible, open-air meetings, and hymn singing. It frowned on drinking and gambling. The name, Methodist, referred originally to members of John and Charles Wesley's Holy Club at Oxford because of the methodical way they lived their lives. They were originally members of the Church of England and a separate Methodist Church did not come officially into existence until after John Wesley's death (*Ess.* I, pp. 387–388).

p. 165. "*rational" and "sensible" in religion*: Richard Whately (1792–1866), fellow of Oriel College Oxford, Anglican Archbishop of Dublin from 1831, and one of Newman's earliest, and for a time, most influential, mentors, maintained that, Christians 'must not expect to learn any thing from revelation, except what is in a *religious* point of view practically important for us to know'. By adopting the 'most *practical* interpretation of each doctrine', we can be fairly certain that it will be the right one (Richard Whately, *Essays on Some of the Peculiarities of the Christian Religion*, Oxford 1825, pp. 215–9). In a letter to Lord John Russell on 16 August 1834, the Whig leader, Lord Melbourne wrote: 'If we are to have a prevailing religion, let us have one that is cool, and indifferent, and such a one as we have got' in Richard Whately (Owen Chadwick, *The Victorian Church, Part One, 1829–1859*, p. 107).

p. 166. *Sisters of Mercy*: nineteenth-century title used to designate female religious communities engaged in corporal works of mercy; such communities were a subsidiary aim of Tractarians, most notably Edward Bouverie Pusey (1800–82), to encourage the Establishment to support them.

p. 166. *St. Philip's daughters in the Acts*: according to Acts 21: 9, Philip the deacon had four daughters each of whom had the gift of prophecy.

p. 166. *the learned Bingham*: Joseph Bingham (1668–1723), Anglican theologian whose ten-volume *Antiquities of the Christian Church* (1708–22) contained a wealth of systematically arranged information on various aspects of the early Church, including its hierarchy, organisation, rites, discipline, calendar and so on. In the preface of an intended second edition, Bingham called for Church unity on the grounds of apostolical succession.

p. 167. *The widows and virgins of the Church . . . under this obligation.*: widows and virgins of the early Church were, however, accorded a special place in the community. Augustine was probably the founder of the first community of nuns in Africa. There had always been virgins who had consecrated their life to God, but they had never lived as a community until one was set up at Hippo.

p. 167. *humicubations*: act of prostrating oneself on the ground, as a sign of repentance and humility.

p. 167. "*single gentlemen*": Newman himself resolved to lead a single life during the autumn of 1816 (*Apo.*, p. 7).

p. 168. *Liguria*: mountainous region between the Arnus and Varus rivers in northern Italy and extending along the north coast of the Ligurian Sea, from Gaul to Etruria (more or less modern Tuscany). Genoa is the chief city of the region.

p. 168. *Alaric*: (*c.* 370–410), Arian King of the Visigoths from around 395. When he sacked Rome in 410, a wave of despair swept over the empire. Ambrose and Jerome were convinced that the world was about to come to an end. The fact is that initial reports of fires, looting, murder and torture were greatly exaggerated. Being a Christian himself, albeit an Arian one, Alaric gave orders that Church personnel and property were not be touched (Michael Grant, *The Fall of the Roman Empire*, London 1990, pp. 188–90). Up till that stage, Rome had resisted foreign invaders for almost 800 years.

p. 169. *Proba*: Anicia Faltonia Proba, grandmother of Demetrias.

p. 169. *Let her that is a widow . . . night and day;*: 1 Timothy 5: 5.

p. 170. *easier for a camel. . . kingdom of heaven*: Matthew 19: 21–24; Mark 10: 25.

p. 170. '*With God is easy what with man is impossible.*': Matthew 19: 26; Mark 10: 27.

p. 170. *Zacchæus*: chief tax collector from Jericho in Jesus' day. We know that he was Jewish because Jesus called him 'son of Abraham'. When Jesus invited himself to dinner at his house, Zacchaeus was so overcome that he made restitution to those he had defrauded and gave half his possessions to the poor (Luke 19: 1–10).

p. 170. '*Charge the rich of this world . . .that they may obtain true life*': 1 Timothy 6: 17–19.

p. 170. *as a lamp in a dark place the morning star arise in our hearts*: 2 Peter 1: 19.

p. 170. '*For Thee my soul . . . no way and no water.*': Psalm 63: 1.

p. 171. '*One ought always to pray, and not to faint.*': Luke 18: 1.

p. 171. '*passed the night in prayer*': Luke 6: 12.

p. 171. '*more largely*': 'more earnestly'; Luke 22: 43.

p. 171. *For He sets our tears . . . is not hid from Him,*: Psalm 38: 9.

p. 172. *Christ's household prayed for Peter and Paul;*: Acts 12: 5.

p. 173. *This celebrated Father . . . general concerns of the Church.*: in spite of advanced old age, Jerome took every opportunity to denounce doctrinal error in any shape or form.

p. 173. "*his eye was not dim, neither were his teeth removed*": Deuteronomy 34: 7.

p. 173. *he addressed to Demetrias a letter*: written in 414.

p. 173. *tract*: brief treatise.

p. 173. *words and ideas in his writing . . . I should shrink*: some of Jerome's polemical works were excessively abusive, bitter and vitriolic. For example, at one stage in his treatise against Jovinian (393) who taught that everyone would be equal in heaven and that marriage was not inferior to virginity, Jerome criticises Jovinian's style as 'so barbarous, and the language so vile and such a heap of blunders, that I could neither understand what he was talking about, nor by what arguments he was trying to prove his points. At one moment he is all bombast, at another he grovels: from time to time he lifts himself up, and then like a wounded snake finds his own effort too much for him'. He accuses Jovinian of discharging 'himself like a sot after a night's debauch' (Jerome, *Against Jovinian*, Book 1).

p. 174. *Probi or Olybrii*: two great Roman families.

p. 174. *Olybrius*: Olybrius was born about AD 325 and elected consul in 379. He married Turrenia Anicia Juliana about 351. Their child, Anicia Faltonia Proba, was the grandmother of Demetrias.

p. 174. *a consul when a boy*: the year was 395.

p. 174. *Happy in his death*: before the fall of Rome in 410.

p. 174. '*They who are clothed in soft garments are in the houses of kings.*': Matthew 11: 8.

p. 174. *their loins girt . . . a leathern belt*: 2 Kings 1: 8; Matthew 3: 4.

p. 174. *Elias, the Lord's forerunner*: Matthew 11: 14; Luke 1: 17.

p. 174. *prophesying in his parent's womb*: Luke 1: 41.

p. 174. *the Judge's voice*: Matthew 11: 7–14.

p. 174. *She admired the ardour of Anna . . . with prayer and fastings.*: Anna was a prophetess and widow in Jesus' time, and daughter of Phanuel from the tribe of Aser. When Mary and Joseph presented Jesus in the Temple, she, together with Simeon, spoke of the Saviour who would redeem Israel (Luke 2: 36–39).

p. 174. *She longed for . . . the gift of prophecy.*: Acts 21: 8–9.

p. 174. *like Esther, a hatred of her apparel*: Esther 14: 16; when Xerxes deposed Queen Vasthi, he choose Esther as his new bride.

p. 175. *Agnes*: young virgin from a noble family who refused to marry a high-profile citizen and who was subsequently beheaded in Rome after being humiliated and tortured. Her martyrdom took place during the reign of the emperor Diocletian (284–305).

p. 175. *Thou didst see thyself as a captive*: reference to the harsh treatment Demetrias and her companions received at the hands of the ruthless Heraclian, Count of Africa. When they first landed in Carthage, he forced them to pay protection money. Jerome described him as one 'who cared for nothing but wine and money, one who under pretence of serving the mildest of emperors [Honorius (395–423)] stood forth as the most savage of all despots' (Jerome, Letter CXXX, para. 7). He unsuccessfully tried to seize imperial power in 413.

p. 175. *liberal Fescennine*: comic, often obscene songs from the town of Fescennia in Etruria, more or less modern Tuscany in northern Italy. Originally, they were fairly crude, rustic affairs, but became more polished and more sophisticated as time went on. They were generally performed at weddings (see Livy, *Ab Urbe Condita*, Book VII, para. 2; Horace, *Epistles*, Book II, part 1, line 145; Catullus, epithalamium (wedding song) for a friend named Mallius, poem lxi, line 27).

p. 175. *God's perfect charity casteth out fear.*: 1 John 4: 18.

p. 175. *Take the shield of faith . . . helmet of salvation;*: Ephesians 6: 14–17.

p. 176. *Their voice was gone*: Virgil, *Aeneid* II, p. 774.

p. 176. *Juliana . . . Proba*: mother and grandmother of Demetrias.

p. 177. '*I humbled my soul in fasting*': Psalm 68: 10.

p. 177. '*I ate ashes as it were bread;*': Psalm 101: 9.

p. 177. '*When they were sick, I put on sackcloth.*': Psalm 34: 13.

p. 177. *Elias . . . is carried off to heaven in a chariot of fire*: 4 Kings (2 Kings) 2: 11.

p. 177. *Moses is fed forty days . . . and converse with God*: Exodus 24: 18; 34: 28.

p. 177. '*Man liveth not by bread alone . . . out of the mouth of God.*': Deuteronomy 8: 3; Matthew 4: 4.

p. 177. *The Saviour of man . . . perfection and life*: John 13: 15; 1 Peter 2: 21.

p. 177. *to fight against the devil*: Matthew 4: 1.

p. 177. *fiery darts of the devil*: Ephesians 6: 16.

p. 177. *prepared by the king of Babylon for the three children*: Daniel 3: 47.

p. 177. *And as at that time . . .mitigated the infinite heat,*: Daniel 3: 25.

p. 178. *Even philosophers have held that 'virtues are a mean, vices extreme;'*: reference to Aristotle's *Nicomachean Ethics*, Book II.

p. 178. *seven sages*: Seven Greeks of the sixth century BC: (1) Solon of Athens who fashioned Athenian law, whose motto was 'know thyself'; (2) Chilo of Sparta, who was celebrated for his maxims ('consider the end'); (3) Thales of Miletus (Ionia, Asia Minor) who taught astronomy; (4) Bias of Priene (Ionia, Asia Minor) who believed that actions make the man; (5) Cleobulus of Lindus (isle of Rhodes) who cautioned people to avoid extremes and respect the golden mean; (6) Pittacus of Mitylene (island of Lesbos) who believed in seizing the moment; (7) Periander of Corinth who believed that nothing was impossible to anyone willing to work hard.

p. 178. '*Nothing too much.*': quote from an early Roman comedy entitled *Andria*, I, i, 61 by Terence (*c.* 195–*c.* 159 BC). The *Andria* itself was one of those Latin plays which Newman adapted for performance by the students of the Birmingham Oratory School from the late 1860s until the year of his death in 1890. Newman himself had taken the part of the slave Davus when at Ealing School in 1816, reading both prologue and epilogue. Andria was the daughter of an Athenian citizen called Chremes.

p. 178. '*without which no man shall see God,*': Hebrews 12: 14.

p. 178. *Imitate your heavenly Spouse;*: Luke 2: 51.

p. 178. '*honourable marriage and the bed undefiled*': Hebrews 13: 4.

p. 178. *till you humble yourself under the mighty hand of God*: 1 Peter 5: 6.

p. 178. '*God resisteth the proud, and giveth grace to the humble.*': 1 Peter 5: 5; James 4: 6.

p. 178. '*Not of him that willeth . . . but of God that showeth mercy.*': Romans 9: 16.

p. 178. *love her . . . she will embrace thee*: Proverbs 4: 6–8.

p. 179. *Pelagius*: see note to p. xiii (*C.F.*).

p. 180. *the Olybrii and Anicii*: two distinguished Roman families.

p. 181. *doctrines contrary to the grace of God*: in the same letter, Augustine writes: 'You see, doubtless, how dangerous is the doctrine in these words, against which you must be on your guard. For the affirmation, indeed, that these spiritual riches can exist only in yourself, is very well and truly said: that evidently is food; but the affirmation that they cannot exist except from you is unmixed poison. Far be it from any virgin of Christ willingly to listen to statements like these. Every virgin of Christ understands the innate poverty of the human heart, and therefore declines to have it adorned otherwise than by the gifts of her Spouse' (Letter CXXXVII, Chapter 2, paragraph 5).

p. 181. *not in season only, but out of season*: 2 Timothy 4: 2.

p. 182. *He surely . . . that which was lost.*: Luke 19: 10.

p. 182. '*What hast thou which thou hast not received?*': 1 Corinthians 4: 7.

p. 182. '*Let every one prove . . . and not in another.*': Galatians 6: 4.

p. 182. '*My glory, and the lifter up of my head.*': Psalm 3: 4.

p. 183. *St. Prosper*: (*c.* 390–*c.* 455), theologian and poet from Aquitaine in south-west France who spent his life defending Augustine's teaching on grace and predestination. In reply to Propers's letters, Augustine wrote *On the Predestination of the Saints* and *On the Gift of Perseverance*. According to Propser, anyone who disagreed with Augustine was a semi-Pelagian, including Vincent of Lerins.

p. 183. *St. Leo*: Bishop of Rome (440–61) and the first pontiff to assume the title of *Pontifex Maximus* ('Supreme Priest'). It was a title previously used by Roman Emperors to indicate that, as civil rulers, they had a right to intervene in ecclesiastical matters. Leo believed in the primacy of Peter the Apostle and his successors. As pope, he opposed Manicheism, Pelagianism, and Nestorianism. The Council of Chalcedon (451) accepted his celebrated *Tome* as the correct interpretation of Christ's incarnation and the union of his human and divine natures. Leo is one of three popes to have the title of 'Great'. Among Leo's surviving writings are 96 sermons and 432 letters, including the celebrated *Tome*, written and dispatched to the Council of Chalcedon (451) setting out the classic Roman view of Christology with its emphasis on the one person of Jesus Christ with a divine and a human nature, united but not mixed. In the summer of 1839, Newman himself was struck by the 'great power' of Leo at the Council of Chalcedon (451) when his orthodox views were vindicated (*L.D.* VII, p. 105; *Apo.*, pp. 114–117; *Diff.* I, pp. 372–374).

p. 183. *This holy and interesting lady*: Demetrias died sometime during the pontificate of Leo the Great (440–61).

p. 183. *Genseric*: (*c.* 390–477), Gaiseric, King of the Vandals and Alani (428–77), and one of the most formidable invaders of the Roman Empire. In 429, he led his people from Spain into Africa, possibly at the request of Boniface, the Roman general and conquered large areas of Roman north Africa. He took Carthage in 439, and dispatched a fleet to Sicily in 440. He dispossessed many Roman landowners and persecuted the clergy, gaining control of the Mediterranean by means of pirate fleets. In 455, he sacked Rome. By 476, his lands included Roman north Africa, Sicily, Sardinia, Corsica, and the Balearic Islands.

p. 184. *Basilica of St. Stephen*: the last we learn of Demetrias is that she financed the building of the basilica in Rome during the reign of Leo the Great (440–61) after the sack of Rome by Genseric in 455. It was rediscovered in 1858.

Chapter X: Martin and Maximus

Synopsis: Even as a child, Martin of Tours dreams of being a monk. At the age of fifteen, his father enlists him in the army where he gives half his cloak to a beggar while on duty at Amiens in Gaul. After seeing a vision of Christ wearing the same cloak, he is baptised. At the age of twenty, he quits the army, settles in Illyrium (Balkans) before being expelled by the local Arian party. He then moves to Milan where he is again expelled by the local Arian bishop. He then moves on to Poitiers where Hilary invites him to set up France's first monastery at nearby Ligugé. He becomes Bishop of Tours around 372, but continues to live as a monk at nearby Marmoutier. He then clashes with Magnus Maximus, rival emperor of the west (383–8), who has Gratian, the legitimate ruler of the west, murdered. Many people, including Martin, consider Maximus a usurper and murderer even though he protests his innocence. Maximus is an orthodox Christian and takes his religious duties seriously, sometimes too seriously. Martin intercedes with Maximus on behalf of some of Gratian's followers who refuse to swear allegiance, and on behalf of Priscillian, Bishop of Avila, who has been accused of heresy and witchcraft. In spite of promises of imperial clemency, Priscillian is beheaded, the first time a Christian is executed for heresy. Martin refuses to have anything to do with the anti-Priscillian party, headed by Felix and Ithacius. To save more lives, Martin agrees to attend the consecration of Felix as Bishop of Trier, a decision which haunts him to his dying day.

p. 185. "*He that lieth in ambush . . . have power over the poor.*": Psalm 9: 9–10.

p. 185. *Maximus*: Magnus Maximus, usurping emperor in the west (383–88) who came from a poor Spanish family which had connections with Theodosius I (379–95). He was a successful commander-in-chief of troops in Britain against the Picts and Scots. His troops, dissatisfied with Gratian who occupied the western throne proclaimed Maximus rival emperor in 383. Maximus then had Gratian murdered by his cavalry commander near Lyons, thus alienating himself from Martin. Maximus was an orthodox Christian who was all to eager to demonstrate it at every opportunity in order to secure the loyalty of the French and Spanish hierarchy.

p. 185. *Martin*: (*c.* 316–97), Martin of Tours, son of non-Christian parents, born in Pannonia (Hungary); when his father, a military tribune, was posted to Pavia, south of Milan, Martin accompanied him; on reaching adolescence, he enlisted in the army as was the custom. His regiment was sent to Amiens in Gaul where he gave half his military cloak to a half-naked beggar, dreaming that night that the beggar was actually Jesus Christ (Sulpicius Severus, *Life of St Martin*, Chapter III). After being baptised and leaving the army, he went to Milan, only to be expelled by Auxentius senior, the powerful Arian Bishop of Milan. By 360, he was with the anti-Arian, Hilary of Poitiers who invited him to set up the first monastery in Gaul at Ligugé outside Poitiers. His reputation for holiness and miracles made him the people's choice for Bishop of Tours around 372. He continued to live as a monk and set up a second monastery at Marmoutier on a tributary of the Loire river. Martin opposed the teachings of Priscillian, Bishop of Avila who taught an extreme of asceticism, who probably practised sorcery and who was condemned by the Council of Saragossa. When Ithacius and some Spanish bishops accused Priscillian of sorcery before the emperor Magnus Maximus (383–8), Martin travelled to Trier, to extricate him from the secular jurisdiction of the emperor. After agreeing to Martin's entreaties, Maximus reneged and ordered Priscillian's execution.

As a consequence, Martin refused to communicate with fellow bishop Ithacius. When, however, he later returned to Trier to ask pardon for two rebel governors, Narses and Leucadius, Maximus agreed to do so on condition that he made peace with Ithacius. To save their lives, Martin agreed to the reconciliation, but afterwards regretted doing so. His life, recorded by friend and historian, Sulpicius Severus (*c.* 360–*c.* 420) became one of the most influential books of the western Church. He is one of the patron saints of France. His feast day is 11 November.

p. 185. *Confessor*: title given in the early Church to anyone who was persecuted for his/her beliefs but did not undergo the actual ordeal of martyrdom. The third-century Church of Roman north Africa believed that confessors had the same spiritual authority and status as bishops and could forgive sins.

p. 185. *Even from British times ... city of Canterbury*;: according to the Venerable Bede (*c.* 673–735), a Church dedicated to the memory of Martin was built at Canterbury in Roman times, long before Augustine's arrival in 597. At the time of Martin's death in 397, it was not customary for churches to be dedicated to saints except the apostles and martyrs whose remains rested in that particular church. In fact, Martin is probably the first Western saint who was not a martyr and to whom churches were dedicated. According to William Thorne's *Chronicle of Saint Augustine's Abbey Canterbury* (1652), 'Ethelbert king of Kent, after the temporal reign which he had held with great vigour for fifty-six years, entered the joys of heavenly eternity on the 24th day of the month of February, and was buried in the porch of St. Martin, inside the church where Queen Bertha lies buried' (Chapter II, §2).

p. 185. *St. George*: popular Christian saint about whom very little is known; he may have been a Roman soldier in the late third or early fourth century who was martyred under Diocletian (284–305) at Lydda in Palestine. According to legend, Lydda was the same place where Perseus, the Greek hero, is said to have rescued Andromeda from the clutches of a sea monster. Some scholars believe that the two stories may have formed the legend of St. George and the dragon. George was declared patron saint of England in the reign of Edward III (1327–77). His feast day is 23 April. Lydda was also the scene where Peter the Apostle cured Aeneas of palsy (Acts 9: 32–34).

p. 185. *St. Nicolas*: Orthodox fourth-century Bishop of Myra in Lycia (south-west corner of Asia Minor), where Paul the Apostle stopped on his way to Rome as a prisoner (Acts 27: 5). Like St. George, very little is known about him. According to legend, he was imprisoned during the

Diocletian persecution, attended the Council of Nicaea (325) and died around 350. In the early sixth century, the emperor Justinian built a church in his honour at Constantinople. Nicholas is also the patron saint of sailors and also the 'Santa Claus' of children everywhere. His feast day is 6 December.

p. 185. *Tours*: city located at the junction of the Loire and Cher rivers in central France. It was first evangelised in the middle of the third century by the missionary Gatien who established a bishopric there. The Christian community remained a minority until Martin became their bishop in the second half of the fourth century. A magnificent basilica was built above his tomb in the latter part of the fifth century, and became a European place of pilgrimage.

p. 185. *St. Perpetuus*: eighth Bishop of Tours (461–91) who built a magnificent cathedral to house Martin's relics. He himself is also buried there.

p. 186. *Pannonia*: one of the most important provinces of the Roman empire in central Europe, southwest of the Danube river. It included parts of modern Austria, Hungary, Slovenia, Croatia, and former Yugoslavia. Its natives were the warlike Illyrians who fell under Rome rule round AD 9. In AD 103, it was divided into Upper and Lower Pannonia. Important centres included Vindobona (Vienna), Aquincum (Budapest) and Sirmium (Mitrovica). Rome abandoned it after the death of Theodosius I in 395.

p. 186. *Pavia*: known as Ticinum in Roman times, and located in Lombardy (northern Italy) on the Ticino river where it flows into the Po.

p. 186. *Sulpicius Severus*: (*c.* 360–*c.* 425), historian and biographer born in Aquitania (south-west France). Martin of Tours was instrumental in his conversion around 394. He wrote a life of Martin detailing his legendry miracles and holy death. He wanted to show that the west could produce a saint as good as any in the east. It has been described as a brilliant piece of propaganda and was a highly popular book in the Latin Church. In old age, he succumbed to Pelagianism for a while but eventually recanted.

p. 187. *Amiens*: capital city of the Somme in northern France whose cathedral is one of the largest Gothic cathedrals in France.

p. 187. *St. Hilary*: (*c.* 315–67), sometimes referred to as 'the Athanasius of the West'. Like Augustine of Hippo, Hilary was well versed in philosophy, particularly Neoplatonism, before his conversion to Christianity around 350. He became Bishop of Poitiers around 353 even though married.

Constantius II exiled him to Phrygia (central Asia Minor) for refusing to condemn Athanasius. It was in exile that he studied eastern theology and wrote his famous treatise on the Trinity. On returning in 360, he invited Martin to set up a monastery at Ligugé near Poitiers. This was the beginning of the monastic movement in France. Four years later, Hilary publicly debated Auxentius senior, Arian Bishop of Milan. Pius IX declared him a Doctor of the Church in 1851. His feast day is 14 January. Newman himself assisted Augustus Short (1802–83), future bishop of Adelaide, in his translation of *St. Hilary on the Trinity* for the *Library of the Fathers* though, in the event, that particular volume was never completed (see *L.D.* VII, pp. 381–3).

p. 187. *Poictiers*: located in central France on the Clain river; was christianised early in the third century and became a bastion of orthodoxy under Hilary in the fourth century. Because of its concentration of important monasteries, it grew into one of the most important religious centres in Gaul.

p. 188. *Illyricum*: see note to p. 42 (*C.F.*).

p. 188. *Auxentius*: (d. 374), native of Cappadocia and the west's most prominent Arian; after Dionysius of Milan was banished by the Arian party in 355, Auxentius was consecrated bishop, even though ignorant of Latin. In 359, he forced many bishops from Illyricum to sign the creed of Ariminum (Rimini). Some western bishops attempted unsuccessfully to persuade him to accept the Nicene Creed. In 364, he was publicly accused of heresy by Hilary of Poitiers and convicted of error in a debate held in Milan by order of the emperor Valentinian I (364–75). He publicly recanted but remained influential enough to drive Hilary out of Milan. Though condemned by a Roman synod in 369, he retained possession of the see until his death, when he was succeeded by the orthodox Ambrose.

p. 190. *Abbey of Marmoutier*: founded by Martin in 372 near Tours on a site bordered by a steep cliff on one side and by a tributary of the Loire river on the other. It became one of the most influential centres in the west. Even after becoming bishop, Martin continued to live there. The abbey had a chequered history, ravaged by Northmen in the ninth century, pillaged by Protestants in the sixteenth century and almost destroyed during the French Revolution in the eighteenth century.

p. 190. *Benedictine rule*: monastic rule drawn up by St. Benedict around 450 for the monks of Monte Cassino south of Rome; it provided for the spiritual and material well-being of the monastery; it was a balanced blend of prayer, study and manual labour with a clearly defined daily routine. By the beginning of the ninth century, the Benedictine rule had become the norm for most monasteries throughout Europe.

p. 190. *Gaul*: the Roman province of Gaul made up of that part of Europe occupied today by southern Holland, Belgium, Luxembourg, France, western Switzerland, Germany west of the Rhine, and northern Italy. There were three major regions: Aquitania to the west, Lugdunensis to the north, and Narbonensis to the east. Julius Caesar first conquered it between 58 BC and 52 BC. The emperor Diocletian (284–305) later divided it up into smaller provinces towards the end of the third century.

p. 190. *Marseilles*: ancient Massilia, located on the Gulf of Lion on the Mediterranean about 863 kilometres (536 miles) south of Paris and about 351 kilometres (218 miles) south of Lyon.

p. 190. *Lyons*: ancient Lugdunum, capital of Gaul, east-central France, located at the junction of the Rhône and Saône rivers.

p. 190. *Vienne*: ancient Vienna, in south-east France, located at the junction of the Rhône river and Gère River; one of the most important cities in Roman Gaul.

p. 190. *Toulouse*: ancient Tolosa, located in the south of France, on the Garonne river, close to the Pyrénées and about halfway between the Bay of Biscay and the Mediterranean Sea.

p. 190. *Tours*: one the first cities in Gaul to be evangelised in the third century, occupying the slice of land between the Loire and the Cher rivers.

p. 190. *Arles*: ancient Arelate, in south-central France, on the Rhône River delta in Provence; in 314, Constantine the Great convened a synod there to condemn Donatism; birthplace of Constantine II (337–40).

p. 190. *Narbonne*: ancient Narbo Martius in the south of France, near the Mediterranean coast; first Roman colony established in transalpine Gaul; later became capital of the Roman province of Narbonensis.

p. 190. *Orleans*: city in north-central France, south-west of Paris on the Loire river.

p. 190. *Paris*: city of ancient Lutetia in north-central France on the Seine river.

p. 190. *Clermont*: city in central France, on the Tiretaine river in the

Auvergne; an episcopal see since the third century, and site of several church councils, including the one of 1095, when Pope Urban II proclaimed the first crusade.

p. 190. *Limoges*: city in west-central France on the Vienne river near which Richard the Lionheart fell in battle in 1199.

p. 190. *and still frequented their idol temples*: superstition was very common among ordinary people in these days. 'Unguents were commonly used in solemn religious rituals of the pagan world for anointing holy stones and statues of the gods. Country folk mouthed cursing and blasphemy as they sowed the fields in the belief that their imprecations . . . would protect the crop from demonic blight, much as obscene songs were sung at weddings to avert infertility' (Henry Chadwick, *Priscillian of Avila: The Occult and the Charismatic in the Early Church*, Oxford 1976, pp. 51–2).

p. 190. *It is difficult to assign the limits of Martin's diocese*: probably the same for most western dioceses of this period.

p. 191. *a powerful sovereign*: Magnus Maximus, usurper and rival emperor of the west, 383–388 and a Spaniard. Maximus had his general of horses (*magister equitum*) Andragathius murder the emperor Gratian at Lyons on 25 August 383. He then set up court at Treves with the intention of invading Italy which was then under the control of the emperor Valentinian II who asked Theodosius I for help. After several battles, Maximus was captured and executed on 28 August 388.

p. 192. *Gratian*: (359–83), son of Valentinian I (364–75), emperor in the west (367–75) from the age of eight, and joint emperor in the west (375–83) from the age of sixteen. Gratian was a pious Christian, interested in theological issues. In 379, he outlawed all heresy and dropped the pagan title of *pontifex maximus* ('supreme priest') from the imperial titles and the ceremonial trappings that went with it. When Gratian heard that Magnus Maximus had crossed the English Channel, Gratian raced to Paris to confront him, but was murdered at Lyon by Maximus' cavalry commander, Andragrathius, who pretended to be a friend. Gratian was only twenty-four and had reigned as sole emperor for less than eight years.

p. 192. *Maximus' general of horse*: Andragrathius who was the emperor's general of horses (*magister equitum*), acting, it seemed, on the orders of Magnus Maximus.

p. 192. *Treves*: see note to p. 154 (*C.F.*).

p. 195. *compared to her who came from the ends of the earth to hear Solomon*: reference to the visit of the Queen of Sheba in 1 Kings 10: 1–2.

p. 195. "*a more blessed thing is it to give rather than to receive*": Acts 20:35.

p. 195. *Priscillianists of Spain*: followers of Priscillian, Bishop of Avila (*c.* 340–*c.* 387), whose strong, ascetic views were attracting a lot of attention in the latter half of the fourth century. Like other movements in the west, Priscillianism 'was accompanied by apocalyptic excitement with the expectation of visions and prophecies' (Henry Chadwick, *Priscillian of Avila: The Occult and the Charismatic in the Early Church*, Oxford 1976, p. 10).

p. 195. *Ithacius*: cruel Bishop of Ossonuba (Faro, southern Portugal) and one of Priscillian's bitterest and most outspoken critics. Sulpicius Severus described him as having 'no worth or holiness about him. For he was a bold, loquacious, impudent, and extravagant man; excessively devoted to the pleasures of sensuality He proceeded even to such a pitch of folly as to charge all those men, however holy, who either took delight in reading, or made it their object to vie with each other in the practice of fasting, with being friends or disciples of Priscillian. The miserable wretch even ventured publicly to bring forward a disgraceful charge of heresy against Martin, who was at that time a bishop, and a man clearly worthy of being compared to the Apostles' (*Life of St. Martin*, Chapter 50).

p. 195. *Priscillian*: (*c.* 340–*c.* 387), controversial Bishop of Avila in central Spain and a Spanish nobleman who was converted to a strict form of Christianity. Because of his disdain for anything physical, many of the hierarchy accused him of being a Manichean. He was condemned as a heretic in 384 by a Church synod at Burdigala (Bordeaux). When he appealed to the emperor Maximus at Trier, he was also charged with witchcraft, found guilty and, despite the protests of Martin of Tours and Ambrose of Milan, executed – the first time a Christian, let alone a bishop, had been executed for heresy. In some parts of Spain, Priscillian was honoured as a martyr.

p. 195. *Egyptian form of . . . formed a party.*: 'For then, for the first time, the infamous heresy of the Gnostics was detected in Spain – a deadly superstition which concealed itself under mystic rites. The birthplace of that mischief was the East, and specially Egypt, but from what beginnings it there sprang up and increased is not easy to explain. Marcus was the first to introduce it into Spain, having set out from Egypt, his birthplace being Memphis. His pupils were a certain Agape, a woman of no mean origin, and a rhetorician named Helpidius. By these again Priscillian was instructed, a man of noble birth, of great riches, bold, restless, eloquent, learned through much reading, very ready at debate and discussion – in fact, altogether a happy man, if he had not ruined an excellent intellect by wicked studies.' (Sulpicius Severus, *Sacred History*, Book II, Chapter XLVI).

p. 195. *A Council condemned them*: a council was held at Saragossa (north-east Spain) in October 380; though summoned, Priscillian and his followers refused to come. So the synod excommunicated four of the leaders, including Priscillian. Although the cruel and impulsive Ithacius was commissioned with enforcing the synod's decrees, it failed to bring him into line. As a result, Pricilllian's followers defiantly ordained him and made him Bishop of Avila in central Spain.

p. 196. *Bordeaux*: ancient city of Burdigala and port in Aquitainia, south-west France, on the Garonne river; with the approval of the usurper Magnus Maximus, a synod of bishops met at Bordeaux and condemned Priscillian as a heretic in 384. As at Saragossa four years earlier, Priscillian refused to attend, convinced that he would not get a fair trial. Instead, he tried to get the trial transferred to Maximus' imperial court at Trier which played right into the hands of the emperor because it gave him a golden opportunity to show the world that, unlike his predecessor, Gratian, he was not going to be soft on heretics and pagans.

p. 196. "*Caesar's to Caesar, and God's to God;*": Matthew 22: 21; Mark 12: 17; Luke 20: 25.

p. 196. "*keep the deposit;*": 1 Timothy 6: 20.

pp. 196–7. *Martin naturally viewed . . . like to inflict.*: according to Martin, appeals from Church synods to the emperor were not allowed by canon 11 of the Council of Antioch (327–28).

p. 198. *Siricius*: pope from 384 to 399.

p. 198. *Narses and Leucadius*: Magnus Maximus had won over most of Gratian's henchmen by threatening to execute anyone who refused to swear allegiance.

p. 199. *Theognistus*: bishop from Gaul who also objected to the Priscillian's execution and refused to talk to anyone connected with it, including Felix of Treves (Trier) and the vicious Ithacius of Ossonoba (Faro, southern Portugal).

p. 201. *They urged him with much earnestness ... but this he refused.*: for Martin, the whole affair had been thoroughly distasteful. In fact, he 'never again attended a synod of bishops, even when its business was of deep concern to him. He used sadly to confess that since the day when he felt forced to join with those polluted men in laying hands on Felix of Trier, he had suffered a loss of charismatic and healing powers' (H. Chadwick, *Priscillian*, p. 147).

p. 202. *a place at the extremity of his charge*: 'In the meantime, a reason sprang up which led him [Martin] to visit the church at Condate [on the road between Autun and Paris]. For, as the clerics of that church were at variance among themselves, Martin, wishing to restore peace, although he well knew that the end of his own days was at hand, yet he did not shrink from undertaking the journey, with such an object in view. He did, in fact, think that this would be an excellent crown to set upon his virtues, if he should leave behind him peace restored to a church' (Sulpicius Severus, Letter III. To Bassula, his Mother-In-Law).

p. 204. *a private friend*: the deacon Aurelius.

p. 204. *They were circulated ... with astonishing rapidity*: a friend told Sulpicius Severus about the popular success of Martin's biography which had spread throughout the empire. 'Paulinus ... was the first to bring it to the city of Rome; and then, as it was greedily laid hold of by the whole city, I saw the booksellers rejoicing over it, inasmuch as nothing was a source of greater gain to them, for nothing commanded a readier sale, or fetched a higher price. This same book ... was already generally read through all Carthage, when I came into Africa ... It has passed through Egypt, Nitria, the Thebaid, and the whole of the regions of Memphis' (Sulpicius Severus, *Dialogues* I, Chapter XXIII).

p. 205. *Huguenots*: French Protestants and members of the Reformed Church established by John Calvin around 1555. In the face of religious persecution, they fled France and sought asylum in Protestant Europe and America in the sixteenth and seventeenth centuries. The origin of the word is obscure. According to French printer and scholar, Henri Estienne (1528–98), in his *Apologie pour Hérodote* (1566), the name itself seems to have originated from the fact that the Protestants of Tours used to meet by night near the gate of the late King Hugo (born 1007) whom they regarded as a spirit which only ventured out at night as they themselves did. According to another tradition, the word was a corruption of the German word 'eidgenossen' meaning sworn companions or confederates. Newman's own mother, Jemima Fourdrinier, came from a refugee family of French Huguenots.

Primitive Christianity

p. 335. *Prefatory Notice*: written by Newman in 1872 to explain that he had written the following chapters between 1833 and 1836 for the *British Magazine* on the premise that the Church of England had a unique place in the Catholic communion and in Apostolical Christianity.

Chapter I: What Does St. Ambrose Say About It?

Section 1: Ambrose and Justina
Synopsis: Because he is too young to rule in his own right, the four-year-old emperor, Valentinian II, is placed under the tutelage of his Arian mother, Justina. She fills the court at Milan with Arian clergy, Arian officials, and an Arian bodyguard of Goths. In March 386, she demands that Ambrose hand over the Portian Church outside the walls of the city to the Arian party for worship. Ambrose refuses point blank. When rioting is about to break out between Ambrose's supporters and imperial guards, court officials become alarmed and dispatch Ambrose to intervene with the promise that no further attempts would be made to seize Church property. On 4 April, the Friday before Palm Sunday, the demand for an Arian church is renewed, this time, Justina demanding the New or Roman Basilica inside the city walls. Again, Ambrose refuses and once again the people rally round him. On the Wednesday of Holy Week before dawn, troops seize the basilica. Instead of confronting them on the spot, Ambrose decides to conduct a service in his own church, but threatens to excommunicate any soldier occupying the other basilica. They abandon the siege and join his congregation. By Good Friday, the imperial court has given up its demands. Now deserted by her soldiers and subjects, an infuriated Justina is forced to admit defeat. Peace is once more restored, but only for the time being.

p. 339. *Ambrose*: (*c.* 339–97), Bishop of Milan from 374 and one of the four traditional Fathers of the western (Latin) Church, alongside Augustine, Jerome and Gregory the Great. Ambrose was born at Trier on the Moselle river in Germany, and son of the Praetorian Prefect of Gaul. He himself was a lawyer and Roman governor of Amelia and Liguria in northern Italy with headquarters in Milan. On the death of the tyrannical Auxentius, Arian Bishop of Milan, in 374, the bishops of the province asked the emperor Valentinian I (364–75) to appoint a successor by imperial decree. He, however, decided that the election must take place in the usual way. Being the newly appointed governor, it was Ambrose's duty to keep law and order while a new bishop was elected. While cautioning peace and moderation to a divided clergy and people in the basilica, a small child cried out 'Ambrose, bishop!'. Whereupon, according to his biographer Paulinus, the entire congregation immediately took up the cry and, to Ambrose's dismay and surprise, he was elected bishop. Even though still a catechumen, they knew that he was a staunch defender of the Nicene Creed. The Arian party offered no objection as he had the reputation of avoiding theological disputes (see *H.S.* I, pp. 339–74).

p. 339. *Justina*: the empress Justina was a dedicated Arian although her husband, Valentinian I (364–75), while he was alive, insisted that she conform to the Nicene Creed. After his death, however, she openly espoused the Arian cause which automatically brought her into conflict with Ambrose. In that same year, her four-year-old son, Valentinian II, was proclaimed joint emperor of the west together his fifteen-year-old brother, Gratian. Justina assumed the role of empress-regent. After Gratian's murder in 383, she begged Ambrose to persuade the usurper Magnus Maximus to stay out of Italy. Ambrose travelled to Treves and convinced Maximus to confine his activities to Gaul, Spain, and Britain, but not Italy. Historians believe that it was the first time that a Christian official was involved in such an exercise against an armed aggressor. Justina later set up a rival Arian bishop of Milan who changed his name to Auxentius, in honour of Ambrose's tyrannical predecessor (see note to p. 346, *P.C.*). After Justina's death, Valentinian renounced Arianism and placed himself under the guidance of Ambrose whom he treated as a second father.

p. 339. *spirit of the times, ... British Constitution has lately undergone*: Newman is referring to a series of reform bills passed by Parliament between 1828 and 1833. They included the repeal of the Test and Corporation Acts of 1828 which allowed dissenters and non-conformists to hold public office; the Catholic Emancipation Act of 1829 which granted political and civil rights to Roman Catholics; the parliamentary Reform Bill of 1832 which gave voting rights to propertied adult males; and the Irish Church Temporalities Bill of 1833 which abolished ten sees in the Anglican Church of Ireland.

p. 340. *our blessed martyr St. Charles*: Charles I, King of England, Scotland and Ireland 1625–49, executed on 30 January by Oliver Cromwell and his followers. He was venerated as a martyr and a special memorial service was added to the Book of Common Prayer by his son, Charles II. 30 January was observed annually as a day of national fasting until 1859.

p. 340. *King George the Good*: George III (1738–1820), whose accession to the throne in 1760 came as a great relief to the Establishment as he was the first Hanoverian monarch to declare himself a loyal Anglican.

p. 341. *Dissenters*: reference to Protestants who refused to accept the re-imposition of bishops and the Prayer Book into the Church of England after the restoration of the monarchy in 1660. They included Baptists, Independents, Presbyterians, Quakers, Congregationalists. The Act of Uniformity of 1662 required all churches to use the Book of Common Prayer, penalising those who refused to obey. The Five Mile Act of 1665 prohibited dissenting ministers from coming within five miles (eight kilometres) of their former parishes. After the Toleration Act of 1689, dissenters were permitted to conduct services in licensed premises and to have their own preachers. The Test Acts of 1673 and 1678 still required civil and military office-bearers to take the oath of allegiance, and to receive the sacrament according to the rites of the Church of England. Dissenters remained duty bound to the two Test Acts until the Test and Corporation Act of 1828 when dissenters (referred more and more to as 'Nonconformists') became eligible for local and state offices. Even then, grievances remained such as church rate, that is, the obligation to pay for the repair of the local established church. 'If church and dissent came to blows as never before and never afterwards in the history of England, a main cause was the tea-cup parochial squabbles of church rate ... The outcry against church rate began only with the struggle for the reform bill at the end of 1830' (Owen Chadwick, *The Victorian Church Part One 1829–1859*, pp. 82–3).

p. 341. *apostolical body*: Anglican bishops 'derive their authority from consecration by other bishops in a line extending back to the first bishops, the Apostles, themselves commissioned by Christ to rule the Church' (*Apo.*, Oxford 1967, critical edition, p. 487); this was known as the doctrine of Apostolic Succession.

p. 342. "*To the poor the Gospel is preached*": Luke 4: 18; 7: 22.

p. 342. "*God hath chosen the poor of this world*": James 2: 5.

p. 342. "*If thou wilt be perfect . . . give to the poor*": Matthew 19: 21.

p. 342. *Becket's letters*: the full title of the collection edited by Newman was: *History of the Contest Between Thomas a Beckett, Archbishop of Canterbury, and Henry II, King of England; Chiefly Consisting of Translations of Contemporary Letters, Extracted From the Printed Edition of the Collection in the Vatican, and from Other Sources.*

p. 342n. *Froude's Remains*: *The Remains of the Late Reverend Richard Hurrell Froude, M.A.* was a collection of journals, letters, sermons etc. of Richard Hurrell Froude (1803–36) edited by Newman and John Keble (1792–1866). To much controversy, the first two volumes appeared in 1838 followed by a further two in 1839. Froude's criticism of the

Reformers aroused a great deal of hostility against the Tractarian party. A close friend of Newman, Froude's death at the age of thirty-three was a grievous loss. 'He was', wrote Newman, 'a high Tory of the Cavalier stamp, and was disgusted with the Toryism of the opponents of the Reform Bill.... He taught me to look with admiration towards the Church of Rome, and in the same degree to dislike the Reformation. He fixed deep in me the idea of devotion to the Blessed Virgin, and he led me gradually to believe in the Real Presence' (*Apo.*, p. 25).

p. 342. *Milan*: modern capital of Cisalpine Gaul about 45 kilometres (13 miles) from the southern foot of the Alps; from 305 to 402, it was the capital of the western Empire and the religious centre of north Italy. In 313, the emperors, Constantine I and Licinius, issued an edict from there granting religious freedom to all. Ambrose was its bishop from 374 to 379. It was badly damaged by the Huns around 450 and again by the Goths in 539. The Lombards finally conquered it in 569. The historian, Baronius, maintained that Barnabas, companion of Paul the Apostle, was the founder of the church of Milan.

p. 342. *Auxentius*: (d. 374), Auxentius senior, native of Cappadocia and one of the leading Arians in the west. In 355, the Arian emperor, Constantius II, elevated him to the see of Milan even though he spoke no Latin and ruled with a rod of iron for twenty years. In 359, he forced several bishops to sign the pro-Arian creed of Ariminum (Rimini in Italy).

p. 343. *a sister*: Marcellina to whom Ambrose dedicated *Three Books Concerning Virgins*.

p. 344. *Basil of Caesarea*: Basil the Great; see note to p. 3 (*C.F.*).

p. 344. *Athanasius of Alexandria*: (*c.* 296–373), Bishop of Alexandria of whom Newman wrote: 'There has been a time in the history of Christianity, when it had been Athanasius against the world, and the world against Athanasius. The need and straitness of the Church had been great, and one man was raised up for her deliverance' (*Dev.* p. 306); see also note to p. 394 (*P.C.*).

p. 344. *Alexandria*: major cultural, economic and political centre founded in 332 BC by Alexander the Great; located on the north-west corner of the Nile delta on a narrow strip of land between the Mediterranean Sea and Lake Mariut (Maretois). After Alexander's death in 323 BC, Ptolemy, one of his generals, founded a dynasty known as the 'Ptolemies' and made Alexandria capital of Egypt. It became a great multicultural centre of trade and celebrated for its library and lighthouse, one of the seven wonders of the ancient world. Cleopatra, last of the Ptolemy rulers, ruled from Alexandria. Egypt became a Roman province in 30 BC. Christianity was first brought to the city by Mark the Evangelist between AD 45 and 62. From the late second century AD, it was famous for its Catechetical School. Alexandria was an important cultural centre of the time, influenced by both Christianity and Hellenism.

p. 345. *Beckett's earthly master*: Henry II, King of England (1154–89) had Thomas Becket murdered in Canterbury Cathedral on 29 December 1170.

p. 345. *Valentinian was dead . . . Justina, his second wife.*: Valentinian I died in 375. His first wife was Marina Severa, mother of Gratian, emperor of the west. His second wife was Justina, mother of Valentinian II. Technically speaking, Valentinian had control of Italy, north Africa and western Illyricum. For all intents and purposes, Justina ruled. She was an Arian and brought up her son as one.

p. 345. *Theodosius*: (347–95), Theodosius I the Great, joint emperor of the east (379–92), ruler of both east and west (394–95) and last emperor to rule an undivided empire. Because of his considerable skill as a soldier, Gratian made him emperor of the east after Valens died fighting the Visigoths in 379. Called the Great, Theodosius was a headstrong, uncompromising supporter of the Nicene Creed. After nearly half a century of Arian emperors, he decreed that the real faith of Christians would be the one professed by the Bishops of Rome and Alexandria. In summoning the first Council of Constantinople (381), he effectively put an end to Arianism. He also issued a decree declaring the Bishop of Constantinople to be second in line after the Bishop of Rome.

p. 346. *a bishop of their persuasion from the East*: Auxentius junior, formerly Mercurinus from Scythia, who was a former Bishop of Durostorum (Silistria) on the lower Danube. He was a favourite of the empress Justina, and set up as a rival bishop to Ambrose by the Arians. He changed his name to Auxentius in memory, so it is said, of Ambrose's Arian predecessor. In 386, he unsuccessfully challenged Ambrose to a public debate at which biased court officials were to be the adjudicators. He also supported the use of the Portian Basilica for Arian worship. Ambrose's refusal to surrender the church ended in a siege of the building, in which Ambrose and his faithful congregation shut themselves up and refused to budge. Ambrose described Auxentius junior as someone 'full of blood and full of murder' ('Sermon Against Auxentius on the Giving Up of the Basilicas', p. 24). The empress eventually abandoned him and made peace with Ambrose.

p. 346. *St. Victor's Church*: Victor Maurus was a native of Mauretania in Roman north Africa in the third century and was thought to have been a soldier in the Praetorian guard who was tortured and decapitated as an old man under the emperor Maximian in Milan around the year 303. A church was later erected over his grave.

p. 346. *Portian Basilica*: located outside the walls, west of Milan.

p. 347. *But in our day ... one Apostolic Church:* as an Anglican evangelical, Newman was initially 'somewhat impatient' of the subject of Apostolical Succession when a friend (William James) spoke to him about it in 1823 'in the course of a walk ... round Christ Church Meadow' (*Apo.*, p. 10). In an 1844 letter to John Keble, he admits that he was less impatient when Richard Hurrell Froude spoke to him about it six years later in 1829 (*Correspondence of John Henry Newman with John Keble and Others, 1839–1845 (K.C.)*, p. 351).

p. 348. "*favour with all the people*": Acts 2: 47.

p. 348. *One man went so far*: among Justina's many attempts to get rid of Ambrose was a plot to have a certain Euthymius rent a house near Ambrose's basilica, and kidnap him. For one reason or another, the plan backfired and Euthymius himself was kidnapped.

p. 349. *imperial hangings:* such hangings probably bore an effigy of the emperor and proclaimed the fact that the New Basilica was now imperial property.

p. 349. *one of the Arian priests*: Castulus; see Ambrose's letter to his sister (Letter XX, p. 5).

p. 349. *All the officers*: 'All the officials of the palace, that is, the recorders, the commissioners, the apparitors [court officers] of the different magistrates, were commanded to keep away from what was going on, on the pretence that they were forbidden to take part in any sedition; many very heavy penalties were threatened against men of position, if they did not surrender the basilica. Persecution was raging, and had they but opened the floodgates, they seemed likely to break out into every kind of violence' (Ambrose, to his sister, XX, p. 7).

p. 349. *place-men:* individuals who hold official government positions.

p. 349. *and men of higher were menaced ... unless the Basilica were surrendered*: In Chapter IV, entitled 'The Penitence of Theodosius', for the 1840 edition, Newman observed: 'There is no sort of doubt, that had the scene been laid in England in the nineteenth century, not to speak in very generosity of the sixteenth, courtliness would have been the order of the day. The Basilica would have been surrendered to the heretics; yet I fear without that change of heart being wrought in prince or prime minister, by a timid policy in the Church to which Valentinian was lead by meeting with resistance. Certainly we have not made great men more religious by letting them have their way' (*Church of the Fathers*, 1840 edition, p. 43).

p. 351. *the New Church ... before the persecution*: assembling in the local Church was a popular way for ordinary citizens to demonstrate and protest.

p. 351. *on the lesson of the day ... from the book of Job*: the congregation would have quickly picked up the fact that Ambrose was referring to the empress Justina when he spoke of the mischief done by women (Job 2: 7–10).

pp. 351–2. "*say a word against God and die*": Job 2: 9.

p. 352. '*When I am weak, then am I strong*': 2 Corinthians 12: 10.

p. 352. *And so ended the dispute for a time*: no more measures were taken by the imperial court that year; on 23 January of the following year, however, Ambrose was horrified to learn of an imperial decree granting Arians freedom to assemble in churches and threatening anyone with the death penalty who interferred. It was probably drawn up by the rival Arian bishop, Auxentius junior.

Section 2: Ambrose and Valentinian
Synopsis: Ambrose is determined to rest his case on divine law while Justina is just as determined to rest her case on civil law. She persuades her son to issue a decree making it a capital offence to interfere with Arian worship. It is promulgated on 21 January 386, and another attempt is made to get possession of the Portian Basilica. Ambrose is ordered to quit Milan but refuses to budge except by force. As he is explaining his reasons to his congregation, soldiers surround his Church, but, afraid of excommunication, they decide to let anyone in but nobody out. To calm his faithful flock and to prevent rioting, Ambrose encourages them to sing hymns until the blockade is lifted. Many of the soldiers join in the singing. He remains in daily peril of his life. Auxentius junior, the rival Arian Bishop of Milan, challenges him to a public debate with court officials acting as adjudicators. Again, he refuses to agree by appealing to the authority of the emperor's father, Valentinian I, who always insisted that, in Church

matters, the clergy ought to sit in judgment on fellow clergy without outside interference.

p. 353. *Valentinian:* although only four years old, Valentinian II (375–92) was declared emperor of the west in 375 by a group of disgruntled staff officers, five days after his half-brother, Gratian, eight years old, was declared emperor of the west. In practice, Valentinian's jurisdiction never extended beyond Italy. He lived in Milan with his mother, Justina, who became the empress-regent. Both were eventually driven out of Italy by the usurper Magnus Maximus in 387 who, in turn, was deposed by Theodosius I a year later. On Justina's death shortly afterwards, Theodosius restored the western empire to Valentinian and persuaded him to renounce Arianism. He became a catechumen and invited Ambrose to baptise him at his palace in Vienne in Gaul, but was murdered before Ambrose had arrived. His body was returned to Milan where Ambrose delivered the funeral oration focusing on the efficacy of the baptism of desire.

p. 353. *Benevolus, the Secretary of State*: 'being firmly attached to the Catholic Church, [Benevolus] refused to write the document, and the empress tried to bribe him by promises of greater honours. He still, however, refused compliance, and, tearing off his belt, he threw it at the feet of Justina, and declared that he would neither retain his present office, nor accept of promotion, as the reward of impiety' (Sozomen, *Ecclesiastical History*, Book VII, Chapter 13). He then retired to Brescia, his native town situated about 90 kilometres (56 miles) east of Milan near the Alps.

p. 354. *if persecuted in one city, flee to another.*: Matthew 10: 23.

p. 354. *The reader shall hear... in a sermon:* present among the congregation was Monica, mother of Augustine, future Bishop of Hippo Regius in Roman north Africa (*Confessions* Book IX, Chapter 15).

p. 355. *Goths*: originally from southern Scandanavia; by the latter half of the second century, they had advanced into what is now Poland; by the early part of the third century, they had advanced to the northern coast of the Black Sea where they spilt into Ostrogoths ('East Goths') settling in the Ukraine, and Visigoths ('West Goths') settling in what is now Romania. In July 251, they defeated and killed Decius, the first Roman emperor to fall in battle. Under the leadership of Alaric (*c.* 391–410), they later invaded Rome in 410 but, contrary to popular opinion, inflicted very little damage and departed after three days.

p. 355. *Naboth*: owner of a vineyard in Jezreel beside the palace of King

Ahab of Samaria, north of Judea; he was a victim of a judicial murder engineered by his wife Jezebel so that Ahab might confiscate his vineyard (3 Kings 21).

p. 355. '*God forbid I should give to thee the inheritance of my fathers!*': 1 Kings 21: 3.

p. 356. '*He who giveth to the poor, lendeth to God.*': Proverbs 19: 17.

p. 356. *the people are misled by the verses of my hymns*: in his *Confessions*, St. Augustine talks about the hymns introduced by Ambrose into Church services at Milan: 'It was then that the practice of singing hymns and psalms was introduced, in keeping with the usage of the Eastern churches, to revive the flagging spirits of the people during their long and cheerless watch. Ever since then the custom has been retained, and the example of Milan has been followed in many other places, in fact in almost every church throughout the world' (*Confessions* Book IX, Chapter 7).

p. 356. '*Their blows are like the arrows of a child*': Psalm 64: 7.

p. 357. *Psalmody*: practice of singing psalms or hymns.

p. 357. *which Ambrose adopted*: known as the Ambrosian Chant in which originally one or two notes were accorded to each syllable; the melody of the *Veni Creator Spiritus* ('Come, creator Spirit') belongs to this tradition. Augustine credited Ambrose with the introduction of antiphonal psalmody, but modern scholars question the claim. On his way to Rome from Milan in 1846, Newman wrote to a friend back home to tell him that he had just visited the 'Church from which St. Ambrose repelled the soldiers of the Arian, and where he and the people passed the night in prayer and psalmody' (*Ward* I, p. 143).

p. 357. *our own collegiate chapels*: Newman is alluding to the system of chapels attached to various Oxford colleges.

p. 358. *St. Laurence*: one of seven Roman deacons martyred under Valerian I (253–60); tradition speaks of him being roasted on a gridiron round 258.

p. 358. *the antiphonal or responsorial.*: alternate singing of verses of the psalms by each half of the congregation; the practice was subsequently adapted by such composers as Johann Sebastian Bach (1685–1750), Felix Mendelssohn (1809–47) and Benjamin Britten (1913–76); 'antiphon' comes from the Greek *antiphona* meaning 'sounding in answer'.

p. 358. *Ignatius*: (*c.* 35–*c.* 115), third Bishop of Antioch (Syria) from around AD 75, succeeding Peter the Apostle and Evodius; he was one of the Apostolic Fathers and was martyred during the reign of the emperor Trajan (98–117). What we know about him comes from the seven epistles which he wrote to various Christian communities in Asia Minor on his way to Rome for execution. He strongly believed that there should be only one bishop for each community so as to minimise internal divisions and to ensure the preservation of Church teaching; see note to p. 402 (*P.C.*).

p. 358. *doxology*: hymn of praise to God; from the Greek words, *doxa* meaning 'praise' and *logos* meaning 'word'; the custom of ending a hymn or rite with such a formula is of Jewish origin. Paul the Apostle uses doxologies constantly (Romans 11: 36; Galatians 1: 5; Ephesians 3: 21). They are also common in the Old Testament (as, for example, Psalm 8: 1). They were addressed to God the Father alone or through Jesus Christ (Roman 16: 27). By the fourth century, it was the custom to use the formula, 'Glory be to the Father, and to the Son, and to the Holy Spirit'. The 'Glory be to the Father' formula is referred to as the minor or lesser doxology, while the 'Gloria in excelsis Deo' of the Eucharist is referred to as the major or greater doxology.

p. 358. *Flavian*: (*c.* 320–404), orthodox Bishop of Antioch who succeeded Meletius in 381, and whose election prolonged the schism in the Eastern Church over the nature of the Trinity. When, Evagrius, an illegally consecrated Bishop of Antioch at the same time, died around 398, Flavian was officially recognised, thus ending the schism which started when Meletius was first expelled from Antioch by the Arian party around 360.

p. 359. *oriental chants, in praise of the Blessed Trinity*: Newman translated Ambrose's *Nunc Sancte Nobis Spiritus* and included it in *Verses on Various Occasions*, p. 245:

> Come, Holy Ghost, who ever One
> Reignest with Father and with Son,
> It is the hour, our souls possess
> With Thy full flood of holiness
> (*V.V.*, first verse, number 140).

p. 360. *which Pope Gregory introduced ... beginning of the seventh century*: traditional music of the Latin rite is generally known as *Gregorian Chant* or *Plainsong*; it was named after Gregory the Great, the first monk to become pope (590–604); what exactly his musical contribution was remains uncertain.

p. 361. *Arian bishop*: Auxentius junior, rival Bishop of Milan; see pp. 342; 346 (*P.C.*).

pp. 362–3. *a service Ambrose ... upon the murder of Gratian*: at first, the usurper Maximus promised Theodosius I to confine himself to Gaul and leave Valentinian II to govern Italy, north Africa and western Illyricum. He soon, however, reneged on his promise not to invade Italy. In desperation, Justina turned for help to Ambrose who agreed to travel to Treves to persuade the usurper Maximus to leave Valentinian alone. As a result of his personal intervention, he succeeded in gaining a temporary reprieve for Justina and the emperor.

Section 3: Ambrose and the Martyrs

Synopsis: The persecution of the Church of Milan comes to an end when the relics of two martyrs, Gervasius and Protasius, are discovered and restore the sight of a blind man called Severus. A huge crowd witnesses the miracle, including Ambrose, Paulinus his secretary and biographer, and Augustine. The translation of the martyrs' relics to the new basilica is a crowning triumph of orthodoxy over Arianism. An increase of converts follows its wake.

p. 364. *Ambrose*: 'It was Ambrose, in his fight to defeat the popular challenge of Arianism, who first systematically developed the cult of relics. Milan was poorly provided in this respect: it had no tutelary martyrs. Rome had the unbeatable combination of St Peter and St Paul; Constantinople acquired Andrew, Luke and Timothy; and during the last fifty or sixty years amazing discoveries had been made at Jerusalem – the body of St Stephen, the head of John the Baptist, the chair of St James, the chains of St Paul, the column used in the scourging of Christ and, since 326, the cross itself ... At the dedication of his new basilica, he [Ambrose] providentially discovered the skeletons of SS Gervasius and Protasius' (Paul Johnson, *A History of Christianity*, London 1990, pp. 105–6).

p. 364. *Martyrs*: Gervasius and Protasius were thought to be the first Christian martyrs (protomartyrs) of Milan under the emperor Nero around the year 64. According to tradition, they were twins, and the children of martyrs, Valeria and Vitalis. Older citizens of Milan remember hearing that Gervasius was flogged to death with lead-tipped scourges while Protasius was beheaded. Their feast day is 19 June.

pp. 365–366. *But if Elisha's bones ... Gervasius and Protasius should not*: Newman claims that 'there exists in matter of fact that very connection and intermixture between ecclesiastical and Scripture miracles, which ...

the richness and variety of physical nature rendered probable' (*Mir.*, p. 161).

p. 366. *dedication*: one of two forms of blessing a church building for the exclusive use of divine worship. Dedication is the simpler form; consecration a more solemn form.

p. 366. *dedication of a certain Church at Milan*: in 386, Ambrose built a basilica at Milan. Asked by his flock to consecrate it in the same way as was done in Rome, he promised to do so if he could get the required relics. According to tradition, he had a dream in which he was shown the spot where martyr's relics could be found. He ordered excavations to be made in the cemetery church of Saints Nabor and Felix, outside the city, and subsequently found the relics of the martyrs Gervasius and Protasius. He transferred them to the church of St. Faustus and, on the following day, into the basilica, which later became known as San Ambrogio Maggiore (St. Ambrose the Greater). Many miracles are said to have taken place, and everyone saw them as a sign from heaven, given at the time of the great struggle between Ambrose and the Arian empress Justina. (*Confessions*, Book IX, Chapter 7).

p. 366. *with the name of "St. Ambrose the Greater"*: originally, the basilica was dedicated to the memory of Gervasius and Protasius, but, after Ambrose's death, it was re-dedicated and became the San Ambrogio Maggiore (St. Ambrose the Greater). In 835, Ambrose's own relics were laid alongside the remains of Gervasius and Protasius. Newman visited it in 1846 while en route to Rome: '... to go into St. Ambrose's Church – where the body of the Saint lies – and to kneel at those relics,' he wrote to Henry Wilberforce back home, 'which have been so powerful, and whose possessor I have heard and read of more than other saints from a boy. It is 30 years this very month, as I may say, since God made me religious, and St. Ambrose in Milner's history was one of the first objects of my veneration' (*Ward* I, p. 139).

p. 366. *Basilica*: from the Greek 'basilikos' meaning 'royal'; name given to important ancient churches built in the fourth century along the lines of Roman public and private halls. One entered the church through a portico, beyond which was an open space with colonnades around it ('atrium') with an entry porch ('narthex') on the far side. The church proper was divided by columns into a nave and two aisles, with an apse at its opening and the bishop's chair placed against the wall beyond. Originally, the word applied to any large public building, such as law courts and commerce.

p. 366. *the church of St. Nabor*: originally the cemetery church of Saints Felix and Nabor, two Roman soldiers who were martyred during the persecution of Diocletian (303). They were beheaded in Lodi, a few kilometres south-east of Milan. Ambrose erected a church over their tomb, now known as the church of Saint Francis. Translation of their relics set a precedent for the future transfer of relics. Their feast day is celebrated on 12 July.

p. 366. *his sister*: Marcellina (*c.* 335–*c.* 398), Ambrose's older and only sister who assisted in pastoral work after his becoming bishop in 374; three years later, Ambrose dedicated a treatise on virginity to her. She was buried in the crypt under the altar of Ambrose's Basilica and honoured as a saint.

pp. 366–337. *ascertained to be Gervasius and Protasius*: see note to pp. 443–6 (*P.C.*).

p. 367. *the neighbouring church of St. Faustus*: now the church of Saints Vitalis and Agricola who were martyred around 304 at Bologna and whose relics Ambrose had transferred to their final resting place in 393. Faustus was crucified during the reign of the emperor Trajanus Decius (249–51).

p. 368. *City of God:* commenced by Augustine in 411, finished around 426, and inspired by a letter from a friend called Marcellinus inquiring whether the fall of Rome in 410 and other disasters were due to emperor Theodosius proclaiming Christianity as the official religion of the Roman empire and whether these catastrophes were the vengeance of the old Roman Gods. The work consisted of twenty-two books in which Augustine contrasts society's search for sexual satisfaction and material goods with the Christian journey towards the city of God. In answering these questions, 'Augustine not only crowned the long tradition of Christian apologetic, but expounded a scheme of Church-State relations which rid educated Western thought of the mirage of apocalypticism' (W.H.C. Frend, *The Early Church: From the beginnings to 461*, p. 207).

p. 369: *Thy Church needs greater guardianship*: among other things, Ambrose would have been referring to his differences of opinion with Justina and Theodosius I over Church-State relations. Later on in 390, Theodosius slaughtered some seven thousand citizens of Thessalonica for assassinating one of his senior officers. For which crime, Ambrose compelled him to do public penance – one of the first instances in which a Roman emperor was forced to bow to the moral authority of the Church.

pp. 369–70. '*These put their trust . . . the Lord our God.*': Psalm 19: 8.

p. 370. *'Jesus, Son of the living Son . . . before the time?'*: Matthew 8: 29.

p. 371. *Paulinus*: secretary and biographer of Ambrose until the latter's death in 397. Paulinus then went to north Africa where he helped Augustine in his campaign against the Pelagians. While there, he wrote a life of Ambrose similar in style to Sulpicius Severus' life of Martin of Tours. Paulinus' Ambrose was a 'man of action, who cut a furrow through his contemporaries: no less than six people suffer crushing divine punishments for standing in his way or for criticising him, among them quite ordinary African clergymen. Paulinus plainly felt that, at the Last Judgment, men would still be divided between those who admired Ambrose, and those who heartily disliked him' (Peter Brown, *Augustine of Hippo*, London 1967, pp. 408–9).

p. 373. *à priori:* literally meaning, *prior to experience*; à priori evidence does not depend for its authority upon empirical evidence as *à posteriori* evidence does.

p. 374. *Tacitus:* Publius Cornelius Tacitus (*c.* AD 55–*c.* 117); one of Rome's greatest historians who was critical of contemporary Rome because of its increasing indolence and loss of spirit and vigour. This idea underpins his two major works, *The Annals of Imperial Rome* and *The Histories*. The original *Annals* covered the Julio-Claudian dynasty from the death of Augustus in AD 14 to the end of Nero's reign in 68 and made up of twelve or fourteen books. The original *Histories* covered the period from the fall of Galba in 69 to the beginning of Vespasian's reign in the same year. Only books 1 to 4 and part of book 5, covering the years 69–70, are extant. In 97, Tacitus rose to the consulship under the emperor Nerva (96–8).

p. 374. *Cæsar:* Gaius Julius Caesar (*c.* 102 – 44 BC) whose commentaries on the Gallic Wars were simple, straightforward, no-nonsense affairs.

Chapter II: What says Vincent of Lerins?

Synopsis: There are many people who seem to think that the *beau idéal* of the Church is about the promotion of good order and sobriety; that clergymen are supposed to be 'reverend' gentlemen with large families going around dispensing 'spiritual consolation' to parishioners, turning a blind eye to differences of doctrinal opinion, and getting on with the more important things in life. The same people also think that the path of doctrinal purity is a broad, all-encompassing highway which can accommodate all types of belief. On the other hand, people like Leo the Great and Gregory Nazianzus would argue that the path to doctrinal purity is a narrow one, and all the better for being narrow; and that there are certain doctrines that every Christian is bound to believe because the Church follows the rule that we must hold as sacred only those truths which have been *always, everywhere and by everybody* believed from the time of the apostles. Antiquity, universality, and consent of the Church Fathers are the real tests of doctrinal purity. Vincent of Lérins develops this rule in his celebrated *Commonitory*.

p. 375. *Tantum religio potuit, etc.,*: 'Such evil deeds could trigger off religion' (Lucretius, *De Rerum Natura*, Book I, line 101). Lucretius (*c.* 99–*c.* 55 BC) was a Roman poet and philosopher. In *De Rerum Natura* ('On the Nature of Things'), he popularised the philosophical theories of Democritus and Epicurus on the origin of the universe with the aim of debunking religious belief. He believed that religion was a human construct triggered off by fear and that the human race would be better off without the yoke of any religion at all (*L.D.* XXVI, p. 389; see *G.A.*, p. 392).

p. 375. *Epicurean*: follower of Epicurus of Samos (342–270 BC) who believed that the essence of life was the pursuit of happiness and that people should fear neither death nor deities nor anything for that matter.

p. 375. *The highest end of Church union ... is quiet and unanimity*: in 1834, Renn Dickson Hampden, then Professor of Moral Philosophy at Oxford, suggested that the Anglican Church is 'neither dogmatic in it spirit ... nor intolerant and sectarian in its zeal, but only desirous of uniting as many hearts and voices as possible in one common confession, without exacting a rigid and impossible uniformity of opinion from individuals members of the society' (Renn Dickson Hampden, *Observations on Religious Dissent*, Oxford 1834, second edition. p. 23). Newman told Hampden that his *Observations* made 'shipwreck of Christian faith' and believed 'that, by its appearance, the first step has been taken towards interrupting that peace and mutual good understanding which has prevailed so long in this place [Oxford] ' and that it was the 'commencement of the assault of Liberalism upon the old orthodoxy of Oxford and England' (*Apo.*, pp. 57–8).

p. 376. *a clergyman is ... by profession a "man of peace"*: Country clergy were 'constant readers of the *Gentleman's Magazine*, deep in the antiquities of the signs of inns, speculations as to what becomes of swallows in winter, and whether hedge-hogs, or other urchins, are most justly accused of sucking milch-cows dry at night' (P. Corsi, *Science and Religion: Baden Powell and the Anglican debate, 1800–1860*, Cambridge 1988, p. 15).

p. 377. "*Propter vitam vivendi perdere causas*": 'for the sake of life to sacrifice life's only end, the only reason for living' (Juvenal, *Satires*, Book VIII, line 84). Juvenal (*c.* AD 55–*c.* 140) was a Roman lawyer and satirist whose angry verses on the lax Roman way of life range from a disgust of poverty, tyranny and affectation to a dislike of Jews and women.

p. 377. *Ananias*: Jewish Christian from Jerusalem; when Christians pooled their resources, Ananias and his wife, Sapphira, withheld theirs. When confronted by Peter the Apostle, they lied and suddenly died within hours of each other (Acts 5: 1–11).

p. 377. *Diotrephes*: local church bishop who was unfavourably mentioned in 3 John 9–10, who loved to dominate and who refused to recognise the authority of John the Apostle.

p. 377. "*a rod*": 1 Corinthians 4: 21.

p. 377. *an English non-juror*: non-jurors were members of the Church of England who, after the Glorious Revolution of 1688, refused to swear an oath of allegiance to William and Mary on the grounds that this would violate their oath to James II. Even though they detested the latter's policies, James was still God's anointed one, and they believed that the oath was inviolable. Several bishops, including the Archbishop of Canterbury, were removed from office. 400 clergy and a number of lay people also refused to take the oath of allegiance. 'The smallness of their numbers proves that their favourite doctrine had outlived its power to command assent, but it is significant that they could force the only High Church schism in the history of the Church of England' (G.R. Cragg, *From Puritanism to the Age of Reason*, Cambridge 1950, p. 182).

p. 378. *over-exactness was the very fault of the fourth and fifth centuries*: according to Renn Dickson Hampden, then Professor of Moral Philosophy at Oxford, the whole corpus of revelation contains facts but 'no *doctrines*'. Doctrines are of human origin and therefore, fallible and flawed. They can be scrutinised and interpreted differently '*without danger to salvation*'. 'This is the view which I take, not only of our Articles at large, but in particular, of the Nicene and Athanasian Creeds' (*The Scholastic Philosophy Considered, in its Relation to Christian Theology*, Oxford 1833, pp. 373–4; 352–3; 378).

p. 378. *even a heathen philosopher*: reference to Aristotle and his *Nicomachean Ethics* (Book II, Chapters VIII–IX).

p. 379. *St. Leo*: Bishop of Rome (440–61); see notes to pp. 183; 337 (*C. F.*).

p. 381. *Quod semper, quod ubique, quod ab omnibus*: that which has been believed 'always [antiquity], everywhere [universality], and by everyone [consent]'.

p. 382. *Vincent of Lerins:* (d. *c.* 450), according to Gennadius of Marseilles (*c.* 490) in his *Catalogue of Illustrious Men* (Chapter LXV): 'Vincentius, by birth a Gaul, a presbyter in a monastery in the island of Lirins [sic], a man learned in the holy Scriptures, and well instructed in the knowledge of the doctrines of the Church, with a view to overthrow the sects of the heretics, composed in elegant and clear language a very powerful dissertation [the *Commonitory*], which, concealing his own name, he entitled PEREGRINUS AGAINST HERETICS. Having lost the greater part of the second book of this work, (the manuscript was stolen,) he recapitulated its substance in a few words, and attached it to the first, and put them forth as one book (AD 434). He died in the reign of Theodosius and Valentinian' (from the preface of the 1837 Oxford translation, p. v).

p. 382. *Lerins*: archipelago of four islands just off the coast of Cannes on the French Riviera. Sainte-Marguerite and Saint-Honorat are its two bigger islands with its two smaller islands of Tradelière and St-Féréol. Today, it is a fifteen-minute boat ride from Cannes to Saint-Honorat and a slightly longer one to Sainte-Marguerite. Honoratus of Arles established a monastery there around the year 400, the first monastery in western Europe. It became a celebrated centre of learning. Its students included Augustine of Canterbury, Hilary of Arles and, probably, Patrick of Ireland. The monastery was secularised during the French Revolution, but reopened as a Trappist monastery in 1871. The island of Sainte Marguerite is the site of the infamous prison in Alexander Dumas's *Man in the Iron Mask*.

p. 382. *famous tract . . . on Heresy*: full title of Vincent's celebrated tract is *The Commonitory For the Antiquity and Universality of the Catholic Faith against the profane Novelties of all Heresies*; derived from the Latin *commonitorius* meaning a 'reminder', an 'aid to memory'. Vincent intended it as a set of simple guidelines for distinguishing doctrinal truth from heresy.

p. 382. *third Ecumenical Council*: held at the city Ephesus (south-west Asia Minor) in 431 at which more than 200 bishops attended and was presided over by Cyril of Alexandria who represented Pope Celestine I. It defined the personal unity of Jesus Christ, declared Mary as Mother of God (*Theotokos*), condemned Nestorius, Bishop of Constantinople and renewed the condemnation of Pelagius.

p. 382. *Nestorius*: Bishop of Constantinople; see note to p. 308 (*T.C.*).

p. 382, 1n. *The Oxford translation of 1837*: sold by J. H. Parker, Oxford and by J.G. and F. Rivington, London. This translation was 'a revision of a version published in 1651, and preserved in the Bodleian [Library, Oxford] ... It has in parts been altered considerably, with the intention of bringing it nearer to the original' (from the preface of the 1837 Oxford translation, pp. v–vi).

pp. 382–4. "*Inquiring often ... priests and doctors together*": these extracts are from the second chapter of the *Commonitory*. It focuses on the twofold test for distinguishing doctrinal truth from heresy, namely, scripture and tradition. Since there have been so many interpretations of scripture, tradition has to be taken into account when interpreting it. We must believe, argued Vincent, that which has been held *always*, *everywhere*, and *by everyone*. In other words, we have to be guided by *universality*, *antiquity*, and *consent*.

p. 383. *Bishop Jebb*: (1775–1833), Bishop of Limerick (1823) who anticipated many of the ideas of Newman and the Oxford Movement. In an appendix to the 1837 translation of the *Commonitory* (pp. 128–9), Jebb is quoted on the relevance of Vincent's views for the Anglican Church of the nineteenth century: 'Such are the views of *Vincentius*. But where, at this day, are those views retained, except in the Church of England? The Protestant Communions on the Continent have not so much as pretended to revere antiquity. The Church of Rome has not been wanting in the pretension; but, instead of revering antiquity, she has idolised herself. The Church of England alone has adopted a middle course; moving in the same delightful path, and treading in the same hallowed footsteps with Vincentius, and the catholic Bishops, and the ancient Fathers: proceeding as far as they proceeded, and stopping where they stopped' (from Bishop Jebb's *Peculiar character of the Church of England. Pastoral Instructions*, p. 293).

p. 383. *Novatian*: rival Bishop of Rome (251–58); although doctrinally orthodox, Novatian was a hardliner when it came to re-admitting into the Church any 'lapsi', that is those who had 'lapsed' (apostatised) during the Decian persecution. In fact, he went as far as to argue that the Church did not have the power to forgive anyone guilty of murder, adultery or apostasy. He was the founder of the first sect that broke away from the early Church on a matter of discipline and not of doctrine. The sect survived until the fifth century.

p. 383. *Photinus*: fourth-century theologian and Bishop of Sirmium (Mitrovica in Kosovo) from around 344 to 351, deposed for his Christological views. His followers (the Photinians) were condemned by the Council of Constantinople (381) and by Theodosius II in 428.

According to Vincent, Photinus believed 'that God is, as the Jews believe, singular and solitary, denying the fulness of the Trinity, not believing that there is any Person of the Word of God, or of the Holy Ghost. . .. Christ was only man, who had his beginning of the Virgin Mary, teaching very earnestly that we ought to worship only the Person of God the Father, and to honour Christ only for man' (*Commonitory*, Oxford 1837, Chapter XII, pp. 33–34).

p. 383. *Sabellius*: early third-century theologian who, in his enthusiasm to preserve the unity of the Godhead, denied the independence of each person of the Trinity. Sabellius 'was a bishop or presbyter in Pentapolis, a district of Cyrenaica [Roman north Africa], included within the territory afterwards called, and then virtually forming, the Alexandrian Patriachate. Other bishops in his neighbourhood adopting his sentiments, his doctrine became so popular among a clergy already prepared for it, or hitherto unpractised in the necessity of a close adherence to the authorized formularies of faith, that in a short time (to use the words of Athanasius) "the Son of God was scarcely preached in the Churches" ' (*Ari.*, p. 118). His followers were referred to as Sabellians. In the west, they became known as Patripassians because they believed that, when Jesus suffered, it was really the Father who was suffering.

p. 383. *Donatus*: schismatic Bishop of Carthage (313–55), whose name is associated with the hardline Donatist movement which divided the Church in north Africa in the fourth and fifth centuries. After the Diocletian persecution (303–11), a split developed in the north African Church over what to do with those who had 'lapsed' (apostatised) during the Diocletian persecution. Hardliners refused to cooperate with any lapsed bishop or priest. Many Numidian bishops declared invalid the ordination of Caecilian the new Bishop of Carthage because the ceremony had included a lapsed bishop in 311. In protest, they consecrated Majorinus who died soon after. They then consecrated Donatus who remained Bishop of Carthage for almost thirty-five years until exiled to Gaul or Spain in 347 where he died. Throughout its brief existence (about 100 years), Donatists claimed they and they alone were the one true church. The rest of Christendom was an evil puppet of a secular state.

p. 383. *Arius*: (*c.* 260–*c.* 336), presbyter and theologian from Alexandria who seems to have been born in Libya and educated at Antioch (Syria). He clashed with his Bishop, Alexander of Alexandria, around 318 when the latter insisted that the Father and the Son were co-eternal and co-equal. Arius believed that the Son was neither co-eternal nor co-equal with the Father and, therefore, not divine. A local synod excommunicated and banished him. He died in the streets of Constantinople around 336.

He was eighty-six years old. 'Sozamen expressly says, that Arius was the first to introduce into the Church the formulae of the "out of nothing," and the "once He was not," that is, the creation and the non-eternity of the Son of God. Alexander and Athanasius, who had the amplest means of information on the subject, confirm his testimony. That the heresy existed before his time outside the Church, may be true, – though little is known on the subject; and that there had been certain speculators, such as Paulus of Samosata, who were simply humanitarians, is undoubtedly true; but they did not hold the formal doctrine of Arius, that an Angelic being had been exalted into a God' (*Ari.*, p. 201).

p. 383. *Eunomius*: (d. *c.* 394), Bishop of Cyzicus (Asiatic side of the Propontis) and one of the leaders of an extreme party within Arianism known as Anomœans; a very capable dialectician who developed much of their theology. His sermons were so boring that his congregation sacked him. Eunomius was even too extreme for the Arian emperor, Constantius II who banished him. 'The proper Arian party did not show itself in the Councils till thirty years after Nicaea, 'under the name of Anomœans, Aetius and Eunomius being its leaders; the Eusebian Councils in the interval were for the most part composed of Semi-Arians' (*T.T.*, p. 147).

p. 383. *Macedonius*: (d. *c.* 362), semi-Arian claimant to the see of Constantinople who competed for the see with the orthodox Peter between 341 and 350 when the latter was exiled to Cucusus in southern Cappadocia by order of the pro-Arian emperor, Constantius II. Macedonius then took over and 'maintained his power by most savage excesses' until he fell out of favour and was himself deposed in 360 (*Ari.*, p. 311). He maintained the position that the Son shared a 'like' substance with the Father but he refused to align himself with the orthodox position that the Son was 'one in being with' the Father. His name was associated with a party that denied the divinity of the Holy Spirit, arguing that the Holy Spirit was a mere creature in the service of the Son, hence their name 'Pneumatomachi' ('those who attack the Spirit').

p. 383. *Apollinaris*: (*c.* 315–*c.* 392), author and staunchly orthodox Bishop of Laodicea in Phrygia from about 361. He is credited with being the first person to work out in any detail the relationship between the human and the divine aspects of Jesus Christ. In his enthusiasm to oppose Arianism, he argued his case for the divinity of Jesus so strongly, that he ended up denying his full humanity, insisting that Jesus had a divine consciousness but not a human one. According to Vincent of Lerins, Apollinaris believed that 'our Saviour in his human body either had not man's soul at all, or at least such a one, as was neither endued with mind nor reason; furthermore he affirmeth, that Christ's body was not taken of the flesh of the holy

Virgin *Mary*, but descended from heaven into the womb of the Virgin, and that, holding doubtfully and inconstantly, some time that it was coeternal to God the Word, some time that it was made of the divinity of the Word; for he [Apollinaris] would not admit two substances in Christ, the one divine, the other human; the one of his father, the other of his Mother …' (*Commonitory*, Oxford 1837, Chapter XII, p. 34).

p. 383. *Priscillian*: Bishop of Avila, north-west of Madrid; see note to p. 195 (*C.F.*).

p. 383. *Jovinian*: see notes to p. 173 (*C.F.*) and p. 401 (*P.C.*).

p. 383. *Pelagius*: fifth-century monk who denied original sin; see note p. xiii (*C.F.*).

p. 383. *Celestius*: friend and follower of Pelagius.

p. 383. *Nestorius*: according to Vincent of Lerins, Nestorius, 'sick of a contrary disease [to Apollinaris], whilst he feigneth a distinction of two substances in Christ, suddenly bringeth in two persons, and with unheard of wickedness will needs have two sons of God, two Christs, one God and another man, one begotten of the Father, another begotten of his mother. And therefore he saith, that the holy Virgin *Mary* is not to be called the mother of God ['Theotokos'] but the mother of Christ ['Christotokos'], because that of her was born not that Christ which is God, but that which was man' (*Commonitory*, Chapter XII, p. 35, Oxford, 1837).

p. 384. *Catholic*: derived from the Greek word 'katholikos' meaning 'universal'; first used by Ignatius of Antioch (Syria) at the beginning of the second century in a letter to the Christian community at Smyrna north of Ephesus. In Chapter VIII of that letter, he says that 'Wherever the bishop shall appear, there let the multitude [of the people] also be; even as, wherever Jesus Christ is, there is the Catholic Church'.

p. 384. *Judaizers*: Jewish Christians of the early Church who claimed that the Mosaic law was binding on all converts (Acts 15; Galatians 2). They were principally divided into Nazarenes and Ebionites.

p. 384. *When, therefore, such men … Apostolic and Catholic doctrine*: reference to Judaizers who were encouraging Paul's converts in Galatia to be circumcised, and to observe other aspects of Jewish law and rituals such as the sabbath, feast days, and food laws. Paul saw them as a threat to 'the truth of the gospel' (Galatians 2: 5).

p. 384. *casting up again the heavenly manna*: reference to the Israelites in the wilderness sighing for forbidden meats (Numbers 21: 5).

p. 385. *Anathema*: meaning something despised, hated, or cursed; originally, the word was reserved in the Hebrew Scriptures for something horrible such as a criminal exposed to public ridicule before being expelled from the community or executed (Deuteronomy 7; 1 Kings 15: 9–23). The early Church adopted the term to signify the expulsion or excommunication of a sinner from the community in order to vindicate justice and to bring offenders to their senses with the enormity of their deeds. For Vincent of Lerins, although anathema meant excommunication, it did not automatically mean eternal damnation.

p. 386. *nominal Christians*: of particular importance to Evangelicals in Newman's day was the great 'invisible' Church of Christ to which God's privileged elect belonged by the grace of conversion and the power of the Holy Spirit. They were the 'real' Christians of the invisible Church as compared 'nominal' Christians who, through baptism, belonged to the visible Church but were not yet one of God's elect.

p. 386. *the noble Ambrose, a high and dry churchman*: in the original 'Letters on the Church of the Fathers' for the *British Magazine*, Newman did not single out Ambrose but 'the Martyr Cyprian, a mere high churchman' (*British Magazine*, "Letters on the Church of the Fathers', No. IX, Volume VI, September 1834, p. 289).

p. 387. '*There must (quoth he) . . . manifest among you.*': 1 Corinthians 2: 9.

p. 388. "*O Timothy . . . about the faith.*": 1 Timothy 6: 20–1.

p. 388. *depositum:* the Church's doctrines are a trust from the apostles to be handed on from generation to generation without alteration, addition, dilution or substitution.

p. 388. *cockle*: Matthew 13: 24–5, 37.

p. 388. *talent*: Matthew 25: 15.

p. 388. *Beseleel*: Exodus 31: 1ff.

p. 389. *basilisk*: legendary snake (Proverbs 23: 32) whose gaze and foul breath were fatal; in some version of the psalms, the word was replaced by viper as in Psalm 90: 13.

p. 389. '*Receive him not . . . his wicked works.*': 2 John: 10–1.

p. 390. *Pelagius:* once again, Vincent of Lerins distances himself from the teaching of Pelagius.

p. 390. *monstrous disciple Celestius*: it has been suggested that, while Vincent of Lerins used the word 'profane' to describe Pelagius, he reserved 'monstrous' for Celestius because the latter was a eunuch.

p. 390. *cruel Novatian*: it has also been suggested that Vincent of Lerins used the word 'cruel' to describe the hardliner, Novatian, because the latter taught that there was no forgiveness of sins after baptism. In fact, Novatian went as far as to argue that the Church had no power to forgive anyone guilty of murder, adultery or apostasy. Once fallen, always fallen.

p. 390. *Simon Magus*: practising magician in Acts 8: 9–24 who became a Christian and then tried to buy Peter's miraculous powers.

p. 390. *Author of evil*: the problem of evil is at the heart of Gnosticism; either God *is not* the creator of evil and therefore good, or God *is* the creator of evil and therefore not good.

p. 390. '*if any man shall preach . . . that which is received*': Galatians 2: 9.

Chapter III: What says the History of Apollinaris?

Synopsis: If the Protestantism of the day, Newman asks, rejects those doctrines which primitive Christianity fought so hard to preserve, then how can it argue that primitive Christianity is basically Protestant in character? The history of Apollinaris the Younger is a classic example of the impossibility of such a claim. After the death of the pro-Arian emperor, Constantius II, the orthodox cause prevails once more and Apollinaris becomes Bishop of Laodicea. Shortly afterwards, the first intimation of doctrinal error later bearing his name surfaces. As it spreads further afield, a synod condemns it in 369, but without mentioning Apollinaris by name. Even Athanasius refuses to associate the heresy with him. After Athanasius' death, Apollinaris begins to reveal his true colours. But, even then, authorities still refuse to believe he has anything to do with it, suggesting that he is using exaggerated language to emphasise a particular point of view. Even when he forms a sect, they continue to condemn the heresy but not the man himself. Finally, a synod in Rome condemns him in 377, followed by another in Antioch in 379 and finally by the Council of Constantinople in 381.

p. 391. *WHAT SAYS THE HISTORY OF APOLLINARIS?*: of the twenty-one letters which Newman wrote for the *British Magazine*, letters XVI and XVII alone were given a title: 'APOLLINARIS'.

p. 391. *Apollinaris*: (*c.* 310–*c.* 390), Apollinaris the Younger was born in Laodicea in Syria. While a lay reader under the local Arian bishop, he himself was orthodox and was later elected Bishop of Laodicea by the Nicene members of the community around 361. In trying to emphasise Christ's divinity, however, he went too far in the opposite direction by denying 'that our Lord was perfect man, or had a rational soul, on the ground that such a tenet interfered with the very notion of the Son coming in human flesh, as introducing a new being or person, or thinking principle, into the Sacred economy. He argued, that *whatever* was joined to the Divine Word [Logos] must be but instrumental and subordinate, and that no entire intelligible nature, such as man's, was or ever could be so' (John Henry Newman, paper on 'Apollinarianism', 22 August 1835, privately printed, p. 3). Apollinaris was condemned by a Roman synod (379) and by the Council of Constantinople (381).

p. 391. *In the judgment of the early Church*: Newman's original introduction to 'Apollinaris' in 1836 for the *British Magazine* began as follows: 'Sir, – No passage of early ecclesiastical history is more painful and more instructive than the fall of Apollinaris into heresy. It becomes so from his high repute for learning and virtue, his intimacy with the great catholic champions of his day, his former services to the church, the temptation which seems to have led to it, the comparative insignificance of his error at first, yet the deplorable defection from the faith at which he, or at least his school, in no long time arrived. He began with the denial of our Lord's human soul, or rather of the intellectual part of it; which he considered was supplied by the Eternal Word incarnate. His object in this was to secure more completely the doctrine of the divinity of our Lord's person, to impress upon the mind that he who came on earth, who taught, acted, and suffered, was God, and not a man, in every thought, word and deed, though acting through and in human nature; and he did so with an especial view of overthrowing Arianism, which denied this essential and singular characteristic of him who had appeared among men in their form and nature...' (*British Magazine*, 'Church of the Fathers', No. XVI, Volume X, July 1836, pp. 35–6; included in the 1840, 1842, 1857 editions but deleted from the uniform edition).

p. 392. *A brief sketch of his history:* Newman prefaced this short paragraph in 1836 for the *British Magazine* with the following observation: ''This was the incredible aberration of a grave, a literary, an aged man, some of whose writings are still extant, and evince a vigour and elegance of mind not inferior to any writer of his day. A sort of shadowy gnosticism seemed to revive in the person of a dialectician, versed in all the accomplishments of Grecian philosophy and rhetoric' (*British Magazine*, 'Church of the Fathers', No. XVI, Volume X, July 1836, p. 36; included in the 1840, 1842, 1857 editions but deleted from the uniform edition).

p. 392. *Berytus*: Beirut, modern capital of Lebanon on the Mediterranean Sea located at the foot of the Lebanon mountains, near Tripoli; an ancient Phoenician city, well known as a trading centre since about 1500 BC. It was an important city under the Seleucids, and increased in importance from about 64 BC under Roman rule. It was in the neighbourhood of Berytus that the story of the epic battle between St. George and the dragon was supposed to have taken place. George is highly honoured throughout the region.

p. 392. *Syrian Laodicea*: seaport in Syria about 186 kilometres (116 miles) south-west of Aleppo. Alexander the Great conquered it in 333 BC after the battle of Issus. Seleceus I renamed it in honour of his mother, Laodicea. It was destroyed by earthquakes in 494 and 555 and rebuilt by the emperor Justinian (527–65); now modern Latakia, one of Syria's busiest and most modern seaports.

p. 393. *Porphory*: (*c.* 232–*c.* 305), prominent Neoplatonist and a follower of Plotinus (*c.* 205–70) whose works were posthumously edited by Porphory into the *Enneads* which contained the foundations of Neoplatonism. In his celebrated, now lost treatise, *Against the Christians*, Porphory attacked Christianity by applying historical criticism to Scripture.

p. 393. *During the reign of Julian*: that is, between 361 and 363.

p. 393. *the two Apollinares*: when the emperor Julian forbade Christians to teach the pagan classics, Apollinaris the Younger and Apollinaris the Elder rewrote much of the Bible in classical form.

p. 393. *Arians*: see note to p. 3 (*C.F.*).

p. 393. *Eunomians*: see note to pp. 78–79 (*C.F.*).

p. 393. *Macedonians*: see note to p. 40 (*C.F.*).

p. 393. *Manichees:* see note to p. 146 (*C.F.*).

p. 393. *Origen*: (*c.* 185–*c.* 253), native of Alexandria, head of its famous catechetical school for twenty years, first systematic theologian of the early

Church, and sometimes criticised for introducing heathen philosophy into the study of the Gospels. After ordination around 230, Origen moved to Caesarea (Palestine) where he opened a school modelled on the Cathechetical School of Alexandria and where Gregory the Wonder-worker was one of his pupils. He spent another twenty years teaching there. He suffered a great deal during the Decian persecution (249–51) and died shortly afterwards in Tyre. Origen was author of the treatise *Contra Celsum* ('Against Celsus') which defended Christianity against Celsus, author of the first philosophical attack on Christianity.

p. 393. *Marcellus*: (*c.* 280–374), Bishop of Ancyra (modern Ankara) and an uncompromising opponent of Arianism. Along with Athanasius of Alexandria, he was one of the leading orthodox figures at the Council of Nicaea (325). Like Apollinaris the Younger, he put so much emphasis on the unity of the Father and the Son in the Trinity that his enemies accused him of Sabellianism. He was deposed from his see in 336 but reinstated in 337, only to be deposed again in 339. He was posthumously condemned at the Council of Constantinople (381).

p. 393. *Millenarians*: individuals who were convinced that Jesus Christ was about to return to earth and reign for 1,000 years before the end of the world. Such a belief was widespread in the early Church.

p. 394. *Athanasius*: According to Newman, Athanasius 'has impressed an image on the Church, which, through God's mercy, shall not be effaced while time lasts' (*U.S.* V, p. 97).

p. 394. *second exile*: Athanasius spent his second exile in Rome, from July 339 to October 346, under the Arian emperor, Constantius II. He was first exiled by Constantine the Great to Trier from July 335 to November 337. He spent the last three periods of exile in the Egyptian desert, first from February 356 to February 362 under Constantius II; then from October 362 to September 363 under Julian the Apostate; and finally from October 365 to January 366 under Valens, last Arian emperor of the east. Throughout his forty-five years as Bishop of Alexandria, Athanasius spent one third of that time in exile. According to Newman in *Arians of the Fourth Century*, thirty of Athanasius' local bishops throughout that time were also exiled and about ninety were stripped of their churches (*Ari.*, p. 331).

p. 394. *Council thereupon held at Alexandria, AD 362*: on return from his third exile in 362, the politically astute Athanasius convened a synod of twenty-one bishops with the aim of bringing about a reconciliation with the Semi-Arian party which, he realised, was very close to the Nicene formula. After years of disagreement and division, the *homoousion* formula of the Nicene Creed was finally accepted. It may have been a small victory in the general fight against Arianism, but it was probably Athanasius' finest hour (*Ari.*, pp. 353 ff.). A decree was also passed 'that such that such bishops as had communicated with the Arians through weakness or surprise, should be recognised in their respective sees, on signing the Nicene formulary; but that those, who had publicly defended the heresy, should only be admitted to lay-communion. No act could evince more clearly than this, that it was no party interest, but the ascendancy of the orthodox doctrine itself, which was the Athanasians' (*ibid.*, p. 359).

p. 397. *Epiphanius*: (*c.* 315–403), orthodox Bishop of Salamis on the island of Cyprus from 367 and a dedicated heresy-hunter who took an active role in the debate against Apollinaris. He was one of the first and most vocal critics of Origen, whom he regarded as the source of all theological error and campaigned to have him condemned.

p. 399. *Eustathius*: (*c.* 300–*c.* 378), Bishop of Sebaste in Pontus who initially supported Arius but moved to a semi-Arian position. He asserted that the Son is *like*, but not the *same* in substance as the Father. His friendship with Basil the Great ended with their disagreement over the divinity of the Holy Spirit. While outwardly welcoming Basil's elevation to the bishopric, Eustathius tried to blacken his name at every opportunity, accusing him of arrogance and Apollinarianism. He remained a thorn in Basil's the Great's side.

p. 399. '*Beware of making many books,*': Ecclesiastes 12: 12.

p. 400. *against Porphyry:* apart from a few fragments, Apollinaris' work against Porphory is not extant; according to St. Jerome, it was 'generally considered as among the best of his works' (Jerome, *Lives of Illustrious Men*, Chapter CIV).

p. 400. *Marcellus and Apollinaris, fell away into heresies of their own*: 'This is what comes', Newman wrote, 'of Reasoning in the province of theology, unless in the first place we enquire our way by Scripture and Tradition, and then proceed to reason under the information thence afforded us' (*T.T.*, p. 309).

p. 400. "*Let him that thinketh he standeth, take heed lest he fall*": 1 Corinthians 10: 12.

p. 400. "*Alas, my brother! round thy tomb . . . To the bright shore of love.*": these two stanzas come from *The Christian Year: Thoughts in Verse for the*

Sundays and Holydays Throughout the Year by John Keble (1792–1868), Oxford 1827, p. 206, written for Eighth Sunday after Trinity. Initially, Newman prefaced the verses with the following remarks in the *British Magazine*: 'It would appear, then, on the one hand, that while there is no antecedent improbability in the notion that the Christian faith is exact and definite, or what liberalists commonly call *technical*, there is, on the other hand, a great body of testimony from the earliest times to prove that so it is. It is for those who still deny it to explain on what ground of argument they resist a truth which satisfies those tests which we commonly use to guide our belief in ordinary matters of conduct. As to Apollinaris, whose history has led to these remarks, let us turn to him, in conclusion, with the following appropriate stanzas ...' (*British Magazine*, 'Church of the Fathers', No. XVI, Volume X, July 1838, p. 41; deleted in the 1840 and subsequent editions).

Chapter IV: And What Say Jovinian and His Companions?
Synopsis: Newman focuses on the commonly held idea of his day that the present Church system, as Anglicans know it, is not genuinely Apostolic; that the present system is a corruption of some lost primitive creed; and that it is foreign to the Gospel. If then, he asks, the present system is not authentically apostolic, *when* did it actually come into existence? The known circumstances of the previous history preclude the possibility of any particular time, however close to the apostles, when there was no Church system. Granting that the present system is actually a corruption of a lost primitive creed, then how could it be a corruption which sprang up everywhere at once? Is it conceivable that we have no evidence that any person retained remnants of that lost system? Is there any evidence of primitive Protestantism in the early Church? If there is, then the best chance of finding it would be in individuals who would best qualify to be called the Luther, Calvin and Zwingli of the fourth century, namely individuals like Aerius, Jovinian and Vigilantius. Unfortunately, however, their lives, when examined, offer no convincing clues that there ever was a lost primitive creed. Thus, Newman concludes, the search for primitive Protestantism in the early Church is a waste of time.

p. 401. *Vincentius*: Vincent of Lerins; see note to p. 382 (*P.C.*).

p. 401. *Jovinian*: (d. *c.* 405), monk from Milan who was condemned as a heretic by synods at Rome and Milan around 390. According to Jerome, Jovinian taught (1) that virginity is not superior to the married state; (2) that abstinence is not spiritually superior to the moderate use of material goods (3) that a person baptised with water and the Holy Spirit cannot commit a sin; (4) that all sins are equal; (5) that there is but one grade of punishment and reward in the next life. According to St. Augustine,

Jovinian also denied the perpetual virginity of Mary. Ambrose, Augustine, Jerome, Pelagius and Siricius I of Rome attacked him. He was eventually exiled by imperial decree; see note p. 173 (*C.F.*).

p. 401. *after the death of St. John*: traditionally dated round the turn of the first century; last of the apostles to die and the only one who was not martyred. He was buried at Ephesus.

p. 401. *a system of Pagan or Jewish origin*: many scholars of Newman's day maintained that any so-called 'revealed' doctrine which had its roots in paganism or Judaism could not possibly be part of divine revelation. For example, Renn Dickson Hampden, one of Newman's contemporaries at Oxford in the 1830s, maintained that the Church's sacramental system is 'utterly repugnant' to the real spirit of Christianity because it had its origins in the early Church and in the 'general belief in Magic' (Renn Dickson Hampden, *Scholastic Theology Considered*, Oxford 1833, pp. 341–2). Newman also criticised another Oxford contemporary, Henry Hart Milman's principle about what qualifies for revelation, namely, that any doctrine claiming to belong to the Gospel, but has its roots in other religions, philosophies and cultures cannot qualify as authentic revelation (see *Ess.* II, pp. 230–1).

p. 402. *Hermas*: one of the disciples at Rome greeted by Paul the Apostle (Romans 16: 14) and believed to be the author of an important book called *The Shepherd* which at one time was included by some in the Bible itself. It consists of a series of prophetic tracts written at a time when many Christians were expecting the end of the world at any moment. It calls for penance and holds out the possibility of forgiveness at least one more time after baptism.

p. 402. *Ignatius with his dogmatism*: (*c.* 35–*c.* 115), third Bishop of Antioch (Syria) whose letter to the Church of Smyrna near Ephesus leaves no doubt that the local bishop is the supreme authority in a diocese and that anyone 'who does anything without the knowledge of the bishop, does [in reality] serve the devil' (Ignatius, *Epistle to the Smyrnaeans*, Chapter IX). He was martyred in Rome during the persecution of the emperor Trajan (98–117).

p. 402. *Irenaeus*: (*c.* 115–*c.* 202), Church Father and orthodox Bishop of Lyons (Lugdunum) in France; he attacked Gnosticism by arguing that he could trace what he taught back to the apostles and could prove what he taught because its roots are found in Scripture. He was the first writer to state that there were only four authentic Gospels. His best known writings are *Against Heresies* and *Proof of the Apostolic Preaching*.

p. 402. *Clement*: (*c.* 150–*c.* 220), head of the famous catechetical school of Alexandria which applied the allegorical method to the Old and New Testaments. According to Newman, the allegorical method of writing was the 'national peculiarity of that literature in which the Alexandrian Church was educated. The hieroglyphics of the ancient Egyptians mark the antiquity of a practice which, in a later age, being enriched and diversified by the genius of their Greek conquerors, was applied as a key both to mythological legends, and to the sacred truths of Scripture' (*Ari.*, p. 57). Although now discounted by modern scholars, the allegorical method was the primary tool of many Church Fathers, including Origen.

p. 402. *Cyprian*: (*c.* 205–58), Bishop of Carthage (*c.* 248) who believed that Christians 'cannot live out of it [the Church], since the house of God is one, and there can be no salvation to any except in the Church' (Letter LXI, para. 4) '... not even the baptism of a public confession and blood can profit a heretic to salvation, because there is no salvation out of the Church' (Letter LXXIII, para. 21). He was martyred during the reign of the emperor Valerian (253–60). Unlike hard-line Donatists, he was in favour of remitting lapsed Christians after a suitable period of penance.

p. 402. *Methodius:* (d. *c.* 311), Bishop of Olympus in Lycia (south-west Asia Minor) and opponent of Origen. Very little is known about him except that he wrote a tract in praise of virginity known as *The Banquet of the Ten Virgins* and written in the form of a Platonic dialogue. It is his only extant work. He was martyred for refusing to sacrifice to the Roman gods.

p. 403. *Luther and Calvin*: Martin Luther (1483–1546), German Protestant Reformer; and John Calvin (1509–1564), French Protestant Reformer; see notes p. 409 (*P.C.*).

p. 403. "*Where was your Church before Luther?*": This was probably the 'most troublesome question of the early seventeenth century, the question which stretched the controversial muscles of the Society of Jesus or of King James' college of theological warriors at Chelsea' (O. Chadwick, *From Bossuet to Newman*, Cambridge 1987, second edition, p. 2).

p. 403. *the art of washing the blackamoor white:* reference to one of the fables of Aesop (sixth century BC), the Greek fabulist, the moral of which is not to waste time pursuing impossible tasks.

p. 404. *Dr. Priestley*: (1733–1804), scientist, political writer and clergyman who was one of the founders of unitarianism; he rejected the doctrine of the Trinity, the Atonement and the inspiration of Scripture.

p. 404. *amanuensis*: secretary; from the Latin *servus a manu* meaning a 'slave at handwriting'; person employed to take down dictation or copy manuscripts.

p. 404. *Socinian*: while not rejecting Christ's supernatural character, Socinians denied his equality with the Father; named after two Italian theologians, Laelius Socinus (1525–62) and his nephew, Faustus Socinus (1539–1604).

p. 405. *modern Socinianism*: Socinianism was a form of unitarianism. Socinians maintained that Jesus was not divine but a human instrument of God, while Arians maintained that Jesus was the first creature, but was neither of the same substance as the Father as orthodox Christians believed, nor was he human as Socinians believed. 'To tell the truth,' Newman commented, 'we think one special enemy to which the American Church, as well as our own, at present lies open is the influence of a refined and covert Socinianism ... Not to the poor, the forlorn, the dejected, the afflicted, can the Unitarian doctrine be alluring, but to those who are rich and have need of nothing, and know not that they are "miserable and blind and naked" ' (*Ess.* I, pp. 347–8).

p. 405. *Puritanism:* extreme form of English Protestantism. Puritans were unhappy with the limitations of the Elizabethan Settlement (1558–59) which, among other matters, dealt with the question whether the Church of England should be seen as Catholic or Protestant. Puritans opted for a Calvinistic form of religion. Their sole authority was the Bible and they rejected traditional forms of worship. Throughout the sixteenth and seventeenth centuries, they were known variously as Presbyterians, Baptists, Separatists and Independents. After the restoration of the monarchy in 1660, they were more commonly known as *Dissenters* or *Nonconformists*.

p. 405. *Erastians*: individuals who believed that the State should control the Church and who took their name from the Swiss theologian, Thomas Erastus (1524–83). According to Newman, the 'doctrinal appellation of "High Church" signifies the teaching which aims at asserting the prerogatives and authority of the Church; but not so much its *invisible* powers as its privileges and gifts as a *visible* body; and, since in the Anglican religion these temporal privileges have always depended on the civil power, it happens accidentally that a partisan of the High Church is almost an Erastian; that is to say, a man who denies the spiritual power pertaining to the Church and maintains that the Church is one of the branches of the civil government' (quoted by Wilfrid Ward in *Kingsley versus Newman, 1864–5*, Oxford 1913, p. xxvii).

p. 405. *Supralapsarians*: individuals who believed in a Calvanistic form of predestination which maintained that God had determined the salvation or damnation of each and every individual before the fall of Adam; term meaning 'above the fall'; also known as antelapsarians ('before the fall').

p. 405. *Independents*: Congregationalists who upheld the independence of the local church; the term was in general use throughout Great Britain until the early part of the nineteenth century.

p. 405. *Sacramentarians*: name used by Martin Luther (1483–1546) for theologians like Zwingli who believed that the bread and wine of the Eucharist represented the body and blood of Christ in a metaphorical rather than in a literal sense. The name was used in the sixteenth century for anyone who denied the real presence of Jesus Christ in the Eucharist.

p. 405. "*Bible religion*": in the *Grammar of Assent*, Newman describes Bible religion as 'both the recognised title and the best description of English religion' of his day; it does not consist in 'rites and creeds, but mainly having the Bible read in Church, in the family, and in private' (*G.A.*, p. 56).

p. 405. *onus probandi*: 'burden of proof'.

p. 405. *Montanist*: disciple of Montanus who founded a prophetic movement in Phrygia in Asia Minor dating from the late second century. Montanus believed that he had received secret information from the Holy Spirit not communicated to the apostles. His followers were extreme ascetics who believed that the second coming of Jesus Christ was just around the corner. The sect was also known as the 'Phrygian heresy'. Newman referred to Montanus as the author of a 'harsh and arrogant discipline' (*Ari.*, p. 16). Its most famous follower was Tertullian (*c.* 160–*c.* 220).

p. 405. *Novatian*: disciple of Novatian, the antipope, who took a hardline stand on the readmission of the lapsed during the Decian persecutions (249–51); see note to p. 383 (*P.C.*).

p. 406. *latitudinarian*: seventeenth-century term applied to broad-minded Anglican theologians (divines) who attached relatively little importance to dogma, church organisation and liturgical practices. According to Newman, this 'party took the side of the revolution of 1688, and supported the Whigs, William III, and the House of Hanover. The spirit of its principles is opposed to extension and proselytism; and, although it has numbered in its ranks remarkable writers among the Anglican theologians, it has had few votaries until ten years ago, when, irritated by the success of the Tractarians, taking advantage of the conversion of some of their principal leaders [including Newman himself] to the Roman Church, and aided by the importation of German literature into England, this party suddenly came before the public view and was propagated among the best educated classes with a rapidity so astonishing that it is almost justifiable to believe that in the coming generation the religious world will be divided between the Deists and the Catholics' (from appendices written by Newman for the French edition of his *Essay on the Development Christian Doctrine* in 1866 and quoted by Wilfrid Ward op. cit., pp. xxiv–xxv).

p. 406. *anabaptist*: originally, a reference to sixteenth-century Continental Protestants who rejected infant baptism. Although never numerous in England, English monarchs from Henry VIII to James I were very suspicious of them and wanted them burnt as heretics.

p. 406. *Erastian*: see note to p. 405 (*P.C.*).

p. 406. *utilitarian*: one who believes that society should be organised to secure the greatest happiness for the greatest number of citizens; generally associated with English philosopher and jurist, Jeremy Bentham (1748–1832).

p. 406. *Athanasius*: Bishop of Alexandria (328–73); see notes to p. 3 (*C.F.*); p. 394 (*P.C.*).

p. 406. *Jerome*: scripture scholar and translator (*c.* 342–*c.* 420); see note to p. 24 (*C.F.*).

p. 406. *Epiphanius*: (*c.* 315–403), Bishop of Salamis (eastern coast of the island of Cyprus); see note to p. 397 (*P.C.*).

p. 406. *Eusebius*: (*c.* 260–*c.* 339), Bishop of Caesarea Maritima, a large deepwater port built by Herod the Great around 10 BC. Eusebius was the first major Church historian and an Arian sympathiser who played a key role in the Council of Nicaea (325). His *Ecclesiastical History* furnished a birdseye view of the early Church from the time of the apostles to the year before the Council of Nicaea (325). He was also key adviser to Constantine the Great whom he baptised before his death in 337. 'A more dangerous adviser Constantine could hardly have selected, than a man thus variously gifted, thus exalted in the Church, thus disposed towards the very errors against which he required especially to be guarded' (see *Ari.*, p. 263). Although Eusebius may not have been the first to write a history of the Church, it is not fragmentary but complete.

p. 406. *Cyril of Jerusalem*: (*c.* 315–68), orthodox Bishop of Jerusalem and Doctor of the Church who succeeded Maximus as bishop (*c.* 350); Cyril was exiled three times from his see (357–58; 360–62; 376–78) when the Arian party was in the ascendant; all in all for a total period of sixteen years. Ironically, his own views about the Nicene formula came under suspicion and no less than Gregory of Nyssa had to vouch for his orthodoxy (see *Ari.*, p. 302). Cyril's main surviving work is a collection of more than twenty catechetical lectures composed for candidates for baptism.

p. 406. *Semi-Arians*: Following the Council of Nicaea (325), Arians soon split into a left-wing faction (Arians) and a right-wing faction (semi-Arians). The left wingers still taught that the Son was of a *different* essence to and even *unlike* the Father, and created out of nothing. Right wingers preferred to say that the Son was not indeed of the *same* essence, yet of *like* essence with the Father. Many actually agreed with the Nicene faith, but were either prejudiced against Athanasius, or saw in the term *of like substance*' shades of Sabellianism. According to Newman, the semi-Arian creed really involved 'contradictions in terms, parallel to those of which the orthodox were accused; – that the Son was born before all times, yet not eternal; not a creature, yet not God; of His substance, yet not the same in substance; and His exact and perfect resemblance in all things, yet not a second Deity' (*Ari.*, p. 299).

p. 407. *sacramentals*: religious practices and objects which were not instituted by Jesus Christ; they included the sign of the Cross, grace before and after meals, vestments, candles, the rosary, Stations of the Cross.

p. 408. *continence kept for God's sake is recorded*: Matthew 18: 12; Luke 15: 4.

p. 409. *Luther*: Martin Luther (1483–1546), German Protestant reformer and theologian who objected to the sale of indulgences, attacked many of the Church's doctrines and proclaimed the sole authority of Scripture.

p. 409. *Calvin*: John Calvin (1509–64), French Protestant reformer and theologian who taught God's absolute transcendence, the depravity of human condition, eternal happiness for a privileged few and the sole authority of Scripture. He established a strict Protestant government in Geneva to enforce Church discipline. His ideas spread to the Netherlands, Scotland, England and New England.

p. 409. *Zwingle*: Ulrich Zwingli (1484–1531), Swiss Protestant reformer who rejected papal authority, clerical celibacy and fasting. For him, the Bible was the only trusted measure of faith.

p. 409. *Aerius*: founder of a fourth-century heretical sect who became jealous when his friend Eustathius was elected Bishop of Sebaste south of Neocaesarea instead of himself around 355. He began publishing grave charges against the new bishop whom he accused of deserting the ascetic life and of amassing riches. Very soon the rupture with Eustathius widened into a rupture with the Church itself. Not only were he and his followers refused admission to all churches, there were denied access to towns and villages. Aerius claimed that bishops and clergy had equal status; denounced the observance of Easter as a relic of Jewish superstition; regarded prayers for the deceased as useless and pernicious; and condemned appointed days of fasting. According to Newman, Aerius anticipated many of the principles enunciated by the Protestant Churches in the sixteenth century.

p. 409. *judaical*: of Jewish origin.

p. 410. *Siricius*: Bishop of Rome (384–99) was steeped in Roman law and referred to himself as the 'heir' of St. Peter in the knowledge that, legally, the title of heir carried with it the full legal force of his predecessors. He was the first pope to issue statements written like imperial edicts carrying the force of law. He presided over a synod around 393 that excommunicated Jovinian for insisting that the Mary lost her virginity when she gave birth to Jesus.

p. 410. *cæteris paribus*: 'all things being equal'.

p. 410. *Simon Magus*: practising sorcerer in Samaria who was baptised by Philip the Deacon. When he saw that many individuals received the Holy Spirit after the imposition of the hands of Peter and John, he offered to buy the power off them, for which Peter severely rebuked him – hence the word 'simony' (Acts 8: 15–24). A tradition surrounding Simon Magus was that he was one of the founders of the Gnostic movement.

p. 410. *Honorius*: succeeded his father, Theodosius I (*c.* 346–95) as emperor of the west (395–423) at the age of twelve while Arcadius, his elder brother, became emperor of the east (395–408).

p. 410. *Dalmatia*: region stretching along the eastern shore of the Adriatic Sea from Croatia in the north to Montenegro in the south and bounded by Bosnia and Herzegovina in the east. Paul the Apostle sent his disciple Titus to Dalmatia (2 Timothy 4: 10), where he established the first Christian see in the city of Salona (modern Split). He was martyred around the year 65.

p. 410. *Vigilantius*: presbyter from south-west Gaul whose negative ideas on ascetic practices became the target of one of Jerome's his most vitriolic attacks in 406. Vigilantius denigrated the growing cult of martyrs and relics, the value of prayers to martyrs, the value of the monastic life and celibacy.

p. 411. *faith and justification*: see note to p. 163 (*C.F.*).

p. 411. *John Wesley*: (1703–91), Anglican Evangelical, founder of the Methodist movement and fellow of Lincoln College, Oxford, where he formed a group of like-minded students which became known as the 'Holy Club' and its members as 'Methodists'. Wesley remained loyal to the Church of England all his life and encouraged his followers to do the same. However, because of increasing pressure, he ordained one of his assistants for work in the USA. It was a practice which he later continued. He maintained that Methodism was a movement within Anglicism.

pp. 411–412. *John Newton*: (1725–1807), captain of a vessel in the African slave trade for about six years; was influenced by the teaching of John Wesley and Thomas à Kempis. He became curate of Olney in Buckinghamshire where he struck up a lifelong friendship with the Evangelical poet, William Cowper (1731–1800). The result was the celebrated *Olney Hymns* produced in 1779. Newton wrote hundreds of hymns, including 'Amazing Grace', one of the most popular in the repertoire.

p. 412. *that faith was trust*: Luther's teaching on 'justification by faith alone' emphasises the element of trust (*fiducia*) in the atoning work of Jesus Christ. According to Newman, it is a belief, 'not only that Christ has died for the sins of the world, but that He has died specially for the individual so believing, and a sense of confident trust in consequence, a claiming as one's own, with full persuasion of its efficacy, what he has done and suffered for all' (*Lectures on the Doctrine of Justification*, p. 8).

p. 412. *Episcopalian*: one who belongs to a Church governed by bishops ('episcopi') such as the Anglican Church, the Episcopal Church in Scotland and the Protestant Episcopalian Church in the USA.

p. 413. *Praxeas*: early proponent of Patripassianism around 200; according to Tertullian, Praxeas taught that it was God the Father who 'was born', that God the Father 'suffered' and that we preach God the Father as 'Jesus Christ'. In doing so, he 'put to flight the Paraclete, and crucified the Father' (Tertullian, *Against Praxeas*, Chapter 1–2). Even popes like Victor I (189–98), Zephyrinus (198–217) and Callistus (217–22) were sympathetic to his ideas.

p. 413. *Noetus*: one of the earliest proponents of Patripassianism which taught that it was the God the Father and not Jesus Christ, who was born, suffered and died. He was condemned by an assembly of presbyters at Smyrna (north of Ephesus in Asia Minor) around 200, was expelled, died soon after and denied a Christian burial.

p. 413. *Sabellius*: see note to p. 383 (*P.C.*).

p. 413. *Catholic or Athanasian doctrine of the Holy Trinity*: reference to the Athanasian creed; a profession of faith used in the western Church, also known as the 'Quicunque Vult' ('Whosoever will be saved'); originally attributed to Athanasius; one of three creeds accepted by Anglicans and Roman Catholics; so called because it embodied the teachings of Athanasius.

Chapter V: And What Do The Apostolic Canons Say?

Synopsis: According to Newman, anyone in search of primitive Protestantism would be hard put to draw a dividing line between an early period of doctrinal purity and a later period of doctrinal corruption so as to put what the Apostles taught on one side and what Church Fathers taught on the other. There is no hard evidence to assume that the Church had once taught a Gospel substantially different from, for example, what is contained in the Apostolical Canons of the Ante-Nicene Church, that is, before the year 325. These Canons were well known to the early Church. In fact, it is a well-documented fact that certain rules and regulations had existed from very early times. Of the eighty-five Apostolical Canons, there is in fact not a single one mentioned in the writings of the Church Fathers which does not belong to this collection. They were constantly alluded to and quoted from many of the synods prior to the Council of Nicaea. They possess genuine ecclesiastical authority and contain no hint or indication of Protestantism.

p. 417. *Apostolical Canons*: collection of ancient rules which, according to tradition, was written by the apostles as guidelines for the day-to-day running of the early Church and entrusted to Clement of Rome who committed them to writing in the first century. One reason for their universal acceptance was that something like them seems to have existed from the dawn of the Church. The first fifty canons are generally attributed to the apostles and the remaining thirty-five to the Ante-Nicene Church. In the main, they deal with the duties and conduct of the clergy while other focus on the duties and conduct of the laity. They represent the earliest canon law of the Church. Their real value and antiquity are still disputed. The Calvinist scholar, Jean Daillé (1594–1670), dated them as no earlier than the fifth century, while some seventeenth-century Anglican divines like William Beveridge and John Pearson maintained that they must have been compiled no later than the end of the second or the beginning of the third century.

p. 417. *heterodoxy*: unorthodox doctrines and opinions.

p. 417. *movement of 1517*: in 1517, Martin Luther (1483–1546) nailed his Ninety-five Theses to the church door at Wittenberg in Germany, thus triggering off the Protestant Reformation throughout Europe. In 1520, Leo X issued a papal bull ('Exsurge Domine') condemning forty-one of his theses, banned his writings and threatened to excommunicate him if he did not recant within sixty days. Luther's reply was to burn the bull together with several Catholic books. He was excommunicated on 3 January 1521.

p. 418. *inosculations*: opening into one another; intimate union.

p. 418. "*when they rose in the morning . . . dead upon the sea-shore*": Exodus 14: 26–31.

p. 418. "*out of the serpent's mouth*": Apocalypse 12: 15.

p. 418. "*lay in the streets of the great city*": Apocalypse 11: 8

p. 418. *ministerial commission:* priesthood.

p. 420. *baptism is not an enlightening*: reference to the Evangelical doctrine about baptismal regeneration, that is, that an individual is regenerated, justified or enlightened through the sacrament of baptism. Influenced by Luther and Calvin, Evangelicals did not subscribe to it. Nor did Newman as an Anglican Evangelical. At the time – around 1824 – he thought that proving it was the real 'burning' theological issue of the day (BOA A.7.1.). An Oxford colleague, Edward Hawkins, took him to task for the severity of his first sermon and its implied rejection of baptismal regeneration. He was critical of Newman's arbitrary division of Christians into converted and unconverted, saved and lost souls. No such dividing line existed and no one, including Newman, had the right to draw one. People may not be as good as they could be, but they were certainly better than they might be. This reminder of Hawkins was the beginning of the end of Newman's attachment to Evangelicalism and its rejection of baptismal regeneration.

p. 420. *the Church was corrupt from 'very' early times indeed*: even Newman's brother, Francis, was convinced that the real apostolical tradition was well and truly corrupt within fifty years of the apostles. That included all the earliest creeds. According to Francis, fourth-century Chrysostom was every inch as bad as, if not worse than the Doctor Wisemans of the nineteenth century (29 April 1840, *L.D.* VII, p. 319). It was in reply to his brother's remarks that Newman first drew up his first defence of doctrinal development which later grew into his celebrated *Essay on the Development of Christian Doctrine* in 1845.

p. 421. *before* AD *50*: that is, before the Council of Jerusalem held by the apostles in AD 49–50 to decide, among other things, whether or not Gentile converts to Christianity must conform with all the prescriptions of the Mosaic law (Acts 15; Galatians 2: 2–10). It was eventually decided in the negative.

p. 421. *Our own divines:* 'our own theologians'; reference to a group of seventeenth-century Anglican theologians which included William Beveridge (1637–1708), Bishop of St. Asaph; John Pearson, Bishop of Chester (1613–86); Richard Hooker (*c.* 1554–1600); John Bramhall (1594–1663), Archbishop of Armagh; and Lancelot Andrewes, Bishop of Winchester (1555–1626); see *Apo.*, pp. 93–4.

p. 421. *before* AD *325*: that is, before the Council of Nicaea.

p. 422. *Bishop Beveridge*: William Beveridge (1637–1708), Anglican divine and Bishop of St. Asaph who published a definitive collection of the *Apostolical Canons* in 1672. In his opinion, some were drawn up by the apostles themselves, while others belong to the second and third centuries. Although High Church, he favoured Calvin's doctrine of predestination – a doctrine which Newman himself temporarily espoused as a young Anglican Evangelical but later rejected (*Apo.*, p.6).

p. 422n. *Pearson*: John Pearson (1613–86), Anglican divine, Lady Margaret Professor of Divinity from 1661, Master of Trinity College, Cambridge, from 1662 and Bishop of Chester from 1673. Among other things, he argued for the authenticity of the Epistles of Ignatius of Antioch (*c.* 35–*c.* 107). His *Exposition of the Creed* (1659) reflects his intimate knowledge of the early Church.

p. 422. *fifteenth chapter of the Acts:* the Council of Jerusalem (*c.* AD 50) whose principal outcome was that Gentile converts to Christianity were not required to conform to all the prescriptions of the Mosaic law, including circumcision (Acts 15; Galatians 2: 2–10).

p. 424. *The Thirty-nine*: the Thirty-nine Articles are the foundation documents of the Church of England; they are a set of doctrinal formulae which defines its position. It is a summary of belief, first issued in 1563. Each article deals with some point raised in current controversies and sets out the Anglican view in broad terms, avoiding narrow definition. An act of Parliament in 1571 ordered all clergy to subscribe to them. The aim was to exclude Roman Catholics and Anabaptists, but not to provide a dogmatic framework of faith like the Nicene Creed. Many of the articles are ambiguously expressed. Articles 1 to 5 focus on such areas as the Trinity; articles 6 to 8 focus on Scripture and the three creeds; articles 9–18 focus on justification, good works and predestination; articles 19 to 36 focus on Church, authority, tradition and the sacraments; and articles 37 to 39 focus on the duties of civil magistrates, almsgiving and the making and breaking of oaths.

p.424. *'the Canon' admits into holy orders*: for example, Canon 1 from the Council of Nicaea (325) states: 'If any one in sickness has been subjected by physicians to a surgical operation, or if he has been castrated by barbarians, let him remain among the clergy; but, if any one in sound health has castrated himself, it behoves that such an one, if [already] enrolled among the clergy, should cease [from his ministry], and that from henceforth no such person should be promoted. But, as it is evident that this is said of those who willfully do the thing and presume to castrate themselves, so if any have been made eunuchs by barbarians, or by their masters, and should otherwise be found worthy, such men the Canon admits to the clergy'.

p. 424. *Antioch*: (341), non-ecumenical Council of Antioch assembled for the dedication of Constantine the Great's Golden Church at Antioch in Syria; the first of several fourth-century councils that tried to modify the Nicene formula with a watered-down version. It was attended by the Arian emperor Constantius II together with about a hundred eastern bishops, most of whom were hostile to Athanasius. About twenty-five disciplinary canons came from this council, but some scholars believe they may have been the product of an earlier council held at Antioch around 330.

p. 424. *Gangra*: (*c.* 343), non-ecumenical Council of Gangra, north-east of Ancyra in Paphlagonia convened with the aim of condemning Eustathius of Sebaste (south of Neocaesarea) for his opposition to Christian marriages and for his exaggerated asceticism. The council introduced more than twenty canons defending the legitimacy of Christian marriage.

p. 424. *Carthage*: reference to several non-ecumenical councils held in Carthage between about 345 and 419 from which one of the earliest collection of canons of the north African Church, including some on celibacy and virginity, have survived.

p. 424. *Alexander:* Bishop of Alexandria (312–28); see note to p. 29 (*C.F.*).

p. 424. *Athanasius*: Bishop of Alexandria (328–73); see note to p. 3 (*C.F.*).

p. 424. *Basil*: Bishop of Caesarea (370–79); see note to p. 3 (*C.F.*).

p. 424. *Julius*: Bishop of Rome (337–52); see note to p. 351 (*T.C.*).

p. 424. *Hampton Court*: Hampton Court Palace located in the upper reaches of the Thames river above Richmond; originally begun by Cardinal Wolsey in 1514 as his private residence, but after his fall from power in 1530 it was confiscated by Henry VIII (1509–47), used as his royal residence and remained so until the time of George II (1727–60). William III (1694–1702) commissioned Christopher Wren (1632–1723) to redesign it. It has been open to the public since 1838, and many of its rooms are now occupied by royal pensioners.

p. 424. *Hampton Court Conference*: convened in 1604 and presided over by James I (1603–25) for the purpose of updating reforms for the Established Church for which Puritan clerics had been petitioning. The King brushed aside their suggestions and declared that the traditional ceremonies would continue; that there would be no provision made for a preaching ministry; and that the existing church order would continue unchanged. The only changes, which did not meet with Puritan approval, were to be made to the Book of Common Prayer. By far, the greatest outcome of the conference was the authorisation of a new translation of the Bible which became known as the King James Version (the Authorised Version). It was published in 1611.

p. 425. *Convocation*: technically referred to as the 'Convocation of the English Clergy', the equivalent in some ways to provincial synods in the early Church. Each ecclesiastical province of Canterbury and York has a Convocation, but the Canterbury gathering is of more importance. Collectively, they have the power to create or modify canon law for the Church of England. Their history and development runs parallel to the development of English constitutional history; its powers and independence, however, were lost at the Reformation; its organisation, retained as a mere form for many years, has been utilised in recent years to give expression to the opinions entertained by the clergy as a body upon questions of the day. Its development can be divided into five stages: (1) before 1295, when it met in diocesan and provincial synods to discuss Church matters; (2) from 1295 until the Reformation when it became a representative body of beneficed clergy ordered to attend Parliament; (3) the

Reformation period when it lost its independence and most of its powers by Henry VIII's Act of Submission (1532) which stipulated that it could meet only by royal command, and that no new canons, constitutions, or ordinances could be enacted without royal permission; (4) The post-Reformation period when it virtually ceased as a deliberative body until 1861; (5) since 1861, when Convocation once more began to act as a deliberative body. In 1969, it was replaced by a general Synod of the Church of England, consisting of bishops, clergy and laity.

p. 426. *exceptio probat regulam:* 'the exception proves the rule'; attributed to Lucius Junius Moderatus Columella, first-century Roman soldier and writer on agriculture; his *De Re Rustica* (12 volumes) covered many facets of country life, including gardening, olive groves, vineyards and animal husbandry.

p. 426. *simoniacal*: describing transactions by which ecclesiastical preferments are bought and sold; from Simon Magus, Acts 8: 15–24.

p. 426. *Gregory*: not to be confused with Gregory of Nazianzus who would have been about ten years old; in the winter of 339, a pro-Arian synod of bishops was held at Antioch and appointed a certain Gregory to replace Athanasius as Bishop of Alexandria, a native of Cappadocia. This particular Gregory studied at Alexandria where Athanasius had treated him with great kindness, though he later helped spread the rumour that Athanasius had murdered Arsenius, Bishop of Hypsela in Upper (southern) Egypt. 'While we were holding,' wrote Athanasius, 'our assemblies in peace, as usual, and while the people were rejoicing in them, and advancing in godly conversation, and while our fellow-ministers in Egypt, and the Thebais, and Libya, were in love and peace both with one another and with us; on a sudden the Prefect of Egypt puts forth a public letter, bearing the form of an edict, and declaring that one Gregory from Cappadocia was coming to be my successor from the court. This announcement confounded every one, for such a proceeding was entirely novel, and now heard of for the first time' (Athanasius, *Encyclical Letter to the Bishops throughout the World*, Part 2).

p. 426. *Arsenius*: the same Arsenius whom Athanasius was accused of murdering (Sozomen, *Ecclesiastical History*, Book II, Chapter XXIII).

p. 426. *Hypsela*: Upper (southern) Egypt.

p. 426, 1n. *The Egyptian Meletius*: fourth-century schismatic Bishop of Lycoplis (near Thebes, east-central region on the Nile) who adopted a hard-line approach to admitting those who had lapsed (apostatised) during the Diocletian persecution (284–305). Because he ordained bishops and clergy for communities abandoned by pastors during the persecution, he was excommunicated and exiled around 306 by Peter, Bishop of Alexandria, who fled to avoid arrest and whom Meletius accused of abandoning his flock. After Peter's martyrdom, Meletius formed his own schismatic Church; see note to p. 121 (*C.F.*).

p. 426, 1n. *Meletius of Antioch*: see note to p. 16 (*C.F.*).

p. 427. "'*The Canon' altogether excludes ... have been twice married.*": 'He who has been twice married after baptism, or who has had a concubine, cannot become a bishop, presbyter, or deacon, or any other of the sacerdotal list' (Canon XVII).

p. 427. "*violation of the Apostolical Canon*": 'If any presbyter or deacon has been excommunicated by a bishop, he may not be received into communion again by any other than by him who excommunicated him, unless it happen that the bishop who excommunicated him be dead' (Canon XXXII).

p. 427. *Eusebius declined being translated ... from the see of Caesarea to Antioch*: 'A bishop is not to be allowed to leave his own parish, and pass over into another, although he may be pressed by many to do so, unless there be some proper cause constraining him, as if he can confer some greater benefit upon the persons of that place in the word of godliness. And this must be done not of his own accord, but by the judgment of many bishops, and at their earnest exhortation' (Canon XIV).

p. 427. *Council of Constantinople,* AD *394*: local synod convened by Nectarius, patriarch of Constantinople, to decide that the deposition of a bishop must henceforth be made by three bishops and not two as originally stipulated by Canon LXXIV.

p. 427. *Gregory Nyssen*: see note to p. 18 (*C.F.*).

p. 427. *Amphilochius*: (*c.* 340–*c.* 395), orthodox Bishop of Iconium, southwest of Nazianzus in Lycaonia from 373; friend of Basil the Great.

p. 427. *Flavian:* orthodox Bishop of Antioch in Syria (381–404).

p. 428. *Virgil's Æneid*: Publius Vergilius Maro (70–19 BC) was born near Mantua in northern Italy, son of a farmer who became one of the most celebrated writers of the early empire. His epic poem, the *Aeneid*, is about the origins of Rome based on Aeneas' flight from Troy following its destruction, and his eventual triumph over his arch-enemy Turnus and the armies of Italy. One of Virgil's aims was to portray the Roman ideals of honour and duty dear to the heart of every Roman citizen.

p. 428. *rhapsodies*: portions of an epic poem adapted for recitation.

p. 430. *Beveridge's*: see note to p. 422 (*C.F.*).

p. 430. *Pearson's*: see note to p. 422 (*C.F.*).

p. 430. *Ussher's*: James Ussher (1581–1656), Archbishop of Armagh, scholar and historian.

p. 430. *Dionysius Exiguus*: Denis the Little, theologian, mathematician, astronomer and monk from the Roman region of the Balkans. He lived in Rome from 500 to 545, compiling papal letters and council records for canon law. His corpus of canon law was the first to gain wide acceptance and formed the foundation of canon law in the Middle Ages. At the head of his collection, he placed the fifty Apostolical Canons which he translated from Greek into Latin around 500. Other items included canons from the Councils of Nicaea (325), Gangra (*c.* 345), Antioch (341) Constantinople (381) and Chalcedon (451). In drawing up a calendar to settle once and for all the date of Easter, he was the first to calculate the Christian era from the birth of Christ, but he made a four–seven year miscalculation. His system is still in use today and is the origin of the terms BC and AD.

p. 430. *John of Antioch*: John III Scholasticus, patriarch of Constantinople (565–77), and author of an important collection of ecclesiastical laws. Though not the first in circulation, his was the first systematic attempt as opposed to merely chronological attempts. In this regard, John's collection was a watershed in the history of canon law.

p. 430. *Emperor Justinian*: (482–565), gifted orthodox Byzantine (eastern) emperor (527–65) who, during his long reign, reclaimed large regions of the western empire from its German conquerors. His codification of Roman law (the *Corpus Juris Civilis*) became one of the foundations of canon law in the west and his greatest accomplishment. It provided stability and unity to a centralised empire and shaped subsequent legal history.

p. 430. *Stephen*: Bishop of Salona (Split in Croatia) who encouraged Dionysius Exiguus to publish his collection of Canons and to whom the preface to them is addressed.

p. 431. *apostolic 'depositum'*: in the original article for the *British Magazine*, Newman preferred to use the phrase 'apostolic revelation' (*British Magazine*, 'Letters on the Church of the Fathers', No. XIX, Volume XI, April 1837, p. 404; included in the 1840 and subsequent editions but altered in the 1868 edition).

p. 434. *of their being found in one compilation*: in the original article for the *British Magazine*, Newman added the following remark: 'On this subject I may quote the decided remark of the dispassionate Mosheim: – : "*The matter of the work is ancient*; for it comprises the customs and rules of the Christians, especially Greek and oriental, in the second and third century; that the form of it is of a later date, divines are mostly agreed.' He [Mosheim] adds, in a note, that the former part of this judgment has been "put beyond all controversy by Bishop Beveridge, a man especially versed in Christian antiquities." (*Ant. Constant. Saes.* i. § 51.)' – (*British Magazine*, 'Letters on the Church of the Fathers', No. XX, Volume XI, May 1837, p. 518; included in the 1840 and subsequent editions but altered in the 1868 edition). The full details of the Mosheim book Newman is referring to are *De Rebus Christianorum ante Constantinum Magnum Commentarii*, part one, section 51, pp. 158–9, Helmstadt 1753. Newman noted on the inside cover of his own copy of *De Rebus Christianorum* that it was from 'the Library of the Rev Hugh James Rose', editor of the *British Magazine*.

p. 435. *composed in uniform style*: typical of the uniform style is, for example, Canon V which states: 'Let not a bishop, presbyter, or deacon, put away his wife under pretence of religion; but if he put her away, let him be excommunicated; and if he persists, let him be deposed'. Again, Canon VI states: 'Let not a bishop, presbyter, or deacon, undertake worldly business; otherwise let him be deposed'.

p. 437. *Cornelius*: Bishop of Rome (251–53) who favored readmitting those who had lapsed (apostatised) during the Decian persecution (249–51) while Novatian, the rival pope, believed that they were eternally damned. The emperor Gallus (251–53) had Cornelius thrown into prison where he died.

p. 437. *Justin Martyr*: (d. *c.* 165), Christian Apologist and martyr who first introduced Newman to the concept of the 'logos spermatikos', that is, the concept that God (the divine Logos) had implanted seeds of divine truth into every age, race, culture and individual from time immemorial. As Newman himself expressed it: 'It would seem, then, that there is something true and divinely revealed, in every religion all over the earth ' (*Ari.*, p. 80).

p. 438, 1n. *Ignatian Epistles in the Author's Essays*: in the second last paragraph of an essay entitled 'Seven Epistles of St. Ignatius', Newman writes: 'Give us, then, but St. Ignatius, and we want nothing more to prove the substantial truth of the Catholic system; the proof of the genuineness and authenticity of the Bible is not stronger; he who rejects the one, ought in consistency to reject the other' (*Ess.* I, p. 261, originally written in 1839).

p. 440. *the following facts about Primitive Christianity*: instead of listing twenty-two separate canons as he did later in *Historical Sketches*, Newman was content with the following observation in his original essay for the *British Magazine*: 'Now, then, let us see what these observances are *on which* the canons build their system, and we shall have some insight into what were considered apostolical at the time these canons were framed ... they take for granted the principle of ministerial superintendence, and the principle of ministerial succession, and consider them both vested in one and the same individual functionary. They take for granted that ordination is necessary, and that it is given by imposition of hands. They presuppose the three orders of bishops, priests, and deacons. They take for granted the one baptism for the remission of sins. They assume that there is an altar and a sacrifice in the visible church under the gospel, and that by "the Lord's appointment." They take for granted the rite of holy communion. They take for granted the practice of excommunication. They speak of heretics, or sectarians, as existing, yet as being in a state of serious disadvantage; they use concerning them the same (what is now called) fierce and contemptuous language which occurs in later centuries. They take for granted a local and diocesan episcopacy. They take for granted an order of precedence among the bishops of each nation. They take for granted that councils are composed of bishops. They take for granted that married men may be clergy – nay, may be bishops. They recognise the observances of celibacy and fasting. They recognise the fast of the great sabbath, or Easter eve, and of Lent, and of Wednesday and Friday. They imply the observance of Easter; they imply the existence of festival days. They recognise the use of churches; and of wax, and of oil, gold and silver vessels, and linen, in the worship, and these as consecrated. They speak of demoniacal possession and exorcism' (*British Magazine*, 'Letters on the Church of the Fathers', No. XXI, Volume XIII, February 1838, pp. 151–2; included in the 1840, 1842 and 1857 editions but modified and re-edited for the uniform edition).

p. 442. *Wesleyans*: members of a Nonconformist Church which started as an Evangelical movement within the Church of England by John Wesley (1703–91) and his brother Charles (1707–88), co-founders of Methodism. There was no break with Anglicanism until after John's death.

p. 442. *Society of Friends*: founded by George Fox (1624–91), former shoemaker from Nottingham who toured the countryside preaching and arguing that consecrated buildings and ordained ministers were irrelevant to individuals seeking God. Initially, Fox formed a group called the 'Friends of Truth' which later became known as the 'Society of Friends' which later became known as 'Quakers'. His principal teaching was that of an inner light, communicated on an individual basis by Jesus Christ. In 1656, Fox and his followers refused to attend Anglican services or pay tithes which resulted in his arrest and trial at which the judge directed Fox 'to quake in the presence of the lord' – hence the name 'Quakers'.

p. 442. *Scotch Kirk*: Presbyterian Church in Scotland, established after 1560 when the reformed church was established as a protest against Mary Queen of Scots (1542–87), then against Charles I (1600–49) after 1637; 'kirk' is the Scottish word for 'church'.

p. 442. *'Record' and 'Patriot'*: the *Record* was a thrice-weekly Evangelical broadsheet which first appeared on 11 January 1828, and for which Newman wrote a series of long letters on 'Church Reform' to get it off the ground (*Apo*. p. 42). The *Patriot* was a Nonconformist broadsheet.

p. 442. *his fourths of October*: 4 October 1835 marked the 300th anniversary of the publication in Zurich of the first complete English Bible ever printed and translated by Miles Coverdale (*c*. 1488–1568), and dedicated to Henry VIII. Coverdale was a former Augustinian friar at Cambridge where he was converted to Protestantism. To escape persecution, he lived abroad from 1528 to 1534. In 1540, he once again fled to the Continent after the fall of his patron Thomas Cromwell (*c*. 1485–1540). He returned home in 1548 and was made Bishop of Exeter in 1551. On the accession of Mary Tudor to the throne in 1553, he was deprived of his see and forced to flee to the Continent a third time. Returning to England the following year, he refused to return to Exeter (see *L.D.* V, p. 147n).

p. 443. *On this subject . . . from a friend:* fellow Oratorian at the Birmingham Oratory, Ambrose St. John (1815–75); see *L.D.* XXVI, pp. 175–6.

p. 443. *Church of St. Ambrogio*: built around 386 by Ambrose and dedicated to Saints Gervasius and Protasius whose relics rest in a crypt below the main altar. The original church has been added to and modified over several generations. In the ninth century, an elaborate altar of gold, silver, jewels and enamel, was built by Volvinus, a master goldsmith. The south bell tower was constructed in the ninth century, and the north tower was added in the twelfth century.

p. 443. *medici*: doctors.

p. 443. *Father Secchi*: a Jesuit.

p. 443. *scurolo*: darkened chamber for prayer and meditation.

p. 443. *corretti*: private cells for prayer and meditation.

p. 444. '*pomum Adami*': Adam's apple.

p. 444. *Archbishop Angelbert*: Archbishop of Milan from 824 to around 860.

p. 445. *Ughelli, Ital. Sacr.*: Ferdinand Ughelli, *Italia Sacra sive de Episcopis Italiae et Insularum adjacentium* . . ., 10 volumes, Venice 1717–22.

p. 445. *golden altar*: the paliotto or high altar was built over a thousand years ago by a master goldsmith named 'Wolvinus' who signed his work and called himself 'Master Phaber' or 'Mister Smith'. The front panel is made entirely of gold, except for the top and bottom mouldings which are made of silver and studded with jewels and enamel. It is divided into three panels which are further divided into smaller ones. The middle panel depicts Jesus surrounded by the twelve apostles. The side panels depict twelve scenes from the life of Christ, including the Annunciation, the Presentation in the Temple, the Crucifixion and the Resurrection. Below the altar is a crypt where the bodies of Ambrose, Gervasius and Protasius repose.

p. 445. *Castellionaeus in his Antiquities of Milan* . . .: J. A. Castellionaeus, 'Mediolanenses Antiquitates ex Urbis Parcoeciis Collectae . . .' in J. G. Graevius, *Thesaurus Antiquitatum et Historiarum*, Vol. III, Leyden 1724, p. i.

p. 445. *Church of St. Lawrence*: one of the churches visited by Newman while en route to Rome in 1846. At 'St. Lawrence's', he wrote back home to Henry Wilberforce, ' we saw the people take off their hats from the other side of the street as they passed along; no one to guard it, but perhaps an old woman who sits at work before the Church door, or has some wares to sell' (*Ward* I, p. 139).

p. 446. *Puricelli's Ambros. Basil. . . . Antiq. Ital. t. 4. part I.*: J. P. Puricelli, 'Ambrosianae Mediolani, Basilicae . . . Descriptio' in J. G. Graevius, *Thesaurus Antiquitatum et Historiarum*, P. Burmann (ed.), Leyden 1722, Vol. IV, p. i.

p. 446. *Paulinus*: a deacon of the Church of Milan, also Ambrose's biographer (see note to p. 371. *P.C.*).

APPENDIX 1

MAPS

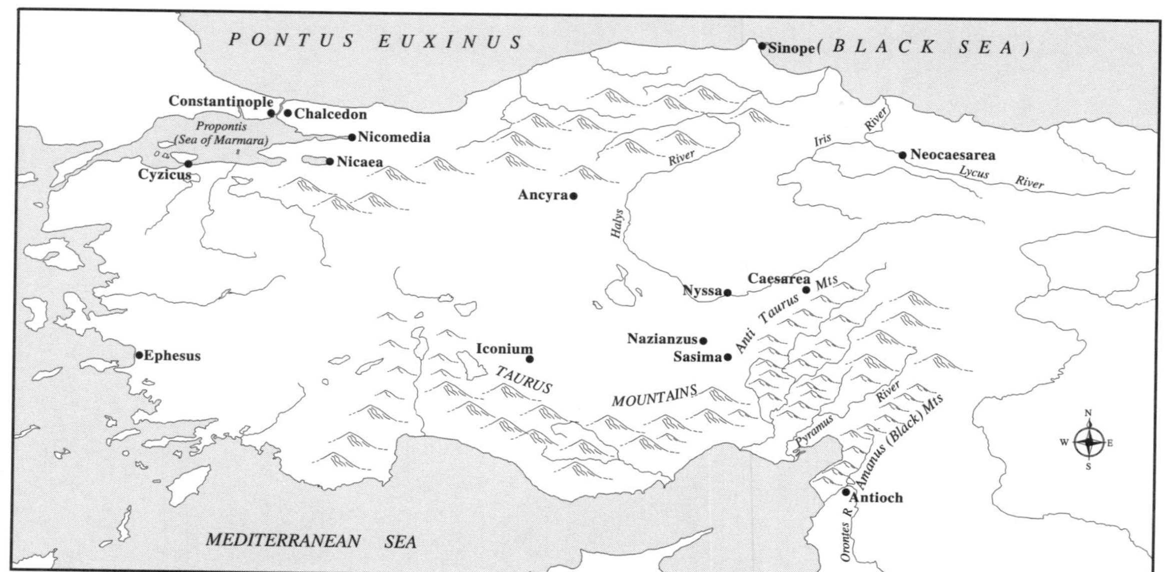

Map 1. Asia Minor: 400 A.D.

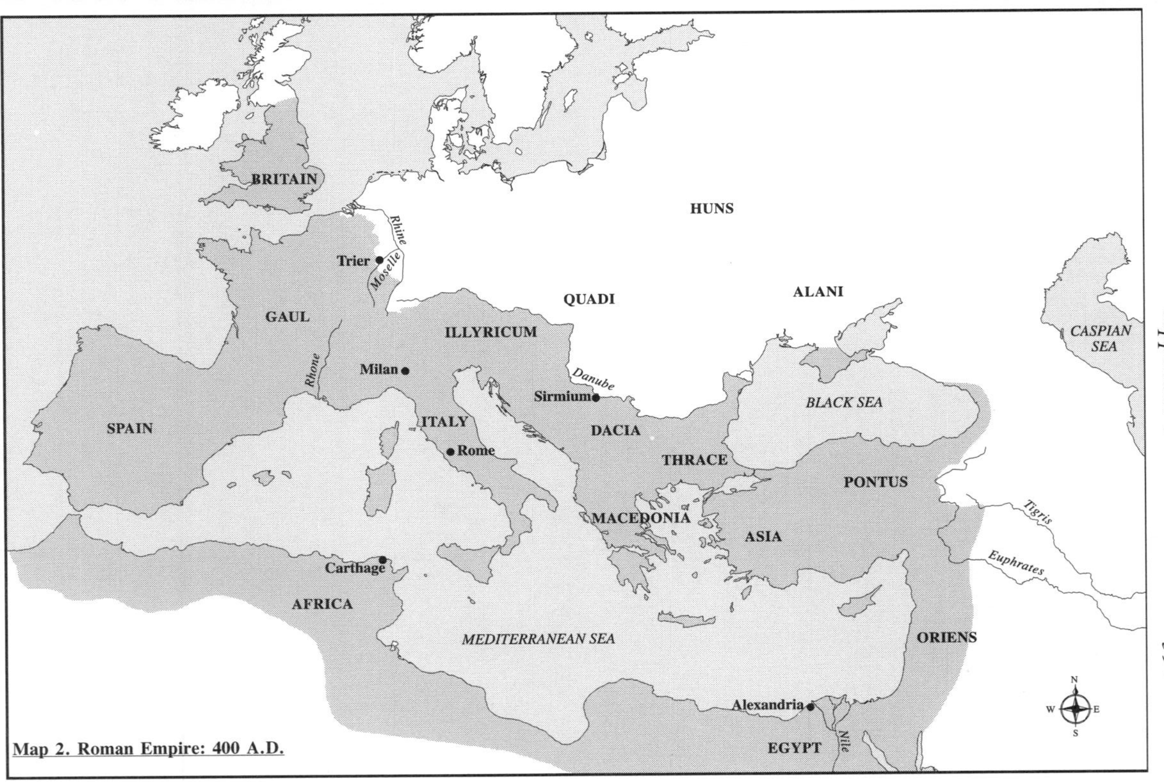

Map 2. Roman Empire: 400 A.D.

APPENDIX 2

ADVERTISEMENT
TO THE FIRST AND SECOND EDITIONS: 1840, 1842[1]

The following sketches, which, with two or three exceptions, have appeared in the *British Magazine*, during 1833 and the following years, do not, as the author is very conscious, warrant a title of such high pretension as that which was there prefixed to them, and is here preserved. But that title will at least show the object with which they were written, viz. to illustrate, as far as they go, the tone and modes of thought, the habits and manners of the early times of the Church.

The author is aware how much a work is open to imperfection, and therefore to criticism, which is made up, in so great a measure as this is, of minute historical details and of translations; nor would he subject himself either to the one or the other, did he not think that the chance of bringing out or recommending one or two of the characteristics of primitive Christianity was the worth the risk of mistakes, which, after all, would but affect himself, and not his readers.

As to the translations, he is very sensible what constant and unflagging attention is requisite in all translation to catch the sense of the original, and what discrimination in the choice of English to do justice to it; and what certainty there is of shortcomings, after all. And further, over and above actual faults, variety of tastes and fluctuation of moods among readers, make it impossible so to translate as to please everyone; and, if a translator be conscious to himself, as he may well be, of viewing either his original or his version differently, according to the season or the feeling in which he takes it up, and finds that he never shall have done with correcting and altering except by an act of self-control, the more easy will it be for him to resign himself to such differences of judgment about his work as he experiences in others.

---

[1] With a few literary corrections.

It should be considered, too, that translation in itself is, after all, but a problem; how, two languages being given, the nearest approximation may be made in the second to the expression of ideas already conveyed through the medium of the first. The problem almost starts with the assumption that something must be sacrificed; and the chief question is, what is the least sacrifice? In a balance of difficulties, one translator will aim at being critically correct, and will become obscure, cumbrous, and foreign; another will aim at being English, and will appear deficient in scholarship. While grammatical particles are followed out, the spirit evaporates; and, while an easy flow of language is secured, new ideas are intruded, or the point of the original is lost, or the drift of the context broken.

Under these circumstances, perhaps, it is fair to lay down that, while every care must be taken against the introduction of new, or the omission of existing ideas in the original text, yet, in a book intended for general reading, faithfulness may be considered simply to consist in expressing in English, the *sense* of the original; the actual words of the latter being viewed mainly as *directions into* its sense, and scholarship being necessary in order to gain the full insight into that sense which they afford; and next, that, where something must be sacrificed, precision or intelligibility, it is better in a popular work to be understood by those who are not critics, than to be applauded by those who are.

In the translations made in this present volume this principle has been moreover taken to justify the omission of passages, and now and then the condensation of sentences, when the extract otherwise would have been too long; a studious endeavour being all along made to preserve the sense from injury.

February 21, 1840.

ADVERTISEMENT
TO THE THIRD EDITION: 1857

The volume here presented to the reader contains some of the earlier compositions of what is called the Oxford or Tractarian, School. They are portions of a Series, which appeared in the *British Magazine* of 1833 and the following years; and they are here reprinted from the Edition of 1842, with such trivial alterations as were rendered necessary by the circumstances under which they were written.

No alterations, however, many or few, can obliterate the polemical character of a work directed originally against Protestant ideas. And this consideration must plead for certain peculiarities which it exhibits, such as its freedom in dealing with saintly persons, the gratuitous character of some of its assertions, and the liberality of many of its concessions. It must be recollected, that, in controversy, a writer grants all that he can afford to grant, and avails himself of all that he can get granted: – in other words, if he seems to admit, it is mainly "for argument's sake;" and if he seems to assert, it is mainly as an "*argumentum ad hominem.*" As to positive statements of his own, he commits himself to as few as he can; just as a soldier on campaign takes no more baggage than is enough, and considers the conveniences of home life as only *impedimenta* in his march.

This being kept in view, it follows that, if the author of this volume allows the appearance of infirmity or error in St. Basil or St. Gregory or St. Martin, he allows it because he can afford to say "*transeat*" to allegations, which, even though they were ever so well founded, would not at all interfere with the heroic sanctity of their lives or the doctrinal authority of their words. And if he can bear to hear St. Antony called an enthusiast without protesting, it is because that hypothesis does not even tend to destroy the force of the argument against the religion of Protestants, which is suggested by the contrast existing between their spirit and his.

Nor is this the sole consideration, on which an author may be justified in the use of frankness, after the manner of Scripture, in speaking of the Saints; for their lingering imperfections surely make us love them more, without leading us to reverence them less, and act as a relief to the discouragement and despondency which may come over those, who, in the midst of much error and sin, are striving to imitate them;— according to the saying of St. Gregory on a graver occasion, "Plus nobis Thomæ ad fidem, quam fides credentium profuit."

And in like manner, the dissatisfaction of Saints, of St. Basil, or again of our own St. Thomas, with the contemporary policy or conduct of the Holy See, while it is no justification of ordinary men, bishops, clergy, or laity, in feeling the same, is no reflection either on those Saints or on the Vicar of Christ. Nor is his infallibility in dogmatic decisions compromised by any personal and temporary error into which he may have fallen, in his estimate, whether of a heretic such as the Pelagius, or of a Doctor of the Church such as Basil. Accidents of this nature are unavoidable in the state of being which we are allotted here below.

As to the translations which this volume contains the author is very sensible, &c. &c. (*as in first and second editions*).

Ladyday, 1857.

ADVERTISEMENT
TO THE FOURTH EDITION: 1868

In the Advertisement to the third Edition of this work, it was implied, that in that Edition, as was the case, portions only were reprinted of the series of Sketches contained in the first and second; but it was not stated what the omissions were, and why they were made. This may now be done at no great expense of words.

Omission then was made of the Chapters on St. Ambrose, on Vincent of Lerins, on Jovinian and his Companions, and on the Canons of the Apostles. Of these the Chapters on St. Ambrose were withdrawn by the author with the hope of rewriting them at some future day with care and pains less unworthy of the great Saint commemorated in them, and because one of them had already been rewritten in his Essay on Ecclesiastical Miracles. The Chapter on the celebrated Treatise of Vincentius had been superseded by the extracts made from that Treatise in one of the Oxford Tracts (*Records of the Church*), and by the Oxford Edition of the whole work. And the Chapters on Jovinian and the rest, and on the Apostolical Canons, though those on the latter subject were carefully done, were rejected on account of their controversial and antiquarian character, which made them uninteresting to the general reader.

It should be added, that besides these omissions, the two Chapters on St. Martin were abridged and brought into one.

March 19, 1868.

APPENDIX 3

CHRONOLOGICAL TABLE: 1840 EDITION

The dates are, for the most part, according to Tillemont.

	A.D.
St. Gervasius and St. Protasius, martyrs under Nero, p. 33	64
St. Hermas writes, p. 316	92
St. Clement of Rome writes, p. 324	97
St. Ignatius, martyr under Trajan, pp. 23. 324	107
St. Justin converted, pp. 324. 339	132
Flight of St. Polycarp from persecution, p. 210	166
Montanus, heretic, pp. 184. 283	171
St. Irenæus, bishop of Lyons, p. 324	177
St. Clement of Alexandria, p. 316	192
Praxeas, heretic at Rome, p. 291	201
Origen, pp. 180. 200. 283; begins to teach	203
Tertullian, pp. 283. 324; turns Montanist, p. 184	about 204
——— writes his treatise against flight in persecution, p. 213	about 211
Noetus, heretic at Ephesus, p. 291	220
Flight of St. Cyprian, St. Gregory, and St. Dionysius, in the Decian persecution, pp. 97. 210, 211. 344	250
St. Antony born, pp. 239. 344. Novatian, schismatic, pp. 149. 283	251
St. Cornelius, bishop of Rome, martyred, p. 324	252
Manichæus, heretic, p. 200	255
Sabellius, heretic, in Africa, p. 291	257
St. Laurence martyred, p. 23	258
Dionysius, bishop of Rome, p. 106	260
St. Antony adopts the solitary life, p. 345	270
St. Antony retires into the desert, p. 349	285
Lactantius, p. 316	303
Nabor and Felix, martyrs at Milan, pp. 32. 39. St. Macrina and her husband in the woods at Pontus, in the Dioclesian persecution, p. 74	304

St. Antony begins to have disciples, p. 368 305
Melitian schism in Egypt, p. 309 306
St. Antony comes to Alexandria to assist the persecuted, p. 378 311
St. Alexander, bishop of Alexandria, p. 305 312
Myrocles, bishop of Milan, p. 19 314
Eusebius, bishop of Cæsarea, p. 285 .... about 315
St. Martin, born in Pannonia, p. 386 316
Arius, driven from Egypt, is received in Palestine, p. 310 319
The forty martyrs of Sebaste in the Licinian persecution, p. 125 320
The first General Council at Nicæa; Arius condemned 325
St. Athanasius, pp. 6. 25. 56. 103. 239. 305; made bishop
of Alexandria 326
St. Gregory and St. Basil born, pp. 87. 117.
Gregory, the Father, made bishop of Nazianzus, p. 117 329
St. Martin enlisted in the army, p. 387 331
Eusebius of Cæsarea declines the see of Antioch, p. 310 332
Apollinaris teaches rhetoric. p. 199 335
St. Martin leaves the army, p. 387 336
St. Julius, pope, p. 305 337
Eusebius of Nicomedia usurps the see of Constantinople, p. 148 338
Eustorgius, bishop of Milan, p. 19 .... about 339
St. Macrina, grandmother to St. Basil, dies, pp. 81. 101.
Council of Gangra, p. 305.
St. Ambrose born in Gaul, p. 5 .... about 340
Gregory of Cappadocia made Arian bishop of Alexandria, p. 309.
Council of Antioch, pp. 305. 321.
Macedonius usurps the see of Constantinople, p. 148 341
St. Cyril delivers his Catechetical Lectures, p. 286.
St. Chrysostom born, p. 344 .... about 347
Flavian's chants at Antioch, p. 23 348
Basil, St. Basil's father dies, p. 74.
St. Emmelia and St Macrina retire from the world, p. 74.
Apollinaris put out of the Church by the Arians, p. 200 349
St. Basil and St Gregory at Athens, p. 118.
St Martin goes to St. Hilary, p. 387.
St. Paul of Constantinople martyred by the Arians, p. 148 350
St. Augustine born, p. 344.
Eustathius bishop of Sebaste, p. 77 354
St. Antony supports St. Athanasius, p. 59.
St. Dionysius of Milan banished, p. 19.
Auxentius, Arian bishop of Milan, pp. 5, 6.
St. Basil leaves Athens, p. 120 355
St. Gregory leave Athens, p. 120.
St Antony dies, pp 58. 344.

St. Martin retires to Milan, p. 388.
St. Hilary of Poictiers banished to the East. p. 388.
St. Basil teaches rhetoric at Cæsarea, p. 124; writes to Apollinaris, p. 205; retires from the world, pp. 58. 124.
Eunomius, the Arian, pp. 59. 85. 149. 176. 200 356

Naucratius, St Basil's brother, drowned, p. 74.
St. Basil goes into the East, pp. 79. 101. 124.
Remains of St. Luke brought to Constantinople, p. 297.
St. Athanasius writes his defence of his flight, p. 211 357

St. Basil retires into Pontus; his chants, pp. 23. 130. 133. 135............ 358

Council of Ariminum, pp. 57. 118.. 359

St. Martin establishes his monastery at Poictiers, p. 388.
Eudoxius usurps the see of Constantinople, p. 148.
St. Basil separates from Dianius, p. 57.
The monks of Nazianzus separate from St. Gregory's father, p. 118 360

St. Gregory ordained priest, pp. 141. 152.
St. Basil returns to Cæsarea, and is ordained priest, p. 58.
Council of Alexandria, p. 200.
Macedonius, heresiarch, pp. 99. 102. 148. 149. 176. 200............ 362

Athanasius of Ancyra conforms, p. 93.
Julian shuts up the Christian schools, pp. 199. 238.
St. Basil, ill-treated by his bishop Eusebius, retires into Pontus, p. 58. 363

St. Athanasius writes the life of St. Antony, pp. 239. 342.
St Gregory reconciles the monks of Nazianzus to his father, pp. 118. 140.. 364

Aerius, heretic, p. 287 .... about 365

Damasus made pope, p. 105.
St. Gregory reconciles St. Basil with his bishop, pp. 62. 135........ 366

St. Epiphanius, pp. 203. 293. 284, bishop of Salamis.
Beginning of the persecution under Valens, p. 91........................ 367

Cæsarius dies.
St. Basil assists St. Gregory in securing his property, p. 135.
Syrian council against the Apollinarians, p. 200 369

Eudoxius, the Arian bishop of Constantinople, dies, p. 148.
Eighty Catholic clergy burnt at sea, pp. 148. 155.
St. Basil raised to the see of Caesarea, pp. 62. 136 370

St. Basil writes to St. Athanasius, p. 103; he resists Valens and Modestus, p. 63, &c; slandered by a monk of Nazianzus, p. 137.
Patricius, Augustine's father, dies a Christian, p. 244.................... 371

St. Martin elected bishop of Tours, p. 389.
St. Gregory, bishop of Nyssa, p. 74.

St. Basil persecuted by the governor of Pontus, p. 69.
Dispute between St. Basil and Anthimus, p. 139.
St. Gregory made bishop of Sasima, p. 141;
complains of St. Basil, p. 143 372

St. Augustine becomes a Manichee, p. 226.
St. Basil falls ill, p. 69;
designs to send St. Gregory Nyssa to Rome, p. 109.
Athanasius dies, [al. A.D. 371,] p. 202 373

Gregory the Father dies, p. 147.
Amphilochius, pp. 68. 71, made bishop of Iconium, pp. 313, 310.
Probus makes St. Ambrose prefect of Liguria, p. 256.
St. Ambrose made bishop of Milan, p. 5.
Marcellus accused of Sabellianism, pp. 110, 200; dies 374

Valentinian I. dies, p. 7.
St. Basil goes into Pisidia and Pontus. p. 72;
enters a protest against Eustathius. p. 78;
complains of Damasus, p. 109 375

Demophilus, Arian bishop of Constantinople, p. 149.
St. Augustine teaches rhetoric at Carthage, p. 231.
Epiphanius engaged on his work on heresies, pp. 203. 289 376

St. Meletius and St. Eusebius, pp. 69. 92, in ill esteem at Rome.
St. Basil writes to St. Ambrose, p. 7.
Apollinaris, heretic, pp. 149. 58. 176; condemned at Rome, p. 203 377

Death of St. Basil, pp. 87. 147, 148.
Accession of Theodosius, pp. 147, 148.
St. Gregory goes to Constantinople, *ib.*
Priscillian begins his heresy, pp. 176. 191 379

Theodosius declares for the Church, p. 147.
St. Eusebius of Samosata killed by an Arian woman.
St. Peter, bishop of Sebaste, p. 74 380

Priscillian made bishop of Avila, p. 405.
Second general Council held at Constantinople, p. 7;
first session, pp. 203. 305.
St. Meletius, president; then St. Gregory, p. 147.
Flavian succeeds St. Melitius at Antioch, p. 311 381

St. Gregory retires to Asia, p. 150;
pronounces oration in praise of St. Basil, p. 145;
passes Lent without speaking, p. 158 382

Maximus assumes the purple; Gratian killed, pp. 7. 29. 401.
St. Ambrose goes on embassy to Maximus, p. 29.
Augustine goes to Rome, pp. 226. 231 383

St. Martin at Treves, is courted by Maximus and his empress, p. 401.
Persecution of St. Ambrose by Justina, p. 4, &c.

St. Augustine goes to Milan, pp. 226. 231.
Council of Bordeaux, p. 406.
Priscillian, heretic, executed, p. 408 384
Second persecution of St. Ambrose by Valentinian II, p. 17.
Maximus defends him, p. 29.
Discovery of the remains of St. Gervasius and St. Protasius, p. 33.
St. Martin's second visit to Treves;
communicates with the Ithacians, p. 409, &c.
St. Augustine converted, p. 240, &c. 386
St. Augustine baptized by St. Ambrose, p. 245.
St. Monica dies, p. 244 387
St. Augustine settles at Thagaste, p. 245 388
St. Gregory Nazianzen dies, p. 147.
Ithacius deposed and banished, p. 408.
St. Augustine ordained priest at Hippo, p. 246 389
Persians come to Milan to see St. Ambrose, p. 256.
Council of Milan against the Ithacians, pp. 47. 408.
Sedition at Thessalonica, p. 44.
Theodosius's penitence, p. 51.
Jovinian, heretic, p. 176; condemned at Rome, p. 288 390
Valentinian II. strangled by Arbogastes, p. 44.
St. Sulpicius Severus introduced to St. Martin, p. 386 392
Council of Constantinople, p. 310. 315 394
Theodosius dies, and Arcadius is emperor, p. 297.
St. Augustine consecrated co-adjutor to Valerius, p. 248 395
St. Sulpicius writes the life of St. Martin, p. 386 396
Council of Carthage, p. 305.
St. Martin dies, p. 397.
St. Ambrose dies 397
St. Ambrose writes his Confessions, pp. 24, 25, 35, 228, &c.
Chrysostom, bishop of Constantinople; his chants, p. 23.
Council of Turin, p. 408.
St. Marcellina, sister to St. Ambrose, dies, p. 5 398
Abbey of Lerins founded, p. 174 401
St. Chrysostom in persecution, p. 257 403
St. Chrysostom in exile. Vigilantius heretic, p. 288 404
St. Sulpicius writes his dialogues, pp. 391, 399, &c.
Pelagius, p. 176, commences his heresy 405
Remains of the prophet Samuel brought from Palestine to Constantinople, p. 297.
St. Jerome writes against Vigilantius, p. 296 406
Rome taken by Alaric, August 24, p. 256 410
St. Augustine writes to Proba, p. 257 411
Paulinus writes the life of St. Ambrose, p. 34 .... about 412

Demetrias devotes herself to religion, p. 263 413
St. Jerome writes to Demetrias, p. 264.
Pelagius writes to Demetrias, p. 272 414
St. Augustine and St. Alypius write to Juliana, p. 273.
Pope Zozimus deceived by Pelagius, *ib*....................................... 417
St. Sulpicius deceived by the Pelagians, p. 413.
Leo an Acolyte, and sent to Carthage 418
St. Jerome dies, p. 263 420
The Semi-Pelagians, vid. p. 277 427
Nestorius, p. 176, made bishop of Constantinople.
The Vandals cross to Africa, p. 209.
St. Augustine writes to Honoratus, p. 216 428
Treatise of unknown author addressed to Demetrias, p. 277.
The Vandals besiege Hippo, p. 222.
Death of St. Augustine, p. 224 430
Third General Council held at Ephesus, pp. 210. 316 431
Vincent of Lerins. p. 174, writes his Commonitorium....................... 434
St. Leo, p. 171. 277, elected pope.. 440
Fourth General Council held at Chalcedon, p. 316 451
Sack of Rome by Genseric, p. 277 455
Demetrias builds the church of St. Stephen, p. 278................. about 456
Gelasius, pope, p. 315 .... about 491
Justinian, emperor, p. 313 527
Dionysius Exiguus, p. 313 533
John of Antioch, Scholasticus, p. 313 564

APPENDIX 4

TEXTUAL VARIANTS

The following list contains a selection only of textual variants contained in the 1840 and 1868 editions of *The Church of the Fathers* as well as contained in the 1859–60 issues of the *Rambler*. Because of space and quantity, minor variations of terms, capitalising, punctuating and spelling have been omitted altogether. The codes denoting each are as follows:

* *The Church of the Fathers* (1840 edition)
** *The Church of the Fathers* (1868 edition)

Chapter I: Trials of Basil

p. 3. 1–5. CHAPTER 1. TRIALS OF BASIL. ... numbered unto me."] * CHAPTER V. BASIL THE GREAT. "Be not afraid of their words, nor be dismayed at their looks, though they be a rebellious house. And thou shalt speak my words unto them, whether they will hear or whether they will forbear; for they are most rebellious." ** CHAPTER I. BASIL THE GREAT. "And thou, O Son of Man, fear them not, neither be thou afraid of their speeches, whereas unbelievers and destroyers are with thee, and thou dwellest with scorpions. Fear not their words, neither be thou dismayed at their looks, for they are a provoking house."

p. 3.6–4.8. As Athanasius was the great champion ... to A.D. 379.] * As Athanasius was the great champion of catholic truth, during the incursions of Arianism upon it, so were Basil and Ambrose, in the East and in the West, the chief instruments in the hands of Providence for repairing and strengthening the bulwarks of the Church, when the fury of the inroad was over. Both had to contend with an Arian sovereign; and both gained their victory by the same means, their popularity with the laity and the vigour of their discipline. From Milan, which had been in heretical possession for twenty years, "round about unto Illyricum," Ambrose preached in the west the gospel of Christ. Basil, whose cares extended from Illyricum down to Egypt, was called to a still more arduous post. These countries had from the first been over-run by the Arians, and were, by the middle of the fourth century, in a deplorable state of religious ignorance. Asia Minor was the especial scene of Basil's labours, first as priest, then as bishop of the church of Cæsarea and Exarch of Cappadocia, from A.D. 358 to A.D. 379.

p. 4. 31. faith of the Church.] * faith of Nicæa.

p. 5. 29. in that day of apostasy, . . . shall see God.] * in that hour of apostasy, by these ascetics, and for which we who now live have reason to be grateful to them.

p. 9. 14–26. he came to Cæsarea.. . . Gregory has preserved] * he came to Cæsarea. There he called before him the prefect Modestus, as he had done in the other cities, and bade him propose to Basil the alternative of communicating with the Arians, or losing his see. Modestus conveyed his pleasure to the bishop, and set before him the arguments which had been already found successful with the inferior sort of men, that it was foolish to resist the times, and to trouble the Church about questions of inconsiderable importance; and he promised him the prince's favour for him and his friends, if he complied. Failing by soft language, he adopted a higher tone. Gregory has preserved

p. 11. 15–21. and heard his sermon. . . . but none of the ministers] * and heard his sermon. Afterwards followed the ceremony of bringing oblations to the altar, in commemoration of the offerings of the Magi. Valens is said to have been much affected by the chants which accompanied the service, and the order which reigned through the congregation, and almost to have fainted away. At length he made an effort to approach the holy table to offer the oblation; but none of the ministers

pp. 11. 23–25. he was kept from falling. . . .It would be a satisfaction] * he was kept from falling. It cannot be too much insisted on that the Church gains the respect of the great, not by courting them, but by treating them as her children. It would be a satisfaction

p. 11. 28–31. the favourable supposition. . . .in great measure,] * the favourable supposition. Yet it was not once only that he trembled before the majestic presence of the exarch of Cæsarea, who ensured for his own provinces an immunity, in great measure, of the sufferings with which the Catholics elsewhere were visited, and so far exerted an influence over him, as to gain some of the best of the imperial lands in the neighbourhood, for the endowment of an hospital which he founded for lepers. ** the favourable supposition. Yet it was not once only that he trembled before the majestic presence of the exarch of Cæsarea. Miracles and supernatural favours are said to have been displayed. Modestus became the saint's friend; Cappadocia was secured, in great measure,

p. 12. 3–5. throughout his province. . . . of the fourth century] * CHAPTER VI. TRIALS OF BASIL. "As a servant earnestly desireth the shadow, and as an hireling looketh for the reward of his work, so am I made to possess months of vanity, and wearisome nights are appointed to me."

On various occasions, before his episcopate, Basil had shown his care for the poor and afflicted. His sale of his lands to alleviate the miseries of a famine, has already been mentioned: he raised funds for erecting and endowing a hospital, near Cæsarea, principally for lepers, whom he treated with a studious familiarity in order to remove the horror at their persons which their malady commonly excited. The buildings also contained accommodation for travellers, and were so extensive as to go by the name of the "New Town." Institutions, such as these, have been ever felt as especially characteristic of Christianity, and St. Basil seems to have succeeded in introducing them throughout his province.

If personal suffering be the providential means of sympathising in the sufferings of others, Basil had abundant opportunities of learning this Christian grace. From his multiplied trials he may be called the Jeremiah or Job of the fourth century, ** CHAPTER II. TRIALS OF BASIL

p. 13. 6–10. or rather sickly. . . . A widow of rank] * or rather unhealthy. What his principal malady was, is told us in the following passage of his history, which sets before us another kind of trial, of which we have already had before us one specimen. – A widow of rank

p. 24. 13–23. Basil did offend, . . . "How." he asks, "shall we attain] * Basil did offend, by behaviour which is specified by a modern historian as the great specimen of his pride. Gregory certainly did not so feel it afterwards, though Gibbon thereupon calls Basil a "haughty prelate," as elsewhere for his resistance to Modestus he reproaches him with "inflexible pride." Indeed, Basil's doctrinal views on the subject of pride have even approved themselves to the fastidious judgment of Protestant controversialists, who, in their warfare with Rome, have often alleged with great satisfaction a passage which it will not be out of place here to quote.

"This is the perfect and absolute glorying in God," says Basil, "when a man is not elated by his own righteousness, but knows himself to be wanting in true righteousness, and justified by faith alone, which is in Christ. And Paul glories in despising his own righteousness and seeking that which is through Christ, a 'righteousness which is of God unto faith, in order that he may know Him, and the power of His resurrection, and the fellowship of His sufferings, being brought into the form of His death, if by any means he may attain unto the resurrection from the dead.' Here is cast down all height of haughtiness; nothing is left to thee for boasting, O man, whose glorying and hope lies in mortifying all that is thine, and living the life to come, which is in Christ; of which we, as having the first fruits, already pursue, living wholly in the grace and gift of God. And God it is 'who worketh in us to will and to do of His good pleasure.' That Pharisee, intrusive and extreme in pride, who not only was confident in himself, but even scoffed at the publican in God's presence, lost the glory of justification for the cause of his pride. Such, too, was the fall of the Israelites; for being elated against the Gentiles, as unclean, they became really unclean, and the Gentiles were cleansed. And the righteous of the one became as a filthy rag: while the iniquity and the ungodliness of the Gentiles was wiped out through faith.

"How, then, shall we attain

Chapter II: Labours of Basil

p. 28. 1–5. CHAPTER II. LABOURS OF BASIL. ... work with my God."] * CHAPTER VII. LABOURS OF BASIL. "Then I said, I have laboured in vain; I have spent my strength for nought, and in vain: yet surely my judgment is with the Lord, and my work with my God." ** CHAPTER III. LABOURS OF BASIL.

p. 28. 16–21. as well as boldness and zeal. ... the majestic Ambrose;] * as boldness and zeal. Such have been many churchmen, in ages whether of more or less religious error. Such seems to have been the intrepid and single-minded Hildebrand, whose misfortune it was (as they tell us who have studied his times) to have to choose between an existing corrupt theology, and the entire abandonment of religion. Such, in a purer age, was the majestic Ambrose;

p. 29. 13–14. and all the sweetness of purity ... Such an one] * and all the sweetness of pureness and integrity. Unlike the first-mentioned weapon of God's designs, such an one

p. 29. 31–34. over the false creed was secured. ... No comparison is,] * the false doctrine was secured. And such, too, we may account the bold and munificent Laud, who was more than forty years old before he quitted Oxford: firm, energetic, unfortunate in his generation, but in the event "the second founder," as one has called him, "of the English Church." No comparison is,

p. 31. 18. by Rome] * by the Latins

p. 36. 3–16. his traditions of Christian truth. . . . other causes unknown.] * his principal traditions of Christian truth. A secret attachment to Sabellian doctrine in the leading persons in the Church seems to have been one chief cause of the opposition shown him; but there were other causes unknown.

p. 45. 8–11. *Ep.* 215.. . . to his friend Eusebius:–] * *Ep.* 215. This is not complimentary to Damasus. In another letter, he says to his friend Eusebius:–

Chapter III: Basil and Gregory

p. 50. 1–4. CHAPTER III. BASIL AND GREGORY. . . . and are sad?"] * CHAPTER VIII. BASIL AND GREGORY. "What manner of communications are these that ye have one to another, as ye walk and are sad?" ** CHAPTER IV. BASIL AND GREGORY. "What are those discourses that you hold one to another, as you walk and are sad?"

p. 50. 15–16. by a divine gift;] * by a divine leading;

p. 52. 6–7. This was about AD 350,] * This was about AD 351,

p. 52. 7–8. twenty-one years of age.] * twenty-two years of age.

p. 62. 23–26. the founder of the monastic . . . had increased the reasons for asceticism,] * the founder of the monastic, that is, the coenobitic discipline in Pontus, a discipline to which the Church gave her sanction as soon as the conversion of the temporal power, by bestowing upon her prosperity for persecution, had increased the reasons for asceticism,

p. 63. 39–64. 3. out of the soul." . . . "Pious exercises nourish the soul] * out of the soul. Let there, then, be a place such as ours, separate from intercourse with men, that the tenour of our exercises be not interrupted from without. Pious exercises nourish the soul

p. 66. 9–12. Basil, on this occasion, . . . as well as at Athens.] * Basil, on this occasion, gained him the interest of the Prefect of Constantinople, and another, whose influence was great at court.

Chapter IV: Rise and Fall of Gregory

p. 75. 1–6. CHAPTER IV. RISE AND FALL OF GREGORY.. . . and not for truth."] * CHAPTER IX. RISE AND FALL OF GREGORY. "O, that I had in the wilderness a lodgingplace of wayfaring men, that I might leave my people and go from them; for they be all adulterers, an assembly of treacherous men." ★★ CHAPTER V. RISE AND FALL OF GREGORY "Who will give me in the wilderness a lodging-place of way-faring men, and I will leave my people and depart from them. Because they are all adulterers, an assembly of transgressors; and they have bent their tongue, as a bow, for lies, and not for truth."

pp. 75. 23–76. 4. into they tabernacles!" – *Orat* 43.... Basil's death found him.] ★ into they tabernacles!" – *Ep*. 20. The English Church has removed such addresses from her services, on account of the abuses to which they have led; and she pointedly condemns what she calls, the Romish doctrine concerning Invocation of Saints, as "a fond thing:" however Gregory, not knowing what would come after his day, thus expressed the yearnings of his heart, and, as we may almost suppose, at the time he thus made them public, had already received an answer to them. He delivered the above-mentioned discourse on his return to Cæsarea from Constantinople, three years after Basil's death; an eventful three years, in which he had been quite a different man from what he was before, though it was all now past and over, and about to be succeeded by a return to the retirement in which Basil's death found him.

p. 78. 17–19. were subjected to ... had embarked.] ★ were subjected to a sentence severer even than our celebrated *præmuniré*, being burned at sea in the ship in which they were embarked.

p. 79. 2–5. whose heretical sentiments ... my fore-going pages.] ★ whose heretical sentiments have been, or will be hereafter, alluded to.

p. 80. 14–17. Their ethical character ... before or after.] ★ Their energy of existence, moral character, talents, acquirements, seems concentrated upon a crisis, and is invisible and silent in the world's annals, both before and after.

p. 83. 22. plain] ★ notorious

p. 84. 25–35. parade and rustle in silk, ... a modern vestry in order.] ★ parade and rustle in silk, and hold forth and lay down the law, and be what is thought dignified and grand; whereas they had no one but "poor, dear, good Gregory," a monk of Nazianzus, a personage, who, in spite of his acknowledged eloquence, was but a child, had no knowledge of the world, no manners, no conversation, and no address; who was flurried and put out in high society, and who would have been singularly ill-adapted to keep a modern vestry in order.

p. 85. 10. though I be parsimonious."] ⋆ though in my narrow circumstances." ⋆⋆ and that by being poor."

p. 88. 14–15. These lines may . . . to the following:–] ⋆ The foregoing lines may have an allusion which introduces us to the following, which are on a subject to which I have already invited the reader's attention, and shall again.

p. 88. 16. As viewing sin, . . . its faintest trace] ⋆ [footnote] Fertur S. Basilii districta sententia. Et mulierem, inquit, ignoro, et virgo non sum. In tantum intellexit incorruptionem carnis non tam in mulieris esse abstinentiâ, quàm in integritate cordis. – *Cassian. Instit.* vi. 19.

p. 92. 11–16. the above rude and free translation . . . I end with] ⋆ the above rude and very free translation, as indeed are all the foregoing; nor is it to the purpose to set forth at length before the reader of the present day a formal defence and recommendation of celibacy, though there is no reason why Gregory should not have his own opinion about it as well as another. I end with

p. 93. 6. And thus I take leave of St. Gregory,] ⋆⋆ And now on taking leave of Gregory, who by his triumphs over Arianism has earned the title of "the Theologian" (which has been given before him to the Evangelist St. John), I am prompted to make him, if he will accept it, a little tribute of affection, unworthy of him, but in his own line. Poets create versifiers, and patrons are best approached in verse. So, as I wish to be his humble client, I beg to be allowed, after joining him at Constantinople, to attend on him and take his blessing in his solitude at Arianzus, in the following lines; and, if my tone in them is of too historico-critical a character to be in keeping with the reverence due to a canonized Saint, all I can say is, that Gregory is dear to me because he is a man, and that, according to my thinking, as I venture in familiarity, I advance in devotion.

GREGORIUS THEOLOGUS.

Peace-loving man, of humble heart and true!
    What dost thou here?
Fierce is the city's crowd; the lordly few
    Are dull of ear.
Sore pain it was to thee, – till thou didst quit
Thy patriarch-throne at length, as though for power unfit.

So works the All-wise, our services dividing
    Not as we ask;
For the world's profit, by our gifts deciding
    Our duty-task.
See in king's courts loth Jeremias plead,
And slow-tongued Moses rule by eloquence of deed.

Yea! thou, bright Angel of the East, didst rear
    The cross divine,
Borne high upon thy liquid accents, where
    Men mocked the sign;
Till that cold city heard thy battle-cry,
And hearts were stirred, and deemed a Pentecost was nigh.

Thou couldst a people raise, but couldst not rule: –
    So, gentle one,
Heaven set thee free, – for, ere thy years were full,
    Thy work was done;
According thee the lot thou lovedst best,
To muse upon the past, – to serve, yet be at rest.

Chapter V: Antony in Conflict

p. 94. 1–5. CHAPTER V. ANTONY IN CONFLICT. ... apple of His eye."] * CHAPTER XVIII. ANTONY IN CONFLICT. "He found him in a desert land, and in the waste howling wilderness; He led him about, He instructed him, He kept him as the apple of His eye. He made him ride on the high places of the earth, that he might eat the increase of the fields; and He made him to suck honey out of the rock, and oil out of the flinty rock." ** CHAPTER VII. ANTONY IN CONFLICT. "He found him in a desert land, in a place of horror and of wilderness; He led him about, and taught him; and He kept him as the apple of His eye; that he might suck honey out of the rock, and oil out of the hard stone."

p. 95. 23. to extravagance,] * to schism,

pp. 95. 29–96. 1. Catholicism does not oppress ... in its decisions,] * true catholicism does not, with the schools of Rome, place us within a strict and rigid creed, extending to the very minutest details of thought, so that a man can never have an opinion of his own; yet, while its creed is short and simple, and it is cautious and gentle in its decisions,

p. 96.4–5. the divine mission of the Church;] * the duty of deference to the Church;

p. 96. 10. "*sensible* Protestants."] * "*sensible* Protestants," as much as that of Romanists.

p. 96. 29–97. 3. the first monk ... Christ sent His Apostles] * the first hermit, whom I had occasion to notice in a former chapter. A hermit's life, indeed – that is, a strictly monastic or solitary life – may be called unnatural, and is not sanctioned by the Gospel. Christ sent His apostles

p. 97. 26. such zeal for it] * our devotion to it

p. 98. 4–6. and had he lived ... Longing for] * had he lived in this day and this country, he would have been exposed to a considerable (though, of course, not insuperable) temptation to become a sectarian. Panting after

p. 98. 13–19. The question is not,... with ardent feelings,] * The question is not whether he would have been justified in so doing; (of course not;) not whether the most angelic temper of all is not that which settles down content with what is every-day (as Abraham's heavenly guests eat of the calf which he had dressed, and as our Saviour went down to Nazareth, and was subject to His parents;) but whether such resignation to worldly comforts is not quite as often at least, the characteristic of a very grovelling mind also, – whether there are not minds between the lowest and the highest, of ardent feelings,

p. 98. 23. the Protestant Establishment] * our established system

p. 98. 28. to dissent,] * to schism,

p. 98. 29. is weakened by the loss.] * is weakened by the loss. For instance, had we some regular missionary Seminary, such an institution would in one way supply the deficiency I speak of.

pp. 98. 30–99. 3. I might be tempted ... if it must be so called.] * I might be tempted to consider him somewhat of an enthusiast; but what I desire to point out to the reader is the subdued and Christian form which his enthusiasm took;

p. 100. 12–13. of some women, ... the single state.] * of some trustworthy female acquaintance, who had devoted themselves to a single life.

p. 101. 31–32. of what Protestants would...of the time,] * of what we should call the enthusiasm of the time,

p. 101. 35. by the high and dry system of the Establishment;] * by the influences of sectarianism;

pp. 101. 37–102. 2. by that monastic system ... methodism and dissent,] * by that Monastic system which, with us, is supplied by methodism and dissent.

p. 107. 26–29. Add to these, ... the evil spirit.] * Add to these, Dan. vii. 3, 4, about the four beasts; Isa. xiii. 21, 22, about satyrs or jackals; and Job xli., about the leviathan, which they interpreted of the evil spirit.

p. 108. 1–2. the prince of the air.] * the prince of the power of the air. ** the prince of this air.

p. 108. 3–5. the family of brute animals, ... Surely there is nothing] * the family of brute animals, the real intelligence of which, if they have no souls, is a supernatural something which makes use of their outward forms as its organs and instruments. If, on the other hand, they have souls, it is natural to attribute to them a moral nature, and a place, however subordinate, in the great conflict which is going on between good and evil. As to the exact connexion between the visible and invisible, the when, where, how, and how far, this it is doubtless idle to attempt to settle; but surely there is nothing

p. 108.14–16. Thus a philosophical view of nature ... same times adopted.] * Here, then, a philosophical view of nature would be considered, in primitive times, to corroborate the method of Scripture interpretation then adopted.

pp. 109. 26–27. On the whole, then, ... I found a narrative,] * On the whole, then, the ancients seem to have considered all that is seen as but a type or instrument of what is unseen, as external indications, to us practically influential, of the Supernatural. This will explain what seems, at first sight, credulity and superstition in many great men. It is objected to them that they *mistook* what is natural for what is above nature; and it is condescendingly observed that, had they lived when "science" had made the advances which it has effected in these enlightened days, such men would not have been exposed to such errors. But, in truth, their theory, whether right or wrong, runs much deeper than we sciolists dream; for they take the *whole of nature*, not certain detached parts of it, to be something supernatural; and the critics in question do not advance one inch towards removing them from their position, by showing a certain *connexion* and *order* between various parts of nature which before seemed unconnected, and by using that connexion for certain present and temporal purposes.

The plain [sic: plane] astronomer speaks as if the sun went round the earth, the physical philosopher as if the earth went round the sun; this may be viewed as a question of practical convenience, the assumption of a theory or fiction necessary as an artifice for arriving at certain practical ends. On the other hand, it does not make the fire from heaven on Sodom less Divine because it came from a volcano; nor, in like manner, need a comet or eclipse be less a sign of tumult and change because it proceeds upon a certain physical law. It is another matter whether it *is* such a sign, – that is a question of *fact*; and to us mortals, who have a difficulty in arriving at facts, it may be a matter of greater or less probability, and of a probability which may be affected by the circumstance of the phenomenon harmonizing or not with the established order of things; but it is one which modern "discoveries" (as they are called) do not, and cannot settle. And, in like manner, since evil spirits are known before now to have entered into brute animals, it is a question of probabilities whether they do now, – whether certain passages in Scripture which seem to assert it, are, or are not, to be understood literally; and supposing I found a narrative,

p. 109. 29. narratives of Scripture] * Scripture doctrine

p. 110. 8–10. in your philosophy."... a very deep subject.] * in your philosophy." What I have been saying comes to this, that there are a number of phenomena in the world, tokens of good and evil, which we may or may not, according as we please, refer to the presence and agency of invisible beings, – such as the course of nature, the accidents of life, the bearing upon us of brute animals, the phantoms which occur in dreams, the influences of the imagination, and the like. If we lived in an age of miracles, the (in that case) acknowledged presence of a supernatural power would lead us, doubtless, to refer many things to it, and reasonably, which otherwise we should have left as we found them; and in proportion as we come near in time or place to miraculous agency, in the same proportion will this persuasion affect us. When, then, we read of Antony's sensible contests with the powers of evil, the abstract probability of these is to be decided by the existence, in his day, of such parallel *facts* as demoniacal possessions, which certainly *are* witnessed unanimously by his contemporaries; and the really superhuman character of what seem like natural occurrences is to be estimated, not by the mere circumstance that they may be brought under natural laws, as demoniacal possessions also may be by the physician, but by the known actual presence of unseen agents to which they may be referred. Antony's conflict in the tombs may be solved into a dream, or into an attack from jackals; yet this only removes the real agent a step further back. Satan may still have been the real agent at the bottom, and have been discerned by Antony through the shadow of things sensible.

I have no wish to trifle or argue subtilly. We are upon a very deep subject.

p. 110. 15–19. extraordinary powers in heathen lands... and the like.] ⋆ extraordinary powers there, whether through or beyond the order of nature. A venerable bishop, who had had to do with heathen lands, once told the writer of these pages, that he did not at all doubt, from his own experience, that Satan had power in them which he has not with us. Certainly there are strange stories among them of sorcerers and the like.

p. 111. 1. material forms,] ⋆ natural objects,

p. 111. 2. imagination,] ⋆ fancy,

Chapter VI: Antony in Calm

p. 112. 1–5. CHAPTER VI. ANTONY IN CALM. ... springs of water."] ⋆ CHAPTER XIX. ANTONY IN CALM. "The wilderness and the solitary place shall be glad for them, and the desert shall rejoice and blossom as the rose, and the parched ground shall become a pool, and the thirsty land springs of water; in the habitations of dragons where each bog shall be grass with reeds and rushes." ⋆⋆ CHAPTER VIII. ANTONY IN CALM. "The land that was desolate and impassible shall be glad, and the wilderness shall rejoice and shall flourish like the lily. And that which was dry land shall become a pool, and the thirsty land springs of water: in the dens where dragons dwelt before, shall rise up the verdure of the reed and the bulrush."

p. 112. 13–18. to manifest Itself. ... of the Revelation.] ⋆ to manifest Itself. I am not denying that there were then in the Church extraordinary and heavenly gifts; but, whatever they were, they were distinct from those peculiar powers which we technically call miraculous.

pp. 113. 25- 114–3. at the utmost. ... Some philosophers came] ⋆ at the utmost. He considered, contrariwise to present notions, that the *consciousness of being* rational was no necessary condition of being rational. I mean, it is the present opinion, that no one can be acting according to reason, unless he reflects on himself and recognises his own rationality. A peasant, who cannot tell *why* he believes, is supposed to have no reason for believing. This is worth noticing, for it is parallel to many others dogmas into which a civilized age will be sure to fall. Antony, on the other hand, considered there was something great and noble in believing and acting on the Gospel, without asking for proof; making experiment of it, and being rewarded by the success of it. He put the arguments for belief, to speak paradoxically, *after*, not *before* believing – that is, he seems to have felt there was a divine spirit and power in Christianity such as irresistibly to commend it to religious and honest minds, coming home to the heart with the same conviction which any high moral precept carries with it, and leaving argumentation behind as comparatively useless, except by way of curiously investigating motives and reasons for the satisfaction of the philosophical analyst. Probably he would not have been at all disconcerted, even could it have proved to him that his cures were the *natural* effect of imagination in the patient; accounting them as rewards to faith, any how, not as evidence to the reason. Perhaps this consideration will tend to solve Paley's difficulty, better than he does himself, why the early Fathers appeal so faintly and scantily to the argument from miracles. That argument is not ordinarily the actual mode by which the mind is subdued to the obedience of Christ.

Some philosophers came

p. 114. 20–23. Again: . . . process of argument.'"] * Again, – "'We prove, not in the persuasive words of Gentile wisdom, as our Teacher says, but we persuade by faith, which vividly anticipates a process through words.' " – §80.

p. 114. 31–33. Christ all-sufficient.'" – Ibid. . . . far from boasting] * Christ all-sufficient.'" – Ibid. As Antony would not be startled at his cures being set down to the power of the imagination, so I conceive he would also have admitted his gift of prescience to be, not miraculous, but the result of deep and continued meditation, acute reflection, and that calmness and dispassionateness of mind which self-denying habits naturally create, aided, of course, by the special evangelical influences of the Spirit, which, in his age, were manifested more fully than in our own. He is far from boasting

p. 116. 4–6. an objector would . . . upon false premisses;] * an objector would urge that this is the very peculiarity of madness, to reason correctly upon false premises;

p. 118. 24–29. in the country of the meek." . . . "Therefore, having now set out] * in the country of the meek."

"Let us, then, apply ourselves to our religious exercise, and not be downcast. We have the Lord to work with us, as it is written. It is well to study the Apostle's saying, 'I die daily.' We shall not sin if we so live as to be dying daily; that is, if we rise as though we should not last till evening, and go to rest as though we should not rise; life being of an uncertain nature, doled out by Providence from day to day. Thus we shall be ever militant and looking forward for the day of judgment; and this more urgent fear and peril of torment will ever rid pleasure of its sweetness, and restore the wavering soul.

"Therefore, having now set out

p. 119. 31–34. of the fourth century. . . . cunning and hypocrisy.] * of the fourth century. Antony was no savage saint, no ostentatious dervise; he had no pomposity or affectation, nothing of cunning and hypocrisy.

pp. 120. 33–121.1. 'Fear not.'" – §35. . . . and active virtue,] * 'Fear not.'" – §35. This might be considered mysticism, but for Antony's constant profession and practice of self-denying and active virtue,

p. 121. 19–26. It has sometimes be objected, . . . For instance:] * It has often been remarked, that the common run of legends and the like fail in point of dignity when they introduce miraculous occurrences. Thus there is something unbecoming, something unlike Scripture, in the account of the flies killed by lightning for settling on a Rabbi's face, or the stones of the heathen temples weeping at the persecution of the Christians. Now Antony's miracles and visions are so far clear of this defect, that had they been ascribed to St. Peter or St. Paul, I conceive they would not have been questioned, evidence being supposed. For instance: –

p. 123. 17–20. the Lord's table." – §82. . . . "The brethren urging him] * the Lord's table." – §82.

It is remarkable what anticipated protests Antony makes against the errors so popular at present in the Roman Church. For instance: the appeal to Scripture, in the narrative of Athanasius, is so frequent and reverential as to be virtual proof of his holding our doctrine of its exclusive authority as the record of necessary truth. Some instances have occurred in the course of the citations made above, to which I add the following by way of illustration: –

When he was at Alexandria, during the Maximian persecution –

"He was like a man in grief, because he did not attain martyrdom; but the Lord was his preserver for the benefit of us and others, in order that he might be to many an instructor in that ascetic life *which he himself had learned from the Scriptures*." – §46.

It is as well that the (so-called) Bible-Christian of this day should be reminded by such remarks as this, that there *are* doctrines which a plain, unlettered, but honest mind, may draw from Scripture over and above that jejune frame-work of words which it is now the fashion to identify with the whole counsel of God.

Again –

"This was his constant commandment to all the monks who came to him – to believe in the Lord, and to love Him; to preserve themselves from evil thoughts and carnal pleasures, and, as it is written in the Proverbs, 'not to be seduced by a full meal'; to flee vain glory; to pray continually; to sing before and after sleep; *to commit to their hearts the Scripture commandments*, and to remember the lives of the saints; so that the soul, being warned by the one, might shape itself into an imitation of the other. . . . Let every one take daily account of his deeds, by day and night; if he has sinned in aught, let him amend; if not, let him not boast, but persevere in what is holy, not be negligent, not condemn his neighbour, nor justify himself (as the blessed Apostle Paul has said) before the Lord come, who searcheth what is secret. For it often happens, that we do not understand ourselves in what we do; we do not know, but the Lord detects all things."– §56.

And, in his last address to the brethren before his death, he says –

"Keep yourselves pure from them [the Arians and Meletians], holding safe the tradition of the Fathers, and, above all, that pious faith in our Lord Jesus Christ, *which ye have learned from the Scriptures*, and have often been *reminded of* by me." – §89.

Again, the tenet of purgatory, in its popular acceptation, is plainly, though indirectly, contravened in the second, not to say the first also, of those visions related above.

And again, in his last instructions before his death, we have a clear protest against superstitions respecting relics, which were at that time spreading in the Church, which he condemns, be it observed, as being in his age not a Catholic, but a local custom of Egypt. This, however, introduces us to the account of his last illness and death, which follows the extract just made. The address, of which it is part, was spoken when he was on a sort of visitation of his brethren, as it may be called. The narrative runs thus: –

"The brethren urging him

pp. 125. 28–126.2. and perhaps in his lifetime . . . let us hear Athanasius:] ⋆ even in his lifetime; which, rhetorical as it may seem, is, after all, a correct representation of the visible change in the world wrought by his example, and affords a pleasing hope that, out of so much of outward manifestation, there was much of the substance of religion within.

p. 126. 14. by the waters." – §44. . . .] ⋆ by the waters." – §44.

I cannot conclude more appropriately than by Herbert's lines on the subject. Speaking of Religion, he says: –

'To Egypt first she came; where they did prove
Wonders of anger once, but now of love.
The Ten Commandments there did flourish, more
Than the ten bitter plagues had done before.
Holy Macarius and great Antony
Made Pharoah, Moses; changing the history.
Goshen was darkness; Egypt, full of lights;

Nilus, for monsters, brought forth Israelites.
Such power hath mighty baptism to produce,
For things misshapen, things of highest use.
How dear to me, O God, thy counsels are!
Who may with thee compare?'
Church Militant, – v. 37, 38.

Chapter VII: Augustine and the Vandals

p. 127. 1–5. CHAPTER VII. AUGUSTINE AND THE VANDALS. . . . face of evil."] * CHAPTER XII. AUGUSTINE AND THE VANDALS. "Lo. Eli sat on a seat by the way-side watching, for his heart trembled for the ark of God." ** CHAPTER IX. AUGUSTINE AND THE VANDALS.

p. 127. 6–9. I began by directing . . . Now, I will put before him,] * I have lately directed my reader's attention to the labours of a missionary bishop, who restored the light of Christianity where it had long been obscured. In my present, I will put before him,

pp. 135. 33- 136. 3. they should undergo."... "Why should men] * they should undergo.

"I understand that a certain bishop has argued, that if our Lord has enjoined flight upon us in persecutions which may ripen into martyrdom, much more is it necessary to flee from barren sufferings in a barbarian and hostile invasion. This is true and reasonable; but in the case of such as have no ecclesiastical office to tie them. For he who awaits, when he might escape, the murderous career of a foe, lest he should desert Christ's ministry, without which, men can neither become nor continue Christians, has attained a greater fruit of charity than he who, after flying not for the brethren's sake, but for himself, and then, being captured, confesses Christ, and accepts martyrdom.

"Why should men

p. 137. 14–20. but to cowardice." ..."O, that there may be] * but to cowardice."

"There is another question which demands consideration. If there is a plain expedience in some ministers flying at the prospect of a sweeping calamity, in order that the remnant of the flock, when the slaughter is over, may still have those who can minister to them, what is to be done in a case where all are likely to perish, unless some escape? What, for instance, if the destruction rages only with the view of reaching the ministers of the Church? "O, that there may be

Chapter VIII: Conversion of Augustine

p. 142. 1–7. CHAPTER VIII. CONVERSION OF AUGUSTINE. . . . of my youth."] * CHAPTER XIII. CONVERSION OF AUGUSTINE. "Thou hast chastised me and I was chastised, as a bullock unaccustomed to the yoke. Turn Thou me and I shall be turned, for Thou art the Lord my God. Surely after that I was turned, I repented, and after that I was instructed, I smote upon my thigh. I was ashamed, yea was confounded, because I did bear the reproach of my youth." ** CHAPTER X. CONVERSION OF AUGUSTINE.

p. 143. 7. the Western Church] * the Latin Church

p. 159. 23–25. Their property was cast . . . whence distribution] * One of their fundamental regulations was the apostolic usage of casting their property into a common stock, whence distribution

p. 159. 27–29. and Augustine took upon himself . . . The consequence naturally was,] * and Augustine took upon himself the task of forming their minds upon those religious principles which they at present held chiefly upon his authority. This design he signified in answer to a friend who wished him to leave Thagaste and join him in a religious retirement elsewhere: "You," he said, "have obtained the gift of dwelling comfortably with your own mind, but my friends about me are but acquiring it, and cannot yet go alone." The consequence naturally was,

pp. 161. 32–162. 1. a religious and clerical community in the episcopal house.] * a religious, or rather a clerical society in the see-house.

Chapter IX: Demetrias

p. 163. 1–4. CHAPTER IX. DEMETRIAS.] * CHAPTER XIV. DEMETRIAS. ** CHAPTER XI. DEMETRIAS.

p. 163. 6–8. a system which, . . . the evangelical dispensation.] * a system which, with all its dangers, (and none could be more sensible of these than he was,) has undoubtedly some especial place in the providential conduct of our dispensation.

p. 163. 14–18. which occasioned them. If a Protestant says . . . and important nevertheless.] * which occasioned them. To say that it may be abused, is only what may be objected with equal force against many Protestant doctrines, such as justification by faith only, which are considered true and important nevertheless.

p. 163. 19–20. and the other charges which he brings against it,] * and the other charges brought against it by ultra-Protestants,

p. 164. 4. his *present* system in which he glories so much,] * our *present* system in which we glory so much,
m

p. 164. 7–18. such a result?... One great purpose] * such a result? If so, it is plain the religious temper of these times is not like that of the primitive Church, the existing liability to certain degeneracies being a sort of index of certain tempers respectively. Clearly, then, whether or not monasticism is right, *we* at least are wrong, as differing in mind and spirit from the first ages of Christianity.

I would maintain then that the monastic life holds a real place in the dispensation of the Gospel, at least providentially.

One great purpose

p. 164. 23–24. in those perilous Arian waters,] * in that noxious Arian "flood"

pp. 164. 31- 165. 12. with his own native air. ... There is another reason.] * with his own native air.

Augustine's monasteries indeed were not meant for this purpose. They were intended as the refuge of Christian piety and holiness, when the increasing spread of religion made the Church more secular. And we may confidently pronounce that such provisions, in one shape or other, will always be attempted by the more serious and anxious part of the community, whenever Christianity is generally professed. In Protestant countries, where monastic orders are unknown, men run into separatism with this object. Methodism has carried off into its own exceptionable discipline many a sincere and zealous Christian, whose heart needed what he found not in the Established Church. This defect in the appointments of the latter is the less excusable, because, I believe, there is no *præmunire* attached to the formation of such a subsidiary system as I am speaking of. That the formation of it requires the most wary judgment, special insight into human nature and Christian truth, and extensive knowledge of history, and, above all, a singular measure of the temper of obedience in those who are to be subjects of it, need scarcely be said; but there is no reason why the English Church should not, from among its members, supply these requisites.

Let it be considered, too, whether there is any other way of evangelizing large towns but that of posting bodies of a monastic character, for the purpose of preaching and visiting, among the dense and ignorant population.

There is another reason

p. 165. 13. convents] ⋆ religious sisterhoods

p. 165. 15. monastic bodies] ⋆ religious fraternities

p. 166. 27. from the time of St. Philip's daughters,] ⋆ from the time of St. Paul and St. Philip's daughters,

p. 167. 17–20. At present ... and "single gentlemen;"] ⋆ At present the only apparent remains among us, at least in the apprehension of the many, of these isolated persons, exist in what are commonly called old maids and single gentlemen;

p. 172. 23–24. or understand." – *Ep*. 130.... settled down in Carthage,] ⋆ or understand." – *Ep*. 130.

These are portions of St. Augustine's letter to Proba, in which his remarks upon set times of prayer must not be understood, contrary to the very drift of his whole advice, as confining their use to what is called their "moral effect", upon the mind; but to mean that, whereas God hears those who are intent on the words they use, not those who are not, we are likely to pray more acceptably, because more attentively, in prayer at set times, than in habitual mental prayer, and in short pointed prayers, than in long addresses.

The exiled ladies seemed to have lived in Carthage,

p. 173. 18–23. there are words and ideas ... his saintly perfection.] ⋆ there are things in his writings and views from which I should shrink; but as the case stands, I shrink rather from putting myself in opposition to something like a judgment of the Catholic world in favour of his saintly perfection.

p. 173. 26–30. And I readily and heartily ... than my human praise.] ⋆ And I am willing to take certain characteristics of this learned and highly-gifted man on faith; and there is, perhaps, need of some exercise of this kind, even in the striking letter from which extracts are now to be made.

p. 180. 12. contrived to baffle the Apostolic see, ...guide of her faith.] ⋆ contrived to mislead the Apostolic see into a defence of him against the Africans, – the very see which St. Jerome, in a part of the foregoing letter not translated, recommends to Demetrias as a safe guide of her faith.

Chapter X: Martin and Maximus

p. 185. 1–4. CHAPTER X. MARTIN AND MAXIMUS. ... over the poor."] ⋆ CHAPTER XX. MARTIN, THE APOSTLE OF GAUL. "Gird Thee with Thy sword upon Thy thigh, O Thou Most Mighty, according to Thy worship and renown; good luck have Thou with Thine honour; ride on because of the word of truth, of meekness, and righteousness; and Thy right hand shall teach Thee terrible things." CHAPTER XXI. MARTIN AND PRISCILLIAN. "Destroy him not; for who can stretch forth his hand against the Lord's anointed and be guiltless? As the Lord liveth, the Lord shall smite him, or his day shall come to die, or he shall descend into battle, and perish." ** CHAPTER XII. MARTIN AND MAXIMUS. "He lieth in ambush, that he may catch the poor man; he will crouch and fall, when he shall have power over the poor."

p. 186. 16–20. Nay, the biographer ... Sulpicius Severus,] * Nay, perhaps more so, for the biographer of St. Martin is not merely a friend, who but sometimes saw him, though a great authority in himself, but a disciple, and intimate, and eye-witness, as well as a man of classical and original mind, – Sulpicius Severus,

p. 187. 15–16. The Divine Vision commanded the youth's attention,] * Christ commanded his notice,

p. 188. 25–26. existed in France. ... He was made bishop of Tours] * existed in France.

St Martin is famous for his alleged miraculous power. Sulpicius's memoir is full of accounts of miracles wrought by him. He is even said to have raised the dead. I cannot deny that a chance reader would regard his life merely as an early specimen of demonology. Whether the works attributed to him were really miracles, and whether they really took place, I leave to the private judgment of each reader of them. What has been said in former chapters applies here; it is difficult to draw the line between real and apparent interruptions of the course of nature; and, in an age of miracles, ordinary events will be exaggerated into supernatural: veneration, too, for an individual, will, at such a time, occasion the ordinary effects of his sagacity or presence of mind to be accounted more than human.

He was made bishop of Tours

pp. 191. 18–202. 31. the Apostle of Gaul. ... between the clergy there.] * the apostle of Gaul; and this function, let it be observed, may account for his having the gift of miracles in the height and fulness in which it is ascribed to him, though this general admission does not oblige us to put credit in each particular statement made concerning its exercise.

It may probably occur to some one to ask how it is that miraculous narratives, such as those which occur in the lives of St. Martin and St. Antony, belong to places removed from the populous thoroughfare of society, and the keen eyes of science. The supernatural incidents in Antony's life, are for the most part the produce of the desert; and in

Martin's they were the persuasives of a barbarous people. The obvious answer is, that towns had already been converted by miracle, and the divine gift travelled onwards. It is remarkable too, that St. Paul did no miracle among the heathens of Athens, and scarcely at Corinth, but among the barbarous Lycaonians who had faith, and the ignorant people of Melita. Nay, as if some unknown law of divine agency were in operation, it is expressly said of our Blessed Lord Himself, that in one place "He did not many mighty works, because of their unbelief." A living writer of great genius has suggested the existence of a parallel law of connexion between barbarous countries and demoniacal influence.

"Many travellers," he says, "who have been conversant with savages, have been fully persuaded that their jugglers actually possessed some means of communication with the invisible world, and exercised a supernatural power which they derived from it. And not missionaries only have believed only have believed this, and old travellers who lived in ages of credulity, but more recent observers, such as Carver and Bruce, whose testimony is of great weight, and who were neither ignorant, nor weak, nor credulous men. What I have read concerning ordeals, also staggers me; and I am sometimes inclined to think it more possible, that where there has been full faith on all sides, these appeals to divine justice may have been answered by Him who sees the secrets of all hearts, than that mode of trial should have been provided so long and so generally, from some of which no person could ever have escaped without an interposition of Providence. ... May it not be, that by such means in dark ages, and among blind nations, the purpose is effected of preserving conscience and the belief of our immortality, without which the life of our life would be extinct? And with regards to the conjurers of the African and American savages, would it be unreasonable to suppose that, as the most elevated devotion brings us into fellowship with the Holy Spirit, a correspondent degree of wickedness may effect a communion with evil intelligences?" [footnote: Southey's Colloquies. Introduction.] If there then be some special Satanic influence in a pagan country, it is not surprising that Christianity should meet it with a correspondent supernatural power on its side.

Martin was not content with destroying the heathen temples; he built churches in their place. At first sight it may be questioned whether the better course would not have been to spare the temples and to consecrate them to Christian uses; but probably they were very rude and miserable buildings, and either not worth preserving, or not capable of a convenient adaptation. In the cities the Church seems to have preserved and retained them; except, indeed, at first, when there was an obvious wisdom to accept the state's permission to destroy them, when their abiding presence would have suggested to the pagans hopes of the future restoration of their idolatry. Add to this, it cannot be denied there was a difference of opinion in the early Fathers, whether, and how far, the fine arts which had been exercised on the temples of idolatry, might lawfully be applied to the service of religion. The conversion of the emperors brought with it into the Church wealth, and the skill to use it; it seemed pious and dutiful to dedicate these gifts to God; and, moreover, a direct fulfilment of the prophecy, that "the glory of Lebanon should come unto" the Church, "to glorify the place of the sanctuary", that "the sons of strangers should build her walls", and the ships of Tarshish bring silver and gold, and that "her windows should be agates, and gates carbuncles;" illustrated too, as this prophecy had been by the offering of the Magi, who brought gold, frankincense, and myrrh, to their divine Lord, when an infant in arms, with temptation and suffering before Him. However, a natural jealousy would be sure to exist in holy men, lest the inward glory of the Gospel should be sacrificed to its material decorations; the Arian or rather the semi-Arian faction had been busy in the erection of churches; and we find Jerome, Epiphanius , and Isidore, not to search deeply into the history of the times, discouraging the spirit which was arising on all sides of them.

For instance, Jerome says, in a letter to Demetrias, which has already come before us, speaking of the disposal of her property; "Let others build churches, incase the walls with marble, transport immense columns, and gild their heads, which cannot feel the precious decoration: let them ornament the folding doors with ivory and silver, and the altars with gold and jewels. I do not blame, I do not dissent; let every one be fully persuaded in his own mind. It is better so to do, than brood over one's store of wealth. But something else is proposed to you; to clothe Christ in the poor, to visit Him in the sick, to feed Him in the hungry, to entertain Him in the houseless, especially in 'the household of faith,' to maintain monasteries of virgins, to have a care of the servants of God, and poor in spirit, who day and night serve your Lord, who, though on earth, imitate the life of Angels, and speak nothing but God's praises, and 'having food and raiment' rejoice in this wealth as desirous of nought besides, that is, if they keep their resolve. Else, if they desire more, they show themselves unworthy too of what is necessary. I speak to a rich virgin, and a noble virgin." – *Ep*. 130.

But to return to St. Martin: one other passage of history shall here be mentioned, if that can so be called which brings before us his departure from this life into the unseen world. Something more of his deeds in the flesh shall be reserved for the next and concluding chapter. He had been at a place, at the extremity of his charge, to settle a quarrel existing between the clergy there.

p. 191. 30–32. The sovereign with whom Martin came into collision was Maximus,] ⋆ As I began, so will I end, with the story of a bishop and a king; but with this addition, that, as in the former case, Ambrose showed how a Christian might be persecuted, so, in this, Martin, and Ambrose too, shall show how a Christian may not persecute. Persecution, indeed, has a variety of meanings, some persons thinking themselves *ipso facto* persecuted, as often as men in power refuse to adopt and promote their opinions. What I mean here by persecution will be clear as I proceed. The sovereign with whom Martin came in contact was Maximus,

p. 193.1–2. but according to his conduct. . . . Maximus asked him,] ★ but according to his conduct. In this behaviour he had been anticipated by St. Ambrose, shortly before, who, on his former embassy to Maximus from Justina, had refused to communicate with him, or with those bishops who had communicated with him.

It was Martin's office to give this military sovereign a second lesson of the spirit of that religion, which, being from heaven, knows not the distinction between man and man. Maximus asked him,

pp. 195. 23–196. 3. The new opinion spread . . . This was the state of things] ★ The new opinions spread through all parts of the country, and that the more, in consequence of indiscreet violence on the part of the metropolitan of Lusitania. Next, a council was held of Spanish and Aquitain bishops, who condemned several of their brethren who had embraced the heresy, and all who should associate with them. The denounced bishops met this proceeding by consecrating Priscillian to the see of Avila; and Idacius, the metropolitan aforesaid, and Ithacius, who were charged with the execution of the synodal decree, retaliated by calling on the civil power to drive the heretics out of the cities. This was what Sulpicius calls a "foul" request; however, by repeated solicitations, Idacius obtained a rescript from Gratian, then emperor, commanding the extermination of the heretics, one and all, not only from churches and cities, but from every country. The heretic bishops made for Rome, with the hope of gaining Damasus; failing with the see of St. Peter, they betook themselves to Milan. Failing equally with Ambrose, they adopted a new line of conduct, bribed the officers of the court, gained a rescript of just an opposite character, commanding their restoration to their churches, and secured its zealous execution. This was the state of things

p. 196. 5–8. against the heretics . . . obliged to fly to Gaul;] ★ against the heretics whom the fallen court had supported.

Ithacius had been obliged to fly to Gaul;

p. 196. 26–28. However, the Ithacians . . . This is the point] ★ However, the Ithacians, having allowed the state to persecute, found it difficult to withstand its right to interfere. This is the point

p. 196. 33. on matters of his own. . . . Martin naturally viewed the Ithacian faction] ★ on matters of his own.

If it is necessary to state in a few words as near as may be what seems to be the doctrine of early times on the subject of persecution, I suppose it would be something like this: that the Church availed herself of the offer of the civil power to confirm her judgments so far as to silence heretical teachers, no difficult matter at a time when the idea of absolute power was fully apprehended, the habit of liberty of speech unknown, and transportation an *ultima ratio*, if the threat of it was not sufficient. The Church having once denounced a doctrine as false, left it to the conscience of the state to prevent its dissemination; but she abhorred cruelty and bloodshed, and denied the state's right of taking direct cognizance of error, and of punishing it as such, or otherwise than as an offence against herself, the divinely appointed teacher of the faith. Martin, then, on every account, viewed the Ithacian faction

p. 201. of great seriousness] * of great piety [footnote: Tillemont, Life of S. Mart. 10.]

pp. 202. 26–205. 26. to the end of his life. . . . "While Martin was praying] *. to the end of his life.

It may not be out of place to append to this passage of St. Martin's history, an account of one of his visions, which seems in various ways to be illustrative, or even mythical of much in it.

"While Martin was praying

PRIMITIVE CHRISTIANITY

Chapter I. What does St. Ambrose Say About it?

p. 339. 2–4. CHAPTER 1. . . . *Ambrose and Justina.*] * CHAPTER I. AMBROSE AND JUSTINA. "No weapon that is formed against thee shall prosper: and every tongue that shall rise against thee in judgment, thou shalt condemn."

p. 353. 1. §2. *Ambrose and Valentinian.*] * CHAPTER II. AMBROSE AND VALENTINIAN. "Look unto Zion, the city of our solemnities: thine eyes shall see Jerusalem a quiet habitation, a tabernacle that shall not be taken down: not one of the stakes thereof shall ever be removed, neither shall any of the cords thereof be broken."

p. 356. 12. they are the poor of Christ's flock;] * they are THE POOR OF CHRIST'S FLOCK; [footnote: Pauperes Christi.]

p. 364. 1. §3. *Ambrose and the Martyrs.*] * CHAPTER III. THE MARTYRS

GERVASIUS AND PROTASIUS. "All Thy garments smell of myrrh, aloes, and cassia, out of the ivory palaces, whereby they have made thee glad."

p. 369. 9. St. Augustine's Confessions,] ★ St. Austin's Confessions,

p. 374. 12–13. Does it give . . .shall we advance?] ★ What alternative shall the Protestant accept? shall we retreat? shall we advance?

Chapter II: What Says Vincent of Lerins?

p. 375. 1–3. CHAPTER II. WHAT SAYS VINCENT OF LERINS?] ★ CHAPTER X. VINCENTIUS OF LERINS. "Though the Lord give you the bread of adversity and the water of affliction, ye shall not thy Teachers be removed into a corner any more, but thine eyes shall see thy Teachers; and thine ears shall hear a Word behind thee, saying, This is the way, walk ye in it, when ye turn to the right hand and when ye turn to the left."

p. 375. 5–9. at the earnestness shown . . . Yet their repeated protests] ★ at the earnestness shown by those ancient bishops who have formed the subject of the foregoing pages, Ambrose, Basil, and Gregory, in defence of the Catholic faith. Ambrose would not give up a Church to the Arians, because their creed was unsound. Basil incessantly importuned the West to interfere in the concerns of the East, for the overthrow of these selfsame Arians. Gregory though he had acquitted himself well, when he consented to be pelted with stones for preaching against these Arians in Constantinople. Yet these repeated protests

p. 378. 18. for that very narrowness.] ★ for that very narrowness. Thus Gregory says:–

> "Strait is the path of truth in very deed,
> Sided with precipice and tightened in;
> And whoso slips away on either hand
> Is dashed adown a deep erratic track."
> Vol. ii. p. 193.

p. 382. 31n. The Oxford translation of 1838 . . . is used in the following extracts.] ★ The Oxford translation of 1837 is used in the following extracts. The whole volume, with appendix, &c., consists of no more than 137 duodecimo pages.

pp. 386. 34–387.5. which I keep to myself. . . . a true and genuine Catholic] ★ which I keep to myself.

However, Vincent does not scruple to treat as severely as a Protestant could desire, some at least of those who commonly are included under the name of Fathers. Let us hear what he says of Origen and Tertullian.

"I suppose that, although I could bring forth many to show this kind of temptation, yet there is almost none which can be compared to the temptation of Origen, in whom were so many gifts, so rare, so singular, so strange, that in the beginning any would have thought that his opinions might have been believed of all men. For if life procureth authority, he was a man of great industry, of great chastity, patience, and labour: if family or learning, who more noble? being in the first place of that house which was honourable for martyrdom, himself afterward for Christ deprived not of his father only, but also spoiled of all his patrimony; and so much he profited in the straits of holy poverty, that, as it is reported, for the confession of Christ's name he often endured affliction. Neither had he only these gifts, all which afterward served for temptation, but also a force of wit, so profound, so quick, so elegant, that he far excelled almost all other whatsoever. A man of such learning and universal erudition, that there were few things in divinity, in human philosophy perhaps almost none, which he had not perfectly attained; who having gotten the Greek tongue, laboured also with success about the Hebrew. And for his eloquence, why should I speak of it? whose language was so pleasant, so soft, so sweet, that in my opinion not words but honey flowed from his mouth. What things were so hard to believe, which with the force of argument he made not plain? what so difficult to bring to pass, which he made not to seem easy? But perchance he maintained his assertions by arguments only, Nay, without question there was never any doctor which used more examples of holy Scripture. But yet haply he wrote not much. No man living more; yea so much, that all his works seem to me not only more than can be read, but even more than can be found; who, not to lack any furtherance to learning, lived also until he was passing old. But yet perchance unfortunate in his scholars. What man ever more happy? for of his nursing grew up doctors and priests without number, yea, confessors and martyrs. Further, who is able to prosecute in words in what admiration he was with all men? in what glory? in what favour? Who that was more zealous of religion, repaired not to him from the furthest parts of the world? What Christian did not venerate him almost as a prophet? What philosopher did not venerate honour him as a master? And how greatly he was reverenced not only of private men, but also of the empire itself, histories do speak, which report that he was sent for of Alexander the emperor's mother, to wit, for the merit of his heavenly wisdom, with the grace whereof he was full, as she was of love to the same. His epistles also testify the same thing, which with the authority of a Christian master he wrote unto Philip the emperor, the first Christian amongst all the Roman princes. And if any man upon our report admitteth not the testimony of a

Christian touching his wonderful knowledge, at least let him receive an heathen confession in the testimony of philosophers. For that impious Porphyry saith, that himself, being but yet, as it were, a boy, moved with his fame, travelled unto Alexandria, where he did see him, being then old, but yet such an one and so learned, as that he had builded him a fortress of universal knowledge. Time would sooner fail me, than I could touch, though briefly, upon those notable gifts which were in that man, all which notwithstanding pertained not only to the glory of religion, but also to the greatness of the temptation. For among how many is there one that would willingly have forsaken a man of such wit, of so deep learning, of so rare grace, and would not sooner have used that saying, that he had rather err with Origen, than believe aright with others? And why should I say more? the matter came to that issue, that, as the end showed, not an usual and common, but a passing dangerous temptation of so great a man, so great a doctor, so great a prophet, carried away very many from soundness of faith: wherefore this Origen, so rare and singular a man, too presumptuously abusing the grace of God, indulging too much his own wit, trusting himself as sufficient, little esteeming the old simplicity of the Christian religion, presuming to be wiser than all other, contemning the traditions of the Church, and the old Fathers' teaching, expounding certain chapters of the Scriptures after a new fashion, deserved that the Church of God should also say of him, 'If there arise up in the midst of thee a prophet;' and a little after, 'Thou shalt not hear (quoth he) the words of that prophet;' and again, 'Because, (quoth he) your Lord God doth tempt you, whether you love him or no.' And surely it is not only a temptation, but also a great temptation, when a man seduceth secretly and by little and little the Church depending upon him, (admiring his wit, knowledge, eloquence, conversation, and grace, nothing suspecting him, nothing fearing him,) suddenly from the old religion to new profaneness. But some will say that Origen's books be corrupted: I will not gainsay it, but rather wish it were so: for that hath been both said and written by some, not only Catholics, but also heretics. But this is now the point we are to consider, that although not he, yet the books passing abroad under his name, are a great temptation, which, full of many hurtful blasphemies, are read and loved, not as the books of others, but as his; so that although Origen gave no cause of originating erroneous doctrine, yet his authority hath been the occasion why the error hath been received. [footnote: The tenets imputed to the Origenists in Vincent's age were these: 1. That the Son of God could not see the Father, nor the Holy Spirit the Son. 2. That the soul had sinned in a pre-existent state, and the body was its prison. 3. That the devil and the fallen spirits would one time repent. 4. That Adam and Eve had no bodies before the fall. 5. That the flesh would not rise again. 6. That the terrestrial paradise was spoken of allegorically. 7. That "the waters above the heavens" were angels, and those above and under the earth, evil spirits. 8. That man by sinning effaced the image of God. – Vide Huet. Origen. ii. 4. §1. n.12. Giesler, Eccles. Hist. vol. i. §33.]

"The case also of Tertullian is the very same with the former: for as Origen is to be thought the best among the Greek doctors, so Tertullian among the Latins without controversy is the chief of all our writers. For who was more learned than he? Who in divinity or humanity more practised? for by a certain wonderful capacity of mind, he attained to, and understood, all philosophy, all the sects of philosophers, all their founders and supporters, all their systems, all sorts of histories and studies. And for his wit, was he not so excellent, so grave, so forcible, that he almost undertook the overthrow of nothing, which either by quickness of wit or weight of reason he crushed not? Further, who is able to express the praises which his style of speech deserves, which is fraught, (I know not how) with that force of reason, that such as it cannot persuade it compels to assent: whose so many words almost are so many sentences; whose so many senses, so many victories. This know Marcion and Apelles, Praxeas and Hermogenes, Jews, Gentiles, Gnostics, and divers others: whose blasphemous opinions he hath overthrown with his many and great volumes, as it had been with thunderbolts. And yet this man after all this, this Tertullian, I say, not holding the Catholic doctrine, that is, the universal and old faith, being far more eloquent than faithful, changing afterwards his mind, at last did that which the blessed confessor Hilary in a certain place writeth of him; 'He discredited (quoth he) with his later error his worthy writings:' and he also was a great temptation in the Church. But hereof I would not say more; only this I will add, that by his defending, against the precept of Moses, for true prophecies the new madness of Montanus springing up in the Church, and those mad dreams about new doctrine of frantic women, he deserved that we should also say of him and his writings, 'If a prophet shall rise up in the midst of thee,' and straight after, 'thou shalt not hear the words of that prophet.' Why so? 'Because (quoth he) your Lord God doth tempt you, whether you love him or no.'

"We ought, therefore, evidently to note by these, so many, so great, and divers others such weighty examples in the Church, and according to the laws of Deuteronomy most clearly to understand, that if at any time any ecclesiastical teacher strayeth from the faith, that God's providence doth suffer that for our trial, whether we love Him or no in our whole heart, and in our whole soul." – Ch. 23, 24.

Vincentius proceeds to speak of the misery of doubting: –

"Which being so, he is a true and genuine Catholic

p. 387. 18–20. may be made manifest among you.' ... "O the miserable state of [waverers]!] ⋆ may be made manifest among you.' As though he should say; This is the cause why the authors of heresies are not straight rooted out by God, that the approved may be made manifest, that is, that every one may appear how stedfastly, faithfully, and constantly, he loveth the Catholic faith. And certain it is, that upon the springing up of any novelty, straightway is discerned both the weight of the corn and the lightness of the chaff; then is that easily blown out of the floor which before lightly remained in the floor; for some by and by fly away, others only shaken, are both afraid to perish, and ashamed to return, remaining wounded, half dead, half alive, like unto those which have drunk so much poison, as neither killeth, nor well digesteth, neither bringeth death, nor yet permitteth to live. O the miserable state of such persons!

p. 388. 3–13. be perfected." – Ch. 25, 26. ... "Who at this day is Timothy,] * be perfected."

"Whereas the Divine Scriptures cry out, 'Do not transfer the bounds which thy fathers have set down:' and 'Do not judge over thy judge;' and, 'The servant will bite him that cutteth the hedge;' and that saying of the Apostle, by which all wicked novelties of all heretics have often been cut in pieces, as it were by a spiritual sword, and always hereafter shall be. [footnote: 1 Tim. vi, 20.] O Timothy, keep the *depositum*, avoiding the profane novelties of voices, and oppositions of falsely-called knowledge, which certain promising have erred about the faith.' " – Ch. 25, 26.

If the general reader has but the twentieth part of the pleasure in perusing, perhaps for the first time, which I have in quoting for the twentieth, he will let me continue a little longer:–

"O Timothy, (quoth he,) keep the *depositum* avoiding profane novelties of voices.' This exclamation O, both showeth foresight, and also argueth charity: for he foresaw certain errors, which beforehand he was sorry for. Who at this day is Timothy,

p. 390. 34–38. to anathematize him." – Ch. 27–34.... a very sorry Protestant.] * to anathematize him." – Ch. 27 – 34.

It is presumed that these extracts have sufficiently explained on what grounds we contend for that exact and strict creed, which we call orthodoxy. According to the doctrine of Vincentius, these grounds are twofold; the ground of Scripture, and the ground of Catholic tradition;– tradition first, then Scripture, in order of perspicuity; Scripture first, then tradition in point of authority; Scripture proving, tradition teaching; tradition interpreting Scripture, Scripture verifying tradition; and the personal mind and will of the individual being the ultimate court of appeal. But here one or two remarks suggest themselves, which will serve to bring this chapter to an end.

What the primitive Church declared to be the faith is plain enough, and a sure guide; but supposing a person alleges that he himself cannot see that primitive doctrine in Scripture, what is to be said in answer to him? Are we to oblige him to accept that doctrine, whether he can see it in Scripture or not? or may he reject it till he sees it in Scripture? If he may reject it, what is the use of tradition? and if he must accept it, where is our reverence for Scripture?

I answer first, that though it is *abstractedly* the right of every individual to verify tradition by Scripture for himself, yet it is not so in *matter of fact*. It is as wrong for the generality of Christians to attempt it, as if there were no right at all. This is evident, even at first sight. Every one *may* be a lawyer, a soldier, or an orator – that is, there is no law of the land against it; yet most men would but bring upon themselves vexation and ridicule if they attempted to be either of the three. Now, it is as certain that the interpretation of Scripture requires qualifications for the due performance of it as pleading or fighting; knowledge of the languages, for instance, does not come by nature. It may, indeed, be urged that a divine illumination is promised us to lead us into the truth; but this is not so easy of proof. Surely no promise of a guidance into truth has been made to each individual, educated or not, and that by means of the bare Greek or Hebrew text; and moreover, as far as we may judge, Almighty God is not wont to effect supernaturally, what may be effected in the way of nature. Now, as to saving faith, considered as a *temper of mind*, this cannot be obtained, except *supernaturally*, on account of Adam's fall; therefore, for the obtaining of *it*, each individual must ask, and may humbly expect, the aid of divine grace. But saving *knowledge*, and of it I am now speaking, though it might be, and has sometimes been, supernaturally vouchsafed, as by inspiration, may also be gained by *natural* means, and therefore it is unlikely that it should be given by divine illumination. Catholic tradition does that which individual examination might do, were men inspired or were they learned. And whereas they are ordinarily neither, this said private inquiry is, in the case of ordinary men, a mistake; and they who attempt to exercise it, are as reasonable and wise as any one who goes out of his depth in any matter of this world.

In the next place, I would say that the juxtaposition of Scripture with tradition is ordinarily but a *negative* comparison of the latter with the former; though it may be, if it so happen, much more. I mean, it must be rather used to see that tradition is not wrong than to prove that it is right. This is the very meaning of the word "test" or "verification;" a test is satisfied if there is no actual disagreement, and does not ask for more. I must explain myself. Scripture has but one sense, undoubtedly; but it does not bring out upon its surface that one sense, in system and fulness; it only implies, and in a certain sense hides it. Be men ever so learned, it requires, besides, a singularly unprejudiced and straightgoing mind to enter into Scripture as it is; to penetrate, and, as it were, become diffused throughout its recesses; and to apprehend "the whole counsel of God" contained in it. Most persons, whatever be their attainments and talents, will mistake its meaning, from not apprehending its entire meaning; and that in opposite ways, from the accident of their opposite circumstances. Catholic tradition, then, has been mercifully given to supply to Scripture what it does not supply to itself, its true interpretation; and since, by the very hypothesis, it is to teach men what otherwise they would not infer from Scripture, there is nothing wonderful in its not at once annihilating, when given, all other inferences from Scripture. That which was before an unknown sense, does not at once become the only conceivable sense. Each man, before, had an interpretation of his own; those private interpretations remain; they do not become impossible, merely because there is found to be an older. The Catholic sense comes as a mediator or arbiter between disputants; and if it at once approved itself to any one party, it could not approve itself to the rest. Tradition supersedes, not reverses, the inferences of private inquirers. All that inquirers can demand to perceive, what they will perceive abundantly is, that the Catholic sense is at least *one* of those senses which Scripture *may* have. They will indeed, in fact, perceive a great deal more; they will have a continually growing perception that it is the one only *true* sense; but, in order to their accepting it, it ought to be enough that they perceive that it is not *excluded* by the text of Scripture from being true. Few men, perhaps, if left to themselves, would see any one sense in Scripture, such as to be sure that it *could* have none other but it; yet I suppose few men, indeed, if they examined diligently, but would also confess, that, whatever other sense it *might* admit, it would, at least, admit the Catholic sense. This, then, is the true mode of verifying or proving the tradition of the Church universal by Scripture, not to insist upon seeing *only* that *one* sense in the text of Scripture which the tradition assigns, but to examine whether there is anything in the text *inconsistent* with that one sense. And now, perhaps, the reader has heard enough of tradition.

Chapter III: What Says The History Of Apollinaris?

pp. 391. 1–392. 24. CHAPTER III. WHAT SAYS THE HISTORY OF APOLLINARIS? ... His father, who bore the same name,] * CHAPTER XI. APOLLINARIS. "Behold, thou art wiser than Daniel; there is no secret that they can hide from thee. By thy great wisdom, and by thy traffic, hast thou increased thy riches, and thine heart is lifted up because of thy riches."

No passage of early ecclesiastical history is more painful and more instructive than the fall of Apollinaris into heresy. It becomes so from his high repute for learning and virtue, his intimacy with the great Catholic champions of his day, his former services to the Church, the temptation which seems to have led to it, the comparative insignificance of his error at first, yet the deplorable defection from the faith at which he, or at least his school, in no long time arrived. He began with the denial of our Lord's human soul, or rather of the intellectual part of it, which he considered was supplied by the Eternal Word incarnate. His object in this was to secure more completely the doctrine of the divinity of our Lord's person, to impress upon the mind that He who came on earth, who taught, acted, and suffered, was God, and not a man, in every thought, word, and deed, though acting through and in human nature; and he did so with an especial view of overthrowing Arianism, which denied our Lord's divinity. His error, slight as it may appear in itself to orthodox Christians of this day, is, at first sight, in one point of view, even slighter still in the judgment of the theologian, who bears in mind that, according to the Catholic creed, our Lord, though perfect man, as far as nature is concerned, is not a man in the sense in which any given individual of the species is such, His person or subsistence not being human, but divine. Apollinaris seemed to say no more than this, that our Lord, not having a human person, had not that particular part of human nature in which personality may be considered to reside – viz., the rational part of the soul. Such was the seemingly trivial character of his doctrinal error; it ended, however, as the history of his school shows us, in no many years, and by no difficult or complicated process, when we come to inspect it, in a variety, or rather an alternative, of the most grievous and wildest tenets – in the belief, on the one hand, that Christ's body was only in appearance flesh; or, on the other, that it was created out of the very substance of Almighty God.

This was the incredible aberration of a grave, a literary, an aged man, some of whose writing are still extant, and evince a vigour and elegance not inferior to any writer of his day. An impious and monstrous gnosticism seemed to revive, in the person of a dialectician, versed in all the accomplishments of Grecian philosophy and rhetoric. A brief sketch of his history, and of the conduct of the Church towards him, may not be out of place in this series of views, as they are intended to be, of ancient Christianity.

His father, who bore the same name,

p. 396. 18–19. he was not outstepping … the teaching of the Catholic Church.] ⋆ he was not outstepping the range which Scripture had prescribed, and the Church Catholic witnessed.

pp. 399. 30–400.18. to escape sin?"– *Ep.* 263, §4. … It is a solemn and pregnant fact,] ⋆ to escape sin? First, there are his theological opinions, supported not by proofs from Scripture, but by human processes. Again, there are his views on the resurrection, made up of fables, or rather of Judaisms; in which he says, that we shall again turn to the legal worship; again be circumcised, keep Sabbath, abstain from meat, offer sacrifices to God, worship in Jerusalem at the temple, and, in short, become Jews for Christians. What can be more absurd? or rather, more foreign to the

Evangelical doctrine? Also, his views of the Incarnation have caused such confusion among my brethren, that few of those who have read them, preserve the ancient marks of piety, but the mass, attending to novelties, have turned aside to questions and contentious speculations of these unprofitable theories."– *Ep.* 264, §4.
It is a solemn and pregnant fact,

p. 400. 21–22. heresies of their own; ... "Let him that thinketh] ⋆ heresies of their own, – Marcellus denied our Lord's personality, Apollinaris His humanity. "Let him that thinketh

Chapter IV: And What Say Jovinian And His Companions?

p. 401.1–2. CHAPTER IV. AND WHAT SAY JOVINIAN AND HS COMPANIONS?] ⋆ CHAPTER XV. JOVINIAN AND HIS COMPANIONS. "And he said unto him, I am a prophet also as thou art, and an Angel spoke unto me by the Word of the Lord, saying, Bring him back with thee into thine house, that he may eat bread and drink water. But he lied unto him."

p. 401. 3–7. Vincentius wrote in the early part... foreign to the pure Gospel,] ⋆ We sometimes hear it said that, true though it be, that the Catholic system, as we Anglicans maintain it, existed in the fourth century, yet that nevertheless it was a system foreign to the pure Gospel,

p. 404. 16–20. which that philosopher opposed. ... Others have gone a step further,] ⋆ which that philosopher opposed. Others denounce St. Barnabas the Apostle as a puerile and nonsensical writer, on the ground of the epistle, which many think is not his, but which these persons are eager in ascribing to him. Others have gone a step further,

p. 404. 22–24. submitting to the Church. ... what quarter of Christendom they will,] ⋆ submitting to the Church.
This, then, is one obstacle in the way of the opponents of the Catholic system: they cannot disconnect it from Apostolic times. Another, which leads to the subject of this paper, is as follows:– That, let them go to what quarter of Christendom they will,

p. 405. 14–16. in the early Church ... so much in favour.] ⋆ in the early Church, of that peculiarity, or *peculiarism*, in religion, (if I may give it a significant appellation,) which is now so much in favour.

p. 405. 21–23. their not being in error, ... I cannot answer] ⋆ their not being in error, that their opinions cannot be found in antiquity. I cannot answer pp. 408. 36–409. 4. of whom more can be made. ... history of Aerius, Jovinian, and Vigilantius,] * of whom more can be made. However, in a hopeless case, as it seems to me, let us turn to what promises best at first sight for modern divinity, – the history of Aerius, Jovinian, and Vigilantius,

p. 409. 7. both by Protestants and their opponents;] * both by ultra-Protestants and their opponents;

pp. 410. 31–411. 1. "What can we require ... of Epiphanius and Jerome.] * "What can you require more than this? Here you have at the time of a great catastrophe, Scriptural truth preserved, as it were, fossile, in the burning matter which destroyed it, in the persecuting language of Epiphanius and Jerome.

p. 412. 13–20. nearer to the Protestant; ... even if a modern wished,] * nearer to the Protestant; though in fact they are little of an argument, even at first sight, against the Catholic, since most of the views and practices which they oppose in the fourth century, had been held in the Church in the first, second, and third.

Further, even if a modern wished,

p. 414. 17–25. to quote Jovinian. ... the Nicene era.] * to quote Jovinian. Why, then, is the fourth century to prove what the second and third disavow? Surely we may fairly ask for pure and primitive heretics, independents of the Apostolic age, before we defer to them, and must not be put off with the dark and fallible protests of the Nicene era.

p. 416. 6–9. There may have been ... in praising celibacy,] * There may have been extreme opinions and extreme acts, over-honour paid to relics, extravagance in praising celibacy,

p. 416. 18–29. but a suspicious orthodoxy. ... and duty of private judgment.] * but suspicious orthodoxy. For the present, then, I give up the search after Protestantism in Antiquity as a failure;– however, before ending the chapter, it may be as well to give a specimen of the kind of answer which the Catholic writers made to these heretics; so I will extract passages from St. Jerome in behalf of fasting against Jovinian, and of the martyrs against Vigilantius. The Scriptural tone of both should be observed.

1. Adam, he observes to Jovinian, received the command in Paradise to observe fast as to one tree, while he ate of the rest. The blessedness of Paradise could not be confirmed to him without abstinence from food. As long as he fasted, he was in Paradise: he ate, and was cast out. How lost

Esau his birthright? for the sake of food, with an impatience which tears would not wash away. Israel, when making for the land flowing with milk and honey, longs after the flesh, gourds, and leeks of Egypt, and despises the food of Angels. Moses, fasting on Sinai for forty days and nights, proved, in the very letter, that man doth not live by bread only, but by every word of God; whereas the full people were the while fashioning their idol. Nor were the tables of the law inscribed a second time without a second fast. What excess has lost, abstinence regained; to show us that as eating forfeited Paradise, fasting recovers it. Elias, after a forty days' fast, saw God in Horeb. Samuel and Hezekiah gained victory over the enemy by a fast; by a fast, Nineveh averted God's wrath; by a fast, impious Ahab delayed it. Hannah, by a fast, gained a son; by fasting, Daniel gained to interpret the king's dream. After an abstinence of three weeks from pleasant meat, an Angel was sent to him. David humbled himself with fasting. The prophet from Judah lost his life from not fasting; and the lion shamed him by not eating the ass. In the New Testament, Anna by fasting gained a sight of her Lord. The Baptist lived on locusts and wild honey. Cornelius fasted, and was rewarded by Baptism. Paul adds fastings to his shipwrecks and perils. Timothy, his disciple, drank water only. "Once," he presently continues, addressing Jovinian, "once, your foot was bare; now it has not only a shoe, but an ornamental one. Then you wore a shaggy tunic and a black vest; you were in mourning garb, pale in face, and rough in hand; now you parade in linen, in silk, in the figured stuffs of Atrebatæ, and the attire of Laodicea. Your cheeks are red; your skin is sleek; your hair is dressed behind and before; your paunch is protuberant; your shoulders are round; your throat is full; and your jaws are so fat that your words are almost strangled. Certainly, in such a contrast of food and clothing, there must be fault on one side or the other. Not that I will impute sin to food or to dress; but that the variation and change for the worse is next door to a reproach." – ii. 21.

2. The same Father is even more energetic in defence of the martyrs against Vigilantius: – "Who, madman, ever at any time, adored the martyrs? who took man for God? did not Paul and Barnabas, when thought to be Jupiter and Mercury by the Lycaonians, who would sacrifice to them, tear their garments, and say they were men? We read the same of Peter, who raised Cornelius when desirous to worship him, saying, 'Rise, for I also am a man.' And do you venture to talk of that 'something or other which we honour by carrying about in a small urn?' I want to know what you mean by 'something or other.' Speak out, and blaspheme freely. 'Some dust or other,' you say, 'wrapped up in precious linen in a small urn.' He grieves that the remains of martyrs have a precious covering, and are not tied up in rags or sackcloth, or cast on the dunghill; that Vigilantius alone may have worshipped in his liquor and his sleep! What! are we sacrilegious in entering the Basilicas of the Apostles? Then was the Emperor Constantius so,

who translated the sacred remains of Andrew, Luke, and Timothy to Constantinople, at which demons howl, yea, the tenants of Vigilantius acknowledge their presence. Sacrilegious, too, is Arcadius, Augustus at this time, who has translated, after so long a period, the bones of the blessed Samuel from Judea into Thrace? All the bishops, not only sacrilegious but infatuate, who carried in silk and gold a vile thing and crumbling ashes. Fools, the people of all the Churches, who met the sacred relics, and received them as joyfully as if they saw the prophet present and alive; so that, from Palestine even unto Chalcedon, swarms of people intermingled continuously, and with one voice resounded the praises of Christ. It seems they were adoring Samuel, not Christ, whose Levite and prophet Samuel was!

"'You reverence the dead, and therefore you blaspheme.' Read the Gospel, 'I am the God of Abraham, Isaac, and Jacob; He is not God of the dead, but of the living.' If, then, they live, they are not shut up in an honourable prison, as you would have it. For you say that the souls of Apostles and martyrs rest either in Abraham's bosom, or under the altar of God, nor can be present from their tombs and where they will. It seems they have a sort of senatorial dignity, not shut up, indeed, with murderers in the most horrible prison, but in free and honourable confinement in isles of the blessed and the Elysian fields! Are you the man to prescribe laws to God? will you put chains on Apostles? so that, till the judgment-day, those are kept in ward, and are not with their Lord, of whom it is written, 'They follow the Lamb, whithersoever He goeth?' If the Lamb be everywhere, they, too, must be considered everywhere who are with the Lamb. And, whereas the devil and the demons range the whole earth, and by their extreme rapidity are everywhere present, shall martyrs, after the outpouring of their blood, be shut up under the altar so as to be unable to leave it?

"You say, in your book, that 'while we live we can pray for each other, but after death no one's prayer for another is to be heard; especially since martyrs, though praying for the vengeance of their own blood, have not availed to obtain it.' If Apostles and martyrs, while in the body, can pray for others, when they ought as yet to be solicitous about themselves, how much rather after their crown, their victory, and their triumph? Paul, the Apostle, says, that two hundred and seventy-six souls in the ship were granted to him; shall Vigilantius, a living dog, be better than a dead lion? So I might rightly argue from Ecclesiastes, could I confess that Paul was dead in spirit. In short, saints are not said to be dead, but asleep.

"We do not light wax tapers in the broad day, as you idly slander us, but to relieve the darkness of night by this substitute; and we watch unto the light, lest, blinded with you, we may sleep in the dark. If any secular men, or at least religious women, through ignorance and simplicity, of whom we may truly say, 'They have a zeal of God, but not according to knowledge;' if such have done this for the honour of martyrs, what do you lose by it? Once, even Apostles complained of the loss of the ointment, but they were reproved by the Lord's voice. Not that Christ needed ointment, nor the martyrs wax lights; and yet that woman so acted in Christ's honour, and her devotion was accepted. And whoever light wax tapers are rewarded according to their faith, as the Apostle speaks, 'Let every one be fully persuaded in his own mind.' Do you call such men idolaters? I do not deny that all of us who believe in Christ have come out of the errors of idolatry: for we are not born, but new-born Christians. And because we once honoured idols, ought we now not to honour God, lest we seem to venerate Him with an honour like that paid to idols? That was done to idols, and therefore was detestable; this is done to martyrs, and therefore is allowable. For even without the remains of martyrs, throughout the Churches of the East, when the Gospel is read, lights are lit, while the sun is bright, not at all to chase away the dark, but as a sign of rejoicing. Whence, too, those Virgins in the Gospel have always their lamps lit. And the Apostles are told to have their loins girded, and burning lights in their hands: and John Baptist is said to be a 'burning and shining light:' that under the type of material light might be signified that Light of which we read in the Psalter, 'Thy word, O Lord, is a lanthorn unto my feet, and a light unto my paths.'" 5–8.

I have already allowed that there are points in Jerome's tone of mind which I receive at the Church's hands without judging; and, again, that superstitions existed in the Church of his day about the holy relics, as, indeed, he seems to grant in the above extract; yet, after all allowances on this, and the other subjects which have come here before us, I do not see that our Protestant brethren gain much by their appeal to the history of Aerius, Jovinian, and Vigilantius.

Chapter V: And What Do The Apostolical Canons Say?

p. 417.1–2. CHAPTER V. ... AND WHAT DO THE APOSTOLICAL CANNONS SAY?] * CHAPTER XVI. CANONS OF THE APOSTLES. "Let Thy Thummin and Thy Urim be with Thy holy one, whom Thou didst prove at Massah, and with whom Thou didst strive at the waters of Meribah; who said unto his father and to his mother, I have not seen him; neither did he acknowledge his brethren, nor knew his own children: for they have observed Thy word and kept Thy covenant."

p. 417. 9–11. to be unscriptural. ... beyond the beaten paths of orthodoxy,] * to be unscriptural. Let the object with which they have been adduced be clearly understood: not thereby directly to prove the truth of those doctrines and practices; but, the hypothesis having been hazarded in some quarters, that *perhaps* those doctrines and practices were an early corruption, and the burden of proving a negative being thrown upon us by men who are better pleased to suggest doubts than to settle anything, we, in our excess of consideration, are going from one quarter to another, prying and extravagating beyond the beaten paths of orthodoxy

p. 417. 23–28. of the Catholic Church. ... The problem before] ⋆ of the Catholic Church.

The more we can vary our witnesses, the better. The consent of Fathers is one sort of witness to Apostolical truth; the accordance of heretics is another; received usage is another. I shall now give, at some length, an instance of the last-mentioned, as afforded in the existence of the Apostolical Canons [footnote: The following account is principally from Bishops Beveridge and Pearson.] and, with that view, I must beg indulgence once in a way, to engage myself in a dry and somewhat tedious discussion.

p. 419. 24–26. Accordingly, Protestants ... was certainly lost;–] ⋆ Whether, however, there be a scarcity of primitive documents or not, I would contend that, supposing the appeal to facts be allowed as a legitimate line of argument, not only there is none for them, but there is enough for us. But the advocates of the creed, by courtesy called Protestantism, do not allow the appeal; they aver that the Apostolic system of the Church was certainly lost,

p. 421. 10–17. address their reason. ... to the general reader.] ⋆ address their reason. With this view I have been inquiring into certain early works, unpopular either in their day or afterwards, to see if any vestige of the hypothetical system in question can be discovered there; for, as to the body of orthodox Fathers, it is pretty well acknowledged that there is nothing ultra-Protestant in them. With this object, then, I have been discussing the Canons called Apostolical.

pp.421. 24–422. 2. These Canons, ... in most parts of Christendom.] ⋆ These Canons were once supposed to be, strictly speaking, Apostolical, and published before A.D. 50. On the other hand, it has been contended that they were composed by some heretic after 450. Our own divines maintain that they were published before 325, and were undoubtedly the digest of Catholic authorities in the course of the second and third, or at the end of the second century, and were received and used in most parts of Christendom.

p. 425. 17–19. of continual obligation; ... But we do know,] ⋆ of continual obligation, yet, in knowing that rules of some kind were in force, we shall possess a fact incompatible with that free-and-easy mode of religion in which ultra-Protestants glory. They glory in being independent; they think it a beauty to be all pulling different ways, and to have as many various rites and regimens as there are tastes and likings in the world. They can be quite sentimental and poetical on the subject; expatiate on the excellence of "agreeing to differ;" descant on the variety of nature, and insist, as philosophers, upon the immateriality of "differences in Church government," while what they call "doctrine" is preserved, or while hearts are one. There is a popular story of a woman fainting on a Sunday, as the whole town was coming from worship, and an Anabaptist providing the chair, and a Quaker a smelling-bottle, and a Roman Catholic a handkerchief, and a Churchman running for a doctor, and the doctor turning out to be a Swedenborgian. It is something of this kind; and then a sagacious father, who seems to have been leading his son round the town instead of taking him to divine service anywhere, points it out to his notice thus:– "See, my boy, what mankind were made to agree in, and what to differ in!" What would the stern old Fathers of Nicæa have said to this? – with their notions of "the Canon," what would they have said to a mixed set of religionists, *zonis solutis*, who glory in having nothing external in common, and who prate about "the superiority of unanimity to uniformity?" Or, as I should rather put it, what do our religionists say to it? or do they get themselves to contemplate the fact, of a vast number of leading men, (to put the matter at the lowest,) from all parts of Christendom, witnessing to the existence of a state of things which they must have known as perfectly as we know what has happened ever since the Reformation, nay, which occupies a less period, and describing circumstances which are quite irreconcilable with modern notions, in the same unhesitating and quiet tone which we should use in speaking of the last three centuries? I believe, when they get themselves to consider it, they are obliged, – they do not scruple, – to say, that an universal corruption, a sudden lapse of the Church, took place *immediately* after the Apostles; though how they can support this hypothesis, when it is narrowly considered, does not appear.

But to return. Even though the Canons we possess were not genuine, and though the Fathers and the Councils which refer to Canons did not mention what was the subject of them, yet the very fact, I say, that there *were* Canons from time immemorial, would be a sufficient confutation of the antithesis now so popular between unanimity and uniformity – it establishes the *principle* of uniformity as being Apostolical. But we do know,

p. 431. 8. apostolic *depositum*;] * apostolic *revelation*;

p. 432. 7–8. and the Decrees of the Popes. ... This, then, seems to be the state of the case] * and the Decrees of the popes. And this conclusion would be abundantly confirmed by a remarkable decree of Pope Gelasius, if it could be trusted as genuine, and which, any how, shows the feelings of the Latins even at a later date. Gelasius is said to have held a council of seventy bishops at Rome, A.D. 494, and to have passed a decree concerning books received in the Church, which may be made to accord to what Dionysius wrote six years later. In this decree, after enumerating the books of the Old and New Testament, the determinations of the four first General Councils, and the works of certain of the Fathers, as being of authority, he proceeds, "But the compositions or teaching of heretics or schismatics are in nowise received by the Catholic and Apostolic Roman Church; of which a few that are extant shall be specified, which are to be avoided by Catholics." Then follows a list of "apocryphal" books, such as the works of Hermas, Clement of Alexandria, Tertullian, Eusebius's History, Lactantius, and, among them, "the Apocryphal Book of Canons of the Apostles." Perhaps the utmost this could be taken to mean would be, that the Book of Canons had never been *received* in the Roman Church. That *some* of the canons were received in it, we know, indeed, from the words of Pope Julius already cited, and from the fact that many of them were incorporated in the decrees of the four General Councils; still the "*body* of canons" may have been peculiar to the East, – as we know, in fact, the traditions of the East and West varied from each other on certain points, as in the questions of the observance of Easter, and of heretical baptism, in the former of which, at least, Apostles themselves seemed to have determined variously. Even if the decree is literally taken to mean, that the Book of Canons is the compilation of heretics, (though, if so, the works of Hermas and Clement of Alexandria are strangely involved in the same imputation,) no serious conclusions will follow. For though the Canons were *put together* by heretics it does not follow that they themselves are heretical; and that a great number are not, we know, from the testimony of the Fathers in their favour, as above insisted on. If indeed, the compiler altered, or suppressed, or invented canons, that is another matter; then he was something more than a compiler; but in merely collecting them, he as little impaired the Canons themselves as Bucer or Peter Martyr would have hurt the doctrine of our Prayer Book, had they collected together in one, without altering, the Catholic devotions of the Church before them. At the same time, if heretics did add to the matter of the Canons, *then* the witness these Canons afford to the primitive religion is still more remarkable. We know, independently of these Canons, what the kind of worship and discipline was which obtained in the Catholic Church; and in these Canons we shall *then* possess an *heretical* testimony to it quite in accordance. In that case, ultra-Protestantism will lose the chance even of heretical support, which was all it had from the first to look for.

But, as the fact really is, this decree of Gelasius' is not genuine. It is not mentioned till three hundred years after its supposed promulgation, and there is reason to believe that Gelasius, so far from rejecting, actually did receive and use the Canons in question. But the discussion of this point would be a deviation from the subject before us.

This, then, seems to be the state of the case

p. 436. 4–8. as a basis for its own. . . . "All who come [to church] to hear] ★ as a basis for its own. The former says, simply, –

"The bishops of every nation are bound to acknowledge the principal among them, and to count him as a head, and to do nothing extraordinary without his advice, but to do those things alone individually which relate to the diocese of each respectively and its towns. He, in turn, must not act without the advice of all."

These plain directions are thus amplified in the Canon of Antioch:–

"The bishops in each province are bound to acknowledge the bishop ruling in the metropolitan see, and that he has the care of the whole province, because all who have business have recourse from every quarter to the metropolis. Whence it has seemed good that he should be first in honour also, and that the other bishops should do nothing extraordinary without him, (according to that most ancient canon which has been in force from our fathers' time,) or such things only as relate to the diocese of each and the places under it. For, each bishop has power over his own diocese to administer it according to his own conscience, and to provide for the whole territory subject to his own city, so as to ordain presbyters and deacons, and to dispose all things with consideration, but to attempt no proceedings beyond this without the metropolitan bishop; and he, in turn, must not act without the advice of the rest."

Or, again, take the following instance; which, when read with the words in brackets, agrees, with but slight exceptions, with the Antiochene, and, without them, with the Apostolical Canon:–

"All who come [to church] to hear

pp. 441. 33–442. 31. These rules furnish us with large portions, . . . the first age of Christianity, or with the last?] ★ Now let us picture to ourselves the irksome position of a modern Protestant in a communion where such points were first principles; with his societies instead of the Church – his committees, boards, and platforms, instead of bishops – his Record or Patriot newspaper instead of councils – his "concerts for prayer" instead of anathemas on heretics and sectaries – his harangues at public meetings instead of exorcisms – his fourths of October instead of festival days – his glorious memories instead of holy commemorations – his cheap religion instead of gold and silver vessels – his gas and stoves for wax and oil – and his denunciations of self-righteousness for fasting and celibacy. Can we doubt that such Canons imply altogether a different notion of Christianity from that which he has been accustomed to entertain? *This*, indeed, would be the very fault he would find with the whole system, – he would say he was not at home in it, or in other words, that there is nothing evangelical in such ecclesiastical regulations; and yet after all quite as much surely as in the rules laid down by St. Paul, as in the fifth, or seventh, or eleventh and twelfth, or fourteenth chapters of his first epistle to the Corinthians; the ninth chapter of his second; or the fourth and fifth of his first to Timothy. I do not mean to allow the essential Gospel doctrines are absent from the Canons, which no one will say who has studied them. But even if they were, such absence is not in point, unless it is a proof that rulers of the Church do not hold doctrines, because they *also* give rules of discipline, and, when giving the latter, do not deliver the former instead. Certain doctrines may be true, and certain ordinances also; the one may be prescribed in Canons, the other taught in Confessions. It does not follow that those who enforce the one do not enforce the other; but it does follow that those who enforce the latter to the exclusion of the former, do not enforce both. Those who enforce the discipline, need not deny the doctrine; but those who think to escape the discipline by professing the doctrine, are more careful of doctrine than the early Church was, and have no congeniality of feeling with times which considered it better to follow out what they had received than to reason against it, "to do these, and not leave the other undone."

Such, then, is a sketch of the main rules of discipline in the primitive Church as they have come down to us, and which I offer for those whom it may concern. They show clearly enough the sort of religion which was then considered Apostolic; not that which *we* should term the "free-and-easy" religion, but what our opponents would call the "formal and superstitious."

APPENDIX 5

CHAPTER IV
THE PENITENCE OF THEODOSIUS.

"Be wise now, therefore, O ye kings; be learned, ye that are judges of the earth. Serve the Lord with fear, and rejoice unto Him with reverence. Kiss the Son, lest He be angry, and so ye perish from the right way."

It is very satisfactory to find that the Christian fortitude of St. Ambrose was not thrown away upon Valentinian. This young prince, who died prematurely, nay, before his baptism, gave signs during several of his last years, of a very altered state of mind towards the Church and her vigorous champion. Such was the fruit of braving the frown of royalty in a good cause. Perhaps St. Ambrose would not have done as much by what men call more prudent conduct; by temporizing and conceding. There is no sort of doubt, that had the scene been laid in England in the nineteenth, not to speak in very generosity of the sixteenth, courtliness would have been the order of the day. The Basilica would have been surrendered to the heretics; yet I fear without that change of heart being wrought in prince or prime minister, by a timid policy in the Church to which Valentinian was led by meeting with resistance. Certainly we have not made great men more religious by letting them have their own way. As for Valentinian, he was cut off under very sad yet interesting circumstances. Being engaged in Gaul in an attempt to reduce the power of Arbogastes, the Frank, who was secretly conspiring against him, he wrote to St. Ambrose to come to him, both to assist him in his negotiations and to baptize. Before Ambrose could arrive, Arbogastes had murdered the emperor.

But, leaving Valentinian, let us turn to the consideration of a still more striking and salutary instance of episcopal vigour, exerted in the case of a more powerful emperor; I mean the conduct of St. Ambrose towards Theodosius, on the occasion of the massacre at Thessalonica. This is the most instructive passage in his history; nay, perhaps in the history of the whole Church; for what sight can be more edifying to the Christian, or more impressive to the world at large, than that of a bishop conscientiously and calmly rebuking a great warrior, and that warrior and sovereign humbly confessing and repenting of his sin?

The circumstances which led to this memorable display of Apostolical severity were as follows:– Theodosius was of a choleric temper, which hurried him on to visit, with the power of an emperor, insults which every one, prince and subject, naturally feels. In the year 390, a tumult took place in Thessalonica on some supposed grievance, such as commonly excites a populace, which ended in the murder of the commander of the imperial forces, who had given the offence, and other officers. The first burst of the emperor's indignation was overcome by the interposition of the clergy, particularly Ambrose; and he promised to pardon the Thessalonians. But his ministers considered the outrage too great to be passed over with safety to the empire: a similar tumult had lately been pardoned at Antioch; and, in the present instance, there had been no tyranny or impolitic rigour on the part of the unfortunate general who had been the victim of the insurrection. So far, their judgment was doubtless right; but the sentence, which they succeeded in recommending to their sovereign, was so shocking, as sufficiently to account for the previous intercession of the Church in behalf of the offenders. The purpose of vengeance was kept secret; the Thessalonians were invited to the circus, which was silently surrounded by soldiery; and, when they expected the races to commence, a signal was given, and a promiscuous massacre followed. It continued for three hours; and 7000, without discrimination of age or sex, are said to have been slaughtered. Theodosius had revoked the cruel order soon after it was given, but too late to prevent its execution.

These events took place in the early spring; and soon afterwards Theodosius returned to Milan. Ambrose had been in the habit of attending the court on its arrival; but now he retired into the country two or three days beforehand. Thence he despatched the following letters to the emperor, who seems to have expressed surprise at his absence:–

"Augustissimo Imperatori THEODOSIO, AMBROSIUS episcopus.

"I bear an affectionate memory of your former friendship towards me, and of your great condescension in so often granting favours to others at my instance. Accordingly, it is not ingratitude that leads me to shun a presence which hitherto has ever been most coveted by me. I will briefly explain to you my reasons for doing so.

"I found that I was forbidden, I alone of your whole court, the natural right of hearing what went on about me, with a view of depriving me of the privilege of speaking. I know you have not unfrequently been displeased at my knowledge of measures which were determined on in your council. Thus I am deprived of this liberty, though the Lord Jesus says that 'there is nothing hid, but shall be made manifest.' However, I acquiesced in the imperial will with all dutifulness; and I took measures for obviating your displeasure, by providing that no news about the imperial statutes should be brought me.

"What else then could I do? Not hear? as if my ears could be closed with the wax which ancient fables speak of? Say what I heard? I could not without hazarding by my words what I feared in your counsels, – some act of blood. Be silent? This would be most wretched of all – to have one's conscience bound and one's lips closed. Is it not written, 'If God's minister fail to speak to the sinner, the latter shall die in his sin; but he shall answer for not speaking?'

"Suffer me, gracious emperor. You have zeal for the faith, I own it; and the fear of God, I confess it; but you have an impetuosity of nature at offenders, which a counsellor may either soothe into compassion, or stimulate till self-government is almost lost. O that those about you were as backward in rousing as they are in appeasing it! I would gladly leave it altogether to your own management; since you can recover yourself, and get the better of this violence of nature by an effort to be merciful.

"I thought it best to leave your own reflections to overcome it, instead of running the risk of increasing it by some public interposition. So I resolved rather to be wanting in my duty towards my office, than in my deference towards my sovereign; and that the world should think me deficient in episcopal vigour rather than that you should accuse my loyalty, so that repressing your anger, you might have free opportunity for determining your course of action. I excused my attendance on the plea of my health, which indeed was severely tried, and which men of merciful minds alone could improve; yet I would rather have died than have been behindhand by a day or two in presenting myself on your arrival. But I knew not what to do.

"A deed has been perpetrated in Thessalonica, which has no parallel in history; which I in vain attempted to prevent; yes, which I protested would be most atrocious, in the frequent expostulations I addressed to you beforehand; nor could I extenuate a deed which you, by your unsuccessful attempts to hinder it, have confessed to be heinous. When the news came, I was engaged in a synod, held on the arrival of the Gallic bishops. All assembled deplored it, none viewed it leniently; your friendship with Ambrose weighed nothing in your favour. Surely the odium of the crime would fall even more heavily on me, should no reconciliation to Almighty God be required of you.

"O emperor, why should you feel shame to act as David acted. – he who was a prophet as well as a king, and a forefather of Christ according to the flesh? A parable was set before him; and, when he found that by it he himself was condemned, he said, 'I have sinned before the Lord.' Take it not ill, then, O emperor, if the same words are used towards you as the prophet used to David – 'Thou art the man.' For if you give due attention to them, and answer 'I have sinned against the Lord,' if you utter that royal and prophetic strain, 'O come, let us worship, and fall down, and kneel before the Lord our Maker,' then it will be said to you, 'Since it repenteth thee, the Lord putteth away they sin: thou shalt not die.'

"I have written this, not to overpower you, but to induce you, by a royal example, to put away this sin from your kingdom, – that is, – by humbling your soul to God. You are a man; temptation has come upon you: get the better of it. Tears and penitence are the only remedy for sin, neither angel nor archangel can take it away; the Lord Himself, who alone can say, 'I am with you always,' even He pardons not except upon penitence.

"I entreat, I demand, I exhort, I admonish; for it sorrows me to think that one, who was a pattern of singular mercy, who was remarkable for clemency, and rescued even individual culprits from their difficulties, should now feel no remorse at the death of a guiltless multitude. Successful as you have been in battle, and great in other aspects, yet it was mercy which crowned all your doings. The devil has envied your chief excellence. Overcome him while you have the means. Add not one sin to another by conduct from which too many suffer.

"For my part, debtor as I am to your clemency in all other things, grateful as I must ever be to it, greater as I have ever thought it than that of all other emperors but one, and unsuspicious though I am as yet of contumacy on your part, still I have apprehension; I dare not offer sacrifice if you resolve to attend. Is that lawful when many innocents have bled, which is not lawful in a solitary murder? I trow not.

"O emperor, I much regret that, in the beginning of this business, I left it to the risk of your temper instead of moving in it myself. When I consider that your pardon is suddenly given, suddenly recalled, as often before, it would appear that you have been overtaken, and I have not averted what it was not right perhaps to anticipate. But thanks be to God, who is pleased to chastise His poor servants lest He lose them altogether. This is my lot in common with the prophets; be it yours in common with the saints.

"Do not I love the father of Gratian more even than my own eyes? Your other innocent children seem to intercede for you also. I mention that beloved youth, not to exclude, but to represent the rest. You have my love, my affection, my prayers. If you have confidence in me, obey me, and allow what I say: if not, make allowance for what I do, in that I prefer God to my sovereign. Gracious emperor, may you and your dear children enjoy everlasting peace."

This letter which is written rather with the familiarity and affection of a friend than with the measured precision of an ecclesiastical censure, is thus summarily treated by the historian Gibbon:– "His epistle is a miserable rhapsody on a noble subject. Ambrose could act better than he could write. His compositions are destitute of taste or genius," – a remark which may be taken as one instance out of many of obliquity of mind or rapidity of judgment in that able writer. In spite of his apparent candour, few persons have been such *practical* haters of Christianity and the Church; and Ambrose was one of those who most especially merited his disgust, by the intrepidity with which he thrust the claims of sacred truth upon the world, – claims, which unbelievers would fain have shut up in the library of the theologian, or within the precincts of consecrated ground.

There is nothing to show how Theodosius bore the remonstrance of Ambrose on the first receipt of it. We next hear of him as attempting to attend divine service at Milan, where Ambrose officiated, having by this time returned to the city. He was met at the entrance by the man of God, who thus addressed him:–

"Surely your majesty is not aware of the heinousness of the slaughter which has taken place. Passion is over; yet reason does not yet estimate the crime. Perchance kingly rule is an obstacle to repentance, and sovereignty prevents reflection. Yet it is as well for a man to feel his perishable nature, and remember that dust is his beginning and his end, in spite of that gorgeous purple which may beguile the heart, but cannot reverse the feebleness of the frame it covers. Your subjects, emperor, are your fellow-creatures; I should rather say, your fellow-servants, – servants of one universal Lord and King, the Maker of the universe. Dare you, then, look upon His shrine, who is Lord of low as well as high? – dare you tread His holy pavement? – dare you stretch forth hands, which are yet reeking with the blood of innocent victims? – dare you receive in them the most holy body of your Lord? – dare you taste His precious blood with lips which have spoken their rage in an unjust slaughter? Go hence; add not a new offence to what is past; submit to the bond which is placed upon you according to the will of the Most High. Take it as medicine to restore your soul."

Theodosius yielded to the voice of the Church; – he retired home, where he remained suspended from Christian communion for eight months.

Christmas was now come, and the emperor made a second attempt to join in public worship, considering doubtless that he had already suffered a sufficient penance for his crime. His minister, Ruffinus, who had been the adviser of the massacre, had found him in tears; and on inquiring the cause of his grief, had been reminded of his state of separation from the Church. "Servants and beggars," said the emperor, "may enter freely to join in prayer; but against me the gates of heaven are shut; for well I know what the Lord has so clearly said, 'Whom ye bind shall be bound in heaven.' " Ruffinus persuaded him to let him go to Ambrose; and Theodosius, impatient at his delay, set out towards the church before his return. When he had got as far as the forum, he was met by his minister, who reported to him the ill success of his mission; on which, with a noble resolution, he declared he would proceed onwards, and undergo the shame which he had deserved.

The bishop's apartments, as has already been noticed, were contained within a range of buildings, of which the Basilica formed a part; and thither, not to the Basilica, Theodosius now betook himself. In the interview which followed, he consented to undergo a public penance; and promised to pass a law that thirty days should, in future, intervene between sentence and execution in all cases of death and confiscation. On these terms he reconciled himself to the Church.

His first appearance in public worship after his absolution, had itself the character of a penance. With all signs of vehement grief, he prostrated himself upon the pavement, and applied the words of the Psalmist to his own situation, – "My soul cleaveth unto the dust: quicken Thou me, according to Thy word." It so happened when the time came for presenting the oblation at the altar, instead of retiring from the chancel, he remained, through forgetfulness, within the rails, according to the custom of the Eastern Church, there to receive the sacrament. Ambrose ventured not to relax one tittle of the stern discipline of the Latins, even to reward a penitent monarch. He sent his archdeacon to signify to him that none but ordained persons were allowed to remain in the sanctuary; on which the emperor promptly retired. Some writers, however, consider that this took place on his first arrival at Milan from the East.

Theodoret adds, that, on his return to Constantinople, one day after making his offering at the altar as usual, he retired, as he had learned from Ambrose, without the rails, and was recalled by the Patriarch Nectarius. Upon this he observed, "Of all whom I have met, Ambrose is the only BISHOP."

Perhaps an unlearned reader might imagine Theodosius some weak prince, such as might be expected in the latter days of Rome, the offspring and the instrument of her degeneracy. For such an one I will quote the unsuspicious evidence of the historian Gibbon: –

"The wisdom of his laws, and the success of his arms, rendered his administration respectable in the eyes both of his subjects and of his enemies. He loved and practised the virtues of domestic life, which seldom hold their residence in the palaces of kings. Theodosius was chaste and temperate; he enjoyed, without excess, the sensual and social pleasures of the table; and the warmth of his amorous passions was never diverted from their lawful objects. The proud titles of imperial greatness were adorned by the tender names of a faithful husband, an indulgent father. His uncle was raised, by his affectionate esteem, to the rank of a second parent.

Theodosius embraced, as his own, the children of his brother and sister; and the expressions of his regard were extended to the distant and obscure branches of his numerous kindred. His familiar friends were judiciously selected from among those persons who, in the intercourse of private life, had appeared before his eyes without a mask; the conscientiousness of personal and superior merit enabled him to despise the accidental distinction of the purple; and he proved, by his conduct, that he had forgotten all the injuries, while he most gratefully remembered all the favours and services, which he had received before he ascended the throne of the Roman empire. The serious or lively tone of his conversation was adapted to the age, the rank, or the character of his subjects whom he admitted into his society; and the affability of his manners displayed the image of his mind. Theodosius respected the simplicity of the good and virtuous; every art, every talent of an useful, even of an innocent nature, was rewarded by his judicious liberality; and, except the heretics, whom he persecuted with implacable hatred, the diffusive circle of his benevolence was circumscribed only by the limits of the human race. The government of a mighty empire may assuredly suffice to occupy the time and abilities of a mortal: yet the diligent prince, without aspiring to the unsuitable reputation of profound learning, always reserved some moments of his leisure for the instructive amusement of reading. History, which enlarged his experience, was his favourite study. ... His disinterested opinion of past events was usefully applied as the rule of his actions; and Theodosius has deserved the singular commendation, that his virtues always seemed to expand with his fortune; the season of his prosperity was that of his moderation; and his clemency appeared the most conspicuous after the danger and success of the civil war. But the emperor showed himself much more attentive to relieve the innocent the innocent than to chastise the guilty. The oppressed subjects of the West, who would have deemed themselves happy in the restoration of their lands, were astonished to receive a sum of money equivalent to their losses; and the liberality of the conqueror supported the aged mother, and educated the orphan daughter of Maximus. A character thus accomplished might almost excuse the extravagant supposition of the orator Pacatus, – that, if the elder Brutus could be permitted to revisit the earth, the stern republican would abjure, at the feet of Theodosius, his hatred of kings; and ingenuously confess, that such a monarch was the most faithful guardian of the happiness and dignity of the Roman people."

Such was the Great Theodosius; – such in his virtues, in his offence, and in his penitence.

CHAPTER XVI
CANONS OF THE APOSTLES

"Let Thy Thummin and Thy Urim be with Thy holy one, whom Thou didst prove at Massah, and with whom Thou didst strive at the waters of Meribah; who said unto his father and to his mother, I have not seen him; neither did he acknowledge his brethren, nor knew his own children: for they have observed Thy word and kept Thy covenant."

Such is the testimony borne in different ways by Origen, Eusebius, and Cyril, Aerius, Jovinian, and Vigilantius, to the immemorial reception, among Christians, of those doctrines and practices which the private judgment of this age considers to be unscriptural. Let the object with which they have been adduced be clearly understood: not thereby directly to prove the truth of those doctrines and practices; but, the hypothesis having been hazarded in some quarters, that *perhaps* those doctrines were an early corruption, and the burden of proving a negative being thrown upon us by men who are better pleased to suggest doubts than to settle anything, we, in our excess of consideration, are going about from one quarter to another, prying and extravagating beyond the beaten paths of orthodoxy, for the chance of detecting some sort of testimony in favour of our opponents. With this object I have fallen upon the writers aforesaid, and since they have been more or less accused of heterodoxy, I thought there was a chance of their subserving the cause of Protestantism, which the Catholic Fathers certainly do not subserve; but they, though differing from each other most materially, and some of them differing from the Church, do not any one of them approximate to the tone or language of the movement of 1517. Every additional instance of this kind goes indirectly to corroborate the testimony of the Catholic Church.

The more we can vary our witnesses, the better. The consent of the Fathers is one sort of witness to Apostolical truth; the accordance of heretics is another; received usage is a third. I shall now give, at some length, an instance of this last mentioned, as afforded in the existence of the Apostolical Canons[1]; and with that view, I must beg indulgence once in a way, to engage myself in a dry and somewhat tedious discussion. These Canons were once supposed to be, strictly speaking, Apostolical, and published before A.D. 50. On the other hand, it has been contended

[1] The following account is principally from Bishops Beveridge and Pearson.

that they were composed by some heretic after 450. Our own divines maintain that they were published before 325, and were undoubtedly the digest of Catholic authorities in the course of the second and third, or at the end of the second century, and were received and used in most parts of Christendom. This view has since been acquiesced in by the theological world, so far as this, to suppose the matter and the enactment of the Canons of the highest antiquity, even though the edition which we possess was not published so early as Bishop Beveridge, for instance, supposes. At the same time it is acknowledged by all parties, that they, as well as some other early documents, have suffered from interpolation, and perhaps by an heretical hand.

They are in number eighty-five, of which the first fifty are considered of superior authority to the remaining thirty-five. What has been conjectured to be their origin will explain the distinction. It was the custom of the early Church, as is well known, to settle in council such points in her discipline, ordinances, and worship, as the Apostles had not prescribed in Scripture, as the occasion arose, after the pattern of their own proceedings in the fifteenth chapter of the Acts; and this, as far as might be, after their unwritten directions, or their practice, or, at least, their mind, or, as it is called in Scripture, their "minding" or "spirit.[2]" Thus it decided upon the question of Easter, upon that of heretical baptism, and the like. And after the same precedent in the Acts, it recorded its decisions in formal decrees, and "delivered them for to keep" through the cities in which its members were found. The Canons in question are supposed to be some of these decrees, of which, first and nearest to the Apostles' times, or in the time of their immediate successors, were published fifty; and in the following age, thirty-five more, which had been enacted in the interval. They claim, then, to be, first, the recorded judgment of great portions of the Ante-Nicene Church, chiefly in the eastern provinces, upon certain matters in dispute, and to be of authority so far as that Church may be considered a representative of the mind of the Apostles; next, they profess to embody in themselves positive decisions and injunctions of the Apostles, though without clearly discriminating how much is thus directly Apostolical, and how much not. I will here attempt to state some of the considerations which show both antiquity and authority, and afterwards use them for the purpose which has led me to mention them.

1. In the first place, it would seem quite certain that, as, on the one hand, councils were held in the primitive Church, so, on the other, they enacted certain Canons. When, then, a collection professing itself to consist of the Ante-Nicene Canons, there is nothing at all to startle us; it only professes to set before us that which we know any how must have

---

[2] φοουημα.

existed. We may conjecture, if we please, that the fact that there were Canons must have suggested and encouraged a counterfeit. Certainly; but though the fact that there were such will account for a counterfeit, it will not account for the original being lost; on the contrary, what is known to have once existed as a rule of conduct, is likely to continue in existence, except under particular circumstances. Which of the two this collection is, the genuine or the counterfeit, must depend on other considerations; but if these be in favour of its genuineness, then this antecedent probability will be an important confirmation.

Canons, I say, must have existed, whether these be the real ones or no; and the circumstance that there were real ones, must have tended to make it difficult to substitute others. It would be no easy thing in our own Church to pass off another set of articles for the Thirty-nine, and obliterate the genuine: Canons are public property, and have to be acted upon by large bodies. Accordingly, as might be expected, the Nicene Council, when enacting Canons of its own, refers to certain Canons as already existing, and speaks of them in that familiar and indirect way which would be natural under the circumstances, and as we speak of our Rubrics or Articles. The Fathers of the Council mention certain descriptions of persons whom "*the Canon* admits into holy orders;" they determine that a certain rule shall be in force, "according to the Canon which says so and so;" they speak of a transgression of the Canon, and proceed to explain and enforce it. Nor is the Nicene the only Council which recognises the existence of certain Canons, or rules, by which the Church was at that time bound. The Councils of Antioch, Gangra, Constantinople, and Carthage, in the same century, do so likewise: so do individual Fathers, Alexander, Athanasius, Basil, Julius, and others.

Now here we have lighted upon an important circumstance, whatever becomes of the particular collection of Canons before us. It seems that, at the Nicene Council, only two centuries and a quarter after St. John's death, about the distance of time we are from the Hampton Court Conference, all Christendom confessed, that from time immemorial it had been guided by certain ecclesiastical rules, which it considered of authority, which it did not ascribe to any particular persons or synods, (a sign of great antiquity,) and which writers of the day assign to the Apostles. I suppose we know pretty well, at this day, what the customs of our Church have been since James the First's time, or the Reformation; and if respectable writers at present were to state some of them, – for instance, that it is the rule of the Protestant Church that the king should name the bishops, that convocation should not sit without his leave, or that Easter should be kept according to the Roman rule, – we should think foreigners very unreasonable who doubted their word. Now, in the case before us, we find the Church Catholic, the first time it had ever met together since the Apostles' days, speaking as a matter of course of the rules to which it had ever been accustomed to defer. If we knew no more than this, and did not know what the rules were, or if, knowing what they were, we yet decide, as we well may, that the particular rules are not of continual obligation, yet, in knowing that rules of some kind were in force, we shall possess a fact incompatible with that free-and-easy mode of religion in which ultra-Protestants glory. They glory in being independent; they think it a beauty to be all pulling different ways, and to have as many various rites and regimens as there are tastes and likings in the world. They can be quite sentimental and poetical on the subject; expatiate on the excellence of "agreeing to differ;" descant on the variety of nature, and insist, as philosophers, upon the immateriality of "differences in Church government," while what they call "doctrine" is preserved, or while hearts are one. There is a popular story of a woman fainting on a Sunday, as the whole town was coming from worship, and an Anabaptist providing the chair, and a Quaker a smelling-bottle, and a Roman Catholic a handkerchief, and a Churchman running for a doctor, and the doctor turning out to be a Swedenborgian. It is something of this kind; and then a sagacious father, who seems to have been leading his son round the town instead of taking him to divine service anywhere, points it out to his notice thus:– "See, my boy, what mankind were made to agree in, and what to differ in!" What would the stern old Fathers of Nicæa have said to this? – with their notions of "the Canon," what would they have said to a mixed set of religionists, *zonis solutis*, who glory in having nothing external in common, and who prate about "the superiority of unanimity to uniformity?" Or, as I should rather put it, what do our religionists say to it? or do they get themselves to contemplate the fact, of a vast number of leading men, (to put the matter at the lowest,) from all parts of Christendom, witnessing to the existence of a state of things which they must have known as perfectly as we know what has happened ever since the Reformation, nay, which occupies a less period, and describing circumstances which are quite irreconcilable with modern notions, in the same unhesitating and quiet tone which we should use in speaking of the last three centuries? I believe, when they get themselves to consider it, they are obliged, – they do not scruple, – to say, that an universal corruption, a sudden lapse of the Church, took place *immediately* after the Apostles; though how they can support this hypothesis, when it is narrowly considered, does not appear.

But to return. Even though the Canons we possess were not genuine, and though the Fathers and the Councils which refer to Canons did not mention what was the subject of them, yet the very fact, I say, that there *were* Canons from time immemorial, would be a sufficient confutation of the antithesis now so popular between unanimity and uniformity – it establishes the *principle* of uniformity as being Apostolical. But we do know, from the works of the Fathers, the *subjects* of these Canons, and that to the number of thirty or forty of them; so that we might form a code, as far as it goes, of primitive discipline, quite independent of the particular Collection which is under discussion. However, it is remarkable that all thirty or forty are found in this collection, being altogether nearly half the whole number, so that the only question is, whether the rest are of the same value of which we know a great proportion of them to be. Further, it is remarkable that *no* Ecclesiastical Canon is mentioned in the historical documents of the primitive era which is not found in the Collection; which shows that, whoever compiled it, the work was done with considerable care. The opponents to its genuineness bring, indeed, several exceptions, as they wish to consider them; but these admit of so satisfactory an explanation as to illustrate the proverb, that *exceptio probat regulam.*

Before going on, however, to consider the whole Collection, let us see in what terms the ancient writers referred to speak of those particular Canons which they cite.

Athanasius speaks as follows:– "*Canons and forms,*" he says, when describing the extraordinary violences of the Arians, "*were not given to the Churches in this day, but were handed down from our fathers well and securely.* Nor again, has the faith had its beginning in this day, but has passed on even to us from the Lord through His disciples. Rouse yourselves, then, my brethren, to prevent that from perishing unawares in the present day *which has been observed in the Churches from ancient times down to us,* and ourselves from incurring a responsibility in what had been intrusted to us." – *Ep. Encycl.* 1. It is remarkable, in this extract, that St. Athanasius accurately distinguishes between the Faith which came from Christ, and the Canons received from the Fathers of old time: which is just the distinction which our divines are accustomed to make.

Again: the Arians, by simoniacal dealings with the civil power, had placed Gregory in the see of Alexandria. Athanasius observes upon this – "Such conduct is both *a violation of the Ecclesiastical Canons*, and forces the heathen to blaspheme, as if appointments were made, not by Divine ordinance, but by merchandise and secular influence." *Ibid.* 2.

Arsenius, bishop of Hypsela, who had been involved in the Meletian[3] schism, and had acted in a hostile way towards Athanasius, at length reconciled himself to the Church. In his letter to Athanasius he promises "to be obedient to *the Ecclesiastical Canon,* according to ancient usage, and never to put forth any regulation, whether about bishops, or any other public ecclesiastical matter, without the sanction of his metropolitan, but to *submit to all the established Canons.*" – *Apol. contr. Arian.* 69.

In like manner, St. Basil, after speaking of certain crimes for which a deacon should be reduced to lay communion, proceeds, "for *it is ancient*

[3] The Egyptian Meletius, from which this schism has its name, must not be confounded with Melitius of Antioch.

Canon, that they who lose their degree should be subjected to this kind of punishment only." – *Ep.* 188. Again – "*The Canon* altogether excludes from the ministry those who have been twice married."

When Arius and his abettors were excommunicated by Alexander of Alexandria, they betook themselves to Palestine, and were re-admitted into the Church by the bishops of that country. On this, Alexander observes as follows:– "A very heavy imputation, doubtless, lies upon such of my brethren as have ventured on this act, in that it is *a violation of the Apostolical Canon*." – *Theod. Hist.* i. 4.

When Eusebius declined being translated from the see of Cæsarea to Antioch, Constantine complimented him on his "observance of the commandments of God, *the Apostolical Canon*, and the rule of the Church." – *Vit. Constant.* iii. 61 – which last seems to mean the regulation passed at Nicaea.

In like manner, Julius, bishop of Rome, speaks of a violation of "*the Apostles' Canons*;" and a Council held at Constantinople, A.D. 394, which was attended by Gregory Nyssen, Amphilochius, and Flavian, of a determination of "*the Apostolical Canons*."

It will be observed, that in some of these instances the Canons are spoken of in the plural, when the particular offence which occasions their mention is only against some one. This shows that they were collected into a code, if, indeed, that need be proved; for, in truth, for various Canons to exist, and to be in force, and yet not to be put together, is just as unlikely as that no collection should be made of the statutes passed in a session of parliament.

With this historical information about the existence, authority, and subject matter of certain Canons in the Church from time immemorial, we should come to many anti-ultra-Protestant conclusions, even if the particular code we possess turn out to have no intrinsic authority. And now let us see how the matter stands as regards this code of eighty-five Canons.

2. If this collection existed *as* a collection in the time of the above writers and councils, then, considering they allude to nearly half its Canons, and that no Canons are anywhere produceable which are not in it, and that they do seem to allude to a collection, and that no other collection is produceable, we certainly could not avoid the conclusion that they referred to *it*, and that, therefore, in quoting parts of it they sanction the whole. If no book is to be accounted genuine except such parts of it as happen to be expressly cited by other writers, – if it may not be regarded as a whole, and what is actually cited made to bear up and carry with it what is not cited, – no ancient book extant can be proved to be genuine. We believe Virgil's Æneid to be Virgil's, because he wrote an Æneid, and because particular passages which we find in it, and in no other book, are contained, under the name of Virgil, in subsequent writers, or in criticisms, or in accounts of it. We do not divide it into rhapsodies, *because* it

exists but in fragments in the testimony of later literature. For the same reason, if the Canons before us can be shown to have existed as one book in Athanasius's time, it is natural to conceive that they are the very book to which he and others refer. All depends on this. If the collection were made after his time, of course he referred to some other; but if it existed in his time, it is more natural to suppose that there was one collection than two distinct ones, so similar, especially since history is silent about their being two.

However, I conceive it is not worth while to insist upon so early a formation of the existing collection. Whether it existed in Athanasius' time, or was formed afterwards, and formed by friend or foe, heretic or Catholic, seems to me immaterial, as I shall by and by show. First, however, I will state, as candidly as I can, the arguments for and against its antiquity *as* a collection.

Now there can be no doubt that the early Canons were formed into one body; moreover, certain early writers speak of them under the name of "the Apostles' Canons," and "the Apostolical Canons." So far I have already said. Now, certain collectors of canons, of A.D. (more or less) 550, and they no common authorities, also speak of "the Apostolical Canons," and incorporate them into their own larger collections; and these which they speak of are the very body of Canons which we now possess under the name. We know it, for the digest of these collectors is preserved. No reason can be assigned why they should not be speaking of the *same* collection which Gregory Nyssen and Amphilochius speak of, who lived a century and a half before them; no reason, again, why Nyssen and Amphilochius should not mean the same as Athanasius and Julius, who lived fifty to seventy years earlier than themselves. The writers of A.D. 550 might be just as certain that they and St. Athanasius quoted the same work, as we, at this day, that our copy of it is the same as Beveridge's, Pearson's, or Ussher's.

The authorities at the specified date (A.D. 550) are three, – Dionysius Exiguus, John of Antioch, patriarch of Constantinople, and the Emperor Justinian. The learning of Justinian is well known, not to mention that he speaks the opinion of the ecclesiastical lawyers of his age. As to John of Antioch, and Dionysius, since their names are not so familiar to most of us, it may be advisable to say thus much, – that John had been a lawyer, and was well versed both in civil and ecclesiastical matters; hence he has the title of Scholasticus; while Dionysius is the framer of the Christian era, as we still reckon it. They both made Collections of the Canons of the Church, the latter in Latin, and they both include the Apostolical Canons, as we have them, in their editions; with this difference, however, (which does not at present concern us,) that Dionysius publishes but the first fifty, while John of Antioch enumerates the whole eighty-five.

Such is the main argument for the existence of the *collection* which we possess, at the end of the third century; viz. that *a* collection being acknowledged at that date, *this* collection is acknowledged by competent authorities at the end of the fifth. On the other hand, when we inspect the language which Dionysius uses concerning them, in his prefatory epistle, we shall find something which requires explanation. His words are these, addressed to Stephen, bishop of Salona:– "We have, in the first place, translated from the Greek what are called the Canons of the Apostles; *which, as we wish to apprise your holiness, have not gained an easy credit from very many persons.* At the same time, some of the decrees of the [Roman] pontiffs, at a later date, seem to be taken from these very Canons." Dionysius must mean, that they were not received *as* the Apostles'; for they were received, or, at least, nearly half of them, is, as I have said, an historical fact, whatever becomes of the collection as a collection. He must mean, that a claim had been advanced that they were to be received as part of the apostolic *revelation*; and he must deny that they had more than *ecclesiastical* authority. The distinction between divine and ecclesiastical injunctions requires little explanation: the latter are imposed by the Church for the sake of decency and order, as a matter of expedience, safety, propriety, or piety. Such is the rule among ourselves, that dissenting teachers conforming must remain silent for three years before they can be ordained; or that a certain form of prayer should be prescribed for universal use in public service. On the other hand, the appointment of the Sacraments is apostolic and divine. So, again, that no one can be a bishop unless consecrated by a bishop, is apostolic; that three bishops are necessary in consecration is ecclesiastical; and, though ordinarily an imperative rule, yet, under circumstances, admits of dispensation. Or again, it has, for instance, in this day, been debated whether the sanctification of the Lord's day is a divine, or an ecclesiastical appointment. Dionysius, then, in the above extract, means nothing more than to deny that the Apostles enacted these Canons; or, again, that they enacted them *as* Apostles; and he goes on to say, that the popes had acknowledged the *ecclesiastical* authority of some of them by embodying them in their decrees. At the same time, his language certainly seems to show as much as this, and it is confirmed by that of other writers, that the Latin Church, though using them separately as authority, did not receive them as a collection with the implicit deference which they met with in the East; indeed, the last thirty-five, though two of them were cited at Nicæa, and one at Constantinople, A.D. 394, seem to have been in inferior account. The Canons of the General Councils took their place, and the Decrees of the popes. And this conclusion would be abundantly confirmed by a remarkable decree of Pope Gelasius, if it could be trusted as genuine, and which, any how, shows the feelings of the Latins even at a later date. Gelasius is said to have held a council of seventy bishops at Rome, A.D. 494, and to have passed a decree concerning books received in the Church, which may be made to accord to what Dionysius wrote six years later. In this decree, after enumerating the books of the Old and New Testament, the determinations of the four first General Councils, and the works of certain of the Fathers, as being of authority, he proceeds, "But the compositions or teaching of heretics or schismatics are in nowise received by the Catholic and Apostolic Roman Church; of which a few that are extant shall be specified, which are to be avoided by Catholics." Then follows a list of "apocryphal" books, such as the works of Hermas, Clement of Alexandria, Tertullian, Eusebius's History, Lactantius, and, among them, "the Apocryphal Book of Canons of the Apostles." Perhaps the utmost this could be taken to mean would be, that the Book of Canons had never been *received* in the Roman Church. That *some* of the canons were received in it, we know, indeed, from the words of Pope Julius already cited, and from the fact that many of them were incorporated in the decrees of the four General Councils; still the "*body* of canons" may have been peculiar to the East, – as we know, in fact, the traditions of the East and West varied from each other on certain points, as in the questions of the observance of Easter, and of heretical baptism, in the former of which, at least, Apostles themselves seemed to have determined variously. Even if the decree is literally taken to mean, that the Book of Canons is the compilation of heretics, (though, if so, the works of Hermas and Clement of Alexandria are strangely involved in the same imputation,) no serious conclusions will follow. For though the Canons were *put together* by heretics it does not follow that they themselves are heretical; and that a great number are not, we know, from the testimony of the Fathers in their favour, as above insisted on. If indeed, the compiler altered, or suppressed, or invented canons, that is another matter; then he was something more than a compiler; but in merely collecting them, he as little impaired the Canons themselves as Bucer or Peter Martyr would have hurt the doctrine of our Prayer Book, had they collected together in one, without altering, the Catholic devotions of the Church before them. At the same time, if heretics did add to the matter of the Canons, *then* the witness these Canons afford to the primitive religion is still more remarkable. We know, independently of these Canons, what the kind of worship and discipline was which obtained in the Catholic Church; and in these Canons we shall *then* possess an *heretical* testimony to it quite in accordance. In that case, ultra-Protestantism will lose the chance even of heretical support, which was all it had from the first to look for.

But, as the fact really is, this decree of Gelasius' is not genuine. It is not mentioned till three hundred years after its supposed promulgation, and there is reason to believe that Gelasius, so far from rejecting, actually did receive and use the Canons in question. But the discussion of this point would be a deviation from the subject before us.

This, then, seems to be the state of the case as regards the collection or edition of Canons, whether fifty or eight-five, which is under consideration. Speaking, not of the Canons themselves, but of this particular publication of them, I thus conclude about it, – that, whether it was made at the end of the third century, or later, there is no sufficient proof that it was of authority; but that it is not very material that it should be proved to be of authority, nay, or to have existed in early times. Give us the Canons themselves, and we shall be able to prove the point for which I am adducing them, even though they were not formed into a collection in early times.

Indeed, it must be confessed, that probability is against this collection having ever been regarded as an authority by the ancient Church. It was an *anonymous* collection; and, as being anonymous, seemed to have no claim upon Christians. They would consider that a collection or body of Canons could only be imposed by a *Council*; and since the Council could not be produced which imposed this in particular, they had no reason to admit it. They might have been in the practice of acting upon this Canon, and that, and the third, and so on to the eighty-fifth, from time immemorial, and that as Canons, not as mere customs, and might confess the obligation of each; and yet might say, "We never looked upon them as a *code*," which should be something complete, and limited to itself. The true sanction of each was the immemorial observance of each, not its place in the collection, which implied a competent framer. Moreover, in proportion as General Councils were held, and enacted Canons, so did the vague title of mere custom, without definite sanction, become less influential, and the ancient Canons fell into disregard. And what made this still more natural, was the circumstance that the Nicene Council did re-enact a considerable number of those which it found existing. It substituted then a definite authority, which, in after ages, would be much more intelligible than what had then become a mere matter of obscure antiquity. Nor did it tend to restore their authority, when their advocates, feeling the difficulty of their case, referred the Collection to the Apostles themselves; first, because this assertion could not be maintained; next, because if it could, it would have seemingly deprived the Church of the privilege of making Canons. It would have made those usages divine which had ever been accounted only ecclesiastical. It would have become a question, whether, under such circumstances, the Church had more right to add to the code of really Apostolic Canons than to Scripture; discipline, as well as doctrine, would have been given by direct revelation, and have been included in the fundamentals of religion.

If, however, all this be so, it follows that we are not at liberty to argue, from one part of this Collection being received, that therefore the other is; as if it were one authoritative work. No number of individual Canons being proved to be of the first age, will tend to prove that the remainder are of the same. It is true: and I do not think it worth while to contest the point. For argument's sake I will grant, that the bond, which ties them into one, is not of the most trustworthy and authoritative description, and will proceed to show, that even those Canons which are not formally quoted by early writers ought to be received as the rules of the Ante-Nicene Church, independently of their being found in one compilation.

3. I have already said, that nearly half of the Canons, as they stand in the Collection, are quoted as Canons by early writers, and thus placed beyond all question, as remains of the Ante-Nicene period: the following arguments may be offered in behalf of the rest:–

(1). They are otherwise known to express *usages* or *opinions* of the Ante-Nicene centuries. The simple question is, whether they had been reflected on, recognised, converted into principles, enacted, obeyed; whether they were the unconscious and unanimous result of the one Christian spirit[4] in every place, or were formal determinations from authority claiming obedience. This being the case, there is very little worth disputing about; for (whether we regard them as being Christian, or in the light of Christian antiquities) if uniform custom was agreeable to them, it does not matter whether they were enacted or not. If they were not, their universal observance is still greater evidence of their extreme antiquity, which, in that case, can be hardly short of the Apostolic age; and we shall refer to them in the existing Collection, merely for convenience' sake, as being brought together in a short compass.

Nay, a still more serious conclusion will follow, from supposing them not to be enactments much more serious than any *we* are disposed to draw. If it be maintained, that these observances did not arise from formal injunctions on the part of the Church, then, it might be argued, the Church has no power over them. As not having imposed, she cannot abrogate, suspend, or modify them. They must be referred to a higher source, even to the inspired Apostles; and their authority is not ecclesiastical, but divine. We are almost forced, then, to consider them enactments, even when not appealed to by ancient writers as such, lest we should increase the authority of some of them more than seems consistent with their subject-matter.

Again, if such Canons as are not appealed to by ancient writers are nevertheless allowed to have been really enacted, on the ground of our finding historically that usage corresponds to them; it may so be that others, about which the usage is not so clearly known, are real Canons also. There is a *chance* of their being genuine; for why, in drawing the line, should we decide by the mere accident of the usage admitting or not admitting of clear historical proof?

(2.) Again, all these Canons or at least the first fifty, are composed in a similar style; there is no reason, as far as the internal evidence goes, why

---

[4] The εκκλησιαστικον φρονημα.

one should be more primitive than another, and many, we know, certainly were in force as Canons from the earliest times.

(3.) This argument becomes more cogent when we consider *what* that style is. It carries with it evident marks of primitive simplicity, some of which I shall instance. The first remark which would be made on reading them relates to their brevity, the breadth of the rules which they lay down, and their plain and unartificial mode of stating them. A good instance of this will be supplied by a comparison of the thirty-fifth Canon with one of a number of Canons passed at Antioch by an Arian council, held A.D. 341, and apparently using the Apostolical Canons as a basis for its own. The former says, simply,–

"The bishops of every nation are bound to acknowledge the principal among them, and to count him as a head, and to do nothing extraordinary without his advice, but to do those things alone individually which relate to the diocese of each respectively and its towns. He, in turn, must not act without the advice of all."

These plain directions are thus amplified in the Canon of Antioch:–

"The bishops in each province are bound to acknowledge the bishop ruling in the metropolitan see, and that he has the care of the whole province, because all who have business have recourse from every quarter to the metropolis. Whence it has seemed good that he should be first in honour also, and that the other bishops should do nothing extraordinary without him, (according to that most ancient canon which has been in force from our fathers' time,) or such things only as relate to the diocese of each and the places under it. For, each bishop has power over his own diocese to administer it according to his own conscience, and to provide for the whole territory subject to his own city, so as to ordain presbyters and deacons, and to dispose all things with consideration, but to attempt no proceedings beyond this without the metropolitan bishop; and he, in turn, must not act without the advice of the rest."

Or, again, take the following instance; which, when read with the words in brackets, agrees, with but slight exceptions, with the Antiochene, and, without them, with the Apostolical Canon:–

"All who come [to church] to hear the [holy] Scriptures read, but do not remain to prayer [with the people,] and [refuse] the holy communion [of the Eucharist] contumaciously, [these] must be put out of the Church, [until, by confession, and by showing fruits of penitence, and by entreaty, they are able to gain forgiveness."]

Now these instances will serve to illustrate the antiquity of the Apostolical Canons in several ways, besides the evidence deducible from the simplicity of their structure. It will be observed that the word "metropolis" into the Canon of Antioch; no such word occurs in that from which it is apparently formed. There it is simply said, "the principal bishop;" or, literally the primus. This accords with the historical fact, that the word metropolitan was not introduced till the fourth century. The same remark might be made on the word "province," which occurs in the Canon of Antioch, not in the other. This contrast is strikingly brought out in two other Canons, which correspond in the two Collections. Both treat of the possessions of the Church; but the Apostolical Canon says simply, "the interests of the Church," "the goods of the Church;" but the Antiochene, composed after Christianity had been acknowledged by the civil power, speaks of "the revenue of the Church," and "the produce of the land." Again, attempts have been made to show that certain words are contained in the Canons before us which were not in use in the ante-Nicene times, but they have in every case failed, which surely may be considered as a positive evidence in favour of their genuineness. For instance, the word "clergy," for the ministerial body, which is found in the Canons, is also used by Origen, Tertullian, and Cyprian. The word "reader," for an inferior order in the clergy, is used by Cornelius, bishop of Rome; nay, by Justin Martyr. "Altar," which is used in the Canons, is the only word used for the Lord's table by St. Cyprian, and. before him, by Tertullian and Ignatius. "Sacrifice" and "oblation," for the consecrated elements, by Clement of Rome, Justin, Irenæus, and Tertullian. This negative evidence of genuineness extends to other points, and surely is of no inconsiderable weight. We know how difficult it is so to word a forgery as to avoid all detection from incongruities of time, place, and the like. A forgery, indeed, it is hardly possible to suppose this Collection to be, both because great part of it is known to be genuine, and because no assignable object would be answered by it; but let us imagine the compiler hastily took up with erroneous traditions, or recent enactments, and joined them to the rest. Is it possible to conceive, under such circumstances, that there would be no anachronisms or other means of detection? And if there are none such, and much more if the compiler, who lived perhaps as early as the fourth century, found none such, (supposing we assume him willing and qualified to judge of them,) nay, if Dionysius Exiguus found none such, what reasons have we for denying that they are the product of those early times to which they claim to belong? Yet so it is; neither rite, nor heresy, nor observance, nor phrase, is found in them which is foreign to the ante-Nicene period. Indeed, the only reason one or two persons have thrown suspicion on them has been, an unwillingness on their part to admit episcopacy, which the Canons assert; a necessity which led the same parties to deny the genuineness of St. Ignatius' epistles. And now I congratulate the reader on having come to the end of a discussion which requires more careful attention than this small work has a right to demand.

CHAPTER XVII
CANONS OF THE APOSTLES

"They shall teach Jacob Thy Judgments, and Israel, Thy law: they shall put incense before Thee, and whole burnt sacrifice upon Thine altar. Bless, Lord, his substance, and accept the work of his hands: smite through the loins of them that arise against him, and of them that hate him, that they rise not again."

From what has been said, it would appear that the Canons called Apostolical come to us under circumstances which make them of especial service in an inquiry which we are desirous of seeing carefully instituted, but which would not suit these pages. Are there discoverable in the records of antiquity any *traces* of that sudden corruption or declension of primitive Christianity which ultra-Protestants say certainly *did* take place, or else Christianity, as we find it in history, would not be so unlike their own Christianity; or, on the other hand, is not this *argument* itself, after all, the real and sole ground of the alleged *fact*, – viz. "Christians *must* necessarily have fallen away, *or else* ultra-Protestantism is not divine." Is the supposed declension proved historically, or is it argued and inferred that it cannot but be so, as being a necessary hypothesis, or key-stone, for reconciling discordant evidence, – viz. ancient facts with modern opinions. In short, is there, or is there not, any ground for the imputation thus cast upon the Christianity of the second and third centuries, beyond the necessity of casting it on the part of the caster, – beyond the duty of self-defence, or the right of self-preservation?

However necessary and becoming as is such a struggle for life, I do not think it will avail the ultra-Protestant who makes it. The problem before him is to draw a line between the periods of purity and alleged corruption, such, as may have all the Apostles on one side, and all the Fathers on the other, which may insinuate and meander through the dove-tailings and inosculations of historical facts, and cut clean between St. John and St. Ignatius, St. Paul and St. Clement; low enough not to encroach upon the book of Acts, yet so high as to be out of the reach of all extant documents besides. And any how, whether he succeeds or not, so much he must grant, that if such a system of doctrine as he would now introduce ever existed in early times, it has been clean swept away as if by a deluge, suddenly, silently, and without memorial; by a deluge coming in a night, and utterly soaking, rotting, heaving up, and hurrying off, every vestige of what it found in the church before cock-crowing; so that "when they rose in the morning" her true seed "were all dead corpses" – nay, dead and buried – but without grave-stone. "The waters went over them; there was not one of them left; they sunk like lead in the mighty waters." Strange antitype, indeed, to the early fortunes of Israel! – then the enemy was drowned, and "Israel saw them dead upon the sea-shore." But now, it would seem, water proceeded as a flood "out of the serpent's mouth," and covered all the witnesses, so that not even their dead bodies "lay in the streets of the great city." Let him take which of his doctrines he will, his peculiar view of self-righteousness, of formality, of superstition, his notion of faith, or of spirituality in religious worship, his denial of the virtue of the sacraments, or of the ministerial commission, or of the visible Church, or his doctrine of the divine efficacy of the Scriptures as the one appointed instrument of religious teaching, and let him consider how far antiquity, as it has come down to us, will countenance him in it. No; he must allow that the supposed deluge has done its work; yes, and has in turn disappeared itself; it has been swallowed up in the earth, mercilessly as itself was merciless.

This representation has been usually met by saying, that the extant records of primitive Christianity are scanty, and that, *for what we know*, what is not extant, had it survived, would have told a different tale. But granting this, the hypothesis that history *might* contain facts which it does not contain, is no positive evidence for the truth of those facts; and this is the question, what is the *positive* evidence that the Church ever believed or taught a Gospel substantially different from that which her extant documents contain? All the evidence that is extant, be it much or be it little, is on our side; ultra-Protestants have none. Is none better than some? Scarcity of records – granting for argument's sake there is scarcity – may be taken to account for ultra-Protestants having no evidence; it will not account for our having all that is to be had; it cannot become a positive evidence in their behalf. That records are few is no argument or presumption in favour of their being worthless.

Whether, however, there be a scarcity of primitive documents or not, I would contend that, supposing the appeal to facts be allowed as a legitimate line of argument, not only there is none for them, but there is enough for us. But the advocates of the creed, by courtesy called Protestantism, do not allow the appeal; they aver that the Apostolic system of the Church was certainly lost, when they know not, how they know not, without assignable instruments, but by a great revolution, – of that they are certain; and then they challenge us to prove it was not so. "Prove," they say, "if you can, that the real and very truth is not so entirely hid from the world as to leave not a particle of evidence betraying it. The very speciousness of your error is, that all the arguments are in your favour. Is it not *possible* that an error has got the place of the truth, and has destroyed all the evidence but what witnesses in its behalf? Is it not possible that all the Churches should everywhere have given up and stifled the scheme of doctrine they received from the Apostles, and have substituted another for it? Of course it is; it is obvious to common sense it may be, is. Well, we say, what *may be, is*; this is our great principle: we say that the Apostles considered episcopacy an indifferent matter, though Ignatius says it is essential. We say that the table is not an altar, though Ignatius says it is. We say there is no priest's office under the Gospel, though Clement affirms it. We say that baptism is not an enlightening, though Justin takes it for granted. We say that heresy is a misfortune, though Ignatius accounts it a deadly sin; and all this because we have a right to interpret Scripture in our own way. We uphold the pure unmutilated Scripture; the Bible, and the Bible only, is the religion of Protestants, and we the only interpreters of it. We claim a sort of parliamentary privilege to interpret laws our own way, and not to suffer an appeal to any court beyond ourselves. We know, and we lament, that all antiquity runs counter to our interpretation; and therefore, the Church was corrupt from *very* early times indeed. But mind, we hold all this in a truly Catholic spirit, not in bigotry. We allow in others the right of private judgment, and confess we, as others, are fallible men. We confess facts are against us, while we claim an indefeasible right to our own opinion. Far be it from us to say, that we are certainly right; we only say, that the whole early Church was certainly wrong. We do not impose our belief on any one; we only say, that those who take the contrary side are Papists, firebrands, persecutors, madmen, zealots, and deserve nothing but contempt and reprobation, as an insult to the nineteenth century."

To such an argument, I am aware, it avails little to oppose historical evidence, of whatever kind. It sets out by protesting against all evidence, however early and consistent, as the testimony of fallible men; yet, at least, the *imagination* is affected by an array of facts; and I am not unwilling to appeal to the imagination of those who refuse to let me address their reason. With this view I have been inquiring into certain early works, unpopular either in their day or afterwards, to see if any vestige of the hypothetical system in question can be discovered there; for, as to the body of orthodox Fathers, it is pretty well acknowledged that there is nothing ultra-Protestant in them. With this object, then, I have been discussing the Canons called Apostolical.

The especial circumstance which recommends these Canons to our notice is this; that they contain what there is reason to consider a fair portrait of the customs and opinions of the ante-Nicene Church. This judgment about them, which depends on historical evidence, is confirmed by the two following considerations: the Canons in question were in a great measure neglected, or at least superseded in the Church, after Constantine's day, especially in the West. Let this be recollected by those who dwell upon the corruptions which they suppose resulted from the

Church's establishment by Constantine, Rome being the fountain-head. Further, there is ground, weak or strong, for suspecting that the *collection* or *edition* of Canons, as we have it, was made by heretics – probably Arians – though they have not meddled with the contents of them. Thus, while the neglect of later times separates these Canons from Romanism, the assent of the Arians, if so, is a second witness, in addition to the judgment and practice of the early Church, in proof of their Apostolical origin. The first ages observe them; even heretics respect them; later and corrupt ages neglect them. Now, the argument to be derived from these Canons, in behalf of the Catholic system, is two-fold: first, from what they *assume*; secondly, from what they *enjoin*. I shall set down some points of detail under each of these heads.

1. First, as to what is implied in the Canons, as if an existing system on which they are built. Let it be observed, they do but contain directions as to particular matters; they do not begin a religion; they do not form a Church; nor are they reformations; they presuppose something existing, recognise it, and carry on its principles into their minute applications or developments. They are but *ecclesiastical* appointments, and assume *Apostolical* appointments as their basis. Here, then, an argument arises in favour of what they assume, for the very reason that they do assume it. That they do not enjoin, but assume it, is not only a stronger evidence of its existence, but even of its importance. It is but a common remark, that indirect notice of facts and events in an historical document is a stronger evidence that they existed, or took place, than direct. But, over and above this, such implication is, in the present case, a stronger evidence also of the authority and moment of the points assumed. For Canons themselves are enacted on the authority of the *Church*; what they assume as principles, and, instead of touching, only attempt to carry out, may seem to depend on an authority higher than the Church, which the Church cannot touch, and to come from the Apostles. This distinction has already been noticed, and is very obvious. For instance, we are accustomed to place the Sacraments among the Divine and Apostolical ordinances which Christ gave, and Christ only can annul; among ecclesiastical, the subordinate rites connected with them, the particular prayers, and the provision about sponsors. Among Divine and Apostolical ordinances, we place the Lord's-day festival; among Ecclesiastical, are Saints' days. Among the Divine, are a number of, more or less, abstract or (what may be called) disembodied rites, to which the Church gives a substance and form – such as public worship, imposition of hands, benedictions, and the sign of the cross, which are first elements of actual ordinances, and the instrumental principles of grace, and are variously applied and dispensed according to the decision of the Church. Hence arise orders of service, the rites of confirmation, absolution, marriage, and the like, which are of a mixed nature, ecclesiastical in form, divine and life-giving in their principle. Now, then,

let us see what these observances are, *on which* the canons build their system, and we shall have some insight into what were considered Apostolical at the time these Canons were framed.

They are such as these: the Canons take for granted the principle of ministerial superintendence, and the principle of ministerial succession, and consider them both vested in one and the same individual functionary. They take for granted that ordination is necessary, and that it is given by imposition of hands. They presuppose the three orders of bishops, priests, and deacons. They take for granted the one baptism for the remission of sins. They assume that there is an altar and a sacrifice in the visible Church under the Gospel, and that by "the Lord's appointment." They take for granted the rite of holy communion. They take for granted the practice of excommunication. They speak of heretics, or sectarians, and of their being in a state of serious disadvantage; they use concerning them the same (what is now called) fierce and contemptuous language which occurs in later centuries. They take for granted a local and diocesan episcopacy. They take for granted an order of precedence among the bishops of each nation. They take for granted that councils are composed of bishops. They take for granted that married men may be clergy – nay, may be bishops. They recognise the observances of celibacy and fasting. They recognise the fast of the great Sabbath, or Easter eve, and of Lent, and of Wednesday and Friday. They imply the observance of Easter; they imply the existence of festival days. They recognise the use of churches; and of wax, and of oil, gold and silver vessels, and linen, in the worship of God, and these as consecrated. They speak of demoniacal possession and exorcism.

These are the usages and the points of discipline which these Canons recognise as established. As to doctrine, besides the sacred truths of the Trinity and Atonement, which are incidentally mentioned, there are the following:– that the Church may not inflict corporal punishments; that to pay for preferment is simony; that unanimity is a chief duty of Christians; that on the bishop solely falls the cure of souls, and its responsibility; that those who serve the altar should live of the altar; that to acknowledge heretics is to associate Christ with Belial; that there is a difference, under the Gospel, between true priests and false priests; that baptism is the cross and death of the Lord; and that persons who fast on festivals fulfil the prophecy in the beginning of the fourth chapter of St. Paul's first Epistle to Timothy.

2. So much on what these Canons *imply*; now, what do they *enjoin*? Here, however, I would observe, lest I should be mistaken, that I do not conceive that the injunctions contained in them have any *direct* binding force on us *as* Canons, but I take them as an historical evidence of the *sort* of religion which was in that age considered as included under the idea of Christianity. They will be found to breathe a certain spirit, very unlike what is now popular, and to be developments of principles which must be

counted false, unless modern received principles are false instead. I shall set down some of them without any care to be systematic:–

It was provided, then, that every bishop should be consecrated by two or three bishops, and the inferior orders always by a bishop; that no bishop, priest, or deacon, should take on him secular cares; that, unless under very extraordinary circumstances and with leave from his brethren, a bishop should not move from see to see; that he should not admit into his diocese the clergy of another; that he should not ordain out of his diocese; that neither bishop, priest, nor deacon might put away his wife on pretext of religion; that a person who married a second time after baptism should not hold any office in the ministry, nor one who had married two sisters, or a niece; that a cleric should not become surety; that neither bishop, priest, nor deacon, might take interest of money; that clergy who had entered the sacred pale single might marry, provided they were only readers or chanters; that no secular influence should interfere with appointment of bishops; that letters of introduction should be required of foreign ecclesiastics; that no suffragan could act in extra-diocesan matters without his metropolitan, nor the metropolitan without his suffragans; that councils should be held twice a year for doctrine and settlement of disputes; that the bishop should have the oversight of all church property, but might not give to his relatives, who, if poor, were to receive the alms of the poor, – nor to himself, unless for his necessary maintenance and that of brethren who were his guests; that the inferior clergy might not move without him; and that a distinction should be preserved between the Church property and his private property, the latter of which he might bequeath to wife, children, relatives, and servants, as he would.

Moreover, these Canons enjoin that no bishop, priest, or deacon, might join in prayer with sectaries[5] much less allow them to perform any ministerial acts; or acknowledge their baptism, sacrifice, or ordination; or re-baptize, or re-ordain, or be re-ordained, or neglect trine immersion, or refuse to restore a penitent; or allow the forged scriptures of the sectaries to be read in church; or ridicule the maim, deaf, blind, or lame; or eat flesh with the blood; or fast on Sundays, or on Saturdays, except Easter eve; or not fast in Lent, and on Wednesday and Fridays, except on account of bodily weakness; or enter a sectarian meeting or synagogue to pray, whether cleric or layman; or apply to common uses consecrated vessels or linen; that such bodily infirmities, and such only, should be a bar to ordination as interfered with ministerial usefulness; that kings and civil magistrates should not be insulted; and household slaves not ordained without the leave of their masters and the grant of freedom.

Now let us picture to ourselves the irksome position of a modern

---

[5] αιφρετικοιζ.

Protestant in a communion where such points were first principles; with his societies instead of the Church – his committees, boards, and platforms, instead of bishops – his Record or Patriot newspaper instead of councils his "concerts for prayer" instead of anathemas on heretics and sectaries – his harangues at public meetings instead of exorcisms – his fourths of October instead of festival days – his glorious memories instead of holy commemorations – his cheap religion instead of gold and silver vessels – his gas and stoves for wax and oil – and his denunciations of self-righteousness for fasting and celibacy. Can we doubt that such Canons imply altogether a different notion of Christianity from that which he has been accustomed to entertain? *This*, indeed, would be the very fault he would find with the whole system, – he would say he was not at home in it, or in other words, that there is nothing evangelical in such ecclesiastical regulations; and yet after all quite as much surely as in the rules laid down by St. Paul, as in the fifth, or seventh, or eleventh and twelfth, or fourteenth chapters of his first epistle to the Corinthians; the ninth chapter of his second; or the fourth and fifth of his first to Timothy. I do not mean to allow the essential Gospel doctrines are absent from the Canons, which no one will say who has studied them. But even if they were, such absence is not in point, unless it is a proof that rulers of the Church do not hold doctrines, because they *also* give rules of discipline, and, when giving the latter, do not deliver the former instead. Certain doctrines may be true, and certain ordinances also; the one may be prescribed in Canons, the other taught in Confessions. It does not follow that those who enforce the one do not enforce the other; but it does follow that those who enforce the latter to the exclusion of the former, do not enforce both. Those who enforce the discipline, need not deny the doctrine; but those who think to escape the discipline by professing the doctrine, are more careful of doctrine than the early Church was, and have no congeniality of feeling with times which considered it better to follow out what they had received than to reason against it, "to do these, and not leave the other undone."

Such, then, is a sketch of the main rules of discipline in the primitive Church as they have come down to us, and which I offer for those whom it may concern. They show clearly enough the sort of religion which was then considered Apostolic; not that which *we* should term the "free-and-easy" religion, but what our opponents would call the "formal and superstitious."

APPENDIX 6

THE MARTYRS GERVASIUS AND PROTASIUS: 1834

BOA D. 6. 2.

1834

<This was the first stage of one of the nos of the Church of the Fathers intended for the British Magazine, but it was rewritten and published in another form. it was returned to me by Mrs Rose, after Rose's death, in 1840. JHN>

I cannot deny that the age in which Ambrose lived was both enthusiastic & superstitious, but then I am not quite sure that enthusiasm & superstition are bad things. I do not wish to speak paradoxes; & hope my reader will not accuse me of such, when I have explained myself. In truth we cannot expect to find the highest tone of mind in any mixed multitude of men, (– and if we must be content with the mass of men being but second-best, though I do not *excuse* any one who is not all he should be, but I take men as they *are*) is it not better that they should be superstitious or enthusiastic, than unbelieving? and every man alive, who is not a full grown Christian, is one or other, or more than one, of these three. Is it not better to grovel in our worship, or to be extravagant in our worship, than to have no worship at all? is it not better to tremble, or to be rapturous, than to be the slave of sensual appetites without remorse, or the deliberate systematic votary of Mammon, or the brutal scoffer or blasphemer? – If this be true, superstition & enthusiasm are not bad things compared with their alternative.

But further superstition & enthusiasm are not discovered in their simple unmixed state, but they are united to real religion. It is a contradiction in terms to speak of a pious infidel: – but superstitious believers, enthusiastic believers are personages we see every day. Nay, may I say it? *all* men (in this frail state) have their share of superstition & enthusiasm; though great on one side of their character, they are little on another, and he is the best man who has purified himself the most entirely from these baser feelings, and whose faith is the most clear & most sober.

And, still further, observe that superstition and enthusiasm are the *paths to* an exalted religious state of mind; or at least superstition is, and enthusiastic superstition, & these are the two principles of action I allude to as common in the age of St Ambrose. As to plain <simple> fanaticism, I am not concerned with it & shall now dismiss the mention of it; and it has advocates enough nowadays without me.

Now if superstition be the antecedent of religion (not that all superstition leads to religion, but certain kinds,) it follows that we must not rudely reject it, but we must treat it tenderly, try to secure and refine its better parts, and keep it all rather than reject it all, if this be in any case the alternative. Superstition (in the sense I am using the word) is *ignorant faith*. The mind sees something or other of the truth; but not distinctly; – just as the eye may see the Sun behind a cloud. – We are sure the sun is there, but we cannot tell the spot; and we admire the whole cloud, & call it glorious, & might go on to account it the source of light; and no one could reason us out of our conviction that light was there, by telling us that clouds were made of water. – Thus, the mind, which is laden with the conscience of sin, prays to the Saints, or submits to grievous penances with a view to expatiate it. The principle is good, but mixed with ignorance; ignorance of the impossibility of any thing created, much less man's imperfect works atoning for his previous guilt. Or to take a better instance, a man (who has heard of the 2nd Commandment) bows down to an image of the Church. He knows God is there present, he worships Him in the cloud. – So again when Apostles wrought miracles, the disciples might mistake what were *not* miracles for miracles, not being skilled to draw the line distinctly between the ordinary & extraordinary works of God; or might attribute the miracle to wrong causes, as the woman who touched the hem of our Lord's garment. Or, when religion has been acknowledged and memorialized <recorded> in the Church, as its permanent witness, the ordinary providences of God *reminding* Christians of its truth mat be mistaken for logical *confirmations* of it; as in cases where natural cures have been taken for supernatural. Nay even in paganism superstition has in it a root of truth; as St Paul's conduct at Athens assures us. It may be observed, he first speaks of the *superstitions* of the people; then, of their *ignorantly* worshipping the True God.

I confess it makes me indignant when I hear, as is so common in this day, some shallow reasoner, who knows little of the wounds and the needs of our fallen nature, compassionating the superstitions of our forefathers, who believed in witchcraft, or had faith in ghosts, or thought the Church could work miracles; and I long to tell him, by way of protest, that I consider such persons indefinitely more advanced in the scale of mind than himself, insomuchas faith is the highest state to which our nature can attain, and he has in him the spirit of unbelief, in spite of his exact knowledge of the social duties, his attainments in the humanities of life, his clearheadedness & candour, and (if it be so) his proficiency in science and his general information. The vulgar mind or the stupid intellect, if it set the thought of God before it, is his superior, for who measures things by the mere standard of *talent*, or by their availableness to the *temporal welfare* of the community.

I know that these considerations, if admitted to be true, make the duty of a Christian Teacher very difficult – for it is no trouble to declaim against the superstitions of the multitude, and to bid one's hearers abjure them, careless of the consequences upon them, and it is a most perplexing task to disentangle, instead of cutting, the knot, to find out where to begin, to find the ends of the thread, and to untwist without fraying them. Let this be born in mind in reading early Church history; and, if we think we have reason to pronounce its great Champions and Luminaries themselves infected with superstition in some of their views, let us remember <reflect> that each fault sees most clearly & blames most unsparingly its opposite, and if we judge them to be superstitious, that they perchance with much better right & reason would determine our thoughts & ways to be profane. This might be the judgment of St Ambrose upon the tracts and periodicals which Societies connected with the Church put forth at the present day, while we are looking with surprise, perhaps with contempt, on the following passage of his history, which took place shortly after the events I last related, & which I shall introduce in his own words[.]

"To the Lady my Sister whom I love better than my eyes and life.

"You know I tell you every thing goes on here, my revered Holy Sister, so I now inform <write to tell> you that we have found the bodies of Martyrs. I lately consecrated a Church [the Ambrosian,] and many were impatient at my not consecrating it with the solemnities which were observed at the consecration of the Roman. I answered, So I will, if I find the remains of martyrs any where. [i.e. which might be placed under the high altar –] As I said this, my heart burned within me, as if by way of presage.

"In short the Lord was merciful. My clergy stood around in deep reverence <awe>, while I bid dig <turn up> the earth before the rails inclosing the tombs of St Felix and St Nabor. The tokens I hoped to see soon discovered themselves. I had with me also the catechumens <candidates for orders>, and the holy martyrs[.]

"Two bodies were exhumated of surprising size, as if they belonged to some primitive age. All the bones were perfect <complete>, and there was much blood by them. For two days following there was a great press of people to see them; after which we placed them in coffins decently, and bought them at the close of day to the Basilica of St Fausta, where we kept vigil, through the night, and held an ordination. Next day we brought them to the Ambrosian; and, during the procession, a blind man recovered his sight. The following is the substance of my discourse to the people...........

"one of the Psalms that has been read in service says, '*Who is as the Lord our God, who hath His dwelling on high, yet beholds the humble* [humbleth Himself to behold the] *things in heaven & earth.* Truly God has looked upon the humble, now that He hath discovered to us the remains of the holy martyrs of His Church hid under the vile clod, whose soul is in heaven, whose body in earth. *Raising the helpless from the earth, & lifting the poor from the dunghill*; ye see how He has placed them among the Princes of His people. Who, think we, are the Princes but Holy Martyrs, to whose number we now add Protasius and Gervasius, who have been long forgotten, and who enrich a Church, which hitherto has been poor in martyrs, though fruitful in her offspring, with the glory and pattern of their sufferings? ......

"There is reason in the common cry that this is a resurrection of the Martyrs; for if they have not literally risen again, to us surely they have risen. Ye know, nay ye yourselves saw how that many were dispossessed of devils; and that very many <more still>, on touching the garment of the Saints, were loosened of the infirmities which had distressed them as though the miracles of the old times were renewed, when an ampler divine influence was poured upon the earth by our Lord's coming, ye see the very shadow of the holy corpses has a general power of healing. How many handkerchiefs are brought to & fro! and garments, indued with a healing power by the very contact of those blessed remains! All feel it as a privilege to touch the very hem of their garment; & whoso touches is made whole.

"Glory to Thee, O Lord Jesus, who hast at this time raised up among us the souls of these Holy Martyrs, now that Thy Church has need of extraordinary aid. .... Old men begin to relate that they formerly heard the names of these Martyrs & read their history. Our city had forgotten her own Martyrs, while she availed herself of foreigners. I know it is from God's mere grace, still surely it is an honor that the Lord Jesus has put on my episcopate, that I, who deserve not to be a martyr, yet should have been the means of gaining these Martyrs for you.

"So let them pass on, victorious victims, to the Holy Place, where lies the Great Sacrifice Himself. But He is on the altar, who suffered for all; they under the altar, for whom He suffered. I had indeed marked out this spot for myself, for surely there should rest the priest where he was used to offer, but I yield to the sacred victims; for them it was destined. Let us bury them in a fit dwelling place <home>, and solemnize the day by the zeal of our devotion.'

"The people cried out to me to put off the burial till the Sunday, & at length gained a delay till next day. Then I addressed them a second time, to this effect: – ......

"'There are those about us, who, according to their wont, grudge you your festival; and from impatience at it, they go on to hate the course of it & are mad enough to deny that virtue in the Martyrs, which the very devils confess. ...... They deny that a blind man has been restored to sight, but he himself denies it not. He says; I see, who aforetime saw not. ...... The man is well known, engaged in the service of the public before his ailment, Severus by name, by trade a butcher. He laid aside his business, when this misfortune befel him. He appeals to the testimony of his former employers; as evidence of the visitation which came upon him, as witnesses and judges of his blindness. He declares that sight was restored to him on touching the fringe of the robe with which the sacred relics are covered.

"'Is not this like the case what we read of in the gospel? ... The Jews asked, How doth thy son see? for he had said, I was blind & now I see; ask others, if not do not credit me, ask indifferent persons, if you suspect my parents of a [sic] understanding with me. So, the perverseness <obstinacy> of these men is worse than the Jews. When they doubted, they went so far as to ask the parents; the Arians examine in secret, but openly deny, believing the fact, but denying its Author."

I venture the following remarks on this letter & the account it contains.

1. First, We have no reason to doubt the *facts* – Ambrose appeals to eyewitnesses, and he affirms that the Arians themselves admits [sic] them; *non operi increduli, sed auctori.*

2. Next, the miracles; which Ambrose so calls, were not miracles in our sense of the word. We define <mean by> a miracle to be an event of that extraordinary nature as attests the presence & favor of God with the parties working it. Now the occurrences which he relates are unusual, but not supernatural; – not even the restoration of sight to one who for a time had lost it. This I shall not attempt to prove here – but refer the reader to *Douglas's Criterion of miracles.* They may be ascribed to the power of the imagination, excited affections, &c.

3. As being *providential* acts, they were to be accepted with humility & thankfulness; and further improved, as confirmations or memorials of God's presence in His Church, a truth *already* known; their use (if we may conjecture) and the use of all more striking providences being to impress and remind, though not to prove.

4. It is certain that Ambrose considered they *proved* that God was on the side of the Church; in other words, that the particular work in which she was then engaged, the defence of our Lord's Divinity was acceptable to Him, i.e. that the doctrine was true.

5. Yet if we consider attentively, we shall find there is not so much difference here between his view and ours, as might seem at first sight. He

would call these miracles *confirmations* of a truth which was already ascertained; or do we think he would have been willing to shut up all previously known evidence from Scripture & tradition, & to *rest* the proof of the doctrine on these? I think not. At the end of his second Sermon he expressly says, in a parallel case, speaking of the Martyrs' acceptance, that the proof of it rests not in the confession of the devils but in their death for Christ's sake. – But, if so, let us reflect how subtle is the difference between *confirming* and *reminding*. Confirmatory arguments are those which are of weight, others being admitted first; in other words they are addressed more commonly to the feelings or imagination than the reasoning faculty. Take e.g. the argument of the Being of a God from the marks of *design* in the creation. Who does not feel its power? Yet who (ordinarily) makes it the *basis* of his belief in a God? He believes that there is a God, and this comes as an argument afterwards, and impresses, and fixes religious convictions on him. It is *in its actual place* but a *confirmatory* argument. Now suppose some 1400 years, when we are as old as the age of Ambrose is now, it should be universally received, as some speculators even now hazard, that the Argument from Design is not logically correct, would that prove all of us to be illogical who have used it? Surely not – for *practically* we have never used it for more than an edifying stimulus to our religious feeling, however we may have accidentally expressed ourselves; so that the utmost which could fairly be proved against us would be that we had spoken laxly, or not sufficiently analysed our own feelings but mistaken an act of the imagination for an act of the reason. Applying this to the case of Ambrose, I would suggest that having his mind filled with an admirable belief in the Church's uprightness in God's sight, he saw the presence of God brought out most vividly in certain passing events, and spoke of impression as if it had been conviction. And this is the case with men daily; &, though often it is the result of mere weakness of intellect, and often of a heated and fanatical temper, yet it will ever be found in men of the most highly gifted imaginations and poetical tastes, whom the common run of critics, that inferior set of clear and hard heads, will call *illogical*. All this of course applies to his addresses to his brethren; when he would make the cures in question an argument to the Arians he *is* illogical.

6. Further, no apology is hence deducible for those fanatics, who (as in our own day) rest their claims of correctness in faith &c on their miracles; for these literally <really>, and not in expression only, make the providences to which they appeal the *proof* of their claims. They have no proof besides them. The Church is the existing monument and evidence of its own pretensions, according to Leslie's argument, but these men have no part in it. They are of yesterday. Providence it is true they meet with; for God makes His Sun to rise on the just & unjust; but these unusual acts, which remind of other privileges to those who have other, belong to no series, nor connect with spiritual gifts, in those who have left the Church.

The imagination, feelings, &c. are often used in God's service, and are sanctified by their use; but in themselves their operations have no power to connect our cause with God's will.

7. Lastly, to recur to the practical subject of inquiring which led to these notices from St Ambrose's history, I must admit that a Church thrown upon the people for support, will always be liable to the impulses of superstition and enthusiasm. But then in alleviation of this objection I remark, first, that there is no help for it, if the aristocracy desert us; so that it is a great thing if we find encouragement under such circumstances, not to look out for such a state of things as the best possible; – and next that such a state is much better than the rationalism & the secularism which would attend on an Erastian compliance with the age, if such must be the price we have to pay for the continuance of the support of the State. And let it be observed we have every thing in our favor in the spirit of the times, which is decidedly opposed to superstition & fanaticism. Our articles too, a safeguard which was wanting to the primitive Church, would restrain all grosser extravagances; and the English character is far different from that of the excitable Italians, and is a warrant that our Prelates will never resemble the actors in those scandalous scenes which have lately been & are still exhibited in the Metropolis.